Summary of BASIC Statements

Statement	Effect	Text Page #
GOTO linenumber	Branches to the specified line number.	487
HOME	Apple MBASIC. Clears the screen.	172
HTAB position	Apple MBASIC. Moves the cursor to horizontal column position on the line.	174
IF condition THEN statement(s) [ELSE statement(s)]	Performs the statement(s) following THEN when the condition evaluates *true*. Performs the statements following the ELSE (if included) when the condition evaluates *false*.	98
INPUT ["prompt";] variable [,variable2,...]	Inputs data from the keyboard. If a prompt is included, it prints before the input occurs.	41
INPUT #filenum, variable [,variable2,...]	Reads data from a sequential data file.	346
KILL "filename"	Deletes a file from disk.	353
LET variable = expression	Evaluates the expression and assigns the result to the variable.	33
LINE [(X.start, Y.start)]—(X.end, Y.end) [,[palette.color] [,B[F]]]	Draws a line in medium- or high-resolution graphics modes.	428
LINE INPUT [;] ["prompt";] stringvariable	Inputs all characters (limit 255) typed at the keyboard. Accepts all characters including commas and colons, until ENTER is pressed.	188
LOCATE row, column [,cursor]	Places the cursor at the row and column position specified. The optional cursor parameter controls the visibility of the cursor.	172
LPRINT items to print	Prints data on the printer. Items are separated by commas or semicolons.	23
LPRINT USING "stringliteral"; items to print LPRINT USING stringvariable; items to print	Prints data on the printer, according to the format specified in the string literal or variable.	78
LSET stringvariable = stringexpression	Left-justifies the string expression in the string variable.	366
MID$(stringvariable, start position, number of characters) = stringexpression	Replaces part of a string variable with the string expression.	181
NAME "old filename" AS "new filename"	Renames a disk file.	353
NEXT [loop index]	Terminates a FOR...NEXT loop.	245

(continued on inside back cover)

Third Edition

Microsoft® BASIC

Using Modular Structure

Third Edition

Microsoft®
BASIC

Using Modular Structure

Julia Case Bradley
Mt. San Antonio College

 Wm. C. Brown Publishers

Book Team

Editor *Kathy Shields*
Developmental Editor *Lisa Schonoff*
Production Editor *Anne E. Gardiner*
Designer *Heidi J. Baughman*
Art Editor *Jess Schaal*
Photo Editor *Michelle Oberhoffer*
Permissions Editor *Marsha McPeek*
Visuals Processor *Amy L. Saffran*

Wm. C. Brown Publishers

President *G. Franklin Lewis*
Vice President, Publisher *George Wm. Bergquist*
Vice President, Publisher *Thomas E. Doran*
Vice President, Operations and Production *Beverly Kolz*
National Sales Manager *Virginia S. Moffat*
Advertising Manager *Ann M. Knepper*
Editor in Chief *Edward G. Jaffe*
Production Editorial Manager *Colleen A. Yonda*
Production Editorial Manager *Julie A. Kennedy*
Publishing Services Manager *Karen J. Slaght*
Manager of Visuals and Design *Faye M. Schilling*

The credits section for this book begins on page 527, and is considered an extension of the copyright page.

Library of Congress Catalog Card Number: 89–082700

ISBN 0–697–07661–X

Printed in the United States of America by Wm. C. Brown Publishers, 2460 Kerper Boulevard, Dubuque, IA 52001

10 9 8 7 6 5 4 3 2

Contents

3 Programs with Loops and Formatted Output   59

4 Adding IF Statements and READ Statements to Programs   97

5 Structured Programming 129

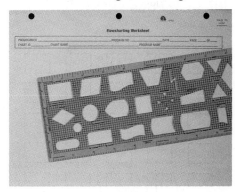

6 Report Design and Subtotals 139

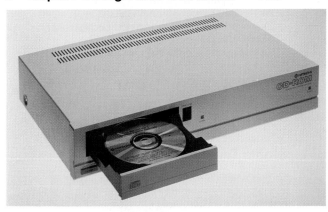

7 Data Validation and Interactive Programs 169

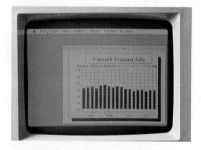

12 Advanced Array Handling 311

14 Random Data Files 369

13 Sequential Data Files 343

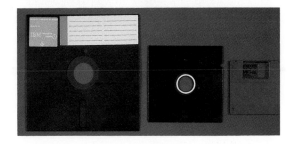

Preface

This textbook is intended for use in an introductory course in BASIC, which assumes no prior knowledge of computers or programming. The fundamentals of programming are taught in a style consistent with current thinking in the computing field. The student programmer will learn good techniques from the start, rather than having to alter habits that are already formed.

This third edition provides updated concepts and terminology as well as some subtle changes to the highly successful and critically acclaimed earlier editions. The menu chapter has been expanded to reflect the growing popularity of menu programs; additional feedback questions have been included, which will help the student apply the concepts learned; and many sections have been enhanced to aid in student understanding.

Structured Programming

The primary feature of the text is the development of well-structured, modular programs. Program modules are implemented with subroutines by the early introduction of the GOSUB statement. Appearing throughout the text are complete example programs that are models of good programming style—meaningful variable names; complete remarks including a dictionary of variable names, program mainline and subroutines; clear, consistent indentation; and control structures limited to the three "proper" constructs—sequence, selection, and iteration. The students are *not* taught to program with the GOTO statement at all.

Microsoft BASIC

The dialect of BASIC chosen is Microsoft BASIC. This selection was made for several important reasons. Microsoft BASIC

1. has the statements allowing for the implementation of the three structured constructs. Specifically, with the inclusion of the IF-THEN-ELSE and WHILE/WEND, programs *can* be written without the use of the GOTO.
2. is the most common version of BASIC in use on microcomputers.
3. is the BASIC supplied with the personal computers manufactured by IBM, DEC, Compaq, Zenith, AT&T, and the many "compatibles," "look-alikes," and "work-alikes."
4. allows formatting of program output with the PRINT USING statement.
5. provides a method for storage and retrieval of data in disk files.

Extensive Appendixes

The inclusion of necessary reference material in the appendixes will do away with the need for most additional, supplementary material generally needed in programming courses. By limiting the dialect of BASIC to that used only on microcomputers running MS-DOS or CP/M, the text can then cover the system commands necessary to operate in those environments. The appendixes include:

1. Edit Mode for Microsoft BASIC (both for the full-screen line editor and the single line editor)
2. BASIC commands
3. MS-DOS and CP/M commands
4. Debugging techniques
5. Discussion and examples of ways to control the special functions of printers
6. Answers to the many feedback questions interspersed throughout the text
7. A list of the reserved words in Microsoft BASIC
8. The ASCII code
9. Error trapping
10. CHAIN and COMMON

Interactive Program Style

The programming emphasis is on interactive program style using menus, good screen design, and input data validation. The INPUT statement is the first method covered for entering data into programs. Not until students are accustomed to interactive programs are the READ and DATA statements covered. Since the majority of software implemented on microcomputers is interactive, it makes sense to learn programming in this manner.

Data File Handling

This text goes well beyond most in the area of data file handling. Chapter 13 covers file concepts and gives extensive coverage of sequential files, including creation, retrieval, and appending data. Chapter 14 covers random data files and shows examples of random and sequential retrieval, updating, and reporting. In chapter 15, indexed files are discussed, and a complete example is included illustrating the creation and maintenance of an indexed file. Sequential file updates are also covered in chapter 15.

Complete Chapter Summaries

At the conclusion of each chapter is a comprehensive list of topics covered in the chapter. During extensive classroom testing of the manuscript, this was one of the most popular features. Although a few of the more advanced students read *only* the summary, most students used the summaries to review the material, for reference to look up topics and terms, and to study for exams. Professors found them a concise source of exam questions.

Program Planning with Flowcharts, Pseudocode, and Hierarchy Charts

The important topic of program planning is covered completely using the three most popular planning tools. Although the trend in the industry is toward dropping the use of flowcharts and switching to either pseudocode or hierarchy charts (or a combination of the two), many students benefit from the visual presentation of program logic afforded by flowcharts. By including all three methods, the student can select the method most beneficial to him or her—and the professor has the choice of methods to use in class.

Significant Changes (improvements) in the traditional sequence of topics

1. *Early coverage of subroutines.* Early (chapter 2) programs are broken into modules using subroutines. Throughout the text programs are written in a modular style, stressing the concept of good module design.

2. *Coverage of looping before selection.* The concept of conditions is presented in the context of controlling loop execution rather than selecting alternate courses of action. The student can easily grasp simple program loops without the necessity of the IF-THEN and IF-THEN-ELSE. With this order of topics, programs can be more meaningful sooner.

3. *Usage of the WHILE/WEND for most program loops.* Until chapter 10, all program loops are formed with the WHILE and WEND. The FOR/NEXT is introduced just before array handling, mainly as an aid to subscript manipulation. Any loop that must be terminated early is always coded with WHILE/WEND, and *never* does execution branch out of a loop with a GOTO or IF-THEN branch.

4. *Early coverage of PRINT USING and LPRINT USING.* The first programs involving program loops (chapter 3) also include formatting the output with LPRINT USING. In this way, the student programmer may create pleasing, properly aligned output.

5. *Early coverage of structured programming guidelines.* The first program examples are coded in a consistent, structured style without giving the complete rationale. Then, as soon as the student has learned enough to understand the terms (chapter 5), a complete coverage of structured programming and top-down programming is presented. This is far superior to having either a late chapter (after the student has developed a programming style) or an early chapter (before the student can understand the terms) devoted to structured programming concepts.

Numerous Examples and Programming Exercises Each chapter has one complete programming example, showing the program planning, program coding, and output. Additionally, many smaller examples are included throughout the text.

Feedback Questions and Exercises Interspersed at appropriate points are thought-provoking questions and exercises to test student learning. Answers are found in an appendix.

BASIC Statements, Commands, and Functions Boxed As each new statement, command, or function is introduced, it is enclosed in a box with its complete format. It is also explained and illustrated with examples which clearly demonstrate its use. These boxes serve as a source of easy reference for the student.

Coverage of Output Report Design A rare topic for BASIC programming textbooks is planning reports. The use of printer spacing charts is covered, along with multiple page output.

Flexibility of Use   This text is ideally suited for the variety of programming courses currently being taught (and those being considered). That "one-semester course in BASIC" is far from standardized, and many colleges and universities offer a second semester of BASIC programming. In many cases, BASIC is introduced in a computer concepts course, and in others, the programming is in an independent course.

The coverage of this text is actually more comprehensive than that of most one-semester courses. This gives the professor some latitude in the selection of topics. Here are some possible variations, using parts of the material presented.

1. *Short course for students with no background.* Spend two or three hours on chapter 1 to give the student an understanding of the hardware and software concepts. Leave out the material on data files and sorting. The course would terminate with chapter 12.

2. *Concepts courses which include BASIC.* Skip chapter 1 (which covers the fundamentals being more completely covered). Use chapters 2, 3, 4, 5, 9, FOR/NEXT from 10, and 11.

3. *One-semester (or quarter) course that has a prerequisite.* Skip chapter 1.

4. *File oriented course.* Cover chapter 14 (random files) early. Some successful courses cover this material before chapter 4, which allows programs to have data file input even before the introduction of selection (IF-THEN).

5. *Advanced course.* The concepts in chapter 7 (interactive programming, screen formatting, data validation) are commonly taught in a second BASIC course. Also, sequential updates and indexing random files (chapter 15) are topics often found in second semester programming courses. Some of the materials in the appendixes make ideal lessons for an advanced course. Error trapping and CHAIN and COMMON statements (appendix I) are generally considered advanced topics, as well as controlling printer functions (appendix H).

6. *Mathematically oriented course.* Cover chapter 10 after chapter 2. Chapter 10 includes the FOR-NEXT statements, functions, and the DEF FN statement.

Supplementary Materials   This text is part of a complete package of course materials.

1. *Instructor's Manual.* Includes chapter outlines, teaching suggestions, test questions, and exercise solutions.

2. *Instructor's Diskette.* Includes a working solution to many programming exercises.

3. *Transparency Masters.*

4. *Testpak.* Computerized version of the test questions contained in the Instructor's Manual.

Acknowledgments

I would like to express my appreciation to the many people who have contributed to the successful completion of this text. Most especially, I want to thank my colleagues and the students of Mt. San Antonio College who helped class test the material in the text and greatly influenced the final form of the manuscript. A special "thank you" goes to David M. Harris of the Toronto School of Business, for his many helpful suggestions. I am also grateful to the reviewers who gave constructive criticism and many valuable suggestions.

Bryan J. Carney—University of Wisconsin, Eau Claire
Louise Darcy—Texas A & M
Maurice Eggen—Trinity University
Jothi Kasiraj—Texas A & M
Norman Lindquist—Western Washington University
George Miller—North Seattle Community College
Lewis D. Miller—Cañada College
Lawrence J. Molloy—Oakland Community College
Donald L. Muench—St. John Fisher College
Keith O'Dell—Olivet Nazarene College
Pasha A. Rostov—California Polytechnic State University at San Luis Obispo
R. Waldo Roth—Taylor University
Sherman Sherrick—William Jewell College
Cherise Vaughn—Enterprise State Junior College
Charles Williams—Georgia State University

We gratefully acknowledge those who responded to our market research survey on the previous edition of this text. Their comments have helped us to make improvements in this edition.

Doug Adams—Merced College
LaVere Adams—Chabot College
Steve Atkins—Surry Community College
Beverly Blaylock—Grossmont College
William R. Chaplin—University of Southern Mississippi
David Dierking—Alpena Community College
Paula H. Gupton—Surry Community College
Alara Lee Hildenbrand—Montgomery College
Russell C. Hollingsworth—Tarrant County Junior College N.E.
Kathy Kimberling—Pierce College
J. W. Lepenski, Sr.—Tarrant County Junior College
Richard Luke—Ricks College
Ronald Osantowski—Gateway Technical Institute
Oscar Poupart—Schoolcraft College
Thomas Roe—South Dakota State University
Evelyn Seils—Ulster County Community College
Glen Stone—South Dakota School of Mines
Michael Wackerly—Delta College
Joseph Waters—Santa Rosa Jr. College

1 Introduction to Computers and BASIC

RUN Command
LIST and LLIST Commands
SAVE Command
LOAD Command
FILES Command
KILL Command
AUTO Command
RENUM Command
PRINT and LPRINT
  Statements

```
Upon completion of this chapter, you
should be able to:

1. Describe the computer and its
   functions.
2. Explain the difference between
   hardware and software.
3. Differentiate between application
   software and operating system
   software.
4. Understand the functions performed
   by interpreters and compilers.
5. Become familiar with the steps in
   program design and development.
6. Draw flowcharts using standard
   flowcharting symbols.
7. Learn to code, enter, and test an
   elementary BASIC program.
```

The Computer

The computer, like a typewriter or calculator, is a tool for solving problems. Once mastered, it can be made to perform marvelous feats on command. Without mastery, it can be like a typewriter or calculator in the hands of a child who has not learned its use—its great potential goes to waste.

Many things must operate together for a computer to do any useful work. Assume you have just purchased a powerful, flexible, accurate, obedient robot. You want the robot to work for you—perhaps scrub the floor, fix the car, wash the dishes, or do math homework.

This robot will do anything you ask, but it doesn't know *how* to do anything for itself. It has no common sense. If you tell the robot to change the spark plugs in the car, it won't know that first it must open the hood. If you remember to tell it to open the hood, you had better be sure to place the steps in the correct sequence. Otherwise, it will attempt to change the spark plugs and *then* open the hood. (At this point, hope that the robot is not strong enough to carry out the task, gets stuck, and sends a message saying, "Not able to carry out the task.")

IBM AT. An IBM AT computer.

In many ways a computer is similar to that obedient, dumb robot. It must be told each step to carry out. Additionally, each step must be carried out in the correct sequence. The computer is not smart enough to know when steps are out of sequence, so it simply follows directions as long as it possibly can. Sometimes the results will not be what are expected, but you can be sure that the computer followed directions exactly.

Did you instruct the robot to remove the spark plugs with a wrench? Did you tell it to check the gap? Exactly how do you think it will replace the old plugs with the new plugs? If it hasn't been told these things, it will either stop or do something strange and unexpected. In either case, the results can be frustrating.

When writing instructions for the computer to solve a problem, you must be certain to compute the result *before* printing it. Since the computer doesn't know the difference, it will do only and exactly what you ask. Depending on your frame of mind, sometimes the results of computer processing can be uproariously funny or infuriating. Frankly, some people get so frustrated with the level of detail required that the programming would be better left to someone else.

Hardware and Software

In our robot story, you could say that you had a powerful robot (the hardware), but without the proper instructions (the software), the robot would not be much help. The same is true for the computer. The computer itself—the circuitry, the case, the keyboard, the screen—are called the *hardware*. While the computer has tremendous power and flexibility, it absolutely *must* have instructions in order to carry out any useful work. Those instructions are the *software,* or the **computer programs.** Computer programs can be thought of as the instructions necessary to convert inputs into outputs.

Lap-top computer. This portable lap-top computer from Hewlett-Packard can be carried around and used anywhere.

TI with graphics on screen. This microcomputer from Texas Instruments is targeted at the business market.

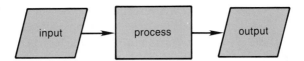

The entire purpose of computer **processing** is to produce some type of **output** (e.g., a report, a computation, a sorted list, a graph). Output may be generated on a screen, a printer, a plotter, a speaker, or some other output device. In order to produce output, there must be processing of the input data. The input to the program may come from the keyboard, from magnetic disk or tape, from a microphone, or from some type of reader such as a bar code reader or card reader. The processing may be arithmetic computations or rearranging, reorganizing, or reformatting data.

The primary goal of this text is to present a method of writing computer software—turning inputs into useful outputs. A basic knowledge of computer hardware is helpful when writing computer instructions.

Hardware

Note the block diagram of a computer. The computer can be seen as a group of components working together. The following sections explain the various components.

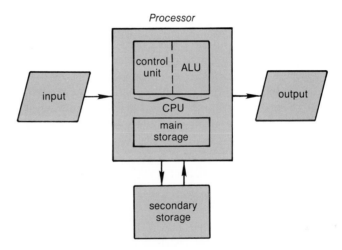

Processor

The main unit of the computer is often called the *processor* or *system unit*. In the block diagram, the two primary components of the processor are the *CPU (Central Processing Unit)* and the *main storage* of the computer.

The CPU, sometimes called the "brain" of the computer, does the actual manipulation of the data. One part of the CPU, called the *ALU (Arithmetic and Logic Unit)*, does all computations and logical operations. Logical operations include such things as determining that one number is greater than another, that one name follows another, or that a condition is *true* or *false*.

Another part of the CPU is the control unit. It is the control unit that controls and coordinates the execution of instructions. The control unit and the ALU working together carry out the instructions of the computer program.

Main Storage

The main storage of the computer can have many different names. The words *storage* and *memory* are used interchangeably when referring to the computer. Main storage may be called *primary storage, internal storage, temporary storage,* or *RAM (Random Access Memory)*.

When a computer is executing a program, main storage must hold the entire program as well as some of the data being operated upon. For this reason, the size of main storage is important. In order to hold a large program, a computer must have a sufficient amount of memory.

Computers are sold with varying amounts of main storage, and often additional memory may be added. Memory size is generally stated in terms of the number of characters that can be stored, where one character equals one letter of the alphabet, one digit of a number, or one of the special symbols such as $, %, *.

In computer terms, the amount of storage needed to hold one character is called a **byte.** A group of 1024 bytes is referred to as one **K** (*K*ilobyte). As a rough guide to computer storage, remember that 1 K holds about one thousand characters, which would be approximately two-thirds of a double-spaced, typewritten page of data.

Typical main storage sizes:

512K bytes—approximately 512,000 characters
640K bytes—approximately 640,000 characters
1M—one megabyte—approximately 1 million characters

Since the entire program and its data must fit into main storage, the computer's memory may be a limiting factor when developing computer programs.

Volatility

As a general rule, you don't need to know how a computer works in order to use one, just as you don't need to understand all of the systems of a car in order to drive. But there are a few pieces of information that will make life easier for you.

One helpful fact to know is that most computer memory is *volatile;* that is, when the power source is removed, the contents of the storage are lost. Any program or data stored in the computer's main storage is gone when the computer is turned off or a power failure occurs. This phenomenon has been the source of many curses and tears by computer users.

Compaq. A portable
microcomputer—
the Compaq Portable III.

Secondary or Auxiliary Storage

Fortunately, there is storage that is nonvolatile—that does *not* lose its memory when the power goes off. This is the type of memory used for long-term storage of data files and programs—the media used to store programs when they are *not* being executed. This is called *secondary storage, auxiliary storage, external storage* (or memory), or sometimes long-term storage.

The two most common forms of secondary storage are magnetic disk and magnetic tape. Within these two groups, the types are further broken down into small disks, large disks, hard-surface disks, floppy disks, and cassette tapes and reel-to-reel tapes of various sizes and shapes. As a BASIC programmer for a personal computer, the storage media you will most likely use is the **floppy disk,** or **diskette,** which comes in several different sizes.

Since it is likely that you will be handling diskettes for storage of programs and data, a few words about the care of disks are in order.

1. The data is stored magnetically, similar to audio tapes. A magnetic field (magnet, power supply, etc.) can erase or scramble your data.
2. *Anything* on the surface of the disk can ruin the data, and maybe even the read/write heads in the disk drive. This means no fingerprints, hairs, lemonade, or cookie crumbs.
3. Heat ruins disks. Leaving a diskette in a hot car is a sure way to destroy it.
4. Pressure can damage a disk. Never allow a disk to be caught by the ring of a binder. Never use a ballpoint pen to write on the disk label.

Read Only Memory (ROM)

There is another type of nonvolatile memory available for computers. This storage resembles main storage with one important difference—the contents of the memory cannot be changed by the computer user. This *ROM* (*Read Only Memory*) is filled with software by the manufacturer. Once inside the computer, the instructions may be executed, but not changed. ROM is actually hardware containing permanently stored software and is sometimes called *firmware.*

Floppies. Three sizes of diskettes used for microcomputers: *A.* 8-inch diskette. *B.* 5¼-inch diskette. *C.* 3½-inch diskette.

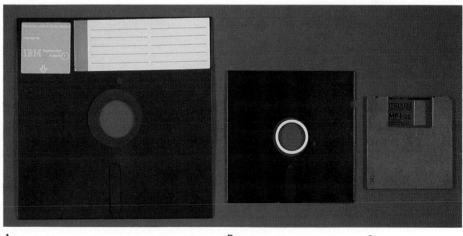

A.   B.   C.

Mac with mouse. A mouse can be used for computer input. As the mouse is moved around the tabletop, the cursor moves on the screen.

Mouse-controlled pointer on screen

Mouse

Light pen. A light pen is a penlike wand attached to the computer by a wire. It can be used to select options from on-screen menus, to point at screen images, and even to draw graphic images.

Computer Input

As you have discovered, main storage must hold the program and some of the data to operate upon. How do these things get into storage? Since all data must be stored electronically, letters, numbers, words, or sounds must first be converted to a form that can be stored. Then these data can be moved into main storage. This conversion to electronic form, sometimes called digitizing, takes place in computer input devices.

The foremost input device is the keyboard. What happens when you press the *A* key on the keyboard? That keypress must be converted into digital electronic pulses that can be stored in computer memory.

Many other input devices are available for personal computers as well as their larger counterparts. Increasingly popular as input devices for personal computers are the joystick and the mouse, along with voice input. Optical scanning devices can digitize drawings, printed pages, or bar codes. Computer input may also come from the more traditional punched cards, magnetic tape, and magnetic disk, or more exotic sources such as thermocouples.

Computer Output

Since the entire reason for using computers is to produce some type of output, it makes sense to examine some of the choices available for that output.

The results of processing will be in main storage (temporarily). You must find a way either to present that information in a human understandable form or to save the information for later reference.

The two most common forms of computer output are the screen display and the printout. However, many others are also available. In this text you will learn to store programs as well as data files on magnetic disk. Computers may also send their output to plotters, tape drives, card punches, voice speakers, and many types of switching devices.

Touchscreen. A touchscreen such as this one from Hewlett-Packard allows the user to input data by merely touching the screen next to a menu choice. Electrical sensors in the glass screen are grounded by this touch, indicating which portion of the screen was selected.

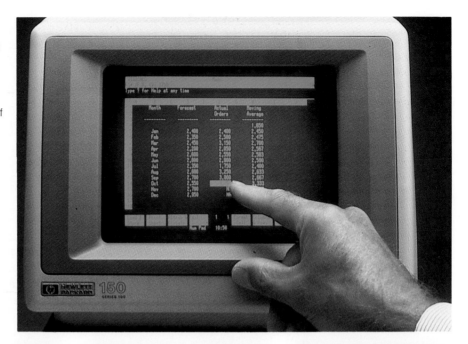

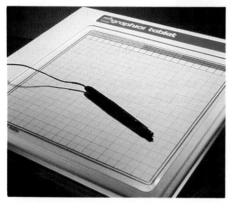

Touch pad. This pad can be used to input characters and graphics. The user draws on the pad, and the characters are interpreted and transferred to the computer.

Joystick. Input from joysticks is very popular for computer games.

Voice input. This microphone is used to provide voice input to a computer.

Software

The instructions to take data from the input devices, manipulate that data, and send it to an output device are called software. Software can be broken down into two broad classifications: (1) *operating system software* (including utilities) and (2) *applications software.*

The necessary software to manage computer operation is called the operating system. This operating system, generally called a **DOS (Disk Operating System),** along with many utility programs, makes up operating system software. Nobody ever bought a computer so that they could use operating system software. People buy computers to produce some desired output. That output is produced by applications software.

Applications software includes accounting programs, games, word processing programs, business applications, scientific applications, medical applications, in fact anything you can name—anything, that is, except the programs to manage the computer itself.

The Operating System

There are many tasks to be done, if an application program is to be run. The disk must first be properly formatted so that programs and data may be stored. A directory must be maintained on the disk to indicate what is there, which parts of the disk are occupied, and which are still available. Programs must be read from the disk into main storage; sequences of characters must be sent from the input devices and to the output devices; and error messages must be sent. The **operating system** performs these, and many more, functions.

You probably will not be surprised to hear that not all operating systems are alike. Although each must solve the same set of problems, each does the job in a slightly different way—disk directories in different locations and in different formats, different codes to indicate similar conditions.

The situation could be compared to that of movie cameras and video recorders. There, the problem is to take pictures, to place them on film or tape, and to reproduce the pictures later. But how many different approaches are there? Different manufacturers use their own techniques and methods. The consumer must choose one, because they are not interchangeable. However, the differences may be mostly technical in nature and not affect the use of the equipment.

You will find the same sort of compatibility, or lack of it, in computer operating systems as in video systems. A video consumer may select from BETA, VHS, video disc, or several other options and have a measure of compatibility. If the user's goal is simply to record and to play back pictures, it makes no difference which is most popular, or how compatible the system will be with others. If the goal is to play tapes produced on other systems, it suddenly becomes important to know what and how much is available in each format.

A computer consumer may select any one of a number of operating systems. Some having more users than others have become more "standard" simply because there are more programs available that are compatible with that system. Some computer manufacturers supply their own operating system with their computers, others purchase a "standard" operating system from a software company and supply that operating system with their computer. Popular operating systems that have been adopted by many manufacturers are MS-DOS (called PC-DOS by IBM), CP/M, Unix, Xenix, and OS/2. These operating systems can be said to be "standard" since they are in use on many different brands of computers.

Operating System Utilities

There are many utility programs that are classified also as operating system software. These utilities exist to make the development, use, and storage of applications software easier or more efficient. Some examples of utilities are: (1) program editors, which provide for entering and changing program lines; (2) copy programs, which will allow entire disks or parts of disks to be copied to another disk or device; (3) debugging aids, which are not for extermination but for finding program errors; (4) disk maintenance programs, which check the validity of data stored on diskette and perhaps make corrections to erroneous data; and (5) compilers and interpreters, which are for application program development and deserve much closer attention.

Compilers, Interpreters, and Programming Languages

The computer does not really speak or understand human language. Although the computer was designed to carry out instructions, those instructions must be in a strange language called *machine language*. The instructions written for the computer must be translated into machine language before the computer can understand or execute them.

For a moment, remember the robot analogy, and imagine that the robot helper speaks, reads, and writes only a strange robot dialect. Any request made of the robot must first be translated into robotese.

Fortunately, there is one person who knows the robot dialect and can translate instructions. The translator understands only precise English and cannot translate any idioms or slang expressions. Instructions must be written carefully. Assume there is a long list of instructions for the robot. How are the instructions going to be translated? The translator will work in either of two methods.

In the first translation mode, the translator converts the first instruction, and the robot executes it. Then the translator translates the next instruction to robot language, and the robot executes it. The entire list is completed, one instruction at a time. If one instruction on the list can't be correctly translated, the robot will perform everything up to that point and stop. If any steps in the list must be repeated, those instructions must be retranslated.

The second method of translation calls for the entire list to be translated before the robot begins. The translator goes through the list, translating and checking. If there is anything in the list that won't properly translate, the translator discovers that before the robot begins. If some of the steps in the list must be repeated, they will need to be translated only once. When the translator is finished with the list, it is handed to the robot, who can now read every word.

Which method is best? That depends on what the task is, how often it must be repeated, and whether it is more advantageous to get started quickly. Translating the whole list before starting will make the execution go much more quickly, but it will take time that perhaps could have been better spent executing instructions. What does all this have to do with computer languages anyway?

Since the computer instructions must be in machine language, a translator is required. That translator is computer software, which reads written instructions and converts them into machine language.

The translator program must be able to understand the written instructions. The instructions must be precise and correct. Many languages have been developed to aid in writing computer instructions. These languages are called computer *programming languages,* and each has strict rules for forming instructions to the computer.

What about the order of translation? Translator programs that convert one instruction at a time are called **interpreters.** Each instruction is executed immediately after it is interpreted. Translator programs that completely translate the entire program to machine code before any execution are called **compilers.** You will find that both methods have their advantages and disadvantages.

Two companies have recently introduced BASIC compilers, which are enjoying considerable popularity. QuickBASIC from the Microsoft Corporation, and Turbo BASIC from Borland International, Inc., are competing in this market. After a few rounds of "top this" revisions, Borland seems to have quit the race, leaving the field to QuickBASIC.

Programming Languages

There are literally hundreds of computer programming languages available for writing instructions to the computer. Each was developed to solve a particular type of problem. Some of the more common programming languages are:

1. BASIC (*B*eginner's *A*ll-purpose *S*ymbolic *I*nstruction *C*ode)—The most popular language in use for microcomputers.
2. FORTRAN (*FOR*mula *TRAN*slation)—The first of the high-level languages, designed for scientific and mathematically oriented programming.
3. COBOL (*CO*mmon *B*usiness *O*riented *L*anguage)—The most popular business language in use for larger computers.
4. Pascal—Increasingly popular with computer scientists, Pascal is known as a highly structured language. Pascal was named after Blaise Pascal, mathematician and inventor of the adding machine.
5. C—Developed by Bell Lab scientists, C is widely used for writing operating systems and utility software.
6. PL/I (*P*rogramming *L*anguage/I)—Developed as an all-purpose language, for both business and scientific applications, and used primarily on large mainframe computers. Subsets of the language are available for use on microcomputers.
7. RPG (*R*eport *P*rogram *G*enerator)—Used primarily for business applications on small business computers.
8. Ada—A relatively new language under development by the U.S. Department of Defense, along with several international organizations and governments. Ada's primary use most likely will be scientific, including missile guidance systems.
9. Assembly language—Included here as a class of languages, since each type of computer has its own assembly language. Assembly is extremely close to machine language and requires an intimate knowledge of the inner working of the computer and the machine's instruction set.

BASIC and Standardization

The language BASIC was developed at Dartmouth College in the 1960s as a simplified method for learning computer programming. The acronym BASIC stands for *B*eginner's *A*ll-purpose *S*ymbolic *I*nstruction *C*ode. Early BASIC had only a fraction of the statements now included in most versions of the language.

As the BASIC language became more popular, new versions were implemented for many different computers. With new implementations came many new additions to the language in order to increase the usefulness of BASIC. Some of the capabilities added to BASIC after its introduction include statements for handling alphabetic data, statements allowing programs to read and write data in disk files, and statements providing a means to give programs better structure. These extensions to the language are both a blessing and a curse. The language is much more powerful and flexible than it once was, but these enhancements have not been uniformly implemented. Now the market abounds with many different versions of BASIC.

There is a group whose mission is to establish standards for the computer industry. The American National Standards Institute (ANSI) has done an admirable job of standardizing COBOL, FORTRAN, and the symbols used for flowcharting.

Unfortunately, ANSI efforts to standardize BASIC came so late in its development that it was an impossible task. A standard was developed and published, but many BASIC language publishers had already gone well beyond the specifications, and have further enhanced their implementations of the language since the list was published.

Which version of BASIC should you learn? Valid arguments can be made for many versions. For this text the version of BASIC written by Microsoft, Inc., was selected for many reasons. Microsoft BASIC

1. is the most common version of BASIC in use on microcomputers.
2. is the BASIC supplied with the personal computers manufactured by IBM, DEC, Compaq, Zenith, AT&T, and the many "compatibles," "look-alikes," and "work-alikes." Most computer manufacturers introducing a computer today include a copy of Microsoft BASIC.
3. allows for the use of long variable names, which make programs more understandable.
4. has statements allowing for more structured programs (specifically the IF-THEN-ELSE and WHILE/WEND).
5. allows formatting of program output with the PRINT USING statement.
6. provides a method for storage and retrieval of data in disk files.

Microsoft BASIC—Interpreted or Compiled?

As mentioned earlier, programming languages may be interpreted (translated one line at a time) or compiled (entire program translated before execution begins).

The BASIC translator appearing on most microcomputers is an interpreter. Interpreting makes program development easier, allowing for minor changes to be made and showing the results more quickly. However, in production environments, interpreted programs run more slowly than compiled programs.

Microsoft BASIC is available in both interpreter and compiler versions. Often applications programs are developed with the interpreted version. Then, when the program is running correctly, it will be compiled for regular use. Programs written in Microsoft BASIC can be compiled using Microsoft's QuickBASIC compiler or their full BASIC compiler. With very few exceptions, most statements will work identically in all three versions.

A First BASIC Program

Following is an elementary computer program, written in the BASIC language.

```
10   REM PROGRAM TO CALCULATE THE AREA OF A ROOM
20   INPUT LENGTH
30   INPUT WDTH
40   LET AREA = LENGTH * WDTH
50   PRINT "THE AREA IS"; AREA
60   END

RUN
? 25
? 35
THE AREA IS 875
```

The individual statements will be examined line by line.

First, notice the **line numbers.** Each BASIC statement begins on a new line, and each line must be numbered. The line numbers indicate the order for the instructions, so each line number must have a higher number than the preceding line. The rule doesn't say how much higher, however. You may number lines 1, 2, 3, 4, 5 or any increment you choose. A handy method is to number by 10s, as in the example. Then, if new statements must be added, there are numbers available for use. To add a new line between lines 10 and 20, you could type a new line and call it 15 or any other number 11 to 19. Line numbers may be from 1 to 5 digits, in the range 1 to 65529.

Line 10 is called a REMark (REM) statement. Remarks are used for program documentation only, to make programs easier for humans to understand. REMs are not translated to machine language or executed by the program. Any time the program is listed, the remarks appear along with the program lines. It is wise to make heavy use of REM statements in programs, and programmers should establish the habit early.

Most versions of Microsoft BASIC allow a second method of writing REM statements, which you will also find in this text. The keyword REM may be replaced by a single quotation mark ('). Line 10 would then read:

```
10   ' PROGRAM TO CALCULATE THE AREA OF A ROOM
```

Lines 20 and 30 are called INPUT statements. Recall the diagram of computer processing.

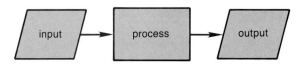

The first step is input. The data must be put into the computer so that it can be operated upon.

Referring back to the example program for a moment, notice the lines

```
RUN
?  25    ← typed by user
?  35    ← typed by user
THE AREA IS 875
```

This is the execution of the program. The computer is carrying out the instructions given in the program lines.

The first question mark is generated by line 20 in the program (INPUT LENGTH). When an INPUT statement is encountered during program execution, a question mark is displayed on the screen. Then execution is suspended while the user types a number. In this case, the number 25 was assigned to LENGTH.

The second question mark was placed there by line 30 (INPUT WDTH). When the user keyed 35, that value was assigned to WDTH.

Line 40 in the program corresponds to the middle box in the diagram of the input-process-output. The LET statement does the processing. In this case, it multiplies the value for LENGTH by the value for WDTH and calls the answer AREA. The names LENGTH, WDTH, and AREA are called **variables,** since the values assigned to those names may be changed.

> *Note:* When choosing variable names, the programmer must avoid a list of "reserved" words. Since the word WIDTH is reserved, the variable was named WDTH. See appendix F for the complete list of reserved words.

The program output is performed by line 50. This will PRINT (display on the screen) both the literal words THE AREA IS and the value calculated for AREA. The program output could be directed to the printer instead of the screen (assuming a printer is attached to the computer) by changing the PRINT statement to LPRINT.

```
50   LPRINT "THE AREA IS"; AREA
```

This program could be executed many times, each with different room sizes.

```
RUN
?  20
?  30
THE AREA IS 600

RUN
?  10
?  30
THE AREA IS 300
```

The last line in the program, END, is the signal that processing is complete.

Program Planning

A series of program planning tasks must be performed before a computer program can be written. A construction crew would not begin building a house until all plans were drawn, and a programmer should not start a computer program until the plans are made. You may find programmers who begin writing the program as soon as they see the problem. You can also find carpenters who begin sawing and hammering without making plans. The analogy is a good one. Generally, the project results will look "slapped together." If the carpenter is experienced and has done this same sort of thing many, many times, chances are good that the project will come out well. A truly experienced programmer also may be able to begin without writing down the plans. In both cases, the reason for success is that the complete plan is really there in the person's head. So, until a programmer attains the level of experience to be able to picture *exactly* how the whole thing fits together, written plans must be made.

Steps in Program Development

1. *Clearly state the problem.* No one can solve a problem if it is not clear exactly what is to be done. The problem statement should have three parts.
   a. The output required.
      A computer program is designed always to produce some desired output. Find out exactly what output is required before proceeding.
   b. The inputs.
      What inputs are available, and what will you need in order to produce the desired output?
   c. The **algorithm** for solution.
      An algorithm is a list of steps necessary to accomplish the task. What processing must be done to get from input to output? This will include any formulas needed for calculations.

2. *Plan the logic of the program.* There are several popular methods for planning program logic. In this book **flowcharts, pseudocode,** and **hierarchy charts** are used. (These terms will be explained in depth in following sections.) In practice, you will probably find that one of these methods works best for you and adopt that method.

   The computer follows directions exactly and in the sequence given. You must be careful to plan each step, making sure the sequence is correct. *The logic should be thoroughly tested, with an operation sometimes called "playing computer," before continuing on to the next step.*

3. *Code the program.* Writing the program statements in a programming language such as BASIC is called coding. The program can be written on plain paper or on a specially designed form called a coding form.

4. *Key the program into the computer.* This generally means to type the program, one line at a time, on the computer keyboard.

5. *Test and debug the program.* Once the program has been keyed into the computer, you are ready to see if it works. When the command RUN is typed, the program begins executing. Did you get the exact output you expected? If the planning was done carefully and well, and no errors were made keying the program, then probably the answer is "yes." But you may want to change the appearance of the output; or maybe the output is *not* correct; or perhaps there was no output at all! If any rules of the BASIC language were broken, there may be error messages from the BASIC interpreter.

   Any programmer will tell you that programmers don't make mistakes, but that their programs sometimes get **bugs** in them. The process of finding and correcting any errors is called **debugging.**

It cannot be emphasized too strongly that *all* computer output must be carefully checked. Too often there are reports of gigantic "computer errors" that resulted in overpayments being made or election results being miscalculated. In most cases, the actual errors were programmer errors. Programmers must thoroughly check every aspect of computer output before allowing a program to be used.

One method of testing programs is to use *test data*. These data have been carefully selected and designed to test all options of a program where expected results are already known.

6. *Complete the documentation.* **Documentation** is used as reference material for computer systems. The documentation includes the program plans (flowchart, hierarchy chart, pseudocode), descriptions of output and input, algorithms for problem solution, program listings, and instructions for the user. Looking back at steps 1 through 5, it is obvious that most of the documentation has already been prepared. The last step is to complete any loose ends and assemble the documentation into a finished product.

Program Planning with Flowcharts, Pseudocode, and Hierarchy Charts

Three methods of planning programs will be presented in this text. As an introduction to program planning, the sample program will be shown in pseudocode, hierarchy chart, and flowchart. (See figures 1.1, 1.2, and 1.3.)

Flowcharts

A flowchart is a graphic, or pictorial, view of the logic of a computer program. It has been said that "one picture is worth a thousand words." Many programmers have found that a flowchart helps to organize their thoughts and produce a well-organized program.

A flowchart is drawn before the program is coded as a planning aid. It also becomes part of the documentation for the completed program as an explanation of the logic. This documentation can be a great aid when modifications must be made to a completed program.

The American National Standards Institute (ANSI) and the International Organization for Standardization (ISO) have each adopted a set of standard flowcharting symbols to be used in computer programming (figure 1.4). This makes flowcharting an effective means of communication between programmers, since all use the same symbols to mean the same thing. (One note here: Just as you can always find people who misuse a spoken language, you may find people who misuse flowcharting symbols.)

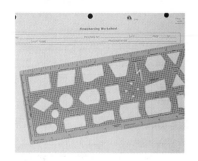

Template. Two basic program design tools: a flowchart template and a flowchart layout form.

Developing Flowcharts

For simple programs, a flowchart may seem superfluous. As programs become more complex, a picture can be an invaluable aid. As the diagram is drawn, often the details of the problem become more apparent. Many times it will become obvious that the boxes should be rearranged for more efficient processing.

When drawing a flowchart, test the logic by "playing computer." This means to step through the program, one line at a time, to determine what the computer output will be. Often there are special conditions that occur only at the beginning of the program or only at the end of the program. Make sure that those steps will always be handled correctly. And, of course, test for the steps that occur in the middle, or main processing, of the program.

There is no rule regarding the language used inside the flowchart symbols. English statements may be used, mathematical formulas, or BASIC statements. The idea is to convey the logic steps and be consistent in language type. (See figure 1.5 for three flowchart examples.)

Input room length

Input room width

Calculate area = length X width

Print area

Figure 1.1
Pseudocode. Pseudocode shows the program logic in English-like statements.

Input room length

Input room width

Calculate area = length X width

Print area

Figure 1.2
Hierarchy chart. A hierarchy chart shows the program organization broken down into individual functions.

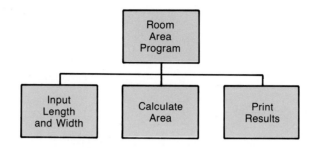

Figure 1.3
Flowchart. A flowchart shows the program logic in pictorial form using standardized symbols.

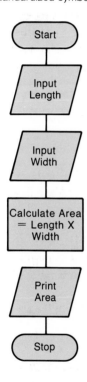

Pseudocode

In pseudocode, natural English statements are used for program planning. The main difference between pseudocode and flowcharts is the lack of pictorial symbols (figure 1.1). Some people find that to be an advantage, others find the written words less clear than the picture.

Pseudocode resembles a cross between a flowchart and the program code. The programmer is free to think about the logical solution to the problem, without being constrained either by selecting the correct symbol or by following the strict syntax rules of the programming language.

There are few rules or standards for the language used in pseudocode. This allows the program planner a great deal of freedom. However, certain conventions have been adopted as an aid to communication.

To be a useful tool, pseudocode should be written as short, imperative statements, with one statement per line. As program logic is developed in this book, the corresponding pseudocode will also be shown. You will find that indentation and alignment of pseudocode lines greatly increase readability and understanding.

These pseudocode examples illustrate the same three programs shown in figure 1.5 as flowcharts.

Sales Tax Computation
Input price
Input tax rate
Calculate tax = price × rate
Print tax
End

Print List of Names
Input name
Loop while name ≠ "END"
    Print name
    Input name
End loop
End

Property Tax Computation
Input property value
If value > 100,000
  then
      calculate tax at 15%
  else
      calculate tax at 12%
Print tax amount
End

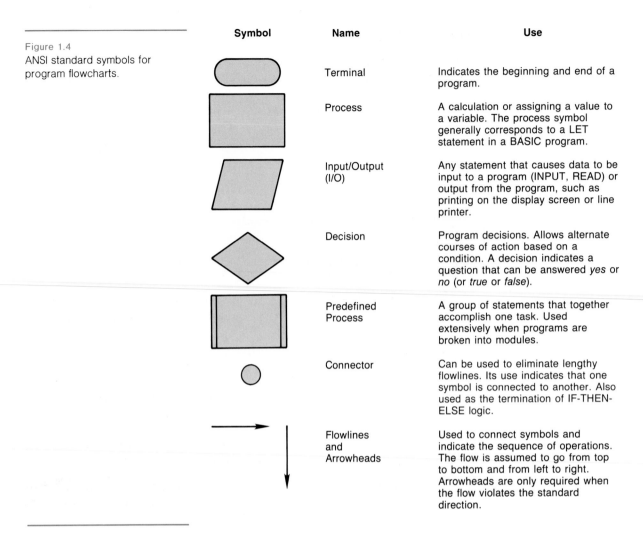

	Symbol	Name	Use
Figure 1.4 ANSI standard symbols for program flowcharts.		Terminal	Indicates the beginning and end of a program.
		Process	A calculation or assigning a value to a variable. The process symbol generally corresponds to a LET statement in a BASIC program.
		Input/Output (I/O)	Any statement that causes data to be input to a program (INPUT, READ) or output from the program, such as printing on the display screen or line printer.
		Decision	Program decisions. Allows alternate courses of action based on a condition. A decision indicates a question that can be answered *yes* or *no* (or *true* or *false*).
		Predefined Process	A group of statements that together accomplish one task. Used extensively when programs are broken into modules.
		Connector	Can be used to eliminate lengthy flowlines. Its use indicates that one symbol is connected to another. Also used as the termination of IF-THEN-ELSE logic.
		Flowlines and Arrowheads	Used to connect symbols and indicate the sequence of operations. The flow is assumed to go from top to bottom and from left to right. Arrowheads are only required when the flow violates the standard direction.

Figure 1.5
Three sample flowcharts. Can you determine what each will do?

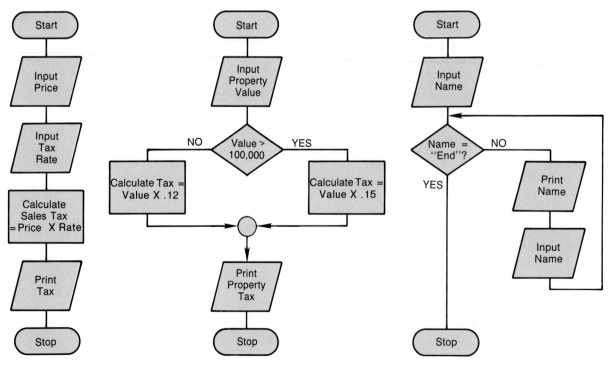

Hierarchy Charts

A hierarchy chart is also called a structure chart or a **VTOC** (*Visual Table Of Contents*). The chart resembles an organization chart in both looks and function (see figure 1.2).

Hierarchy charts are useful when writing programs in a modular fashion. Since you won't learn about modular programming until chapter 2, the presentation of techniques for drawing hierarchy charts will be postponed until that time.

Developing an Example Program

Recall the room area problem presented earlier. This time, each step in program development will be shown.

1. *Clearly state the problem in terms of output, input, and processing.*

   OUTPUT: The area of the room, in square feet
   INPUT: The length and width of the room, in feet
   PROCESSING: Calculate area = length × width

2. *Plan the logic.* For this example, both a flowchart and pseudocode will be used (see figure 1.6). In actual practice, you will choose the one that works best for you.

3. *Code the program.* Coding forms make the process easier. Figure 1.7 is a program coded on coding forms.

4. *Key the program into the computer.* Before beginning a new program, always type the command NEW. This will remove any prior program from the computer's memory.

   For the program lines, first type the line number, then the BASIC statement. At the end of each line, press the ENTER/RETURN key.

5. *Test and debug the program.* To test the program, type the command RUN (with *no* line number). The statements in the program will be executed, one at a time.

Figure 1.6
Flowchart and pseudocode for example program.

Flowchart

Pseudocode

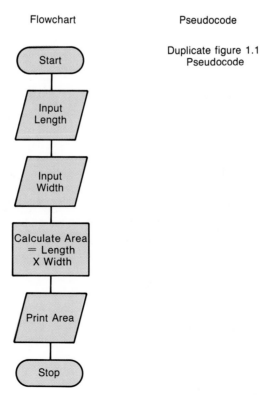

Duplicate figure 1.1
Pseudocode

Figure 1.7
Program coded on coding form.
Any eighty-column layout form
can be an aid in coding a
program.

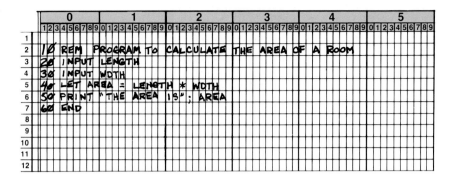

Making the Computer Perform

Running a Program

The RUN Command

```
RUN
```

The RUN command instructs the computer to execute the statements in the program. Type the word RUN without a line number.

Program Errors

Did the program produce the expected output? Exactly? You may need to use a calculator to check the computer output. Is the spacing correct? Check each detail of the output. If the output is not correct, the program may have a *logic error*.

Perhaps the program did not produce what was expected at all. Often, the following message will appear:

SYNTAX ERROR IN line number

For example, if the message SYNTAX ERROR IN 10 was printed, that would mean there was something wrong with line 10 in the program. SYNTAX ERROR means that the rules of the BASIC language have been broken. The error may be caused by a typographical error or a misuse of the statements.

Sample Syntax Errors

```
10   RIM PROGRAM TO CALCULATE THE AREA OF A ROOM
20   INPUT LENGTH
30   INPUT WDTH
40   LET AREA = LENGTH * WDTH
50   PRINT "THE AREA IS"; AREA
60   END

RUN
SYNTAX ERROR IN 10


10   REM PROGRAM TO CALCULATE THE AREA OF A ROOM
20   INPUT LENGTH
30   INPUT WDTH
40   LET AREA = LENGTH * WDTH
50   PRNT "THE AREA IS"; AREA
60   END

RUN
SYNTAX ERROR IN 50
```

Have you spotted the errors in the two preceding programs? In the first example, REM was misspelled, and in the second, PRINT was misspelled.

Sample Logic Errors

Can you find the logic errors in these three programs?

```
10   REM PROGRAM TO CALCULATE THE AREA OF A ROOM
20   INPUT LENGTH
30   INPUT WDTH
40   LET AREA = LENGTH * WDTH
50   PRINT "THE AREA IS"; A
60   END

RUN
? 25
? 35
THE AREA IS 0


10   REM PROGRAM TO CALCULATE THE AREA OF A ROOM
20   INPUT LENGTH
30   INPUT WDTH
40   LET AREA = LENGTH + WDTH
50   PRINT "THE AREA IS"; AREA
60   END

RUN
? 25
? 35
THE AREA IS 60

10   REM PROGRAM TO CALCULATE THE AREA OF A ROOM
20   INPUT LENGTH
30   INPUT WDTH
40   PRINT "THE AREA IS"; AREA
50   LET AREA = LENGTH * WDTH
60   END

RUN
? 25
? 35
THE AREA IS 0
```

In these three examples, there were no syntax errors. The BASIC interpreter was able to translate and execute each statement in the program, but the results were not correct. Before reading any further, see if you can find the logic error in each example.

In the first example, the result on line 40 was called AREA. Then the computer was told to print the value, not of AREA, but A. Although it is perfectly legal to call a variable A, since no value was assigned to A, its value is zero.

In the second example, the arithmetic operation was incorrectly specified. LENGTH should be multiplied by WDTH, not added.

The error in the third example may be a little more difficult to see. Recall the earlier discussion about the sequence of instruction execution. The statements are executed one at a time in the order given. When the PRINT statement was executed, the value of AREA was still zero. AREA was not actually calculated until *after* it was printed.

Correcting the Errors

There are two distinct methods for making changes in a program statement: (1) replace the entire line, or (2) change the existing line with *edit mode*. Since editing is different for different implementations of BASIC, edit mode will be covered in appendix B.

For now, the program can be corrected by retyping the line in error. With the cursor on a new line, type the line number and the complete, corrected line. It is not necessary to physically place the statement in its correct sequence. The computer will replace the statement in memory with the corrected line by line number.

To see a list of the program statements, type LIST. The line in error will be replaced by the new, corrected line. If the program listing is to appear on the printer rather than the screen, type LLIST.

When you are satisfied that the program has been corrected, RUN it again. You may type RUN or LIST as often as desired.

Adding and Removing Lines

Additional lines may be added to the program at any point. If you want a new line to appear between lines 30 and 40, type a new line and give it a number between 30 and 40 (like 35).

Lines may be easily removed from the program by typing the line number and the ENTER/RETURN key. For example, to remove line 40, type:

```
40<ENTER>
```

LIST the program again, and line 40 is gone.

Format of BASIC Statements and Commands

Throughout this text, new statements will be introduced. In order to maintain consistency and to conform to the manuals published by computer vendors, some conventions have been adopted.

1. Words in capital letters are *keywords* and must be typed as they appear. They may be entered in upper- or lowercase, but BASIC will convert them to uppercase.
2. Items appearing in square brackets ([]) are optional.
3. An ellipsis (. . .) indicates an item may be repeated as many times as desired.

The LIST and LLIST Commands—General Form

```
LIST  [line1] [-[line2]]
LLIST [line1] [-[line2]]
```

The LIST and LLIST commands will list the entire program or only the specified lines. LIST displays the program on the screen, while LLIST gives hard-copy output (on the printer).

For both the LIST and LLIST commands, a period (.) may be used to indicate the current line number.

The LIST and LLIST Command—Examples

LIST	List the entire program
LIST 40-100	List lines 40 to 100, inclusive
LIST 40-	List all lines, beginning with 40
LIST -60	List all lines up to and including 60
LLIST	List the entire program on the printer
LLIST 10-.	List all lines from 10 to the current line, on the printer
LLIST 30	List line 30 only, on the printer

Saving and Reloading a Program

Once a program has been completed and is running correctly, what then? You may want to save the program on diskette so that it can be run sometime in the future.

If a program is to be saved, it needs a name. The name chosen will be used to store the program. It will also be used in the future when the program is to be run again.

The rules for naming programs (files) are specified by the DOS (*D*isk *O*perating *S*ystem) being used. Using MS-DOS or CP/M, a program name may be from one to eight characters long, followed by an optional period and up to three-character extension. When the extension is omitted (the recommended practice), BASIC will supply an extension of .BAS.

Sample Filenames for Programs

```
PROGRAM1.BAS      PROG1.BAS
A.PGM             PROG.1
```

The SAVE Command—General Form

```
SAVE "filename"
```

The SAVE command will cause a program to be written on the currently logged disk drive.

The SAVE Command—Examples

```
SAVE "MYPROG"       File will be called MYPROG.BAS
SAVE "PROG1.TST"
SAVE "B:MYPROG"     Saves MYPROG.BAS on drive B
```

In the future, when you want to run the program again, the LOAD command is used.

The LOAD Command—General Form

```
LOAD "filename"
```

The LOAD Command—Examples

```
LOAD "MYPROG"
LOAD "PROG1.TST"
LOAD "B:MYPROG"        Find the program on drive B:
```

When the LOAD command is given, the program will be read from the currently logged disk drive and loaded into the computer's memory. At that point, the program can be LISTed, RUN, or changed.

For both the SAVE and LOAD commands, if the extension is omitted, BASIC will supply the extension .BAS.

Viewing the Files Stored on a Diskette

To see the names of the files stored on a diskette, use the FILES command.

The FILES Command—General Form

```
FILES
```

The FILES Command—Example

```
FILES

AUTOEXEC.BAT   BASIC   .COM   MYPROG   .BAS
PROG1    .TST   NAMES   .DAT   PROGRAM2.BAS
```

Changing or Removing a Program File on the Diskette

The program on diskette is written only when a SAVE command is given. Assume that a program is LOADed and major changes are made to the program in memory. There are now two versions of the program—the one in memory and the one on the disk. The program on the disk will *not* be automatically changed as changes are made to the program in memory. If the new version is to be saved, it must be SAVEd again. Otherwise, the version on the disk will remain unchanged. When you SAVE the new version, you may call it by the same name (it replaces the old one) or give it a new name. If a new name is given, both versions will be on the disk.

To completely remove a program from the disk, use the KILL command.

The KILL Command—General Form

```
KILL  "filename"
```

The KILL Command—Examples

```
KILL  "MYPROG.BAS"
KILL  "PROG1.TST"
KILL  "B:MYPROG.BAS"
```

There is one important difference between the KILL command and the SAVE and LOAD commands. For KILL, the extension *must* be given. If the file was SAVEd without an extension, add .BAS to the name when KILLing it.

There are two additional commands that will come in handy when entering program lines: AUTO and RENUM.

The AUTO Command—General Form

```
AUTO  [beginning line number] [,increment]
```

AUTO will automatically generate the next line number, after each program line has been entered. AUTO entered alone will begin numbering at line 10 and increment by 10. To cancel AUTO mode, hold down the CTRL key and press the BREAK key at the same time (or CTRL-C on some systems).

The AUTO Command—Examples

```
AUTO          Begin with line 10 and increment by 10
AUTO 400,2    Begin with line 400 and increment by 2
AUTO 50       Begin with line 50 and increment by 10
AUTO ,20      Begin with line 10 and increment by 20
```

The RENUM Command—General Form

```
RENUM  [new line number][,old line number][,increment]
```

The RENUM command renumbers the entire program or partial program. When renumbering only part of a program, you may specify the starting line, but not the ending line. The entire program will be renumbered, beginning with the line named.

RENUM by itself will renumber the entire program with line numbers that begin with 10 and are incremented by 10.

The RENUM Command—Examples

RENUM	Renumbers entire program, beginning with line 10, incrementing by 10
RENUM 500,100,2	Gives line number 100 a new number of 500, increments by 2
RENUM 500,100	Gives line number 100 a new number of 500, increments by 10

Beginning a New Program

Each time you begin a new program, it is a good idea to clear the memory of any prior program. This is especially true if you are sharing computers in a lab—at times people leave programs in memory, which can cause problems for your program.

To completely remove any program in memory, use the NEW command.

The NEW Command—General Form

NEW	Clear program from memory

BASIC Statements and Commands

You may have noticed a difference in the terminology between *statements* and *commands*.

BASIC statements are those that are entered with line numbers for later execution. The INPUT, LET, PRINT, LPRINT, and END are examples of BASIC statements.

BASIC commands are entered without line numbers for immediate action. When the command RUN is typed, execution of the program begins immediately.

BASIC Commands Covered in this Chapter

NEW	Clear any prior program from memory
RUN	Begin program execution
LIST	Display the program lines on the screen
LLIST	List the program on the printer
SAVE "filename"	Place the program in memory onto the disk
LOAD "filename"	Read the named program from the disk and place it in memory
FILES	Print a directory of the files on the disk
KILL "filename"	Delete a program from the disk
AUTO	Automatically generate line numbers
RENUM	Renumber a program in memory

BASIC Commands vs. Operating System Commands

It must be noted that all of the commands listed are BASIC commands; that is, you are "talking to" the BASIC interpreter. The BASIC interpreter must be loaded into memory and be active for these commands to take effect. There is another, different set of commands that communicate with the operating system. See appendix A for a list of operating system commands.

Formatting Program Output with the PRINT Statement

Many techniques for formatting computer output will be presented in later chapters. For now, there is one simple method of controlling output placement with PRINT and LPRINT statements.

The PRINT and LPRINT Statements—General Form

```
line number  PRINT  items to print
line number  LPRINT  items to print
```

The only difference between the PRINT and LPRINT statements is that PRINT displays its output on the display screen, while LPRINT places output on the printer (assuming one is connected to the computer). All comments about PRINT also apply to LPRINT. The "items to print" may be literals (the actual characters to print) or variables. They may be separated by semicolons or commas (and in some cases, spaces).

The PRINT and LPRINT Statements—Examples

```
                   literal            variable
10 PRINT "THE LENGTH IS"; LENGTH
50 LPRINT "LENGTH", "WIDTH", "AREA"
80 PRINT A;B;C
```

Vertical Spacing

To achieve vertical spacing in computer output, the PRINT statement may be used without any "items to print." This effectively prints blank lines and places the output in the desired location.

```
200    PRINT "TOP LINE"
210    PRINT
220    PRINT
230    PRINT "FOURTH LINE"
RUN
TOP LINE


FOURTH LINE
```

Horizontal Spacing—Semicolons and Commas

In the sample program shown earlier, both the literal "THE AREA IS" and the value of the variable AREA were printed.

```
50    PRINT "THE AREA IS"; AREA
```

Any mix of literals and variables can be included on a print statement, as long as each literal is enclosed in quotation marks.

```
50    PRINT "THE AREA OF A ROOM"; LENGTH; "FEET BY"; WDTH;
          "FEET IS"; AREA; "SQUARE FEET"
```

When RUN with this statement, the example program would produce this output:

```
RUN
? 20
? 30
THE AREA OF A ROOM 20 FEET BY 30 FEET IS 600 SQUARE FEET
```

Placing semicolons between elements to print cause no extra spaces to appear between the items.

```
100    PRINT "HELLO"; "MARTHA"
RUN
HELLOMARTHA
```

If a space is desired between literals, a space may be included within the literal.

```
120    PRINT "HELLO "; "MARTHA"
RUN
HELLO MARTHA
```

or

```
140    PRINT "HELLO   "; "  HARRY"
RUN
HELLO    HARRY
```

There is one exception to this spacing rule. When the element to print is a number (variable), spaces are left between the items. When printing numeric values, BASIC leaves one space after each number and allows one print position for the sign of the number. If the number is negative, the position is taken by the minus sign. When the number is positive, the sign is suppressed, and a blank space precedes the numeric output.

```
200    LET TEAM = 6
210    PRINT "TEAM NUMBER"; TEAM
RUN
TEAM NUMBER 6
              ↑
              ⋮
            Space for sign
```

Numeric values may also be printed directly, without the use of variables.

```
310    PRINT "TEAM NUMBER"; 6
RUN
TEAM NUMBER 6
```

To print a series of numbers:

```
400    PRINT 2; 4; 6; 8; 10
RUN
 2   4   6   8   10
```

These numbers printed with two spaces between them—one for the sign and one for the trailing space supplied by BASIC. Now try two more examples:

```
500    PRINT 2; 4; 6; 8        600    PRINT 2; 4; 6; 8;
510    PRINT 10; 12            610    PRINT 10; 12
RUN                           RUN
 2   4   6   8                 2   4   6   8   10   12
 10   12
```

Can you see the difference? Notice the trailing semicolon on line 600. After printing 2 4 6 8, the internal print pointer stays on the same line. So when the next PRINT is executed, the 10 appears right after the 8.

Using Print Zones for Spacing

Spacing on the line can also be controlled by taking advantage of the *print zones*, which BASIC has defined as fourteen columns wide. Using a comma between elements causes the internal print pointer to move to the start of the next zone before printing. When the item to print is a literal, it will be printed at the start of the zone. If the item to print is a numeric value, one space will precede the number (for the sign). Figure 1.8 is a print zone layout.

```
700    PRINT "ONE", "TWO", "THREE"
710    PRINT 1, 2, 3
RUN
ONE            TWO            THREE
 1              2              3
```

A comma may also be used at the end of a PRINT line. This causes the internal print pointer to move to the start of the next print zone. The next item to print will appear on that same line.

```
800    PRINT "HOW", "NOW",
810    PRINT "BROWN", "COW"
RUN
HOW            NOW            BROWN          COW
```

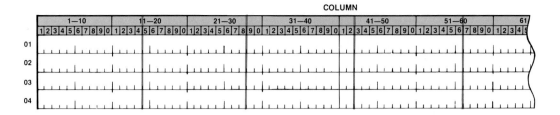

Figure 1.8
Print zones. Each zone is
fourteen columns wide.

Print zones function in a manner similar to the TAB key on a typewriter. It advances a variable number of spaces to the next preset position. This allows for aligning columns of data.

```
900    PRINT ,"SOCKS", "BRAVES"
910    PRINT
920    PRINT ,"ALEXANDER", "TOM"
930    PRINT ,"JOE", "KENNY"
940    PRINT ,"PASCUAL", "KIM"
RUN
                 SOCKS          BRAVES

                 ALEXANDER      TOM
                 JOE            KENNY
                 PASCUAL        KIM
```

There are five print zones defined on the standard eighty-character line. If a command is given to advance to a zone beyond the end of a line, printing "wraps around"; that is, it advances to the next line and continues using the print zones.

```
1000    PRINT "A", "B", "C", "D", "E", "F", "G"
RUN
A               B               C               D               E
F               G
```

Feedback

What will print for each of these program segments? Try to determine the results by hand, then enter them into the computer to verify your results.

1. `100 PRINT "HALF A LOAF ";`
    `110 PRINT "IS BETTER THAN NONE"`

2. `200 PRINT "HALF,", "MY EYE"`

3. `300 PRINT "HAWKS";0, "DOVES";0`

4. `400 PRINT 1,2,3,4,5,6,7,8,9,10`

5. `500 PRINT 1,`
    `510 PRINT 2,`
    `520 PRINT 3,`
    `530 PRINT 4,`
    `540 PRINT 5,`
    `550 PRINT 6,`
    `560 PRINT 7,`
    `570 PRINT 8,`
    `580 PRINT 9,`
    `590 PRINT 10`

Find the syntax errors in the following program segments.

6. `10 RAM PROGRAM TO PRINT MY NAME`
    `20 PRINT "MY NAME IS JOHN JOHNSON"`

7. `50 ' PROGRAM TO PRINT THE NUMBERS FROM 1 TO 5`
    `60 PRINT 1: 2: 3: 4: 5`

```
8.  100 REM INPUT AND PRINT A NUMBER
    110 INPUT 1
    120 PRINT 1

9.  200 REM INPUT, PROCESS, OUTPUT
    210 INPUT ANUM
    220 LET ANUM = ANUM * 2
    230 PT ANUM
    240 END
```

Each of these program segments has at least one logic error, since the program will not do what the remarks claim. How can each error be corrected?

```
10.  300 REM INPUT AND PRINT A PERSON'S AGE
     310 INPUT A
     320 PRINT AGE
     330 END

11.  350 REM PRINT THE NUMBERS FROM ONE TO THREE
     360 PRINT ONE; TWO; THREE

12.  400 REM PRINT NUMBERS, ALL ON THE SAME LINE
     410 PRINT 2,4,6,8,10,12,14,16,18,20

13.  500 REM CALCULATE AND PRINT THE SUM OF TWO NUMBERS
     510 INPUT NUM1
     520 INPUT NUM2
     530 PRINT SUM
```

Summary

1. The computer is a tool for solving problems.
2. A computer needs instructions to be given in the correct sequence in order to do any task.
3. Software is the instructions the machine is given to follow.
4. Computer hardware is the physical components, such as the keyboard, screen, printer, disk drives, and internal circuitry.
5. The reason for employing a computer for a task is to produce some desired output. A computer program (software) consists of the instructions necessary to convert inputs into the desired outputs.

Input → Processing → Output

6. The hardware of the computer includes input devices, output devices, storage (or memory), the CPU (Central Processing Unit), and assorted circuitry.
7. The CPU includes the ALU (Arithmetic and Logic Unit) and the control unit. The ALU executes the instructions, doing the arithmetic and logical functions. The control unit coordinates and directs the execution of instructions.
8. Computer main storage is also called primary storage, internal storage, or RAM (Random Access Memory).
9. Main storage must hold the program being executed and the data being operated upon.
10. A larger main storage size may be needed to store larger programs.
11. Main storage is measured in bytes, where one byte equates to one character. One K is 1024 bytes of storage. The amount of RAM is generally given in the number of K bytes, such as 640 K bytes.
12. Most main storage is volatile, which means that the contents are lost when the power source is removed.
13. Secondary storage is nonvolatile and can be used for long-term storage of data.
14. Secondary storage is also called auxiliary storage or external storage.
15. The most popular forms of secondary storage are magnetic disk and magnetic tape.

16. ROM (*Read Only Memory*) is hardware that has software permanently stored inside.
17. Input devices include the keyboard, optical readers, scanners, punched cards, the joystick, mouse, magnetic disk, and magnetic tape.
18. Output devices are used to present computer results in a human readable form.
19. Output devices include the display screen, printers, plotters, speakers, card punches, magnetic disk, and magnetic tape.
20. Software can be broken into two types: (1) operating system software, and (2) applications software.
21. Applications software includes all programs written to meet the needs of the end user, such as accounting programs, games, word processing, applications in business, science, medicine, law, and research.
22. Operating system software includes the *Disk Operating System* (DOS) and utility programs designed to aid in the development and use of applications programs.
23. The most popular operating system for microcomputers is MS-DOS from Microsoft (which is also IBM's PC-DOS).
24. Operating system utility programs are available to aid in the development, storage, use, and maintenance of applications software.
25. Instructions to the computer must be translated to machine language (or machine code) before the instructions can be executed. The translation is done by a compiler or interpreter.
26. With an interpreter, program statements are translated and then executed, one at a time. However, with a compiler, the entire program is translated before any statements are executed.
27. There are many programming languages available. Some of the most popular are BASIC, FORTRAN, COBOL, Pascal, C, RPG, and Assembly language.
28. Many different versions of BASIC are in use, some offering more features than others. This book will concentrate on Microsoft BASIC.
29. BASIC may be either interpreted or compiled. Generally, program development is done with an interpreter. If execution speed is needed, the completed program may be compiled.
30. BASIC program statements must each have a line number. The line numbers are used to indicate the sequence of instructions and must be in ascending order.
31. The REM statement in BASIC allows for remarks within the program. The primary purpose of REMs is for program documentation and to make the program easier for humans to understand. REMs are not translated to machine language.
32. The general pattern of computer programs is

Input $\longrightarrow$ Processing $\longrightarrow$ Output

The BASIC statement presented for the input operation was INPUT. The statement to accomplish the processing was the LET statement. The program output was performed by the PRINT statement. The LPRINT may be used for output on the printer, rather than the display screen.
33. The steps in program development are:
   a. Clearly state the problem, in terms of its output, input, and processing.
   b. Plan the program logic with a flowchart, hierarchy chart, or pseudocode.
   c. Code the program.
   d. Key the program into the computer.
   e. Test and debug the program.
   f. Complete the documentation.
34. There is a set of standard flowcharting symbols used for drawing a pictorial representation of the program logic.

35. A flowchart is used for planning purposes and is drawn before the program is coded. Flowcharts are also used to document completed programs.
36. Pseudocode is English statements that are "like code." In writing pseudocode, the programmer need not be concerned with language syntax rules or flowchart symbols.
37. A hierarchy chart resembles an organization chart and shows the organization of program functions.
38. Once a BASIC program has been planned, coded, and entered into the computer, it can be executed with the RUN command.
39. The two types of program errors that may occur are syntax errors and logic errors.
40. Syntax errors are caused by incorrectly using the elements of the language.
41. When there are no syntax errors but the program output is incorrect, the cause is a logic error.
42. Program errors are called bugs; locating and correcting the errors is called debugging the program.
43. The LIST command prints a program listing on the display screen; the LLIST sends the listing to the printer.
44. Programs may be saved on a diskette with the SAVE command.
45. A program saved on diskette may be reloaded into memory with the LOAD command.
46. To remove a program from diskette, use the KILL command.
47. The AUTO command will automatically number program lines.
48. The RENUM command will cause the program in memory to be renumbered.
49. The NEW command clears any previous program from the computer's memory.
50. BASIC *statements* are entered with line numbers for later execution. BASIC *commands* are entered without line numbers for immediate execution.
51. The PRINT and LPRINT statements can print combinations of literals and variables.
52. Vertical spacing can be achieved by printing blank lines, that is, including a PRINT statement with no items named for printing.
53. Horizontal spacing on a line can be controlled by the use of semicolons and commas between the items to print.
54. A semicolon between elements on a PRINT statement will cause the items to be printed next to each other. The internal print pointer remains in the position immediately following the last item printed.
55. A comma between elements to print causes the internal print pointer to move to the next print zone before the next item is printed.
56. Each print zone is fourteen positions wide.

Programming Exercises

For each of the programming assignments, plan the program with a flowchart or pseudocode. Include REMs indicating your name, the exercise number, the date, and the purpose of the program.

1.1. Write a program to produce the following output. Use the print zones for the columns of data.

```
TEAM RECORD

NAME            AGE

PATRICIA         18
RONALD           20
MARIA            21
TIEN             19
KENNETH          22
```

1.2. Write a program that will output the following information: your name, address, major, and reason for studying BASIC programming. Include print statements for the screen and printer, and nicely format your output, using both semicolons and commas for spacing.

1.3. Write a program that will produce address labels for you and two other people. The labels will be printed "three up," which means that the three labels are next to each other, horizontally. All three are printed at the same time. Place your own name on the leftmost label, and use the name of two friends or acquaintances for each of the others.

Output must appear on the screen as well as the printer.

SAMPLE PROGRAM OUTPUT:

```
JERRY JAMISON         GEORGE GARNER         SILVIA SAUCEDO
127 CANYON DRIVE,     881 ELGIN COURT,      410 E. GLADSTONE,
CHINO, CA 91710       ONTARIO, CA 91764     WALNUT,CA 91789
```

1.4. Write a program that will input three numbers and print the sum and average of the numbers with appropriate labels. The program should work for *any* three numbers. Run the program several times with different numbers for each run.

Use LPRINT to show the output on the printer as well as the screen.

1.5. Write a program with a title and headings to print your three favorite TV programs, the day of the week they air, and the time they air. Use print zones for the columns of data.

1.6. Write a program to produce the following output using print zones.

```
    PERFECT PICTURE INC.
    STORE #        SALES GOAL

    _____        _____

    LA-021         4525
    LA-023         3121
    LA-151         3769
    LA-221         2987
```

1.7. Write a program to produce the following output using print zones.

```
THE PROGRAM THAT
            PRODUCED THIS OUTPUT
                        SHOWS THAT I KNOW HOW
            TO EFFECTIVELY USE
PRINT ZONES.
```

1.8. Write a program that will compute gallons per hour of gas used on a trip.

INPUT: The number of gallons used and the number of hours the trip took will be input from the keyboard.
OUTPUT: Print the number of gallons used per hour with an appropriate label.
PROCESS: Calculate gallons per hour = gallons/hours.

1.9. Write a program to convert pints into quarts.

INPUT: The number of pints will be input from the keyboard.
OUTPUT: Print the calculated number of quarts.
PROCESS: Calculate quarts = pints / 2.

1.10. Write a program to convert miles to kilometers.

INPUT: The number of miles will be input from the keyboard.
OUTPUT: Print the computed number of kilometers.
PROCESS: Calculate kilometers = miles * 1.61

2

Modular Programs with Calculations and Strings

LET Statement
INPUT Statement
GOSUB Statement
RETURN Statement

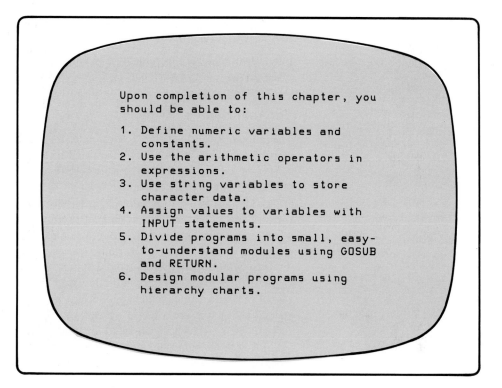

```
Upon completion of this chapter, you
should be able to:

1. Define numeric variables and
   constants.
2. Use the arithmetic operators in
   expressions.
3. Use string variables to store
   character data.
4. Assign values to variables with
   INPUT statements.
5. Divide programs into small, easy-
   to-understand modules using GOSUB
   and RETURN.
6. Design modular programs using
   hierarchy charts.
```

Numeric Variables

As you saw in chapter 1, numeric values can be referred to by a name. These names are called *variable names,* since the actual number referred to is changeable. Picture each variable as a scratch pad with a name. Different values can be placed on the scratch pad. In this example, the variable (or scratch pad) is called AMT.

```
10   LET AMT = 100
```

AMT
100

After execution of this statement, AMT has a value of 100. You could print the value of AMT, use AMT in a calculation, or change AMT to any other chosen numeric value.

```
20   LET AMT = -1.25
```

AMT
-1.25

Line 20 will change the value of AMT to −1.25. The effect of the LET statement is to assign a value to a variable.

Variable Names

The language of BASIC has a set of rules for naming variables. In addition, there are naming guidelines dictated by good programming practice.

The naming rules in Microsoft BASIC are more flexible than for most versions of BASIC. In the more restrictive rules of "standard" BASIC, variable names can be a maximum of two **characters** in length, where the first character must be a letter of the alphabet. The second character, if present, must be a numeric digit (0–9). This allows for names like A, B, X1, X2, X3. This rule explains the look of many BASIC programs with unintelligible variable names.

In Microsoft BASIC, variable names may be as long as desired. However, only the first forty characters are actually used. The first character must be a letter. The rest of the name can be made up of letters, numeric digits, and the period (.). No other special characters are allowed. (Later you will learn about the use of some characters—$ % ! #—that have a special meaning in BASIC.)

A variable name cannot be a **reserved word** (see appendix F for a list of reserved words), but a reserved word may be embedded in a variable name. Thus LET is not a valid variable name, but LETTUCE is acceptable. Some valid variable names are:

```
A                          INTEREST
TOTAL                      TYPE1
RATE.OF.PAY                R2D2
NUMBER.OF.PIECES.OF.PIE
```

Invalid variable names:

```
1TOT  (must begin with a letter)
A*    (special characters are not allowed)
END   (reserved word)
```

Good programming practice dictates that meaningful names should be used for variables. When reading a program, names such as RATE, DISCOUNT, TAX, and BONUS are descriptive and easy to understand. Names such as A, X, Y, D1, and T2 are much harder to decipher. Anyone who has attempted to read and to understand a program written by someone else (or even their own program after a lapse of a few months) will appreciate the value of descriptive variable names. Often, those who employ programmers prohibit the use of single character variable names.

Feedback

Which of the following is/are valid numeric variable names? For any that are invalid, give the reason.

```
PORCUPINE.PIE        ETC...          2A
COUNT#1              A2              PRINT
```

Numeric Constants

The actual numbers assigned to variables are called **constants.** In the example

```
10   LET AMT = 100
```

AMT is the variable, and 100 is the constant.

Constants are formed with combinations of the numeric digits (0–9) and an optional decimal point. An operational sign ($+$ or $-$) may precede the number, but it is optional for positive numbers. No other characters are allowed in constants, which rules out the use of commas, dollar signs, or percent signs. Examples of valid numeric constants are

25	$+47$	$+47.0$
$-.00025$	-47	$+47.$
2500.25	-47.5	

Examples of invalid numeric constants are

25%	(no special symbols are allowed)
1,250.50	(no commas are allowed)
\$1.25	(no special symbols)
15$-$	(the sign must precede the number)

LET Statements

You have seen several examples of numbers being assigned to variables. In the example

```
10   LET AMT = 100
```

the constant 100 is assigned to the variable AMT. LET statements always operate from right to left; that is, the value appearing on the right side of the equal sign is assigned to the variable on the left of the equal sign. It is often helpful to read the equal sign as "be replaced by." The example above would read, "Let the value stored in AMT be replaced by 100."

The equal sign used in the LET statement does *not* imply equality. The operation indicated by the equal sign is actually *assignment.* A perfectly valid assignment statement is LET $X = X + 1$. If the equal sign here actually meant "is equal to," it would be difficult to find a value of X to satisfy the equation.

The LET Statement—General Form

```
line number LET  variable = variable
line number LET  variable = constant
line number LET  variable = arithmetic expression
```

LET statements must always have a variable name to the left of the equal sign. However, the value on the right side of the equal sign may be another variable, a constant, or an arithmetic expression.

The LET Statement—Examples

```
50 LET PROFIT = SALES
60 LET BALANCE = 10000
70 LET SUM = NUM1 + NUM2 + NUM3
80 LET TOTAL = TOTAL + AMT
```

In line 50, the current value of the variable SALES is assigned to the variable PROFIT.

In line 60, the constant 10000 is assigned to the variable BALANCE.

In line 70, the expression on the right of the equal sign is evaluated (that is, the *current* values of NUM1, NUM2, and NUM3 are added together), and the result is assigned to the variable SUM.

Line 80 will take the current value of TOTAL, add AMT, and assign the results to TOTAL. The effect is to add AMT to TOTAL.

Note: The word LET is optional. The example LET statements may be written:

```
50   PROFIT = SALES
60   BALANCE = 10000
70   SUM = NUM1 + NUM2 + NUM3
80   TOTAL = TOTAL + AMT
```

Arithmetic Expressions

In the preceding example, NUM1 + NUM2 + NUM3 is called an *expression*. Expressions are formed with combinations of variables and constants using **arithmetic operators.**

Arithmetic Operators

It is important to determine the order in which operations will be performed. Consider the expression 3 + 4 * 2. What is the result? If the addition is done first, the result is 14. However, if the multiplication is done first, the result is 11.

The **hierarchy of operations** or *order of precedence* in arithmetic expressions (refer to table 2.1), from highest to lowest is

1. exponentiation
2. multiplication and division
3. addition and subtraction

In the previous example, the multiplication is done before the addition, and the result is 11. To change the order of evaluation, use parentheses: (3 + 4) * 2 will yield 14 as the result. One set of parentheses may be used inside another set. In that case, the parentheses are said to be **nested.** For example:

```
((SCORE1 + SCORE2 + SCORE3)/3) * 1.2
```

Extra parentheses can always be used for clarity. The expressions 2 * COST * RATE and (2 * COST) * RATE are equivalent, but the second may be more easily understood.

Table 2.1.
Arithmetic operators.

Operator	Meaning	Example	Explanation
+	addition	A + B	add together the current value of A and the current value of B
−	subtraction	A − B	subtract the value of B from the value of A
*	multiplication	A * B	multiply the value of A times the value of B
/	division	A / B	divide the value of A by the value of B
$\wedge$	exponentiation	A $\wedge$ B	raise the value of A to the power of B

When there are multiple operations at the same level (such as multiplication and division), the operations are performed from left to right. The example: 8 / 4 * 2 yields 4 as its result, not 1. The first operation is 8 / 4, then 2 * 2 is performed.

The process of evaluation of an expression is done in this order:

1. All operations within parentheses are evaluated first. If there are multiple operations within the parentheses, the operations are performed according to the rules of precedence.
2. All exponentiation is done. If there are multiple exponentiation operations, they are performed from left to right.
3. All multiplication and division is done. Multiple operations will be performed from left to right.
4. All addition and subtraction is done from left to right.

Although the precedence of operations in BASIC is the same as in algebra, take note of one important difference: there are no implied operations in BASIC. The following expressions would be valid in mathematics, but they are not valid in BASIC:

Mathematic Notation	Equivalent BASIC Expression
2A	2 * A
3 (X + Y)	3 * (X + Y)
(X + Y) (X - Y)	(X + Y) * (X - Y)

A word about spacing. The spaces between the operators and variables are optional. The expression 2*A is equivalent to 2 * A as well as   2   *   A.

Rounding and Functions

BASIC supplies many **functions** that may also be used in expressions. The INT function is used for a variety of purposes, including rounding numbers. (See chapter 10 for a list of more functions.) The purpose of the INT function is to find the largest integer (whole number). For a positive number, the effect is to truncate (chop off) all digits to the right of the decimal point, thus making a whole number (or integer). (For the effect on negative numbers, see the discussion in chapter 10.) This example is how a program for finding the largest integer would look:

```
10   REM MAKE AN INTEGER OF A DECIMAL FRACTION
20   LET FRAC = 1.995
30   LET WHOLE = INT(FRAC)
40   PRINT WHOLE
RUN
1
```

The INT function can be used as a tool to round to as many decimal places as desired. When rounding a number, look to the next digit to the right of the desired place value. If the digit to the right is 5 or more, increase the digit immediately to its left by 1. If that right digit is not as large as 5, drop it and all digits to its right. Note these examples of rounding:

2.82549 rounded to the nearest whole number is 3
        rounded to the nearest tenth is   2.8
        rounded to the nearest hundredth is   2.83
        rounded to the nearest thousandth is 2.825
        rounded to the nearest ten-thousandth 2.8255

These are the steps necessary to round a number using the INT function:

1. Move the decimal point to the correct location (with multiplication).
2. Add .5 to the number.
3. Truncate all digits to the right of the decimal point, using the INT function.
4. Move the decimal point back to the starting location (with division).

This is how to round 2.82549 to the nearest hundredth using the four steps.

1. `2.82549 * 100 = 282.549`
2. `282.549 + .5 = 283.049`
3. `INT(283.049) = 283`
4. `283/100 = 2.83`

The program to round 2.82549 would be similar to this:

```
10   REM ROUND A NUMBER
20   LET NUM = 2.82549
30   LET NUM1 = INT(NUM + .5)              'NEAREST WHOLE NUMBER
40   LET NUM2 = INT(NUM * 10 + .5) / 10    'NEAREST TENTH
50   LET NUM3 = INT(NUM * 100 + .5)/ 100   'NEAREST HUNDREDTH
60   LET NUM4 = INT(NUM * 1000 + .5)/1000  'NEAREST THOUSANDTH
70   LET NUM5 = INT(NUM * 10000 +.5)/10000 'NEAREST TEN-
                                                   THOUSANDTH
80   PRINT NUM1, NUM2, NUM3, NUM4, NUM5
RUN
3          2.8        2.83       2.825      2.8255
```

Feedback

What will be the result of evaluation of these expressions?

X	Y	Z
2	4	3

1. `X + Y ^ 2`
2. `8 / Y / X`
3. `X * (X + 1)`
4. `X * X + 1`
5. `Y ^ X + Z * 2`
6. `Y ^ (X + Z) * 2`
7. `(Y ^ X) + Z * 2`
8. `((Y ^ X) + Z) * 2`

Which of the following are valid statements? For those that are invalid, give the reason.

9. `100 LET AVG = (NUM1 + NUM2 + NUM3) / 3`
10. `110 LET 10 = TEN`
11. `120 LET MINE = YOURS`
12. `130 LET COUNT = COUNT + 1`
13. `140 LET APPLES + ORANGES = SALAD`
14. `150 LET ANS = NUM(NUM − 1)`
15. `160 LET RESULT = (X+Y)/((X-Y)^2)`

String Variables

In addition to storing numeric values in variables, strings of alphabetic characters, special characters, and digits can also be stored. Variables that store alphanumeric data such as this are called *string variables* and are named differently from numeric variables.

String variable names must have a dollar sign as the last (rightmost) character of the variable name. The remaining rules for string variable names are the same as those for numeric variables. Following is a summary of naming rules for string variables. Variable names:

1. must be terminated by a dollar sign ($).
2. may be any length, with only the first forty characters being significant.
3. may use combinations of letters, digits, and periods.

4. must begin with a letter.
5. must not be a reserved word such as LET or PRINT. Using LET$ as a variable name will cause a syntax error.

Values may be assigned to string variables with the LET statement.

```
10   LET NAM$ = "PORKY DUCK"
20   PRINT NAM$
RUN
PORKY DUCK
```

One string variable may also be assigned to another string variable.

```
60   LET LAST$ = FIRST$
```

String Literals

In the above example, "PORKY DUCK" is called a *string literal*. String literals are also sometimes called *string constants* or *quoted strings*. When assigning a string literal to a string variable, quotation marks must enclose the literal. Valid string literals may be up to 255 characters and include combinations of alphabetic characters, special characters, blank spaces, and numeric digits.

```
50    LET DAY$ = "MONDAY"
100   LET CODE$ = "#402"
200   LET CURSE$ = "%&#*/%!"
300   LET HEADING$ = "  ACCOUNT NUMBER          NAME "
500   LET TITLE$ = " M O N T H L Y    R E P O R T "
600   LET ACCT.NUM$ = "0550"
```

String literals are not stored in the same way that numeric constants are stored. Notice in line 600 above that the string literal is all numeric. It is not possible to do any arithmetic operations with ACCT.NUM$, and when printed, the left zero will not be suppressed. When a string literal is stored, the characters are stored one at a time, as individually coded characters. So "0550" is stored as a coded zero, five, five, zero. When the numeric constant 0550 is stored in a numeric variable, the value is actually five hundred fifty.

```
600   LET ACCT.NUM$ = "0550"
610   LET ACCT.NUM  = 0550
620   PRINT ACCT.NUM$
630   PRINT ACCT.NUM
RUN
0550
 550
```

Feedback

Determine which are valid string variable names and which are invalid. For the invalid names, give the reason. Try them on the computer to see which ones will generate error messages.

1. A$
2. PAY.CLASS$
3. $PERSON
4. ANSWER1$
5. ANSWER$1
6. PRINT$

Which of these are valid statements? Give the reason for any which are invalid.

7. 500 LET PAY.CLASS = "M"
8. 510 LET SSNO$ = 550-51-5257
9. 520 LET SIGN$ = "$"
10. 530 LET "SAMMY" = PERSON$

INPUT Statements

Using LET statements to assign values to variables is a useful tool. However, if the data value must be changed, the LET statement in the program must be changed. In actual practice, changing the program for each set of values is cumbersome. BASIC provides a powerful statement that allows values to be entered during program execution and to be placed into program variables.

The INPUT Statement—Elementary Form

```
line number INPUT variable name
```

The INPUT Statement—Examples

```
100    INPUT RATE
200    INPUT ANSWER$
```

When an INPUT statement is encountered during the RUN, execution pauses, and the program waits for the data to be typed at the keyboard. A question mark is displayed on the screen as a signal that an input is expected. Any valid constant can be typed in response to the input prompt. The value keyed in will be assigned to the variable named on the INPUT statement.

```
100    INPUT RATE
```

When this statement is run, the program will print a question mark and pause, awaiting entry of a numeric constant.

```
RUN
?          (execution paused)
```

When the **user** enters a constant and presses the RETURN key, that value is placed in the variable RATE.

```
100    INPUT RATE
RUN
? .08 ◄——keyed by user
```

RATE
.08

The INPUT statement can also be used to input string data. The variable named must be a string variable. The data entered by the user may optionally be enclosed with quotation marks.

```
200    INPUT MONTH$
RUN
? JUNE ◄——keyed by user
```

MONTH$
JUNE

Prompting INPUT

Whenever data input is expected during the run of the program, the user must be informed what to enter. Having only a question mark appear each time data are requested could be confusing and perhaps even infuriating. One way to **prompt** the user for the correct input is to place a PRINT statement immediately before the INPUT statement.

```
90     PRINT "ENTER THE RATE OF INTEREST"
100    INPUT RATE
RUN
ENTER THE RATE OF INTEREST
? .08 ◄——keyed by user
```

If it is desirable to place the question mark generated by the INPUT statement on the same line as the prompt message, a semicolon can be placed after the PRINT statement.

```
90    PRINT "ENTER THE RATE OF INTEREST";
100   INPUT RATE
RUN
ENTER THE RATE OF INTEREST?  .08 ◄──keyed by user
                            ┃___placed by INPUT
```

It is important that the type (numeric or string) of the data entered be the same as the type of the variable named. More specifically, if inputting into a numeric variable, a valid numeric constant must be entered. If an invalid response is entered, the unfriendly message REDO FROM START will appear.

Since numeric digits are valid characters in a string literal, a number *can* be entered into a string variable.

Invalid INPUT into
a Numeric Variable
```
300 INPUT TYPE
RUN
? CASHEW
REDO FROM START
```

Valid INPUT into a
Numeric or String Variable
```
400 INPUT DEPT.NUM
410 PRINT DEPT.NUM
RUN
? 010
  10

500 INPUT DEPT.NUM$
510 PRINT DEPT.NUM$
RUN
? 010
  010
```

Example Program

Program Listing

```
110 REM CALCULATE SIMPLE INTEREST ON A DEPOSIT
120 REM
130 REM          VARIABLES USED:
140 REM
150 REM          RATE            RATE OF INTEREST, DECIMAL FORM
160 REM          DEPOSIT         AMOUNT DEPOSITED
170 REM          YEARS           LENGTH OF TIME DEPOSIT DRAWS
                                 INTEREST
180 REM          INTEREST        SIMPLE INTEREST FOR PERIOD
190 REM          VALUE           ENDING VALUE OF DEPOSIT
200 REM

400 REM ************** DATA INPUT *******************
410 PRINT "ENTER THE INTEREST RATE, IN DECIMAL FORM";
420 INPUT RATE
430 PRINT "ENTER THE AMOUNT OF DEPOSIT";
440 INPUT DEPOSIT
450 PRINT "ENTER THE NUMBER OF YEARS";
460 INPUT YEARS

500 REM ************** CALCULATIONS *****************
510 LET INTEREST = DEPOSIT * RATE * YEARS
520 LET VALUE = DEPOSIT + INTEREST

600 REM ************** PROGRAM OUTPUT ***************
610 PRINT
620 PRINT
630 PRINT "THE INTEREST IS        ";INTEREST
640 PRINT "THE ENDING BALANCE IS  ";VALUE
650 END
```

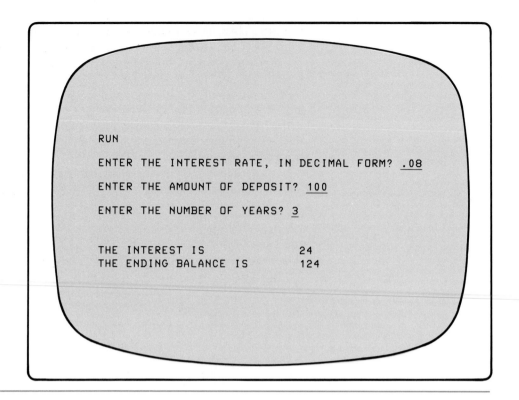

```
RUN

ENTER THE INTEREST RATE, IN DECIMAL FORM? .08

ENTER THE AMOUNT OF DEPOSIT? 100

ENTER THE NUMBER OF YEARS? 3


THE INTEREST IS          24
THE ENDING BALANCE IS    124
```

The example program can be rerun as often as needed with different values substituted for the deposit, rate, and number of years.

Combining Literals with INPUT Statements

INPUT statements in Microsoft BASIC can also be used to print a literal message before the INPUT occurs. This would allow combining the PRINT and INPUT statements from the example program and simplify the programming of INPUT statements.

```
220 INPUT "ENTER INTEREST RATE"; RATE
::
::
RUN

ENTER INTEREST RATE? ____ ◄—value placed here will
                              be assigned to RATE
```

When this statement is executed, the message ENTER INTEREST RATE will first be printed, then the question mark. Execution will pause awaiting keyboard entry of the value to be placed in the variable RATE.

As a further variation on this same statement, it is possible to suppress the question mark, which is printed to indicate that input is requested. By using a comma in the INPUT statement in place of the semicolon, the message will be printed and INPUT occur without the question mark.

```
220  INPUT "ENTER INTEREST RATE ", RATE
::                              ┃_____notice, extra space
::
RUN

ENTER INTEREST RATE ____  ◄—value placed here will
                              be placed in RATE
                   ┃_____notice, no question mark
```

The extra blank space included at the end of the literal prompt in line 220 is helpful but not required. When the prompt line is printed on the CRT, the cursor remains at the space immediately following the last character printed. Then when the user begins to key in the response, it will appear run together with the prompt message. The blank space included in the literal prompt will separate the words and improve the appearance of the input dialogue.

The INPUT Statement—General Form

```
line number  INPUT  [;] ["literal prompt";] variable name(s)
line number  INPUT  [;] ["literal prompt",] variable name(s)
```

The INPUT Statement—Examples

```
60 INPUT "ENTER RATE, DEPOSIT AMOUNT, AND NUMBER OF YEARS,
   SEPARATED BY COMMAS ", RATE, DEPOSIT, YEARS

80 INPUT "WHO ARE YOU"; NAM$

90 INPUT "HOW MANY DO YOU WANT"; NUM

100 INPUT; "ENTER RATE ", RATE
```

Line 60 in the example shows one INPUT to enter values for three variables. When the program is run, the user must take great care to enter three constants, to enter in the correct order, and to separate by commas. BASIC is not forgiving of an inexperienced user. The REDO FROM START message is printed in response to too few constants, too many constants, illegal characters embedded in the constants, or missing commas. Since one of the objectives in writing good programs is to make programs clear and easy to use (user friendly), it is obvious that multiple variables on the INPUT statement will only be used in exceptional circumstances.

When multiple variable names are placed on an INPUT statement, commas are required in two separate locations. The programmer must separate the variable names by commas. The user, when running the program, must separate the individual data items with commas.

```
60   INPUT "ENTER RATE, DEPOSIT AMOUNT, AND NUMBER OF YEARS,
     SEPARATED BY COMMAS ", RATE, DEPOSIT, YEARS
::
::
RUN

ENTER RATE, DEPOSIT AMOUNT, AND NUMBER OF YEARS, SEPARATED
BY COMMAS .08, 100, 3    ←—all three entered by user
```

RATE		DEPOSIT		YEARS
.08		100		3

Another technique is available for INPUT statements, as shown in the example line 100.

```
100   INPUT; "ENTER RATE ", RATE
         ↑_____ extra semicolon
```

The extra semicolon in line 100 immediately following the word INPUT serves the same function as a semicolon placed at the end of a PRINT statement; that is, after the input (or print) is completed, no carriage return or linefeed is sent. The next item to be printed will print on the same line, immediately following the last item printed.

Example Program

The use of INPUT statements can greatly increase the flexibility of programs. Each run of the program can have different values for the variables.

Program Listing

```
110 REM PROGRAM TO CALCULATE THE AVERAGE OF THREE TEST SCORES
120 REM
130 REM          VARIABLES USED:
140 REM
150 REM          STUDENT$          NAME OF STUDENT
160 REM          TEST1             SCORE FOR TEST 1
170 REM          TEST2             SCORE FOR TEST 2
180 REM          TEST3             SCORE FOR TEST 3
190 REM          AVG               TEST AVERAGE
200 REM

400 REM ************** DATA INPUT ***************************
410 INPUT "ENTER STUDENT NAME  ", STUDENT$
420 INPUT "SCORE FOR TEST 1    ", TEST1
430 INPUT "SCORE FOR TEST 2    ", TEST2
440 INPUT "SCORE FOR TEST 3    ", TEST3

500 REM *************** CALCULATIONS ************************
510 LET AVG = (TEST1 + TEST2 + TEST3) / 3

600 REM *************** PROGRAM OUTPUT **********************
610 PRINT
620 PRINT "THE AVERAGE FOR "; STUDENT$; " IS"; AVG
630 END
```

Sample Program Output

```
RUN

ENTER STUDENT NAME  GEORGE PORGE
SCORE FOR TEST 1    100
SCORE FOR TEST 2    80
SCORE FOR TEST 3    90

THE AVERAGE FOR GEORGE PORGE IS 90
```

Without changing the program, the user can rerun it.

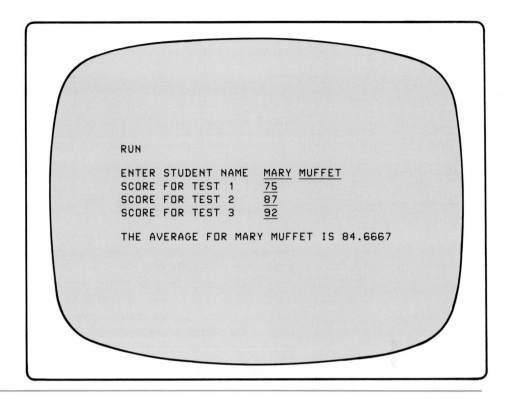

```
RUN

ENTER STUDENT NAME   MARY MUFFET
SCORE FOR TEST 1     75
SCORE FOR TEST 2     87
SCORE FOR TEST 3     92

THE AVERAGE FOR MARY MUFFET IS 84.6667
```

String Delimiters

A potential for error exists when string variables are input. When entering the data, the user may or may not use quotation marks around the literal. Commas are used as **delimiters** to separate literals. So, if a comma is needed within the string, quotation marks *must* be used.

```
10   INPUT "ENTER STUDENT NAME ", STUDENT$
20   PRINT STUDENT$
::
::
RUN
ENTER STUDENT NAME CROCKETT, DAVEY
?REDO FROM START
```

In this case, the comma was taken as a delimiter between two fields. The computer saw DAVEY as a second field of input when none was required and refused to cooperate.

```
10   INPUT "ENTER STUDENT NAME ", STUDENT$
20   PRINT STUDENT$
::
::
RUN
ENTER STUDENT NAME "CROCKETT, DAVEY"
CROCKETT, DAVEY
```

The comma is the only special character that causes problems in string literals. Any other character may be included in the literal input without requiring quotation marks.

```
10    INPUT "WHAT IS THE PROBLEM"; PROBLEM$
20    PRINT "THAT'S TOO BAD ABOUT "; PROBLEM$
::
::
RUN
WHAT IS THE PROBLEM? THE #$%&**! COMMAS
THAT'S TOO BAD ABOUT THE #$%&**! COMMAS
```

An important thing to remember is that the value entered for an INPUT must match the type of variable defined on the INPUT statement. The REDO FROM START message will be given if this rule is not followed.

```
250    INPUT "ENTER NAME AND AGE ", NAMES$, AGE
::
::
RUN
ENTER NAME AND AGE 25, SALLY MORRIS
?REDO FROM START
```

The number 25 was first placed in NAMES$ without any problem. Remember, digits are legal characters in a string literal, but SALLY MORRIS cannot be placed in the numeric variable AGE.

Another important point to notice about the previous example is that it is perfectly legal to have both string variable names and numeric variable names in one INPUT statement. As long as the user enters correctly the values in the proper order, it will all work out correctly. Again, this is not considered good programming practice, since it requires a lot from the user and introduces an unnecessary potential for errors.

```
300    INPUT "ENTER PRODUCT NUMBER, DESCRIPTION, UNIT PRICE
       AND QUANTITY, SEPARATED BY COMMAS ", NUMBER, DESC$,
       PRICE, QUANTITY
::
::
RUN
ENTER PRODUCT NUMBER, DESCRIPTION, UNIT PRICE AND QUANTITY,
SEPARATED BY COMMAS 125, TORCH, 9.75, 12
```

NUMBER	DESC$	PRICE	QUANTITY
125	TORCH	9.75	12

Feedback

1. Write the statements necessary to input a class name and class count.
2. Write the statements necessary to input and print out a name and address.
3. Write the INPUT statement necessary to input this value into DAT$.

DAT$
JAN. 15, 1940

Modular Programming

As programs become larger and more complex, it becomes more difficult to write clear, understandable solutions that work correctly. The goal of **modular programming** is to break up the program into small parts that are more easily understood. Then planning, coding, and testing can be done on these small, relatively simple units, rather than on one large, complex body of code. Remember the adage Divide and Conquer!

Programmers must develop the skill and the ability to look at a large problem and to decompose it into individual functions. The alternative is a phenomenon called "spaghetti code." Once a programmer has learned to modularize programs, programs will be coded more quickly, will be more likely to work correctly, and will certainly be easier to read and to be maintained by others.

Virtually all computer scientists recommend modular programming. The only disagreement seems to be at what point a programmer should begin writing what are called "subroutines." Many wait until programs become hopelessly complex. Then, introducing subroutines can save the day. The more practical approach is to begin using subroutines early. As programs become more complex, if correct habits are already in place, the programmer doesn't need to be "rescued." The solution to the problem is at hand.

Subroutines

A **subroutine** is a group of statements intended to accomplish an individual task. For example, all INPUT statements may be placed together in a subroutine. Another subroutine might contain all calculations for the program. Or, if the calculations become more complex, they may be divided into multiple subroutines, each one accomplishing a specific portion of the whole.

Subroutine Used for Report Headings

Main Program

```
100    GOSUB 500          'transfer control to line 500
110    ::                 'continue with rest of program
       ::
```

Subroutine

```
500    REM ********** SUBROUTINE TO PRINT HEADINGS **********
510    LPRINT ,, "CLUB ROSTER"
520    LPRINT
530    LPRINT
540    LPRINT "NAME",, "ADDRESS",, "TELEPHONE"
550    LPRINT
560    RETURN
```

When this program is run, execution proceeds one statement after another until line 100 is reached. At line 100, control is transferred to line 500; that is, line 500 will be executed after line 100. The statements in the subroutine, lines 500–560 will be executed in order. When line 560 is reached, control is transferred back to the statement immediately following the GOSUB. So line 110 will be executed after line 560. Program execution will then continue with any statements following line 110.

The GOSUB Statement — General Form

```
line number GOSUB statement number
```

The GOSUB Statement — Example

```
50   GOSUB   200
```

The RETURN Statement — General Form

```
line number RETURN
```

The RETURN Statement — Example

```
250   RETURN
```

Each time a GOSUB is encountered during program execution, control passes to the statement named on the GOSUB. The statements in the subroutine are then executed. When a RETURN is encountered, control passes back to the statement immediately following the GOSUB.

Subroutines may be called from more than one location in a program and may be called any number of times. A subroutine may be called from within another subroutine, which is called *nesting* subroutines. In fact, you may nest as many levels of subroutines as you wish in Microsoft BASIC.

Feedback

1. Why would anyone want to use subroutines?
2. When a RETURN statement is executed, to what statement does execution "return"?
3. What do you think would happen if a RETURN statement were encountered in program execution, but there was no GOSUB? (Try it to see.)
4. What is the limit to the number of subroutines that may be in one program?
5. Play computer. What will be the output when these program segments are executed? Watch for syntax and logic errors.

```
a. 100 PRINT "HELLO FROM LINE 100"
   110 GOSUB 200
   120 PRINT "HELLO FROM LINE 120"
   130 GOSUB 200
   140 PRINT "HELLO FROM LINE 140"
   150 END
   200 PRINT "HELLO FROM LINE 200"
   210 RETURN
```

```
b. 300 PRINT "START HERE"
   310 GOSUB 350
   320 PRINT "FINISH HERE"
   330 END
```

```
c. 400 PRINT "PRINTED BY LINE 400"
   410 GOSUB 500
   420 PRINT "PRINTED BY LINE 420"
   430 END
   500 PRINT "PRINTED BY LINE 500"
   510 GOSUB 540
   520 PRINT "PRINTED BY LINE 520"
   530 RETURN
   540 PRINT "PRINTED BY LINE 540"
   550 GOSUB 580
   560 PRINT "PRINTED BY LINE 560"
   570 RETURN
   580 GOSUB 610
   590 PRINT "PRINTED BY LINE 590"
   600 RETURN
   610 PRINT "PRINTED BY LINE 610"
   620 RETURN
```

```
d. 100 ' CALCULATE THE SUM OF 3 NUMBERS
   110 '
   120 ' NUM1      FIRST NUMBER
   130 ' NUM2      SECOND NUMBER
   140 ' NUM3      THIRD NUMBER
   150 '
   160 ' **** MAINLINE ****
   170 GOSUB 300     'INPUT NUMBERS
   180 GOSUB 400     'CALCULATE SUM
   190 GOSUB 500     'PRINT RESULTS
   200 '
```

```
300 ' **** INPUT NUMBERS ****
310 INPUT "ENTER FIRST NUMBER ", NUM1
320 INPUT "ENTER SECOND NUMBER ", NUM2
330 INPUT "ENTER THIRD NUMBER ", NUM3
340 RETURN
350 '
400 ' **** CALCULATE SUM ****
410 LET SUM = NUM1 + NUM2 + NUM3
430 '
500 ' **** PRINT RESULTS ****
510 PRINT "THE SUM IS"; SUM
520 RETURN
```

Forming Modular Programs—The Program Mainline

When a program is written with individual tasks in subroutines, a **mainline,** or *control program,* is needed. This control program is sometimes called the *program outline,* as it presents an overview of the program tasks. Another term sometimes used for the program mainline is the *driver.*

Example Program:
The Interest Program Written with Subroutines

Program Listing

```
10 REM CALCULATE SIMPLE INTEREST ON A DEPOSIT
20 REM
30 REM          VARIABLES USED:
40 REM
50 REM          RATE           RATE OF INTEREST, DECIMAL FORM
60 REM          DEPOSIT        AMOUNT DEPOSITED
70 REM          YEARS          LENGTH OF TIME DEPOSIT DRAWS
                               INTEREST
80 REM          INTEREST       SIMPLE INTEREST FOR PERIOD
90 REM          VALUE          ENDING VALUE OF DEPOSIT,
                               INCLUDING INTEREST
100 REM
200 REM ************* PROGRAM MAINLINE **************
210 GOSUB 300                  ' INPUT DATA
220 GOSUB 400                  ' CALCULATIONS
230 GOSUB 500                  ' PROGRAM OUTPUT
240 END                        ' END OF PROGRAM
250 '
300 REM ************* INPUT DATA *******************
310 INPUT "ENTER INTEREST RATE, IN DECIMAL FORM ", RATE
320 INPUT "ENTER THE AMOUNT OF DEPOSIT          ", DEPOSIT
330 INPUT "ENTER THE NUMBER OF YEARS            ", YEARS
340 RETURN
350 '
400 REM ************* CALCULATIONS *****************
410 LET INTEREST = DEPOSIT * RATE * YEARS
420 LET VALUE = DEPOSIT + INTEREST
430 RETURN
440 '
500 REM ************* PROGRAM OUTPUT ***************
510 PRINT
520 PRINT "THE INTEREST IS                 ";INTEREST
530 PRINT "THE ENDING BALANCE IS           ";VALUE
540 RETURN
550 REM *********** END OF PROGRAM ****************
```

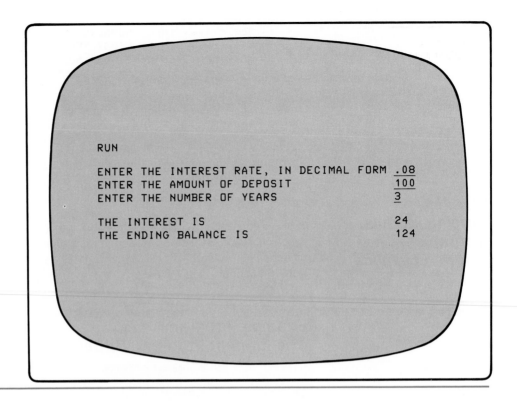

```
RUN

ENTER THE INTEREST RATE, IN DECIMAL FORM .08
ENTER THE AMOUNT OF DEPOSIT               100
ENTER THE NUMBER OF YEARS                 3

THE INTEREST IS                          24
THE ENDING BALANCE IS                    124
```

Notice how the program mainline is the outline of the tasks to be performed. The mainline controls execution of each task. Also note the addition of line 240, the END statement. This is the logical end, or the finish of execution of the program. This is necessary, so that execution does not "fall through" and accidentally enter a subroutine.

Another new item was added in the preceding example. The single quotation mark (') for remarks was added on the end of a program line. This allows a remark to explain a statement and is recommended for GOSUB statements. Good documentation standards require remarks throughout a program to explain the logic. In fact, as programs become more complex, an increasing number of program statements will require remarks.

Modular Program Planning

There are several popular methods used for planning modular programs. Pseudocode or flowcharts may be used, with a slight modification for the subroutines; or, hierarchy charts may be used. The preceding example program will be shown using all three methods.

Pseudocode

When tasks are to be performed by a subroutine, show those statements indented below the main heading.

1. Input data
   1.1   Prompt and input rate, deposit amount, and number of years
2. Calculations
   2.1   Calculate interest = deposit * rate * years
   2.2   Calculate ending balance = deposit + interest
3. Output
   3.1   Print interest and ending balance

Figure 2.1
A modular flowchart.

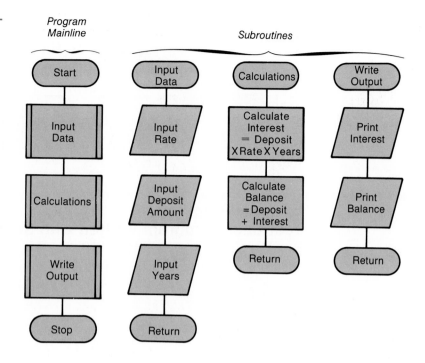

Flowcharts

Modular flowcharts can be drawn using the *predefined process* symbol.

This symbol indicates that a particular function is to be performed, generally a series of statements that together accomplish a task. Use the predefined process symbol to indicate that a subroutine is to be executed. The subroutine itself will be flowcharted individually.

Use the terminal symbol to show the beginning and end of a subroutine. At the start of the subroutine, label the terminal symbol with the functional name of the subroutine (i.e., Print Headings, Compute Volume, Compute Mean). The ending terminal should contain the word RETURN (figure 2.1).

Hierarchy Charts

Many programmers who write modular programs prefer to plan their programs with hierarchy charts. An example of a hierarchy chart can be seen in figure 2.2. A hierarchy chart is used to plan and show program structure. It is constructed much like an organization chart. At the highest level (indicated by *A*), the entire program is shown. At the next level (*B*), the program is separated into its major functions. The mainline (main control module) will be coded directly from this *B* level on the chart. Any functions that are further broken down are shown at another (lower) level. The **modules** can be broken into smaller and smaller parts until the coding for each function becomes straightforward and often obvious.

Many programmers use a hierarchy chart to plan the overall structure of a program. Then, when the individual modules are identified, flowcharting or pseudocode will be used to plan the details of the logic.

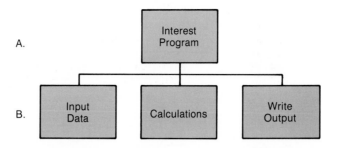

Figure 2.2
Hierarchy chart. Level *A* shows
the entire program, which is
broken down into major program
functions on the *B* level. A more
complicated program would be
further broken down into lower
levels.

A. Interest Program

B. Input Data | Calculations | Write Output

Example Program:
Test Score Program Written with Subroutines

Hierarchy Chart   Refer to figure 2.3.

Flowchart   Refer to figure 2.4.

Figure 2.3
Program hierarchy chart for the
test score program. The chart
shows the three program
modules.

Figure 2.4
Program flowchart for the test
score program. This program
inputs a person's name and three
test scores. It then calculates and
rounds the average score and
prints it along with the name.

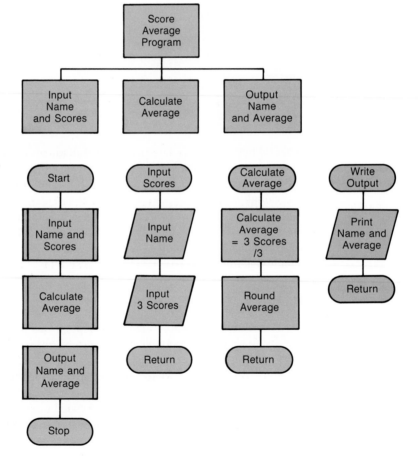

Program Listing

```
110 REM PROGRAM TO CALCULATE THE AVERAGE OF THREE TEST SCORES
120 REM
130 REM          VARIABLES USED:
140 REM
150 REM          STUDENT$          NAME OF STUDENT
160 REM          TEST1             SCORE FOR TEST 1
170 REM          TEST2             SCORE FOR TEST 2
180 REM          TEST3             SCORE FOR TEST 3
190 REM          AVG               TEST AVERAGE
200 REM
210 '
300 REM *************** PROGRAM MAINLINE ********************
310 GOSUB 400                      ' DATA INPUT
320 GOSUB 500                      ' CALCULATIONS
330 GOSUB 600                      ' PROGRAM OUTPUT
340 END                            ' END OF PROGRAM
350 '
400 REM ************** DATA INPUT ***************************
410 INPUT "ENTER STUDENT NAME  ", STUDENT$
420 INPUT "SCORE FOR TEST 1    ", TEST1
430 INPUT "SCORE FOR TEST 2    ", TEST2
440 INPUT "SCORE FOR TEST 3    ", TEST3
450 RETURN
460 '
500 REM *************** CALCULATIONS ***********************
510 LET AVG = (TEST1 + TEST2 + TEST3) / 3
520 LET AVG = INT(AVG + .5)
530 RETURN
540 '
600 REM *************** PROGRAM OUTPUT *********************
610 PRINT
620 PRINT "THE AVERAGE FOR "; STUDENT$; " IS"; AVG
630 RETURN
640 REM *************** END OF PROGRAM *********************
```

Summary

1. A numeric variable holds a numeric value, which can be changed during execution of the program.
2. Numeric variable names are composed of letters, numeric digits, and the period. The names may be as short as one character or as long as desired, with only the first forty characters being significant. The first character of the variable name must be a letter of the alphabet.
3. Numeric constants are values that do not change.
4. Numeric constants are the actual numbers (digits) used in a program.
5. A numeric constant is made up of the numeric digits (0–9), and an optional decimal point. The sign of the number (+ or −) may also be included, if it precedes the digits.
6. No special characters ($, % #) may be included in a numeric constant.
7. Values can be assigned to variables with the LET statement.
8. The LET statement operates from right to left. The value on the right side of the equal sign is placed in the variable named on the left side of the equal sign.
9. A variable name must appear on the left side of the equal sign. On the right side of the equal sign, there may be another variable, a constant, or an arithmetic expression.
10. Since the equal sign means assignment, not equality, the statement LET ANS = NUM1 + NUM2 should read: LET ANS *be replaced* by NUM1 + NUM2.
11. Arithmetic expressions are used to perform calculations and are formed with combinations of variables, constants, and the arithmetic operators (+ − * / ∧).

12. Parentheses may be used to control the order of execution of operations. When one set of parentheses is enclosed inside another set, they are said to be nested.
13. The hierarchy of operations is:
    a. calculations within parentheses;
    b. all exponentiation, from left to right;
    c. all multiplication and division, from left to right;
    d. all addition and subtraction, from left to right.
14. The INT function truncates all digits to the right of the decimal point.
15. The INT function can be used to round numbers.
16. String variables are used to store alphabetic characters, special characters, and numeric digits.
17. String variable names must have a dollar sign as the rightmost character.
18. String literals are made up of alphabetic characters, blank spaces, special symbols, and numeric digits.
19. In most instances, string literals must be enclosed in quotation marks.
20. Although strings may hold numeric digits, no calculations may be done with strings.
21. A second way of assigning a value to a variable is with the INPUT statement.
22. When an INPUT statement is encountered during the run of a program, execution pauses and awaits keyboard entry. The value entered on the keyboard will be assigned to the variable named on the INPUT statement.
23. The INPUT statement may be used to input both numeric and string data.
24. When a numeric variable is named on an input statement, only valid numeric constants may be entered.
25. A literal prompt may be included on an INPUT statement. This is usually to inform the user what to enter.
26. Multiple variables may be requested with one INPUT statement, but this is usually considered poor programming.
27. When multiple variables are requested, the user must exactly match the number and type of data items.
28. Programs should be broken into small, easy-to-understand parts. These small parts are called modules.
29. Subroutines can be used to code program modules.
30. The GOSUB statement is used to call a subroutine.
31. The RETURN statement is placed at the end of a subroutine. When the RETURN statement is encountered in program execution, control is transferred back to the statement following the GOSUB that called the subroutine.
32. A subroutine may be called multiple times and may be called from more than one location in the program.
33. Subroutines may be nested; that is, one subroutine may call another subroutine, which may call another subroutine. Each RETURN transfers control back to the line following the most recent GOSUB.
34. Modular programs are generally written with a mainline and subroutines.
35. Modular programs can be planned with pseudocode, flowcharts, or hierarchy charts.
36. Subroutines are flowcharted with the predefined process symbol.
37. Hierarchy charts are similar to organization charts and show the structure of a program.
38. The top level of a hierarchy chart shows the entire program. The next-lower level shows the major program functions. Each major function is then broken down into smaller parts until each contains only one function and can be easily coded.
39. Many programmers draw hierarchy charts to identify the program modules and flowchart the individual modules.

Each of these exercises should be written as a modular program with a program mainline and subroutines. Plan the program with a modular flowchart, pseudocode, or a hierarchy chart. Run the program with the test data provided as well as additional data that you make up.

2.1. The stopping distance for a moving automobile can be calculated for any given rate of travel.

INPUT: The speed of the car, in miles per hour.
OUTPUT: The distance needed to stop the car, in feet.
PROCESSING: The formula for stopping distance is:

$$\text{STOPPING DISTANCE IN FEET} = \text{VELOCITY} * 2.25 + \frac{\text{VELOCITY} \wedge 2}{21}$$

Where 2.25 is a factor for the time necessary to perceive and react to the situation, and 21 is a friction factor for stopping. Round the answer to the nearest foot.

SAMPLE PROGRAM OUTPUT:

```
VELOCITY? 25
THE DISTANCE REQUIRED TO STOP IS 86 FEET
```

TEST DATA: 25, 40, 55, 70

2.2. In retail sales, it is important for the manager to know the average inventory figure and the turnover of merchandise.

INPUT: Beginning inventory, ending inventory, cost of goods sold.
OUTPUT: The average inventory in dollars and the turnover in number of times the inventory was turned over.
PROCESSING: The values can be calculated from these formulas:

$$\text{Average inventory} = \frac{\text{Beginning inventory} + \text{Ending inventory}}{2}$$

$$\text{Turnover} = \frac{\text{Cost of goods sold}}{\text{Average inventory}}$$

Round the turnover to the nearest tenth.

SAMPLE PROGRAM OUTPUT:

```
BEGINNING INVENTORY = 58500
ENDING INVENTORY =    47000
COST OF GOODS SOLD =  400000
AVERAGE INVENTORY =   52750
TURNOVER =            7.6
```

TEST DATA:

Beginning	Ending	Cost of Goods Sold
58,500	47,000	400,000
75,300	13,600	515,400
3,000	19,600	48,000

2.3. Calculate and print the area of a triangle.

INPUT: The base and height of the triangle.
OUTPUT: The area of the triangle.
PROCESSING: The formula for calculations:

$$\text{Area} = 1/2 * (\text{Base} * \text{Height})$$

SAMPLE PROGRAM OUTPUT:

```
ENTER BASE OF TRIANGLE   3
ENTER HEIGHT OF TRIANGLE 4

THE AREA IS              6
```

TEST DATA:

Base	Height
4.5	6.2
10	15
1	1

2.4. A local recording studio rents its facilities for $200 per hour. The management charges only for the number of minutes used.

INPUT: Name of the group and number of minutes used.
OUTPUT: Print the name of the group and the total charges on both the screen and the printer.
PROCESSING: Calculate the per-minute cost as 1/60 of the hourly rate. Round the charges to the nearest cent.

SAMPLE PROGRAM OUTPUT:

```
NAME OF GROUP? THE BIRDDOGS
NUMBER OF MINUTES? 45

TOTAL CHARGES = $ 150
```

SAMPLE PRINTER OUTPUT:

```
THE CHARGES FOR THE BIRDDOGS ARE $ 150
```

TEST DATA:

Group	Minutes
Pooches	95
Hounddogs	5
Mutts	480

2.5. Determine the future value of an investment at a given interest rate for a given number of years.

INPUT: Amount of investment, the interest rate (as a decimal fraction), and the number of years the investment will be held.
OUTPUT: The future value of the investment.
PROCESSING: The formula for calculations is:

$$\text{Future value} = \text{Investment amount} * (1 + \text{interest rate})^{\wedge} \text{years}$$

Where the interest rate is a decimal value (8 1/2% is entered as .085)
Convert the decimal rate to percent for output.
(Percentage = interest rate * 100)
Round the future value to the nearest cent.

SAMPLE PROGRAM OUTPUT:

```
ENTER AMOUNT OF INVESTMENT        1000.00
ENTER INTEREST RATE, DECIMAL FORM .125
NUMBER OF YEARS                   5
THE FUTURE VALUE OF $ 1000 INVESTED AT 12.5% FOR
 5 YEARS IS $ 1802.03
```

TEST DATA:

Amount	Rate	Years
2,000.00	.15	5
10,000.00	.185	5
1,234.56	.10	1

2.6. Calculate the shipping charge for a package, if the shipping rate is $0.12 per ounce.

INPUT: Package identification number (a six-digit code that contains letters and numbers) and the weight of the package in pounds and ounces.
OUTPUT: The shipping charge on both the screen and the printer.
PROCESSING: Find the total number of ounces (16 ounces in a pound) and multiply by .12 to find the charge.

SAMPLE PROGRAM OUTPUT:

```
ENTER PACKAGE ID   K2576C
WEIGHT - POUNDS 3
          OUNCES 12

THE CHARGE FOR 60 OUNCES IS $ 7.2
```

SAMPLE PRINTER OUTPUT:

```
PACKAGE ID       WEIGHT         CHARGE
K2576C             3 LB. 12 OZ.   $ 7.2

|(zone 1)         |(zone 2)       |(zone 3)
```

TEST DATA:

ID	Weight
L5496P	0 lb. 5 oz.
J1955K	2 lb. 0 oz.
Z0000Z	1 lb. 1 oz.

2.7. Convert the temperature given in degrees Fahrenheit to the corresponding value in degrees Celsius.

INPUT: Temperature in degrees Fahrenheit.
OUTPUT: Temperature in degrees Celsius.
PROCESSING: The formula for conversion:

Celsius = 5/9 * (Fahrenheit — 32)
Round the temperature to the nearest whole number

SAMPLE PROGRAM OUTPUT:

```
TEMPERATURE IN DEGREES FAHRENHEIT? 75
TEMPERATURE IN DEGREES CELSIUS IS 24
```

TEST DATA: 32, 90, 212

2.8. The charges for a rental car at the local agency are $15 per day, plus $0.12 per mile. Print an invoice for rental customers.

INPUT: Customer name, address, city, state, zip code, beginning odometer reading, ending odometer reading, and number of days the car was used.
OUTPUT: Print a customer bill, similar to the sample shown on the next page.
PROCESSING: Subtract the beginning odometer reading from the ending odometer reading to find the miles driven. Multiply the miles driven by .12, and add the daily charge (15 * number of days). Round the charges to the nearest cent.

SAMPLE PROGRAM OUTPUT:

```
CUSTOMER NAME                    IVAN TERRIBLE
STREET ADDRESS                   2601 DISTANT STREET
CITY                             NOWHERE
STATE                            CA
ZIP CODE                         91711

BEGINNING ODOMETER READING       35202.5
ENDING ODOMETER READING          35700.9
NUMBER OF DAYS                   3

CHARGES                          $ 104.81
```

SAMPLE PRINTER OUTPUT:

```
                    AWESOME CAR RENTALS
                    CUSTOMER INVOICE

IVAN TERRIBLE
2601 DISTANT STREET
NOWHERE, CA 91711

NUMBER OF DAYS        MILES DRIVEN        TOTAL CHARGE
 3                      498.4             $ 104.81
```

TEST DATA:

	Beginning	Ending	Days
(You make up names	1,520.1	1,542.3	1
and addresses)	20,425.2	20,619.0	2
	50,402.5	53,212.2	5

2.9. Write a program to determine the discount and sale price of any item input.

INPUT: The description of the item, the base price, and the percentage of discount to be given will be entered from the keyboard.
OUTPUT: Print the description of the item, the base price, the sale price, and the discount.
PROCESS:
   1. Discount = base price * percent of discount / 100.
   2. Sale price = base − discount.

2.10. Write a program to input five numbers and find the mean.

INPUT: Five numbers will be input from the keyboard.
OUTPUT: Print the calculated mean with the appropriate label.
PROCESS: Calculate the mean = sum of numbers / 5.

2.11. Write a program to calculate the slope of a line.

INPUT: The X and Y coordinates of two points on a line will be input from the keyboard.
OUTPUT: The slope of the line.

PROCESS: Calculate the slope $= \dfrac{Y_2 - Y_1}{X_2 - X_1}$

Note: Slope is the measure of the steepness of a line. X_1 and Y_1 are the coordinates for point 1, X_2 and Y_2 are the coordinates for point 2.

2.12. Write a program to input the titles of your three favorite books and their authors. Print a title, headings, the titles, and the authors. Output should be to both the screen and the printer.

2.13. Write a program to calculate net pay.

> INPUT: Gross pay will be input from the keyboard.
> OUTPUT: Calculated net pay, identified by an appropriate literal.
> PROCESS: Net pay = gross pay − deductions.
>> Deductions:
>>> 1. FICA = .0715 * gross pay
>>> 2. FED = .14 * gross pay
>>> 3. STATE = .09 * gross pay

2.14. Write a program to calculate an employee's net pay, and print a budget report based on the percentages given.

> INPUT: The employee's name and dollar amount of sales earned this month will be input from the keyboard.
> OUTPUT: Print an appropriate title and headings. Print the base pay, amount of sales, amount of commission, gross pay, deductions, net pay, and the dollar amount that can be spent on housing, food and clothing, entertainment, and miscellaneous items.
> PROCESS:
>> 1. Gross pay = $900 a month + 6% commission on all sales over $200.
>> 2. Commission = (total sales − $200) * 6%.
>> 3. Net pay = gross pay − deductions.
>> 4. Deductions = 18% of gross pay.
>> 5. Housing = 30% of net pay.
>> 6. Food and clothing = 15% of net pay.
>> 7. Entertainment = 50% of net pay.
>> 8. Miscellaneous items = 5% of net pay.

> TEST DATA:
>> Base pay = $900
>> Sales = $1200

> SAMPLE OUTPUT:

```
                        BUDGET REPORT FOR Joan Cooley
Base Pay     Sales      Commission     Gross     Deductions
  900         1200          60          960        172.8

Net
787.2

Housing         = 236.16
Food/Clothing   = 118.08
Entertainment   = 393.6
Miscellaneous   = 39.36
```

2.15. The Perfect Picture company has created a bonus program to give its employees some incentive. Each store has a sales goal to reach. For every dollar the store makes over the goal, the employees of that store receive 15% of sales. The amount each employee receives is based upon the percentage of hours they worked of the total hours the store was open. (There are two employees per store and no more than one employee working at any given time.) Write a program that will print a summary report for one store.

> INPUT: Input from the keyboard the store number, name of employee 1, name of employee 2, total hours worked for employee 1, total hours worked for employee 2, store's sales goals, and actual sales.
> OUTPUT: Print a title and column headings. Detail output will consist of store number, sales goal, actual sales, amount of sales over goal, each employee's name, number of hours each employee worked, and bonus amount each employee earned.

PROCESS:
1. The store's bonus will be calculated as (actual sales − sales goal) * 15%. Round the bonus to the nearest whole number.
2. Each employee's percent of the bonus is calculated as their hours divided by the total store hours.
3. For each employee, multiply the bonus earned for the store by the percent calculated in step 2 above. Round the amount to the nearest cent.

SAMPLE PROGRAM OUTPUT:

```
            Monthly Bonus Summary Report

Store #        LA-021
Store Goal     3800
Sales          4300
Store Bonus    75


Employee          Hours Worked      Bonus Earned

Anita Bonita         150              36.53
Mitzi Micro          158              38.47
```

3

Programs with Loops and Formatted Output

WHILE Statement
WEND Statement
OR Operator
AND Operator
NOT Operator
TAB Function
SPC Function
PRINT USING Statement

Upon completion of this chapter, you
should be able to:

1. Write program loops using the WHILE
   and WEND statements.
2. Use the relational and logical
   operators.
3. Terminate INPUT loops by asking a
   question.
4. Understand and use priming INPUT
   statements.
5. Control loop execution with
   counters.
6. Accumulate sums.
7. Format printed output with the TAB
   and SPC functions.
8. Produce well-formatted output with
   the PRINT USING and LPRINT USING
   statements.

Loops

Until now, each of the practice programs has only been able to process a single set of data. There has been no way to go back and repeat the same steps without rerunning the program. The computer is capable of repeating a group of instructions multiple times, without the necessity of rerunning the program for each set of new data. This process of repeating a series of instructions is called *looping*. The group of repeated instructions is called **loop.**

```
10     REM    CALCULATE THE AREA OF A ROOM
20     LET ANS$ = "YES"
30     WHILE ANS$ = "YES"
40         INPUT "ENTER LENGTH"; LENGTH
50         INPUT "ENTER WIDTH"; WDTH
60         LET AREA = LENGTH * WDTH
70         PRINT "THE AREA IS "; AREA
80         PRINT
90         INPUT "DO YOU WISH TO CONTINUE"; ANS$
100    WEND
110    PRINT
120    PRINT "BYE"
130    END
```

The new BASIC statements forming the loop are the WHILE (line 30) and WEND (pronounced WHILE END, line 100). Any time the program logic calls for repeating one instruction or a group of instructions, the WHILE and WEND are the way to accomplish the task.

The program lines 30–100 form a loop and will be executed repeatedly until the user enters something other than YES to the question (in line 90) DO YOU WISH TO CONTINUE?

The WHILE Statement—General Form

```
line number   WHILE  <condition>
```

The WHILE Statement—Examples

```
250    WHILE COUNT < 10
400    WHILE ANS$ = "YES"
650    WHILE GUESS$ <> "COW"
```

Each WHILE statement must have a corresponding WEND.

The WEND Statement—General Form

```
line number   WEND
```

The WEND Statement—Example

```
300    WEND
```

In execution, each time a WHILE is encountered in a program, a condition is evaluated. If the condition is *true,* the statements in the loop are executed. When the WEND is encountered, control is again passed to the WHILE, and the condition is again evaluated. If the condition is *true,* the loop is executed again. If the condition is *false,* control will pass to the next statement following the WEND.

Conditions

Control of the loop execution is based on a *condition*. To form the conditions, there are six **relational operators** (table 3.1) used to compare two values. The result of the comparison is either *true* or *false*.

Symbol	Relation Tested	Examples		
>	greater than	AMT	>	NUM
		ITEM$	>	"STAR"
<	less than	COUNT	<	10
		ITEM$	<	CHOICE$
=	equal to	SUM	=	TOTAL
		NAM$	=	"BASIC"
<>	not equal to	CHOICE	<>	100
		BIG$	<>	LARGE$
>=	greater than or equal to	NUM	>=	GUESS
		PART$	>=	ID$
<=	less than or equal to	AMT	<=	LIMIT
		STRING1$	<=	STRING2$

Table 3.1.
The six relational operators.

The conditions to be tested can be formed with numeric variables and constants, string variables and constants, and arithmetic expressions. However, it is important to note that comparisons must be made on "like types"; that is, strings can be compared only to other strings, and numeric values can be compared only to other numeric values, whether a variable, constant, or arithmetic expression.

Comparing Numeric Variables and Constants

When numeric values are involved in a test, an algebraic comparison is made; that is, the sign of the number is taken into account. Therefore, -20 is less than 10, and -2 is less than -1.

Even though an equal sign ($=$) means replacement in a LET statement, in a relation test the equal sign is used to test for equality. For example, the statement

```
WHILE PRICE = MAX
```

is interpreted to mean "is the current value stored in PRICE equal to the current value stored in MAX?"

Some Sample Comparisons

ALPHA	BRAVO	CHARLIE
5	4	−5

Condition	Evaluates
ALPHA = BRAVO	False
CHARLIE < 0	True
BRAVO > ALPHA	False
CHARLIE <= BRAVO	True
ALPHA >= 5	True
ALPHA <> CHARLIE	True

Comparing Strings

String variables can be compared to other string variables or string literals enclosed in quotation marks. The comparison begins with the leftmost character and proceeds one character at a time from left to right. As soon as a character in one string is not

Figure 3.1
ASCII Collating sequence
(American Standard Code for
Information Interchange). For a
more complete list of the ASCII
code, see appendix C.

ASCII CODE	CHARACTER	ASCII CODE	CHARACTER	ASCII CODE	CHARACTER
32	SPACE	64	@	96	'
33	!	65	A	97	a
34	"	66	B	98	b
35	#	67	C	99	c
36	$	68	D	100	d
37	%	69	E	101	e
38	&	70	F	102	f
39	'	71	G	103	g
40	(	72	H	104	h
41	)	73	I	105	i
42	*	74	J	106	j
43	+	75	K	107	k
44	,	76	L	108	l
45	–	77	M	109	m
46	.	78	N	110	n
47	/	79	O	111	o
48	0	80	P	112	p
49	1	81	Q	113	q
50	2	82	R	114	r
51	3	83	S	115	s
52	4	84	T	116	t
53	5	85	U	117	u
54	6	86	V	118	v
55	7	87	W	119	w
56	8	88	X	120	x
57	9	89	Y	121	y
58	:	90	Z	122	z
59	;	91	[	123	{
60	<	92	\	124	¦
61	=	93	]	125	}
62	>	94	^	126	~
63	?	95	–	127	DEL

equal to the corresponding character in the second string, the comparison is terminated, and the string with the lower ranking character is judged less than the other.

The determination of which character is less than another is made based on the code used to store characters internally in the computer. The code, called the **ASCII code** (pronounced ask-key), has an established order (called the collating sequence) for all letters, numbers, and special characters. Note in figure 3.1 that *A* is less than *B, L* is greater than *K,* and all numeric digits are less than all letters. Some special symbols are lower than the numbers and some are higher, and the blank space is lower than the rest of the characters shown.

PERSON1$	PERSON2$
JOHN	JOAN

The condition PERSON1$ < PERSON2$ evaluates *false*. The *A* in JOAN is lower ranking than the *H* in JOHN.

WORD1$	WORD2$
HOPE	HOPELESS

The condition WORD1$ < WORD2$ evaluates *true*. When one string is shorter than the other, it can be considered that the shorter string is padded with blanks to the right of the string, and the blank space will be compared to a character in the longer string.

C$	D$
300ZX	PORSCHE

The condition C$ < D$ evaluates *true.* When the number 3 is compared to the letter *P,* the 3 is lower, since all numbers are lower ranking than all letters.

Feedback

Determine which conditions will evaluate *true,* and which ones *false.*

L	M	N	P$	R$
5	5	−5.5	DATA10A	DATA10B

1. L >= M
2. N < 0
3. N < M
4. L <> M
5. L + 2 > M * 2

6. P$ < R$
7. P$ <> R$
8. P$ > "D"
9. "2" <> "TWO"
10. "$" <= "?"

Compound Conditions

Compound conditions, which allow more than one condition to be tested, can be formed using the **logical operators.**

Logical Operators	*Example*
OR—If one or the other condition is true, or both are true, the entire condition is true.	NUM = 0 OR NUM = 5
AND—Both conditions must be true for the entire condition to be true.	NUM >= 1 AND COUNT <= 10
NOT—Reverses the condition, so that a true condition will evaluate false and vice versa.	NOT COUNT = 0

The OR Operator—Example

```
40    INPUT "ENTER A NUMBER BETWEEN 1 & 10 ", NUM
50    WHILE NUM < 1 OR NUM > 10
60        INPUT "VALUE NOT IN RANGE 1-10, PLEASE RE-ENTER ", NUM
70    WEND
```

If the value of *NUM* is less than 1 or greater than 10, then the message will print. *Note that the NUM must be repeated in the second condition.* If this were written IF NUM < 1 OR > 10, BASIC would *not* assume that you meant NUM > 10, but produce a SYNTAX ERROR.

When a compound condition contains an OR, the two conditions are tested independently. Then if one condition *or* the other is true, the entire condition evaluates true.

The AND Operator—Example

```
140    WHILE ANS$ <> "YES" AND ANS$ <> "NO"
150        INPUT "ENTER 'YES' OR 'NO'", ANS$
160    WEND
```

In this example, if ANS$ contains *neither* YES nor NO, then the condition will be true. If ANS$ contains NO, then the first condition is true, the second condition is false, and the entire condition is false. The compound condition also evaluates false if ANS$ contains YES.

When two conditions are joined by AND, each condition is evaluated independently. Then, if both conditions are true, the entire compound condition is true. If one or the other is false, the entire condition tests false.

The NOT Operator—Example

```
40   WHILE NOT RESPONSE$ = "QUIT"
50      GOSUB 1000     'CALCULATE
60      GOSUB 2000     'PRINT
70      INPUT "ENTER NEXT ONE ('QUIT' TO END)", RESPONSE$
80   WEND
```

In the example, if RESPONSE$ holds anything other than QUIT the condition evaluates true. The NOT operator reverses the truth of a condition and applies only to the condition it precedes.

The use of the NOT operator is generally confusing and difficult to evaluate and is therefore not recommended. Conditions usually can be constructed without the use of NOT (e.g., RESPONSE$ <> "QUIT" rather than NOT RESPONSE$ = "QUIT"). Refer to figure 3.2 for the outcomes of use of logical operators.

Combining the Logical Operators

Combinations of AND and OR can be used in a single compound condition. When the operators are combined, the order of evaluation becomes important. The condition surrounding the AND is evaluated first, then the condition surrounding the OR is tested.

```
200     WHILE SCORE >= 0 AND SCORE <= 100 OR SCORE = 999
```

If the SCORE entered is in the range 0–100 or if 999 is entered, then the entire condition is true.

	Evaluated First			*Evaluated Second*			
SCORE	SCORE >= 0	AND	SCORE <= 100	AND Cond.	OR	SCORE = 999	Entire Cond.
0	TRUE	AND	TRUE	TRUE	OR	FALSE	TRUE
90	TRUE	AND	TRUE	TRUE	OR	FALSE	TRUE
100	TRUE	AND	TRUE	TRUE	OR	FALSE	TRUE
200	TRUE	AND	FALSE	FALSE	OR	FALSE	FALSE
−1	FALSE	AND	TRUE	FALSE	OR	FALSE	FALSE
999	TRUE	AND	FALSE	FALSE	OR	TRUE	TRUE
1000	TRUE	AND	FALSE	FALSE	OR	FALSE	FALSE

Compound conditions can be useful, but should only be used when thoroughly understood. Multiple ANDs, ORs, and NOTs may be used when necessary. The logic should be carefully worked out for all possible combinations before use. Parentheses may be used to alter the order of evaluation, with the conditions within the parentheses being evaluated first. Extra use of parentheses can also make the statement easier to understand.

Figure 3.2
Effect of logical operators (truth tables).

	First Condition	
OR	T	F
Second Condition T	T	T
F	T	F

	First Condition	
AND	T	F
Second Condition T	T	F
F	F	F

Condition	NOT Condition
T	F
F	T

Example: Parentheses used to clarify, but not alter, the sequence of operations:

```
200   WHILE (SCORE >= 0 AND SCORE <= 100) OR SCORE = 999
```

Example: Parentheses used to alter the sequence of operations:

```
500   WHILE (NUM < 1 OR NUM > 10) AND NUM <> 999
```

Feedback

Determine which conditions will test *true,* and which *false.*

A	B	C$
10	15	M

1. A = B OR C$ = "M"
2. A = B AND C$ = "M"
3. A = 10 OR B = 15 AND C$ = "F"
4. (A = 10 OR B = A) AND C$ = "F"
5. (A = 10 OR B = 10) AND C$ = "M"
6. For what value(s) of X would this condition be true?

    X < 1 AND X > 10

7. For what value(s) of Y would this condition be true?

    Y >= 1 AND Y <= 10

Example Program: Conversion of Miles to Kilometers

Program Listing

```
1000 REM PROGRAM TO CONVERT MILES TO KILOMETERS
1010 '
1020 '              PROGRAM VARIABLES
1030 '              MILES            DISTANCE IN MILES
1040 '              KM               DISTANCE IN KILOMETERS
1050 '              ANS$             ANSWER TO QUESTION
1060 '
2000 '*************** PROGRAM MAINLINE ***********************
2010 CLS                            'CLEAR THE DISPLAY SCREEN
2020 LET ANS$ = "Y"                 'INITIALIZE THE FIELD
2030 WHILE ANS$ = "Y"
2040     GOSUB 3000                 'INPUT MILES
2050     GOSUB 4000                 'CONVERT
2060     GOSUB 5000                 'PRINT RESULTS
2070     INPUT "ANOTHER CONVERSION (Y/N)"; ANS$
2080 WEND
2090 END
2100 '
3000 '*************** INPUT MILES ****************************
3010 PRINT
3020 INPUT "ENTER DISTANCE IN MILES ", MILES
3030 PRINT
3040 RETURN
3050 '
4000 '*************** CONVERT ********************************
4010 LET KM = MILES * 1.6
4020 RETURN
4030 '
5000 '*************** PRINT RESULTS **************************
5010 PRINT MILES; "MILES IS EQUIVALENT TO"; KM; "KILOMETERS"
5020 PRINT
5030 RETURN
5040 '*************** END OF PROGRAM *************************
```

Sample Program Output

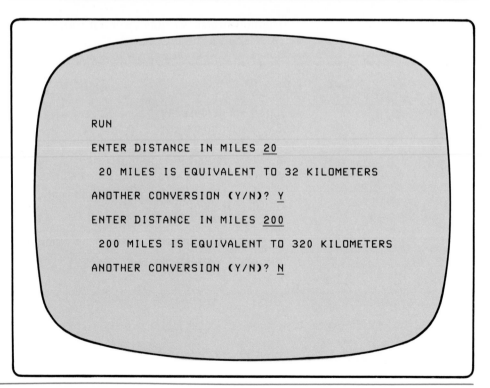

```
RUN

ENTER DISTANCE IN MILES 20

 20 MILES IS EQUIVALENT TO 32 KILOMETERS

ANOTHER CONVERSION (Y/N)? Y

ENTER DISTANCE IN MILES 200

 200 MILES IS EQUIVALENT TO 320 KILOMETERS

ANOTHER CONVERSION (Y/N)? N
```

Loop Indentation

Notice in the conversion program that the statements in the loop (lines 2040–2070) have been indented. This is done to improve the readability of programs. As the complexity of a program increases, good indentation practice becomes more and more important.

The WHILE and WEND statements should be aligned with each other. This clearly indicates the beginning and end of the loop. Then all statements within the loop should be indented and aligned with each other. The precise number of spaces to indent is not important. Some programmers prefer two spaces, others pick a convenient TAB location. The important thing is to be consistent.

If you ever find yourself making changes in another person's program, or even returning to one of your own after a time delay, you will quickly appreciate the importance of good, consistent indentation practices for readability and understanding.

Endless Loops

Care must be taken when programming loops so that an *endless loop* does not occur.

```
10    REM   AN ENDLESS LOOP
20    WHILE NUM <> 10
30        PRINT "HELLO"
40    WEND
```

In this example, there is no way for NUM to become equal to 10, so the condition will always be *true*. This program will continue printing HELLO until one of two things occurs: (1) you turn off the power to the computer, or (2) you learn to interrupt a program on your computer. Simultaneously pressing the CTRL and C (or CTRL-BREAK) keys works for most computers; investigate yours. Try entering the endless loop program, run it, and make sure you can stop it. Then vow not to write that kind of program yourself.

Here is a cleaned up version of the loop program.

```
10    REM   A PROPER LOOP
20    WHILE NUM < 10
30        PRINT "HI THERE, HANDSOME"
40        LET NUM = NUM + 1
50    WEND
```

How many times will the PRINT statement be executed?

Terminating Loops

A loop must always have a way to terminate by using a variable that changes value within the loop. Then the loop condition will be tested again after each **iteration** (execution of the body of the loop). Three common ways of controlling loop exits are (1) questioning the user (e.g., Do you wish to continue?); (2) testing for a particular input value; and (3) using a counter.

Asking a Question to Terminate the Loop

When data is being input from the keyboard, the program can ask the question DO YOU WISH TO CONTINUE?, ARE THERE MORE DATA ITEMS?, or some such question. Then the program can test the value of the data input. Since it is not practical to test for all possible answers (YES, NO, NOPE, Y, N, NO THANKS, YES I DO, etc.), it is best to suggest the desired responses:

```
DO YOU WISH TO CONTINUE (Y/N)?
ARE THERE MORE DATA (YES/NO)?
```

Check for the affirmative response to continue program execution. (Later you will learn to make sure that the response matches one response or the other. If not, you will rerequest input.)

```
400    REM *** ENTER AND PRINT NAMES AND DISTANCES ***
410    LET ANS$ = "YES"
420    WHILE ANS$ = "YES"
430        INPUT "ENTER NAME      ", NAM$
440        INPUT "ENTER DISTANCE ", DIST
450        LPRINT NAM$,,DIST
460        PRINT
470        INPUT "ARE THERE ANY MORE TO ENTER (YES/NO)"; ANS$
480    WEND
```

Notice the addition of line 410, where ANS$ was set to YES to begin. Without this statement, the loop would not be executed even once. Since the condition (ANS$ = "YES") is tested before the first execution of the loop, and the value of ANS$ would most likely *not* be equal to YES, control would pass to the next statement after the WEND. If ANS$ had not been used previously in the program, it would contain the value of the **NULL string** (no characters assigned to ANS$).

Terminating Loops with a Particular Data Value

Many times a certain value in a field will be used to terminate an INPUT loop. Some common ways to end loops are:

```
100    INPUT "ENTER NAME (TYPE 'QUIT' TO END) ", NAM$
500    INPUT "ENTER SCORE (ZERO TO QUIT) ", SCORE
```

When using a predetermined value to end a loop, there are several things to remember. Be sure to choose an ending value that will make sense to the user. Some common ending values are QUIT, END, EOD (*End Of D*ata). Also, make certain that the terminating data requested is a valid constant for the field named on the INPUT statement. When inputting numeric data, you cannot request the word END, but you can select a value that is not a possible value for the field. Zero might or might not be a suitable value to use depending on the data to be entered—perhaps −1 or 999 would be suitable.

```
700    INPUT "ENTER GOLF SCORE (-1 TO QUIT) ", SCORE
800    INPUT "ENTER SALES AMOUNT (0 TO QUIT) ", SALE
```

Priming INPUT

Consider the timing of the condition test in a WHILE loop. The condition is tested at the top of the loop. Each time the WEND is encountered, control is passed back to the WHILE, and the condition is tested again. In order to keep from executing the body of the loop again after the user has entered the terminal value, the INPUT statement should immediately precede the condition test. Therefore, the INPUT should be the *last* statement in the loop, just before the WEND.

```
310    WHILE NAM$ <> "END"
320        GOSUB 1000    'CALCULATIONS
330        GOSUB 2000    'PRINT RESULTS
340        INPUT "ENTER NAME (TYPE 'END' TO QUIT) ", NAM$
350    WEND
```

This technique will work for all data items starting with the second INPUT. One more statement is needed to complete the logic. That statement is called the *priming INPUT*. It serves to get things going, to "prime the pump."

```
300    INPUT "ENTER NAME (TYPE 'END' TO QUIT) ", NAM$
310    WHILE NAM$ <> "END"
320        GOSUB 1000    'CALCULATIONS
330        GOSUB 2000    'PRINT RESULTS
340        INPUT "ENTER NAME (TYPE 'END' TO QUIT) ", NAM$
350    WEND
```

Example Program:
A Variation on the Conversion Problem

Program Listing

```
1000 REM PROGRAM TO CONVERT MILES TO KILOMETERS
1010 '
1020 '          PROGRAM VARIABLES
1030 '          MILES              DISTANCE IN MILES
1040 '          KM                 DISTANCE IN KILOMETERS
1060 '
2000 '*************** PROGRAM MAINLINE *********************
2010 CLS
2020 GOSUB 3000                    'INPUT MILES
2030 WHILE MILES >= 0
2050     GOSUB 4000                'CONVERT
2060     GOSUB 5000                'PRINT RESULTS
2070     GOSUB 3000                'INPUT MILES
2080 WEND
2090 END
2100 '
3000 '*************** INPUT MILES **************************
3010 PRINT
3020 INPUT "ENTER DISTANCE IN MILES (NEGATIVE NUMBER TO QUIT) ",
MILES
3030 PRINT
3040 RETURN
3050 '
4000 '*************** CONVERT ******************************
4010 LET KM = MILES * 1.6
4020 RETURN
4030 '
5000 '*************** PRINT RESULTS ************************
5010 PRINT MILES; "MILES IS EQUIVALENT TO"; KM; "KILOMETERS"
5020 RETURN
5030 '*************** END OF PROGRAM ***********************
```

Sample Program Output

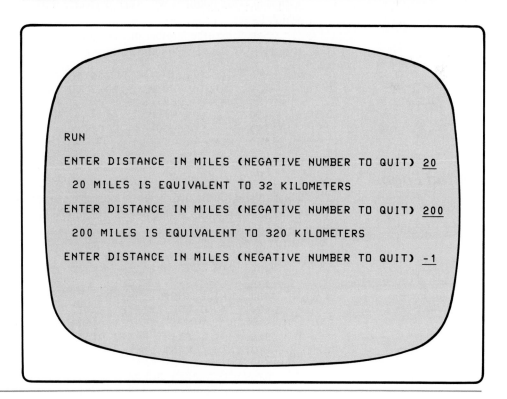

```
RUN

ENTER DISTANCE IN MILES (NEGATIVE NUMBER TO QUIT) 20

  20 MILES IS EQUIVALENT TO 32 KILOMETERS

ENTER DISTANCE IN MILES (NEGATIVE NUMBER TO QUIT) 200

  200 MILES IS EQUIVALENT TO 320 KILOMETERS

ENTER DISTANCE IN MILES (NEGATIVE NUMBER TO QUIT) -1
```

Counter-Controlled Loops

When a loop must be executed a given number of times, a variable can be used as a **counter.** For each execution of the loop, the counter is incremented by 1. The condition on the WHILE statement can then test for the terminal value needed.

```
200   REM *** PRINT 10 ROWS ***
210   LET COUNT = 0
220   WHILE COUNT < 10
230       LPRINT "-------------------------------------"
240       LET COUNT = COUNT + 1
250   WEND
```

PROGRAM EXECUTION:

```
VALUE OF
COUNT
 1    -----------------------------------
 2    -----------------------------------
 3    -----------------------------------
 4    -----------------------------------
 5    -----------------------------------
 6    -----------------------------------
 7    -----------------------------------
 8    -----------------------------------
 9    -----------------------------------
10    -----------------------------------
```

Or, an alternate solution:

```
300   REM *** PRINT 10 ROWS ***
310   LET COUNT = 10
320   WHILE COUNT > 0
330       LPRINT "-------------------------------------"
340       LET COUNT = COUNT - 1
350   WEND
```

Either of these methods will work perfectly well. It is strictly a matter of preference which to use.

Sometimes the number of iterations of a loop must be variable. One possibility is to INPUT the value for the counter before beginning the loop.

```
100   REM  *** PRINT A VARIABLE NUMBER OF ROWS ***
110   INPUT "HOW MANY ROWS TO PRINT"; COUNT
120   WHILE COUNT > 0
130       LPRINT "-------------------------------------"
140       LET COUNT = COUNT - 1
150   WEND
```

Nested Loops

Often it will be necessary to place one loop inside another loop. These are called **nested loops**. A situation in which nested loops are needed is when input data must be checked for a valid response. If the user enters an invalid response, continuous requests must be made for a valid response. Whenever program statements must be repeated, a WHILE loop is needed.

```
400   REM *** ENTER AND PRINT NAMES AND DISTANCES ***
410   LET ANS$ = "YES"
420   WHILE ANS$ = "YES"
430       INPUT "ENTER NAME      ", NAM$
440       INPUT "ENTER DISTANCE ", DIST
450       LPRINT NAM$,,DIST
460       PRINT
470       INPUT "ARE THERE ANY MORE TO ENTER? (YES/NO) ",ANS$
475       '*** CHECK THE ANSWER FOR A VALID RESPONSE ***
480       WHILE ANS$ <> "YES" AND ANS$ <> "NO"
490           INPUT "PLEASE ENTER 'YES' OR 'NO' ", ANS$
500       WEND
510   WEND
```

Or, as a further variation, the inner loop can be used to ask the question every time.

```
400   REM *** ENTER AND PRINT NAMES AND DISTANCES ***
410   LET ANS$ = "YES"
420   WHILE ANS$ = "YES"
430       INPUT "ENTER NAME       ", NAM$
440       INPUT "ENTER DISTANCE ", DIST
450       LPRINT NAM$,,DIST
460       PRINT
470       LET ANS$ = " "
475       '*** KEEP INPUTTING UNTIL "YES" OR "NO" ENTERED ***
480       WHILE ANS$ <> "YES" AND ANS$ <> "NO"
490         INPUT "ARE THERE ANY MORE TO ENTER? (YES/NO) ", ANS$
500       WEND
510   WEND
```

Microsoft BASIC will allow nesting to as many levels as desired, as long as these rules are followed.

1. Each WHILE must have a WEND.
2. Each WEND will be matched with the last unmatched WHILE statement (regardless of any indentation). This means that an inner loop must be completely contained within an outer loop.

Good programming practice requires proper indentation of WHILE loops. This is especially important with nested loops.

```
WHILE <condition 1>
    loop statements for loop 1
    WHILE <condition 2>
        loop statements for loop 2
        WHILE <condition 3>
            loop statements for loop 3
        WEND
        more loop statements for loop 2
    WEND
    more loop statements for loop 1
WEND
```

Feedback

1. Code a BASIC loop that will print your name five times (one PRINT statement executed five times).
2. Write a BASIC loop that will print the numbers 1–10. This should be done with one PRINT statement executed multiple times. (PRINT X, where X changes in value for each iteration of the loop.)
3. Write a BASIC loop that will continuously input and print the names of contest participants, until QUIT is entered in place of the name.
4. How many times will the PRINT be executed?

```
10   WHILE ZED <> 0
20       PRINT ZED
30       LET ZED = ZED + 1
40   WEND
```

5. What will print? Try this with several different values for AMT, such as 5, 10, 1, 0.

```
10   INPUT AMT
20   WHILE AMT > 0
30       PRINT "*";
40       LET AMT = AMT - 1
50   WEND
```

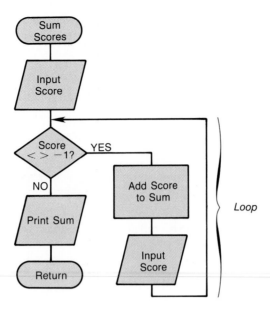

Figure 3.3
Flowchart for summation in a
loop. The statements in the loop
will be repeated until -1 is input
for the score.

Accumulating Sums

A common task in programming is summing numbers. Earlier, three test scores were added with these statements:

```
10    INPUT TEST1
20    INPUT TEST2
30    INPUT TEST3
40    LET SUM = TEST1 + TEST2 + TEST3
```

What if there had been twenty scores, or 500? Imagine the program necessary to input 500 scores and add them up! How would a program work if the exact number of scores were unknown?

Fortunately, there is a simple solution to the problem—loops. The scores can be input one at a time until all scores are entered. Of course, each time the INPUT statement in the loop is executed, a new score will replace the previous score. It is not necessary to save each individual score. What is needed is the total, so each score may be added into the total as it is input. In this way, a running total is kept. Then, after all scores have been entered, the total can be printed (see figure 3.3). The statements in the loop will be repeated until -1 is input for the score.

It should be noted that at the start of program execution, BASIC sets all numeric variables to zero. This eliminates the need for the initialization step required in many programming languages.

```
500    REM*** SUM VARIABLE NUMBER OF TEST SCORES ***
510    PRINT "ENTER TEST SCORES, (-1 TO QUIT)"
520    INPUT SCORE
530    WHILE SCORE <> -1
540         LET SUM = SUM + SCORE
550         INPUT SCORE
560    WEND
570    PRINT " THE SUM IS "; SUM
580    RETURN
```

To trace the execution of the program statements, enter scores of 100, 75, 90, 85, and −1 to end (see figure 3.4).

Figure 3.4
Summation in a loop.

Beginning of program	SCORE 0	SUM 0
After execution of line 520 (Priming INPUT)	SCORE 100	SUM 0
540 LET SUM = SUM + SCORE	SCORE 100	SUM 100
550 INPUT SCORE	SCORE 75	SUM 100
540 LET SUM = SUM + SCORE	SCORE 75	SUM 175
550 INPUT SCORE	SCORE 90	SUM 175
540 LET SUM = SUM + SCORE	SCORE 90	SUM 265
550 INPUT SCORE	SCORE 85	SUM 265
540 LET SUM = SUM + SCORE	SCORE 85	SUM 350
550 INPUT SCORE	SCORE -1	SUM 350
FINAL - TO PRINT	SCORE -1	SUM 350

Figure 3.5

Flowchart of subroutine to
average scores. The scores are
summed and counted in the loop.
Then after all scores are entered,
the average can be calculated by
dividing the sum by the count of
the scores.

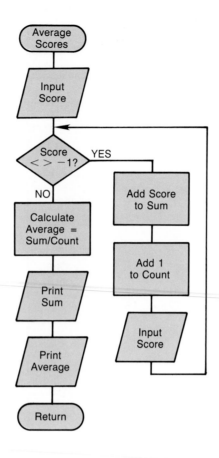

Averaging

To know the average of the scores, it is also necessary to know the number of scores entered. This can be accomplished with a counter in the loop. In figure 3.5, note how the scores are summed and counted in the loop. Then after all scores are entered, the average can be calculated by dividing the sum by the count of the scores.

```
500    REM*** AVERAGE VARIABLE NUMBER OF TEST SCORES ***
510    PRINT "ENTER TEST SCORES, (-1 TO QUIT)"
520    INPUT SCORE
530    WHILE SCORE <> -1
540         LET SUM = SUM + SCORE
545         LET COUNT = COUNT + 1
550         INPUT SCORE
560    WEND
565    LET AVG = SUM / COUNT
570    PRINT " THE SUM IS "; SUM
575    PRINT " THE AVERAGE IS "; AVG
580    RETURN

RUN
```

Line Number	Screen Display	Value of Score	Value of Sum	Value of Count
510	ENTER TEST SCORES, (-1 TO QUIT)	0	0	0
520	?100	100	0	0
530		100	0	0
540		100	100	0
545		100	100	1
550	? 75	75	100	1
560		75	100	1

Line Number	Screen Display	Value of Score	Value of Sum	Value of Count
530		75	100	1
540		75	175	1
545		75	175	2
550	? 90	90	175	2
560		90	175	2
530		90	175	2
540		90	265	2
545		90	265	3
550	? 85	85	265	3
560		85	265	3
530		85	265	3
540		85	350	3
545		85	350	4
550	? -1	-1	350	4
560		-1	350	4
530		-1	350	4
565		-1	350	4
570	THE SUM IS 350	-1	350	4
575	THE AVERAGE IS 87.5	-1	350	4

Planning Programs with Loops

When planning the logic of a program, a good practice is to number each logic step. A relatively clear way to plan loop logic is to give the loop one number. Then for each step in the loop use the loop's number, a decimal point, and a sequential number within the loop. This is similar to an outline form.

1. Initialize variables
2. Print headings
3. Priming input
4. Loop until end of data
   4.1 Add to totals
   4.2 Print a line
   4.3 Input next data
5. Print totals
6. Stop

Figure 3.6
Flowchart for a single loop. The statements in the body of the loop are repeated as long as the condition (More Data?) is true.

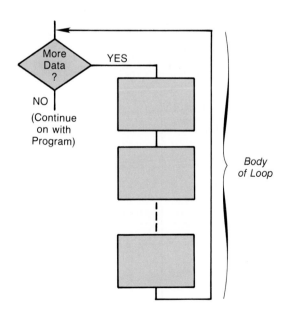

Flowcharting Loops

When flowcharting a loop, the decision comes first. The decision determines whether or not the loop should be executed again. A decision is flowcharted with the diamond-shaped symbol (see figure 3.6). The question within the symbol is stated as a question that can be answered YES or NO, TRUE or FALSE. The statements in the body of the loop are repeated as long as the condition (MORE DATA?) is true.

Output Formatting

Creating program output that is pleasing, properly spaced, and aligned has sometimes been a difficult task. BASIC has several statements and functions to assist in the formatting process. Those presented in the sections to follow are TAB, SPC, PRINT USING, and LPRINT USING.

The PRINT Functions— TAB and SPC

TAB

The placement of variables and constants on the screen or printer can be controlled by the use of the TAB function. It is similar to the tabs used on a typewriter.

A layout form can be a helpful tool in planning program output (see figures 3.7 and 3.8).

```
100   PRINT TAB(25) "WEEKLY SALES"
110   PRINT
120   PRINT TAB(10) "NAME" TAB(40) "AMOUNT"
130   PRINT
140   PRINT TAB(6) NAM$ TAB(40) AMT
::
::
RUN
                              WEEKLY SALES


          NAME                          AMOUNT

          SAM   TONG                     25.25
```

The TAB function can only be used in PRINT and LPRINT statements. The keyword TAB is followed by an open parentheses (no intervening space allowed), then the desired position number, a closing parentheses, and the data item to print. That data item may be a variable, a constant, or an expression.

Figure 3.7
Layout showing TAB locations.

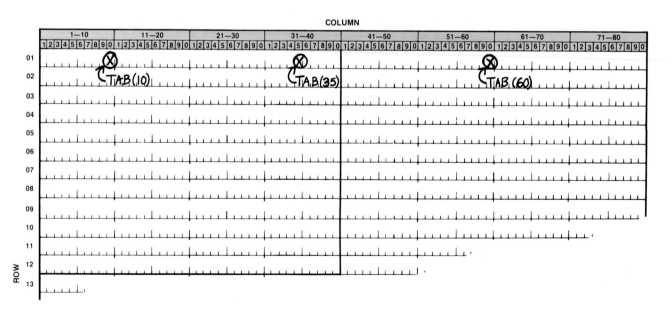

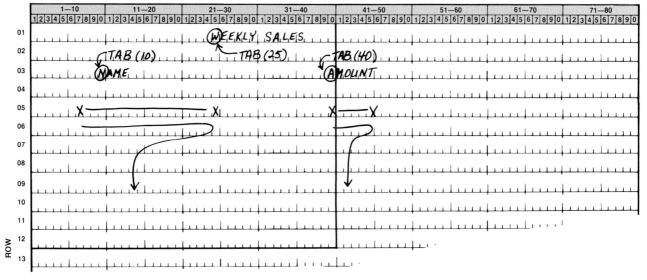

Figure 3.8
TAB example.

The position to occupy is an absolute position. That is, the first position on the line is TAB(1), and the twentieth position is TAB(20). The TAB location is limited by the line length of the video display or by the line length of the printer used. The position number may be a constant, variable, or arithmetic expression in the range 1–255. Any fractional values will be rounded up.

When the PRINT is executed, the internal print pointer moves to the position specified in the TAB, then the data value is printed in that exact position. A semicolon may be used between the TAB and data value (many other versions of BASIC require it), but watch out for the comma! A comma in a PRINT statement always means "go to the next zone," and the effects of the TAB will be lost. Do not use commas with TABs.

The TAB Function—General Form

| line number | PRINT TAB(position) [;] items to print |
| line number | LPRINT TAB(position) [;] items to print |

The TAB Function—Examples

```
60    PRINT TAB(20) "UNDERWATER REPORT"
100   LPRINT TAB(5) "NAME = ";NAMES$;TAB(40) "CLASS = ";CLASS$

20    LET T1 = 5
30    LET T2 = 20
40    LET T3 = 45
50    LET T4 = 60
60    LET T5 = 66
200   LPRINT TAB(T1);ITEM;TAB(T2);DESC$;TAB(T3);PRICE;TAB(T4);
      QUANTITY;TAB(T5);TOTAL

400   LET SPOT = SPOT + COLUMN
410   PRINT TAB(10 + SPOT); FIGURE
```

It is a good practice to use variables for the TAB position. Then, report layouts may be changed more easily.

If a TAB position is given that has already been passed on that line, BASIC will go to that TAB position on the next line to print.

```
140   PRINT TAB(10) "POSITION 10" TAB(5) "POSITION 5"
::
::
RUN
              POSITION 10
        POSITION 5
```

SPC

Another function that can control horizontal spacing on the line is SPC. SPC differs from TAB in that TAB moves the print pointer to an absolute position on the line, but SPC moves the pointer a given number of spaces on the line (relative to the preceding item printed).

```
10   PRINT "ACCOUNT NUMBER"; SPC(5); "BALANCE"
::
::
RUN
ACCOUNT NUMBER     BALANCE
```

The SPC Function—General Form

```
line number    PRINT SPC(number of characters)[;] items to print
line number    LPRINT SPC(number of characters)[;] items to print
```

```
20   PRINT TAB(20) "COSTS = " SPC(4) COST
100    LPRINT NAM$;SPC(3);ADDR$;SPC(3);CITY$;SPC(3);STATE$
```

Like the TAB, SPC can be used only in PRINT and LPRINT statements. The number of characters to space may be a variable, constant, or arithmetic expression in the range 1–255. SPC may appear multiple times on one PRINT line to control spacing all across the line.

Formatting Output with PRINT USING and LPRINT USING

A powerful aid to formatting screen and printer output is the USING option of the PRINT and LPRINT statements. The PRINT USING statement will provide for "editing" data such as

1. alignment of decimal points.
2. exact alignment of columns of data.
3. rounding to any desired number of decimal places.
4. forcing right zeros to print in decimal fractions.
5. placement of commas, dollar signs, plus signs, and minus signs in numeric values.
6. exact horizontal spacing of both numeric and string data for printed lines.

All options shown for the PRINT USING are also available for the LPRINT USING.

The PRINT USING Statement—General Form

```
line number    PRINT USING "string literal"; items to print
line number    PRINT USING (string variable); items to print
```

```
50    PRINT USING " ###     ###.##     #,###.##"; ITEM, PR, TOT
RUN
 250      14.50     1,450.00


100   LET N$ = "###,###.##"
110   PRINT USING N$; 12.5
120   PRINT USING N$; 1.365
130   PRINT USING N$; .111
140   PRINT USING N$; 12345
RUN
       12.50
        1.37
        0.11
   12,345.00
```

Editing Numeric Data

The formats for numeric values are defined by using the number sign (#), the decimal point, and the comma. The number of symbols used will determine the length and format of the results. Notice in the second example of the PRINT USING statement decimal points are aligned in the results, each output number has two digits to the right of the decimal point, and short numbers have been padded with right zeros and the long numbers (1.365 and .111) were rounded to print in the print image.

Editing Strings

Strings may also be printed with PRINT USING statements. The backslash character (\)* is used to show the beginning and end of an edited string. The backslash characters are included in the length of the string. In the example, there are six blank spaces between the backslashes, so the printed string length is eight characters. Any string longer than the edit image will be truncated when printed (see the results of the example following).

```
200    LET D$ = "\        \    ###.##"
210    PRINT USING D$; "SAM"; 4.5
220    PRINT USING D$; "JANET"; 25
230    PRINT USING D$; "HORNSWAGGLED"; 1
RUN
SAM              4.50
JANET           25.00
HORNSWAG         1.00
```

The **print image,** or string used for formatting the data, can be a literal (as in the first two examples following) or a variable (third example following). The combination of special characters used in the print image will determine the format of the data printed. When there are multiple items to print, they may be separated by semicolons or commas.

```
200    LET D$ = " ###.#    ###.#    ###.#"
210    PRINT USING D$; R1, R2, R3

100    PRINT USING "### \        \    ##,###.##"; NUM, DES$, AMT
10    LET PRIZE = 1000
20    PRINT USING "##,###.##"; PRIZE
RUN
1,000.00
```

*Microsoft BASIC for the TRS-80 uses percent signs (%) rather than backslashes.

Rounding

One of the advantages of the PRINT USING is that numeric values will be rounded to the specified number of digits in the format.

```
100   LET SHOW = 1.625
110   PRINT USING "  #    #.#    #.##    #.###    #.####"; SHOW,
        SHOW, SHOW, SHOW, SHOW
RUN
  2    1.6    1.63    1.625    1.6250
```

Defining Entire Print Lines Including Literals

Print images may contain formatting characters for multiple items along with literals to be printed on a line. The spacing in the print image will define the exact horizontal spacing on the printed line.

```
150   LET T$ = "TOTAL JOKES = ### -- TOTAL DUDS = ###"
160   PRINT USING T$; JOKE.TOT, DUD.TOT
RUN
TOTAL JOKES = 125 -- TOTAL DUDS =   1
```

Formatting PRINT Images

Each print image should contain one specification for each variable to be printed. The variables will be placed into the specifications on the line on a one-for-one basis. The variable type (numeric or string) must correspond.

```
100   LET D$ = "  ##.#   ##.#    \        \   ## "
110   PRINT USING D$; NUM1, NUM2, ST$, NUM3
```

In line 100, four specifications are shown for data. Then in line 110, four variables are named in the correct order (numeric, numeric, string, numeric).

```
250   LET A$ = "  THE GROSS IS #,###.##    THE NET IS #,###.## "
260   PRINT USING A$; GROSS, NET
```

Line 250 specifies two literals to print, exactly as shown ("THE GROSS IS" and "THE NET IS"). Additionally, two numeric specifications are included for formatting the two variables GROSS and NET. Assuming that GROSS has a value of 1000 and NET has a value of 800, the output of line 260 would be:

```
THE GROSS IS 1,000.00    THE NET IS   800.00
```

Short Numeric Formats

```
10   LET G$ = "###.#"
20   PRINT USING G$; 1000
30   PRINT USING G$; 999.95
40   PRINT USING G$; 1000000
RUN
%1000.0
%1000.0
%1000000.0
```

When the format given for a number is too short for the value, a percent sign is printed first, then the entire value. This will often cause columns of data to be mis-aligned. Whenever there is a percent sign at the beginning of the printed output, the first suspicion should be an inadequate numeric format.

Placement of PRINT Images in the Program

Each program module should perform one, and only one, function. Setting up all print images for the program is a good example of a group of statements that together accomplish one task. Since a print image must be defined before the first time it is used, it makes sense to set up all print images at the start of the program in a step called initialization.

A further advantage to defining all print images in one subroutine is that it is easy to see that columns are aligned—headings will appear above the correct column of data, and totals will be exactly aligned below their columns.

Example Program: Using PRINT Images

Program Listing

```
10 REM **** EXAMPLE USING PRINT IMAGE LINES ************
20 REM ************ MAINLINE **************************
30 GOSUB 1000              'SET UP PRINT IMAGES
40 GOSUB 2000              'PRINT HEADINGS
45 GOSUB 3000              'DETAIL LOOP
50 GOSUB 4000              'PRINT TOTAL
60 END
70 '
1000'********** SET UP PRINT IMAGES ****************
1010 LET H$ = "      NAME                AMOUNT "
1020 LET D$ = "    \             \       ###.## "
1030 LET T$ = "            TOTAL =      #,###.## "
1040 RETURN
1050 '
2000'************* PRINT HEADINGS ******************
2010 LPRINT H$
2020 LPRINT
2030 RETURN
2040 '
3000'************* DETAIL LOOP ********************
3010 INPUT "ENTER NAME ('QUIT' TO END) ", NAM$
3020 WHILE NAM$ <> "QUIT"
3030     INPUT "ENTER AMOUNT GIVEN ", AMT
3040     LET TOTAL = TOTAL + AMT
3050     LPRINT USING D$; NAM$, AMT
3060     INPUT "ENTER NAME ('QUIT' TO END) ", NAM$
3070 WEND
3080 RETURN
3090 '
4000'************* PRINT TOTAL *******************
4010 LPRINT
4020 LPRINT USING T$; TOTAL
4030 RETURN
```

```
        NAME                    AMOUNT


     MAJOR GENERAL               2.75
     COLONEL CHICKEN            12.00
     PRIVATE PUNCH               4.01

            TOTAL  =            18.76
```

Feedback

What output will result for each of these examples? Check your answers with the computer.

1. 1000 LET D$ = " ##   ##.#   ##.##   ##.### "
   1010 LET NUM = 25.3964
   1020 PRINT USING D$; NUM, NUM, NUM, NUM

2. 600 LET P$ = "\   \ ##"
   610 PRINT USING P$; "FROGS", 10
   620 PRINT USING P$; "TOADS", 5
   630 PRINT USING P$; "POLLIWOGS", 75

3. 700 LET T$ = " THE SCORE IS ## FOR THE \   \"
   710 PRINT USING T$; 12; "ROVERS"
   720 PRINT USING T$; 6; "BRAVES"
   730 PRINT USING T$; 125; "AMAZING AMAZONS"

4. 500 LET R$ = " \   \ SPENT ###.## ON \   \ "
   510 LET MONEY = 2
   520 LET KID$ = "JOEY"
   530 LET TREAT$ = "GUM"
   540 PRINT USING R$; KID$, MONEY, TREAT$

5. 800 LET A$ = " ### NEEDED BY \   \ "
   810 LET DAT$ = "12/25/95"
   820 LET AMT = 3.5
   830 PRINT USING A$; DAT$, AMT

Extended Numeric Editing

Numbers may also be edited with dollar signs, asterisks, and plus and minus signs. Dollar signs may be "fixed" at a particular location on the line or may be caused to "float."

Dollar Signs

Dollar signs may be placed in print images in one of two different ways.

1. The sign can be *fixed*—that is, it will always appear in the location defined.
2. A *floating dollar sign* will be printed to the left of the first significant digit of the number (first nonzero digit).

Fixed Dollar Sign One dollar sign in the print image will fix the dollar sign.

```
50   PRINT USING "$##,###.##";25
RUN
$      25.00
```

Floating Dollar Sign Two dollar signs in the print image will cause the sign to be printed in the first position to the left of the formatted number.

```
60   PRINT USING "$$#,###.##";25
RUN
     $25.00
```

Since one dollar sign must always be printed by this print image, the largest number that can be printed in this image has five digits to the left of the decimal point (99,999).

Plus and Minus Signs

Without any help from a print image, positive numbers are printed without a sign, and negative numbers are printed with a leading minus sign. By using a print image, the sign may be printed at either end of the number, and plus signs may be forced to print.

The printing of the sign is controlled by the sign used in the print image. Using a plus sign will force a sign to print on all numbers—a plus sign for positive numbers and a minus sign for negative numbers. Using a minus sign in the image will cause a sign to be printed for negative numbers only.

Trailing Signs The sign placed at the right end of the format specification will cause the sign to trail the formatted number.

```
90    P$ = "###.#-      ###.#+"
100   PRINT USING P$; 10,10
110   PRINT USING P$; -50.65, -50.65
120   PRINT USING P$; .22, .22
RUN
 10.0         10.0+
 50.7-        50.7-
  0.2          0.2+
```

Leading Signs A plus sign placed at the left end of the format specification will cause the sign to be printed preceding (leading) the formatted number. However, a minus sign cannot be used on the left of a format specification.

```
40    LET S$ = "+###.##      ###.##"
50    PRINT USING S$; 10, 10
60    PRINT USING S$; -1.555, -1.555
70    PRINT USING S$; -100, -100
RUN
 +10.00      10.00
  -1.56      -1.56
-100.00    %-100.00
```

Asterisk Check Protection

Two asterisks in a format specification specify *check protection.* All spaces to the left of the number will be filled with asterisks.

```
130    LET C$ = "**##,###.##"
140    PRINT USING C$; 1000
150    PRINT USING C$; 1.25
RUN
***1,000.00
*******1.25
```

Combining a Floating Dollar Sign with Check Protection

To combine the floating dollar sign and asterisk check protection, use two asterisks and one dollar sign (**$).

```
160    LET D$ = "**$#,###.##"
170    PRINT USING D$; 50
180    PRINT USING D$; 2542.22
RUN
*****$50.00
**$2,542.22
```

Number of Characters Printed

Each of the formatting characters (# , $. * + −) counts as one character. The floating dollar sign and asterisk check protection character are each considered one digit position. If the number to be printed is too long, the editing characters will not print.

```
10    LET L$ = "**$,###.##"
20    PRINT USING L$; 10
30    PRINT USING L$; 1000
40    PRINT USING L$; 10000
50    PRINT USING L$; 100000
60    PRINT USING L$; 1000000
RUN
****$10.00
*$1,000.00
$10,000.00
%$100,000.00
%$1,000,000.00
```

Editing String Data

Strings can be formatted to a specified length with the backslash character. The number of print positions used will be the number of spaces between the backslashes plus two, since the backslash characters are included in the length. Long strings will be truncated to fit the format, and short strings will be filled with blank spaces.

```
300    LET K$ = "\  \    \    \  \         \"
310    LET V$ = "ABCDEFGHIJ"
320    PRINT USING K$; V$; V$; V$
RUN
ABCD    ABCDEF  ABCDEFGHIJ
```

Printing Variable Length Strings

When the entire string should be printed, regardless of the length, the ampersand (&) is used.

```
240    LET L$ = "& ## ####"
250    PRINT USING L$; "MAY", 15, 1940
260    PRINT USING L$; "DECEMBER", 1, 1990
RUN
MAY  15   1940
DECEMBER   1 1990
```

Repeated PRINT Images

```
200    PRINT USING "##,### "; 25; 10000; 235
RUN
       25  10,000   235
```

One print image is used to format all three numeric values. When the print image does not contain enough numeric specifications, the image is repeated. When this technique is used, it is advisable to include blank spaces within the image to control horizontal spacing between numeric values.

Feedback

What output will result for each of these examples?

```
1.    500 LET E$ = "**$#,###.##"
      510 PRINT USING E$; 1
      520 PRINT USING E$; 250000
      530 PRINT USING E$; .599
      540 PRINT USING E$; 999.999
      550 PRINT USING E$; 123456789
2.    600 LET NUM1 = 4
      610 LET NUM2 = -50.45
      620 LET NUM3 = -100.63
      630 LET NUM4 = 0
      640 PRINT USING " ###.#- "; NUM1, NUM2, NUM3, NUM4
      650 PRINT USING " ###.#+ "; NUM1, NUM2, NUM3, NUM4
      660 PRINT USING " +##.## "; NUM1, NUM2, NUM3, NUM4
      670 PRINT USING " $$##,###.## "; NUM1, NUM2, NUM3, NUM4
      680 PRINT USING "  $##,###.## "; NUM1, NUM2, NUM3, NUM4
```

Combining TABs and PRINT Images

It is permissible to combine TAB with PRINT USING, but only one TAB function may be used per line.

```
90    PRINT TAB(20) USING "##.##   ##"; TOTAL, COUNT
```

Notice the placement of the TAB between the PRINT and USING.

Feedback

Can you name any advantages of using a variable rather than a literal for the print image?

Programming Example: Jog-a-Thon Fund-Raising Drive

A jog-a-thon has been planned for a fund-raising drive. What is needed is a program to keep track of the runners and the donations they have earned. Each runner has received pledges of a certain amount of money for each lap run. After the event has been run, the amount each runner has earned for the cause must be calculated.

At the conclusion of the report, the program should show the totals of the amount pledged, the number of laps run, and the amount earned. Also, the organizers would like to know the average amount pledged per runner, the average number of laps run, and the average amount earned.

Input

1. Runner's name
2. Amount pledged per lap (for that runner)
3. Number of laps run

Output (printer)

1. All three input fields
2. Amount earned (one runner)

Calculations

1. Amount earned = amount pledged * laps run
2. Total the amount pledged, laps run, and amount earned
3. Count the number of runners
4. Average the amount pledged, laps run, and amount earned

Pseudocode

1. Initialize print images
2. Print headings
3. Input runner name (priming input, name only)
4. Loop until END entered
    4.1   Input amount pledged and laps run
    4.2   Calculations
        4.2.1   Calculate amount earned
        4.2.2   Add to 3 totals
        4.2.3   Add 1 to count
    4.3   Output on printer
        4.3.1   Name, amount pledged, laps run, amount earned
    4.4   Input next runner name
5. Total calculations
    5.1   Average 3 fields
6. Print totals

Hierarchy Chart

Refer to figure 3.9.

Flowchart

Refer to figure 3.10 (pp. 87–88).

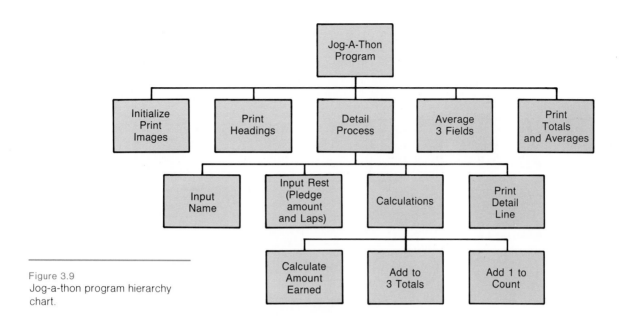

Figure 3.9
Jog-a-thon program hierarchy chart.

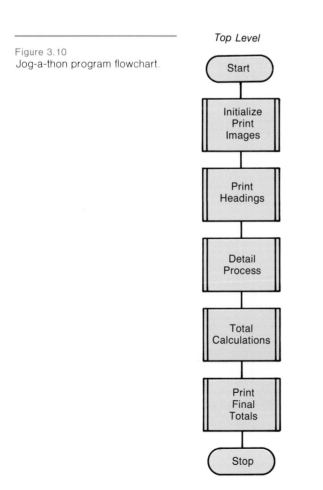

Figure 3.10
Jog-a-thon program flowchart.

Top Level

Figure 3.10—*Continued*

Second Level

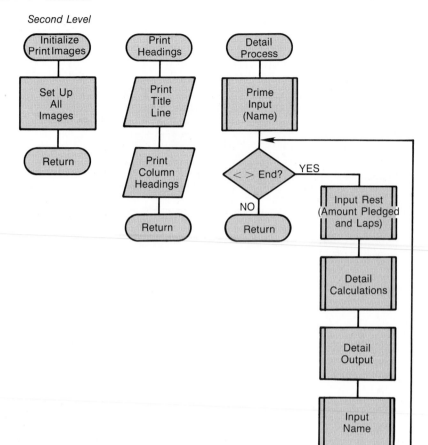

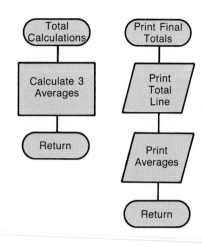

Third Level

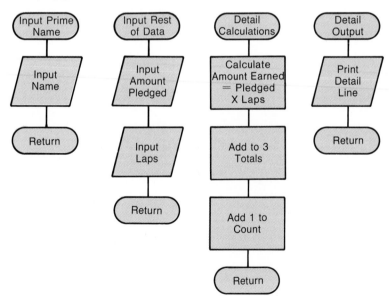

Chapter 3

Example Program

```
1000 '        PROGRAM TO KEEP TRACK OF THE DONATIONS FOR THE JOG-A-THON
1010 '
1020 '          PROGRAM VARIABLES
1030 '
1040 '          RUNNER$            NAME OF RUNNER
1050 '          PLEDGE            AMOUNT PLEDGED PER LAP
1060 '          LAPS              NUMBER OF LAPS RUN
1070 '          EARNED            AMOUNT EARNED/ ONE RUNNER
1080 '          TOT.LAPS          TOTAL NUMBER OF LAPS
1090 '          TOT.PLEDGE        TOTAL OF PLEDGE COLUMN
1100 '          TOT.EARNED        TOTAL OF EARNED COLUMN
1110 '          COUNT             COUNT OF NUMBER OF RUNNERS
1120 '          AVG.PLEDGE        AVERAGE AMOUNT PLEDGED PER LAP
1130 '          AVG.LAPS          AVERAGE NUMBER OF LAPS PER RUNNER
1140 '          AVG.EARNED        AVERAGE AMOUNT EARNED PER RUNNER
1150 '          T$, H1$, H2$
1160 '          D$, TL$, S1$      PRINT IMAGES
1170 '          S2$, S3$
1180 '
2000 '******************** PROGRAM MAINLINE ********************
2010 GOSUB 3000                'INITIALIZE PRINT IMAGES
2020 GOSUB 4000                'PRINT HEADINGS
2030 GOSUB 5000                'DETAIL LOOP
2040 GOSUB 9000                'TOTAL CALCULATIONS
2050 GOSUB 9500                'PRINT TOTALS
2060 END
2070 '
3000 '**************** INITIALIZE PRINT IMAGES ****************
3010 LET T$  = "       J O G - A - T H O N   D O N A T I O N S"
3020 LET H1$ = "       RUNNER              AMOUNT      LAPS        AMOUNT"
3030 LET H2$ = "                           PLEDGED     RUN         EARNED"
3040 LET D$  = "\                 \    ###.##       ###      #,###.##"
3050 LET TL$ = "       TOTALS          #,###.##   ##,###     ##,###.##"
3060 LET S1$ = "       AVERAGE PLEDGED PER LAP    ###.##"
3070 LET S2$ = "       AVERAGE LAPS RUN           ##.#"
3080 LET S3$ = "       AVERAGE EARNINGS           ###.##"
3090 RETURN
3100 '
4000 '******************** PRINT HEADINGS ********************
4020 LPRINT T$                 'TITLE LINE
4030 LPRINT
4040 LPRINT H1$                'FIRST HEADING LINE
4050 LPRINT H2$                'SECOND HEADING LINE
4060 LPRINT
4070 LPRINT
4080 RETURN
4090 '
5000 '****************** MAIN DETAIL LOOP ******************
5005 CLS                       'CLEAR SCREEN FOR INPUT
5010 GOSUB 6000                'INPUT RUNNER NAME
5020 WHILE RUNNER$ <> "END"
5030     GOSUB 6500            'INPUT THE REST FOR ONE RUNNER
5040     GOSUB 7000            'CALCULATE
5050     GOSUB 8000            'OUTPUT
5060     GOSUB 6000            'INPUT RUNNER NAME
5070 WEND
5080 RETURN
5090 '
6000 '***************** INPUT RUNNER NAME ******************
6010 INPUT "ENTER RUNNER NAME (TYPE 'END' TO QUIT) ", RUNNER$
6020 RETURN
6030 '
```

```
6500 '*************** INPUT REST FOR ONE RUNNER ***************
6510 PRINT
6520 INPUT "AMOUNT PLEDGED PER LAP ", PLEDGE
6530 PRINT
6540 INPUT "NUMBER OF LAPS RUN    ", LAPS
6550 PRINT
6560 RETURN
6570 '
7000 '**************** CALCULATIONS ***********************
7010 LET EARNED = PLEDGE * LAPS
7020 LET TOT.EARNED = TOT.EARNED + EARNED
7030 LET TOT.PLEDGE = TOT.PLEDGE + PLEDGE
7040 LET TOT.LAPS = TOT.LAPS + LAPS
7050 LET COUNT = COUNT + 1
7060 RETURN
7070 '
8000 '**************** DETAIL OUTPUT ***********************
8010 LPRINT USING D$; RUNNER$, PLEDGE, LAPS, EARNED
8020 RETURN
8030 '
9000 '***************** TOTAL CALCULATIONS *****************
9010 LET AVG.PLEDGE = TOT.PLEDGE / COUNT
9020 LET AVG.LAPS = TOT.LAPS / COUNT
9030 LET AVG.EARNED = TOT.EARNED / COUNT
9040 RETURN
9050 '
9500 '***************** PRINT FINAL TOTALS *****************
9510 LPRINT
9520 LPRINT USING TL$; TOT.PLEDGE, TOT.LAPS, TOT.EARNED
9530 LPRINT
9540 LPRINT
9550 LPRINT USING S1$; AVG.PLEDGE
9560 LPRINT USING S2$; AVG.LAPS
9570 LPRINT USING S3$; AVG.EARNED
9580 RETURN
9590 '****************** END OF PROGRAM *******************
```

Sample Program Output

```
RUN
ENTER RUNNER NAME (TYPE 'END' TO QUIT)  RANDY

AMOUNT PLEDGED PER LAP  2.50

NUMBER OF LAPS RUN       30

ENTER RUNNER NAME (TYPE 'END' TO QUIT)  SUZANNE

AMOUNT PLEDGED PER LAP  1.50

NUMBER OF LAPS RUN       40

ENTER RUNNER NAME (TYPE 'END' TO QUIT)  JOEY

AMOUNT PLEDGED PER LAP  3.50

NUMBER OF LAPS RUN       20

ENTER RUNNER NAME (TYPE 'END' TO QUIT)  END
```

Sample Printer Output

```
     J O G - A - T H O N   D O N A T I O N S

     RUNNER              AMOUNT     LAPS     AMOUNT
                         PLEDGED    RUN      EARNED


     RANDY                2.50       30       75.00
     SUZANNE              1.50       40       60.00
     JOEY                 3.50       20       70.00

     TOTALS               7.50       90      205.00


     AVERAGE  PLEDGED PER LAP     2.50
     AVERAGE  LAPS RUN           30.0
     AVERAGE  EARNINGS           68.33
```

Summary

1. When one or more program statements are repeated, a loop is formed.
2. A loop is programmed with the WHILE and WEND (While End) statements.
3. Each WHILE must have a WEND.
4. When a WHILE statement is executed, the condition is tested. If the condition is true, the statements in the body of the loop are executed. Each time a WEND is encountered, the condition is again tested, and the loop is re-executed if the condition is true.
5. When the condition is false, execution continues with the next statement following the WEND.
6. The condition in a WHILE statement is formed using one or more of the six relational operators: > (greater than); < (less than); = (equal); <> (not equal); >= (greater than or equal); <= (less than or equal). These operators may be combined with the logical operators AND, OR, and NOT to form compound conditions and may be grouped by using parentheses.
7. Good, consistent indentation is important for program understandability and maintenance. Each WHILE and WEND should be aligned, and the statements in the loop should be indented and aligned with each other.
8. A statement must be included in each loop that will cause the loop to terminate; otherwise, endless loops will result.
9. Loops containing INPUT statements may ask a question to determine whether the statements should be re-executed.
10. INPUT loops often are terminated by the user entering a particular value to indicate the end of data. These values must match the type of variable being input (string or numeric).
11. When using a specific value to terminate the loop, the INPUT should be the last statement in the loop (before the WEND). In order to start the execution, a priming INPUT is used.
12. Counters can be used to control the number of iterations of a loop.
13. WHILE loops may be nested to any level.
14. Each WEND will be matched with the last unmatched WHILE, regardless of indentation.
15. When totals are required for a listing, a running total is accumulated. During each iteration of the loop the current values are added into the totals.
16. List totals are generally printed after the main processing loop is completed.
17. When planning a loop with pseudocode, follow indentation and numbering guidelines.

18. A flowchart for a WHILE loop shows the decision first, and then the statements in the body of the loop. The logic flow returns to the decision after each execution of the loop.

19. The PRINT USING and LPRINT USING statements are the most powerful of the formatting statements.

20. All options of the PRINT USING are also available with LPRINT USING.

21. The PRINT USING can be used to insert dollar signs, commas, asterisks, plus signs, and minus signs. It can align decimal points, round numbers, and force the printing of zeros to the right of the decimal point.

22. The string used to format the printing is called a print image, and it may be a literal or a variable.

23. A dollar sign used in a numeric format may be either fixed or floating. One dollar sign is a fixed sign, which will appear in the exact position placed. Two dollar signs in the format define a floating dollar sign, which will print immediately to the left of the number.

24. A plus sign placed in a numeric format will cause the sign of the number to print. The sign may be placed at the left or the right of the number.

25. A minus sign may be placed at the right of a numeric format. The printed output will have a minus sign for negative numbers, a blank for positive numbers.

26. Asterisk check protection is implemented with two asterisks in the numeric format.

27. When the print image is too short—that is, when there are not enough specifications for the variables named—the image will be repeated.

28. Any number to be printed that is too long for its format will print with a percent sign to the left of the number.

29. Strings can be printed with PRINT USING by using backslashes or an ampersand. The backslash method will print a specified number of characters for each string. An ampersand for formatting will print a variable length string.

Programming Exercises

Each of the following exercises should be written as a modular program with a program mainline and subroutines. Plan the program with a modular flowchart, pseudocode, or hierarchy chart. Run the program with the test data provided, as well as other data that you design. Any rounding of results should be accomplished with the (L)PRINT USING statement.

3.1. Modify the program in exercise 2.2 (merchandise turnover problem, p. 53) to have a program loop. The program should keep requesting new values for beginning inventory, ending inventory, and cost of goods sold, and keep printing the appropriate figures for average inventory and turnover. A negative number entered for beginning inventory will end the program. Accumulate and print totals for beginning inventory, ending inventory, and cost of goods sold.

Format the output with a title and column headings for beginning inventory, ending inventory, cost of goods sold, average inventory, and turnover. Align the total fields on the decimal point beneath the corresponding columns.

3.2. Modify the program in exercise 2.1 (automobile stopping distance problem, p. 53) to print a table of speeds and stopping distances. Print one line for each velocity, in 5-mph increments, from 30 mph to 80 mph. Round the stopping distances to the nearest tenth [use (L)PRINT USING]. Print an appropriate title on the report and the message END OF REPORT at the bottom of the list.

INPUT: None. Use a counter for the speeds.
SAMPLE PROGRAM OUTPUT:

```
                  AUTOMOBILE STOPPING DISTANCE TABLE
    SPEED (MPH)        DISTANCE REQUIRED TO STOP (FEET)
        30                      110.4
        35                      137.1
        40                      166.2
        45                      197.7
        50                      231.5
        55                      267.8
        60                      306.4
        65                      347.4
        70                      390.8
        75                      436.6
        80                      484.8
END OF REPORT
```

3.3. Modify the program in exercise 2.4 (recording studio charges, p. 54) to calculate charges for all groups for an entire day. Keep requesting the name of a new group until END is entered for group name. Accumulate and print totals of the minutes used and the charges made. Format the report with a title and column headings. Each detail line should show Group Name, Number of Minutes, and Charges. The total line will show the total for Number of Minutes and Charges.

3.4. Compute the factorial for any integer.

INPUT: An integer (N) should be requested. After the output, continue requesting integers for calculation until zero is entered.
OUTPUT: Print the message

```
N! = xxxxxxxx
```

PROCESSING: The factorial is calculated as

$$N \times (N-1) \dots \times 2 \times 1$$
$$\text{Example: } 5! = 5 \times 4 \times 3 \times 2 \times 1$$

TEST DATA: 10, 5, 25, 0

3.5. Modify the program in exercise 2.8 (car rental invoice, p. 55) to print multiple invoices. After each invoice is printed, ask the question: ANOTHER INVOICE TO PRINT? As long as the user enters YES, print another invoice. Any answer other than YES will terminate the program. Format the output with (L)PRINT USING.

3.6. The Computer Club needs to keep a membership list with member names and telephone numbers.

INPUT: Names and telephone numbers will be input during program execution.
OUTPUT: Print a nicely formatted listing with appropriate title and column headings. Each detail line will consist of a member name and telephone number. At the end of the report, print the number of members with an identifying literal, such as

```
NUMBER OF MEMBERS = XX
```

PROCESSING: Accumulate a count of the number of members.

3.7. Modify the program in exercise 3.6 to include a data validity check. For each iteration of the loop, ask the question: ANOTHER MEMBER (Y/N)?. If any response other than Y or N is entered, print a message and allow the response to be re-entered. As a further variation, consider the possibility of lowercase letters as well as uppercase (Y or y, N or n).

3.8. Write a program to create a grocery list on the printer. Continue inputting items until QUIT is entered.

INPUT: Items for the grocery list will be input from the keyboard.
OUTPUT: The list of items should be printed on the printer.

3.9. Modify the program in exercise 2.15 (employee bonus program, p. 57) to handle multiple stores. Request input until QUIT is entered for the store number. Use print images to format your output.

3.10. Write a program that will input a number and print the number, the square of the number, and the cube of the number. Continue the operation until 999 is entered.

3.11. Write a program that will request the length and width of a rectangle until 0 is entered for either the length or the width. You will then print the area and the perimeter for each set of inputs.

INPUT: The length and width will be input from the keyboard.
OUTPUT: The area and perimeter will be printed with appropriate labels.
PROCESS:
  1. Area = length * width.
  2. Perimeter = (length + width) * 2.

3.12. Write a program to create two lists for a potluck dinner party you are planning. The first list will be a guest list, and the second list will be an itemization of things to be brought.

INPUT: For the guest list, guest names should be input from the keyboard until QUIT is entered. For the second list, items to bring should be entered until QUIT is entered.
OUTPUT: Print an appropriate title for each list. Also, print the total number of people invited on the guest list.
PROCESS: Keep a count of the total number of people invited.

3.13. Using nested WHILE/WEND loops, write a program to create a baseball statistics sheet for baseball teams until QUIT is entered for the team name and the player's name. Each team has twelve players.

INPUT: Input a team name. Then, for that team, input player's name, player's number, total home runs, total at bats, and total singles. At the conclusion of one team, input the next team name and players on that team.
OUTPUT: Team name, player's name, player's number, total home runs, total at bats, total singles, and the player's two averages will be output to the printer.
PROCESS:
  1. Calculate first average $= \dfrac{\text{total singles}}{\text{total at bats}}$
  2. Calculate second average $= \dfrac{\text{total at bats}}{\text{total singles}}$

3.14. Using nested WHILE/WEND loops, write a program to create a sheet of test results for multiple classes. Each student will have five test scores.

INPUT: Name of class, teacher, student's name, and test grades will be input from the keyboard. End a class group when QUIT is entered for student name. End processing when QUIT is entered for teacher name.

OUTPUT: Name of class, teacher, student's name, test grades, test average and the class score average will be output to the printer.

PROCESS:

1. Calculate test average for each student $= \dfrac{\text{total for all tests}}{\text{number of tests}}$

2. Calculate class score average $= \dfrac{\text{total of all test scores for class}}{\text{number of students} * \text{number of tests (5)}}$

SAMPLE OUTPUT FOR ONE CLASS:

```
Class name: Basket Weaving
Teacher: Mrs. Twine


Student Name           Test 1   2    3    4    5       Average
_____                                            _____


Steve Campbell          80   93   90  100   95          91.6
Chris Conley            79   80  100  100   80          87.8
Dean Cummings           63   50   55   60   80          61.6
Teresa Foss             75   78   80   90  100          84.6
Tricia Mills            85   90   95  100   83          90.6
Shawn Nelson            82   78   40   55   60          63.0
Albert Plucker          57   65   83   84   97          77.2
Jon Snow                98  100   85   80   84          89.4
Jim Spencer             76   81   91   88   59          79.0
Eric Stone             100  100   95  100   98          98.6

Class Score Average = 82.3
```

3.15. The Kiwi Karate Studio needs to purchase some GIs, belts, and weapons for its students. The GIs and belts are bought from one company and the weapons are bought from another. Write a program to create two purchase orders using the data given below.

INPUT: The date, name and address of vendor, karate studio name and address, and the sample data on the following page will be input from the keyboard.

OUTPUT: Make up appropriate title and column headings. Include the date, name and address of vendor, karate studio name and address, item description, price, subtotal, tax, and total will be output to the printer.

PROCESS:
1. Extended price = price * quantity.
2. Subtotal = sum of extended price column.
3. Tax = subtotal * .065.
4. Total = tax + subtotal.

TEST DATA:
PURCHASE ORDER 1:

Description	Price	Quantity
Size 1 GI	$65	5
Size 2 GI	$65	8
Size 3 GI	$65	10
Size 4 GI	$65	20
Size 5 GI	$65	7
Size 6 GI	$65	5
Brown belt	$20	10
Black belt	$18	15
Orange belt	$16	15
Blue belt	$14	20
Green belt	$12	30
White belt	$10	30

PURCHASE ORDER 2:

Description	Price	Quantity
Samurai sword	$50	25
Nunchucks	$15	30
Manrici	$20	30
Scye	$15	20
Joto	$5	40

4

Adding IF Statements and READ Statements to Programs

IF-THEN-ELSE Statement
READ Statement
DATA Statement
RESTORE Statement

```
Upon completion of this chapter, you
should be able to:

1. Program alternate actions based on
   a condition using IF-THEN and IF-
   THEN-ELSE statements.
2. Nest IF statements for more
   complicated selection problems.
3. Use READ and DATA statements.
4. Properly structure loop programs
   using a priming READ and
   terminating data.
5. Understand the function of the
   RESTORE statement.
```

The programs presented thus far have executed a single sequence of actions—not realistic for computer applications. One powerful asset of the computer is the ability to make decisions and to take alternate courses of action based on the outcome.

A decision made by the computer is formed as a question: Is a given condition true or false? If it is true, do one thing; if it is false, do something else.

like: IF   the sun is shining   (condition)
            THEN go to the beach   (action to take if condition is true)
            ELSE go to class   (action to take if condition is false)

or: IF   you don't succeed   (condition)
            THEN try, try again   (action to take if condition is true)

Notice in the second example, no action is specified if the condition is not true.

IF-THEN-ELSE

Note the following example:

```
10   '****** AN AGREEABLE PROGRAM ******
20   INPUT "DO YOU LIKE THIS CLASS?"; ANS$
30   IF ANS$ = "YES"
        THEN PRINT "SO DO I"
        ELSE PRINT "NEITHER DO I"
```

The condition ANS$ = "YES" will be tested. If the content of the variable ANS$ is equal to YES, then the condition evaluates *true,* and the first PRINT will be executed. If ANS$ has *any* value other than YES, then the condition is *false,* and the second PRINT will be executed. Too bad if ANS$ contains SURE DO.

Study this example:

```
110  '*** GIVE DISCOUNT OF 5% ON A SALE LESS THAN $100, OR A
120  '        DISCOUNT OF 10% WHEN SALE IS $100 OR MORE ******
130  INPUT "ENTER AMOUNT OF SALE"; AMOUNT
140  IF AMOUNT < 100
        THEN LET DISC = AMOUNT * .05
        ELSE LET DISC = AMOUNT * .10
150  LET TOTAL = AMOUNT - DISC
160  PRINT "THE DISCOUNT IS "; DISC
170  PRINT "THE TOTAL IS    "; TOTAL
180  RETURN
```

Here the variable AMOUNT will be tested to see if it is less than 100. Any amount less than 100 will cause the condition to be true, and a 5 percent discount calculated. If the condition is not true (an amount 100 or more), a 10 percent discount will be calculated. (What happens on exactly 100?) Figure 4.1 illustrates the discount selection.

The IF-THEN-ELSE Statement—General Form

```
line number IF <condition> THEN <statement(s)>
    ELSE <statement(s)>
```

The IF-THEN-ELSE Statement—Example

```
50 IF X > Y
      THEN PRINT "X IS GREATER"
      ELSE PRINT "X IS NOT GREATER"
```

If the value of X is greater than the value of Y, then the condition X > Y is true, and the first PRINT is executed. In any other case (including X = Y), the condition is false, and the second PRINT is executed.

Figure 4.1
The discount selection. When the
amount is less than 100, a 5%
discount is given. For an amount
100 or more, a 10% discount is
given.

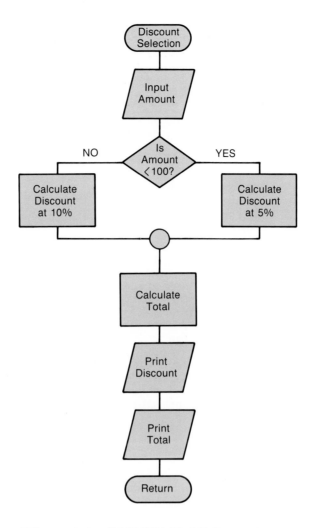

Effect of the IF-THEN-ELSE Statement

In an IF statement, when the condition is *true,* only the THEN clause is executed. THEN may be followed by one or more statements to be executed. When the condition is *false,* only the ELSE clause, if present, is executed.

Conditions for IF Statements

There is no difference between the conditions used in WHILE statements and the conditions used in IF statements. In both instances, the conditions are formed with combinations of the relational operators ($>$, $>=$, $<$, $<=$, $=$, $<>$), the logical operators (AND, OR, NOT), and the parentheses (). Compound conditions may be used in IF statements:

```
200   IF SCORE >= 80 AND SCORE <= 90
          THEN PRINT "YOUR GRADE IS B"
```

Indentation

The examples shown on multiple lines are aligned and indented for clarity. This form has been shown to improve readability and understandability of programs, and it has been adopted as standard by many programming groups. To achieve the spacing, press CTRL-RETURN (CTRL-J or ALT-J on some systems) at the end of each line (instead of RETURN or ENTER). The CTRL-RETURN causes a "line feed" without a "carriage return" and allows the statement to be continued. Do not press RETURN/ENTER until the entire statement is complete.

```
150   IF SIDES > 3 <CTRL-RETURN>
         THEN GOSUB 200 <CTRL-RETURN>
         ELSE GOSUB 300 <RETURN>
```

Note: If the CTRL-RETURN combination does not work for you, check your BASIC version number. Microsoft version 3.20 (and 3.21) introduced a bug in the software that makes the editor send a "line feed" *and* "carriage return" when CTRL-RETURN is pressed. Earlier versions of BASIC work correctly, as do later versions, beginning with version 3.22.

IF Statement Examples

Statement	*Comparison*

50 IF AMOUNT > QUOTA
    THEN GOSUB 1000
    ELSE GOSUB 2000
	Variable/variable

100 IF SCORE <> (NUM1 + NUM2)/2 THEN LET SCORE = 0	Variable/expression
150 IF DIFF < 0 THEN PRINT "NEGATIVE VALUE"	Variable/constant
210 IF COUNT + 1 = MAX - 1 THEN GOSUB 300	Expression/expression
600 IF SUM - CHECK > 0 THEN GOSUB 1200	Expression/constant
750 IF 2 >= 3 THEN PRINT "HOW DID THAT HAPPEN?"	Constant/constant
800 IF PERSON$ = "SAMMY" THEN PRINT "HI THERE, SAMMY!"	Variable/literal
850 IF NAM$ <> PRIOR.NAM$ THEN GOSUB 2000	Variable/variable

A word of warning: Due to the way decimal values are stored internally in the computer, two values may appear to be equal, but will not test equal in a relation test. If X holds 1 and Y holds .9999999, both fields will print as 1 but will test unequal. This problem can be surmounted by testing for a minute difference between the two. Since the only interest is in the difference between the two numbers, not which one is larger, use the Absolute Value function (see chapter 10). To test for "equality," try

```
100   IF ABS(X - Y) < .00001
         THEN PRINT "CLOSE ENOUGH"
```

For a further discussion of accuracy in Microsoft BASIC, see chapter 10.

Example Program: Using IF Statements

Program Listing

```
100 '    PROGRAM TO ASSIGN A LETTER GRADE FROM A NUMERIC SCORE
110 '       USING THE SCALE
120 '           90 - 100 = A
130 '           80 -  89 = B
140 '           70 -  79 = C
150 '           60 -  69 = D
160 '              <  60 = F
170 '
180 '           PROGRAM VARIABLES
190 '
200 '           SCORE           NUMERIC SCORE
210 '           GRADE$          LETTER GRADE
220 '
500 '*************** PROGRAM MAINLINE ************************
510 GOSUB 1000          'INPUT THE SCORE
520 GOSUB 2000          'ASSIGN THE GRADE
530 GOSUB 3000          'PRINT THE GRADE
540 END
550 '
```

```
1000 '*************** INPUT THE SCORE ***************************
1010 CLS                     'CLEAR THE SCREEN
1020 INPUT "ENTER THE NUMERIC SCORE ", SCORE
1030 RETURN
1040 '
2000 '**************** ASSIGN THE GRADE ***********************
2010 IF SCORE >= 90
        THEN LET GRADE$ = "A"
2020 IF SCORE >= 80 AND SCORE <= 89
        THEN LET GRADE$ = "B"
2030 IF SCORE >= 70 AND SCORE <= 79
        THEN LET GRADE$ = "C"
2040 IF SCORE >= 60 AND SCORE <= 69
        THEN LET GRADE$ = "D"
2050 IF SCORE < 60
        THEN LET GRADE$ = "F"
2060 RETURN
2070 '
3000 '**************** PRINT THE GRADE *********************
3010 PRINT
3020 PRINT
3030 PRINT "YOUR GRADE IS "; GRADE$
3040 RETURN
3050 '**************** END OF PROGRAM **********************
```

Sample Program Output

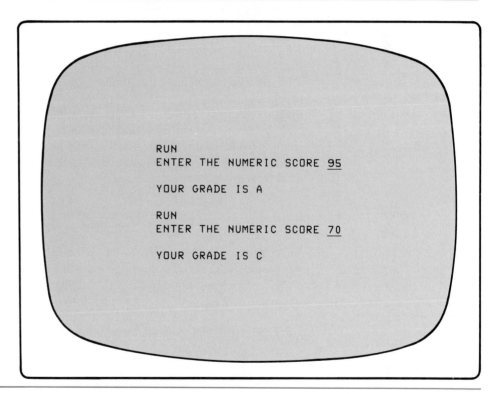

```
RUN
ENTER THE NUMERIC SCORE 95

YOUR GRADE IS A

RUN
ENTER THE NUMERIC SCORE 70

YOUR GRADE IS C
```

Feedback

Assume that FROGS = 10, TOADS = 5, POLLIWOGS = 6 What will print for each of these statements?

1. IF FROGS > POLLIWOGS
    THEN PRINT "THE FROGS HAVE IT"
2. IF FROGS > TOADS + POLLIWOGS
    THEN PRINT "IT'S THE FROGS"
    ELSE PRINT "IT'S THE TOADS & POLLIWOGS"
3. IF POLLIWOGS > TOADS AND FROGS <> 0 OR TOADS = 0
    THEN PRINT "IT'S TRUE"
    ELSE PRINT "IT'S FALSE"

4. Write the BASIC statements necessary to input the price of apples and the price of oranges. Then print either "THE APPLES COST MORE" or "THE ORANGES COST MORE".

Multiple Statements for THEN or ELSE

Sometimes more than one statement is necessary when the condition is *true* (or *false*), as shown in the accompanying flowchart.

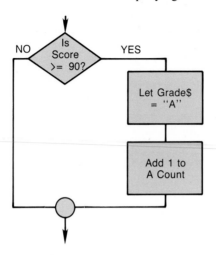

This situation can be handled in more than one way, and the choice *may* depend on the computer used. One solution is to use multistatement lines. Alternatively, subroutines may be used to execute multiple statements.

BASIC allows multiple statements to be placed on one line as long as the statements are separated by colons (:). The only limit is the 255-character line length. At times, it may be convenient to use multistatement lines to execute more than one statement for a given condition.

```
2040    IF SCORE >= 90
            THEN LET GRADE$ = "A":
                LET A.COUNT = A.COUNT + 1
```

Notice that the second statement for the line (LET A.COUNT = A.COUNT + 1) was placed on the next line down and aligned with the first statement (LET GRADE$ = "A"). This was accomplished with a CTRL-RETURN after the colon. When one statement number will have multiple BASIC statements, *always* use the CTRL-RETURN to place each individual statement on a line by itself. This will greatly improve the clarity and understandability of your programs.

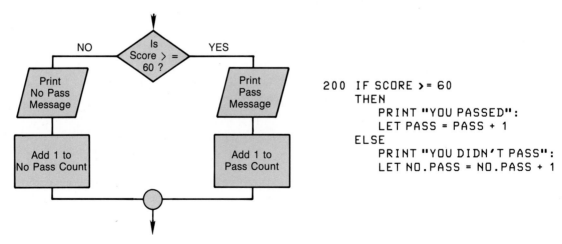

One Small Fly in the Ointment—System Dependent Differences

The indentation shown for the preceding IF-THEN-ELSE statement is the preferred form. It is clear and easy to follow. Most versions of Microsoft BASIC will allow for this indentation. The exception to the rule is the IBM-PC BASIC. In IBM-PC BASIC, the CTRL-RETURN (or CTRL-J) actually causes sufficient blank spaces to be inserted to achieve the line spacing. This will quickly use up the 255 characters allowed in one BASIC line. Most other versions of Microsoft BASIC including GWBASIC insert only one character for the "line feed," which will allow more characters for the line. Since the standard screen width is eighty characters, the longest statement allowed on an IBM-PC is three lines, plus fifteen characters on the fourth line.

Coding the previous pass/fail logic shown previously for the IBM-PC offers two choices—neither quite as nice as the preferred form.

Version 1 (IBM-PC)

```
700   IF SCORE >= 60
         THEN PRINT "YOU PASSED": LET PASS = PASS + 1
         ELSE PRINT "YOU DID NOT PASS": LET NO.PASS = NO.PASS + 1
```

Version 2 (IBM-PC)

```
800   IF SCORE >= 60
         THEN GOSUB 900
         ELSE GOSUB 950
::
::
900   '*********** SCORE >= 60 ********************
910   PRINT "YOU PASSED"
920   LET PASS = PASS + 1
930   RETURN
940   '
950   '*********** SCORE < 60 ********************
960   PRINT "YOU DID NOT PASS"
970   LET NO.PASS = NO.PASS + 1
980   RETURN
```

Example Program:
The Grade Program with Multistatement Lines

Program Listing

```
100 '    PROGRAM TO ASSIGN LETTER GRADES FROM NUMERIC SCORES.
110 '      THIS VERSION WILL INCORPORATE A LOOP TO INPUT MULTIPLE
120 '    SCORES AND KEEP A COUNT OF THE OCCURRENCES OF EACH GRADE.
130 '      GRADES ARE ASSIGNED USING THIS SCALE:
140 '
150 '           90 - 100 = A
160 '           80 -  89 = B
170 '           70 -  79 = C
180 '           60 -  69 = D
190 '            <  60 = F
200 '
210 '           PROGRAM VARIABLES
220 '
230 '           SCORE           NUMERIC SCORE
240 '           GRADE$          LETTER GRADE
250 '           ANS$            ANSWER FOR LOOP CONTROL
260 '           A.COUNT         COUNT OF A GRADES GIVEN
270 '           B.COUNT         COUNT OF B GRADES GIVEN
280 '           C.COUNT         COUNT OF C GRADES GIVEN
290 '           D.COUNT         COUNT OF D GRADES GIVEN
300 '           F.COUNT         COUNT OF F GRADES GIVEN
310 '           T$, D$          PRINT IMAGES
320 '
```

```
1000 '**************** PROGRAM MAINLINE **********************
1010 CLS
1020 GOSUB 2000              'INITIALIZE PRINT IMAGES
1030 LET ANS$ = "Y"
1040 WHILE ANS$ = "Y"
1050     GOSUB 3000              'INPUT THE SCORE
1060     GOSUB 4000              'ASSIGN AND COUNT THE GRADE
1070     GOSUB 5000              'PRINT THE GRADE
1080     INPUT "ANY MORE DATA? (Y/N) ", ANS$
1090 WEND
1100 GOSUB 6000              'PRINT THE FINAL COUNTS
1110 END
1120 '
2000 '************** INITIALIZE PRINT IMAGES *****************
2010 LET T$ = " TOTALS"
2020 LET D$ = " &    ##"
2030 RETURN
2040 '
3000 '**************** INPUT THE SCORE **********************
3010 INPUT "ENTER THE NUMERIC SCORE ", SCORE
3020 RETURN
3030 '
4000 '*********** ASSIGN AND COUNT THE GRADE ***************
4010 IF SCORE >= 90
         THEN LET GRADE$ = "A":
             LET A.COUNT = A.COUNT + 1
4020 IF SCORE >= 80 AND SCORE <= 89
         THEN LET GRADE$ = "B":
             LET B.COUNT = B.COUNT + 1
4030 IF SCORE >= 70 AND SCORE <= 79
         THEN LET GRADE$ = "C":
             LET C.COUNT = C.COUNT + 1
4040 IF SCORE >= 60 AND SCORE <= 69
         THEN LET GRADE$ = "D":
             LET D.COUNT = D.COUNT + 1
4050 IF SCORE < 60
         THEN LET GRADE$ = "F":
             LET F.COUNT = F.COUNT + 1
4060 RETURN
4070 '
5000 '***************** PRINT THE GRADE *********************
5010 PRINT
5030 PRINT "YOUR GRADE IS "; GRADE$
5040 RETURN
5050 '
6000 '*************** PRINT FINAL COUNTS ********************
6010 PRINT
6020 PRINT
6030 PRINT T$
6040 PRINT
6050 PRINT USING D$; "A", A.COUNT
6060 PRINT USING D$; "B", B.COUNT
6070 PRINT USING D$; "C", C.COUNT
6080 PRINT USING D$; "D", D.COUNT
6090 PRINT USING D$; "F", F.COUNT
6100 RETURN
6110 '**************** END OF PROGRAM **********************
```

Sample Program Output

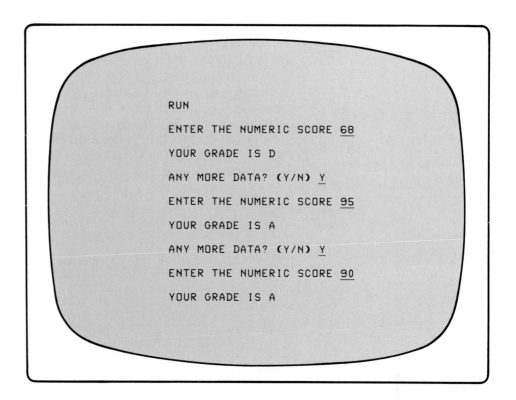

```
RUN
ENTER THE NUMERIC SCORE 68
YOUR GRADE IS D
ANY MORE DATA? (Y/N) Y
ENTER THE NUMERIC SCORE 95
YOUR GRADE IS A
ANY MORE DATA? (Y/N) Y
ENTER THE NUMERIC SCORE 90
YOUR GRADE IS A
```

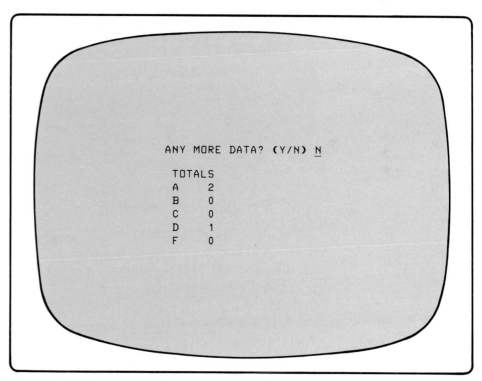

```
ANY MORE DATA? (Y/N) N
   TOTALS
A      2
B      0
C      0
D      1
F      0
```

Finding the Highest or Lowest Value in a List

Using IF statements, it becomes a simple task to find the highest or lowest value of a series. In this example, a series of names, along with the score for each, will be INPUT. At the end, the name of the person having the highest score, along with his score, will be printed out. Note that ties are not allowed in this solution.

The key to this technique is the two variables: HIGH.SCORE and HIGH.NAM$. For each score input, the current score will be compared to the high score. When the current score is larger than the score stored in HIGH.SCORE, the current score is placed in HIGH.SCORE, and the name of the person who achieved that score is placed in HIGH.NAM$. In order to assure that the first score will be placed in high score to start, HIGH.SCORE should be initialized to a number lower than the lowest possible score.

```
500  '******** FIND HIGHEST VALUE FROM ALL THOSE INPUT ********
510  LET HIGH.SCORE = -1          'INITIALIZE TO LOW VALUE
520  LET ANS$ = "Y"
530  WHILE ANS$ = "Y"
540     INPUT "NAME   ", NAM$
550     INPUT "SCORE  ", SCORE
560     IF SCORE > HIGH.SCORE
            THEN LET HIGH.SCORE = SCORE:
                 LET HIGH.NAM$ = NAM$
570     PRINT
580     INPUT "ANOTHER SCORE (Y/N)"; ANS$
590     PRINT
600  WEND
610  PRINT "THE HIGHEST SCORE WAS"; HIGH.SCORE; ", EARNED BY ";
         HIGH.NAM$
620  END
RUN
NAME  LOU LOW
SCORE 12

ANOTHER SCORE (Y/N)? Y

NAME  HANK HIGH
SCORE 95

ANOTHER SCORE (Y/N)? Y

NAME  MARK MIDDLE
SCORE 50

ANOTHER SCORE (Y/N)? N

THE HIGHEST SCORE WAS 95 , EARNED BY HANK HIGH
```

The lowest score can be found in a similar manner. In this case, the comparison variable (LOW.SCORE) will be initialized to a value higher than the highest allowable score. This will assure that the first score input will be placed into the LOW.SCORE field.

```
600  '******** FIND LOWEST VALUE FROM ALL THOSE INPUT ********
610  LET LOW.SCORE = 101          'INITIALIZE TO HIGH VALUE
620  LET ANS$ = "Y"
630  WHILE ANS$ = "Y"
640     INPUT "NAME   ", NAM$
650     INPUT "SCORE ", SCORE
660     IF SCORE < LOW.SCORE
            THEN LET LOW.SCORE = SCORE:
                 LET LOW.NAM$ = NAM$
670     PRINT
680     INPUT "ANOTHER SCORE (Y/N)"; ANS$
690     PRINT
700  WEND
710  PRINT "THE LOWEST SCORE WAS"; SCORE; ", EARNED BY ";
         LOW.NAM$
720  END
```

```
RUN
NAME  LOU LOW
SCORE 12

ANOTHER SCORE (Y/N)? Y

NAME  HANK HIGH
SCORE 95

ANOTHER SCORE (Y/N)? Y

NAME  MARK MIDDLE
SCORE 50

ANOTHER SCORE (Y/N)? N

THE LOWEST SCORE WAS 12 , EARNED BY LOU LOW
```

Feedback

Write the BASIC statements that will test the current value of K. When K is greater than zero, the message THE ACCOUNT IS POSITIVE should be printed, K reset to zero, and K.COUNTER incremented by one. When K is zero or less, print the message THE ACCOUNT IS NOT POSITIVE (do not change the value of K or increment the counter).

Nested IF Statements

Remember that in an IF statement, a condition is evaluated. Then a series of statements can be executed if the condition is true, and another series of statements can be executed if the condition is false.

Often it is desirable to have another IF statement as one of the statements to be executed when the condition is true. A second IF can be included in the THEN portion of the statement, in the ELSE portion, or both. Combining IF statements in this way is called *nesting IF statements*.

Figure 4.2 shows the coding and flowchart for a nested IF statement. This will add 1 to one of four counts.

Figure 4.2
Multiple statements for THEN and ELSE. This will add 1 to one of four counts.

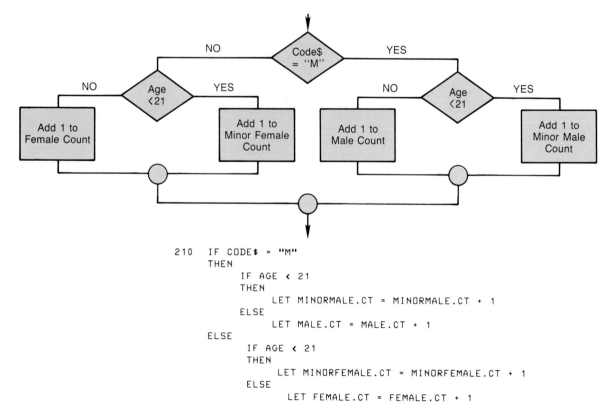

```
210   IF CODE$ = "M"
      THEN
            IF AGE < 21
            THEN
                  LET MINORMALE.CT = MINORMALE.CT + 1
            ELSE
                  LET MALE.CT = MALE.CT + 1
      ELSE
            IF AGE < 21
            THEN
                  LET MINORFEMALE.CT = MINORFEMALE.CT + 1
            ELSE
                  LET FEMALE.CT = FEMALE.CT + 1
```

When nesting IF statements, the inner IF should always have an ELSE. This is necessary because BASIC will always match an ELSE with the last unmatched THEN. The indentation is for human understanding only. BASIC will ignore the indentation and match THENs with ELSEs on a one-for-one basis.

Incorrect Example:

```
250   IF CODE$ = "M"
      THEN
            LET MALE.CT = MALE.CT + 1:
            IF AGE < 21
            THEN
                  LET MINORMALE.CT = MINORMALE.CT + 1
      ELSE
            LET FEMALE.CT = FEMALE.CT + 1:
            IF AGE < 21
            THEN
                  LET MINORFEMALE.CT = MINORFEMALE.CT + 1
```

An insidious BUG exists here! When will 1 be added to the FEMALE count?

More on System Differences

Note that the indentation shown for nested IF statements is not possible on the IBM-PC due to the CTRL-RETURN problem described earlier. The only way to use the nested IF on the IBM-PC is to run the statements all together. This is extremely poor programming and is not recommended. The alternative is to place the statements in subroutines.

Version 1 (IBM-PC)—Nested IF Statement—A Poor Example

```
210   IF CODE$ = "M" THEN IF AGE < 21 THEN LET MINORMALE.CT = MINORMALE.CT +1 ELSE
LET MALE.CT = MALE.CT + 1 ELSE IF AGE < 21 THEN LET MINORFEMALE.CT = MINORFEMALE
.CT + 1 ELSE LET FEMALE.CT = FEMALE.CT +1
```

Version 2 (IBM-PC)—Nesting IF Statements with Subroutines—The Preferred Choice

```
210   IF CODE$ = "M"
            THEN GOSUB 500
            ELSE GOSUB 600
  ::
  ::
500   '******** MALE CODE ********
510   IF AGE < 21
            THEN LET MINORMALE.CT = MINORMALE.CT + 1
            ELSE LET MALE.CT = MALE.CT +1
520   RETURN
530   '
600   '******** FEMALE CODE *******
610   IF AGE < 21
            THEN LET MINORFEMALE.CT = MINORFEMALE.CT + 1
            ELSE LET FEMALE.CT = FEMALE.CT + 1
620   RETURN
```

Notes on Decision Making and Structured Programming

Guidelines for good structured programs require that programs and program segments have only one entry point and one exit point. To comply with this rule, program statements cannot be allowed to "branch around" indiscriminately. It is for this reason that neither the GO TO nor the "IF condition THEN branch" have been introduced. Although it is possible to write well-structured programs with these statements, the majority of beginning programmers start writing "spaghetti code" when introduced to these statements. The resulting programs are often difficult to debug and expensive to maintain. For these reasons, it is strongly recommended that all decision statements follow the form shown in this chapter.

Planning Program Decisions

Before beginning to code a program in BASIC, the logic should always be planned carefully. This planning can be in the form of a flowchart, pseudocode, hierarchy chart, or one of several other planning methods.

Flowcharts

When planning with flowcharts, always show the decision symbol and two possible courses of action (one for *true,* one for *false*). There will be statement(s) to execute when the condition is true, and there may be other statement(s) to execute when the condition is false. After these statements, the logic flow must return to a common point (the one exit point) before continuing with the program. It is suggested that the question in the decision symbol be stated so that it has a YES and a NO for the two possible courses of action.

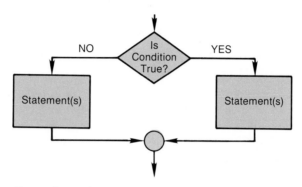

Pseudocode

When planning IF-THEN-ELSE logic with pseudocode, indentation should be in the same form as in BASIC code.

    IF condition
        THEN statement(s) to be executed when true
        ELSE statement(s) to be executed when false

When there are no statements to execute when the condition is false, use this form:

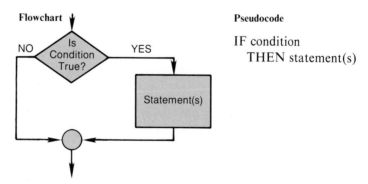

Flowchart

Pseudocode

    IF condition
        THEN statement(s)

Hierarchy Charts

Hierarchy charts show neither the selection process nor the control structures needed to implement the logic. Only the modules are shown. When there are two modules and only one will be executed for each run of the program, show the two modules, but not the selection. Figure 4.3 shows the form for a hierarchy chart and a flowchart of an example with two modules.

The introduction of the IF statement adds new and powerful logic capabilities to programs. The next topic to be introduced will not add logical functions; instead, it will give a little more flexibility in offering another way to do a familiar task.

Figure 4.3
A. Hierarchy chart showing two modules. *B.* Flowchart showing two modules.

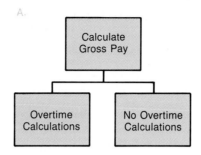

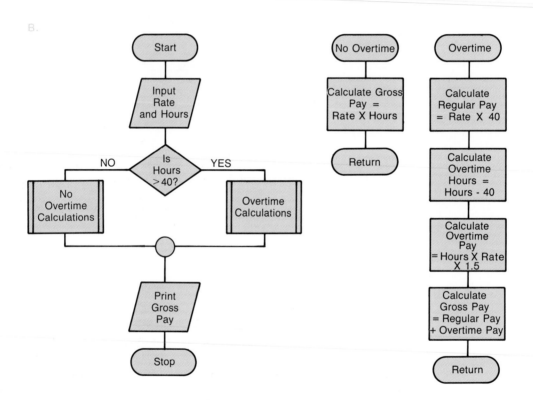

The READ and DATA Statements

Two methods have been shown for assigning a value to a variable—the LET and INPUT statements. There is a third method—READ and DATA statements.

Using READ and DATA allows for all data to be entered before program execution. This can save time and trouble for the user when running the program, especially when there is a large amount of data to enter. However, the results of the program will be exactly the same each time it is run. Here is an example calculating gas mileage.

```
10   '**** CALCULATE GASOLINE MILEAGE ****
20   READ MILES, GALLONS
30   LET MILEAGE = MILES / GALLONS
40   PRINT "MILES ="; MILES ,"GALLONS ="; GALLONS,
       "MILEAGE ="; MILEAGE
50   DATA 265, 10
80   END

RUN

MILES = 265 GALLONS = 10 MILEAGE = 26.5
```

The READ statement causes the first DATA value (265) to be placed in the variable MILES and the second DATA value (10) to be placed in the second variable, GALLONS.

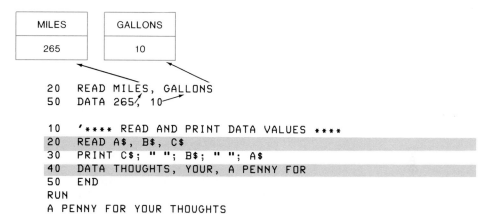

```
10   '**** READ AND PRINT DATA VALUES ****
20   READ A$, B$, C$
30   PRINT C$; " "; B$; " "; A$
40   DATA THOUGHTS, YOUR, A PENNY FOR
50   END
RUN
A PENNY FOR YOUR THOUGHTS
```

In the preceding example, THOUGHTS was assigned to the variable A$, YOUR was placed into the variable B$, and A PENNY FOR was placed in the variable C$. Blank spaces included as part of a string constant will be included as long as the spaces are not leading or trailing. To include leading or trailing spaces, quotation marks must enclose the string constant.

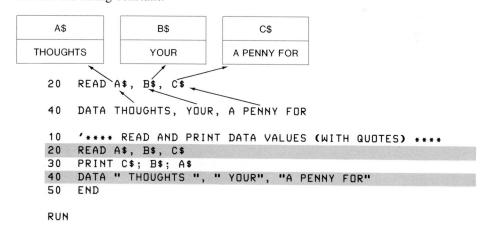

```
10   '**** READ AND PRINT DATA VALUES (WITH QUOTES) ****
20   READ A$, B$, C$
30   PRINT C$; B$; A$
40   DATA " THOUGHTS ", " YOUR", "A PENNY FOR"
50   END

RUN

A PENNY FOR YOUR THOUGHTS
```

Note in the following example that if a comma is needed as part of a string constant, quotes are required. This is necessary because commas are delimiters (separaters) between the constants. To include colons in a constant also requires quotes.

```
10  '**** READ A PERSON'S NAME AND THREE TEST SCORES ****
20  '        AND PRINT OUT THE AVERAGE SCORE
30  READ NAM$, TEST1, TEST2, TEST3
40  LET AVERAGE = (TEST1 + TEST2 + TEST3)/ 3
50  PRINT "THE AVERAGE SCORE FOR "; NAM$; " IS"; AVERAGE
60  DATA "MARTIN, JOAN", 84, 67, 92
70  END

RUN

THE AVERAGE SCORE FOR MARTIN, JOAN IS 81
```

The READ Statement—General Form

line number READ list of variables, separated by commas

The READ Statement—Example

50 READ A, B, C

The DATA Statement—General Form

line number DATA list of constants, separated by commas

The DATA Statement—Example

100 DATA 1.25, 3.5, -20

Note that the data statement example could have been written as two or three lines with the same results:

```
100  DATA 1.25            or        100  DATA 1.25, 3.5
110  DATA 3.5                       110  DATA -20
120  DATA -20
```

Rules for READ and DATA Statements

1. The variables in READ statements must be matched by corresponding values in DATA statements.
2. READ statements contain one or more variable names separated by commas.
3. DATA statements contain one or more constants separated by commas.
4. The DATA values are assigned to variables with the READ statement on a one-to-one basis.
5. Items in the DATA list must be constants, either numeric values or character strings, and the type of value must agree with the variable type specified on the READ. If the types do not agree, a SYNTAX ERROR will occur.
6. Character strings do not require quotation marks unless:
   a. they contain significant leading or trailing blanks. (Leading or trailing blanks will be ignored if the string is not quoted. Why do you suppose that is?)
   b. a comma or colon appears in the string.
7. DATA statements are nonexecutable and may be placed anywhere in the program.
8. A DATA statement may contain as many constants as will fit on one program line (255 characters), and any number of DATA statements may appear in a program.
9. The READ statement accesses the DATA values in order by line number. All DATA constants in the program may be thought of as one continuous list of items, regardless of how many items are on a line or where the lines are placed in the program.

10. As READ statements are executed, values are taken, one after another, from the data list. The BASIC interpreter keeps track of the current element in the DATA list, even though the READ and DATA statements may be widely separated.

11. For every variable in a READ list, there must be a corresponding constant in DATA statement. If there are not enough data items to satisfy the READ, an OUT OF DATA error will occur. However, no error will occur if there are more elements in the DATA list than in the READ list.

Placement of READ and DATA Statements

Since DATA statements are nonexecutable, they may be placed anywhere in the program. Many programmers place all DATA statements at the beginning of the program or in a separate module placed at the physical end of the program just before the END statement. It generally works well to place the DATA statements in modular programs at the conclusion of the module that contains the READ. The goal is to make the DATA statements easy to find and easy to change when necessary, as well as to keep the logic of the program clean and easy to follow.

Comparison of READ/DATA, INPUT, and LET Statements

Using READ/DATA statements has an advantage over using LET statements and constants in calculations—there is more flexibility in the program. The data is easier to locate and change. However, the programs using READ/DATA statements cannot be considered **interactive** (or *conversational* between the user and the program). If nonprogrammers are going to run the program and make changes in the data values, the INPUT statement is preferable.

Many programs will have use for both READ/DATA and INPUT statements. When a large quantity of data is to be entered—perhaps a long list of words or a table of values that seldom change—READ and DATA statements will relieve the user of the task of entering all data for every program run. The data need be entered only once before program execution. Errors in the data can easily be corrected, and the data can be processed more than once without having to be retyped. READ/DATA can be useful for testing programs when multiple test runs must be made.

Using READ/DATA in a Loop

When data is read into a variable, it replaces whatever is already there. So when a READ is placed in a loop, a new value will be assigned to the variable for each execution (iteration) of the loop.

```
10   '**** READ AND DATA STATEMENTS IN A LOOP ****
20   WHILE NAM$ <> "END OF DATA"
30        READ NAM$, ADDR$
40        PRINT NAM$, ADDR$
50   WEND
60   DATA ANN DOE, 1234 BAKER ST., BRUCE LEE, 457 HIGH ST.,
     HOPE SEW, 222 BANK ST., END OF DATA, NO ADDRESS
70   END

RUN
ANN DOE        1234 BAKER ST.
BRUCE LEE      457 HIGH ST.
HOPE SEW       222 BANK ST.
END OF DATA    NO ADDRESS
```

First execution of line 30

NAM$	ADDR$
ANN DOE	1234 BAKER ST.

Second execution of line 30

NAM$	ADDR$
BRUCE LEE	457 HIGH ST.

Third execution of line 30

NAM$	ADDR$
HOPE SEW	222 BANK ST.

Fourth execution of line 30

NAM$	ADDR$
END OF DATA	NO ADDRESS

Priming READ

Although the program works exactly as intended, the last line of output is not appealing. In order to have the program stop after the last READ without printing the contents of NAM$ and ADDR$, the logic will have to be changed. What is wanted is to have the condition, NAM$ <> "END OF DATA", tested *after* the READ but *before* the PRINT. The way to accomplish this is to place the READ *last* in the loop. Then, immediately after execution of the READ, the condition will be tested. Since NAM$ *will* be equal to END OF DATA, the condition will evaluate *false,* control will pass to the next statement following the WEND, and the program will stop without printing END OF DATA on the list.

```
10    '**** READ AND DATA IN A LOOP - A BETTER WAY ****
20    READ NAM$, ADDR$
30    WHILE NAM$ <> "END OF DATA"
40        PRINT NAM$, ADDR$
50        READ NAM$, ADDR$
60    WEND
70    DATA ANN DOE, 1234 BAKER ST., BRUCE LEE, 457 HIGH ST.,
      HOPE SEW, 222 BANK ST., END OF DATA, NO ADDRESS
80    END

RUN
ANN DOE         1234 BAKER ST.
BRUCE LEE       457 HIGH ST.
HOPE SEW        222 BANK ST.
```

As you can see, this approach requires a *priming READ*. The initial READ (line 20) will be executed only once at the beginning of the program. After that, the READ within the loop will take care of all reading. The purpose of the first READ is to start the process, or "prime the pump."

Data Terminators

Another principle can be observed from the preceding sample program. How many names and addresses is this program capable of reading and printing? You could insert as many pairs of names and addresses as desired, as long as END OF DATA, NO ADDRESS is last. Of course, the data can continue on many DATA statements, and the only limit will be the amount of main storage the computer has allocated for the program. The data item END OF DATA is generally called a **data terminator.** Sometimes data terminators are also called **trailers, trailer data, sentinels,** or **flags.**

The data terminator is generally selected by the programmer. There is no reason not to have selected a string of Xs, a certain name, or "*" as the terminator. As long as the condition in the WHILE statement checks for the same value as placed last in the data list, the program will find the value and stop on command.

Considering the way READ and DATA statements work, explain why NO ADDRESS appears after END OF DATA. How could the program be modified so that NO ADDRESS is not needed?

The RESTORE Statement

The data in the DATA list may be reread from the beginning by use of the RESTORE statement.

```
10   READ A, B
20   RESTORE
30   READ C, D
40   PRINT A, B, C, D
50   DATA 25, 50
60   END

RUN

25               50               25               50
```

The RESTORE Statement—General Form

```
line number RESTORE
```

The RESTORE Statement—Example

```
150 RESTORE
```

RESTORE returns the internal pointer back to the beginning of the program. Any subsequent READ will then reread the data from the beginning.

Feedback

1. Some of the following problems have syntax errors, others will not do what was intended. Identify each error, determine what type of error it is, and tell how to correct it.

   a. 10 READ NAM1$, SCORE1, NAM2$, SCORE2
      20 PRINT NAM1$, NAM2$
      30 PRINT SCORE1, SCORE2
      40 DATA JOHN, MARTHA, 4, 5
   b. 110 READ X, Y, Z
      120 PRINT X, Y, Z
      130 DATA 100, 200
   c. 50 READ NAM$, DAT$
      60 PRINT NAM$, DAT$
      70 DATA HUMPTY DUMPTY, JAN. 15, 1990
   d. 10 READ A, B
      20 PRINT B, A
      30 DATA 40, -21, 25, 16
   e. 200 WHILE F$ <> "END"
      210   READ F$
      220   PRINT F$
      230 WEND
      240 DATA APPLES, PEACHES, PLUMS, PEARS, BANANAS, END

2. Write the READ and DATA statements to assign these values to the variables.

ST.TIME$	END.TIME$
1:25	2:45

3. Write the statements necessary to read and print a series of words until END is read. At the end of the list, print a count of the number of words printed. Do *not* print or count the word END.

Programming Example

A Little League team wants to print a list of the players along with their batting averages. In addition, it would be helpful to know the overall team batting average, team totals for total number of official times at bats, and number of hits. As an added incentive, each week the program will print out the name and average of the player with the highest average and player with the lowest average.

Batting average is calculated as the number of hits divided by the number of official times at bat multiplied by 1000 (hits / at bats * 1000).

Input

Read each player's name, number of official times at bats, number of hits (use READ/DATA).

Output

1. Print the team name at the top of the page, and identify each column of output.
2. For each player, print the name, times at bats, number of hits, and batting average.
3. Print a total below the columns for times at bats and hits.
4. Print the player's name and batting average for the player who had the highest average and the one with the lowest average.

Calculations

1. Calculate the batting average for each player (hits / at bats * 1000).
2. Calculate a team batting average (total hits / total at bats * 1000).

Pseudocode

1. Initialize variables
    1.1 LET high average = −1
           LET low average = 1001
    1.2 Initialize print images
2. Print title and column headings
3. Detail processing loop
    3.1 Priming READ, name, at bats, and hits
    3.2 Loop until "END" entered
          3.2.1 Calculations
                Batting average:
                IF at bats > 0
                    THEN batting average = hits / at bats * 1000
                    ELSE batting average = 0
                Add at bats and hits to totals
          3.2.2 Find lowest and highest average
                IF average < lowest average so far
                    THEN save average and name as lowest
                IF average > highest average so far
                    THEN save average and name as highest
          3.2.3 Print a line
          3.2.4 READ next name, at bat, and hits
4. Calculate team average
    total hits / total at bats * 1000
5. Write totals
    5.1 Print total line
    5.2 Print high average and name
    5.3 Print low average and name

Hierarchy Chart

Refer to figure 4.4 for the hierarchy chart.

Flowchart

Refer to figure 4.5 for the flowchart (pp. 117–18).

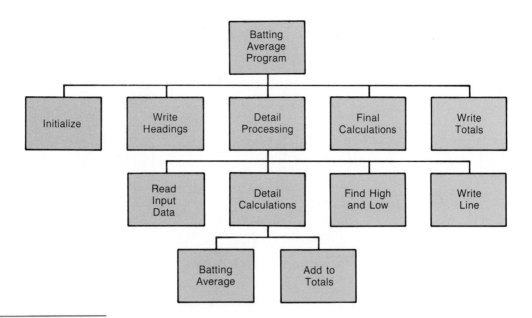

Figure 4.4
Hierarchy chart for batting
average program.

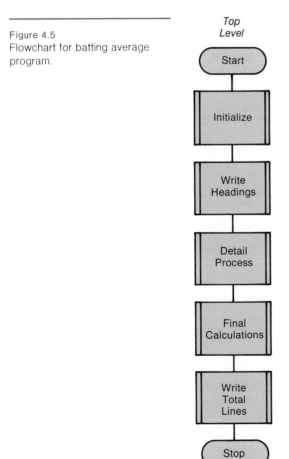

Figure 4.5
Flowchart for batting average
program.

Figure 4.5—*Continued*

Second Level

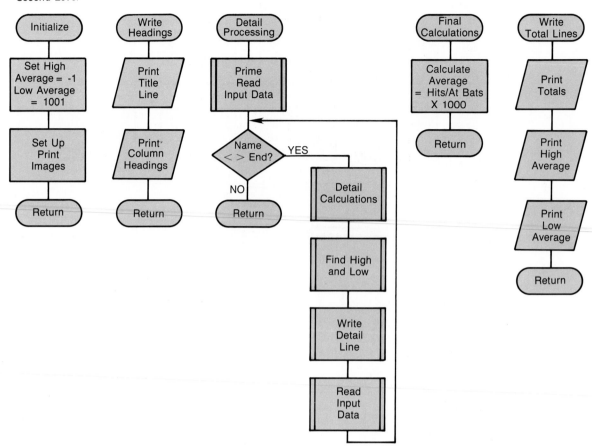

Third Level

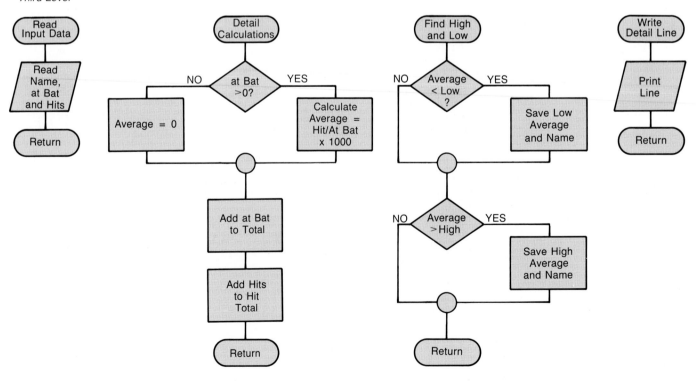

```
100 ' PROGRAM TO CALCULATE BATTING AVERAGE FOR EACH PLAYER ON THE TEAM,
110 '    CALCULATE THE TEAM BATTING AVERAGE, AND PRINT OUT THE NAME OF
120 '    THE PLAYER WITH THE HIGHEST BATTING AVERAGE, AND THE LOWEST
130 '
140 '                    PROGRAM VARIABLES
150 '
160 '   NAM$            PLAYER'S NAME
170 '   ATBAT           NUMBER OF TIMES AT BATS
180 '   HIT             NUMBER OF HITS
190 '   TOT.ATBAT       TEAM TOTAL OF NUMBER OF TIMES AT BATS
200 '   TOT.HIT         TEAM TOTAL OF NUMBER OF HITS
210 '   AVERAGE         BATTING AVERAGE
220 '   HIGH.AVERAGE    HIGHEST AVERAGE ON THE TEAM
230 '   LOW.AVERAGE     LOWEST AVERAGE ON THE TEAM
240 '   HIGH.PLAYER$    NAME OF PLAYER WHO ACHIEVED HIGH AVERAGE
250 '   LOW.PLAYER$     NAME OF PLAYER WHO ACHIEVED LOW AVERAGE
260 '   T$,H$,D$,TL$, PRINT IMAGES
270 '     S1$,S2$
280 '
290 '
500 '**************** PROGRAM MAINLINE ********************
510 GOSUB 1000                      'INITIALIZE VARIABLES
520 GOSUB 1500                      'WRITE HEADINGS
530 GOSUB 2000                      'DETAIL PROCESSING LOOP
540 GOSUB 6000                      'FINAL CALCULATIONS
550 GOSUB 7000                      'WRITE FINAL TOTALS
560 END
570 '
1000 '*************** INITIALIZE VARIABLES *****************
1010 LET HIGH.AVERAGE = -1
1020 LET LOW.AVERAGE = 1001
1040 LET T$  = "           Y E L L O W   S O C K S"
1050 LET H$  = "   PLAYER                AT BATS    HITS    AVERAGE"
1060 LET D$  = "\                    \     ###       ##      ###"
1070 LET TL$ = "   TOTALS                  ####      ###     ###"
1080 LET S1$ = "   HIGH BATTING AVERAGE = ### BY \            \"
1090 LET S2$ = "   LOW  BATTING AVERAGE = ### BY \            \"
1100 RETURN
1110 '
1500 '**************** WRITE HEADINGS *********************
1510 LPRINT
1520 LPRINT   T$          'PRINT TITLE LINE
1530 LPRINT
1540 LPRINT   H$          'HEADING LINE
1550 LPRINT: LPRINT       'TWO BLANK LINES
1560 RETURN
1570 '
2000 '*************** DETAIL PROCESS LOOP ******************
2010 GOSUB 3000               'PRIMING READ
2020 WHILE NAM$ <> "END"
2030    GOSUB 4000                  'CALCULATIONS
2040    GOSUB 4500                  'FIND HIGH AND LOW
2050    GOSUB 5000                  'WRITE DETAIL LINE
2060    GOSUB 3000                  'READ NEXT DATA
2070 WEND
2080 RETURN
2090 '
3000 '************ READ INPUT DATA *********************
3010 READ NAM$, ATBAT, HIT
3020 DATA KIRK BRAGGART, 20, 9
3030 DATA ROBERT ABLE, 15, 5
3040 DATA IAN BROTHER, 10, 3
3050 DATA SUZY SLEEPER, 12, 2
3060 DATA DON TREADER, 16, 4
3070 DATA RANDY RUNNER, 7, 1
3080 DATA MICHELLE ANGEL, 16, 7
3090 DATA TIM CODY, 8, 2
3100 DATA END, 0, 0
3110 RETURN
3120 '
```

```
4000 '*************** DETAIL CALCULATIONS ********************
4010 IF ATBAT > 0
        THEN LET AVERAGE = INT(HIT / ATBAT * 1000)
        ELSE LET AVERAGE = 0
4020 LET TOT.ATBAT = TOT.ATBAT + ATBAT
4030 LET TOT.HIT = TOT.HIT + HIT
4040 RETURN
4050 '
4500 '*************** FIND HIGH AND LOW ********************
4510 IF AVERAGE < LOW.AVERAGE
        THEN LET LOW.AVERAGE = AVERAGE:
            LET LOW.PLAYER$ = NAM$
4520 IF AVERAGE > HIGH.AVERAGE
        THEN LET HIGH.AVERAGE = AVERAGE:
            LET HIGH.PLAYER$ = NAM$
4530 RETURN
4540 '
5000 '*************** WRITE DETAIL LINE ********************
5010 LPRINT USING D$; NAM$, ATBAT, HIT, AVERAGE
5020 RETURN
5030 '
6000 '*************** FINAL CALCULATIONS ********************
6010 LET AVERAGE = INT(TOT.HIT / TOT.ATBAT * 1000)
6020 RETURN
6030 '
7000 '*************** WRITE TOTAL LINES ********************
7010 LPRINT
7020 LPRINT USING TL$; TOT.ATBAT, TOT.HIT, AVERAGE
7030 LPRINT: LPRINT
7040 LPRINT USING S1$; HIGH.AVERAGE, HIGH.PLAYER$
7050 LPRINT USING S2$; LOW.AVERAGE, LOW.PLAYER$
7060 RETURN
7070 '*************** END OF PROGRAM ********************
```

Sample Program Output

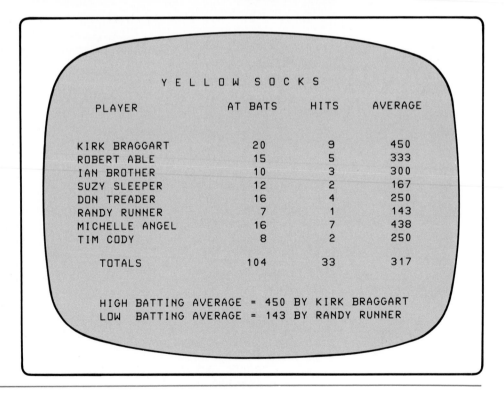

```
              Y E L L O W   S O C K S

    PLAYER              AT BATS     HITS      AVERAGE


    KIRK BRAGGART          20         9          450
    ROBERT ABLE            15         5          333
    IAN BROTHER            10         3          300
    SUZY SLEEPER           12         2          167
    DON TREADER            16         4          250
    RANDY RUNNER            7         1          143
    MICHELLE ANGEL         16         7          438
    TIM CODY                8         2          250

    TOTALS                104        33          317


    HIGH BATTING AVERAGE = 450 BY KIRK BRAGGART
    LOW  BATTING AVERAGE = 143 BY RANDY RUNNER
```

Summary

1. The selection process is implemented with the IF-THEN-ELSE. A condition is evaluated. When the condition is true, one course of action is taken; when the condition is false, another course of action is taken.

2. The conditions for IF statements are formed with the six relational operators: > (greater than); < (less than); = (equal); <> (not equal); >= (greater than or equal); <= (less than or equal). These operators may be combined with the logical operators AND, OR, and NOT, and with parentheses to form compound conditions.

3. Good indentation practices are important for producing programs that are clear and understandable.

4. There is a choice of two techniques when multiple statements are needed for the *true* or *false* conditions. The logic can be coded either with subroutines or with multistatement lines (within the bounds of a 255-character line).

5. IF statements may include other IF statements. These are called nested IF statements. When nesting IF statements, be certain that each inner IF contains an ELSE so that errors do not occur.

6. In nested IF statements, each ELSE is matched with the last unmatched THEN. Proper indentation can help for understanding of the logic, but the BASIC interpreter will match each ELSE and THEN on a one-for-one basis.

7. As the logic of programs becomes more complicated, proper indentation becomes more and more important.

8. Programs should be readable from "top to bottom" with no jumping around. In order to discourage unstructured code, no branch instructions will be used.

9. Programs must always be planned before the coding begins. Flowcharting, pseudocode, or hierarchy charts can be used for the planning step.

10. In hierarchy charts, only the individual modules are shown, not the control structure. IF statements are not indicated on the chart. The various actions to take *are* indicated.

11. READ and DATA statements can be used to assign values to variables.

12. An advantage that READ/DATA may have over INPUT statements is that all data can be entered before program execution.

13. A disadvantage of READ/DATA compared to INPUT is that the program will not be interactive. Nonprogrammers cannot be expected to change values in DATA statements.

14. READ/DATA can be more flexible than LET statements for assigning values to variables. DATA statements can be grouped together, making the values easier to locate and change than LET statements.

15. READ statements are executable, while DATA statements are not. The READ must be placed in the proper sequence for the logic of the program. The DATA statements may be placed anywhere.

16. It is recommended that the DATA statements be placed in a group, either at the beginning of the program or in the READ subroutine.

17. When a READ statement is executed, a value is placed into the variable or variables named, one at a time. Always the next unused value from the list of DATA values will be assigned to the next variable named on a READ statement.

18. The variable named on the READ and the corresponding value listed on the DATA statement must agree in type; that is, a numeric variable must receive a numeric value, and a string variable must receive a string value.

19. String values placed in DATA statements do not require quotation marks around them unless the value contains a comma or a colon, or there are leading or trailing blank spaces that must be included as part of the string.

20. A special item of data, called a data terminator, is usually placed at the end of a data list.

21. The data terminator is used to end the READ loop.

22. The data terminator may be any value and is chosen by the programmer.

23. A priming READ is generally required before a loop containing READ or INPUT statements. The loop condition is retested at the bottom of the loop, so the READ or INPUT statement should be last. Then the data terminator will be found by the condition test, and no further processing will be done on the termination data.
24. The RESTORE statement allows the DATA values in a program to be reread. Following execution of a RESTORE statement, the next READ executed will take its value from the first DATA statement in the program.

Programming Exercises

Each of these programs should be written as a modular program with a program mainline and subroutines. Plan the program with a modular flowchart, pseudocode, or hierarchy chart. Program remarks listing the program variables are required. Test your program with two or three different sets of data, making sure that it will perform correctly with any data. In most cases, data may be entered with either READ/DATA or with INPUT statements.

4.1. Piecework workers are paid by the piece. Often, workers who produce a greater quantity of output are paid at a higher rate.

1–199 pieces completed	$.50 each
200–399	.55 each (for all pieces)
400–599	.60 each
600 or more	.65 each

INPUT: For each worker, input the name and number of pieces completed. Data may be entered with READ or INPUT statements.

OUTPUT: Print an appropriate title and column headings. There should be one detail line for each worker, which shows the name, the number of pieces, and the amount earned. Compute and print totals of the number of pieces and the dollar amount earned.

PROCESSING: For each person, compute the pay earned by multiplying the number of pieces by the appropriate price. Accumulate the total number of pieces and the total dollar amount paid.

SAMPLE PROGRAM OUTPUT:

```
            PIECEWORK WEEKLY REPORT

    NAME                PIECES      PAY

    JOHNNY BEGOOD        265       145.75
    SALLY GREAT         650       422.50
    SAM KLUTZ           177        88.50
    PETE PRECISE        400       240.00
    FANNIE FANTASTIC    399       219.45
    MORRIE MELLOW       200       110.00

    TOTALS             2091      1226.20
```

TEST DATA: Test your program with the data shown in the sample output, as well as with another set of data that you make up.

4.2. Modify the program in exercise 4.1 to compute and print the following information. At the conclusion of the list, print additional lines naming the person with the greatest number of pieces and with the least number of pieces. Also, print the average number of pieces for all workers.

4.3. A battle is raging over the comparative taste of Prune Punch and Apple Ade. Each taste tester rates the two drinks on a scale of 1–10 (10 being best). The proof of the superiority of one over the other will be the average score for the two drinks.

INPUT: For each tester, input (or read) the score for each of the two drinks.

OUTPUT: Print a title and headings above the columns of scores. Then print one line on the report for each tester that shows their rating for each drink. At the bottom of the report, print the overall (average) score for each drink. Then print one line declaring the winner based on the comparative scores.

PROCESSING: Average the scores for each drink and round to the nearest tenth of a point. The winning drink will be the one with the highest average.

TEST DATA:

Prune Punch	Apple Ade
8	9.5
2	10
9	4
7.5	8.2
6	5

4.4. The local library has a summer reading program to encourage reading. A chart will be kept with the readers' names and bonus points earned.

INPUT: Each reader's name and number of books read. Use INPUT or READ.

OUTPUT: Print a title and headings over the columns of data. Each detail line will show the name, number of books read, and number of points earned. Print totals for the number of books and the number of points. Also, print the average number of points for all readers.

PROCESSING: Assign points according to this schedule. The first three books are worth 10 points each. The next three books are worth 15 points each. All books over six are worth 20 points each.

TEST DATA:

Name	Number of Books
SAM SONG	4
LINDA LOU	2
P. DEXTER	8
K. C. SMITH	6

4.5. Modify the program in exercise 4.4 to include the name of the winner (assume that no ties are allowed).

4.6. The Fox family is planning a large family reunion and wishes to accumulate some statistics on the size and distribution of the group.

INPUT: Input the name and age of each person attending. Use INPUT or READ statements.

OUTPUT: Print a title and headings over the columns of data. Print one line for each attendee showing the name and age. The average age should be printed along with the number of persons in each age group.

PROCESSING: Accumulate the number of family members in each of these groups:

<20
20–39
40–59
60–79
>79

TEST DATA: Make up a series of names and ages or use the list below. Be sure to include ages that fall on the boundaries, such as 39 and 40, 59 and 60.

Name	Age
GRANDPA	80
GRANDMA	79
AUNT VIXEN	60
MAMA	21
PAPA	20
CUBBY	1

4.7. Write a program to compute your checking account balance for one month's transactions.

INPUT: The first input should be the bank balance from the previous month. Then deposits, checks, or service charges will be entered at the keyboard. The user should be prompted to enter D, C, S, or E (for *D*eposit, *C*heck, *S*ervice charge, or *E*nd), and the amount of the transaction.

OUTPUT: Print a statement with a title and column headings, showing the beginning balance, each transaction as it is applied, and a current balance.

PROCESSING: Add deposits to the balance, subtract checks and service charges.

TEST DATA:

Beginning balance	$20.05
Check	15.00
Deposit	50.50
Check	45.57
Check	5.00
Deposit	60.00
Service charge	6.00
End	

4.8. Add error checking to the program in exercise 4.7. If any code other than D, C, S, or E is entered, print a message and reprompt for input. Continue checking the input until a correct code is entered.

4.9. Modify your program of exercise 4.7 or 4.8 to compute and print the following additional information: The total number of deposits and dollar total of deposits, the total number of checks, and dollar total of the checks.

4.10. Modify your program of exercise 4.7 (or 4.8 or 4.9) to not allow payment of any check not covered by sufficient funds. If there is not enough money to cover a check, it will be rejected with the message INSUFFICIENT FUNDS, and a service charge of $10 will be charged to the account. Make up additional data to test these routines.

4.11. A salesperson earns a weekly base salary plus a commission when sales are at or above quota. Write a program that will input the weekly sales and calculate the amount of pay.

INPUT: Use READ statements to establish the base pay, the quota, and the commission rate (these will apply to all salespersons). Then, for each salesperson, INPUT the name, social security number, and amount of sales.

OUTPUT: Print the salesperson's name, social security number, sales, commission, and total pay. When the salesperson has not earned a commission, omit the commission line. Do not print a line for commission = 0. After all sales have been entered, print report totals showing total sales, total commissions, and total pay.

PROCESSING: Compare the sales to the quota. When the sales are equal to or greater than the quota, calculate the commission by multiplying the sales by the commission rate. Each salesperson will receive the base salary, plus the commission if one has been earned. Round the commission to the nearest cent.

SAMPLE PROGRAM OUTPUT:

```
NAME  =               SANDY SMUG
SOC. SEC. NUMB =      123-45-6789
SALES =                 1,000.00
COMMISSION =              150.00
PAY   =                  400.00


NAME  =               SAM SADNESS
SOC. SEC. NUMB =      222-22-2222
SALES =                  999.99
PAY   =                  250.00


NAME  =               JOE WHIZ
SOC. SEC. NUMB =      555-55-5555
SALES =                 2,000.00
COMMISSION =              300.00
PAY   =                  550.00


TOTAL SALES =           3,999.99
TOTAL COMMISSIONS =       450.00
TOTAL PAY =             1,200.00
```

TEST DATA: Be sure to change the data to make certain your program will produce correct results with any values for quota, commission rate, base pay, and sales amounts. Use these values to test the program.

QUOTA = 1000
COMMISSION RATE = .15
BASE PAY = 250

4.12. Calculate and print a customer sales invoice. Separate totals will be accumulated for taxable and nontaxable items, the tax will be calculated, and an invoice total will be calculated.

INPUT: Input the item description, the quantity sold, the unit price, and whether or not the item is taxable. Alternately, READ and DATA statements may be used for the program input.

OUTPUT: Print an appropriate title and column headings at the top of the invoice. There should be one line in the body of the invoice for each item purchased. Each line should show (in this order) the quantity, item description, unit price, extended price, and the letters TX for any taxable item. At the bottom of the invoice, print the total of taxable items, the sales tax, the total of nontaxable items, and the invoice total.

PROCESSING: For each item of input, multiply the quantity times the unit price to obtain the extended price. Accumulate separate totals for taxable items and nontaxable items. After all data for one customer has been input and printed, calculate the sales tax at 6 percent (.06) times the taxable total. Do not calculate tax on each individual item. The total of taxable items, the sales tax, and the total of nontaxable items should be added together to produce the invoice total.

TEST DATA: Test your program with the following data. Also, create different data to thoroughly test your program. Test it with only taxable items, and only nontaxable items. Turn in at least two invoices—one with the data exactly as shown, another with data that you create.

Quantity	Description	Unit Price	Taxable
2	NAPKINS	.59	YES
1	POTATO CHIPS	1.69	NO
2	SODA POP	.69	NO
3	BOWL	1.29	YES
1	PRETZELS	.89	NO

SAMPLE PROGRAM OUTPUT USING TEST DATA:

```
          YOUR COMPANY NAME HERE

          CUSTOMER INVOICE

QUANTITY     DESCRIPTION      UNIT PRICE  PRICE

   2         NAPKINS                .59    1.18  TX
   1         POTATO CHIPS          1.69    1.69
   2         SODA POP               .69    1.38
   3         BOWL                  1.29    3.87  TX
   1         PRETZELS               .89     .89

                   TAXABLE ITEM TOTAL   5.05
                   SALES TAX             .30
                   NONTAXABLE TOTAL     3.96
                                       -----
                   INVOICE TOTAL        9.31
```

4.13. Write a program that will calculate the current value of a portfolio of stocks. Given the stock name, number of shares, and the purchase price per share, input the current price per share. From that data, calculate and print the current value for each stock, the gain or loss, and the percentage gain or loss. Additionally, each of those figures is to be calculated for the portfolio as a whole.

INPUT: Stock name, number of shares, and original purchase price will be read from DATA statements. The current price per share of each stock will be INPUT from the keyboard.

OUTPUT: The output will be a printed report, with appropriate title and column headings centered over the columns of data. For each stock, print the name, number of shares, original price per share, current price per share, current value, the dollar amount of gain or loss, and the percent gain or loss. At the end of the report, print the total dollar valuation of the portfolio, the overall gain or loss, and the overall percentage gain or loss.

PROCESSING:

1. For each stock read, input the current price per share.
2. Calculate the original value of the stock as the original price per share times the number of shares.
3. Calculate the current value of the stock as the current price per share times the number of shares.
4. Calculate the gain or loss as the current value minus the original value.
5. Calculate the percent gain or loss as the gain or loss divided by the original value.
6. Accumulate totals of the current value of the stocks and the overall dollar gain or loss.

7. Calculate the overall (portfolio) gain or loss as the total current value minus the total original value.
8. Calculate the overall percentage gain or loss for the portfolio as the overall gain or loss divided by the total original value.

TEST DATA:

	From DATA Statements		*INPUT During Program Run*
STOCK	# SHARES	ORIG PRICE	CURRENT PRICE
AT&T	200	35	38
IBM	100	120	118
APPLE	50	20	22
WANG	20	30	21

For a second run of the program, consider finding *today's* price for each of the stocks.

4.14. Write a program that will produce a summary of the amounts due for Pat's Auto Repair Shop.

INPUT: Using DATA statements, enter job number, customer name, amount charged for parts, and hours of labor for each job. Use DATA statements for the tax rate and the hourly labor charge also, so that the program may be easily adapted if either changes. Current charges are $30 per hour for labor and 6 percent (.06) for the tax rate.

OUTPUT: Print a report with a title and column headings. Each detail line will consist of the job number, customer name, amount charged for parts, amount for labor, the sales tax, and the total charges for that customer. All dollar amounts will be rounded to the nearest cent and printed with decimal points aligned. Print a total line, indicating totals for parts, labor, tax, and customer total. The total fields must be decimal point aligned beneath the corresponding columns.

PROCESSING: Sales tax is charged on parts but not on labor. Multiply the amount for parts by the tax rate to determine the amount of sales tax. The labor charge is calculated as the hourly rate times the number of hours worked. The customer total is the sum of the amounts charged for parts, labor, and sales tax. Report totals must be accumulated for parts, labor, tax, and customer total.

TEST DATA:

tax rate = .06
labor charge = $30/hour

(job number, customer name, parts, hours of labor)
125, HARRY BUTLER, 27.50, 1.5
126, LEE HERNANDEZ, 45.37, 2.1
127, IAN GORDON, 1.75, 5.2
000, END, 0, 0

SAMPLE PROGRAM OUTPUT USING TEST DATA:

```
                   PAT'S AUTO REPAIR SHOP

   JOB        CUSTOMER        PARTS      LABOR     TAX      TOTAL
 NUMBER         NAME

   125      HARRY BUTLER      27.50      45.00    1.65      74.15
   126      LEE HERNANDEZ     45.37      63.00    2.72     111.09
   127      IAN GORDON         1.75     156.00     .11     157.86

            TOTALS            74.62     264.00    4.48     343.10
```

4.15. Write a program using DATA statements to print a list of students, the college attended, and their ages.

INPUT: Use the test data below for your DATA statements.

OUTPUT: Print a title and headings over the columns of data. Each detail line will contain the student's name, the college attended, and age.

TEST DATA:

Name	College	Age
Dave Drive	Facetious University	25
Tricia Scudder	Swain College	20
Jane Adams	Rakish University	27
Lynn Steen	Ludicrous University	21
Anita Bonita	Charm College	37
Mary Berry	Outlandish College	18
Eric Pavy	Juvenile College	29
Brian Dudlin	Arachnid University	31
Mitzi Micro	Jaunty University	19
Judy Judlin	Convexity College	34

5

Structured Programming

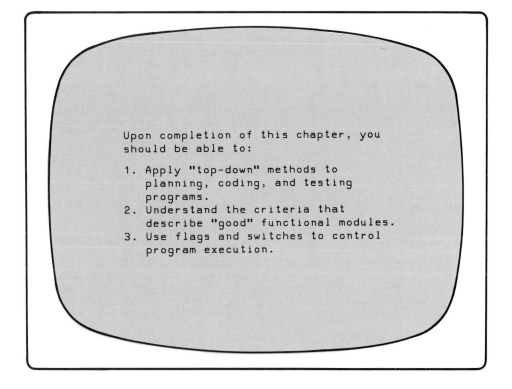

Upon completion of this chapter, you should be able to:

1. Apply "top-down" methods to planning, coding, and testing programs.
2. Understand the criteria that describe "good" functional modules.
3. Use flags and switches to control program execution.

Top-Down Programming

The term **top-down** is often used to describe well-structured, modular programs. Looking at the hierarchy chart in figure 5.1, you can visualize the top-down concept. First look at the entire program (or system of programs). Begin breaking the program into its functional parts. The process continues until, at the lowest level, relatively simple logic remains.

Top-down programming has three parts: (1) plan the program with the top-down approach; (2) code the program—mainline first, then the subroutines; and (3) test the program in a top-down manner.

Top-Down Testing

In a large and complex program, *top-down testing* can save much time and effort. The program mainline is written first, and perhaps some of the subroutines. Other subroutines will be *stubbed in* (a dummy module written), so that the program can be tested. The overall program structure can be tested and debugged early in program development. Then, one at a time, individual subroutines may be added. If the program fails at any point, the most likely cause will be the last subroutine added.

Module Stubbing

As a simple example, the chapter 4 programming example (p. 116) will be shown with some modules stubbed in. Although the program is relatively small to actually be a candidate for stubbing, you will see that for complicated programs this could be helpful. Assume that the programmer was asked to begin coding the program, but the precise calculations to be done were uncertain. All the calculations could be left for later.

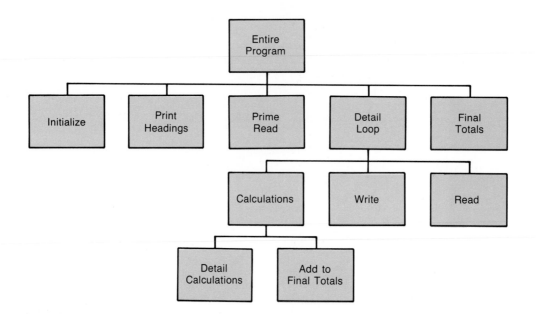

Figure 5.1
Hierarchy chart showing top-down organization.

Example Program:
Module Stubbing for Top-Down Testing

Program Listing

```
100 ' PROGRAM TO CALCULATE BATTING AVERAGE FOR EACH PLAYER ON THE TEAM,
110 '    CALCULATE THE TEAM BATTING AVERAGE, AND PRINT OUT THE NAME OF
120 '    THE PLAYER WITH THE HIGHEST BATTING AVERAGE, AND THE LOWEST
130 '
140 '                   PROGRAM VARIABLES
150 '
160 ' NAM$           PLAYER'S NAME
170 ' ATBAT          NUMBER OF TIMES AT BATS
180 ' HIT            NUMBER OF HITS
190 ' TOT.ATBAT      TEAM TOTAL OF NUMBER OF TIMES AT BATS
200 ' TOT.HIT        TEAM TOTAL OF NUMBER OF HITS
210 ' AVERAGE        BATTING AVERAGE
220 ' HIGH.AVERAGE   HIGHEST AVERAGE ON THE TEAM
230 ' LOW.AVERAGE    LOWEST AVERAGE ON THE TEAM
240 ' HIGH.PLAYER$   NAME OF PLAYER WHO ACHIEVED HIGH AVERAGE
250 ' LOW.PLAYER$    NAME OF PLAYER WHO ACHIEVED LOW AVERAGE
260 ' T$,H$,D$,TL$,  PRINT IMAGES
270 '   S1$,S2$
280 '
290 '
500 '***************** PROGRAM MAINLINE *********************
510 GOSUB 1000                   'INITIALIZE VARIABLES
520 GOSUB 1500                   'WRITE HEADINGS
530 GOSUB 2000                   'DETAIL PROCESSING LOOP
540 GOSUB 6000                   'FINAL CALCULATIONS
550 GOSUB 7000                   'WRITE FINAL TOTALS
560 END
570 '
1000 '*************** INITIALIZE VARIABLES *****************
1010 LET HIGH.AVERAGE = -1
1020 LET LOW.AVERAGE = 1001
1040 LET T$ = "              Y E L L O W   S O C K S"
1050 LET H$ = "   PLAYER              AT BATS      HITS      AVERAGE"
1060 LET D$ = "\                    \       ###        ##        ###"
1070 LET TL$ = "   TOTALS                   ####       ###        ###"
1080 LET S1$ = "   HIGH BATTING AVERAGE = ### BY \              \"
1090 LET S2$ = "   LOW  BATTING AVERAGE = ### BY \              \"
1100 RETURN
1110 '
1500 '***************** WRITE HEADINGS ********************
1510 LPRINT
1520 LPRINT T$            'PRINT TITLE LINE
1530 LPRINT
1540 LPRINT H$            'HEADING LINE
1550 LPRINT: LPRINT       'TWO BLANK LINES
1560 RETURN
1570 '
2000 '************** DETAIL PROCESS LOOP *****************
2010 GOSUB 3000                  'PRIMING READ
2020 WHILE NAM$ <> "END"
2030    GOSUB 4000               'CALCULATIONS
2040    GOSUB 4500               'FIND HIGH AND LOW
2050    GOSUB 5000               'WRITE DETAIL LINE
2060    GOSUB 3000               'READ NEXT DATA
2070 WEND
2080 RETURN
2090 '
```

```
3000 '************ READ INPUT DATA (SHORT DATA LIST) **********
3010 READ NAM$, ATBAT, HIT
3020 DATA KIRK BRAGGART, 20, 9
3030 DATA ROBERT ABLE, 15, 5
3100 DATA END, 0, 0
3110 RETURN
3120 '
4000 '**************** DETAIL CALCULATIONS ********************
4010 '           ******* STUB MODULE ********
4020 LET AVERAGE = 350
4030 RETURN
4050 '
4500 '*************** FIND HIGH AND LOW *********************
4510           ******* STUB MODULE ********
4520 LET LOW.AVERAGE = 300
4530 LET HIGH.AVERAGE = 400
4540 LET LOW.PLAYER$ = "LOW GUY"
4550 LET HIGH.PLAYER$ = "HIGH GUY"
4560 RETURN
4570 '
5000 '*************** WRITE DETAIL LINE ********************
5010 LPRINT USING D$; NAM$, ATBAT, HIT, AVERAGE
5020 RETURN
5030 '
6000 '*************** FINAL CALCULATIONS ******************
6010           ******* STUB MODULE *******
6020 LET AVERAGE = 365
6030 RETURN
6040 '
7000 '************** WRITE TOTAL LINES *******************
7010 LPRINT
7020 LPRINT USING TL$; TOT.ATBAT, TOT.HIT, AVERAGE
7030 LPRINT: LPRINT
7040 LPRINT USING S1$; HIGH.AVERAGE, HIGH.PLAYER$
7050 LPRINT USING S2$; LOW.AVERAGE, LOW.PLAYER$
7060 RETURN
7070 '************** END OF PROGRAM ********************
```

Structured Programming

Structured programming is one step beyond modular programming with guidelines for "good" modules and "poor" modules. The structured programming guidelines also define "proper" flow of control and coding standards (such as indentation). In many large programming projects for which statistics have been kept, it has been shown that structured programming has many demonstrable advantages over the old-style, unstructured programs.

1. Programs are more reliable. Fewer bugs appear in testing and later operation.
2. Programs are easier to read and understand.
3. Programs are easier to test and debug.
4. Programs are easier to maintain.

Most commercial programming shops report that at least 50 percent of programmer time is spent making changes and corrections in existing programs rather than developing new programs (some report more than 90 percent maintenance). Anything that will save time in correction and maintenance can save a company considerable money. It is easy to see why most commercial shops hiring programmers insist on structured programming techniques.

The current **definition of structured programming** includes standards for program design, coding, and testing that are designed to create proper, reliable, and maintainable software. These standards include coding guidelines and rules for flow of control and module formation.

Structured Coding Guidelines

The *structured coding guidelines* are designed to make programs more readable and easier to understand.

1. Use meaningful variable names.
2. Code only one statement per line.
3. Use REMarks to explain program logic.
4. Indent and align all statements in a loop.
5. Indent the THEN and ELSE actions of an IF statement.

Flow of Control

In 1964, Italians Bohm and Jacopini proved mathematically that any program logic can be accomplished with just three control structures. Within a few years, studies were done declaring the GOTO statement to be harmful to good programming. In fact, in comparisons of selected large programming projects, there was a direct correlation between the number of GOTO statements and program bugs found.

BASIC was not designed as a structured language, but some of the current additions to the language now permit the programmer to adhere to the *three "proper" constructs*. All programming can be done with combinations of these three constructs.

Three "Proper" Constructs for Structured Programs

1. *SEQUENCE*—Statements are executed one after another in sequence.

```
50   INPUT NUM
60   LET TOTAL = TOTAL + NUM
70   PRINT TOTAL
```

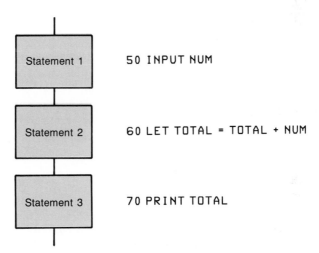

2. *SELECTION*—Choosing one course of action or another. In BASIC, the selection control is implemented with the IF-THEN-ELSE.

```
80 IF NUM > 10
   THEN
     PRINT "LIMIT EXCEEDED"
   ELSE
     LET COUNT = COUNT - NUM
```

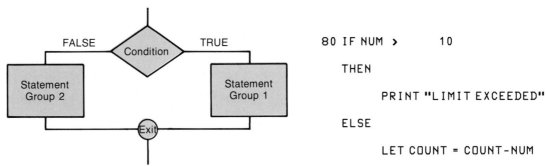

3. *ITERATION*—This is the loop structure. The BASIC statements learned for looping are the WHILE/WEND.

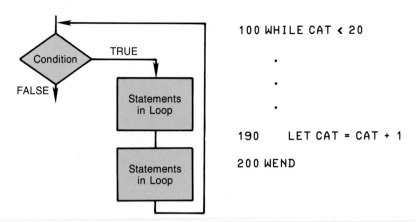

```
100 WHILE CAT < 20
      .
      .
      .
190     LET CAT = CAT + 1
200 WEND
```

Structured Module Design Considerations

One Entry, One Exit

The primary rule for program modules is that each module must have only one entry point and one exit point. So, even though BASIC will allow a GOSUB to a line number within a subroutine and will allow multiple RETURN statements, such violations of the "one-entry, one-exit" rule should be avoided.

The "Black Box" Concept

A "black box" (program module) is designed to accomplish a task. Generally, some data is input to the module, a transformation occurs, and data is output from the module. The details of what happens within the "black box" are not important to the overall program. What *is* important is that for a given input, the module will reliably produce the correct output. That module could be replaced by another—perhaps in another language such as assembler—without changing the rest of the program. It is important that each module "stand alone."

Module Cohesion

Choosing the correct statements to combine into modules is an important skill for programmers to develop. "Good" or "bad" module design is often an elusive concept when beginning to modularize programs.

Cohesion refers to the internal strength of a module. It is an indication of how closely related each of the statements in a module are to one another. As cohesion is increased, module independence, clarity, maintainability, and portability are increased.

The "best" modules are those that accomplish one task; and all statements in the group relate to that one function. Some examples of good, functional modules would be:

    detail calculations
    total calculations
    subtotal calculations
    validate input data
    print headings

When other statements are "thrown in" because "they need to be done also" or "that's what comes next," the cohesion of a module is destroyed.

In order to improve the cohesion of modules, resist the urge to lump the PRINTs with the calculations or to group together all program preliminaries such as initializing variables, printing headings, and doing priming READ.

It is not always possible to isolate each function into a module, especially in small programs. Such an attempt can cause many one-line modules. But one-line modules are not forbidden and are often preferable to an uncohesive, poor, utility module.

Module Coupling

Coupling refers to the connections, or interfaces, between modules. As a general rule, modules should be loosely coupled; that is, what goes on inside one module should not affect the operation in other modules.

The control for execution of program modules must "come from above." Looking at a hierarchy chart, a lower level module cannot determine what a higher level module should do—or even a module at the same level. For example, do not allow the detail read routine to determine that it is time to do final total calculations. That decision must be made by the mainline.

When a decision will determine which function to perform, place that decision at as high a level as possible.

Poor Construction	*Preferable Construction*
50 GOSUB 100	
60 GOSUB 200	50 IF CODE$ = "A"
::	THEN
100 IF CODE$ = "A"	GOSUB 100
THEN	ELSE
::	GOSUB 200
::	
110 RETURN	
200 IF CODE$ <> "A"	
THEN	
::	
::	
210 RETURN	

The decision to perform a function should not be made after calling the subroutine, but should be made at the higher level, if possible.

At times it is necessary to have lower ranking modules make a determination that will alter the program flow of control. Those lower modules may place values in variables that will be checked at a higher level. The variables used for this type of control are called switches or flags.

Using Switches and Flags

Sometimes you want to know "How did it go?" after an operation is complete. Was the data valid or invalid? Was this the end of data? Was a particular key pressed? A common practice is to use a variable to indicate the status of the operation. Some programmers refer to these variables as **switches,** others call them **flags.**

A switch (or flag) is nothing more than a variable that is allowed to have one of two values. Commonly, a numeric variable is used. Then a value of 1 means the switch is "on," and a value of 0 indicates the switch is "off." Many programmers prefer to use a string variable for the switch field. Then the two values would be Y and N for YES and NO, or T and F for TRUE and FALSE.

Use of a switch field generally requires three steps. The first step is to initialize the field—to know its initial state. Then, the switch will be set to indicate a condition. At a later point, the switch field can be tested to see how it was set.

Switches are commonly used in well-structured programs. However, care must be taken to observe proper flow of control. The preferred usage is to have the lower ranking module set the switch to indicate the condition. Then the higher ranking module will check the switch field to determine the correct subroutine to execute.

Example Program Segment:
General Form for Using Switches

Program Listing

```
500 '****** GENERAL FORM FOR USE OF A SWITCH *************
510 LET SWITCH = 1              'SET ON (OR OFF) TO START
520 GOSUB 700                   'SET VALUE IN SUBROUTINE
530 IF SWITCH = 1
        THEN ...                'STILL ON - SELECT COURSE OF ACTION
540 ::
    ::
```

Example Program Segment:
Selection of Correct Subroutine with a Switch

Program Listing

```
1000 '****** SELECTION OF CORRECT SUBROUTINE WITH SWITCH ****
1010 LET REASONABLE.FLAG = 1         'SET SWITCH ON
1020 GOSUB 5000                      'CALCULATE PAY
1030                                 'SELECT COURSE OF ACTION,
1040                                 ' BASED ON REASONABLE.FLAG
1050 IF REASONABLE.FLAG = 1
        THEN GOSUB 6000
        ELSE GOSUB 7000
1060 ...
::
::
5000 '************* CALCULATE PAY ***************************
5010 LET PAY = HOURS * RATE
5020 IF PAY > MAX.PAY
        THEN LET REASONABLE.FLAG = 0
5030 IF PAY > (2*PRIOR.PAY)
        THEN LET REASONABLE.FLAG = 0
5040 IF PAY < 0
        THEN LET REASONABLE.FLAG = 0
5050 RETURN
5060 '
6000 '*********** PRINT PAYCHECK ***************************
6010 ...
::
::
6998 RETURN
6999 '
7000 '********** UNREASONABLE PAY ***********************
7010 PRINT "ERROR IN PAY CALCULATIONS"
7020 RETURN
```

Example Program Segment: Loop Control with a Switch

```
2000 '****** KEEP AT IT UNTIL GOOD CODE FIELD ENTERED ******
2010 LET SWITCH = 0              'SET SWITCH OFF TO BEGIN
2020 WHILE SWITCH = 0
2030      GOSUB 3000             'INPUT VALID SELECTION
2040 WEND
::
::
3000 '********** INPUT VALID SELECTION ********************
3010 INPUT "ENTER SELECTION CODE (A, D, F) ", CODE$
3020 ' ** SWITCH SET ON FOR VALID DATA **
3030 IF CODE$ = "A" OR CODE$ = "D" OR CODE$ = "F"
          THEN LET SWITCH = 1
3040 RETURN
```

Feedback

1. What is the difference between the terms "top-down programming" and "structured programming"?
2. It would seem that coding a program as concisely as possible would be a desirable trait. Why not use one- or two-character variable names?
3. Consider a subroutine that adds to subtotals, prints a detail line, and reads the next data. Would this be a "good" subroutine? If not, is it an example of poor coupling or poor cohesion?

Summary

1. A hierarchy chart can be a useful tool for planning structured programs.
2. The entire program is shown at the highest level of a hierarchy chart. Then at each lower level, the program is further broken down into smaller and smaller parts.
3. Top-down programming applies to program design, coding, and testing.
4. In top-down design, the program is planned from the overall view first, then broken down into individual parts.
5. Top-down coding suggests that the main part (or top) of the program be written first. Details (or bottom level) can be added later.
6. In top-down testing, the program is tested and debugged in the midst of top-down coding. The overall structure of the program can be tested by "stubbing in" lower level modules.
7. Structured programming is a tool for creating proper, reliable, and maintainable software.
8. Structured programming includes rules for module formation, for flow of control, and for coding.
9. Coding guidelines include standards for naming variables, use of REMarks, indentation, and alignment. The purpose of the rules is to make programs more readable and understandable.
10. Module formation rules include:
    a. One entry, one exit.
    b. Good cohesion—The statements of a module should be grouped together because they all contribute to one program function.
    c. Loose coupling—The statements in one module cannot be allowed to affect, alter, or interfere with those in any other module.
    d. Decisions for control must be made at the highest level possible.

11. There are three "proper" constructs for programming logic:
    a. sequence
    b. selection
    c. iteration
12. Sequence refers to executing one statement after another in sequence.
13. In selection, alternate courses of action are taken, depending on a condition. In BASIC, the selection construct is formed with IF-THEN-ELSE.
14. Iteration refers to program loops. Whenever a statement or group of statements is to be repeated, use the WHILE/WEND.
15. A variable may be used as a switch (sometimes called a flag). A value of 1 in the field generally means the switch is ON, and 0 means the switch is OFF. This technique allows one module of the program to set the switch to indicate a condition. Then, in another module, the value of the switch variable can be checked to determine what that condition was. As a general rule, switches will be used to pass status information to a higher ranking module for determining flow of control.

Programming Exercises

5.1. Write a program to create an inventory list for your collection of model cars using the top-down approach in planning, coding, and testing the program. Code the main module and the detail module, and create stub submodules for the initialization, title, headings, read, calculations, output, and totals.

OUTPUT: Print a message such as HEADING ROUTINE for each GOSUB in the main module.

5.2. Code the initialization, title, and heading subroutines for the car inventory program in program 5.1. You will need a heading for manufacturer's number, year, make, model, description, and price.

5.3. Code and debug the read, calculation, output, and total subroutines for the car inventory program in exercise 5.1.

INPUT: Input can come from INPUT statements or READ/DATA statements. Use the test data below.
OUTPUT: Print a title, column headings, manufacturer's number, year, make, model, description, price, and total price on the printer and on the screen.
PROCESS: Calculate the total price = sum of all purchase prices.
TEST DATA:

Manufact #	Yr	Make	Model	Description	Price
BMR-R79	49	FIAT	500B	GILLETTE RAZOR	7.99
HOTWELS-34	57	CHEVY	NOMAD	4/DR STATION WAGON	12.95
MATCHBX-878	73	FORD	BRONC	3/DR 4X4 RED SPARE WHL	25.99
MATCHBX-72	69	BUIK	CENTY	YELLOW TAXI	1.49
BRM-R88	34	BUGAT	TY575	RACER, BLACK	35.00
MATCHBX-25	80	LINCO	MRKIV	WHITE, LIMOUSINE	14.99
LESNEY-Y42	82	CHEVY	MALBU	4/DR GREEN PASSENGER	1.99
HASBRO-119	75	AMC	GRMLN	2/DR SEDAN, YELLOW	1.69
TABY-6332	71	TOYOT	CELIC	2/DR SEDAN, BLUE	2.99
BMR-SY238	36	ROLRY	SYLVC	4/DR SEDAN, SILVER-GRAY	60.00

6

Report Design and Subtotals

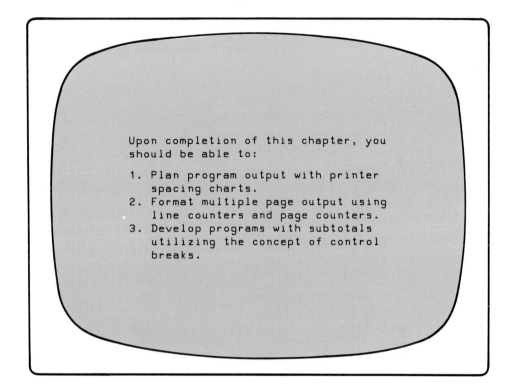

Upon completion of this chapter, you should be able to:

1. Plan program output with printer spacing charts.
2. Format multiple page output using line counters and page counters.
3. Develop programs with subtotals utilizing the concept of control breaks.

Planning Output with Printer Spacing Charts

When designing the format of printed output, a *printer spacing chart* (or *print chart*) can be a valuable tool. The lines have been drawn to the standard scale, so it is easy to see how the completed output will look. Coding the print images in a program is far easier once a print chart has been drawn. See figure 6.1 for a typical printer spacing chart.

Printers vary a great deal in their specifications. Before designing output for any particular printer, a programmer should check the line length, horizontal spacing, and vertical spacing. It can be extremely discouraging to plan all program output for 132-character lines and then to find that the printer has only 80-character lines.

The horizontal spacing of a printer is generally stated in the number of *characters per inch (CPI)*, with 10 CPI being the most common. The most common line lengths are 80 characters, 120 characters, and 132 characters.

Vertical spacing is measured in *lines per inch (LPI)*, with 6 lines per inch being the most common. Many of the larger printers attached to mainframe computers have a switch, which allows printing at 6 LPI or 8 LPI. Many of the popular printers for personal computers allow selection of line width in increments of 1/72 inch or even 1/216 inch.

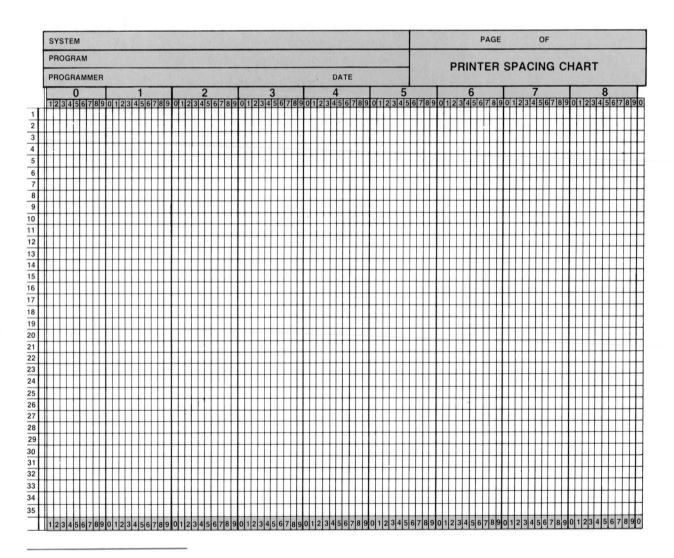

Figure 6.1
Sample printer spacing chart.

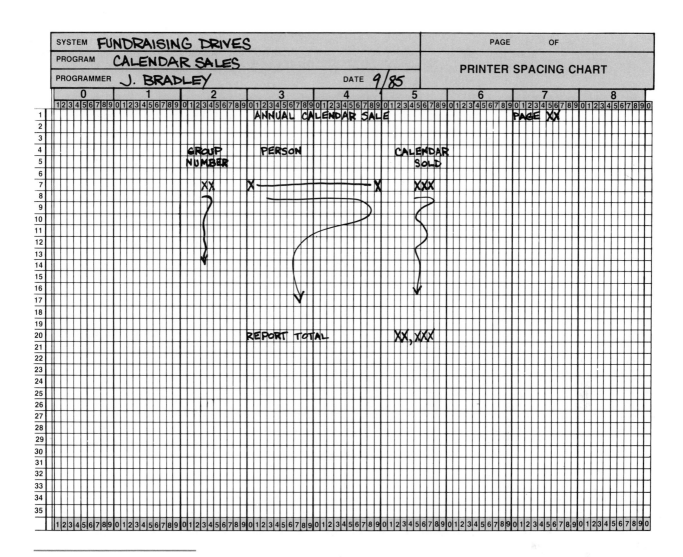

Figure 6.2
Completed printer spacing chart.

If a programmer doesn't know what type of printer will be used for output, the safest practice is to plan for an 80-character line with 6 lines per inch. For standard 8 1/2-by-11-inch paper, this will allow for 66 lines of 80 characters (which would fill the entire sheet).

Some recommendations for planning output (refer to figure 6.2):

1. Allow 1 inch at the top of the paper above the title.
2. Allow at least 1 inch at the bottom of the sheet for a margin. (Subtracting 12 lines for top and bottom margin leaves 54 lines for printing.)
3. Center the title and triple space (2 blank lines). Consider adding the date and identification of the program that produced the output to the title line.
4. Generally 1 or 2 lines are needed for column headings, plus 1 blank line before the first detail line. (Subtract 6 lines for title, headings, and blank lines—leaving 48 lines for printing the detail lines.)
5. Decide where the data will appear for detail lines before placing the column headings. Plan the number of characters for each field, including edit characters (commas, decimal points, dollar signs). Then decide on the number of spaces to allow between columns of data, and center the detail data on the 80-character line. Columns of data too close together (2 or 3 spaces) are difficult to read. Columns too far apart (more than 10) cause difficulties for many people in visually aligning the data fields.

6. Once the detail line has been drawn on the chart, *then* center the headings above the columns of data. A slight abbreviation is acceptable if the meaning is clear. It is better to allow 2 (or even 3) lines of column headings than to code cryptic headings.

7. Draw wavy lines below the columns of data to show that more lines will be printed. Single spacing of detail lines is assumed unless a note appears to the contrary.

8. When totals are needed, indicate the spacing below the last line of detail data. Always make sure the total fields are decimal point aligned beneath their columns of data.

9. Will the report fit on one page? After subtracting the lines for the total line and spacing, there will be about 45 or 46 lines left for detail data. If the data is likely to require more than that, multiple pages are required. If it is possible to fit the report on one page with modest modification, it is probably a good idea.

10. If multiple pages are required, add the page number to the title line.

Multiple Page Output

When a report must be printed on multiple pages, additional program logic is required. The detail lines must be counted as they are printed. When the page is filled, the paper must be advanced to the top of the next page, a page number and headings printed, and the lines on the new page counted.

Two counters must be added to a program that prints multiple pages. A **line counter** is needed to count the number of detail lines printed, and a **page counter** must be kept in order to print the page number on each page. The line counter must be re-initialized for each new page, while the page counter must begin at 1 and keep incrementing. As each detail line is printed, it must be counted. When the count goes over the specified number of lines, a page break occurs.

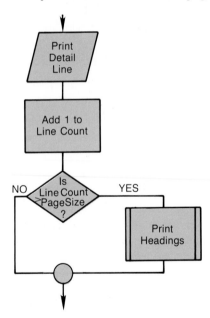

Figure 6.3
Flowchart of heading subroutine.

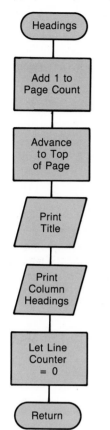

The heading subroutine must do several things (figure 6.3):

Increment the page counter
Advance to the top of the next page
Print the headings
Reset the line counter to zero (for the next page)

Question: How do you make the printer advance to the top of the page?
Answer: Two ways.

1. There are 66 lines on a page, and you know how many have been printed. So, print the correct number of blank lines to advance to the top of the page.
2. Trickier but better. Most printers respond to a special, nonprinting character, called the form-feed, by advancing to the top of the next page. The character is the twelfth code in the ASCII coding sequence and can be sent to the printer with this statement:

```
LPRINT CHR$(12);
```

The trailing semicolon keeps the internal print pointer on the first line, rather than allowing it to advance one more line.

There is one small catch to this—how does the printer know where the top of the next page is? When the printer is powered on (or reset), it establishes *that* line as top-of-form. It keeps its own internal counter as it prints lines. So, each time it receives the form-feed character [CHR$(12)], it advances to a point 66 lines from the last top-of-form. Obviously, if the paper is not set correctly in the beginning, the page breaks will be misplaced.

Note: For more information about controlling the printer with special characters, see appendix H.

Coding the Heading Module

```
2000  '***************** PRINT HEADINGS *********************
2010  LET PAGE.CT = PAGE.CT + 1      'ADD TO PAGE COUNTER
2015  LPRINT CHR$(12);              'ADVANCE TO TOP OF PAGE
2020  LPRINT USING T$; PAGE.CT       'PRINT TITLE LINE
2030  LPRINT:LPRINT
2040  LPRINT H1$                     'PRINT COLUMN HEADINGS
2050  LPRINT H2$
2060  LPRINT
2070  LET LINE.CT = 0                'RESET LINE COUNTER
2080  RETURN
```

The logic of the program will need to be altered to provide for the printing of headings when interspersed in the detail lines. In prior programs, the headings were always printed from the program mainline before the detail loop was begun. Now, the line counter must be tested in the detail loop. When the number of lines printed indicates the page is full, the heading module must be executed.

Programming Example

This program must print a summary of the calendars sold for the annual fund-raising drive. In order to demonstrate multiple page output without including great quantities of data, the number of lines per page has been set to 10.

Input

(from DATA statements)

1. Group number
2. Name of person
3. Number of calendars sold

Output

(on printer)

1. Report with title, column headings, and multiple page output.
2. For each person, print the group number, name, and number of calendars sold.
3. A report total is required for the total number of calendars sold.

Calculations

Add all calendar sales.

Pseudocode

Main Program

1. Initialize
   Print images and maximum page size
2. Print headings—for first page
3. Detail process
   - 3.1 Prime read
   - 3.2 Loop until end of data
     - 3.2.1 Calculations—add to total
     - 3.2.2 Print a line
           Add to line counter
     - 3.2.3 If line counter > maximum allowed
               then print headings
     - 3.2.4 Read next data
   - 3.3 End loop
4. Print final total

Heading Subroutine

1. Add to page counter
2. Advance to top of page
3. Print title and column heading lines
4. Reset line counter to zero

Flowchart

Figure 6.4 reflects the calendar sales flowchart form.

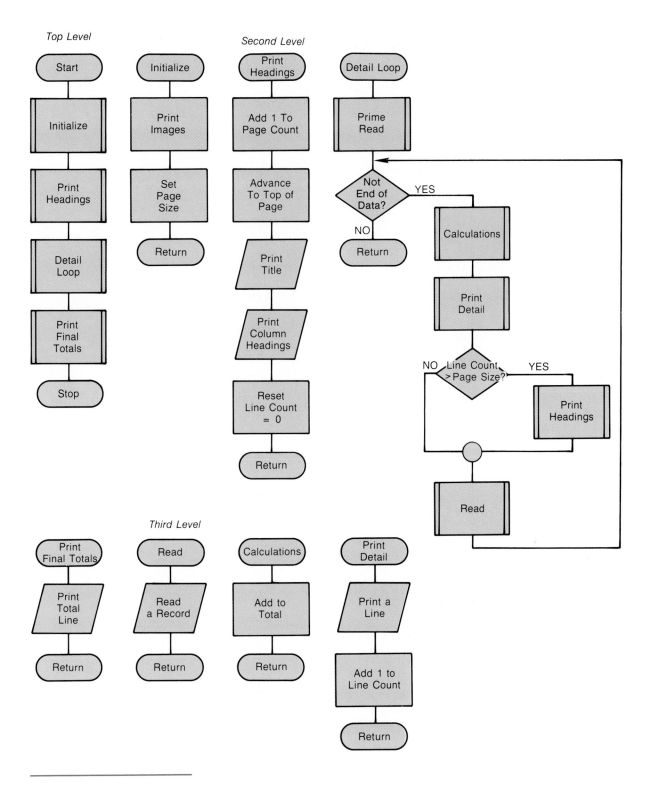

Figure 6.4
Calendar sales program
flowchart.

```
100 'PROGRAM TO REPORT ON THE ANNUAL CALENDAR SALE DRIVE
110 ' INCLUDES MULTIPLE PAGE BREAKS, WITH THE NUMBER OF
120 ' LINES PER PAGE SET TO 10 TO DEMONSTRATE PAGE COUNTER
130 '
140 '                VARIABLES USED
150 '     GROUP$            GROUP NUMBER
160 '     PER$              NAME OF PERSON
170 '     CAL               CALENDARS SOLD
180 '     CAL.SUBTOT        GROUP SUBTOTAL
190 '     CAL.TOT           REPORT TOTAL
200 '     LINE.CT           LINE COUNT
210 '     PAGE.CT           PAGE COUNT
220 '     MAX.LINES         MAXIMUM NUMBER OF LINES PER PAGE
230 '     T$,H1$,H2$,D$     PRINT IMAGES
240 '     ST$,RT$
250 '
500 '************** PROGRAM MAINLINE *************************
510 GOSUB 1000                    'INITIALIZE PRINT IMAGES
520 GOSUB 2000                    'PRINT HEADINGS
530 GOSUB 3000                    'DETAIL LOOP
540 GOSUB 7000                    'PRINT FINAL TOTALS
550 END
560 '
1000 '***************** INITIALIZE ***************************
1010 LET T$ = "                        ANNUAL CALENDAR SALE    PAGE ##"
1020 LET H1$ = "         GROUP       PERSON              CALENDARS"
1030 LET H2$ = "         NUMBER                            SOLD"
1040 LET D$ = "          \\            \            \        ###"
1050 LET RT$ = "                        REPORT TOTAL        ##,###"
1060 LET MAX.LINES = 10    'SET PAGE SIZE FOR SHORT PAGE TO DEMONSTRATE
1070 RETURN
1080 '
2000 '**************** PRINT HEADINGS ************************
2010 LET PAGE.CT = PAGE.CT + 1 'ADD TO PAGE COUNTER
2020 LPRINT CHR$(12);            'ADVANCE TO TOP OF PAGE
2030 LPRINT USING T$; PAGE.CT  'PRINT TITLE LINE
2040 LPRINT:LPRINT
2050 LPRINT H1$                  'PRINT COLUMN HEADINGS
2060 LPRINT H2$
2070 LPRINT
2080 LET LINE.CT = 0             'RESET LINE COUNTER
2090 RETURN
2100 '
3000 '*************** DETAIL LOOP ****************************
3010 GOSUB 4000                  'PRIME READ
3020 WHILE GROUP$ <> "00"
3030    GOSUB 5000               'CALCULATIONS
3040    GOSUB 6000               'PRINT A LINE
3050    IF LINE.CT >= MAX.LINES
           THEN GOSUB 2000       'PRINT HEADINGS
3060    GOSUB 4000               'READ
3070 WEND
3080 RETURN
3090 '
```

```
4000 '***************** READ DATA ************************
4010 READ GROUP$, PER$, CAL
4020 DATA 1A,CLEO THORPE,4,1A,BERTHA THOMAS,6,1A,KARL BETTS,3
4030 DATA 1B,ANTHONY HOFFMAN,12,1B,DAVID YOUNT,4,2A,PHILLIP TIBBS,6
4040 DATA 2B,VICTOR PROCTOR,15,2B,PAUL PARSONS,25,2B,BRENDA MILLER,18
4050 DATA 3A,RALPH MAY,6,3A,DEANNA MC CLURE,10,3A,FLOYD SWANSON,20
4060 DATA 3A,STEVE SUTTON,3,3A,BARBARA KIDWELL,12,3A,KENNETH KING,22
4070 DATA 3B,PAUL DEMPSEY,25,3B,RUBY BAILEY,12,4A,BILL WILKINSON,10
4080 DATA 4A,RUSSELL BUTLER,21,4A,CHARLES CAIN,15,4B,HARVEY CALDWELL,6
4090 DATA 5A,EILEEN FAY,9,5A,ALLEN FARMER,14,5B,ARTURO HERNANDEZ,13
4100 DATA 5B,BERNICE HENDERSON,7,5B,LARRY HOLT,30,5B,WADE LEE,25
4110 DATA 00,00,00
4120 RETURN
4130 '
5000 '**************** CALCULATIONS **********************
5010 LET CAL.TOT = CAL.TOT + CAL
5020 RETURN
5030 '
6000 '**************** PRINT A LINE **********************
6010 LPRINT USING D$; GROUP$, PER$, CAL
6020 LET LINE.CT = LINE.CT + 1
6030 RETURN
6040 '
7000 '**************** PRINT FINAL TOTALS *****************
7010 LPRINT
7020 LPRINT USING RT$; CAL.TOT
7030 RETURN
7040 '**************** END OF PROGRAM ********************
```

Sample Program Output

```
              ANNUAL CALENDAR SALE                PAGE 1

     GROUP        PERSON              CALENDARS
     NUMBER                           SOLD


      1A          CLEO THORPE             4
      1A          BERTHA THOMAS           6
      1A          KARL BETTS              3
      1B          ANTHONY HOFFMAN         12
      1B          DAVID YOUNT             4
      2A          PHILLIP TIBBS           6
      2B          VICTOR PROCTOR          15
      2B          PAUL PARSONS            25
      2B          BRENDA MILLER           18
      3A          RALPH MAY               6
```

```
              ANNUAL CALENDAR SALE                PAGE 2

     GROUP        PERSON              CALENDARS
     NUMBER                           SOLD


      3A          DEANNA MC CLURE         10
      3A          FLOYD SWANSON           20
      3A          STEVE SUTTON            3
      3A          BARBARA KIDWELL         12
      3A          KENNETH KING            22
      3B          PAUL DEMPSEY            25
      3B          RUBY BAILEY             12
      4A          BILL WILKINSON          10
      4A          RUSSELL BUTLER          21
      4A          CHARLES CAIN            15
```

```
                    ANNUAL CALENDAR SALE                    PAGE 3

     GROUP           PERSON                 CALENDARS
     NUMBER                                    SOLD


      4B        HARVEY CALDWELL                 6
      5A        EILEEN FAY                      9
      5A        ALLEN FARMER                   14
      5B        ARTURO HERNANDEZ               13
      5B        BERNICE HENDERSON               7
      5B        LARRY HOLT                     30
      5B        WADE LEE                       25

                REPORT TOTAL                  353
```

Feedback

1. When multiple pages are needed, how will the printed output look if the line counter is not reset to zero in the heading routine?
2. Can you think of any reason why it might be better to advance to the next page by printing a form-feed character (ASCII code 12) rather than printing blank lines?
3. How many lines can be printed on a standard 8 1/2-by-11-inch paper?
4. What is the difference between detail lines and any other lines printed?

Subtotals with Control Breaks

Another technique often required for reports is printing subtotals. For the programming example for calendar sales, subtotals can be printed at the end of each group before beginning the next group. At the end of the entire list, the report totals can be printed.

Sample Program Output

```
                    ANNUAL CALENDAR SALE                    PAGE  1

     GROUP           PERSON                 CALENDARS
     NUMBER                                    SOLD


      1A        CLEO THORPE                     4
      1A        BERTHA THOMAS                   6
      1A        KARL BETTS                      3

                SUBTOTAL                       13

      1B        ANTHONY HOFFMAN                12
      1B        DAVID YOUNT                     4

                SUBTOTAL                       16

      2A        PHILLIP TIBBS                   6

                SUBTOTAL                        6

      2B        VICTOR PROCTOR                 15
      2B        PAUL PARSONS                   25
      2B        BRENDA MILLER                  18

                SUBTOTAL                       58

                REPORT TOTAL                   93
```

Figure 6.5
Flowchart of the subtotal
subroutine.

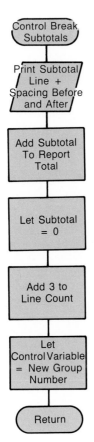

There is a field controlling the totaling process to determine when subtotals are required. (In this case, group number controls the totals.) As long as the group number stays the same, detail lines are printed and totals are accumulated. As soon as the group number changes, subtotals are required. The field controlling the process is called the **control variable.** When the contents of the field change and subtotals are printed, this is called a **control break.**

When a control break occurs, several steps must take place:

1. The subtotals are printed (generally along with spacing before and after the subtotal line).
2. The subtotal fields are added into the report totals.
3. The subtotal fields are reset to zero (so that the next group subtotals will be correct).
4. The extra lines are added to the line counter.
5. The control variable is reset for the next group.

Figure 6.5 shows a flowchart of the subroutine needed when a control break occurs.

How do you know when it's time to print the subtotals? The only way to know that the last item in the group has been printed is to read the next record and to find that the group number is different. So, after each read, ask the question, "Is this group number different from the last one?" But if you use the statement

```
READ GROUP$, ...
```

the new group number replaces the old one, and a comparison cannot be made. For this reason, another variable is required to hold the previous group number.

```
READ GROUP$, ...
IF GROUP$ <> GROUP.SAVE$
    THEN GOSUB 2000          'CONTROL BREAK
```

In the flowchart of the control break subroutine (figure 6.4), the contents of GROUP.SAVE$ was altered so that the next group would use the new value as its control variable. Once this process gets going, it will work well. One problem remains—for the first group, GROUP.SAVE$ will not have the correct value. Subtotals will print the first time the comparison is made. To solve this one last problem, the first group number is placed into the save field immediately after the priming READ.

```
3000  '**************** DETAIL LOOP ********************
3010  GOSUB 4000                'PRIME READ
3020  LET GROUP.SAVE$ = GROUP$  'SAVE FIRST GROUP NUMBER
3030  WHILE GROUP$ <> "00"
3040     GOSUB 5000             'CALCULATIONS
3050     IF LINE.CT > MAX.LINES
             THEN GOSUB 2000     'PRINT HEADINGS
3060     GOSUB 6000             'PRINT A LINE
3070     GOSUB 4000             'READ
3080     IF GROUP.SAVE$ <> GROUP$
             THEN GOSUB 6500     'SUBTOTALS
3090  WEND
3100  RETURN
   ::
6500 '**************** SUBTOTAL BREAK ********************
6510  LPRINT
6520  LPRINT USING ST$; CAL.SUBTOT    'PRINT SUBTOTAL LINE
6530  LPRINT
6540  LET CAL.TOT = CAL.TOT + CAL.SUBTOT  'ADD TO REPORT TOTAL
6550  LET CAL.SUBTOT = 0        'RESET SUBTOTAL TO ZERO
6560  LET LINE.CT = LINE.CT + 3 'ADD TO LINE COUNTER
6570  LET GROUP.SAVE$ = GROUP$  'SAVE NEW GROUP NUMBER
6580  RETURN
```

One important point must be made. The input data *must* be in order by group number. Otherwise, subtotals would occur every time another group number was read.

The Page Headings

The alert reader may have noticed a change in the placement of the line counter test (line 3050 preceding). This is largely a matter of aesthetics. If the last detail line of one group happens to be the last line on the page, the choice can be to have the subtotals appear in the bottom margin or as the first line on the new page. Generally, it is not considered good form to begin a page with subtotals. In order to keep from printing headings between the last detail line and the subtotal line, the decision has been placed *before* the PRINT.

Example Program: Calendar Sales

The program for calendar sales is ready to be shown in its entirety.

Pseudocode

Main Program
1. Initialize
       Print images and line count
2. Detail process
    2.1   Prime read
    2.2   Save group number
    2.3   Loop until group = 00
        2.3.1   Calculations—add to subtotal
        2.3.2   If line counter > maximum allowed
              then print headings
        2.3.3   Print a line
              Add to line counter
        2.3.4   Read next data
        2.3.5   If new group
              do subtotals
    2.4   End loop
3. Print final totals

Subtotal Subroutine

1. Print subtotal line with space before and after
2. Add subtotal to report total
3. Reset subtotal to zero
4. Add 3 to line counter
5. Save group number

Hierarchy Chart

Refer to figure 6.6 for the chart.

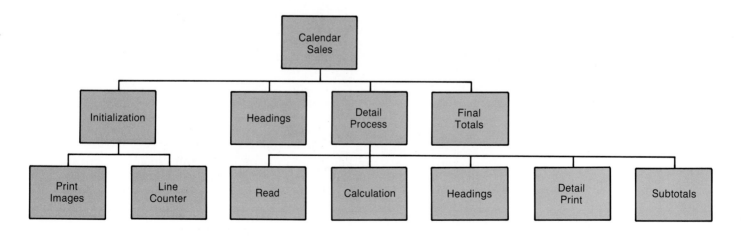

Figure 6.6
Calendar sales program hierarchy chart.

Refer to figure 6.7 for the flowchart.

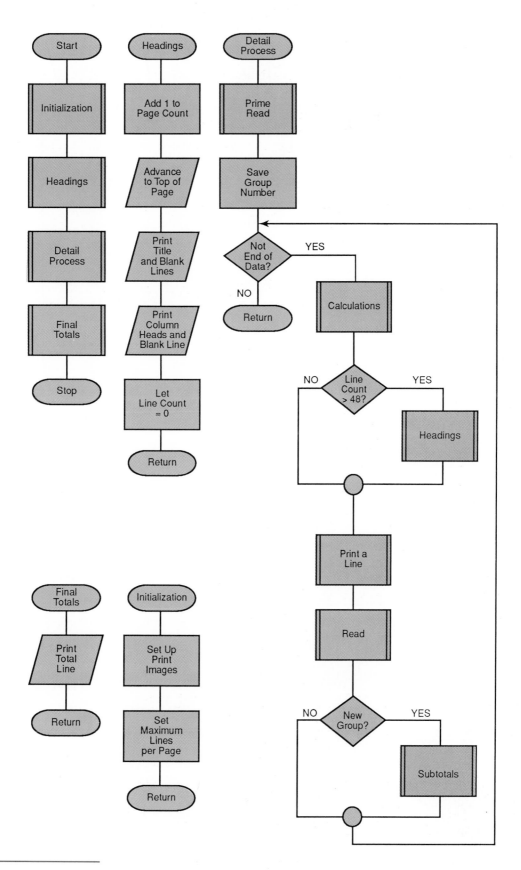

Figure 6.7
Calendar sales program flowchart
using control breaks.

Figure 6.7—*Continued*

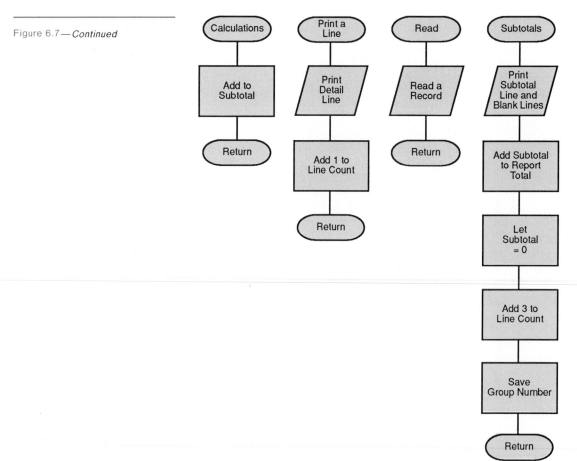

Program Listing

```
100 'PROGRAM TO REPORT ON THE ANNUAL CALENDAR SALE DRIVE
110 '     INCLUDES PAGE BREAKS AND CONTROL BREAKS, ALONG
120 '     WITH MULTIPLE PAGE OUTPUT
130 '
140 '          PROGRAM VARIABLES
150 '    GROUP$           GROUP NUMBER
160 '    PER$             NAME OF PERSON
170 '    CAL              CALENDARS SOLD
180 '    CAL.SUBTOT       GROUP SUBTOTAL
190 '    CAL.TOT          REPORT TOTAL
200 '    LINE.CT          LINE COUNT
210 '    PAGE.CT          PAGE COUNT
220 '    MAX.LINES        MAXIMUM NUMBER OF LINES PER PAGE
230 '    GROUP.SAVE$      PREVIOUS GROUP NUMBER
240 '    T$,H1$,H2$,D$    PRINT IMAGES
250 '    ST$,RT$
260 '
500 '************** PROGRAM MAINLINE ***************************
510 GOSUB 1000                    'INITIALIZE PRINT IMAGES
520 GOSUB 2000                    'PRINT HEADINGS
530 GOSUB 3000                    'DETAIL LOOP
540 GOSUB 7000                    'PRINT FINAL TOTALS
550 END
1000 '***************** INITIALIZE ***************************
1010 LET T$ = "                        ANNUAL CALENDAR SALE    PAGE ##"
1020 LET H1$ = "              GROUP        PERSON                CALENDARS"
1030 LET H2$ = "             NUMBER                                SOLD"
1040 LET D$ = "              \\          \                    \  ###"
1050 LET ST$ = "                        SUBTOTAL              #,###"
1060 LET RT$ = "                        REPORT TOTAL         ##,###"
1070 LET MAX.LINES = 48
1080 RETURN
1090 '
```

```
2000 '***************** PRINT HEADINGS *********************
2010 LET PAGE.CT = PAGE.CT + 1
2020 LPRINT CHR$(12);                'ADVANCE TO TOP OF PAGE
2030 LPRINT USING T$; PAGE.CT
2040 LPRINT:LPRINT
2050 LPRINT H1$
2060 LPRINT H2$
2070 LPRINT
2080 LET LINE.CT = 0
2090 RETURN
2100 '
3000 '***************** DETAIL LOOP *********************
3010 GOSUB 4000                      'PRIME READ
3020 LET GROUP.SAVE$ = GROUP$        'SAVE FIRST GROUP NUMBER
3030 WHILE GROUP$ <> "00"
3040    GOSUB 5000                   'CALCULATIONS
3050    IF LINE.CT >= MAX.LINES
           THEN GOSUB 2000           'PRINT HEADINGS
3060    GOSUB 6000                   'PRINT A LINE
3070    GOSUB 4000                   'READ
3080    IF GROUP.SAVE$ <> GROUP$
           THEN GOSUB 6500           'SUBTOTALS
3090 WEND
3100 RETURN
3110 '
4000 '***************** READ DATA *********************
4010 READ GROUP$, PER$, CAL
4020 DATA 1A,CLEO THORPE,4,1A,BERTHA THOMAS,6,1A,KARL BETTS,3
4030 DATA 1B,ANTHONY HOFFMAN,12,1B,DAVID YOUNT,4,2A,PHILLIP TIBBS,6
4040 DATA 2B,VICTOR PROCTOR,15,2B,PAUL PARSONS,25,2B,BRENDA MILLER,18
4050 DATA 3A,RALPH MAY,6,3A,DEANNA MC CLURE,10,3A,FLOYD SWANSON,20
4060 DATA 3A, STEVE SUTTON,3,3A,BARBARA KIDWELL,12,3A,KENNETH KING,22
4070 DATA 3B,PAUL DEMPSEY,25,3B,RUBY BAILEY,12,4A,BILL WILKINSON,10
4080 DATA 4A,RUSSELL BUTLER,21,4A,CHARLES CAIN,15,4B,HARVEY CALDWELL,6
4090 DATA 5A,EILEEN FAY,9,5A,ALLEN FARMER,14,5B,ARTURO HERNANDEZ,13
4100 DATA 5B,BERNICE HENDERSON,7,5B,LARRY HOLT,30,5B,WADE LEE,25
4110 DATA 00,00,00
4120 RETURN
4130
5000 '***************** CALCULATIONS *********************
5010 LET CAL.SUBTOT = CAL.SUBTOT + CAL
5020 RETURN
5030 '
6000 '***************** PRINT A LINE *********************
6010 LPRINT USING D$; GROUP$, PER$, CAL
6020 LET LINE.CT = LINE.CT + 1
6030 RETURN
6040 '
6500 '***************** SUBTOTAL BREAK *********************
6510 LPRINT
6520 LPRINT USING ST$; CAL.SUBTOT            'PRINT SUBTOTAL LINE
6530 LPRINT
6540 LET CAL.TOT = CAL.TOT + CAL.SUBTOT 'ADD TO REPORT TOTAL
6550 LET CAL.SUBTOT = 0                      'RESET SUBTOTAL TO ZERO
6560 LET LINE.CT = LINE.CT + 3               'ADD TO LINE COUNTER
6570 LET GROUP.SAVE$ = GROUP$
                                             'SAVE NEW GROUP NUMBER
6580 RETURN
6590 '
7000 '***************** PRINT FINAL TOTALS *********************
7010 LPRINT
7020 LPRINT USING RT$; CAL.TOT
7030 RETURN
7040 '***************** END OF PROGRAM *********************
```

```
                    ANNUAL CALENDAR SALE    PAGE 1

        GROUP           PERSON              CALENDARS
        NUMBER                                SOLD

         1A         CLEO THORPE                  4
         1A         BERTHA THOMAS                6
         1A         KARL BETTS                   3

                    SUBTOTAL                    13

         1B         ANTHONY HOFFMAN             12
         1B         DAVID YOUNT                  4

                    SUBTOTAL                    16

         2A         PHILLIP TIBBS                6

                    SUBTOTAL                     6

         2B         VICTOR PROCTOR              15
         2B         PAUL PARSONS                25
         2B         BRENDA MILLER               18

                    SUBTOTAL                    58

         3A         RALPH MAY                    6
         3A         DEANNA MC CLURE             10
         3A         FLOYD SWANSON               20
         3A         STEVE SUTTON                 3
         3A         BARBARA KIDWELL             12
         3A         KENNETH KING                22

                    SUBTOTAL                    73

         3B         PAUL DEMPSEY                25
         3B         RUBY BAILEY                 12

                    SUBTOTAL                    37

         4A         BILL WILKINSON              10
         4A         RUSSELL BUTLER              21
         4A         CHARLES CAIN                15

                    SUBTOTAL                    46

         4B         HARVEY CALDWELL              6

                    SUBTOTAL                     6

         5A         EILEEN FAY                   9
         5A         ALLEN FARMER                14

                    SUBTOTAL                    23
```

```
                        ANNUAL CALENDAR SALE   PAGE 2

       GROUP          PERSON                 CALENDARS
       NUMBER                                   SOLD


        5B       ARTURO HERNANDEZ              13
        5B       BERNICE HENDERSON             7
        5B       LARRY HOLT                   30
        5B       WADE LEE                     25
                 SUBTOTAL                     75


                 REPORT TOTAL                353
```

Feedback

1. When subtotals are printed, why is it called a *control break?*
2. What changes would need to be made in the program if there were two fields that needed subtotals and report totals?
3. Code the additional lines necessary to print the average number of calendars sold for each group (on the group subtotal line) and the average for the entire report (on the report total line).
4. Sometimes a third (or fourth) level of subtotals is needed. Consider the situation in which the groups are divided into divisions. What changes would be necessary in the program to print group subtotals, division subtotals, and report totals?

Summary

1. Printer spacing charts are used to plan program output.
2. The most common horizontal spacing for personal computer printers is 80-character lines (10 characters per inch).
3. The most common vertical spacing for printers is 6 lines per inch.
4. It is considered good practice to leave 1 inch at the top and bottom of the page for printed output.
5. The detail line spacing should be determined before the column headings are placed on the print chart.
6. Column headings should not be abbreviated in a way that makes their meaning unclear.
7. If multiple pages will be needed, add page numbers to the report.
8. When multiple pages are needed, the program will need line counter and page counter fields.
9. The line counter field is used to count the detail lines printed. When the counter becomes greater than the specified number of lines, a new page is needed.
10. The tasks of the heading routine are to: (1) advance to the next page; (2) increment the page counter; (3) print the title and column headings; and (4) reset the line counter to zero.
11. Advancing to the next page can be accomplished by printing blank lines or printing a form-feed character (ASCII code 12).
12. The printing of subtotals is also called control breaks.
13. The field controlling the subtotal process is called the control variable.
14. In order to compare the control variable for the current record to that of the previous record, a "save" field is required.
15. When the current control variable is different from the previous one, subtotals are printed.

Each of these programming assignments is to use line and page counters and to have multiple page output. A printer spacing chart must be prepared to document the report layout.

Note: The program output must *exactly* match the layout shown on the printer spacing chart.

6.1. Write a program to produce a report of the gross earnings of employees.

INPUT: The input data will be read from DATA statements. The data consists of the employee's name, the department number, hourly pay rate, and the number of hours worked.

OUTPUT:

1. Print an appropriate title and column headings at the top of each page of the report. The title should be centered on the title line. The title line must include the page number. The column headings must be meaningful and be aligned over the columns of data.

2. Each detail line is to include the employee's name, department number, hourly pay rate, number of hours worked, regular hours, overtime hours, regular pay, overtime pay, and gross pay.

3. Print a total of 20 detail lines per page.

4. At the end of the report, print a total line that includes totals of the number of hours worked, regular hours, regular pay, overtime hours, overtime pay, and total gross pay. The totals must be properly aligned below the detail line columns.

5. The data will fit (barely) on an 80-character line. If you are using a printer with a wider carriage and paper, you may take advantage of the width by placing these statements in your program.

```
line number WIDTH "LPT1:",132 'Set line length to 132 characters
line number WIDTH "LPT1:",80  'Set it back to 80 characters
```

Many dot matrix printers are capable of printing in smaller, condensed print. To print a longer line in condensed print, add these lines to your program. See appendix H, Controlling Printer Functions, for more explanation.

```
line number WIDTH "LPT1:", 132 'Set line length to 132 characters
line number LPRINT CHR$(15);   'Turn on condensed mode
```

And at the conclusion of the program, add these lines:

```
line number WIDTH "LPT1:", 80 'Set line length back to normal
line number LPRINT CHR$(18);    'Reset to normal characters
```

CALCULATIONS:

1. Calculate the regular pay for each employee. The first forty hours worked are the regular hours. The regular pay is to be calculated by multiplying regular hours times the hourly pay rate. Round the pay to the nearest cent.

2. Calculate the overtime pay for each employee. Any hours worked in excess of forty hours are the overtime hours. The overtime pay rate is to be equal to the hourly pay rate times 1.5. Overtime pay is to be calculated by multiplying overtime hours by the overtime pay rate. Round the pay to the nearest cent.

3. The gross pay is calculated as the sum of the regular pay and the overtime pay.

4. Accumulate report totals of the number of hours worked, regular hours, overtime hours, regular pay, overtime pay, and gross pay.

TEST DATA:

Name	Dept. No	Pay Rate	Hours Worked
FRANK BENSON	10	6.50	25.5
BETTY BERGMAN	10	6.85	40.0
ROGER BROWN	10	7.75	45.0
TONY CHAVEZ	12	6.75	32.25
ELLA COURTNEY	12	8.25	39.75
PAUL DERBY	15	5.50	41.0
EDWARD DUNLAP	20	10.75	15.5
LOUISE ERICKSON	20	7.95	40.5
HENRY GARCIA	20	8.10	40.0
MAX GOODRICH	20	9.00	1.0
CRAIG HILL	20	6.75	40.0
BEN ISAACSON	22	7.35	50.0
BRIAN KING	22	10.05	40.0
MARY LAMONT	22	8.65	40.0
NIEN LE	24	7.60	36.0
COLLEEN MARTIN	24	7.60	39.5
TIEN NGUYEN	24	8.25	20.25
HENRY OKADA	24	6.85	40.0
LEON PITTMAN	24	11.00	25.0
DON RIDGEWAY	24	8.25	23.0
LILLIAN SALINAS	28	12.00	40.0
THOMAS SHIPLEY	28	9.25	40.0
ANNA TAYLOR	28	7.85	40.0
PETER ULRICH	30	8.10	49.5
DAVID VERDUGO	31	7.60	42.0
END OF DATA	00	0.00	0.0 (not to be printed)

6.2. Modify the program in exercise 6.1 to include control breaks. For each department, print subtotals of the number of hours worked, regular hours, overtime hours, regular pay, overtime pay, and the gross pay. Double-space (1 blank line) before and after each subtotal line. The extra blank lines are to be counted as detail lines when determining page size.

6.3. Write a program using control breaks to produce a student grade report.

INPUT: The input will consist of the student number, the student name, the course code, the course title, number of units, and letter grade. The input data will be included on DATA statements within the program.

OUTPUT:
1. Print an appropriate title and column headings at the top of each page of the report. The title should be centered on the title line. The title line must include the page number. The column headings must be meaningful and be aligned over the columns of data.
2. A detail line is to be printed for each input record. The first line for each student will contain the student name and number, but the subsequent lines for that student will not. In addition to the name field, each detail line is to include the student ID, the course code, course title, number of units, and the letter grade.
3. A student total line (control break) is to be printed for each student. Leave 1 blank line before and after the total line.
4. Print a total of 10 detail lines per page. The blank lines before and after the student total lines are to be counted as detail lines for determining page size.
5. At the end of the report, double-space (1 blank line) and print a total line that includes the total number of units completed for all students. Double-space again and print a line showing the average number of units completed per student.

CALCULATIONS:
1. Accumulate the total number of units for each student.
2. Accumulate the total number of units for all students.
3. Calculate the average number of units for all students (total units / number of students).

TEST DATA:

Name	ID	Course Code	Title	Units	Grade
DAVID BASSETT	1462	0814	SYSTEMS ANALYSIS	3	B
DAVID BASSETT	1462	0813	DATA PROCESSING	3.	A
DAVID BASSETT	1462	2625	DATA PROCESSING LAB	.5	A
DAVID BASSETT	1462	1823	ENGLISH	3	C
OSCAR FERNANDEZ	2145	2015	BASIC PROGRAMMING	3	B
OSCAR FERNANDEZ	2145	2016	BASIC PROGRAMMING LAB	1	A
MARIA GREEN	2452	1823	ENGLISH	3	B
MARCIA KNIGHT	3665	3333	ALGEBRA	4	B
MARCIA KNIGHT	3665	0814	SYSTEMS ANALYSIS	3	A
MARCIA KNIGHT	3665	4244	ACCOUNTING	4	B
LE NIEN	4891	0813	DATA PROCESSING	3	B
LE NIEN	4891	2625	DATA PROCESSING LAB	.5	B
LE NIEN	4891	3333	ALGEBRA	3	A
LE NIEN	4891	4244	ACCOUNTING	4	B
CHRIS REEVES	5678	3333	ALGEBRA	3	D

END OF DATA

SAMPLE PROGRAM OUTPUT USING TEST DATA:

```
              REPORT TITLE                              PAGE 1

STUDENT                    COURSE
NAME            ID         CODE    TITLE               UNITS   GRADE

DAVID BASSETT   1462       0814    SYSTEMS ANALYSIS     3.0    B
                1462       0813    DATA PROCESSING      3.0    A
                1462       2625    DATA PROCESSING LAB  0.5    A
                1462       1823    ENGLISH              3.0    C

                           TOTAL UNITS                  9.5


OSCAR FERNANDEZ 2145       2015    BASIC PROGRAMMING    3.0    B
                2145       2016    BASIC PROGRAMMING LAB 1.0   A

                           TOTAL UNITS                  4.0

MARIA GREEN     2452       1823    ENGLISH              3.0    B

                           TOTAL UNITS                  3.0
::
::
::

          TOTAL UNITS FOR ALL STUDENTS                 XXX.X

          AVERAGE NUMBER OF UNITS PER STUDENT           XX.X
```

6.4. Write a program using control breaks to produce a sales summary for charter hours booked for yachts.

INPUT: The program input may be read from DATA statements or INPUT statements. For each yacht, enter the length, the rate per hour, and the number of hours chartered.

OUTPUT: Print an appropriate title, column headings, and detail lines for each ship. Detail lines include the yacht type, length, hourly rate, hours chartered, and the total revenue for those hours chartered. Print subtotals for each yacht type and report totals at the end of the report. Subtotals and totals are to be printed for the charter hours column and charter revenue column.

PROCESSING: The charter revenue for each ship is calculated as the hourly rate times the number of hours chartered. Accumulate subtotals and totals for charter hours and charter revenue.

TEST DATA:

Type	Size	Rate	Charter Hours
Ranger	22	95.00	24
Ranger	22	69.00	12
Wavelength	24	69.00	6
Wavelength	24	89.00	12
Catalina	27	160.00	24
Catalina	27	99.00	6
Catalina	30	190.00	12
Catalina	30	225.00	24
Coronado	32	230.00	24
Hobie	33	192.00	33
Hobie	33	235.00	24
Hobie	33	137.00	6
Hobie	33	235.00	24
C & C	34	290.00	24
C & C	34	175.00	6
Catalina	36	185.00	6
Catalina	36	320.00	24
Hans Christian	38	400.00	24
Hans Christian	38	250.00	6
Excaliber	45	550.00	24
Excaliber	45	295.00	6

SAMPLE PROGRAM OUTPUT USING TEST DATA:

```
YACHT TYPE              SIZE    RATE    CHARTER     REVENUE

RANGER                   22     95.00    24.0     $2,280.00
RANGER                   22     69.00    12.0        828.00

        RANGER SUBTOTAL                   36.0      3,108.00

WAVELENGTH               24     69.00     6.0        414.00
  ::                     ::     : :        ::          ::
  ::                     ::                ::          ::

        REPORT TOTAL                     XXX.X    $XXX,XXX.XX
```

6.5. The local video arcade is sponsoring a summer team competition and is planning to give trophies to the members of the winning team. Also, the highest individual score on each team will earn a medal. There is one individual grand prize for the person with the highest score. Each team may have up to three players, and any number of teams may enter the contest.

INPUT: For each player, input the team number, the player's name, and the number of points scored. Data may be entered with INPUT statements or READ/DATA.

OUTPUT: Print a report with appropriate title and column headings. Each detail line will show the player name and points scored. The first detail line for each team must also indicate the team number. At the conclusion of each group, print the team total for points scored. Also, print the name of the player with the highest score for that team.

At the end of the report, print:

1. the team number of the winning team;
2. the number of points scored by the winning team; and
3. the name of the individual with the highest score.

PROCESSING: Accumulate the total points scored for each team. Also, determine the highest-scoring contestant on each team and the highest-scoring individual for the entire contest.

SAMPLE PROGRAM OUTPUT:

```
                    THE SUMMER GAMES
                 VIDEO ARCADE SHOOTOFF

       TEAM     NAME                        POINTS

        1       ACE BRADLEY                 10,000
                RICHARD OCHOA                9,100
                JAY JOHNSTON                 5,050

                TOTAL POINTS                24,150


                TEAM WINNER - ACE BRADLEY

        2       CHRIS JACKSON               11,100
                KEN RYAN                     8,990
                ::
                ::


THE WINNING TEAM IS TEAM # XX WITH XXX,XXX POINTS

THE WINNING INDIVIDUAL IS XXXXXXXXXXXXX WITH XXX,XXX POINTS
```

6.6. Write a program to create a dues report for the Women's Club.

INPUT: Input will come from the test data below.

OUTPUT: Output should be to the printer. Print a title, column headings, member's name, number of years as a member, amount due, total number of members, and total amount due. Print a page number on each page, with only 10 detail lines per page.

PROCESS:

1. If the person has been a member longer than six years, dues are $800.
2. If the person has been a member for six years or less, dues are $1200.
3. Count the total number of members.
4. Accumulate a sum of all dues owed.

TEST DATA:

Member Name	Years of Membership
Judy Niles	2
Elaine Norton	4
Mary Percel	7
Sarah Rivera	8
Beatrice Udell	10
Anita Ashley	1
Janice Wills	5
May Wong	3
Kim Smith	2
Louise Olsen	1
Jane Adams	11
Holy Johnstone	4
Sheree Drake	6
Lisa Kayhill	8
Susan Zank	9
Michelle Brown	12

Member Name	Years of Membership
Mandy Goodwill	2
Denise Jones	1
Carol Lang	1
Joanne Miller	4

6.7. Write a program to create a hospital billing report for Stateside Hospital.

INPUT: Use DATA statements for the patient's name, number of days in the hospital, and type of room. Use the test data below.

OUTPUT:

1. Output may be to the screen or the printer.
2. Print a title and page number on each page.
3. Print column headings for the patient's name, number of days, room type, and total bill.
   A. Room types are as follows:
      1. Intensive care
      2. Private
      3. Double
4. Print 10 detail lines per page.
5. Print a count of the total number of patients.
6. Print the total billing amount.

PROCESS:

1. Intensive care = $355 a day.
2. Private = $275 a day.
3. Double = $150 a day.
4. Calculate the amount due for each patient.
5. Accumulate a report total of the amount due to the hospital.

TEST DATA:

Name	Days	Room Type
Greg Scott	3	I
John Nelson	12	I
Sally Goldsmith	14	P
Carol Dunckon	2	I
Kim Agnew	1	D
Tom Jones	7	D
Richard Hernandez	15	D
Deon Moore	18	I
Gail Kidd	17	I
Ray Redstone	12	P
Steve Sillo	6	P
Scott Brown	2	P
Peggy Smith	5	D
Sue Johnson	7	I
Martha Miller	21	P
Jaime Robinson	6	D
Pearl Russ	4	I
Diane Hanley	3	I
Mike Williams	19	D
Duane Nichols	14	D

6.8. Write a program using control breaks to produce a transaction list for the Yin-Yan Wholesale Company.

INPUT: Department number, transaction date, and amount of the order will come from DATA statements. Use the sample data below.

OUTPUT: Make up a title and column headings for the department number, transaction date, and amount of order. Print department subtotals and a report total for the amount field. Display the output on the screen.

PROCESS:
1. Accumulate a subtotal of the amount field, by department.
2. Accumulate a report total of the amount field.

TEST DATA:

Dept. #	Trans. Date	Amount, in dollars
100	1–21–86	6.75
100	1–21–86	14.85
100	2–21–86	21.21
100	2–28–86	8.21
119	3–05–86	121.83
119	3–21–86	19.50
119	4–10–86	21.50
121	5–01–86	12.75
121	5–21–86	100.21
142	5–22–86	53.47

6.9. The Kafkaesque Bank wants to know which group of customers has the most money in the bank. Write a program using control break logic to print a customer listing.

INPUT: Customer code, customer name, and amount of money in the bank.

OUTPUT: Print a title and column headings for the customer code, customer name, and amount of money. Print subtotals and report totals for the amount column.

PROCESS:
1. Accumulate a subtotal on the amount column, by customer code.
2. Accumulate a report total of the amount column.

TEST DATA:

Code	Name	Amount, in dollars
A	Andy Adams	500
A	Lisa Anderson	150
A	Loni Adler	50
B	Steve Brown	300
B	John Bone	173
B	Scott Burges	75
J	Sally Jensen	20
J	Tom Jones	275
M	Anita Millsap	10
M	Michelle Millspaugh	510
M	Jane Miller	100
S	Jim Setella	83
S	Mike Stone	321
S	Trish Sapp	25

6.10. You have a stamp collection and you want to print a list broken down into groups. The three groups are plants, people, and miscellaneous.

> INPUT: Type of stamp, name of stamp, first day of issue, and the face value will come from DATA statements. Use the sample data below.
>
> OUTPUT: Make up an appropriate title and column headings for the type of stamp, name of stamp, first day of issue, and the face value. Print a subtotal for the face value field.
>
> PROCESS: Accumulate a subtotal and report total of the face value amount for each of the three types of stamps.
>
> TEST DATA:

Type	Name	Issue Date	Face Value in dollars
Plant	Agave	12–11–81	.20
Plant	Barrel Cactus	12–11–81	.20
Plant	Saguaro	12–11–81	.20
Misc	Ballooning	3–31–83	.20
Misc	In Flight	3–31–83	.20
Misc	Building A Snowman	8–28–82	.20
Misc	Lend A Hand	4–20–83	.20
People	Nathaniel Hawthorne	7–08–83	.20
People	Nikola Tesla	9–21–83	.20
People	Dr. Mary Walker	6–10–82	.20

6.11. Looney Toon Grocers needs to track its inventory on a monthly basis. Management needs a report on this inventory, by department. Print a report showing, by department, the inventory item, its unit cost, the quantity on hand, and the inventory cost, plus the total inventory cost.

> INPUT: Input will come from DATA statements. Use the test data on the following page.
>
> OUTPUT:
> 1. The output of this program is a report printed on the screen.
> 2. Print a title, with a page number and column headings.
> 3. Print 15 detail lines per page. These 15 lines must include the subtotal lines.
> 4. Print the fields in the following order, from left to right:
>
> Department Number
> Inventory Item
> Quantity On Hand
> Unit Price
> Inventory Cost

5. Double-space before and after printing the inventory cost for each department. Include the department number in the subtotal output line.

PROCESS:
1. For each item, calculate the inventory cost by multiplying the quantity on hand by the unit cost.
2. Calculate a subtotal by department of inventory cost.
3. Accumulate the sum of the total inventory cost.

TEST DATA:

Inventory Item	Dept. #	Quantity	Unit cost, in dollars
American cheese	14	50	1.92
Salted butter	14	41	2.53
Swiss cheese	14	32	3.55
Cider	17	20	1.98
Chowchow	17	40	3.02
Prunes	17	62	2.51
Sweet potatoes	17	72	3.38
Ketchup	21	80	1.75
Tapioca	21	94	3.50
Beans	21	81	3.20
Peas	21	42	2.53
Olives	21	32	3.15
Whipping cream	26	20	1.98
Brooms	26	72	4.95
Fly paper	26	61	2.56
Zinc bucket	26	52	3.65
Dog biscuits	28	50	1.05
Condensed milk	28	41	3.65
Apples	28	83	2.67
Apricots	28	22	5.06
Cocoa	35	90	1.61
Ceylon tea	39	30	1.10
Coffee	39	13	2.05
Dates	39	41	3.03
Figs	42	50	1.85
Raisins	42	72	2.45
Apple sauce	42	12	3.50
Crackers	53	60	1.95
Lemon extract	53	74	3.47
Noodles	53	31	4.05
Macaroni	53	12	2.60

6.12. The Sales Manager for the Far-Out Sales Company needs to track the sales amount and the commissions paid to the sales force for each sales office. Generate the following report showing, by sales office, the amount of commissions paid and the dollar amount of sales. Also, include report totals for amount of commissions and the dollar amount of sales.

INPUT: Input will come from DATA statements. Use the test data below.
OUTPUT:
1. Print the title SALES COMMISSION REPORT and a page number at the top of each page.
2. Use appropriate column headings above each column of output. Underline the headings with equal signs, then double-space.
3. Display 12 detail lines per page.
4. Leave a blank line before and after each subtotal line.
5. Display the detail data in the following sequence from left to right.
    a. Sales Region
    b. Sales Office Number
    c. Salesperson Name
    d. Sales Amount
    e. Commission Amount
6. Display the report totals under the appropriate columns of data, and align the decimal points with the detail data.

PROCESS:
1. Compute a 10 percent commission for each salesperson.
2. Accumulate Sales Office totals for sales amount and commission amount.
3. Accumulate report totals for sale amounts and commission amounts.

TEST DATA:

Salesperson Name	Office #	Sales Amount, in dollars	Sales Region
Andy Atom	14	134.08	50
Brian Brown	14	145.16	41
Claudia Cool	14	170.56	32
Deon Done	19	189.54	20
Eric Espinosa	19	243.19	62
Frank Ferry	19	244.37	72
Greg Green	21	251.27	80
Hank Hanna	21	303.31	94
Isabel Isha	21	305.58	81
Jane Jones	21	340.61	42
Kevin Kline	21	341.47	32
Leon Lang	26	391.03	20
Molly Moore	26	432.21	50
Nina Nelson	26	443.21	72
Olivia Oston	42	456.98	12
Penny Pamper	42	490.07	71
Quinn Quiery	42	521.04	21
Randy Rich	42	525.14	83

6.13. Write a program with multilevel control breaks to produce a list of books on cassette available to the blind. The first-level control break will be for fiction or nonfiction. The second-level control break will be the subject category.

INPUT: The type of book (fiction or nonfiction), the subject category, the author, the title of the book, and the shelf number will be input using DATA statements. Use the test data below.

OUTPUT: Print a title and appropriate column headings, the type of book, subject category, author, title of book, shelf number, subtotal for each subject, a total of nonfiction and fiction books, and a report total of all books.

PROCESS: Keep a subtotal for each subject category, a total of nonfiction books, a total of fiction books, and a report total of all books.

TEST DATA:

Type	Subject	Author	Title	Shelf #
F	Best-sellers	Anita Brokner	Hotel Du Lac	RC-21510
F	Best-sellers	John Fowles	A Maggot	RC-22954
F	Best-sellers	Robert Moss	Moscow Rules	RC-21509
F	Fantasy	Richard Adams	Maia	RC-21237
F	Fantasy	Michael Ende	Momo	RC-22829
F	Occult	Harriet Waugh	Kate's House	RC-22652
F	Occult	F. Paul Wilson	The Tomb	RC-22793
F	Religion	James Kavanaugh	The Celibates	RC-23389
F	Religion	Michael Delahaye	On the Third Day	RC-22277
F	Romance	Sandra Kitt	Adam and Eve	RC-23209
F	Romance	Edna Maye Manley	Agatha	RC-22636
F	Humor	Norma Levinson	The Room Upstairs	RC-22401
F	Humor	Maggie Brooks	Loose Connections	RC-22853
F	Humor	Jill McCorkle	July 7th	RC-22222
F	Science Fiction	Frederik Pohl	Black Star Rising	RC-23663
F	Science Fiction	William Sleator	Interstellar Pig	RC-22792
NF	Business	Michael Drosnin	Citizen Hughes	RC-21530
NF	Business	David Sinclair	Dynasty	RC-22259
NF	Business	Mark Singer	Funny Money	RC-23712
NF	Humor	Frank B. Gilbreth	Cheaper by the Dozen	RC-23282
NF	Humor	Bill Adler	Kid's Letters to President Reagan	RC-22848
NF	Women	Geraldine A. Ferraro	Ferraro: My Story	RC-23725
NF	Women	Karen Armstrong	Beginning the World	RC-22572
NF	Philosophy	Lewis Mumford	The Conduct of Life	RC-22264
NF	Philosophy	Mortimer Adler	Ten Philosophical Mistakes	RC-22827
NF	Education	Sara Gilbert	How to Take Tests	RC-23232
NF	Education	Eda LeShan	When Your Child Drives You Crazy	RC-23361

6.14. Write a program using multilevel control breaks to print a list of local gyms and their members. The first-level control break should be on the name of the gym. The second-level control break should be on sex (male or female). The third-level control break should be on age (under 25, 25 and over).

INPUT: Gym name, member name, sex, age, weight, and phone number will come from the test data below.

OUTPUT: Print a title and column headings, gym name, member name, sex, age, weight, phone number, and a subtotal of the number of members of each of the three levels of control breaks.

PROCESS:

1. Accumulate a subtotal of the number of members at each of the three levels of control breaks.

2. On the first level control break (gym name) advance to a new page.

TEST DATA:

Gym	Member Name	Sex	Age (yr)	Weight (lb)	Phone #
Ersatz	Sue Stone	F	19	123	123–4287
Ersatz	Jenny Scott	F	21	105	467–8221
Ersatz	Rose Jones	F	23	110	867–4289
Ersatz	Molly Mist	F	18	125	966–4037
Ersatz	Holly Howe	F	24	130	862–3090
Ersatz	Lynn Long	F	25	121	334–0712
Ersatz	Kim Smith	F	30	150	332–0021
Ersatz	Debbie Doe	F	50	143	167–0072
Ersatz	John Jones	M	19	175	963–0421
Ersatz	Scott Miller	M	21	200	331–0021
Ersatz	Steven Brown	M	23	150	966–0404
Ersatz	Larry Show	M	43	189	967–0000
Ersatz	James Randal	M	67	178	339–0421
Licit	Vira Osmond	F	21	110	334–0202
Licit	Sandra Long	F	24	130	334–0212
Licit	Gaynel Sillo	F	19	110	332–0264
Licit	Joelle Derlap	F	27	100	960–0215
Licit	Jeannie Jones	F	30	137	960–1245
Licit	Mike Moore	M	23	170	962–0405
Licit	Jerry Sandoval	M	24	189	339–0211
Licit	Tom Tone	M	37	175	421–1234
Licit	Tim Short	M	40	183	330–1001
Fetid	Cathy Nelson	F	21	105	331–0219
Fetid	Sonia Song	F	19	142	967–0121
Fetid	Jackie Smith	F	24	189	337–7123
Fetid	Tricia Scudder	F	18	120	960–1234
Fetid	Nora Nomes	F	23	163	301–1243
Fetid	Randy Rich	M	24	152	961–1111
Fetid	Tony Hernandez	M	21	110	333–4444
Fetid	Tommy Foss	M	18	125	900–0000
Fetid	Doug Donley	M	85	129	312–3456

6.15. Write a program using control break logic to print a list of animals broken down into type, and phylum.

INPUT: Type, name, phylum, class, order, and family will be input using DATA statements. Use the test data below.

OUTPUT: Print a title and column headings, type, name, phylum, class, order, family, a subtotal for each type, a subtotal for each phylum within each type, and a grand total of all animals.

PROCESS:
1. Accumulate a subtotal count for each type of animal.
2. Accumulate a subtotal count for each phylum within each type.
3. Accumulate a grand total of all animals.

TEST DATA:

ANTHROPODS

Name	Phylum	Class	Order	Family
Bed Bug	Anthropoda	Insecta	Hemiptera	Cimicidae
Wart-Biter	Anthropoda	Insecta	Orthoptera	Tettigoniidae
Comet	Anthropoda	Insecta	Lepidoptera	Saturniidae
Goat Moth	Anthropoda	Insecta	Lepidoptera	Cossidae
Ant Lion	Anthropoda	Insecta	Neuroptera	Myrmeieonidae

WORMS

Name	Phylum	Class	Order	Family
Tapeworm	Platyheiminthes	Cestoda	Cyclophyllidae	Taeniidae
Flatworm	Platyheiminthes	Turbellaria	Tricladida	Bipalidae
Ribbon Worm	Nemertini	Anopla	Heteronemertini	Lineidae

MOLLUSCS

Name	Phylum	Class	Order	Family
Sea Ear	Mollusca	Gastroposa	Diotocardia	Haliotidae
Squid	Mollusca	Cephalopoda	Decapoda	Loliginidae
Paper Nautilus	Mollusca	Cephalopoda	Octopoda	Argonautidae
Periwinkle	Mollusca	Gastroposa	Monotocaroia	Littorinidae
Music Volute	Mollusca	Gastroposa	Monotocaroia	Volutidae

ECHINODERMS

Name	Phylum	Class	Order	Family
Basket Star	Echinodermata	Ophiuroidea	Euryalae	Euryalidae
Sea Cucumber	Echinodermata	Holothuroidea	Dendrochirotida	Cucumariidae

AMPHIBIANS

Name	Phylum	Class	Order	Family
Olm	Vertebrata	Amphibia	Urodeia	Proteidae
Flying Frog	Vertebrata	Amphibia	Anura	Rhacophoridae

REPTILES

Name	Phylum	Class	Order	Family
Blind Snake	Vertebrata	Reptilia	Squamata	Typhlopidae
Flying Dragon	Vertebrata	Reptilia	Squamata	Agamidae

7

Data Validation and Interactive Programs

CLS Statement
LOCATE Statement
SPACE$ Function
STRING$ Function
LEN Function
LEFT$ Function
RIGHT$ Function
MID$ Function and
  Statement
VAL Function
STR$ Function
INSTR Function
CHR$ Function
ASC Function
INKEY$ Function
INPUT$ Function
LINE INPUT Statement
DATE$ Function
TIME$ Function

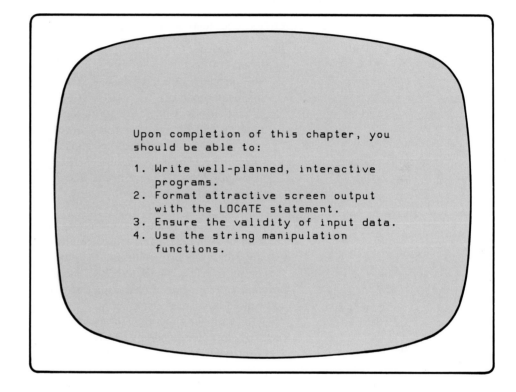

```
Upon completion of this chapter, you
should be able to:

1. Write well-planned, interactive
   programs.
2. Format attractive screen output
   with the LOCATE statement.
3. Ensure the validity of input data.
4. Use the string manipulation
   functions.
```

User Friendly?

When writing computer programs, it should be assumed that the user (person who runs the program) will *not* be the programmer. Therefore, the programmer must strive to make the input dialogue clear and easy to understand. If the user makes mistakes or causes the program to malfunction, it must be assumed that the programmer is at fault. In this chapter, you will learn to "idiot proof" programs.

Guidelines for Interactive Programs

1. Make all program output clear, choosing terms the user will understand. *Never* use computerese. Use descriptive words rather than program variable names for INPUT prompts. If you had never run a program before, which would you rather see?

    ENTER BG __

    or

    ENTER BEGINNING BALANCE __

2. Design the layout of the screen so there will be no question about what is expected.
    a. Use menus, if possible, whenever there is a choice of options (see chapter 9 for menu programs).
    b. Whenever possible, place data in the same location every time. This requires that the screen *not* be allowed to scroll the print statements. This precise screen placement is accomplished with the LOCATE statement.
    c. Choose one area of the screen—perhaps the bottom line—to use for error messages. After the error has been corrected, clear the message. (Again, the LOCATE statement will help.)
3. Check the input data for validity. Many errors made by users can be caught at the point of entry. Finding and correcting the error early can often keep the program from producing erroneous results or "blowing up" during execution. Careful programmers include validity checking as a means of self-protection. It is better to reject bad data than to spend time attempting to debug the program only to discover (sometimes after hours or days) that the problem was caused by a "user error."

    In computer circles, you often hear the term, **GIGO** (*G*arbage *I*n, *G*arbage *O*ut). The accuracy of any program is only as good as the data it is given. The only way to hope to produce output that is not garbage is to make sure that garbage isn't allowed to enter.

    If the user was supposed to enter 3 and entered 4 instead, the program will not be able to detect the error as long as 4 is also a valid response. When there are only certain responses allowed, the program *can* check.

    In the following sections you will learn to check for these types of errors:
    a. reasonableness, or range checking
    b. matching a predetermined value, or code checking
    c. verifying that numeric fields are truly numeric
    d. consistency
    e. check digit calculations
4. Ask someone unfamiliar with computers to test your programs. Allow the tester to enter any values, to make sure your programs can function correctly, to identify the errors, and to not "blow up." Remember, a good programmer makes it easy to enter correct data and difficult to make mistakes.

Validity Checking

1. *Reasonableness, or range checking.* Numbers must be in a certain range, such as ID numbers less than 100 or hours in the range 0–100 (total hours a person could work in a week). Sometimes an upper (or lower) limit will be placed on amounts, such as checks written.

```
10    '************ VALIDATE RANGE ********************
20    INPUT "ENTER A NUMBER FROM 1-100 ", NUM
30    WHILE NUM < 1 OR NUM > 100
40       INPUT "NUMBER MUST BE BETWEEN 1 AND 100, REENTER ", NUM
50    WEND
60    RETURN
```

2. *Matching a predetermined value, or code checking.* Code only values of M (male) or F (female) allowed in a field, or perhaps a list of acceptable values in a field. This situation was handled earlier when checking for a YES or NO response.

```
100   '*************** VALIDATE CLASS CODE ****************
110   INPUT "ENTER CLASS CODE ", CODE$
120   WHILE CODE$ <> "FR" AND CODE$ <> "SO"
         AND CODE$ <> "JR" AND CODE$ <> "SR"
130       INPUT "ONLY VALUES FR, SO, JR, SR ALLOWED ", CODE$
140   WEND
150   RETURN
```

3. *Verifying that numeric fields are truly numeric.* Many operations require valid numeric data. Of course, BASIC can do the checking. The statement

```
10    INPUT "ENTER A NUMBER", NUM
```

requests input of a numeric constant. If the user presses the wrong key or enters a comma, a dollar sign, or a percent sign, what should happen? As it stands, the BASIC message ?REDO FROM START will be printed. This is apt to confuse the noncomputer person running the program, as well as mess up a carefully formatted screen. A much better solution is to input numbers as strings so that anything is allowed. Then, in the program, check for valid numeric values and print a friendly message for invalid data. The BASIC statements to accomplish the checking will be covered in the upcoming section on string manipulation functions along with a way to convert strings to numbers.

4. *Consistency.* Check the consistency of one data item against another. This could include checking that the ending date of a series is later than the starting date; that the return time for a flight is after the departure time; that the returns of an item don't exceed the sales of that item; that date fields are checked for the correct number of days in each month; or that a baseball player is not awarded more hits than the number of times at bat.

```
200   INPUT "NUMBER OF TIMES AT BAT ", ATBAT
210   INPUT "NUMBER OF HITS ", HITS
220   IF HITS > ATBAT
         THEN PRINT "ERROR: THE NUMBER OF HITS CANNOT
         EXCEED THE NUMBER OF TIMES AT BAT"
```

5. *Check digit calculations.* When accounting is primarily based on ID numbers such as credit card processing, a great potential for error exists. A one-digit error or a simple transposition can result in the wrong party receiving charges or credits. Many different schemes have been developed to check the validity of ID numbers. Each usually involves an arithmetic operation on the digits of the number. Then the result of the operation will be added as an extra digit to the ID number. An example of a check digit calculation will be shown later in this chapter in figure 7.5.

Output Formatting

There are several functions available for formatting output. Some, like TAB and SPC, may be used for screen or printer output. The most powerful formatting statement, LOCATE, can only be used on the screen. Note that Microsoft BASIC for the Apple uses the VTAB and HTAB statements in place of the LOCATE (see p. 174).

Clearing the Screen

The first step in creating well-formatted screens is generally to clear the screen. The CLS statement will clear the screen and place the **cursor** in the upper left corner. (Apple's version of Microsoft BASIC uses the HOME statement in place of CLS.)

The CLS Statement—General Form

```
line number CLS
```

The CLS Statement—Example

```
100   CLS
```

Precise Cursor Placement

The LOCATE statement is used to place the cursor at any spot on the video display screen. It is generally executed just prior to a PRINT or INPUT statement. The placement is to an absolute row and column position—not relative to the previous location of the cursor.

The LOCATE Statement—General Form

```
line number LOCATE  [row],[col][,cursor]
```

Row and *col* are integer values that specify the exact location on the screen for the cursor. The acceptable values of *row* and *col* will depend on the screen size of the computer in use. For a standard screen of 24 rows and 80 columns, *row* can have any value 1–24 and *col* must be in the range 1–80. Any fractional values for *row* or *col* will be rounded up.

The third parameter on the LOCATE statement controls the visibility of the cursor. If the value of CURSOR is 0, then the cursor will not be visible. If CURSOR is 1, the cursor is on. If the parameter is omitted, the cursor remains as it was.

The LOCATE Statement—Examples

```
50    LOCATE 1,1
60    PRINT "THIS IS THE UPPER LEFT-HAND CORNER"

100   LET ROW = 4
110   LET COL = 20
120   LOCATE ROW, COL
130   PRINT "THIS WILL APPEAR AT VERTICAL POSITION 4,
      HORIZONTAL POSITION 20"
```

Figure 7.1 shows the cursor position at LOCATE 4,20. Other manipulations are possible. Either the row or the column may be omitted. In that case, the current value is used.

```
700   LOCATE N
```

Move the cursor to row N, keeping the same column.

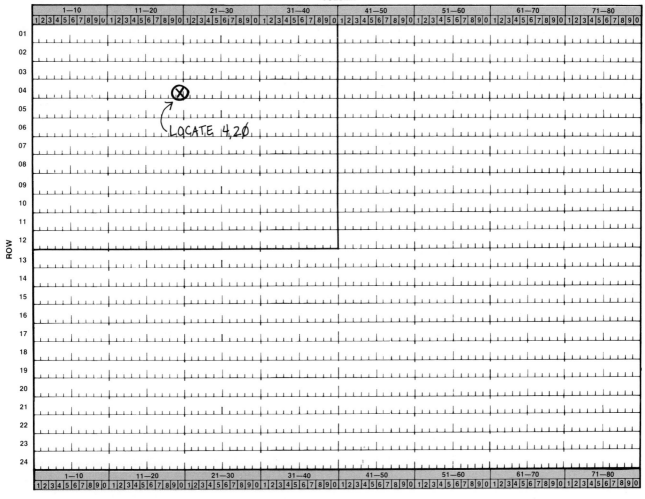

Figure 7.1
Screen layout showing cursor location. The statement LOCATE 4,20 will place the cursor at row 4, column 20 on the screen.

```
800   LOCATE ,C
```

Move the cursor to column C, without changing the current row.

```
500   LOCATE ,,0
```

This will make the cursor invisible, and leave it where it was.

Be aware that executing a LOCATE and PRINT will not clear the screen prior to execution. Any old data will remain where it was with the exception of the new characters printed. This can be disconcerting at times, if you are expecting to completely replace data on the screen. When a short string is printed in the same location as a longer one, for example, the excess characters from the first string will still appear. It may be necessary to erase areas of the screen by printing a string of blank spaces.

```
200   '*** BLANK OUT LINE ON SCREEN ***
210   LOCATE 5,10
220   PRINT "                              "
225   '*** NOW INPUT AT THE SAME LOCATION ***
230   LOCATE 5,10
240   INPUT "NAME: ", NAM$
```

This will move the cursor to row 5, column 10 and blank out the space on the line. (Most likely there was another name in the spot from a prior iteration of the program.) Then in line 230, the cursor is placed back in the same spot. The input prompt "NAME:" will begin on line 5, column 10.

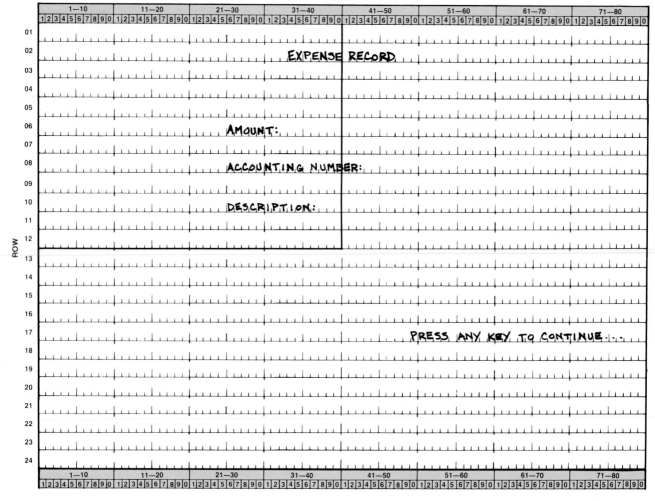

Figure 7.2
Data entry form drawn on the
screen. Input will always appear
in the same location.

There can be many advantages to having the line not clear when new data is printed. A data entry form can be constructed on the screen with titles for all fields (see figure 7.2). Those titles can remain in place, with only the data fields changing. Try drawing a box on the screen and change the contents of that box. LOCATE will handle these situations beautifully.

Cursor Placement for the Apple

Placing the cursor in Apple's version of Microsoft BASIC is accomplished with VTAB (for the row) and HTAB (for the column). A combination of these two statements will move the cursor to an absolute row and column position on the screen. The VTAB and HTAB statements are executed just prior to a PRINT, which will place the data in the exact location designated.

Most of the comments made about the LOCATE also apply to the VTAB and HTAB (with the exception of the invisible cursor). Any data already on the screen will remain. The only changes will be in the actual print positions that have new data printed in them.

```
200    '*** BLANK OUT LINE ***
210    VTAB 5
220    HTAB 10
230    PRINT "
235    '*** NOW INPUT AT THE SAME SPOT ***
240    VTAB 5
250    HTAB 10
260    INPUT "NAME: ", NAM$
```

174   Chapter 7

Feedback

1. Using the LOCATE (or VTAB and HTAB) statement, write the statements necessary to print your name in the exact center of a clear screen.
2. Using the LOCATE statement (or VTAB and HTAB), write the statements necessary to clear the screen and draw a box in the center of the screen. Then place the cursor inside the box and INPUT a number.

String Manipulation to Assist Screen Formatting

Joining Strings— Concatenation

Strings may be joined together by using the plus sign (+) to form longer strings. This joining is called **concatenation.**

```
10   LET A$ = "THEY SHOOT HORSES"
20   LET B$ = "DON'T THEY?"
30   LET C$ = A$ + ", " + B$
40   PRINT C$
RUN
THEY SHOOT HORSES, DON'T THEY?
```

String Manipulation Functions

BASIC supplies many *functions* that provide a means for performing operations. The functions presented thus far include INT, TAB, and SPC. A function can be thought of as a prewritten subroutine, which accomplishes one operation. Functions do not themselves have line numbers, but are used within other BASIC statements (such as LET and PRINT), which do have line numbers.

SPACE$

The SPACE$ function is similar to the SPC function, since both produce a series of spaces. But SPACE$ does not have the limitation of always having to be included in a PRINT or LPRINT statement. SPACE$ may also be used to assign blank spaces to a string variable.

The SPACE$ Function—General Form

```
SPACE$(number of spaces)
```

The SPACE$ Function—Examples

```
10   PRINT SPACE$(15) "THIS IS IT"
40   LET EMPTY$ = SPACE$(40)
90   LET DRAW$ = "XXX"+SPACE$(20)+"XXX"+SPACE$(20)+"XXX"
```

STRING$

Another function, which resembles SPACE$ and may prove useful in formatting output, is STRING$. This function produces a series of identical characters of the desired length.

The STRING$ Function—General Form

```
STRING$(length, character)
```

```
10   PRINT STRING$(40,"*")


50   LET STAR$ = STRING$(40,"*")


20   '**** UNDERLINE COLUMNS OF DATA ****
30   LET COLWIDTH = 15
40   LET LINECHAR$ = "_"
50   LET LIN$ = STRING$(COLWIDTH, LINECHAR$)
60   PRINT TAB(10); LIN$; SPC(5); LIN$; SPC(5); LIN$
```

The first example will print forty asterisks on the screen. The second example assigns a string of forty asterisks to the variable STAR$, presumably to print at a later point in the program. The technique shown in the third example can be used to underline columns of data.

The length specified in the STRING$ function may be a constant, a numeric variable, or an arithmetic expression. The character to duplicate may be given as a string literal, as a string variable, or as the number indicating the position in the ASCII coding sequence. For example, the ASCII code number for the asterisk is 42, so the first example given could have been written

```
10   PRINT STRING$(40,42)
```

Both statements have the same effect.

```
10    '******* A PRETTY SCREEN, BY ANY NAME ************
20    LET LIN$ = STRING$(80,"*")
30    LET BORDER$ = "**" + SPACE$(76) + "**"
35    CLS
40    PRINT LIN$;
50    PRINT LIN$;
60    LET ROW = 3
70    WHILE ROW < 22
80        PRINT BORDER$;
90        LET ROW = ROW + 1
100   WEND
110   PRINT LIN$;
120   PRINT LIN$;
130   LOCATE 12,36
140   PRINT "HI, MOM"
```

What do you think the result would be if the semicolons were not placed at the end of each PRINT?

Formatting a Screen for Data Entry

When designing the layout for a screen, a layout form can be extremely helpful. See the example in figure 7.3. To use the form for data entry, these steps are necessary.

1. Draw the form on the screen.
2. Input the data.
3. Clear the data areas on the screen.

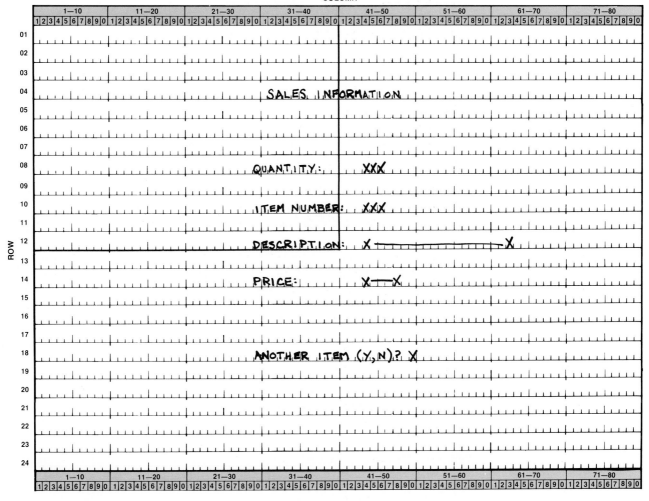

Figure 7.3
Using a screen layout to design a
data entry screen.

Example Program:
Inputting Data Using a Formatted Screen

Program Listing

```
100 ' PROGRAM TO DEMONSTRATE FORMATTED SCREEN DATA ENTRY
110 '    INPUTS DATA FROM SCREEN AND PRINTS A SIMPLE REPORT
120 '
130 '        PROGRAM VARIABLES
140 '        QUAN      QUANTITY
150 '        ITEM      ITEM NUMBER
160 '        DESC$     ITEM DESCRIPTION
170 '        PRICE     ITEM PRICE
180 '        ANS$      ANSWER - TO CONTINUE
```

```
500 '****************** PROGRAM MAINLINE ********************
510 GOSUB 1000            'PRINT FORM ON SCREEN
520 LET ANS$ = "Y"        'SET TO BEGIN LOOP
530 WHILE ANS$ = "Y" OR ANS$ = "y"
540     GOSUB 2000        'INPUT DATA FROM SCREEN
550     GOSUB 3000        'CALCULATIONS
560     GOSUB 4000        'PRINT DETAIL LINE
570     GOSUB 5000        'CLEAR DATA FIELDS ON SCREEN
580   WEND
590 END
1000 '***************** PRINT FORM ON SCREEN ******************
1010 CLS
1020 LOCATE 4,32
1030 PRINT "SALES INFORMATION"
1040 LOCATE 8,30
1050 PRINT "QUANTITY:"
1060 LOCATE 10,30
1070 PRINT "ITEM NUMBER:"
1080 LOCATE 12,30
1090 PRINT "DESCRIPTION:"
1100 LOCATE 14,30
1110 PRINT "PRICE:"
1120 LOCATE 18,30
1130 PRINT "ANOTHER ITEM (Y/N)"
1140 RETURN
1150 '
2000 '***************** INPUT DATA FROM SCREEN ****************
2010 LOCATE 8,44
2020 INPUT "", QUAN
2030 LOCATE 10,44
2040 INPUT "", ITEM
2050 LOCATE 12,44
2060 INPUT "", DESC$
2070 LOCATE 14,44
2080 INPUT "", PRICE
2090 LOCATE 18,48
2100 INPUT ANS$
2110 RETURN
2120 '
3000 '****************** CALCULATIONS ***********************
3010 LET TOTAL = QUAN * PRICE
3020 RETURN
3030 '
4000 '***************** PRINT DETAIL LINE *******************
4010 LPRINT QUAN, ITEM, DESC$, PRICE, TOTAL
4020 RETURN
4030 '
5000 '************** CLEAR DATA AREAS ON SCREEN **************
5010 LOCATE 8,44
5020 PRINT SPACE$(10)
5030 LOCATE 10,44
5040 PRINT SPACE$(10)
5050 LOCATE 12,44
5060 PRINT SPACE$(30)
5070 LOCATE 14,44
5080 PRINT SPACE$(10)
5090 LOCATE 18,48
5100 PRINT SPACE$(10)
5110 RETURN
5120 '***************** END OF PROGRAM ********************
```

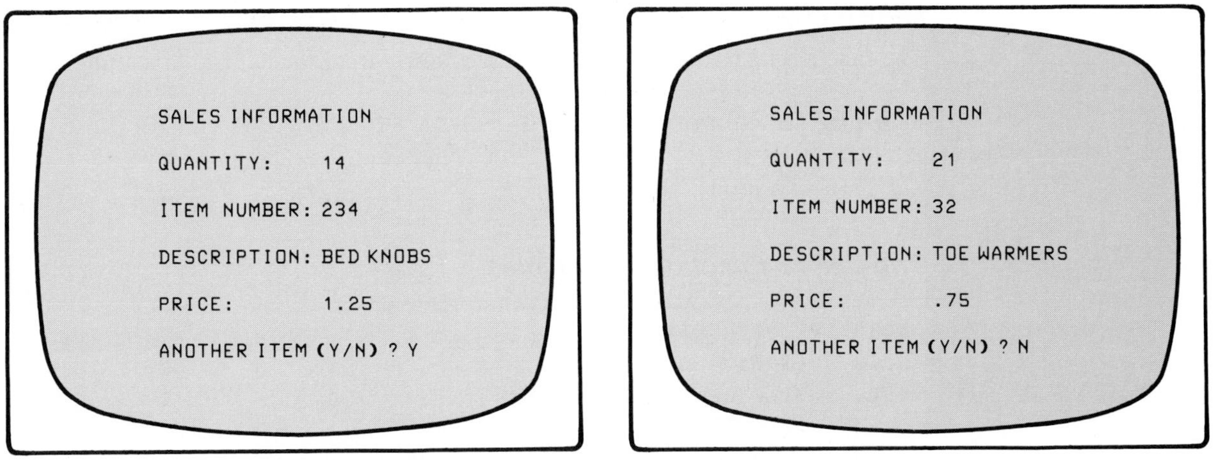

```
SALES INFORMATION

QUANTITY:    14

ITEM NUMBER: 234

DESCRIPTION: BED KNOBS

PRICE:      1.25

ANOTHER ITEM (Y/N) ? Y
```

```
SALES INFORMATION

QUANTITY:    21

ITEM NUMBER: 32

DESCRIPTION: TOE WARMERS

PRICE:       .75

ANOTHER ITEM (Y/N) ? N
```

Figure 7.4
Screen output produced by
sample program.

Notice the INPUT statements in the subroutine at line 2000. The "empty prompt" was used to eliminate the question mark generated by an INPUT statement. See figure 7.4 for screen output.

More String Manipulation

When checking for valid input data, it is important to be able to check each individual character. Numeric data should be input as a string, checked for validity, and then converted to numeric form. The tools to implement this validity checking are presented in the sections following.

LEN

The number of characters in a string can be found with the LEN function.

The LEN Function—General Form

```
LEN(string)
```

The LEN Function—Examples

```
100   LET COUNT = LEN(A$)
150   PRINT TAB(20-LEN(C$)); C$
300   LET VLINE$ = STRING$(LEN(K$), "-")
```

Line 150 will right-justify C$ at print position 20. Line 300 will assign to VLINE$ a series of dashes the same length as K$.

Any spaces embedded within a string are counted in the length of the string.

```
500   LET A$ = "PEACE OF MIND"
510   LET A = LEN(A$)
520   PRINT "THE LENGTH OF "; A$; " IS"; A
RUN
THE LENGTH OF PEACE OF MIND IS 13
```

LEFT$

The function LEFT$ is used to extract characters from the left end of a string.

The LEFT$ Function—General Form

```
LEFT$(string, number of characters)
```

The LEFT$ Function—Examples

```
1000    PRINT LEFT$(A$,N)
3050    LET B$ = LEFT$(A$,4)
4000    WHILE LEFT$(X$,1) = "Y"
```

The LEFT$ function returns a string of the specified length.

```
Assume that P$ = "WASTE NOT WANT NOT"
Then LEFT$(P$,1) is W
     LEFT$(P$,5) is WASTE
     LEFT$(P$,9) is WASTE NOT
```

A common use for LEFT$ is in checking a response when YES or NO is requested.

```
50    INPUT "DO YOU WISH TO CONTINUE"; ANS$
60    WHILE LEFT$(ANS$,1) = "Y"
::
::
```

This will allow entry of Y or YES (or YEP or YESSIREE).

RIGHT$

This function is used to extract characters from the right end of a string.

The RIGHT$ Function—General Form

```
RIGHT$(string, number of characters)
```

The RIGHT$ Function—Examples

```
50     LET B$ = RIGHT$(D$,4)
100    IF RIGHT$(X$,2) = "ED"
       THEN ...
```

Each of these "picks off" characters from the right end of the string.

```
If P$ = "WASTE NOT WANT NOT"
then RIGHT$(P$,1) is T
     RIGHT$(P$,3) is NOT
     RIGHT$(P$,7) is ANT NOT
```

MID$

The MID$ function extracts characters from anywhere within a string. The starting location is given, and a count of the number of characters wanted.

The MID$ Function—General Form

```
MID$(string, starting location [,number of characters])
```

The MID$ Function—Examples

```
700    LET S$ = MID$(R$,2,4)
950    PRINT MID$(K$,B,N)
1010   IF MID$(D$,2,1) = ","
          THEN ...
5000   LPRINT MID$(N$,LEN(N$)/2)
```

When the third argument (number of characters) is missing, as in line 5000 above, the MID$ function returns the rest of the string, beginning at the starting location.

```
If T$ = "A STITCH IN TIME SAVES NINE"
then MID$(T$,3,6)     is STITCH
     MID$(T$,8,6)     is H IN T
     MID$(T$,18,4)    is SAVE
     MID$(T$,18)      is SAVES NINE
     MID$(T$,5,4)     is ITCH
```

Notes on string functions

1. If the starting location or number of characters is a fractional value, it will be rounded to the nearest whole number.
2. If the number of characters specified for LEFT$ or RIGHT$ is greater than the number of characters in the string, the entire string is returned.

MID$ Statement

MID$ may be used as a function or as a statement. When used as a statement, MID$ appears on the left of the equal sign in an assignment statement. It is used to replace characters in strings.

```
40    LET D$ = "WATER"
50    MID$(D$,2,4) = "INE "
```

WATER is changed into WINE

Leaving out the space in "INE " gives a three character replacement, and WATER becomes WINER. The replacement will never increase the length of a string.

```
60    LET F$ = "WINE"
70    MID$(F$,2,4) = "ATER"
```

F$ changes from WINE to WATE

VAL

The VAL function is used to convert a string value into a numeric value. The number 123 can be assigned to a numeric variable or a string variable.

```
10    LET V = 123
20    LET V$ = "123"
```

In order to do any arithmetic operations with the value, however, the numeric variable must be used.

The VAL Function—General Form

```
VAL(string)
```

The digits in the string will be converted to their numeric value. If there is a mixture of numeric digits and other characters in the string, VAL starts its conversion at the left and continues until the first nonnumeric character is found. In the event the first character of the string is not numeric, zero will be returned. The VAL function will accept a leading sign (if present), a decimal point, and the ten numeric digits (0–9).

The VAL Function—Examples

```
50    LET AMT = VAL(A$)
100   IF VAL(S$) = 0
        THEN PRINT "NOT A VALID NUMBER"
200   PRINT TAB(40-LEN(N$)); VAL(N$)
```

Statement: 100 PRINT VAL(A$)

Value of A$	Printed
"1234"	1234
"+1.2B"	1.2
" -4C"	-4
"1 2 3"	123
"ABC"	0

An important use of the VAL function occurs during data validation. In order to properly check for *any* input values, numeric digits must be input into strings. After the validation, the data must be converted to a numeric variable for computations.

```
100   INPUT "ENTER NUMBER", NUM$
110   GOSUB 500              'VALIDATE NUMBER
120   LET NUM = VAL(NUM$)
```

(*Note:* The coding for the validation will be shown shortly.)

STR$

STR$ does the reverse operation of VAL. STR$ takes a numeric value and converts it into a string. The primary use for this function is to allow for the use of the string manipulation functions such as LEN or MID$.

The STR$ Function—General Form

```
STR$(numeric expression)
```

The STR$ Function—Examples

```
400   LET K$ = STR$(K)
500   LET L = LEN(STR$(AMT))
```

Line 500 may return a slightly different value than expected. When AMT is converted to a string, the first character is reserved for the sign. If AMT is a negative number, the first character is a minus sign. When AMT is a positive number, the first character is a blank. In either case (blank or —), that first character is included in the length of the string.

Numeric data can now be INPUT as a string and checked for valid numeric characters, one digit at a time. To determine the number of digits to check, use the LEN function. For checking each character, the MID$ function allows selection of each digit individually. Once the data has been determined to be numeric, the VAL function will be used to place the digits into a numeric variable.

Example Subroutines: Numeric Validity Checking

Program Listing

```
100 '******* INPUT NUMERIC DATA INTO STRING AND VALIDATE ********
110 LET VALID.SW = 0              'SET SWITCH OFF TO ENTER LOOP
120 WHILE VALID.SW = 0           'CONTINUE UNTIL DATA PASSES TEST
130    INPUT NUM.AMT$            'INPUT INTO STRING
140    LET VALID.SW = 1          'ASSUME DATA GOOD UNTIL PROVEN BAD
150    GOSUB 500                 'VALIDATE AMOUNT
160    IF VALID.SW = 0
          THEN GOSUB 600         'PRINT ERROR MESSAGE
170 WEND
180 LET NUM.AMT = VAL(NUM.AMT$) 'CONVERT VALIDATED AMT TO NUMERIC
190 PRINT NUM.AMT
200 RETURN
210 '
500 '************ VALIDATE THE AMOUNT ************************
510 LET P = LEN(NUM.AMT$)        'FIND THE NUMBER OF DIGITS TO CHECK
520 WHILE P > 0 AND VALID.SW = 1
530    IF MID$(NUM.AMT$,P,1)<"0" OR MID$(NUM.AMT$,P,1)>"9"
          THEN VALID.SW = 0 'SET SWITCH FOR BAD CHARACTER
540    LET P = P - 1            'CHECK NEXT CHARACTER
550 WEND
560 RETURN
570 '
600 '********** PRINT ERROR MESSAGE ************************
610 LOCATE 22,5
620 PRINT "INVALID NUMERIC AMOUNT ENTERED";
630 LOCATE 24,50
640 PRINT "PRESS ENTER TO CONTINUE";
650 INPUT X$                     'WAIT FOR ENTER KEY
660 CLS                          'CLEAR THE MESSAGES
670 RETURN
```

More Handy String Functions

INSTR

The INSTR function searches a string for the occurrence of a second string. The value returned is the position within the first string where the second string begins.

The INSTR Function—General Form

```
INSTR([starting position,] string, string to search for)
```

The starting position may be omitted, in which case the entire string is searched. When the search is unsuccessful—that is, the second string is not found within the first string—the function returns zero.

The INSTR Function—Examples

```
3000   LET POINTER = INSTR(PRIMARY$,SEARCH$)
4000   LET C = INSTR(N,NAM$,",")
```

INSTR may be used to count the occurrences of a substring (the second string) within the primary string.

Example Program:
Counting Occurrences of a Substring within a String

```
100 '*** COUNT OCCURRENCES OF SUBSTRING WITHIN A STRING ***
110 INPUT "STRING"; A$
120 INPUT "SUBSTRING"; B$
130 LET P = 1                 'P IS START POSITION TO CHECK
140 LET N = -1                'INITIALIZE N TO ENTER LOOP
150 WHILE N <> 0
160      LET N = INSTR(P,A$,B$)
170      IF N <> 0
             THEN LET COUNT = COUNT + 1
180      LET P = N + 1
190 WEND
200 PRINT B$; " OCCURRED"; COUNT; "TIMES IN "; A$

RUN
STRING? ABRACADABRA
SUBSTRING? A
A OCCURRED 5 TIMES IN ABRACADABRA

RUN
STRING? ABRACADABRA
SUBSTRING? BRA
BRA OCCURRED 2 TIMES IN ABRACADABRA
```

At times, it is necessary to reverse the name within a string. If the name is stored as SMITH, JOHN, it may be preferrable to print JOHN SMITH. Assume that names are stored LAST-NAME, FIRST-NAME. Use a combination of the string functions to place the names in the form FIRST-NAME LAST-NAME.

Example Program: Reversing Name Position

```
10 '*** REVERSE POSITION OF NAMES ***
15 ' P USED AS A POINTER TO THE POSITION OF THE COMMA
20 READ NAM$
30 WHILE NAM$ <> "END"
40      LET P = INSTR(NAM$, ",")
50      LET NAM2$ = MID$(NAM$,P+2) + " " + LEFT$(NAM$,P-1)
60      PRINT NAM$, NAM2$
70      READ NAM$
80 WEND
90 DATA "LAST, FIRST", "JONES, PAT", "HORTON, ERIC", "END"

RUN

LAST, FIRST    FIRST LAST
JONES, PAT     PAT JONES
HORTON, ERIC   ERIC HORTON
```

CHR$

The CHR$ function returns one character specified by its number in the ASCII coding sequence. This can be useful when a character is required that is not on the keyboard of the computer you are using.

The CHR$ Function—General Form

CHR$(code number)

The CHR$ Function—Examples

```
240    PRINT CHR$(7)
400    PRINT CHR$(34); "HELLO,"; CHR$(34); " HE SAID"
```

These two examples show solutions to problems frequently encountered. Line 240 prints character 7, which is the bell (or speaker) on most computers. This will cause the bell to sound—perhaps for an error condition or a game. The second example, line 400, solves a sticky problem. Since quotation marks are used to surround literals in a PRINT statement, how do you actually print quotation marks when needed? ASCII code 34, the quotation mark, does just what is wanted. The following two statements will give the same results, since ASCII code 65 is the letter A.

```
100    PRINT CHR$(65)
110    PRINT "A"
```

ASC

The ASC function does the opposite operation of CHR$. For any character, it will return the ASCII code number.

The ASC Function—General Form

```
ASC(character)
```

The ASC Function—Examples

```
20    IF ASC(C$) < 32
          THEN PRINT "UNPRINTABLE CHARACTER"
150   IF ASC(D$) < 48 OR ASC(D$) > 57
          THEN PRINT "NOT A VALID NUMERIC DIGIT"
```

The ASC function returns the decimal number corresponding to the character's position in the ASCII code. Referencing the chart in appendix C, all code numbers less than 32 are nonprinting control characters. There are times these codes need to be sent to a terminal or printer, however. Code 12 is a form-feed character. When the statement

```
100    LPRINT CHR$(12)
```

is executed, most printers will advance to the top of the next page (assuming the paper is correctly set).

With INPUT responses, it is sometimes necessary to check for both uppercase and lowercase characters. If a user enters *y*, it won't be equal to *Y*. One way to handle the problem is to convert lowercase characters to uppercase.

On the chart of ASCII codes, the set of lowercase letters is located above the uppercase—precisely 32 positions above. The code for any lowercase letter minus 32 will give the corresponding capital letter.

```
290    '** CONVERT LOWERCASE TO UPPERCASE **
300    INPUT ANS$
310    LET A = ASC(ANS$)
320    IF A > 96 AND A < 123
          THEN LET ANS$ = CHR$(A-32)
```

BASIC has two ways to allow characters to be input from the keyboard without the necessity of pressing RETURN/ENTER. These two statements, INKEY$ and INPUT$, have some things in common. Both return the key pressed as a string character, and neither **echoes** (displays) that character on the screen. This could be handy for passwords when screen display is not wanted. Both statements also cause the cursor to become invisible. To overcome that inconvenience, use the LOCATE statement. Recall from the discussion of LOCATE that LOCATE ,,1 makes the cursor visible.

There are some important differences between INKEY$ and INPUT$. INKEY$ does not halt program execution, but simply checks to see if there has been any key pressed lately. This could be useful for game playing, when the player presses keys during execution of the program. INPUT$ *does* halt program execution, similar to the INPUT statement. Another significant difference is that INPUT$ allows for input of multiple characters, while INKEY$ inputs a single keyboard character.

The INKEY$ Function—General Form

```
line number LET string variable = INKEY$
```

When INKEY$ is used, the keyboard buffer is checked. If any key has been pressed, its value is placed into the variable named in the LET statement. The string returned will have a length of 0, 1, or 2 characters:

0—If no key has been pressed, the null string (of zero length) is returned.
1—The actual character pressed on the keyboard is placed in a one-character string.
2—Two-character strings are returned when the key pressed was one of the special control keys such as the cursor movement keys. See your system manual for this option.

The INKEY$ Function—Example

```
20   LET X$ = INKEY$
```

Since INKEY$ does not halt program execution, it is often used in a loop.

```
600   '**** KEEP PRINTING UNTIL A KEY IS PRESSED ******
610   PRINT "PRESS ANY KEY TO STOP PROGRAM"
620   LET A$ = ""              'INITIALIZE TO NULL STRING
630   WHILE A$ = ""
640      PRINT "TEST OF THE EMERGENCY BROADCASTING SYSTEM"
650      LET A$ = INKEY$
660 WEND
```

Line 630 could also be written as:

```
630   WHILE LEN(A$) = 0
```

The INPUT$ Function—General Form

```
LET string variable = INPUT$(number of characters)
```

INPUT$ will halt program execution and await the number of keystrokes specified. When the characters have been pressed, the string will then be assigned to the variable named. The RETURN/ENTER key is not required.

The INPUT$ Function—Examples

```
 40   LET V$ = INPUT$(1)
 90   LET K$ = INPUT$(N)
120   LET R$ = INPUT$(4)
```

When a screen full of data has been printed, the user needs a chance to read it before continuing. Print the message PRESS ANY KEY TO CONTINUE to allow the user to control execution. The INPUT$ function accomplishes this task nicely.

```
450   PRINT "PRESS ANY KEY TO CONTINUE"
460   LET X$ = INPUT$(1)
470   CLS
```

(continue with program)

In this example, X$ is a **dummy variable,** since it doesn't matter what value it has, and it won't be used anywhere else.

Inputting Strings of Data with the INPUT$ Function

Since INPUT$ does not echo the characters on the screen, it may be necessary for the program to do so.

```
800   '*** KEYBOARD ENTRY OF A STRING USING INPUT$ *****
810   LOCATE ,,1                  'TURN ON THE CURSOR
820   LET P$ = ""                 'NULL STRING, TO BEGIN LOOP
830   WHILE P$ <> CHR$(13)        'CHECK FOR RETURN KEY
840       LET P$ = INPUT$(1)      'GET ONE CHARACTER
850       PRINT P$;               'ECHO ON SCREEN
860       IF P$ <> CHR$(13)
              THEN LET Q$ = Q$+P$ 'TACK CHARACTER ON TO
                                   ACCUMULATE STRING
880   WEND
890   PRINT Q$
```

More on Numeric Validity Checking

You now have more tools that will allow greater flexibility in numeric validity checking. Some programmers prefer to print an error message or sound the bell as an inappropriate key is pressed; others wait for the return key. Another approach is to "throw away" any bad characters and only accept the good ones.

Example Program: Checking for "Good" and "Bad" Characters

Program Listing

```
110 '********* CHECK EACH CHARACTER AND IGNORE BAD ONES *******
120 LOCATE ,,1                'SET CURSOR TO VISIBLE
130 LET INVAR$ = ""           'CLEAR OUT STRING TO BEGIN
140 LET C$ = INPUT$(1)        'GET FIRST CHARACTER TO GET STARTED
150 WHILE C$ <> CHR$(13)      'CHECK FOR RETURN CHARACTER
160     IF ASC(C$) >= 48 AND ASC(C$) <= 57
            THEN GOSUB 220    'GOOD CHARACTER
170     LET C$ = INPUT$(1)
180 WEND
190 LET INVAR = VAL(INVAR$) 'CONVERT STRING TO NUMERIC VAR.
200 PRINT INVAR             'LET'S SEE OUR GOOD NUMBER
210 RETURN
215 '
220 '*********** SAVE AND PRINT GOOD CHARACTER ***************
230 LET INVAR$ = INVAR$ + C$'TACK CHARACTER ONTO STRING
240 PRINT C$;               'ECHO ON SCREEN
250 RETURN
```

```
110 '** CHECK EACH CHARACTER AND SOUND BELL FOR BAD ONES*******
120 LOCATE ,,1              'SET CURSOR TO VISIBLE
130 LET INVAR$ = ""         'CLEAR OUT STRING TO BEGIN
140 LET C$ = INPUT$(1)      'GET FIRST CHARACTER TO GET STARTED
145 WHILE C$ <> CHR$(13)    'CHECK FOR RETURN CHARACTER
150     IF ASC(C$) >= 48 AND ASC(C$) <= 57
            THEN GOSUB 300
            ELSE GOSUB 400
170     LET C$ = INPUT$(1) 'GET NEXT KEYBOARD CHARACTER
180 WEND
190 LET INVAR = VAL(INVAR$) 'CONVERT STRING TO NUMERIC VAR.
200 PRINT INVAR             'LET'S SEE OUR GOOD NUMBER
210 RETURN
220 '
300 '*********** SAVE AND PRINT GOOD CHARACTER *****************
310 LET INVAR$ = INVAR$ + C$'TACK CHARACTER ONTO STRING
320 PRINT C$;               'ECHO ON SCREEN
330 RETURN
340 '
400 '************ BAD CHARACTER *********************
410 PRINT CHR$(7);          ' RINGS THE BELL
420 RETURN
```

If the preference is to wait until the entire input is entered before printing the error message, use the INPUT statement. Check the characters with MID$. See the example shown earlier in this chapter (p. 183).

Inputting Strings with the LINE INPUT Statement

Microsoft BASIC provides another statement for inputting data that may prove useful in some situations. An entire line of characters (including commas and quotation marks) may be input into a string variable with the LINE INPUT statement. All characters entered at the keyboard are assigned to the string variable until the ENTER key is pressed.

The LINE INPUT Statement—General Form

```
line number LINE  INPUT  [;] ["literal prompt";] stringvariable
```

The LINE INPUT Statement—Examples

```
200   LINE INPUT ADDRESS$
300   LINE INPUT "ENTER ADDRESS "; ADDRESS$
400   LINE INPUT; "ENTER A SENTENCE"; SENT$
```

Each of these examples will assign to the variable named all characters entered until the ENTER key is pressed. The extra semicolon in line 400 suppresses the line feed and carriage return, which normally occur following keyboard entry. This might be helpful with formatted screens to prevent scrolling.

Retrieving the Date and Time

For those computers having a clock, the current system date and time can be retrieved by a BASIC program. Naturally, the computer operating system must have been set previously to the correct date and time.

The DATE$ Function—General Form

```
LET string variable = DATE$
```

DATE$ is a variable that returns the current date in a ten-character string in the form mm–dd–yyyy. The first two digits are the month, then a dash, then two digits for the day, another dash, and the year in the form 19xx.

For example, if the date is July 4, 1998, then DATE$ will return 07–04–1998.

The DATE$ Function—Examples

```
 50   LET DA$ = DATE$
100   PRINT DATE$
```

Parts of the date may be used for other operations.

```
100   LET YR$ = RIGHT$(DATE$,4)
110   LET DAY$ = MID$(DATE$,4,2)
```

Or, if the values are needed in a numeric operation:

```
100   LET YR = VAL(RIGHT$(DATE$,4))
110   LET DAY = VAL(MID$(DATE$,4,2))
```

The TIME$ Function—General Form

```
LET string variable = TIME$
```

The variable TIME$ will return an eight-character string in the form hh:mm:ss, in twenty-four-hour notation. The first two characters (hh) represent the hour (00–23); mm represents the minutes (00–59); ss represents the seconds (00–59).

When the TIME$ function is executed, the current value of the system clock will be placed in the variable. If it is 8:01 A.M., TIME$ will yield 08:01:00. For 8:01 P.M., you will see 20:01:00.

The TIME$ Function—Examples

```
 50   LET T$ = TIME$
100   PRINT TIME$
190   LET SEC$ = RIGHT$(TIME$,2)
```

Parts of the time may be accessed:

```
100   LET HR = VAL(LEFT$(TIME$,2))
110   LET MIN = VAL(MID$(TIME$,4,2))
120   LET SEC = VAL(RIGHT$(TIME$,2))
130   LET TOT.SEC = SEC + MIN * 60 + HR * 360
```

Feedback

1. When might it be necessary to use this statement?

   ```
   100   LOCATE ,,1
   ```

2. How many ways can you think of to print a line of forty equal signs on the screen?
3. How can you find out the number of digits in a numeric variable?
4. What is the most likely situation to require the use of the VAL function?
5. Name one reason for using INKEY$ rather than INPUT.
6. Name one reason for using INKEY$ rather than INPUT$.
7. Name one reason for using INPUT$ rather than INKEY$.
8. Write the statements necessary to READ this series of words (until END is encountered) and print each word right-justified at column 30.

   ```
   100   DATA FIG, WATERMELON, PINEAPPLE, PLUM, MANGO, END
   ```

9. What will print when these statements are executed?

```
60   LET A$ = "GOOD GRIEF"
70   PRINT MID$(A$,4,1) + MID$(A$,2,1) + LEFT$(A$,1)
```

10. Write the statements necessary to print all characters following the period in P$. Assume that there will always be one and only one period in the string.

11. Write the statements necessary to print all characters following the period in P$. This time, do not assume that there will always be a period. If there is no period in the string, print nothing.

12. Write the statements necessary to advance the printer paper to the top-of-form.

13. Using INPUT$, keep inputting characters until an asterisk is entered. Echo all characters except the asterisk on the screen.

Check Digit Calculation

Many credit card companies and other institutions use a check digit to ensure validity of the account numbers. The check digit calculation is designed to catch errors in keying such as transpositions or misstrikes.

Many different algorithms have been devised for generating check digits. The general plan is to perform a calculation on the digits of the ID number. Then, the results of that calculation are appended to the ID number as an extra digit. Each time an ID number is used, the calculation can be performed to verify that the number is valid. (See figure 7.5.)

Table 7.1 summarizes the string manipulation functions.

Figure 7.5
Check digit calculation.

SAMPLE CHECK DIGIT ALGORITHM

1. Double every other digit
2. Add the digits together
3. Use the right-most character of the sum as the check digit.

ID NUMBER	CHECK DIGIT CALCULATION	NEW ID NUMBER
45261	$4 + (5 \times 2) + 2 + (6 \times 2) + 1 = 29$	452619
54261	$5 + (4 \times 2) + 2 + (6 \times 2) + 1 = 28$	542618
45621	$4 + (5 \times 2) + 6 + (2 \times 2) + 1 = 25$	456215

Table 7.1.
Summary of string manipulation functions.

Key: X$= string expression; variable, literal, or combinations including string functions
n= numeric expression; variable, constant, or arithmetic expression
pos= numeric expression, indicating a position within the string
C$= string character, either variable or literal

ASC(X$)	Returns the number corresponding to the ASCII code for the first character of X$. Reverse of CHR$ function.
CHR$(n)	Returns the string character that corresponds to the ASCII code n. Reverse of ASC function.
DATE$	Retrieves the system date, as a ten-character string in the form mm–dd–yyyy.
INKEY$	Allows keyboard entry of a single character without the RETURN key being pressed. Does not halt program execution.
INPUT$(n)	Allows keyboard entry of n characters without the RETURN key being pressed. Halts program execution to await entry.
INSTR([pos,]X$,X2$)	Searches for the occurrence of the substring X2$ in X$, starting at position *pos*. If *pos* is omitted, the start position is 1. Returns a numeric value that is the position where the substring begins; returns 0 if the substring is not found.
LEFT$(X$,n)	Returns the leftmost n characters of X$.
LEN(X$)	Returns the length of X$ (a count of the number of characters in the string).
MID$(X$,pos[,n])	Extracts n characters from X$, starting at position *pos*. When n is omitted, the rest of the string, beginning at position *pos*, is returned.
RIGHT$(X$,n)	Returns the rightmost n characters of X$.
SPACE$(n)	Returns a string of blank spaces of n length.
STR$(n)	Returns the string value of the numeric expression. Used to convert numeric values to strings. Reverse of VAL function.
STRING$(n,C$)	Returns a string of length n, filled with the character named. The character may be a variable, a literal enclosed in quotes, or the ASCII code for the character.
TIME$	Retrieves the system time as an eight-character string in a twenty-four-hour format, in the form hh:mm:ss.
VAL(X$)	Returns the numeric value of X$. Used to convert strings to numeric values. Reverse of STR$ function.

As a memory aid, it should be noted that all function names containing a dollar sign return a string value, and those function names not containing a dollar sign return a numeric value.

Example Subroutines: Check Digit Calculation

Each time an ID number is entered, the program will calculate the check digit. If it matches, the ID number passes; if not, an error message is generated.

Program Listing

```
10 '********* CHECK DIGIT CALCULATION **********************
20 LET VALID.SW = 0                    'SWITCH OFF TO START
30 WHILE VALID.SW = 0
40     INPUT "ENTER ID NUMBER ", IDNO
60     GOSUB 2000                  'CHECK VALIDITY
70     IF VALID.SW = 0
          THEN PRINT "INVALID ID NUMBER, REENTER "
80 WEND
90 RETURN
95 '
2000 '**************** VALIDITY CHECK ************************
2020 LET ID$ = STR$(IDNO)
2030 LET D1 = VAL(MID$(ID$,2,1))
2040 LET D2 = VAL(MID$(ID$,3,1))
2050 LET D3 = VAL(MID$(ID$,4,1))
2060 LET D4 = VAL(MID$(ID$,5,1))
2070 LET D5 = VAL(MID$(ID$,6,1))
2080 LET D6 = VAL(MID$(ID$,7,1))
2090 LET CHECK = D1 + (D2*2) + D3 + (D4*2) + D5
2095 LET CHECK = VAL(RIGHT$(STR$(CHECK),1))
2100 IF CHECK = D6
        THEN VALID.SW = 1
2130 RETURN
```

Programming Example

As an example of an interactive program with screen formatting and validity checking, a math drill program will be developed. The user will be asked to enter the number to be practiced. Then the entire set (1–12) will be produced. A correct answer will produce the message RIGHT, while an incorrect (or invalid) response will cause TRY AGAIN to appear. The user will be allowed to quit (by entering Q) after each problem. When the set (1–12) is complete, the user may select a new set or quit.

This program is one that suggests many further enhancements, such as multiple messages and random selection of the problems. These will be left as an exercise for the programmer. (The random number function, RND, in chapter 10 could prove helpful.)

Input

1. Number to select problem set (validate for numeric and 1–12)
2. Answer to problem (validate for numeric)

Output

1. The problem
2. Messages for right or wrong answer

Processing

1. Check for correct answer
2. Validate all input
3. Hold messages on screen until a key is pressed
4. Blank out all messages

Pseudocode

Main Program

1. Print title
2. Select number
3. Math drill
4. Print ending message

Select Number Subroutine

2.1   Input a number
2.2   Loop until number found valid
      2.2.1   Validate number
      2.2.2   If not valid
              then print a message
                  re-enter number
2.3   End loop

Math Drill Subroutine

3.1   Loop until "Q" entered (once for each set)
      3.1.1   Begin problems in set with 1
      3.1.2   Loop until problem 12 or "Q" entered
            3.1.2.1 Print problem on screen
            3.1.2.2 Input the answer
            3.1.2.3 Validate answer
            3.1.2.4 If answer correct
                    then print "RIGHT"
                    else print "TRY AGAIN"
            3.1.2.5 Wait for keypress
            3.1.2.6 Clear out message areas
      3.1.3   End loop for set
      3.1.4   Choose a new set
3.2   End drill loop

Hierarchy Chart   See figure 7.6.

Figure 7.6
Hierarchy chart for math drill
program.

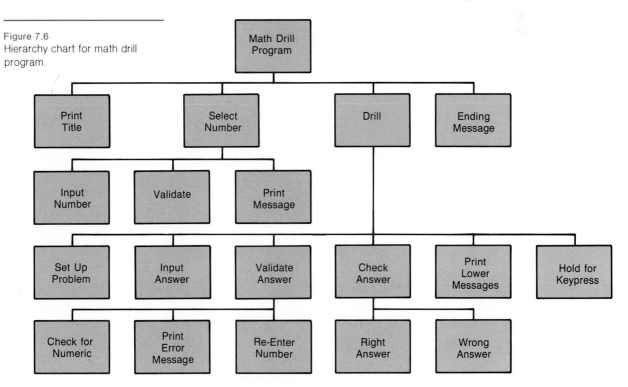

Flowchart　　　　　　Refer to figure 7.7.

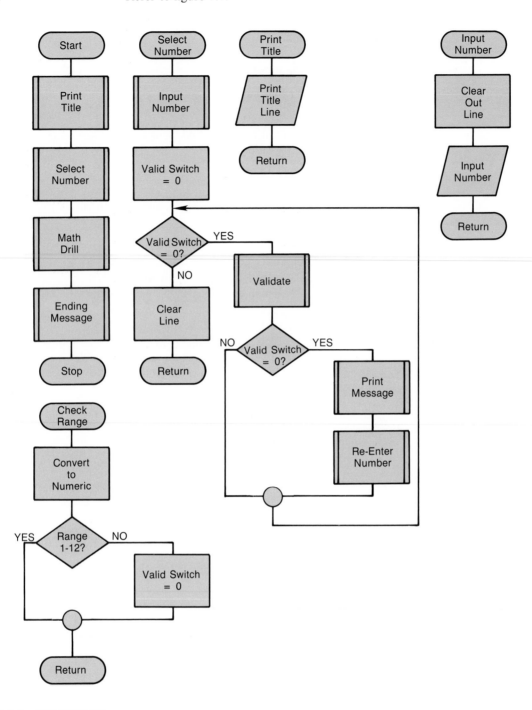

Figure 7.7
Flowchart for math drill program.

Figure 7.7—*Continued*

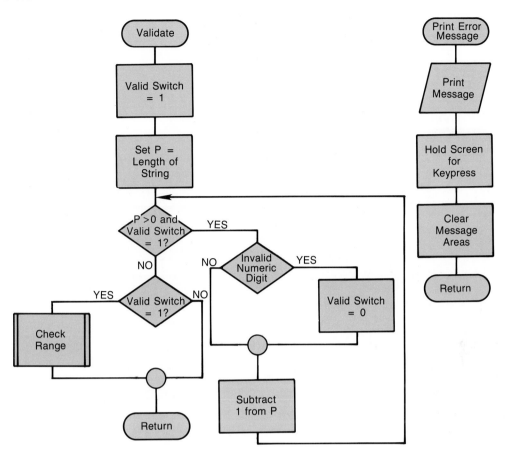

Figure 7.7—*Continued*

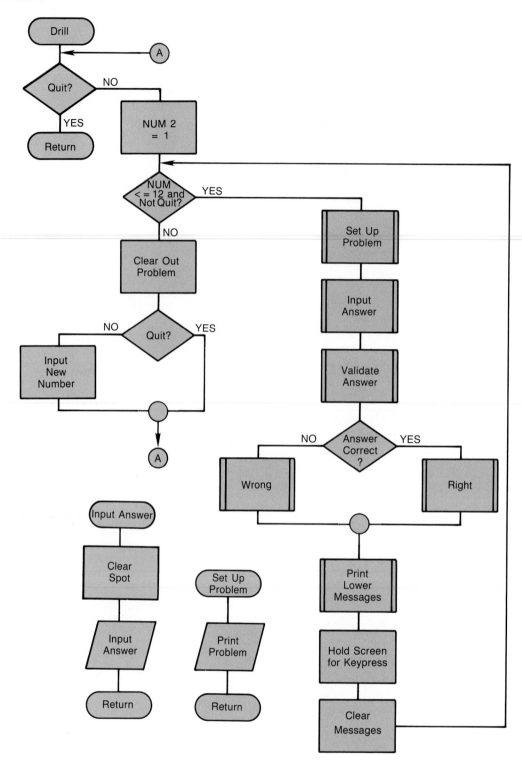

Chapter 7

Figure 7.7—*Continued*

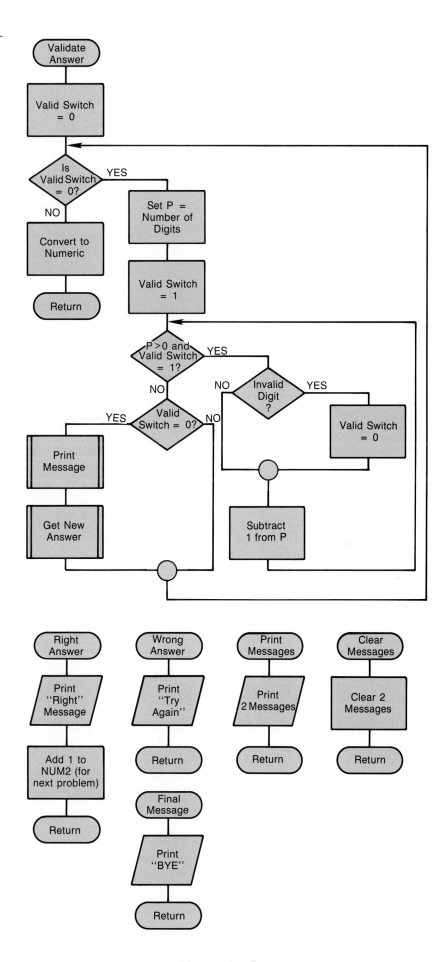

```
100 '  INTERACTIVE PROGRAM TO PRACTICE MULTIPLICATION TABLES
110 '    ALL SCREENS FORMATTED TO NOT ALLOW SCROLLING
120 '
130 '              PROGRAM VARIABLES
140 '              NUM1$       NUMBER TO USE FOR MULTIPLIER--STRING
                              FORM
150 '              NUM1        NUMBER TO USE FOR MULTIPLIER--NUMERIC
                              FORM
160 '              NUM2        SECOND NUMBER
170 '              P           DIGIT POSITION FOR CHECKING NUMBER
180 '              ANS$        ANSWER TO PROBLEM--STRING FORM
190 '              ANS         ANSWER TO PROBLEM--NUMERIC FORM
200 '              RES$        RESPONSE TO MESSAGE FOR QUIT
210 '              VALID.SW    SWITCH FOR VALIDITY CHECKING
220 '
500 '*************** PROGRAM MAINLINE ***********************
510 GOSUB 1000                    'PRINT TITLE
520 GOSUB 2000                    'SELECT NUMBER
530 GOSUB 4000                    'DO DRILL
540 GOSUB 9000                    'SAY GOODBYE
550 END
1000 '*************** PRINT TITLE ************************
1010 CLS
1020 LOCATE 2,20
1030 PRINT "M U L T I P L I C A T I O N    T A B L E S"
1040 RETURN
1050 '
2000 '*************** SELECT NUMBER ************************
2010 GOSUB 2400                    'INPUT A NUMBER
2020 LET VALID.SW = 0              'SET OFF TO ENTER LOOP
2030 WHILE VALID.SW = 0
2040     GOSUB 2600                'VALIDATE NUMBER
2050     IF VALID.SW = 0
            THEN GOSUB 2900:
                 GOSUB 2400        'PRINT MESSAGE AND RE-ENTER NUMBER
2060 WEND
2070 LOCATE 8,22
2080 PRINT SPACE$(40)              'CLEAR OUT THE LINE
2090 RETURN
2100 '
2400 '*************** INPUT THE CHOSEN NUMBER ******************
2410 LOCATE 8,22
2420 PRINT SPACE$(40)              'CLEAR OUT THE LINE
2430 LOCATE 8,22
2440 INPUT "WHAT NUMBER DO YOU WANT TO PRACTICE"; NUM1$
2450 RETURN
2460 '
2600 '*************** VALIDATE NUMBER ***********************
2610 LET VALID.SW = 1             'ASSUME OK UNTIL PROVEN BAD
2620 LET P = LEN(NUM1$)           'FIND NUMBER OF DIGITS TO CHECK
2630 WHILE P > 0 AND VALID.SW = 1
2640     IF MID$(NUM1$,P,1) < "0" OR MID$(NUM1$,P,1) > "9"
            THEN LET VALID.SW = 0 'SET SWITCH TO SHOW BAD DATA
2650     LET P = P - 1            'CHECK NEXT DIGIT
2660 WEND
2670 IF VALID.SW = 1
        THEN GOSUB 2800           'CHECK RANGE (1-12)
2680 RETURN
2800 '*************** CHECK RANGE ***********************
2810 LET NUM1 = VAL(NUM1$)        'CONVERT TO NUMERIC
2820 IF NUM1 < 1 OR NUM1 > 12
        THEN LET VALID.SW = 0     'SET SWITCH FOR BAD DATA
2830 RETURN
2840 '
```

```
2900 '*************** PRINT ERROR MESSAGE *********************
2910 LOCATE 11,29
2920 PRINT "I CAN'T DO THAT NUMBER"
2930 LOCATE 13,32
2940 PRINT "I ONLY KNOW 1-12"
2950 GOSUB 8000                    'PRINT ENDING MESSAGE
2960 LET RES$ = INPUT$(1)          'GET ONE CHARACTER FROM KEYBOARD
2970 GOSUB 8500                    'CLEAR OUT MESSAGES
2980 LOCATE 11,29
2990 PRINT SPACE$(22)              'CLEAR ERROR MESSAGE AREAS
3000 LOCATE 13,32
3010 PRINT SPACE$(16)
3020 RETURN
3030 '
4000 '****************** DO THE DRILL ***********************
4010 WHILE RES$ <> "Q"             'KEEP GOING UNTIL Q ENTERED
4020    LET NUM2 = 1               'START DRILL AT 1
4030    WHILE NUM2 <= 12 AND RES$ <> "Q"
4040       GOSUB 5000              'SET UP PROBLEM
4050       GOSUB 6000              'INPUT THE ANSWER
4060       GOSUB 6500              'VALIDATE ANSWER
4070       IF ANS = NUM1 * NUM2
              THEN GOSUB 7000
              ELSE GOSUB 7500
4080       GOSUB 8000             'PRINT BOTTOM MESSAGES
4090       LET RES$ = INPUT$(1) 'GET ONE CHAR FROM KEYBOARD
4100       LOCATE 12,35
4110       PRINT SPACE$(9)        'CLEAR OUT MESSAGE
4120       GOSUB 8500             'CLEAR OUT BOTTOM MESSAGES
4130    WEND
4140    LOCATE 9,35
4150    PRINT SPACE$(15)          'CLEAR OUT PROBLEM
4160    IF RES$ <> "Q"
           THEN GOSUB 2000        'INPUT A NEW NUMBER FOR DRILL
4170 WEND
4180 RETURN
4190 '
5000 '***************** SET UP PROBLEM ********************
5010 LOCATE 9,35
5020 PRINT NUM1; "X"; NUM2; "="
5030 RETURN
5040 '
6000 '***************** INPUT THE ANSWER ******************
6010 LOCATE 9,44
6020 PRINT SPACE$(10)              'CLEAR OUT THE SPOT
6030 LOCATE 9,44
6040 INPUT ANS$                    'INPUT THE ANSWER
6050 RETURN
6500 '*************** VALIDATE ANSWER *********************
6510 LET VALID.SW = 0             'TO BEGIN LOOP
6520 WHILE VALID.SW = 0
6530    LET P = LEN(ANS$)          'FIND NUMBER OF DIGITS TO CHECK
6540    LET VALID.SW = 1           'SET TO GOOD BEFORE CHECK
6550    WHILE P > 0 AND VALID.SW = 1
6560       IF MID$(ANS$,P,1) < "0" OR MID$(ANS$,P,1) > "9"
              THEN LET VALID.SW = 0
6570       LET P = P - 1
6580    WEND
6590    IF VALID.SW = 0
           THEN GOSUB 7500:
                GOSUB 6000          'PRINT MESSAGE AND GET NEW ANSWER
6600 WEND
6610 LET ANS = VAL(ANS$)            'VALID NUMERIC VALUE
6620 RETURN
6630 '
```

```
7000 '****************** RIGHT ANSWER *********************
7010 LOCATE 12,35
7020 PRINT "RIGHT!"
7030 LET NUM2 = NUM2 + 1          'GO ON TO NEXT NUMBER
7040 RETURN
7050 '
7500 '***************** WRONG ANSWER ********************
7510 LOCATE 12,35
7520 PRINT "TRY AGAIN"
7530 RETURN
7540 '
8000 '********* PRINT MESSAGES AT BOTTOM OF SCREEN ************
8010 LOCATE 21,46
8020 PRINT "PRESS ANY KEY TO CONTINUE ..."
8030 LOCATE 23,50
8040 PRINT "PRESS Q TO QUIT ..."
8050 RETURN
8060 '
8500 '*********** CLEAR OUT BOTTOM MESSAGES ******************
8510 LOCATE 21,46
8520 PRINT SPACE$(30)
8530 LOCATE 23,50
8540 PRINT SPACE$(20)
8550 RETURN
8560 '
9000 '****************** SIGN OFF *********************
9010 CLS
9020 LOCATE 10,38
9030 PRINT "GOODBYE"
9040 RETURN
```

Sample Program Output

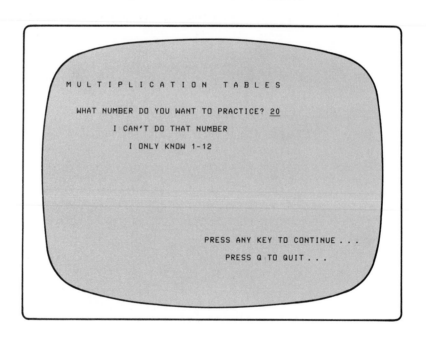

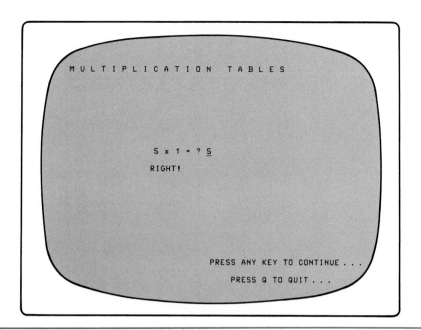

```
M U L T I P L I C A T I O N   T A B L E S




              5 x 1 = ? 5
              RIGHT!




                                    PRESS ANY KEY TO CONTINUE . . .
                                      PRESS Q TO QUIT . . .
```

Summary

1. "Good" programs make it easy for users to enter correct data and difficult for them to make errors.
2. Program output should be in terms that a noncomputer person will understand. Never use computer jargon or program variable names in program output.
3. Format screen output pleasingly, with each item of data in the same location each time it appears.
4. Check input data for validity whenever possible.
5. GIGO means *Garbage In, Garbage Out.* Good validity checking can keep most garbage out of programs.
6. Range checking involves checking high and/or low limits for input values.
7. Many times data input must match preset values such as codes. Input data can be checked to verify that a match is found.
8. Try to shield the user from cryptic system errors such as **REDO FROM START** or **TYPE MISMATCH**. Whenever possible, allow the user to enter any value as a response. Then, have the program trap any errors and print friendly explanations.
9. Many times the value of one field can be compared to another for consistency.
10. A technique used for verifying the validity of ID numbers is called check digit calculation.
11. Ask an inexperienced computer user to test your programs.
12. The CLS statement will clear the screen and place the cursor in the upper left corner.
13. The LOCATE statement is a powerful statement for formatting screen output. The internal print pointer is moved to an absolute row and column position on the screen.
14. LOCATE is generally used just prior to a PRINT statement.
15. Placing program output with the LOCATE statement does not erase the screen. This allows for placing new data intermixed with output previously written.
16. The visibility of the cursor can also be controlled with the LOCATE statement.
17. BASIC has many functions for manipulating string data.
18. Strings may be joined together, or added, in an operation called concatenation.
19. The SPACE$ function returns a string of blank spaces of the specified length.

20. A string of identical characters of any length (up to 255 characters) may be generated with the STRING$ function.
21. The LEN function can be used to determine the length of a string.
22. There are three functions that provide a means to extract a substring from a larger string. These are LEFT$, RIGHT$, and MID$.
23. LEFT$ returns a given number of characters from the left end of a string, while RIGHT$ takes characters from the right end of the string.
24. MID$ provides a way to extract any number of characters from anywhere in the string.
25. The VAL function is used to convert a string into its numeric equivalent. A popular use for VAL is in the editing of input data. Numeric input can be INPUT into strings, validated, and then converted to numeric variables.
26. STR$ converts a numeric expression into a string. STR$ is the opposite operation of VAL.
27. In order to search for the occurrence of one string (called the substring) within another string, the INSTR function is used. INSTR can search for one single character, for a whole word, or for a longer series of characters and spaces.
28. To use the CHR$ function, you must provide an ASCII code number. The function returns the corresponding character.
29. To use the ASC function, you specify a character. The ASC function returns the corresponding ASCII code number. ASC and CHR$ perform opposite operations.
30. There are two functions that provide a way to read the keyboard without requiring the RETURN/ENTER key. These two functions are INKEY$ and INPUT$. Neither function echoes the character on the screen.
31. INKEY$ takes a character from the keyboard buffer without halting program execution. If no character has been pressed, a null string (empty string) is returned. INKEY$ is generally used in a loop to keep checking for a keypress.
32. INPUT$ halts program execution and awaits keyboard entry, similar to the INPUT statement. For INPUT$, the number of characters to return is specified, while INKEY$ always returns one character.
33. The LINE INPUT statement can input any characters, including commas and quotes, into a string variable.
34. The system date and time can be retrieved with the DATE$ and TIME$ functions.

Programming Exercises

7.1. Modify the program in exercise 6.3 (student grade report, p. 157) to request input data from the keyboard, rather than use DATA statements. Verify that student ID, course ID, and number of units are valid numeric digits. The only acceptable values for the letter grade are A, B, C, D, F, I (incomplete), or W (withdrawal). The acceptable range for number of units is .5 to 5.0.

Design test data to verify that all data is correctly validated and that any error messages are cleared from the screen after the data is corrected.

7.2. Modify the program in exercise 6.1 (employee gross pay report, p. 156) to input the number of hours worked. Verify that the number of hours is a valid numeric value. Company policy does not allow working more than 50 hours per week. Verify that the hours do not exceed 50. DATA statements will still be used to enter the employee name, department number, and pay rate. Design test data to verify that all input data is correctly validated and that any error messages are cleared from the screen after the data is corrected.

7.3. Write an interactive program that will count the number of words in a sentence. The user will be prompted to type a sentence terminated by a period (*not* the ENTER key). Use the INPUT$ function to input characters, one at a time, until the period is entered. Each character must be echoed (printed) on the screen. Count the number of words (by checking for a blank character).

When the entire sentence has been entered, print the sentence on the printer along with the word count. Continue inputting and printing sentences until the ENTER key is pressed.

SAMPLE PROGRAM OUTPUT:

```
TYPE A SENTENCE, TERMINATED BY A PERIOD.
     The quick brown fox jumped over the lazy dog's
back and ran after the three little pigs.
WORD COUNT = 17
```

7.4. Modify the program in exercise 7.3 to allow the user to erase a character by pressing the backspace key. (Hint: The backspace key sends CHR$(8) to the program.) To erase a character on the screen, a blank character must be printed.

7.5. Write a program that will find all words in a list beginning with a selected prefix (one or more characters).

INPUT: The user will be prompted to enter the prefix (letter or letters) for which to search. Read the list of words from DATA statements.
OUTPUT: Print the list of words that begin with the requested prefix. At the conclusion of the list, print the count of the words found.
PROCESSING: Count the number of words that begin with the selected prefix. After the count is printed, the user should be given the opportunity to enter a new prefix and to begin the search again.
TEST DATA: List of words for DATA statements.
     ANIMALS, ANT, TAN, AUNT, ANTEATER, BANTER, LANTERN, PLEASANT
PROGRAM EXECUTION: Search for all words beginning with *A*, then search for the words beginning with *ANT*.

7.6. Write a program that will count all occurrences of the letter combination *ON* in a list of words.

INPUT: The list of words will be read from DATA statements.
OUTPUT: A count of the number of times the letters *ON* are found in the list.
PROCESSING: After reading each word, check for all occurrences of the *ON* combination. If the letter combination *ON* appears more than once in a word, it should be counted each time.
TEST DATA: List of words for DATA statements.
     CONVERT, TON, BUN, NOPE, NONE, ONLY, ONE, ONION, AND, MARTIAN, MOON, MOUNTAIN

7.7. Write a program that will count the number of times one particular letter appears in a paragraph. The paragraph may be entered with a LINE INPUT statement. (Recall that the maximum length of a string variable is 255 characters.)

INPUT: Request the paragraph and the search character.
OUTPUT: A count of the number of times the selected letter appears in the paragraph.
TEST DATA: Test your program by counting the number of times the letter *P* appears in this paragraph:
     PETER PIPER PICKED A PECK OF PICKLED PEPPERS. A PECK OF PICKLED PEPPERS, PETER PIPER PICKED. IF PETER PIPER PICKED A PECK OF PICKLED PEPPERS, WHERE'S THE PECK OF PICKLED PEPPERS PETER PIPER PICKED?

7.8. Write a program that will produce the following output by using the LEFT$ function.

```
O
ON
ONO
ONOM
ONOMA
ONOMAT
ONOMATO
ONOMATOP
ONOMATOPO
ONOMATOPOE
ONOMATOPOEI
ONOMATOPOEIA
```

7.9. Write a program using the MID$ and INSTR functions that will print only the last name when you input the first name, middle initial, and the last name.

7.10. Write a program using the STRING$ function to produce the following output. Erase the screen when a key is pressed.

```
**
****
******
********
**********
************
**************
****************
```

7.11. Write a program using the MID$ function to produce the following output.

```
FUSSBUDGET
USSBUDGET
SSBUDGET
SBUDGET
BUDGET
UDGET
DGET
GET
ET
T
```

7.12. Write a program to print all of the characters from CHR$(128) to CHR$(255) on the screen.

7.13. Write a program to check input for a valid password. Use data validation to allow only alphabetic input.

INPUT: A password will be input from the keyboard.
OUTPUT: Print the message "VALID PASSWORD" or "INVALID PASSWORD" on the screen depending on the input.
PROCESS: Use the INPUT$ function to validate input data. Make sure the input word is a valid password from the list.

VALID PASSWORDS

SPUD	KARATE	SHORT
BANANA	WORK	SWEET
HELP	FAST	WORD

7.14. Modify the program in exercise 2.15 (Perfect Picture bonus program, p. 57) to include data validation.

INPUT: The store number, name of employee number 1, name of employee number 2, total hours worked for employee number 1, total hours worked for employee number 2, store's sales goal, and actual sales will be input from the keyboard.

OUTPUT: See exercise 2.15.

PROCESS:
1. Use the INPUT$ function and validate the input.
2. Total hours worked, store's sales goal, and actual sales goal should be validated as numeric fields.
3. Allow for the backspace or back arrow keys to be pressed in order to correct mistakes.

7.15. Write a program that produces a customer account number that consists of the first three digits of the last name, the first two digits of the first name, the zip code, and the last four digits of the address.

INPUT: Customer name, address, city, state, zip code, and phone number will be input from the keyboard.

OUTPUT: The customer name and account number should be printed on the screen with appropriate headings.

PROCESS: All data should be validated.

8 Text Graphics and Music

WIDTH Statement
KEY Statement
COLOR Statement
BEEP Statement
PLAY Statement

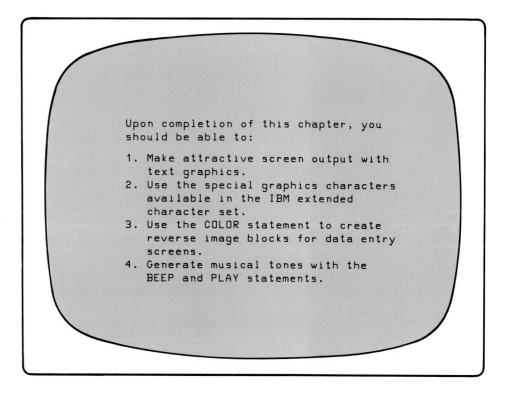

Upon completion of this chapter, you
should be able to:

1. Make attractive screen output with
   text graphics.
2. Use the special graphics characters
   available in the IBM extended
   character set.
3. Use the COLOR statement to create
   reverse image blocks for data entry
   screens.
4. Generate musical tones with the
   BEEP and PLAY statements.

Text Graphics

There is more than one way to draw a picture. In this chapter, we will create graphics with text characters such as letters, digits, and special characters such as % # *] [. We will also use some additional characters called the IBM Extended Graphics Character Set.

Another way to draw pictures is to draw with individual dots (called **pixels**). Pixel graphics are covered in chapter 16.

The Text Screen

Until this point we have used a screen size of twenty-four lines of eighty characters each. But that is not the only choice. The twenty-fifth line on the screen that normally holds the function key definition may be cleared and used for program output with the KEY OFF statement. Note that line twenty-five will not scroll like lines 1–24. Whatever you print on the twenty-fifth line will "stay put," in a manner similar to the function key indications that normally appear.

The number of characters per line is selectable. We may choose to have either the normal eighty characters or forty larger ones. The WIDTH statement controls the number of characters on a line.

Characters may be placed anywhere on the screen with combinations of LOCATE and PRINT statements. You may refer to chapter 7 for a review of the LOCATE statement.

The WIDTH Statement—General Form

```
line number   WIDTH 40
        or
line number   WIDTH 80
```

The WIDTH Statement—Examples

```
100 WIDTH 40 'Change display screen to 40-column mode
200 WIDTH 80 'Change display screen to 80-column mode
```

Simple graphics may be created by printing letters on the screen.

Example Program:
Creating Graphics with Characters

Program Listing

```
100 ' Create graphics with characters
110 '
120 CLS:KEY OFF            'Clean screen
130 WIDTH 40               'Select wide characters
140 PRINT
150 PRINT " H     H  EEEEE  L       L           000   "
160 PRINT " H     H  E      L       L          0   0  "
170 PRINT " HHHHH  EEEE    L       L          0     0 "
180 PRINT " H     H  E      L       L          0   0  "
190 PRINT " H     H  EEEEE  LLLLL  LLLLL       000   "
200 END
```

Program Output

Note: Wide characters appear on the screen, but not on the printer.

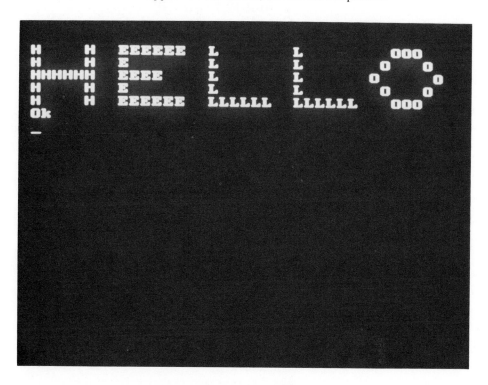

The Extended Graphic Character Set

The standard ASCII character set is made up of 128 characters. Some computer and printer manufacturers have developed their own, nonstandard additions to the ASCII code, to take advantage of special features of the hardware or to create special shapes to be used for foreign language symbols, mathematical symbols, and graphics. The IBM Extended Graphics Character Set, available with Microsoft BASIC, allows for many special shapes to be printed in text mode. See appendix C for a complete list of these special characters. Although the special characters are not on the keyboard, they may be printed by using the CHR$ function.

> *Note:* Not all printers are capable of printing the extended graphics characters. The printer must be dot matrix and support the IBM character set. Some printers have several modes and require a special control code to enable the IBM set. See your printer manual and appendix H for sending control codes.

Sample Graphics Characters

```
100 ' Some of the graphics characters available in text mode
110 PRINT CHR$(191), CHR$(192), CHR$(193), CHR$(247), CHR$(219)
120 PRINT CHR$(194), CHR$(195), CHR$(168), CHR$(224), CHR$(225)
130 PRINT CHR$(3),   CHR$(4),   CHR$(5),   CHR$(6),   CHR$(251)
```

Lines, boxes, and pictures can be drawn using combinations of the graphics characters.

Example Program:
Creating a Box with Graphic Characters

Program Listing

```
100 ' PROGRAM TO DISPLAY A BOX ON THE SCREEN,
110 '    USING SPECIAL GRAPHICS CHARACTERS
120 '
130 '                    PROGRAM VARIABLES
140 '    UPLFT$           UPPER LEFT CORNER
150 '    UPRGT$           UPPER RIGHT CORNER
160 '    LOLFT$           LOWER LEFT CORNER
170 '    LORGT$           LOWER RIGHT CORNER
180 '    VERT$            VERTICAL LINE
190 '    HORIZ$           HORIZONTAL LINE
200 '    MARGIN           DISTANCE TO TAB TO CENTER THE BOX
210 '    LINES            COUNTER FOR HEIGHT OF BOX
220 '
300 '******** INITIALIZE PRINT STRINGS *************************
310 LET UPLFT$ = CHR$(201)
320 LET UPRGT$ = CHR$(187)
330 LET LORGT$ = CHR$(188)
340 LET LOLFT$ = CHR$(200)
350 LET VERT$  = CHR$(186)
360 LET HORIZ$ = CHR$(205)
400 '*************** SET UP BOX SIZE ************************
410 INPUT "Enter width in characters (1-79)"; WIDE
420 INPUT "Enter height in characters"; TALL
430 LET MARGIN = (80 - WIDE)/2
440 WIDTH 80
500 '**************** PRINT THE BOX ***********************
510 CLS
520 PRINT TAB(MARGIN); UPLFT$ + STRING$(WIDE-2,HORIZ$) + UPRGT$
530 LET TALL = TALL - 2      'SUBTRACT FOR TOP AND BOTTOM LINES
540 WHILE TALL > 0
550     PRINT TAB (MARGIN); VERT$ + SPACE$(WIDE-2) + VERT$
560     LET TALL = TALL - 1
570 WEND
580 PRINT TAB(MARGIN); LOLFT$ + STRING$(WIDE-2,HORIZ$) + LORGT$
590 END
```

Program Output

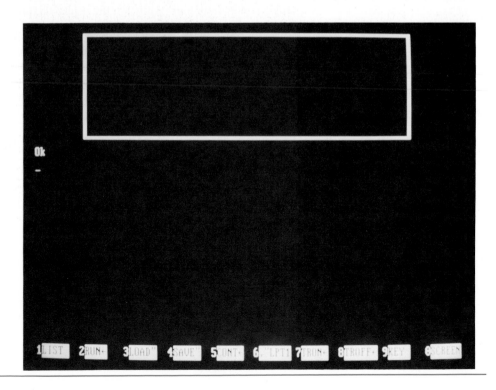

Using Graphics Characters to Draw a Figure

This program uses a selectable graphics character to draw a figure. The shape of the figure is stored in DATA statements, in which each pair of numbers denotes a starting position and number of characters. Note that a screen layout form was used to plan the output.

Example Program:
A Company Logo Drawn with Graphics Characters

Program Listing

```
100 ' Draw a picture with characters
110 '
120 LET PIC$ = CHR$(178)          'Select character to draw with
130 CLS:KEY OFF                    'Clean screen
140 READ START, LENGTH
150 WHILE START <> 0 AND LENGTH <> 0
160    PRINT TAB(START);
170    WHILE LENGTH > 0
180       PRINT PIC$;
190       LET LENGTH = LENGTH - 1
200    WEND
210    READ START, LENGTH
220 WEND
230 '*************** DATA FOR COMPANY LOGO ******************
240 DATA 18,5,17,7,16,3,21,3,14,4,21,26,14,3,21,26,14,4,21,3
250 DATA 40,5,16,7,36,11,18,4,36,5,44,4,36,2,39,2,43,2
260 DATA 46,2,0,0
```

Program Output

Using the Extended Graphics Characters with Function Keys

The functions assigned to the function keys are changeable by the programmer. Any character string up to fifteen characters long may be assigned to each key. Then when the function key is pressed, the corresponding characters are returned, just as if they had been typed at the keyboard. It is often useful to assign the commands most often used to the function keys. But another use presents itself: Characters may be assigned to function keys that cannot usually be typed, since they are not on the keyboard. The following program demonstrates the use of function keys as graphics keys. It only makes us regret that we can define no more than ten keys this way.

Example Program:
Using the Function Keys for Graphics Symbols

Program Listing

```
100 '
110 ' Program to assign special graphics symbols to the
120 ' function keys. This provides an easy way to include
130 ' graphics symbols in programs.
140 '
150 ' Run this program, and watch the key definition at the
160 ' bottom of the screen change. Then, whenever you would
170 ' like to include the graphic symbol, press the corre-
180 ' sponding function key. The symbols may be included in
190 ' REMarks (like these), screen or printer output (if your
200 ' printer supports the character set), or anywhere a
210 ' string constant is appropriate. Of course, you may
220 ' select any characters you wish from the 255 possible.
230 '
240 KEY 1, CHR$(201)              'BOX UPPER LEFT CORNER
250 KEY 2, CHR$(200)              'BOX LOWER LEFT CORNER
260 KEY 3, CHR$(187)              'BOX UPPER RIGHT CORNER
270 KEY 4, CHR$(188)              'BOX LOWER RIGHT CORNER
280 KEY 5, CHR$(186)              'BOX VERTICAL LINES
290 KEY 6, CHR$(205)              'BOX HORIZONTAL LINES
300 KEY 7, CHR$(228)              'GREEK SYMBOL
310 KEY 8, CHR$(241)              'PLUS OR MINUS SIGN
320 KEY 9, CHR$(227)              'PI
330 KEY 10, CHR$(171)             'ONE HALF
340 NEW                           'CLEAR PROGRAM FROM MEMORY
```

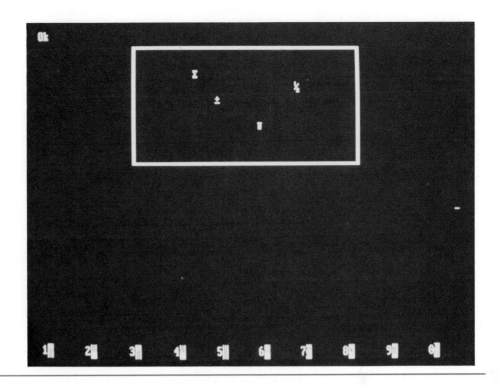

The KEY Statement—General Form

```
line number   KEY OFF
line number   KEY ON
line number   KEY keynumber, "character string"
              KEY LIST
```

The KEY Statement—Examples

```
100   KEY OFF                    'Turn off display of function keys
200   KEY ON                     'Turn on display of function keys
300   KEY 1,"LIST"               'Assign LIST command to Key One
400   KEY 2,"RUN"+CHR$(13)       'Assign RUN + Carriage Return
                                  to Key Two
500   KEY 3,CHR$(219)            'Assign block graphic character
                                  to Key Three
KEY LIST                         'Display a listing of current Function
                                  key assignments
```

Note that the KEY statement may have line numbers and be executed during the program run, or may be issued from command mode. Each key may have up to fifteen characters assigned to it, but only the first six will display on the function definition line (line 25). Even though the display may be turned off (KEY OFF), the function keys are still available for use.

A Bar Chart Program, Drawn with Graphic Characters
This simplified Bar Chart program demonstrates the use of graphic characters to make solid bars. A more comprehensive version, including scaling and colored bars is found in Chapter 16.

Example Program:
A Bar Chart Using Text Graphics

Program Listing

```
100 '   Program to print a bar chart, using graphic text
        characters
110 '
120 '                    Program Variables
130 '   PIC$             Character used to print bars for chart
140 '   MONTH$           Names of months, from DATA list
150 '   HOWMANY          Number of hamburgers sold for each month
160 '   COUNT            Counter for loop
190 '
500 '********************** MAINLINE ************************
510 LET PIC$ = CHR$(219)          'SELECT PRINT CHARACTER
520 GOSUB 600                     'PRINT HEADING
530 GOSUB 700                     'PRINT DETAIL DATA
540 GOSUB 900                     'PRINT SCALE
550 END
600 '****************** PRINT HEADING ********************
610 CLS
620 LOCATE 4,25: PRINT "HAMBURGER SALES"
630 PRINT:PRINT:PRINT
640 RETURN
700 '**************** PRINT A BAR CHART ******************
710 READ MONTH$, HOWMANY
720 WHILE MONTH$ <> "END"
730    PRINT MONTH$; TAB(10)              'MONTH NAME
740    LET COUNT = 1
750    WHILE COUNT <= HOWMANY
760       PRINT PIC$;                     'PRINT THE BAR
770       LET COUNT = COUNT + 1
780    WEND
790    PRINT:PRINT
800    READ MONTH$, HOWMANY
810 WEND
820 RETURN
830 '
1000 '******************** PRINT SCALE ********************
1010 PRINT TAB(9);CHR$(179);                'START SCALE LINE
1020 LET COUNT = 1
1030 WHILE COUNT <= 14
1040    PRINT STRING$(4,196);CHR$(179);  'SEGMENTS OF LINE
1050    LET COUNT = COUNT + 1
1060 WEND
1070 PRINT TAB(5);
1080 LET COUNT = 0
1090 WHILE COUNT <= 70
1100    PRINT USING "   ##"; COUNT;       'PRINT NUMBERS
1110    LET COUNT = COUNT + 5
1120 WEND
1130 RETURN
1140 '
1150 '***************** DATA FOR HAMBURGER SALES **************
1160 '* Caution: numbers must be < 72 in this program.
1170 '*Scaling to graph variable size data appears in chapter 16
1180 DATA JUNE,40,JULY,70,AUGUST,55,SEPTEMBER,30,END,0
1190 '***************** END OF DATA ************************
```

Program Output

Color for Black-and-White Monitors

Although a black-and-white monitor cannot display in color, it can use the COLOR statement to control reverse image (black characters on a white background), underlined characters, high intensity, and invisible text (black on black). Not all display adapters and monitors respond in the same way to these statements. Try this program on yours.

Note: Color graphics are covered in chapter 16.

Example Program:
Color in Black and White

Program Listing

```
200 ' Demonstrate use of COLOR statement for B&W monitors
210 CLS
220 COLOR 0,7              'REVERSE IMAGE
230 PRINT "THIS IS REVERSE IMAGE"
240 COLOR 15,0             'HIGH INTENSITY
250 PRINT "THIS IS HIGH INTENSITY"
260 COLOR 1,0              'UNDERLINE
270 PRINT "THIS TEXT IS UNDERLINED"
280 COLOR 23,0             'BLINKING
290 PRINT "THIS IS A BLINKING LINE"
300 COLOR 31,0             'BLINKING HIGH INTENSITY
310 PRINT "THIS BLINKING LINE IS HIGH INTENSITY"
320 COLOR 7,0              'NORMAL WHITE ON BLACK
330 PRINT "ENTER YOUR PASSWORD ";
340 COLOR 0,0              'INVISIBLE
350 INPUT PASSWORD$
360 COLOR 7,0              'BACK TO NORMAL WHITE ON BLACK
370 PRINT PASSWORD$
380 END
```

Example Program:
Using Reverse Image Blocks for Data Entry

Program Output

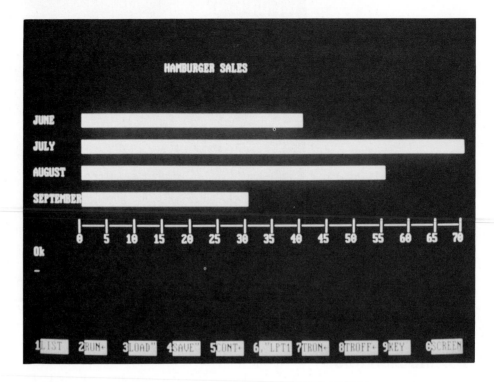

**Reverse Image
for Data Entry**

When a user enters data into a screen, it is important to make the process as clear and easy as possible. One technique used for professional programs is to place a block on the screen where data is to be typed. This gives a clear indication of the location and length of required data. Printing spaces in reverse image gives a good-looking data entry block. In the example program segment that follows, note the technique used when the backspace key is pressed by the user.

Program Listing

```
100 ' Use reverse image for data entry areas
110 '        Uses COLOR statement on monochrome monitors
120 '
130 '*********** PRINT DATA ENTRY FORM *************************
140 CLS: KEY OFF                         'CLEAN SCREEN
150 LOCATE 10,20: PRINT "Name:"
160 LOCATE 12,20: PRINT "Telephone:"
170 COLOR 0,7                            'TURN ON REVERSE IMAGE
180 LOCATE 10,40: PRINT SPACE$(20);      'PRINT A BAR FOR NAME
190 LOCATE 12,40: PRINT SPACE$(15);      'PRINT A BAR FOR TELEPHONE
200 '************* INPUT NAME ***********************************
210 LOCATE 10,40,1                       'PLACE CURSOR FOR ENTRY
220 LET NAM$ = ""
230 LET IN$ = INPUT$(1)                  'GET ONE CHARACTER
240 WHILE IN$ <> CHR$(13)                'CHECK FOR RETURN KEY
250    IF IN$ <> CHR$(8)
          THEN GOSUB 300                 ,HANDLE GOOD CHARACTER
          ELSE GOSUB 400                 'HANDLE BACKSPACE CHARACTER
260    LET IN$ = INPUT$(1)               'GET ONE CHARACTER
270 WEND
280 COLOR 7,0                            'RETURN TO NORMAL PRINT
290 END
300 '**************** GOOD CHARACTER ****************************
310 PRINT IN$;                           'ECHO CHARACTER ON SCREEN
320 LET NAM$ = NAM$ + IN$                'TACK ONTO LONG STRING
330 RETURN
400 '**************** BACKSPACE CHARACTER ENTERED **************
410 LET NAM$ = LEFT$(NAM$, LEN(NAM$)-1)  'REMOVE ONE CHARACTER
420 PRINT CHR$(29);                      'MOVE CURSOR BACK
430 PRINT " ";                           'PRINT A SPACE
440 PRINT CHR$(29);                      'REPLACE CURSOR
450 RETURN
```

Program Output

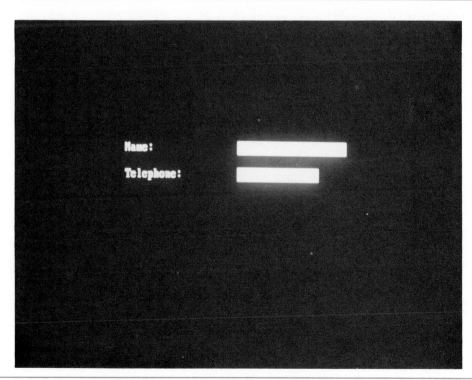

Music

There are several statements available to make sounds. You may use the BEEP statement, which does just as the name implies. Or you may use more sophisticated statements like SOUND, PLAY, or ON PLAY to create more elaborate sounds. Music may be played in the background (at the same time other statements are executing) or in the foreground (completing execution before any other statements are executed). In this chapter we will cover only BEEP and some functions of PLAY. Consult the BASIC manual for more functions.

The BEEP Statement—General Form

```
line number   BEEP
```

The BEEP Statement—Examples

```
100   BEEP                  'Beep the speaker
110   PRINT CHR$(7);        'Exactly same effect as BEEP
200   IF VALID.SW <> 1
         THEN BEEP          'Beep on invalid data
```

You may select actual notes to play with the PLAY statement. Note that PLAY is an option of the advanced version of BASIC, so you will need either BASICA or GWBASIC.

The PLAY Statement—General Form

```
line number   PLAY string
```

The PLAY statement takes its instructions from the characters included in the string, which may be a literal or variable. The choices for this "tune definition language" are shown in figure 8.1.

Figure 8.1
Tune definition for the PLAY statement.

Tune Definition Language for the PLAY Statement

A to G, with optional ♯ , +, or −
   Plays the indicated note. A sharp is indicated by ♯ or
   +, a flat by −.

O n
   Changes octave for the notes that follow. There are 7 octaves, numbered 0 to 6.
   The default is Octave 4. Octave 3 begins with middle C.

L n
   Sets the length for the notes that follow.
   L1 Whole note
   L2 Half note
   L4 Quarter note (the default)
   L8 Eighth note

P n
   Pause (rest). The pause lengths are similar to the note lengths shown above.

T n
   Sets the number of quarter notes in a minute, which may range from 32 to 255,
   with default of 120.

MF
   Plays music in the foreground (the default). This means that no other statements
   will be executed until the music is finished.

MB
   Music plays in the background, during execution of other statements. The notes
   (up to 32) are placed in a buffer, and program execution continues.

N n
   Plays a specific note, where n may range from 0 to 84. This is an alternate way of
   selecting a note, rather than its octave (O n) and letter designation (A–G). Zero
   represents a "rest," and the notes 1 to 84 select the possible notes in 7 octaves.

The PLAY Statement—Examples

```
100 PLAY "O3 CDEFGAB O4 C"        'Scale in octave 3,
                                    ending with C of octave 4
200 PLAY "MB O2 GFE-FGGG"         'Mary Had a Little Lamb
300 PLAY "C C+ D D+ E F F+ G G+ A A+ B"  'All notes in the
                                    fourth octave
400 PLAY "L2 N40 L1 N42"          'Note 40 as a half-note,
                                    note 42 as a whole-note
```

Feedback

1. How can you determine whether your printer is capable of printing the graphics characters?
2. How can the COLOR statement be used on a black-and-white monitor?
3. Why would it be unwise to draw a pie chart with text graphics?

Summary

1. Graphics may be created with text characters printed on the screen or printer.
2. The WIDTH statement can select either 40 or 80 characters per line on the screen.
3. There is a set of 128 graphics characters that may be displayed on the screen, as well as on some printers. Since these characters are not on the keyboard, they must be specified using the CHR$ function.
4. The KEY statement can be used to change the keystrokes associated with each of the ten function keys.
5. Black-and-white monitors are capable of displaying characters in reverse image, blinking, and high-intensity. These functions are controlled with the COLOR statement.
6. BEEP sounds the computer's speaker.
7. Musical notes are played with the PLAY statement. A special "tune definition language" defines the notes to play.

Programming Exercises

8.1. Draw the word "CUTE" on the screen using the WIDTH and PRINT statements.

8.2. Using any graphic character you wish, draw a square on the screen.

8.3. Write a program to print ten graphic characters on the screen and beep after each one has been printed.

8.4. Use the PLAY statement to write a program to play all the notes in the third octave.

8.5. Write a program to create an input screen for the calculation of the markup on an item.

INPUT: Item description, retail selling price, and the cost of the item will be input from the keyboard. Use reverse image for the input fields.
OUTPUT: The item description, retail selling price, cost of the item, and the markup should be printed on the printer.
PROCESS:
   1. Calculate markup = retail selling price − cost.

8.6. Write a program to create an input screen for the calculation of markup based on cost and the percentage of markup based on selling price.

INPUT: Item description, cost of item, and percentage of cost to be marked up will be input from the keyboard.

OUTPUT: Print the item description, cost of the item, percentage it was marked up, the amount of markup, and the selling price on the printer.

PROCESS:
1. Use reverse image for the input fields.
2. Markup = percent * cost.
3. Selling price = cost + markup.
4. Markup as a percent of selling price = markup / selling price.

8.7. Write a program to create a bar chart that represents the demand of refrigeration units (in thousands) per quarter. The x-axis will indicate year-quarters for three years (e.g., Year 1, Quarter 1, Quarter 2, Quarter 3, Quarter 4; Year 2, Quarter 1, etc.). The y-axis will be the number of refrigeration units in demand in thousands. The y-axis will increase by 20,000 each step and go from 0 to 200.

Read the demand for each of four quarters for three years, and plot the values.

8.8. Draw a picture of the American flag, without stars, on the screen.

8.9. Write a program using the PLAY statement to play one of your favorite songs. While the song is playing, the title of the song, the composer, the year it was written, and the words to the song should be printed on the screen.

8.10. Modify the program in exercise 7.1 (student grade report, p. 202) to use reverse image for the data input fields on the screen. Allow entry of the backspace key to correct errors.

8.11. Modify the program in exercise 7.2 (employee gross pay report, p. 202) to use reverse image for the data input fields on the screen. Allow entry of the backspace key to correct errors.

9 Menus

ON...GOSUB Statement

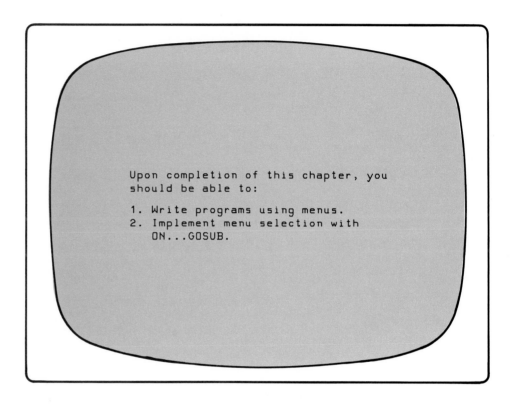

Upon completion of this chapter, you should be able to:

1. Write programs using menus.
2. Implement menu selection with ON...GOSUB.

Menu-Based Programs

An increasingly popular technique for interactive programs is the **menu.** Whenever the user has a choice to make, a menu is usually the best way to present the options available. Menus can be presented at any level of the program. In fact, many well-organized programs present successively lower levels of menus. Examples of menus abound in word processing programs, data base processing, and operating systems software, to name a few.

Top Level Menu

```
          MENU

     1. APPETIZERS
     2. SALADS
     3. MAIN COURSES
     4. VEGETABLES
     5. DESSERTS

     ENTER CHOICE 3
```

Second Level Menu (After 3—MAIN COURSES chosen on above menu)

```
        MAIN COURSE MENU

     1. SEAFOOD
     2. CHICKEN DISHES
     3. MEATS
     4. VEGETARIAN DISHES

     ENTER CHOICE 2
```

Third Level Menu (After 2—CHICKEN DISHES chosen on second level)

```
        CHICKEN DISH MENU

     1. CHICKEN AND DUMPLINGS
     2. FRIED CHICKEN
     3. ROASTED CHICKEN
     4. CASHEW CHICKEN
     5. CHICKEN RIPPLE ICE CREAM

     ENTER CHOICE _
```

Menus can provide the user with many choices. The options can become more narrow on each level, until an exact match is made. Printing a menu is a straightforward task. Any combination of the print formatting statements may be used, such as LOCATE, TAB, SPC.

Plan the menu to be user-friendly. Always arrange the menu screen to be pleasing to view, centered on the screen, with plenty of blank space. Too many choices can be confusing. When there are many options, it is far better to break the choices into groups and to present smaller menus.

Example Program: Printing a Menu Using TABs

Program Listing

```
500 '******** PRINT A MENU USING TABS ***************
510 CLS
520 PRINT TAB(35) "PRINT MENU"
530 PRINT:PRINT:PRINT:PRINT
540 PRINT TAB(27) "1. PRINT OUTPUT ON SCREEN"
550 PRINT
560 PRINT TAB(27) "2. PRINT OUTPUT ON PRINTER"
570 PRINT
580 PRINT TAB(27) "3. QUIT"
590 PRINT:PRINT:PRINT
600 PRINT TAB(22) "ENTER CHOICE (1-3)";
610 INPUT CHOICE
620 RETURN
```

Example Program: Printing a Menu Using LOCATE

Program Listing

```
500 '******** PRINT A MENU USING LOCATE ************
510 CLS
515 LOCATE 5,35
520 PRINT "PRINT MENU"
530 LOCATE 10,27
540 PRINT "1. PRINT OUTPUT ON SCREEN"
550 LOCATE 12,27
560 PRINT "2. PRINT OUTPUT ON PRINTER"
570 LOCATE 14,27
580 PRINT "3. QUIT"
590 LOCATE 18,22
600 PRINT "ENTER CHOICE (1-3)";
610 INPUT CHOICE
620 RETURN
```

Sample Program Output

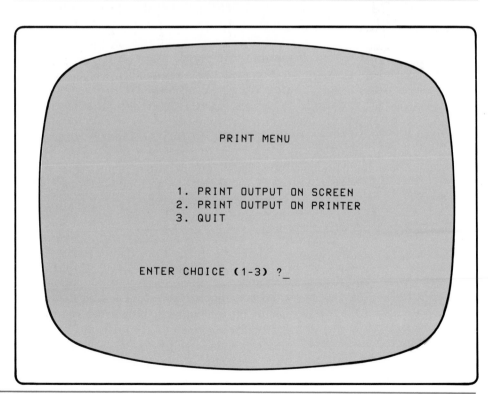

After displaying the menu and inputting the choice, the program must execute the correct subroutine. This could be accomplished with IF statements.

```
200   GOSUB 500          'DISPLAY MENU
210   IF CHOICE = 1
         THEN GOSUB 1000
220   IF CHOICE = 2
         THEN GOSUB 2000
230   IF CHOICE = 3
         THEN GOSUB 3000
```

However, BASIC provides an ideal statement for implementing the selection process—the ON . . . GOSUB.

```
200 GOSUB 500           'DISPLAY MENU
210 ON CHOICE GOSUB 1000, 2000, 3000
```

ON...GOSUB

The ON...GOSUB statement will execute one of several different subroutines, depending on the value of the variable named. In the example above, if the current value of the variable CHOICE is 1, then the subroutine at line 1000 will be executed. If CHOICE = 2, then the subroutine at line 2000 will be executed. When CHOICE = 3, the subroutine at line 3000 will be executed. If CHOICE contains 0 or any rounded value larger than 3, none of the subroutines will be executed, and execution will "fall through" to the next statement following the ON...GOSUB.

The ON...GOSUB Statement—General Form

line number ON numeric expression GOSUB list of line numbers

The numeric expression is used to determine which subroutine to execute. For example, if the value of the expression is 5, then execution will branch to the fifth line number in the list. If the value of the expression is 10, then the tenth subroutine named will be executed.

The numeric expression should be an integer in the range 0–255. BASIC will round the expression, if necessary. If the rounded value of the numeric expression is zero or greater than the number of lines listed, BASIC will proceed to the next statement following the ON...GOSUB. When the value is negative or greater than 255, an ILLEGAL FUNCTION CALL message will be printed.

The ON...GOSUB Statement—Examples

```
500   ON N GOSUB 1000, 2000, 1000, 1000, 2000
600   ON VAL(CHOICE$) GOSUB 2000, 4000, 3000, 5000, 6000,
      7000, 9000, 9000, 9000
700   ON R/2 GOSUB 1200, 1400
```

In each of these examples, the numeric expression will be evaluated. Then, if the value is 1, the first subroutine named will be executed. If the value is 2, the second subroutine named will be executed. In line 600, if the value of CHOICE$ is 6, control will pass to the sixth statement number in the list (7000). When the RETURN statement in the subroutine is encountered, control will pass back to the statement immediately following the ON...GOSUB. Figure 9.1 shows a flowchart of the logic of the ON...GOSUB.

Figure 9.1
Flowchart of ON . . . GOSUB.
One subroutine will be executed
depending on the value of the
arithmetic expression.

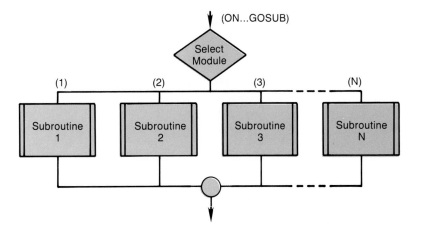

Figure 9.2
Hierarchy chart of a menu
program.

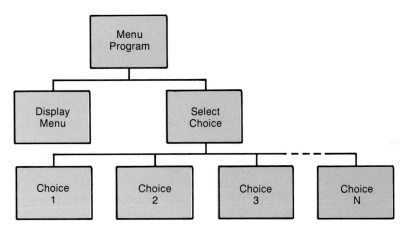

Writing a Menu Program

The top level of a menu program will display the menu and select the correct subroutine to execute. (See the hierarchy chart of a menu program in figure 9.2.) Each time one of the subroutines is completed, the menu should be redisplayed. The menu display and selection must therefore be placed in a loop.

```
100    '******* MAINLINE OF A MENU PROGRAM *************
110    LET CHOICE = 0
120    WHILE CHOICE <> 5          '5 IS ENDING VALUE
130        GOSUB 1000            'PRINT MENU & INPUT CHOICE
140        ON CHOICE GOSUB 2000, 4000, 6000, 8000
150    WEND
160    PRINT "END OF PROGRAM"
170    END
```

Feedback

1. What do you think is the most common use for the ON...GOSUB statement?
2. `10 ON C GOSUB 100, 50, 625, 400`
   When this statement is executed, what will happen if C has a value of 3? Of 0? Of 5? Of −1?
3. When using the ON...GOSUB statement, where do the RETURN statements belong?
4. When a RETURN statement is encountered after execution of an ON...GOSUB, to what location does execution return?

A Simple Menu Program

As an example of a simple menu program, a series of choices will be given to display price lists for various services.

Top Level Menu:

1. Haircuts
2. Perms
3. Hair color
4. Manicures
5. Quit

Output

Screens showing four different classes of services: Haircuts, perms, hair coloring, and manicures

Input

Number for selection of desired price list

Pseudocode

1. Loop until "Quit" chosen
   1.1 Display menu and input selection
   1.2 Execute corresponding subroutine to print list
2. Stop

*** Subroutines for each choice ***

1. Clear the screen
2. Print the title
3. Print the price list
4. Hold for a keypress
5. Return

Hierarchy Chart

Refer to figure 9.3 for the hierarchy chart.

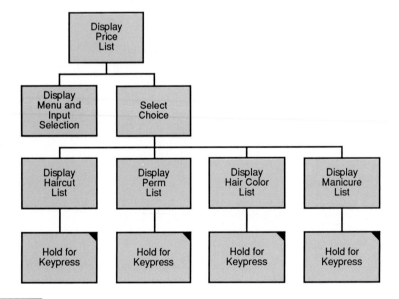

Figure 9.3
Hierarchy chart for a menu program. The symbols with shaded corners indicate that the module is shared.

Flowchart   Refer to figure 9.4 for the flowchart.

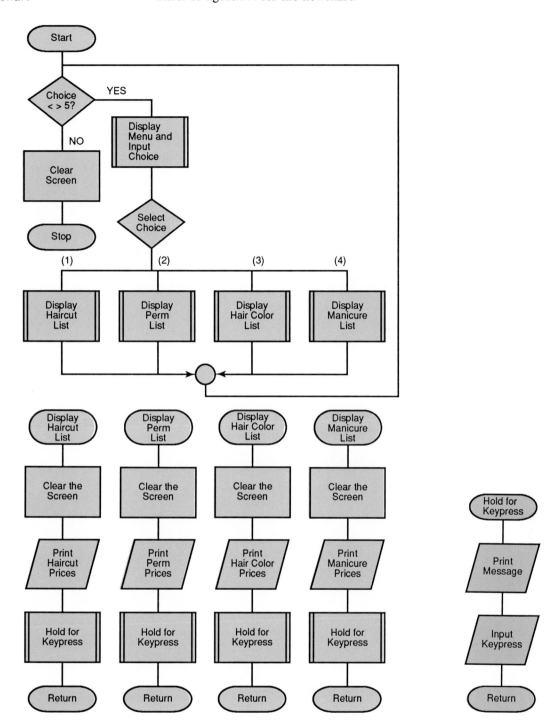

Figure 9.4
Flowchart for a price list menu
program.

```
100 '       SIMPLE MENU PROGRAM
110 '       Program will display a menu, and display one of four
120 '       price lists, depending on the selection made by the user
130 '
140 '              Program Variables
150 '
160 '    CHOICE$        Menu selection in string form
170 '    CHOICE         Menu selection in numeric form
180 '    DUMMY$         Holds keystroke from "Press any key"
190 '
200 ' ***************** Program Mainline ******************
210 '
220 WHILE CHOICE <> 5  'Check for Quit option
230     GOSUB 500           'Display menu and input selection
240     ON CHOICE GOSUB 1000, 2000, 3000, 4000
250 WEND
260 CLS
270 END
280 '
500 '***********Display Menu and Input Selection ************
510 '
520 CLS
530 PRINT
540 PRINT
550 PRINT TAB(33); "SALLY'S SALON"
560 PRINT
570 PRINT TAB(35); "Price List"
580 PRINT
590 PRINT
600 PRINT TAB(33); "1.  Haircuts"
610 PRINT
620 PRINT TAB(33); "2.  Perms"
630 PRINT
640 PRINT TAB(33); "3.  Hair color"
650 PRINT
660 PRINT TAB(33); "4.  Manicures"
670 PRINT
680 PRINT TAB(33); "5.  Quit"
690 PRINT
700 PRINT
710 PRINT
720 PRINT TAB(30); "Enter your choice ";
730 INPUT "", CHOICE$              'Input into string
740 LET CHOICE = VAL(CHOICE$)      'Convert to numeric
750 RETURN
760 '
```

```
1000 '****************** Haircuts ******************
1010 '
1020 CLS
1030 PRINT
1040 PRINT
1050 PRINT TAB(28); "SALLY'S SUPER HAIRCUTS"
1060 PRINT
1070 PRINT
1080 PRINT TAB(30); "Short hair:   $10.00"
1090 PRINT
1100 PRINT TAB(30); "Long hair:    $15.00"
1110 PRINT
1120 PRINT TAB(30); "No hair:      $20.00"
1130 GOSUB 5000                      'Hold for a keypress
1140 RETURN
1150 '
2000 '******************* Perms ********************
2010 CLS
2020 PRINT
2030 PRINT
2040 PRINT TAB(31); "SALLY'S SUPER PERMS"
2050 PRINT
2060 PRINT
2070 PRINT TAB(30); "Super curly:   $40.00"
2080 PRINT
2090 PRINT TAB(30); "Medium curly:  $50.00"
2100 PRINT
2110 PRINT TAB(30); "No curls:      $60.00"
2120 GOSUB 5000                       'Hold for a keypress
2130 RETURN
2140 '
3000 '******************** Hair Color ************************
3010 '
3020 CLS
3030 PRINT
3040 PRINT
3050 PRINT TAB(29); "SALLY'S SUPER COLORS"
3060 PRINT
3070 PRINT
3080 PRINT TAB(30); "Blond:        $20.00"
3090 PRINT
3100 PRINT TAB(30); "Brunette:     $25.00"
3110 PRINT
3120 PRINT TAB(30); "Redhead:      $30.00"
3130 GOSUB 5000                          'Hold for a keypress
3140 RETURN
3150 '
```

```
4000 '******************** Manicures ********************
4010 '
4020 CLS
4030 PRINT
4040 PRINT
4050 PRINT TAB(28); "SALLY'S SUPER MANICURES"
4060 PRINT
4070 PRINT
4080 PRINT TAB(30); "Manicure:    $5.00"
4090 PRINT
4100 PRINT TAB(30); "Polish:     $5.00"
4110 PRINT
4120 PRINT TAB(30); "Pedicure:   $10.00"
4130 GOSUB 5000                        'Hold for a keypress
4140 RETURN
4150 '
5000 '************* Hold for a keypress *************
5010 '
5020 LOCATE 22,20
5030 PRINT "Press any key to continue . . ."
5040 LET DUMMY$ = INPUT$(1)
5050 RETURN
```

Sample Program Output

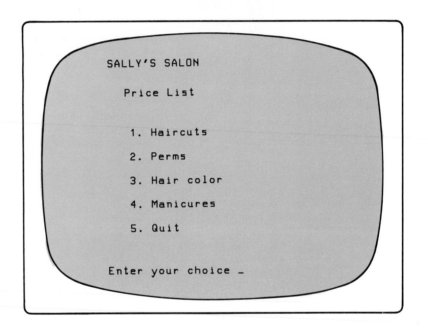

```
SALLY'S SALON

   Price List


      1. Haircuts

      2. Perms

      3. Hair color

      4. Manicures

      5. Quit


   Enter your choice _
```

```
        SALLY'S SUPER HAIRCUTS


     Short hair:  $10.00

     Long hair:  $15.00

     No hair:     $20.00


Press any key to continue . . .
```

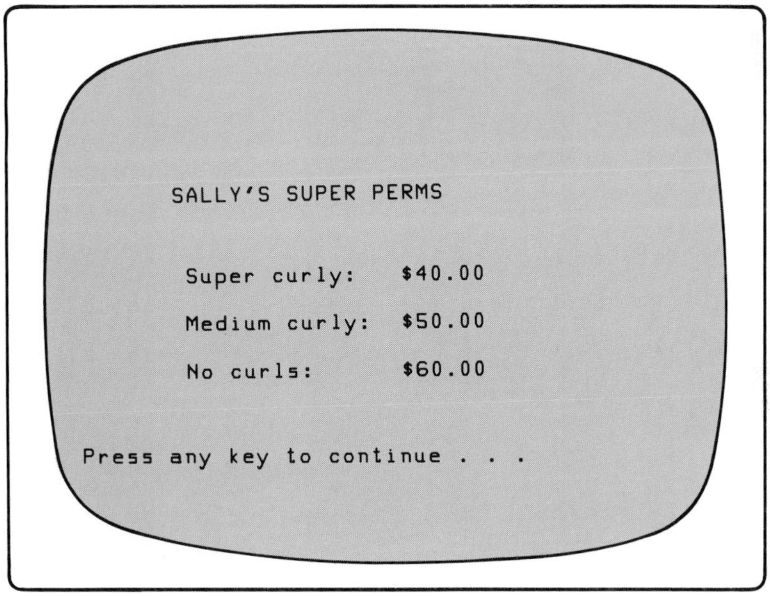

```
        SALLY'S SUPER PERMS


    Super curly:   $40.00

    Medium curly:  $50.00

    No curls:      $60.00


Press any key to continue . . .
```

```
SALLY'S SUPER COLORS


    Blond:      $20.00

    Brunette:   $25.00

    Redhead:    $30.00


Press any key to continue . . .
```

```
SALLY'S SUPER MANICURES


    Manicure:      $5.00

    Polish:        $5.00

    Pedicure:     $10.00

Press any key to continue . . .
```

Another Approach to Menus—The INSTR Function

Sometimes menu selections are made with letters rather than numbers. In this menu, the user responds by entering the first character of the chosen item. Note that the only acceptable responses are N, P, S, or Q.

```
SELECTION MENU


N)AMES ONLY
P)HONE NUMBERS
S)ELECTIVE LIST
Q)UIT

SELECTION?_
```

Executing the correct subroutine may be done in one of two ways. Certainly a series of IF statements will work.

```
200  IF SEL$ = "N"
         THEN GOSUB 5000
210  IF SEL$ = "P"
         THEN GOSUB 6000
220  IF SEL$ = "S"
         THEN GOSUB 7000
```

However, a combination of the INSTR function and the ON...GOSUB can be used for a slick solution.

Recall that INSTR(ST$,SUBST$) searches the primary string (first string named) for the occurrence of the substring (second string named). The value returned is the *numeric* position where the substring is found. This numeric value could be used for the ON...GOSUB if it could be arranged that the first character in the primary string was the first item on the menu. The second character in the primary string would be the second item on the menu, and so on.

```
100   LET ST$ = "NPSQ"
::
::
200   INPUT SEL$
::
::
400   ON INSTR(ST$,SEL$) GOSUB 5000, 6000, 7000, 8000
```

When SEL$ = "S" then INSTR(ST$,SEL$) = 3—since *S* is the third letter in ST$. The third line number named—7000—will be used for the GOSUB.

What if the user enters an invalid response, and the substring is not found in the primary string? Recall that in this case, INSTR returns the value zero. The ON...GOSUB then will *not* execute any subroutine. The statement immediately following the ON...GOSUB will be executed. When reading the sample program following, be sure to determine what will occur if the user enters an invalid response.

One more point should be noted. Generally a program will not execute a subroutine for the final choice on the menu (QUIT or STOP). The termination choice is used to end the program execution from the mainline. In the example shown, the Q (QUIT) option has been omitted from the primary string.

Example Program:
Menu Selection Using Alphabetic Characters

Program Listing

```
1000 ' PROGRAM FRAMEWORK FOR MENU SELECTION USING ALPHABETIC
1010 '    CHARACTERS FOR THE SELECTION
1020 '
1030 '          SEL$     MENU SELECTION (FROM KEYBOARD)
1040 '          ST$      SELECTION STRING, TO HOLD THE FIRST
1050 '                   CHARACTER OF EACH MENU CHOICE
1060 '
2000 '***************** MAIN PROGRAM *************************
2010 GOSUB 3000                    'INITIALIZE SELECTION STRINGS
2020 WHILE SEL$ <> "Q"
2030     GOSUB 4000                'PRINT MENU
2040     ON INSTR(ST$,SEL$) GOSUB 5000,6000,7000
2050 WEND
2060 END
3000 '*************** INITIALIZE *****************************
3010 LET SEL$ = "GO"
3020 LET ST$ = "NPS"                   'THREE MENU CHOICES, OTHER THAN
                                        QUIT
3030 RETURN
3040 '
4000 '***************** PRINT MENU ***********************
4010 CLS
4020 LOCATE 5,30
4030 PRINT "SELECTION MENU"
4040 LOCATE 10,31
4050 PRINT "N)AMES ONLY"
4060 LOCATE 12,31
4070 PRINT "P)HONE NUMBERS"
4080 LOCATE 14,31
4090 PRINT "S)ELECTIVE LIST"
4100 LOCATE 16,31
4110 PRINT "Q)UIT"
4120 LOCATE 20,31
4130 INPUT "SELECTION"; SEL$
4140 RETURN
4150 '
5000 '************* STUB MODULE FOR NAMES ONLY **************
5010 PRINT "NAMES ONLY "
5020 LET X$ = INPUT$(1)          'HOLD FOR KEYPRESS
5030 RETURN
5040 '
6000 '************* STUB MODULE FOR PHONE NUMBERS ***********
6010 PRINT "PHONE NUMBERS "
6020 LET X$ = INPUT$(1)          'HOLD FOR KEYPRESS
6030 RETURN
6040 '
7000 '************* STUB MODULE FOR SELECTIVE LIST **********
7010 PRINT "SELECTIVE LIST"
7020 LET X$ = INPUT$(1)          'HOLD FOR KEYPRESS
7030 RETURN
```

Programming Example:
Menu for Personal Telephone Listing

A program is needed to keep personal telephone numbers. On demand, it must be able to print the list on the screen or the printer. A useful feature would allow the user to specify the area code, then print only those matching.

In the interest of brevity, the example program has been written with only those options named. Many other useful features quickly come to mind and are left for the programmer to add as further enhancements. Possible additions include selection by name—perhaps by the first letter of the name. As the size of the list grows, you will need to add multiple page breaks. A long list printed on the screen would scroll by too quickly to be read, so a good technique is to print one full screen of data and request the user to PRESS ANY KEY TO CONTINUE. This allows time to read the first set before continuing.

Output

1. Complete list on the screen
2. Selective list (one area code) on the screen
3. Complete list on the printer
4. Selective list (one area code) on the printer

Input

1. List of names and phone numbers (in DATA statements)
2. Selection—screen or printer
3. Selection—"all" or area code

Pseudocode

1. Initialize variables
2. Loop until "QUIT" Chosen
    2.1   Display menu
    2.2   Input and validate choice
    2.3   Execute correct subroutine
        2.3.1   Print list on screen
        2.3.2   Print list on printer
3. Stop

** PRINT LIST ON SCREEN SUBROUTINE **

1. Allow choice of area code or all
    1.1   Input area code
    1.2   Validate
2. Print headings
3. Priming read—name
4. Loop until name = "END"
    4.1   Read phone number
    4.2   If match on area code or all chosen then print detail line
    4.3   Read next name
5. Hold screen output until a key is pressed
6. Return

Hierarchy Chart   Refer to figure 9.5 for the chart.

Flowchart   Refer to figure 9.6 (pp. 237–38) for the flowchart.

Printer Spacing Chart   Refer to figure 9.7 (pp. 239–42).
and Screen Layouts

Figure 9.5
Hierarchy chart for personal
telephone listing program.

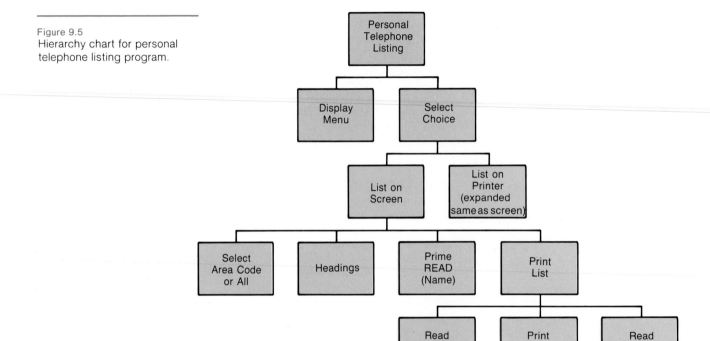

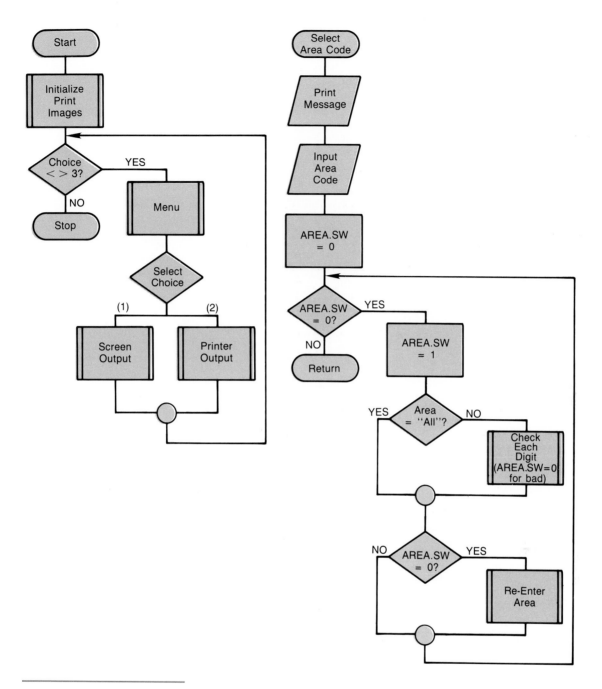

Figure 9.6
Flowchart for personal
telephone listing program.

Figure 9.6—*Continued*

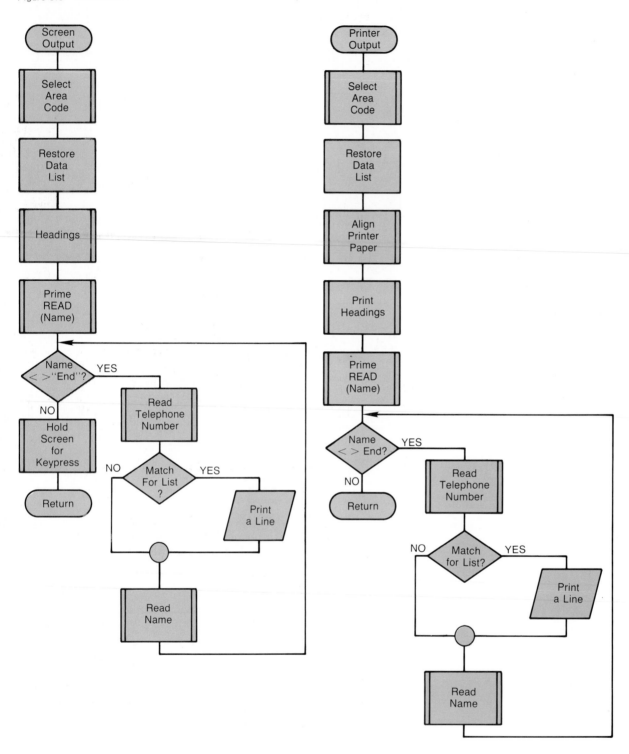

Figure 9.7
Screen and printer layouts for
personal telephone listing
program.

Figure 9.7—*Continued*

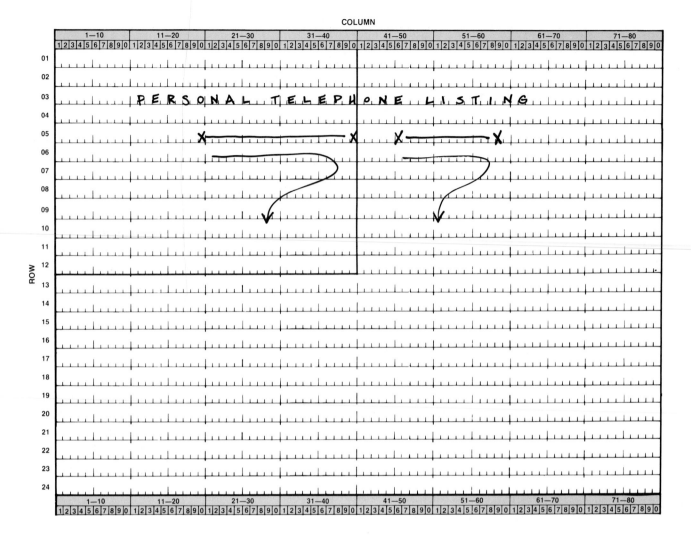

Figure 9.7—*Continued*

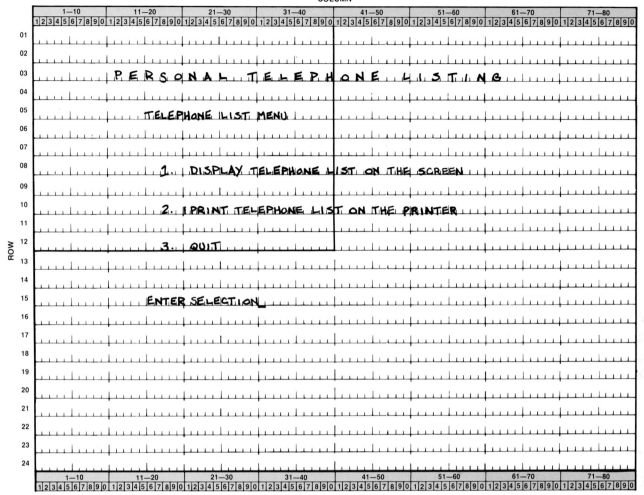

Figure 9.7 — *Continued*

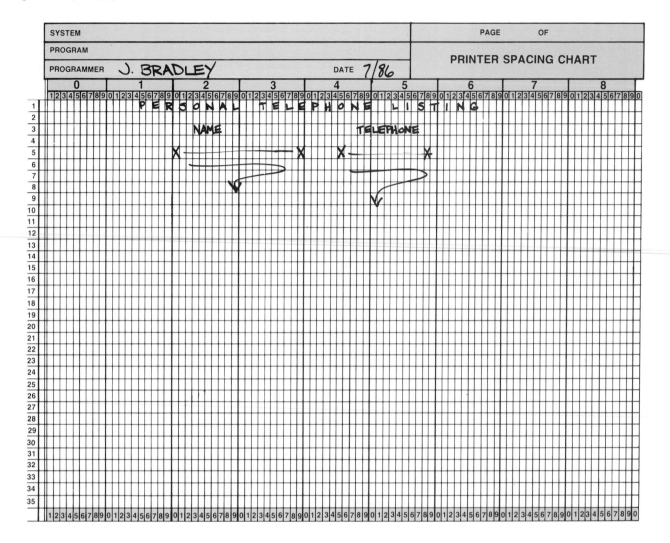

```
100 '           PROGRAM TO PRINT TELEPHONE NUMBER LISTS
110 '            LISTS WILL BE PRINTED IN THEIR ENTIRETY OR
120 '            SELECTED BY AREA CODE
130 '
140 '                    PROGRAM VARIABLES
150 '       NAM$              NAME
160 '       TEL$              TELEPHONE NUMBER
170 '       CHOICE            MENU CHOICE FOR MAIN MENU
180 '       AREA.SW           SWITCH TO INDICATE GOOD DATA FOR
190 '                           AREA CODE
200 '       CK                COUNT OF DIGITS TO CHECK
210 '       AREA$             AREA CODE FOR SELECTIVE LIST
220 '       PT$               PRINT IMAGE FOR PRINTER TITLE
230 '       PD$               PRINT IMAGE FOR DETAIL LINE
240 '       D$                DUMMY VARIABLE
250 '
1000 '**************** PROGRAM MAINLINE ************************
1010 GOSUB 3000                    'INITIALIZE PRINT IMAGES
1020 LET CHOICE = 0
1030 WHILE CHOICE <> 3
1040     GOSUB 2000                'PRINT MAIN MENU
1050     ON CHOICE GOSUB 4000, 8000
1060 WEND
1070 END
1080 '
2000 '************ DISPLAY MAIN MENU **************************
2010 GOSUB 3500                    'PRINT MAIN TITLE
2020 LOCATE 5,26
2030 PRINT "TELEPHONE LIST MENU"
2040 LOCATE 8,18
2050 PRINT "1. DISPLAY TELEPHONE LIST ON THE SCREEN"
2060 LOCATE 10,18
2070 PRINT "2. PRINT TELEPHONE LIST ON THE PRINTER"'
2080 LOCATE 12,18
2090 PRINT "3. QUIT"
2100 LOCATE 15,16
2110 PRINT "ENTER SELECTION ";
2120 LET CHOICE = 0
2130 WHILE CHOICE < 1 OR CHOICE > 3
2140     LOCATE 15,36,1          'SET CURSOR
2150     LET CHOICE = VAL(INPUT$(1)) 'ALLOW ANY INPUT, BUT
                                      CONVERT TO NUM.
2160 WEND
2170 RETURN
2180 '
3000 '***************** INITIALIZE PRINT IMAGES ***************
3010 LET PT$ = "    NAME                        TELEPHONE"
3020 LET PD$ = "\                  \        \                  \"
3030 RETURN
3040 '
3500 '*********** PRINT MAIN TITLE FOR ALL SCREENS ***********
3510 CLS
3520 LOCATE 3,12
3530 PRINT "P E R S O N A L   T E L E P H O N E   L I S T I N G"
3540 RETURN
3550 '
```

```
4000 '*********** PRINT TELEPHONE LIST ON SCREEN **************
4010 GOSUB 5000                    'SELECT AREA CODE TO PRINT
4020 RESTORE                       'START AT TOP OF DATA
4030 GOSUB 3500                    'PRINT HEADING ON SCREEN
4040 LOCATE 7,1                    'SET CURSOR FOR FIRST DETAIL LINE
4050 GOSUB 7000                    'READ FIRST NAME
4060 WHILE NAM$ <> "END"
4070    GOSUB 7500                 'READ PHONE NUMBER
4080    IF AREA$ = "ALL" OR AREA$ = MID$(TEL$,2,3)
           THEN PRINT TAB(20) USING PD$; NAM$, TEL$
4090    GOSUB 7000                 'READ NAME
4100 WEND
4110 GOSUB 6000                    'ALLOW TIME TO SEE LIST
4120 RETURN
4130 '
5000 '**** SELECT ONE AREA CODE OR ALL TO PRINT ***************
5010 GOSUB 3500                    'MAIN TITLE
5020 LOCATE 5,25
5030 PRINT "SELECT AREA CODE TO PRINT"
5040 LOCATE 7,25
5050 PRINT "OR TYPE " CHR$(34) "ALL" CHR$(34) " ";
5060 INPUT AREA$
5070 LET AREA.SW = 0               'SET OFF TO ENTER LOOP
5080 WHILE AREA.SW = 0
5090    LET AREA.SW = 1            'SET IT FOR GOOD DATA BEFORE CHECK
5100    IF AREA$ <> "ALL"
           THEN GOSUB 5200         'CHECK THE DIGITS
5110    IF AREA.SW = 0
           THEN GOSUB 5500         'REENTER AREA CODE
5120 WEND
5130 RETURN
5140 '
5200 '*********** CHECK DIGITS OF AREA CODE ******************
5210 LET CK = 1
5220 WHILE CK <= 3
5230    IF MID$(AREA$,CK,1) < "0" OR MID$(AREA$,CK,1) > "9"
           THEN LET AREA.SW = 0    'SET SWITCH OFF (BAD DATA)
5240    LET CK = CK + 1
5250 WEND
5260 RETURN
5270 '
5500 '************ REENTER AREA CODE ***********************
5510 LOCATE 15,24
5520 PRINT "ENTER " CHR$(34) "ALL" CHR$(34) " OR AREA CODE";
5530 LOCATE 7,39
5540    PRINT "        "           'CLEAR OUT PRIOR ENTRY
5550 LOCATE 7,39
5560 INPUT AREA$                   'INPUT AT SAME SPOT ON SCREEN
5570 RETURN
5580 '
6000 '******** ALLOW TIME TO SEE SCREEN BEFORE CLEARING *********
6010 LOCATE 24,40
6020 PRINT "PRESS ANY KEY TO CONTINUE";
6030 LET D$ = INPUT$(1)            'WAIT FOR ANY KEY PRESS
6040 RETURN
6050 '
7000 '**************** READ A NAME ***********************
7010 READ NAM$
7020 RETURN
7030 '
```

```
7500 '**************** READ TELEPHONE NUMBER ******************
7510 READ TEL$
7520 RETURN
7530 '
8000 '************** PRINT LIST ON PRINTER ********************
8010 GOSUB 5000                    'CHOOSE AREA CODE
8020 RESTORE                       'START AT TOP OF DATA
8030 GOSUB 9000                    'ALIGN PAPER
8040 GOSUB 9600                    'PRINT HEADING ON PRINTER
8050 GOSUB 7000                    'READ FIRST NAME
8060 WHILE NAM$ <> "END"
8070    GOSUB 7500                 'READ PHONE NUMBER
8080    IF AREA$ = "ALL" OR AREA$ = MID$(TEL$,2,3)
            THEN LPRINT TAB(20) USING PD$; NAM$, TEL$
8090    GOSUB 7000                 'READ NAME
8100 WEND
8110 RETURN
8120 '
9000 '************ ALIGN PAPER ON PRINTER *********************
9010 LOCATE 20,10
9020 PRINT "ALIGN PAPER TO TOP OF PAGE, AND PRESS RETURN WHEN READY"
9030 LET D$ = ""                   'INITIALIZE TO ENTER LOOP
9040 WHILE D$ <> CHR$(13)          'CHECK FOR RETURN CHARACTER
9050    LET D$ = INPUT$(1)         'GET ONE CHARACTER FROM KEYBOARD
9060 WEND
9070 RETURN
9080 '
9600 '************ PRINT TITLES ON PRINTER ********************
9610 LPRINT TAB(15)
"P E R S O N A L   T E L E P H O N E   L I S T I N G"
9620 LPRINT
9630 LPRINT TAB(20) PT$
9640 LPRINT
9650 RETURN
9660 '
10000 '*************** DATA BEGINS HERE ***********************
10010 DATA JOHNNY HARRINGTON,(414) 555-2145
10020 DATA SUZIE WONG,(714) 555-4598
10030 DATA TIEN NGUYEN, (818) 555-4295
10040 DATA SCOTT HERRON, (213) 555-6214
10050 DATA RUBEN LOPEZ, (213) 555-2222
10060 DATA SANDRA WASHINGTON, (714) 555-2722
10070 DATA CURT KIRSCH, (714) 555-8118
10080 DATA MELINDA ROBB, (213) 555-4321
10090 DATA END
10100 END
```

Sample Program Output

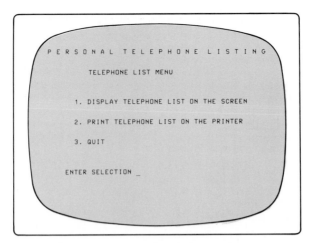

```
P E R S O N A L   T E L E P H O N E   L I S T I N G

        TELEPHONE LIST MENU


     1. DISPLAY TELEPHONE LIST ON THE SCREEN

     2. PRINT TELEPHONE LIST ON THE PRINTER

     3. QUIT


  ENTER SELECTION _
```

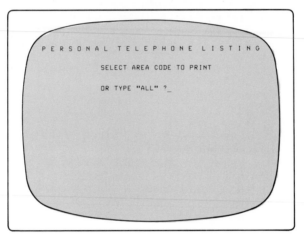

```
P E R S O N A L   T E L E P H O N E   L I S T I N G

       SELECT AREA CODE TO PRINT

       OR TYPE "ALL" ?_
```

Sample Printer Output

```
P E R S O N A L    T E L E P H O N E    L I S T I N G
        NAME                    TELEPHONE

    JOHNNY HARRINGTON       (414) 555-2145
    SUZIE WONG              (714) 555-4598
    TIEN NGUYEN             (818) 555-4295
    SCOTT HERRON            (213) 555-6214
    RUBEN LOPEZ             (213) 555-2222
    SANDRA WASHINGTON       (714) 555-2722
    CURT KIRSCH             (714) 555-8118
    MELINDA ROBB            (213) 555-4321

P E R S O N A L    T E L E P H O N E    L I S T I N G
        NAME                    TELEPHONE

    SUZIE WONG              (714) 555-4598
    SANDRA WASHINGTON       (714) 555-2722
    CURT KIRSCH             (714) 555-8118
```

Summary

1. Menus are a good way to present program choices to the user.
2. Often, several levels of menus will allow a user to quickly make precise choices.
3. The ON...GOSUB statement provides a means to selectively execute one subroutine from many choices.
4. In the ON...GOSUB statement, a list of statement numbers is given. When the value of the control variable is 1, control passes to the first named line number. When the control variable contains 2, control passes to the second line number; a 3 sends execution to the third line number, and so forth. If the value of the control variable is zero or greater than the number of subroutines named, control passes to the statement immediately following the ON...GOSUB.
5. The effect of the ON...GOSUB is similar to the GOSUB; that is, control passes to the first statement in the subroutine and continues sequentially until a RETURN is encountered. The RETURN statement returns execution to the next statement after the ON...GOSUB.
6. For menu selection by a letter rather than a number, the INSTR function may be used in conjunction with the ON...GOSUB.
7. Hierarchy charts are helpful in planning menu programs.

Programming Exercises

9.1. Write a menu program that will print various formulas and do calculation, if requested.

Menu Choices
  1. Calculate the area of a triangle
  2. Calculate the area of a rectangle
  3. Calculate the area of a circle
  4. Calculate the volume of a cube
  5. End the program

For each menu choice, clear the screen and print the formula for the calculation. Then ask the user if a computation is desired. If the answer is affirmative, prompt for each necessary value. Then calculate and print the requested value. After each menu choice, the menu should be redisplayed.

Formulas
  1. Area of a triangle $= 1/2 \times$ base $\times$ height
  2. Area of a rectangle $=$ length $\times$ width
  3. Area of a circle $= \pi \, (3.1416) \times$ radius^2
  4. Volume of a cube $=$ length $\times$ width $\times$ depth

9.2. Write a menu program to convert currency. The menu must offer at least four choices in addition to the choice to end the program. You may use the menu choices suggested or select other currencies for the conversion.

Suggested Menu Choices
  1. Convert U.S. dollars to British pounds
  2. Convert British pounds to U.S. dollars
  3. Convert U.S. dollars to Canadian dollars
  4. Convert Canadian dollars to U.S. dollars
  5. End the program

After the user selects a menu choice, clear the screen and prompt for the amount to be converted. Then print the converted amount with identifying literals. After each choice, the menu should be redisplayed. Find the current conversion rate or use the (outdated) rates below.

Conversion Rates
1 U.S. dollar = 1.1330 British pounds
1 British pound = .8826 U.S. dollars
1 U.S. dollar = .7531 Canadian dollars
1 Canadian dollar = 1.3277 U.S. dollars

9.3. Write a menu program to perform various conversions for cooking. For each choice, clear the screen and request the number to be converted. After printing the converted value, redisplay the menu.

Menu Choices
1. Tablespoons to teaspoons
2. Teaspoons to tablespoons
3. Cups to tablespoons
4. Tablespoons to cups
5. Cups to quarts
6. Quarts to cups
7. Quarts to gallons
8. Gallons to quarts
9. Quit

Formulas
1 tablespoon = 3 teaspoons
1 teaspoon = 1/3 tablespoon
1 cup = 16 tablespoons
1 tablespoon = 1/16 cup
1 cup = 1/4 quart
1 quart = 4 cups
1 quart = 1/4 gallon
1 gallon = 4 quarts

9.4. Write a menu program to list the "best" colleges to attend for a particular major.

Menu Choices
1. Computer Information Systems
2. Computer Programming
3. Business Economics
4. Photography
5. Quit

After the user selects a menu choice, clear the screen and print the list of colleges. After each choice, the menu should be redisplayed. Use DATA statements for the college names.

Colleges
1. Computer Information Systems
   a. University of Twilight Zone
   b. Bogus University
   c. State Polymetric University
   d. College of the Loafers
   e. University of the Atlantic

2. Computer Programming
   a. California Long-term College
   b. San Rose State University
   c. Romona State University
   d. Southern State University
   e. Bogus University
3. Business Economics
   a. Champain College
   b. Golden Bate University
   c. Holy Verbs College
   d. University of Sandy Beach
   e. Woodpecker University
4. Photography
   a. Art Center College
   b. Cooks Institute
   c. Coma Linda University
   d. Bills College
   e. University of Twilight Zone

9.5. Write a menu program to do various conversions.

Menu Options
1. Change a percentage to a decimal fraction
2. Change a percentage to a common fraction
3. Change a decimal to a percent
4. Change a common fraction to a percent
5. Quit

After the user has made a selection, clear the screen and display the conversion. Hold the screen for a keypress. After a key has been pressed, redisplay the menu.

Conversions
1. Percent to decimal fraction
   Divide number by 100
   Example: 25% = .25
2. Percent to a common fraction
   Make the number the numerator of a fraction that has 100 as its denominator
   Example: 50% = 50/100
3. Decimal to a percent
   Multiply number by 100
   Example: .375 = 37.5%
4. Common fraction to a percent
   Divide the numerator by the denominator and multiply by 100
   Example: 2/5 = 40%
   Note: Input the numerator and denominator separately.

10

Additional Control Structures and Numeric Functions

FOR / NEXT Statements
RND Function
RANDOMIZE Statement
DEF FN Statement

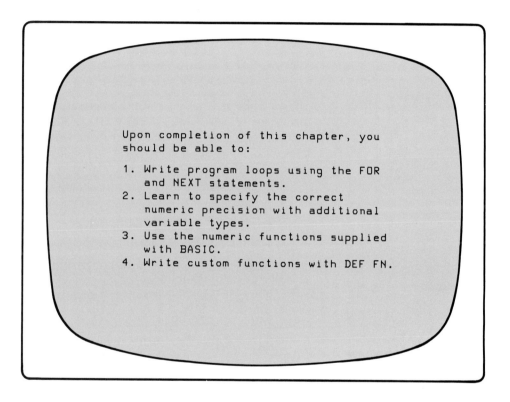

Upon completion of this chapter, you should be able to:

1. Write program loops using the FOR and NEXT statements.
2. Learn to specify the correct numeric precision with additional variable types.
3. Use the numeric functions supplied with BASIC.
4. Write custom functions with DEF FN.

Figure 10.1

Flowchart of a counter-controlled
loop. The counter variable must
be initialized, incremented, and
tested for the final value.

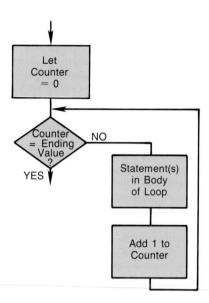

FOR/NEXT Loops

If you pause and look back at the programs written thus far, it becomes obvious that most require loops. Until now the WHILE/WEND statements were used for all loops, and this could continue. But for the counter-controlled loop there is an easier way. Since looping is so common, BASIC provides a statement to automate the counter-controlled loop.

A counter-controlled loop generally has three elements (see figure 10.1).

1. Initialize the counter
2. Increment the counter—in the loop
3. Test the counter—to determine when it is time to quit

```
500  '********* COUNTER-CONTROLLED WHILE LOOP *********
510  LET COUNT = 0                    'INITIALIZE
520  WHILE COUNT < 10                 'TEST
530      PRINT COUNT
540      LET COUNT = COUNT + 1        'INCREMENT
550  WEND
560  PRINT "END OF LIST"


600  '******** COUNTER-CONTROLLED FOR/NEXT LOOP *******
610  FOR COUNT = 1 TO 10              'INITIALIZE AND TEST
620      PRINT COUNT
630  NEXT COUNT                       'INCREMENT
640  PRINT "END OF LIST"
```

When the FOR statement (line 610) is reached during program execution, several things occur. The variable, COUNT, is established as the loop counter, and is initialized to 1. The final value for the COUNT (10) is also declared.

Execution is now "under control of" the FOR statement. After the value of COUNT is set, it is tested to see if COUNT is greater than 10 (the final value). If not, the statements in the body of the loop are executed—in this case, only the PRINT statement. The NEXT statement causes COUNT to be incremented by 1. Then control passes back to the FOR statement. Is the value of COUNT greater than 10? If not, the loop is again executed. When the test is made and COUNT *is* greater than 10, control passes to the statement immediately following the NEXT (line 640).

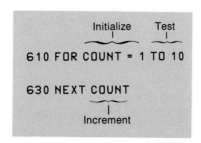

```
                    Initialize    Test
                        |          |
                    ⌣⌣⌣⌣⌣      ⌣⌣⌣⌣⌣
    610 FOR COUNT = 1 TO 10

    630 NEXT COUNT
        ⌣⌣⌣⌣⌣⌣⌣⌣⌣⌣
             |
          Increment
```

The loop written with the FOR and NEXT statements has exactly the same effect as the WHILE loop. In fact, all loops could be written with the WHILE and WEND with no loss of programming capability. But FOR/NEXT offers a handy, concise way of doing the same thing and is the *only* loop control structure available in some dialects of BASIC. As you can see, two fewer statements are needed to code the loop with FOR/NEXT than with WHILE/WEND.

The FOR and NEXT Statements—General Form

```
line number FOR  loop index = initial value TO test value [STEP increment]
                  : :
                  : :  (Body of loop)
                  : :
line number NEXT [loop index]
```

The *loop index, initial value,* and *test value* may be constants, variables, or numeric expressions. The optional word STEP may be included, along with the value to be added to the loop index for each iteration of the loop. When the STEP is omitted, the increment is assumed to be 1.

The FOR and NEXT Statements—Examples

```
50    FOR INDEX = 2 TO 100 STEP 2
200   FOR COUNT = START TO ENDING STEP INCR
450   FOR NUM = A - B TO A + B
500   FOR X = 1 TO LEN(A$) STEP 1
800   FOR RATE = .05 TO .25 STEP .05
900   FOR COUNTDOWN = 10 TO 0 STEP -1
```

Each of these FOR statements will also have a corresponding NEXT statement, which must follow the FOR. All statements between the FOR and the NEXT are considered to be the body of the loop and will be executed the specified number of times.

Line 50 will count from 2 to 100 by 2. The statements in the body of the loop will be executed 50 times—once with INDEX = 2, once with INDEX = 4, once with INDEX = 6, and so forth.

When the comparison is done, the program checks for *greater than* the test value—not equal to. When INDEX = 100 in the preceding example, the body of the loop will be executed one more time. Then, at the NEXT statement, INDEX will be incremented to 102, the test made, and control will pass to the statement following the NEXT. If the value of INDEX were to print (or be used in any way) *after completion* of the loop, its value would be 102.

Using Variables to Control Loop Execution

It may be handy at times to input the beginning, ending, or increment values.

Example Program: Variables for Loop Control

Program Listing

```
400 '****** TEMPERATURE CONVERSION **********************
410 PRINT "CONVERSION FROM DEGREES FAHRENHEIT TO CELSIUS"
420 INPUT "ENTER LOWEST TEMPERATURE, IN FAHRENHEIT ", LOW
430 INPUT "ENTER HIGHEST FAHRENHEIT TEMPERATURE    ", HIGH
440 INPUT "ENTER VALUE FOR INCREMENT              ", INCR
450 FOR FAHREN = LOW TO HIGH STEP INCR
460    LET CELSIUS = 5/9 * (FAHREN - 32)
470    PRINT USING "##.#    ##.#"; FAHREN, CELSIUS
480 NEXT FAHREN
490 PRINT "END OF LIST"
500 END
```

Sample Program Output

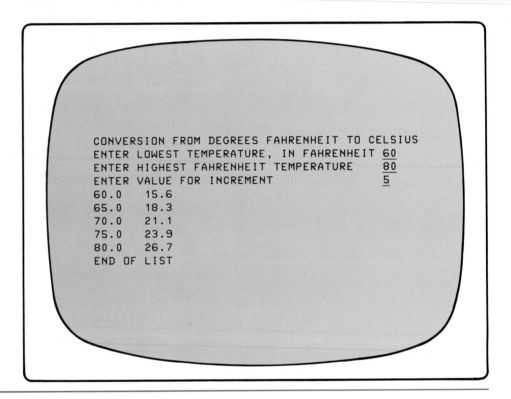

```
CONVERSION FROM DEGREES FAHRENHEIT TO CELSIUS
ENTER LOWEST TEMPERATURE, IN FAHRENHEIT 60
ENTER HIGHEST FAHRENHEIT TEMPERATURE    80
ENTER VALUE FOR INCREMENT               5
60.0   15.6
65.0   18.3
70.0   21.1
75.0   23.9
80.0   26.7
END OF LIST
```

Negative Increment, or Counting Backward

The value for STEP may be a negative number. This has the effect of decreasing the loop index rather than increasing it. When the STEP is negative, BASIC will test for *less than* the test value instead of greater than.

```
700  '*********** COUNT BACKWARDS *******************
710  FOR COUNT = 10 TO 0 STEP -1
720     PRINT COUNT
730  NEXT COUNT
740  PRINT "BLAST OFF"
```

Condition Satisfied before Entry

At times, the terminal value will be reached before entry into the loop. In that case, the statements in the body of the loop will not be executed even once.

```
1000   '********* AN UNEXECUTABLE LOOP ****************
1010   LET TERM = 5
1020   FOR COUNT = 6 TO TERM
1030      PRINT "THIS WILL NEVER PRINT"
1040   NEXT COUNT
RUN
OK
```

Indentation

For ease of reading and debugging, the loop should be easily recognizable. Align the FOR and NEXT statements to show the beginning and end of the loop. The statements in the body of the loop should be indented and aligned with each other.

Flowcharting FOR/NEXT Loops

The logic of a FOR/NEXT loop is identical to a counter-controlled WHILE loop and may be flowcharted in the same way. Figure 10.2 shows the ANSI standard symbols used to flowchart a FOR/NEXT loop.

A nonstandard symbol has been developed to indicate a FOR/NEXT loop. Figure 10.3 illustrates the specialized FOR/NEXT symbol. Although the symbol is not included in the standards, it does have widespread use.

Figure 10.2
ANSI standard flowcharting symbols used to plan a FOR/NEXT loop.

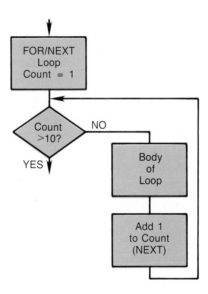

Figure 10.3
Nonstandard FOR/NEXT flowcharting symbol.

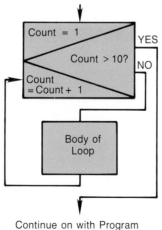

Notes on Loops and Structured Programming

Consistent with the philosophy of this text, nothing has been said about branching into or out of FOR/NEXT loops. Good program modules have one entry point and one exit point. Therefore, a loop will always be entered at the top and exited at the bottom.

Many times it is desirable to end a counter-controlled loop before the test value is reached. BASIC does allow branching out, but structured programming guidelines do not. *If you need to terminate a loop early, always use a WHILE loop rather than a FOR/NEXT loop.* According to the rules of BASIC, if execution branches out of a FOR/NEXT loop prior to normal termination, the variable used for the loop index will retain its current value. BASIC does *not* allow branching into the body of the loop. Execution must always begin with the FOR statement.

Altering the Values of the Control Variables

Once the FOR loop has been entered, the values for beginning, ending, and increment have already been set. Changing the value of the variables within the loop will have no effect on the number of iterations of the loop. Many texts admonish against changing the values within the loop. However, Microsoft BASIC just ignores you if you try.

```
100   '** BAD EXAMPLE--CHANGING THE CONTROL VARIABLES **
110   LET FINAL = 5
120   LET INCR = 1
130   FOR INDEX = 1 TO FINAL STEP INCR
140      PRINT INDEX
150      LET FINAL = 10
160      LET INCR = 2
170   NEXT INDEX

RUN
1
2
3
4
5
```

INDEX will still go from 1 to 5, even though FINAL and INCR were changed within the loop. It should be obvious that changing the values is not possible and that the preceding coding is highly undesirable.

The value that BASIC *will* allow you to change within the loop is the index variable. Again an admonition: This is considered poor programming!

```
200   '******* POOR PROGRAMMING ************************
210   FOR NUM = 1 TO 10 STEP 1
220      PRINT NUM
230      LET NUM = NUM * 2
240   NEXT NUM
250   PRINT "AFTER LOOP TERMINATION, NUM =" NUM

RUN
1
3
7
AFTER LOOP TERMINATION, NUM = 15
```

The clue to the strange output here is to recall, step-by-step, what happens during execution. Each time line 230 is reached, the value of NUM will double. Each time line 240 is executed, 1 will be added to the current value for NUM.

Calculating the Number of Iterations

At times it is useful to quickly calculate the number of times a loop will be executed. Use this handy formula:

Number of iterations = (test value − initial value)/increment + 1
Examples:

```
100 FOR INDEX = 50 TO 100 STEP 1
```

Number of iterations = $(100 - 50) / 1 + 1 = 51$

```
200 FOR COUNTER = .5 TO 20 STEP .5
```

Number of iterations = (20 − .5) / .5 + 1 = 40

```
300 FOR COUNT = −10 TO 10 STEP .1
```

Number of iterations = (10 − −10) / .1 + 1 = 201

Feedback

1. Identify the statements that are correctly formed and those which have errors. For those with errors, state what is wrong and how to correct it.

   a. ```
      20 FOR N = 3.5 TO 6, STEP .5
      50 NEXT N
      ```
   b. ```
      100 FOR A = B TO C STEP D
      150 NEXT D
      ```
   c. ```
      200 FOR 4 = 1 TO 10 STEP 2
      250 NEXT FOR
      ```
   d. ```
      300 FOR K = 100 TO 0 STEP -25
      350 NEXT K
      ```
   e. ```
      400 FOR N = 0 TO -10 STEP -1
      450 NEXT N
      ```
   f. ```
      500 FOR X = 10 TO 1
      550 NEXT X
      ```

2. Write a FOR/NEXT loop to print the numbers counting by 3, from 3 to 100.

3. Using a FOR/NEXT loop, write the statements necessary to print "THIS IS A LARK" ten times.

4. What will be the output when each of these program segments is executed?

   a. ```
      10 FOR REC = 1 TO 5
      20   READ ITEM$, PRICE
      30   LET TOT = TOT + PRICE
      40   PRINT ITEM$, PRICE
      50 NEXT REC
      60 PRINT ,TOT
      70 DATA BICYCLE,150,TRAIN,65,BALL,1.50,NERD,.27
      80 DATA GAME,6.95,BOX,4,END,0
      ```
   b. ```
      100 READ X,Y,Z
      110 FOR INDEX = X TO Y STEP Z
      120     PRINT INDEX
      130 NEXT INDEX
      140 DATA 10,15,2
      ```
   c. ```
      50 READ TERM
      60 FOR COUNT = 1 TO TERM
      70   PRINT "*";
      80 NEXT COUNT
      90 DATA 8.5
      ```

5. How many times will the body of the loop be executed for each of these examples? What will be the value of the loop index after normal completion of the loop?

   a. ```
      150 FOR K = 2 TO 11 STEP 3
      ```
   b. ```
      200 FOR B = 10 TO 1 STEP -1
      ```
   c. ```
      400 FOR S = 3 TO 6 STEP .5
      ```
   d. ```
      450 FOR A = 5 TO 1
      ```
   e. ```
      500 FOR L = 1 TO 3
      ```

Nesting FOR/NEXT Loops

FOR/NEXT loops may be nested; that is, one loop may be placed inside another loop. The inner loop must be completely contained within the outer loop with no overlap. Each loop must use a unique variable name for the loop index.

Example Program: Nested Loops

Program Listing

```
400 '*************** NESTED LOOPS ********************
410┌FOR OUTER.INDEX = 1 TO 5
420│   PRINT "OUTER LOOP" OUTER.INDEX
430│  ┌FOR INNER.INDEX = 1 TO 3
440│  │   PRINT TAB(6); "OUTER INDEX =" OUTER.INDEX;
450│  │   PRINT "INNER INDEX =" INNER.INDEX
460│  └NEXT INNER.INDEX
470└NEXT OUTER.INDEX
```

Sample Program Output

```
        OUTER LOOP 1
              OUTER INDEX = 1 INNER INDEX = 1
              OUTER INDEX = 1 INNER INDEX = 2
              OUTER INDEX = 1 INNER INDEX = 3
        OUTER LOOP 2
              OUTER INDEX = 2 INNER INDEX = 1
              OUTER INDEX = 2 INNER INDEX = 2
              OUTER INDEX = 2 INNER INDEX = 3
        OUTER LOOP 3
              OUTER INDEX = 3 INNER INDEX = 1
              OUTER INDEX = 3 INNER INDEX = 2
              OUTER INDEX = 3 INNER INDEX = 3
        OUTER LOOP 4
              OUTER INDEX = 4 INNER INDEX = 1
              OUTER INDEX = 4 INNER INDEX = 2
              OUTER INDEX = 4 INNER INDEX = 3
        OUTER LOOP 5
              OUTER INDEX = 5 INNER INDEX = 1
              OUTER INDEX = 5 INNER INDEX = 2
              OUTER INDEX = 5 INNER INDEX = 3
```

When the nested loop program is run, the inner loop will be executed three times for each iteration of the outer loop. At line 410, the outer loop is initialized and OUTER.INDEX is set to 1. With OUTER.INDEX still at 1, the inner loop is begun, and INNER.INDEX is set to 1. The body of the inner loop is executed (line 440) and the inner NEXT (line 460). INNER.INDEX is incremented and tested. Since it is not greater than 3, the inner loop is re-executed. The outer NEXT will not be executed for the first time until the inner loop is completely satisfied. Then, when OUTER.INDEX has a value of 2, the inner loop is re-initialized and must be completely satisfied before OUTER.INDEX can go to 3.

In *nested FOR/NEXT loops,* the inner loop variable varies faster than the outer loop variable. This can be compared to the hands of a clock, on which the minute hand travels faster than the hour hand.

```
1000    '***** PROPERLY NESTED LOOPS ****
1010┌ FOR I = 1 TO 10
1030│     ┌FOR K = I TO 10
1050│     └NEXT K
1150│     ┌FOR L = 1 TO I
1160│     │   ┌FOR M = L TO 0 STEP -1
1200│     │   └NEXT M
1250│     └NEXT L
1300└NEXT I
```

Notice that each nested loop is completely contained within its outer loop. There is no crossing over. Also observe that I, the outermost loop index, is used as an initial value on line 1030 and as a final value on line 1150. The loop index L is also used as an initial value on an inner loop. This technique is perfectly acceptable and is often a slick solution to programming problems. It is important, however, that each loop have its own, unique loop index.

```
2000   '***** IMPROPERLY NESTED LOOPS *****
2010   FOR I = 1 TO 10
2020        FOR K = 1 TO 2
2030   NEXT I
2040        NEXT K
2050        FOR M = L TO 0 STEP -1
2060   FOR L = 1 TO I
2070        NEXT M
2080   NEXT L
```

On execution, these loops would produce the error NEXT WITHOUT FOR.

Example Program: Print Multiplication Tables

One application of nested loops is to print multiplication tables.

Program Listing

```
800 '************** PRINT MULTIPLICATION TABLES *********
805 '                 USING NESTED LOOPS
810 LET P$ = " ### :"            'INITIALIZE PRINT IMAGES
811 LET D$ = " ### "
815 CLS
820 PRINT "    :    0    1    2    3    4    5    6    7    8    9    10"
825 PRINT " -------------------------------------------------------------"
830 FOR ROW = 0 TO 10
840     PRINT USING P$; ROW;
850     FOR COL = 0 TO 10
860         LET PROD = ROW * COL
870         PRINT USING D$; PROD;
880     NEXT COL
890     PRINT
900 NEXT ROW
910 END
```

Sample Program Output

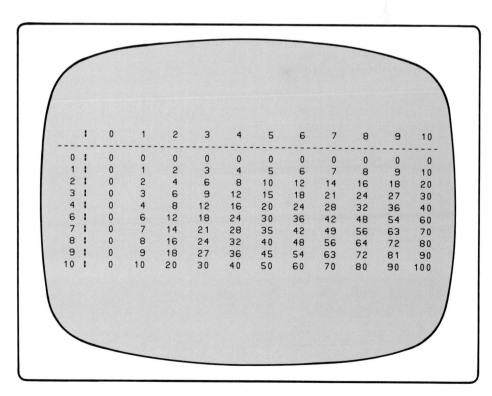

Feedback

1. What will print when the following program segment is run?

```
50   FOR COUNT = 2 TO 6 STEP 3
60       FOR INDEX = 1 TO 3
70           PRINT COUNT, INDEX
80       NEXT INDEX
90   NEXT COUNT
```

2. a. What will print when the following program segment is run?
   b. What is the purpose of the PRINT on line 560? What would the output look like if it were removed?

```
510   FOR ROW = 1 TO 5
520       READ NUM
530       FOR STAR = 1 TO NUM
540           PRINT "*";
550       NEXT STAR
560       PRINT
570   NEXT ROW
580   DATA 5,2,10,6,1
```

Programming Example

The local children are on a fund-raising drive. Since none of the children excels in arithmetic, it was decided to print a chart to show the price for multiple items including tax. In order to keep the program flexible, the tax rate, description, and price of the items will be entered with DATA statements.

Input

1. Tax rate
2. Item description (for each of four items)
3. Item price (for each of four items)

Output

Refer to figure 10.4 for output layout.

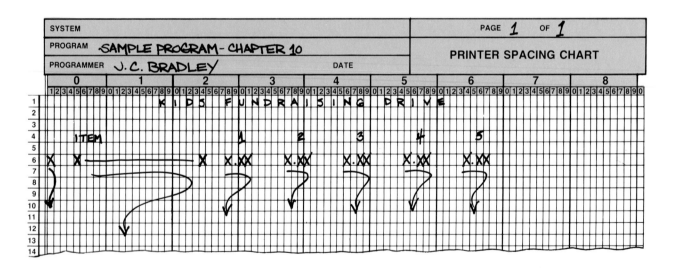

Figure 10.4
Output layout for fund-raising tax table program.

Processing

For each of four items:

Compute the price of 1, 2, 3, 4, and 5 items, including tax

= (price * quantity) * (1 + rate)

Pseudocode

1. Initialize
   1.1   Print headings
   1.2   Initialize print images
2. Print table
   For each of 4 items
   2.1   Read description and price
   2.2   Print description and price
   2.3   For each of 5 quantities
       2.3.1   Calculate total including tax
       2.3.2   Print total
   2.4   Print blank line
3. End

Hierarchy Chart

Refer to figure 10.5 for the chart.

Figure 10.5
Hierarchy chart for fund-raising
tax table program.

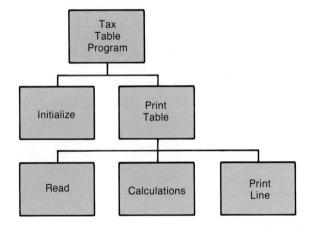

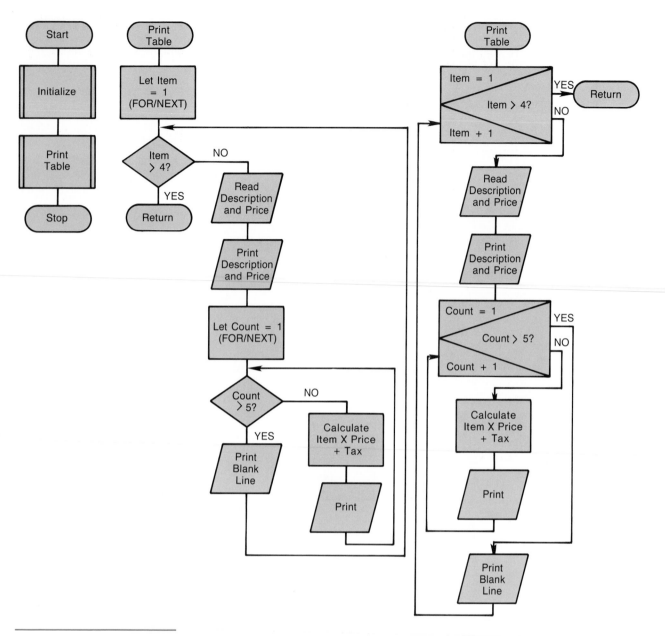

Figure 10.6
Flowchart of fund-raising tax table
program.

Flowchart   Refer to figure 10.6 for the flowchart.

Program Listing

```
110 '  PROGRAM FOR THE KIDS' FUNDRAISING DRIVE
120 '    PRINT A CHART WHICH SHOWS EACH ITEM BEING SOLD,
130 '    ALONG WITH THE PRICE, FOR 1-5 QUANTITY, INCLUDING TAX
140 '
150 '        PROGRAM VARIABLES
160 '            RATE           TAX RATE (DECIMAL FRACTION)
170 '            DESC$          DESCRIPTION OF ITEM
180 '            PRICE          PRICE OF EACH ITEM
190 '            TOT            CALCULATED TOTAL, INCLUDING TAX
100 '            ITEM           ITEM NUMBER, USED TO COUNT
210 '            COUNT          NUMBER OF ITEMS SOLD
220 '
```

```
490 '****************** PROGRAM MAINLINE *****************************
500 GOSUB 1000                        'INITIALIZE
510 READ RATE                         'TAX RATE TO APPLY TO ALL PURCHASES
520 GOSUB 2000                        'PRINT TABLE
530 END
540 '
1000 '********************** INITIALIZE ***************************
1010 CLS
1020 PRINT "        K I D S   F U N D R A I S I N G    D R I V E"
1025 PRINT:PRINT
1030 PRINT "    ITEM                1        2        3        4        5"
1035 PRINT
1040 LET I$ = "#   \                       \   "
1045 LET D$ = "  ##.##   "
1050 RETURN
1060 '
2000 '********************** PRINT WHOLE TABLE ********************
2020 FOR ITEM = 1 TO 4
2025     READ DESC$, PRICE
2030     PRINT USING I$; ITEM, DESC$;
2040     FOR COUNT = 1 TO 5
2050         LET TOT = (COUNT * PRICE) * (1 + RATE)
2060         PRINT USING D$; TOT;
2070     NEXT COUNT
2080     PRINT
2090 NEXT ITEM
2100 RETURN
2110 '
3000 '***************** DATA BEGINS HERE ************************
3010 DATA .06                         'TAX RATE
3020 DATA CANDY BAR, .75, FUDGE COOKIES, 1.25, OATMEAL COOKIES, 1.00,
          MACAROONS,1.45
3030 END
```

Sample Program Output

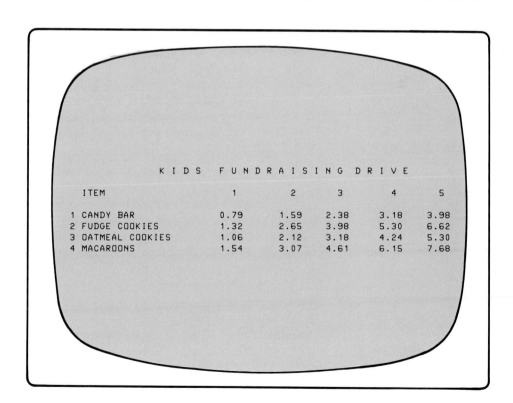

```
              K I D S   F U N D R A I S I N G  D R I V E


    ITEM                  1         2         3         4         5

 1 CANDY BAR            0.79      1.59      2.38      3.18      3.98
 2 FUDGE COOKIES        1.32      2.65      3.98      5.30      6.62
 3 OATMEAL COOKIES      1.06      2.12      3.18      4.24      5.30
 4 MACAROONS            1.54      3.07      4.61      6.15      7.68
```

Numeric Precision

The **precision** of a number refers to the number of digits that can be stored accurately. The numeric variables used thus far are called *single-precision* variables. Due to the space allocated for variables, each variable can hold up to seven digits (six accurately). Any numbers with more than six significant digits will not be held accurately.

```
10   LET A = 112233445566
20   PRINT USING " ###,###,###,#### ";A
RUN
112,233,500,000
```

The first six digits here are correct; the seventh digit is not even correctly rounded. The error here is 54,434. Is that close enough? For some applications, maybe yes. For others, it could be a disaster.

To increase the storage allocated for variables, and also the number of digits held, declare variables to be *double-precision*. A double-precision variable will hold up to seventeen digits (sixteen accurately).

The storage in the computer is measured in bytes, where one byte will hold one alphanumeric (ASCII) character when strings are being stored. When numbers are being stored in computer memory, the numbers are converted to their binary value. If 123 is stored as a number, you won't find an ASCII coded 1, 2, 3. Instead, the numeric value for one hundred twenty-three is converted to binary and held in the standard size for a numeric variable. Recall from chapter 7 that the functions STR$ and VAL are used to convert from one form to the other.

The standard size for a single-precision numeric variable is four bytes. Whether zero is being stored or 1,000,000, it still takes four bytes. Double-precision variables always take eight bytes of storage.

There is also a third type of numeric variable—**integers** (whole numbers). Integers take two bytes of storage, and can hold any whole number in the range -32768 to $+32767$.

The way to specify the type of variable wanted is in the choice of variable names. You already found that a dollar sign as the rightmost character declared a string variable. Now learn to explicitly declare integer variables with a percent sign (%), double-precision variables with a number sign (#), or single-precision with an exclamation point (!) as the rightmost character of the variable names. Table 10.1 summarizes the variable types and codes.

When the type of variable to use is not specified, BASIC sets up and uses single-precision variables. For most applications, this is fine, and there is little reason to change.

The occasions to consider changing variable types include:

1. When accuracy is needed for large numbers. Whenever more than six digits must be held, double-precision is needed.
2. For large programs, when storage space is at a premium. Sometimes it may be necessary to use the smallest size consistent with usage. Two notes on size:
   (1) For large programs, the CHAIN operation may be the best solution.
   (2) The programmer time spent attempting to make a program smaller generally costs more than purchasing additional main storage, if available. However, the Microsoft BASIC interpreter will only use 64K bytes of memory, even if more is present.

Table 10.1.
Explicitly declaring variable types.

Variable Type	Character to Declare Type	Number of Bytes of Storage Allocated
String	$	1 for each character (0 to 255)
Integer	%	2
Single-precision	!	4
Double-precision	#	8

3. When execution speed is an issue. Although the speed improvement is generally negligible, it *can* make a difference. Computations done with integers are faster than those done with either single or double precision. Single-precision computations are done more quickly than double-precision. (If speed is really an issue, the program should be compiled, rather than interpreted.)

Example Programs: Comparison of Execution Speeds for Single-Precision and Integer Variables

Program Listing

```
10 '**** TIME A LOOP WITH SINGLE-PRECISION VARIABLES ****
20 LET START = VAL(RIGHT$(TIME$,2))
30 FOR COUNT = 1 TO 10000
40 NEXT COUNT
50 LET FINISH = VAL(RIGHT$(TIME$,2))
60 IF START > FINISH
      THEN LET FINISH = FINISH + 60
70 LET ET = FINISH - START
80 PRINT "ELAPSED TIME = " ET
90 END
RUN
ELAPSED TIME = 15
```

Program Listing

```
10 '******* TIME A LOOP WITH INTEGER VARIABLES *********
20 LET START = VAL(RIGHT$(TIME$,2))
30 FOR COUNT% = 1 TO 10000
40 NEXT COUNT%
50 LET FINISH = VAL(RIGHT$(TIME$,2))
60 IF START > FINISH
      THEN LET FINISH = FINISH + 60
70 LET ET = FINISH - START
80 PRINT "ELAPSED TIME = " ET
90 END
RUN
ELAPSED TIME = 11
```

Counters on FOR/NEXT loops are good candidates for integers. This loop program was tested on an IBM-PC using an integer count and a single-precision count. The integer loop took 11 seconds, the single-precision loop took 15 seconds.

Feedback

1. When would it be a good idea to use integer variables?
2. Name one advantage of using double-precision numeric variables rather than single-precision.
3. Name one advantage of using single-precision variables over double-precision variables.

Binary Fractions and Accuracy

The accuracy of fractional numbers is one of the stickiest issues in computer programming. It is expected that when the computer does computations, the answers must be accurate. Right? Wrong! Although a complete explanation of the binary number system, binary fractions, and computer storage is beyond the scope of this text, a little technical discussion is necessary to understand the occasional strange output.

In our decimal number system, some fractions cannot be held accurately and must be rounded. For example, consider

$$1/3 = .33333 \text{ (nearly)}$$
$$\text{and } 2/3 = .66667 \text{ (almost)}$$

The numbers stored in the computer memory are held, not in decimal, but in binary. In the binary number system, there are some fractions that cannot be held accurately.

Additional Control Structures and Numeric Functions

Unfortunately, those inaccurate fractions are some like 1/10 and 1/100. This means that decimal fractions holding dollars and cents will not be exact. Try taking $1.00, subtracting 100 pennies from it, and checking for zero. It won't be zero. Close, but not zero.

```
100   '*********** GIVE AWAY 10 PENNIES **************
110   PRINT "I STARTED WITH .10"
120   FOR WAD = .10 TO 0 STEP -.01
130      PRINT "I GAVE AWAY 1 PENNY, THEN I HAD"; WAD
140   NEXT WAD
RUN
I STARTED WITH .10
I GAVE AWAY 1 PENNY, THEN I HAD 9.000001E-02
I GAVE AWAY 1 PENNY, THEN I HAD 8.000001E-02
I GAVE AWAY 1 PENNY, THEN I HAD 7.000001E-02
I GAVE AWAY 1 PENNY, THEN I HAD 6.000001E-02
I GAVE AWAY 1 PENNY, THEN I HAD 5.000001E-02
I GAVE AWAY 1 PENNY, THEN I HAD 4.000002E-02
I GAVE AWAY 1 PENNY, THEN I HAD 3.000002E-02
I GAVE AWAY 1 PENNY, THEN I HAD 2.000002E-02
I GAVE AWAY 1 PENNY, THEN I HAD 1.000001E-02
I GAVE AWAY 1 PENNY, THEN I HAD 1.490116E-08
```

The values for WAD are printed in **E** (**exponential**) notation, which is similar to scientific notation. The last printed value, 1.490116E–08, means "move the decimal point eight positions to the left." This gives .00000001490116, which is extremely close to zero (especially in dealing with pennies).

What to Do?

What action the programmer should take depends on the desired results. If the concern is the appearance of the output, PRINT USING is the solution. Since numbers are rounded to fit the print image, the program can be written to print the "right" numbers.

```
100   '*********** GIVE AWAY 10 PENNIES **************
110   PRINT "I STARTED WITH .10"
120   FOR WAD = .10 TO 0 STEP -.01
130      PRINT "I GAVE AWAY 1 PENNY, THEN I HAD";
135      PRINT USING " .##"; WAD
140   NEXT WAD
RUN
I STARTED WITH .10
I GAVE AWAY 1 PENNY, THEN I HAD .09
I GAVE AWAY 1 PENNY, THEN I HAD .08
I GAVE AWAY 1 PENNY, THEN I HAD .07
I GAVE AWAY 1 PENNY, THEN I HAD .06
I GAVE AWAY 1 PENNY, THEN I HAD .05
I GAVE AWAY 1 PENNY, THEN I HAD .04
I GAVE AWAY 1 PENNY, THEN I HAD .03
I GAVE AWAY 1 PENNY, THEN I HAD .02
I GAVE AWAY 1 PENNY, THEN I HAD .01
I GAVE AWAY 1 PENNY, THEN I HAD .00
```

Be aware of the accuracy problem in computations, also. If a WHILE loop had been used and tested for zero, an endless loop would have been created.

```
100   '*********** AN ENDLESS LOOP ******************
110   LET WAD = .10
120   WHILE WAD <> 0
130      LET WAD = WAD - .01
135      PRINT WAD
140 WEND
```

Sometimes you may need to check for a "close," rather than an exact, figure.

```
120   WHILE ABS(WAD) > .001
```

This loop will be terminated when the value of WAD gets close to zero.

Another possible solution is to always calculate with whole numbers. You can convert all decimal values to a whole number of pennies. Then, just before printing results, you will have to divide by 100. With this method you will never have to check for "close"; the results of all intermediate calculations will be accurate, and columns of dollars and cents will add up correctly.

```
200 '****** Use pennies only for calculations *********
210 INPUT "Enter dollar amount"; DOLLARS
220 LET CENTS = INT(DOLLARS * 100)

230 GOSUB 500              'Calculations using CENTS

240 '********* Print out results of calculations ******
250 LET DOLLARS = CENTS / 100
260 PRINT USING " $##,###.##"; DOLLARS
```

Numeric Functions

Many numeric functions are included in BASIC. Some have already been used, such as INT and ABS. Most of the common functions are listed in table 10.2.

Random Numbers— RND and RANDOMIZE

The function RND returns a number between 0 and 1. This means that any number from 0 to 1 (but not 0 or 1) is just as likely to come up as any other. RND is popular for use in games, as well as problems in probability and queuing theory.

The RND Function—General Form

```
RND
```

The RND Function—Examples

```
10    LET X = RND
90    LET NUM = INT(RND*10)
200   PRINT RND
```

Table 10.2.
Numeric functions.

Function	Value Returned
ABS(X)	The absolute value of X. $\lvert X \rvert = X$ if $X >= 0$ $\lvert X \rvert = -X$ if $X < 0$
ATN(X)	The angle in radians whose tangent is X. The result will be in the range $-\pi/2$ to $+\pi/2$.
CINT(X)	The integer closest to X (rounded).
COS(X)	The cosine of X, where X is in radians.
EXP(X)	The value of e raised to the power X ($e = 2.718282...$).
FIX(X)	The integer portion of X (truncated).
INT(X)	The largest integer $<= X$.
LOG(X)	The natural logarithm of X, where $X > 0$.
RND	A random number in the range 0–1 (exclusive).
SGN(X)	The sign of X. -1 if $X < 0$ 0 if $X = 0$ 1 if $X > 0$
SIN(X)	The sine of X where X is in radians.
SQR(X)	The square root of X where X must be $>= 0$.
TAN(X)	The tangent of X where X is in radians.

Here are ten random numbers generated by RND.

```
10    '********** GENERATE RANDOM NUMBERS **************
20    FOR COUNT = 1 TO 10
30        PRINT RND
40    NEXT COUNT
50    END
RUN
 .7151002
 .683111
 .4821425
 .9992938
 .6465093
 .1322918
 .3692191
 .5873315
 .1345934
 .9348853
```

To generate numbers in a range 1–N:

```
LET NUM = INT(RND * N + 1)
```

```
10    '****** GENERATE NUMBERS IN A GIVEN RANGE ********
20    INPUT "HIGHEST NUMBER"; LIMIT
30    FOR INDEX = 1 TO 10
40        LET X = INT(RND * LIMIT + 1)
50        PRINT X

60    NEXT INDEX

RUN
HIGHEST NUMBER? 10
 8
 7
 5
 10
 7
 2
 4
 6
 2
 10
```

Unfortunately, the numbers are not really random. Every time the program is executed, the same sequence of "random" numbers is generated. To generate a different series of random numbers for each program run, the RANDOMIZE statement is used (once) at the beginning of the program. This is called *seeding* the random number generator.

The RANDOMIZE Statement—General Form

```
line number RANDOMIZE  [numeric expression for seed]
```

The RANDOMIZE Statement—Examples

```
10     RANDOMIZE

100    INPUT "ENTER A NUMBER BETWEEN 1 AND 100", SEED
110    RANDOMIZE SEED

150    RANDOMIZE VAL(RIGHT$(TIME$,2))
```

RANDOMIZE can be used with or without the optional numeric expression. When the expression is omitted (line 10), BASIC suspends program execution and requests the seed from the keyboard.

```
Random Number Seed (-32768 to 32767)?__
```

The second example (lines 100 and 110) is a nicer way to request the seed from the user. The numbers 1–100 are not really required, but may seem less confusing to some users than −32768 to 32767.

The example on line 150 uses the internal clock for the seed as a way of selecting a different seed for each program run.

Example Program:
Using Random Numbers in a Guessing Game

Program Listing

```
600 '*************** GUESSING GAME *********************
610 CLS                             'CLEAR THE SCREEN
620 RANDOMIZE VAL(RIGHT$(TIME$,2))  'SEED RANDOM NUMBER
                                     GENERATOR
630 LET NUM = INT(RND * 100 + 1)    'GENERATE RANDOM NUMBER
640 INPUT "I'M THINKING OF A NUMBER BETWEEN 1 AND 100--YOUR
GUESS";GUESS
650 WHILE GUESS <> NUM
660      IF GUESS > NUM
             THEN PRINT "TOO HIGH, GUESS AGAIN";
             ELSE PRINT "TOO LOW, GUESS AGAIN";
670      INPUT GUESS
680 WEND
690 PRINT "RIGHT ON!"
700 END
```

Sample Program Output

```
I'M THINKING OF A NUMBER BETWEEN 1 AND 100--YOUR GUESS? 50
TOO HIGH, GUESS AGAIN? 20
TOO LOW, GUESS AGAIN? 35
TOO LOW, GUESS AGAIN? 40
TOO HIGH, GUESS AGAIN? 37
TOO LOW, GUESS AGAIN? 38
RIGHT ON!
```

Table 10.3.	Function	Return for Values of X			
INT, FIX, and CINT functions.		X = 1.5	X = −1.5	X = 1.4	X = −1.4
	INT(X)	1	−2	1	−2
	FIX(X)	1	−1	1	−1
	CINT(X)	2	−2	1	−1

Converting to Integers—INT, FIX, and CINT Functions

```
1000   LET A = INT(X)
1200   LET B = FIX(X)
1400   LET C = CINT(X)
```

Each of these three functions will convert a **real number** (with digits to the right of the decimal point) to a whole number. Each does the conversion in a little different fashion.

Number Line

INT produces the largest integer not greater than X (the argument). Negative values of X return the next lowest integer. The largest integer will be to the left on the number line (more negative). INT(−1.5) returns −2.

FIX truncates (chops off) all digits to the right of the decimal point. For negative arguments, FIX returns the next larger (less negative) number, which is to the right on the number line. FIX(−1.5) returns −1.

CINT rounds up to the nearest integer and thus could go in either direction on the number line. CINT(−1.4) returns −1, CINT(−1.5) returns −2. Table 10.3 shows a summary of these functions.

Arithmetic Functions— ABS, SGN, SQR

```
200   LET A = ABS(X)
300   LET B = SGN(X)
400   LET C = SQR(X)
```

Each of these functions returns a real number based on the value of X.

ABS is the absolute value function, written as :X: in mathematics. ABS has the effect of stripping the sign from a number. For a positive X, it will return X; for a negative X, it will return −X. ABS will always return the positive representation of the argument.

SGN is the sign function. It can be used to determine the sign (positive, negative, or zero) of any argument. SGN returns −1 for negative numbers, +1 for positive numbers, and 0 for zero.

SQR is the square root function. It will return the square root of any positive argument. A negative argument generates the error message: ILLEGAL FUNC-TION CALL. Table 10.4 summarizes the ABS, SGN, and SQR functions.

Table 10.4. ABS, SGN, and SQR functions.	Function	Return for Values of X			
		X = 1.5	X = −1.5	X = 0	X = 4
	ABS(X)	1.5	1.5	0	4
	SGN(X)	1	−1	0	1
	SQR(X)	1.224745	ERROR	0	2

Table 10.4.
ABS, SGN, and SQR functions.

```
200  '*** CONVERT NEGATIVE NUMBERS FOR SQR FUNCTION ******
210  INPUT X
220  IF SGN(X) = -1
        THEN LET Y = SQR(ABS(X))
        ELSE LET Y = SQR(X)
```

The sign of a number can be used for an ON...GOSUB statement. Adding 2 to the value returned (−1,0,+1) will give the proper numbers for branching (1,2,3).

```
400  '****** USE THE SIGN OF A NUMBER FOR BRANCHING ******
410  ON SGN(X) + 2 GOSUB 1000, 2000, 3000
```

Exponential and Trigonometric Functions

```
100  LET A = SIN(X)
200  LET B = COS(X)
300  LET C = TAN(X)
400  LET D = ATN(X)
500  LET E = LOG(X)
600  LET F = EXP(X)
```

These functions can be used to solve mathematic and trigonometric problems. The trigonometric functions operate with angles measured in radians, rather than degrees. To convert from degrees to radians, multiply by $\pi/180$, where $\pi = 3.14159$.

Example Program: Use of SIN, COS, and TAN

To convert from degrees to radians, use this formula.

$$RADIANS = DEGREES * (3.14159/180)$$

Program Listing

```
10  '****** DEMONSTRATE THE USE OF SIN, COS, AND TAN ************
20  '   DEG                 ANGLE MEASURED IN DEGREES
30  '   RAD                 ANGLE MEASURED IN RADIANS
40  '   D$                  PRINT IMAGE
50  '
60  GOSUB 400              'INITIALIZE
70  WHILE DEG <> -1
80      LET RAD = DEG * (3.14159/180)
90      PRINT USING D$; DEG, RAD, SIN(RAD), COS(RAD), TAN(RAD)
100     READ DEG
110 WEND
120 END
130 '
200 '**************** DATA GOES HERE ********************
210 DATA 0, 30, 45, 60, 90, -1
220 '
400 '**************** INITIALIZE ************************
410 CLS
420 LET D$ = "   ###     ##.###     #.####     #.####     ###,###.####"
430 PRINT   " DEGREES RADIANS     SINE      COSINE            TANGENT"
440 PRINT
450 READ DEG
460 RETURN
```

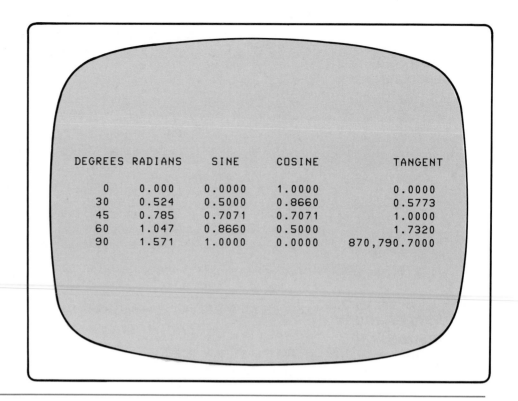

DEGREES	RADIANS	SINE	COSINE	TANGENT
0	0.000	0.0000	1.0000	0.0000
30	0.524	0.5000	0.8660	0.5773
45	0.785	0.7071	0.7071	1.0000
60	1.047	0.8660	0.5000	1.7320
90	1.571	1.0000	0.0000	870,790.7000

The EXP function returns the mathematical number e (2.718282) raised to the power of X.

```
10   LET Y = EXP(4)
```

yields Y = 54.59815

The LOG function returns the natural log and is the inverse of the EXP function.

```
20   LET Z = LOG(54.59815)
```

yields Z = 4

User-Defined Functions

In addition to the built-in functions, you can define your own functions. Any calculations done with **user-defined functions** can also be done without them. However, defining a relationship in a function can simplify programming. This is especially true when a complicated operation must be done in more than one location in the program.

```
10   '*********** FUNCTION TO ROUND TO 2 DECIMAL PLACES *****
20   DEF FN ROUND(X) = FIX(X * 100 + .5 * SGN(X)) / 100
:::
200  '***** USE THE FUNCTION IN VARIOUS LOCATIONS **********
210  LET AMT = FN ROUND(AMT)
:::
500  PRINT FN ROUND(A), FN ROUND(B), FN ROUND(C)
:::
600  LET TAX = FN ROUND(SALE * .065)
```

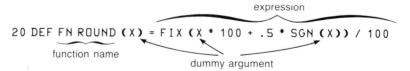

20 DEF FN ROUND (X) = FIX (X * 100 + .5 * SGN (X)) / 100

expression

function name

dummy argument

Line 20 defines a function called FN ROUND. X is called a *dummy argument,* since it is holding the place for the actual argument. When the function is called later in the program, the actual argument named is substituted for X in the function definition. The expression on the right side of the equal sign is the operation to be carried out each time the function is referenced.

When line 210 is executed, the current value for AMT will be rounded. AMT takes the place of X in the function expression.

When line 500 is executed, the function FN ROUND is referenced three times, each time with a different argument. A, B, and C will each be rounded according to the rule named in the DEF FN statement.

When line 600 is executed, first SALE will be multiplied by .065, then the result rounded by the function FN ROUND.

The DEF FN Statement—General Form

line number DEF FN name(argument(s)) = expression

The naming of the function follows the rules for naming variables. The function name will be FN + the name given. The type of function (numeric or string) is defined by the name given.

There may be multiple arguments named (or none). The arguments that appear in the function definition serve only to define the function. They don't bear any relationship to any program variables that may have the same name.

```
300   '***** STRING FUNCTION TO PRINT A PATTERN **********
310   DEF FN PT$(A$) = STRING$(5,A$)+SPACE$(5)+STRING$(5,A$)
320   LET A$ = "B"
330   PRINT FN PT$("=")
```

This will print:

```
=====     =====
```

The A$ = "B" statement (line 320) has no effect on the function. The argument of the function is the equal sign ("="), which was passed when the function was called.

An **argument** is data that is passed to the function. The variables named in the expression may or may not appear as arguments. However, the function may reference (use in calculations) variables that are not named as arguments. When a variable is an argument, the value of the argument is supplied when the function is called. When the variable is not an argument, the current value of the variable will be used.

Example Program: Variable Used in Function Expression

Program Listing

```
10 '***** VARIABLE USED IN FUNCTION EXPRESSION ********
20 DEF FN PN$(X$) = STRING$(SIZE,X$)+ SPACE$(SIZE*2) +
                    STRING$(SIZE,X$)
30 LET P$ = "#"
40 FOR SIZE = 1 TO 10
50     PRINT FN PN$(P$)
60 NEXT SIZE
```

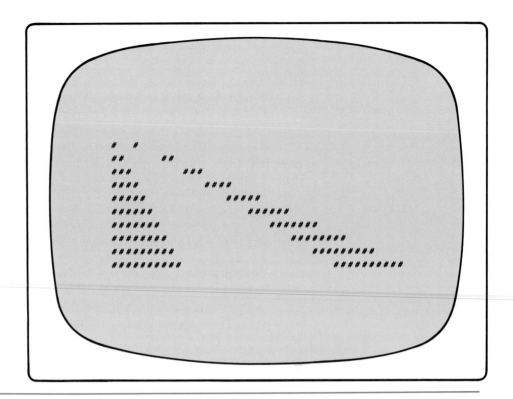

Functions with No Arguments

Although most versions of BASIC require at least one argument for functions, Microsoft does not. There may be occasions when no arguments are required.

```
50    DEF FN SEC = VAL(LEFT$(TIME$,2)) * 3600 +
                    VAL(MID$(TIME$,4,2))
                    * 60 + VAL(RIGHT$(TIME$,2))
100   '****************** TIME A LOOP ********************
110   LET START = FN SEC         'GET STARTING TIME
120   ::                         'LOOP GOES HERE
      ::
200   LET FINISH = FN SEC        'GET ENDING TIME
210   LET ELAPSED.TIME = FINISH - START
```

Functions with Multiple Arguments

One function may be defined with multiple arguments, as long as the function is called with the same number of arguments. The arguments may be any precision numeric variables or string variables. No matter what the precision of the arguments, a numeric function will always return a single-precision number.

```
240   '*** FUNCTION TO CENTER STRING ON ANY LENGTH LINE ***
250   DEF FN CENT$(X$,L) = SPACE$((L-LEN(X$))/2) + X$
        .
        .                                        line length
        .
400   PRINT FN CENT$(HD$,80)
500   LPRINT FN CENT$(HD$,120)
```

This function will center a string on whatever length line is specified. The function (FN CENT$) is a string function. The function name is defined with a dollar sign, so the value returned will be a string. It is perfectly acceptable to have both string and numeric arguments, as long as the number, type, and order of arguments on the function reference exactly match those on the DEF FN statement. The actual arguments are substituted for the dummy arguments on a one-for-one basis depending on their position.

```
100   DEF FN AVG(A,B,C,D) = (A + B + C + D) / 4
500   LET AVERAGE = FN AVG(SCORE1,SCORE2,SCORE3,SCORE4)
700   LET A = FN AVG(T1,T2,T3,T4)
```

Referencing User-Defined Functions

In a program, user-defined functions are referenced (called) in the same way as built-in functions. The function must always be referenced by its full name (including FN) and may appear in any expression.

```
100   LET Y = INT(FN X(A) / FN Y(A))
200   PRINT TAB(FN A(K)); K
300   LET STRANGE = SQR(ABS(FN R(Z)))
```

Order of Execution

The DEF FN statement must be executed before any reference to the function is made. The general practice is either to place all function definitions at the beginning of the program or to place them in an initializing subroutine (much better for modular programs).

Hierarchy of Operations

Functions rank above parentheses and exponentiation in the hierarchy of operations. If functions are used within other functions, the innermost operations are performed first.

```
490   '***** EXAMPLE TO SHOW ORDER OF OPERATIONS *************
500   LET WHAT = SQR(INT(ABS(A / B)) * 2) + A ^ 2
                      │    │    │  │      │    │   │
                      5    3    2  1      4    7   6
```

Feedback

1. Evaluate the following functions:
   a. INT(2.1)   e. SQR(-9)
   b. FIX(2.1)   f. ABS(4)
   c. CINT(2.1)   g. ABS(-4)
   d. SQR(9)   h. SGN(-4)

2. What will print?
   a.
   ```
   10 DEF FN K(A) = SQR(ABS(A))
   20 LET A = 9
   30 LET B = -25
   40 PRINT FN K(B)
   ```
   b.
   ```
   20 DEF FN A(X,Y,Z) = (X+Y+Z)/3
   80 PRINT FN A(10, 20, 30)
   ```
   c.
   ```
   100 DEF FN LN$(C$) = C$+" "+C$+" "+C$+" "+C$
   110 PRINT FN LN$("*")
   ```
   d.
   ```
   250 DEF FN UC$(A$) = CHR$(ASC(A$) -32)
   300 READ RES$
   310 DATA Yes Please
   320 FOR CT = 1 TO LEN(RES$)
   330     LET R$ = MID$(RES$,CT,1)
   340       IF ASC(R$) >= 97 AND ASC(R$) <= 122
                  THEN MID$(RES$,CT,1) = FN UC$(R$)
   350 NEXT CT
   360 PRINT RES$
   ```

3. What is a dummy argument?
4. How many operations may be done in the expression of a DEF FN statement?
5. Can you think of a good application for user-defined functions that was not mentioned in the chapter?

Summary

1. Loops that are controlled by a counter have three distinct steps. The counter must be initialized, incremented, and tested for completion.
2. The FOR and NEXT statements can be used to control the execution of a loop.
3. In the FOR statement, the counter variable is established and initialized. Also, the increment amount is defined.
4. The initial value, test value, and increment may be numeric constants, variables, or arithmetic expressions.
5. If the test condition is true before entry into the loop, the body of the loop will not be executed at all.
6. The NEXT statement marks the bottom of the loop. When NEXT is reached during execution, the counter is incremented, and control is passed back to the FOR statement to test the condition again.
7. The condition is tested for "greater than" the final value. In the case of a negative increment, the test is for "less than."
8. FOR/NEXT loops may be nested to any level.
9. When nesting FOR/NEXT loops, the inner loop must be completely contained within the outer loop.
10. The loop index for the inner loop is incremented faster than the outer loop index.
11. Single-precision numeric variables hold up to seven digits, six accurately.
12. Double-precision numeric variables can hold up to seventeen digits, sixteen accurately.
13. Integer variables hold whole numbers in the range -32768 to 32767.
14. Numeric variables that are not explicitly defined default to single-precision.
15. To explicitly define the type of variables, the rightmost character must be % for integers, ! for single-precision, # for double-precision, and $ for string variables.
16. The unit of measurement for computer storage is the byte. Integer variables take two bytes, single-precision variables take four bytes, double-precision variables take eight bytes, and string variables take one byte for each character stored.
17. The correct selection of variable type can affect the accuracy of the program, the speed of execution, and the program size.
18. Fractional numbers may not be stored accurately due to the nature of binary fractions.
19. When using fractional values, it may be necessary to check for "close" rather than exact numbers.
20. Many numeric functions are available in BASIC. A function performs the prescribed operation using the value passed as the argument.
21. The RND function returns a "random" number between 0 and 1 (exclusive).
22. To generate random numbers in the range 1–N, use the formula INT(RND * N + 1).
23. Every run of the program generates the same series of "random" numbers, unless the RANDOMIZE statement is used.
24. The functions INT, FIX, and CINT convert fractions to whole numbers, each in a little different manner.
25. INT returns the largest integer not greater than the argument. Negative numbers return the next lower integer.
26. FIX returns the integer portion of the argument by truncating all digits to the right of the decimal point. Negative numbers return the next higher integer.

27. CINT returns the nearest integer determined by rounding. Negative numbers may return a higher or lower number, whichever is closer.
28. ABS returns the absolute value of the argument.
29. SGN is used to determine the sign of a number. SGN returns -1 for a negative argument, $+1$ for a positive argument, and 0 for a zero argument.
30. SQR returns the square root of a positive argument.
31. The trigonometric functions, SIN, COS, TAN, and ATN operate on angles measured in radians.
32. The exponential functions EXP and LOG perform opposite operations using natural logarithms.
33. Additional functions can be defined by the programmer.
34. User (programmer)-defined functions are established with the DEF FN statement.
35. The DEF FN statement consists of the function name, the argument(s), and an expression that establishes the operation to be performed.
36. The variable(s) named as arguments in the DEF FN statement are called dummy arguments, since they are not actual program variables. The dummy arguments are used to indicate the operation to perform on the actual arguments.
37. Functions have higher priority than exponentiation in the hierarchy of operations for evaluating expressions.

Programming Exercises

10.1. Write a program that will print a table for conversion between pounds and kilograms.

INPUT: None
OUTPUT:
1. Print an appropriate title and column headings centered over the columns of data.
2. Print one detail line for each weight in pounds, beginning with .5, in increments of .5, ending with 20 pounds.
CALCULATIONS:
1. Use a FOR/NEXT loop to control the processing. The index of the loop must be the number of pounds. (Hint: Use .5 as the STEP.)
2. The formula for conversion:
1 pound is approximately equal to .45 kilograms

10.2. Write a math drill program for elementary school students, allowing a choice of addition, subtraction, multiplication, or division. The selection of problem type is to be presented to the user as a menu. After the completion of one group of problems, the menu must be redisplayed.

MENU: Clear the screen and present a centered menu. The choices should be (1) Addition, (2) Subtraction, (3) Multiplication, (4) Division, and (5) Quit.
INPUT: Input the name of the student and the menu selection. After each problem is presented, the student's answer must be input.
OUTPUT: Present each problem on the screen. After the user's response, print a message that indicates whether the answer was correct or incorrect. Clear the problem and any messages before presenting the next problem.
PROCESSING:
1. The numbers for the problems are to be generated with the RND function. Use digits 0–9 for operands.
2. Each group should present ten problems.

3. If the user gives an incorrect answer three times for one problem, print the correct answer and proceed to the next problem. (Give encouraging messages.)
4. Subtraction problems must not require a negative answer.
5. Division problems will have integer answers (in the range 0–9).
6. No problem will require division by zero.
7. At the end of a group of problems, indicate how many were answered correctly on the first attempt. Then redisplay the menu (after a reasonable pause).
8. Validate the number input for menu item choice. The only valid response is a number in the range 1–5.

10.3. Print a table showing X, X², X³, and $\sqrt{X}$, for X = 1 to 10. A FOR/NEXT loop must be used to increment X.

INPUT: None
OUTPUT: Complete this table.

X	X²	X³	$\sqrt{X}$
1	1	1	1.000
2	4	8	1.414
3	9	27	1.732
.	.	.	.
.	.	.	.

10.4. If one cent were placed in an investment that doubles in value each day, what would be the value of the investment at the end of thirty days? Write a program (using a FOR/NEXT loop) that calculates and prints the value of the investment for each of thirty days.

INPUT: None
OUTPUT: Complete the output shown.

```
DOUBLE OR NOTHING INVESTMENT COMPANY

DAY              VALUE OF INVESTMENT

1                     .01
2                     .02
3                     .04
.                      .
.                      .
.                      .
```

10.5. On a clear day, you can see forever (almost). The distance you can see depends on your altitude while viewing and can be determined by this formula:

$$\text{distance in miles} = \text{SQR(altitude)} * 1.22$$

Write a program that will print a table of distances from an altitude of 1,000 feet to 10,000 feet in increments of 1,000 feet. Use a FOR/NEXT loop for the altitude with a step of 1000.

```
        VIEWING DISTANCES

ALTITUDE               DISTANCE

  1,000                  38.6
  2,000                  54.6
  3,000                  66.8
    .                      .
    .                      .
    .                      .
```

10.6. Simulate a coin toss twenty times, and count the number of heads and the number of tails thrown. Use the RND function. Assume that any value $> .5$ is heads, the rest tails. Be sure to use the RANDOMIZE statement, so that each program run will produce different results.

INPUT: A random number seed.
OUTPUT: For each run, print the number of heads and the number of tails produced.

10.7. Some line printers can only print uppercase characters. Write a program that will print address labels, converting all lowercase letters to uppercase.

INPUT: During program execution, request input of a name, address, city, state, and zip code. Continue inputting and printing until END is entered for the name.
OUTPUT: Print one address label for each person. The labels will be printed "one-up," which means that each label is directly below the preceding one. The most commonly used labels have room for five printed lines, with one more line lost between labels. Therefore a new label should begin every six lines (one inch). All alphabetic output must be uppercase.

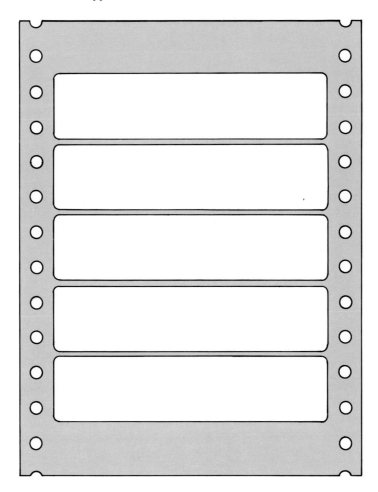

PROCESSING: Using a FOR/NEXT loop, check each character of the input strings. Any lowercase letters must be converted to uppercase.

10.8. Write a program that will randomly place dots on the screen until a key is pressed.

10.9. Write a program to randomly place squares made with graphics symbols on the screen until a key is pressed.

10.10. Write a program to print a list of ten random numbers between 1 and 100. Print the numbers on the screen.

10.11. Write a program to print the absolute value, square root, and square of any number input from the keyboard.

10.12. Use a FOR-NEXT loop to total the numbers from 1 through 100. Print the numbers on the screen.

10.13. Modify program 3.15 (karate studio purchase orders, p. 95) to use FOR/NEXT loops instead of WHILE/WEND loops.

10.14. Write a program using FOR/NEXT loops to find the standard deviation and midrange of a set of fifty numbers.

INPUT: The fifty numbers will come from DATA statements.
OUTPUT: Print the standard deviation, the midrange, and the 50 numbers on the printer.
PROCESSING:

1. Standard deviation = square root of $\dfrac{n(\text{sum of } x^2) - (\text{sum of } x)^2}{n(n-1)}$

2. Midrange = $\dfrac{\text{highest score} + \text{lowest score}}{2}$

10.15. Write a program to print addition, subtraction, multiplication, and division tests. Use FOR-NEXT loops to print fifty problems per page and use the RANDOMIZE statement so each test is different.

INPUT: Choose an option from a menu: addition, subtraction, multiplication, division, or quit.
OUTPUT: Print a title, a place for the student's name and score, and fifty problems on the printer. Format the output using print images.

11

Single-Dimension Arrays

DIM Statement

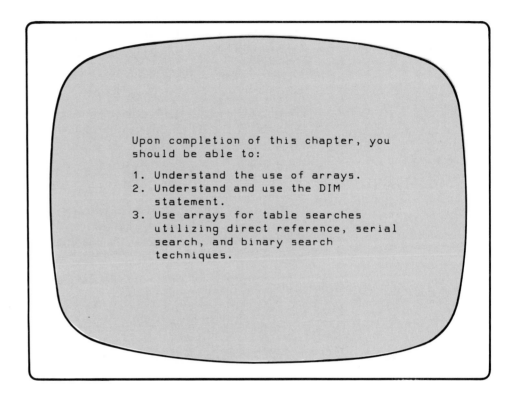

Upon completion of this chapter, you
should be able to:

1. Understand the use of arrays.
2. Understand and use the DIM
   statement.
3. Use arrays for table searches
   utilizing direct reference, serial
   search, and binary search
   techniques.

When you are programming, very likely you will find times that you want to hold multiple values for a variable. In situations where you need to compare, sort, or rearrange a series of values, you must have all the values available in variables at the same time. When you need to input a series of values, such as scores, and have all those values available after input is finished, a problem arises. As you know, whenever data is input in a loop, each new value for a variable replaces the previous value. In this chapter you will learn to use **arrays** to overcome this problem, holding each new input value without destroying the old.

```
10    '************* AVERAGE SCORES *************************
20    INPUT SCORE
30    WHILE SCORE <> -1
40         LET COUNT = COUNT + 1
50         LET TOT = TOT + SCORE
60         INPUT SCORE
70    WEND
80    LET AVG = TOT/COUNT
90    PRINT "AVERAGE SCORE = " AVG
```

Although each score is accumulated in the loop, the individual scores are no longer available to the program after the loop is complete. Sometimes these scores may need to be available again later in the program. A common operation is to compute the variance for each score, which is the measure of how far an individual score is from the average [variance = ABS(average − score)]. For that operation, we would need to input the scores once to find the average and then input them a second time to compute the variance.

A second solution could be to give every score a unique variable name, so that all are available after completion of the loop. For this approach, the number of scores must be known ahead of time. In the interest of simplicity, six scores are used for the example.

```
500    '******* CALCULATE VARIANCE FOR SIX SCORES *********
510    INPUT SCORE1
520    INPUT SCORE2
530    INPUT SCORE3
540    INPUT SCORE4
550    INPUT SCORE5
560    INPUT SCORE6
570    LET AVG = (SCORE1+SCORE2+SCORE3+SCORE4+SCORE5+SCORE6)/6
580    PRINT "VARIANCE FOR" SCORE1 " IS" ABS(AVG-SCORE1)
590    PRINT "VARIANCE FOR" SCORE2 " IS" ABS(AVG-SCORE2)
600    PRINT "VARIANCE FOR" SCORE3 " IS" ABS(AVG-SCORE3)
610    PRINT "VARIANCE FOR" SCORE4 " IS" ABS(AVG-SCORE4)
620    PRINT "VARIANCE FOR" SCORE5 " IS" ABS(AVG-SCORE5)
630    PRINT "VARIANCE FOR" SCORE6 " IS" ABS(AVG-SCORE6)
640    RETURN
```

This program does solve the problem. The individual scores were retained in memory by giving each a unique variable name. With a little work, a search could find the highest score, print that one first, then the next highest, and so forth, to produce a sorted list. Stop and picture the program required to handle 30 scores, or 100 scores.

Fortunately, there is a much better way. To hold related multiple variables, use an array. An array is a series of individual variables, all referenced by the same name.

Programming
with Arrays

> An ARRAY can be defined as a series (or a group) of variables that are all referred to by one name.

In mathematics, multiple scores could be noted:

S_1 S_2 S_3 S_4 . . . S_N

In BASIC, an array may be referenced in much the same way:

```
SC(1), SC(2), SC(3), SC(4), SC(5), SC(6)
```

These are read SC sub one, SC sub two, SC sub three, and so forth.

Each individual variable is called an *element* of the SC array. The individual elements, also called **subscripted variables,** are treated the same as any other variable used and may be used in any statement such as LET, PRINT, INPUT, and READ.

```
LET SC(1) = 5

LET TOT = TOT + SC(4)

READ SC(2)

INPUT SC(5)

PRINT SC(1), SC(2), SC(3), SC(4)
```

Subscripts

The real advantage of arrays is not realized until variables are used for **subscripts** in place of the constants.

```
LET SC(N) = 5

LET TOT = TOT + SC(INDEX)

READ SC(INDEX)

INPUT SC(SC.SUB)

PRINT SC(K), SC(K+1), SC(K+2), SC(K+3)
```

Subscripts may be constants, variables, or numeric expressions. Although the subscripts must be integers, BASIC will round any noninteger subscript. The problem to compute the variance for six scores becomes much easier.

```
700  '******** INPUT SCORES AND COMPUTE AVERAGE *************
710  FOR COUNT = 1 TO 6
720      INPUT SC(COUNT)
730      LET TOT = TOT + SC(COUNT)
740  NEXT COUNT
750  LET AVG = TOT/6              'CALC AVERAGE
755  '
760  '*********** COMPUTE AND PRINT VARIANCE ***************
770  FOR COUNT = 1 TO 6
780      LET VARIANCE = ABS(AVG - SC(COUNT))
790      PRINT "THE VARIANCE FOR" SC(COUNT) " IS" VARIANCE
800  NEXT COUNT
810  RETURN
```

For the statement   `INPUT SC(COUNT)`

When COUNT = 1   `INPUT SC(1)`

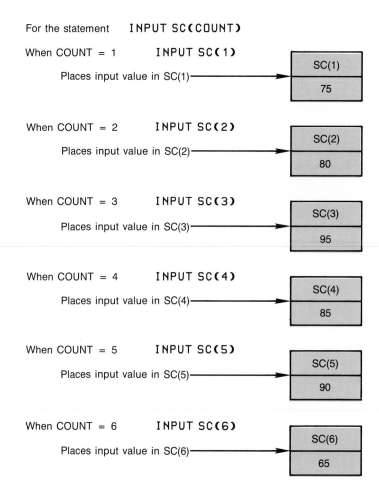

   Places input value in SC(1)

When COUNT = 2   `INPUT SC(2)`

   Places input value in SC(2)

When COUNT = 3   `INPUT SC(3)`

   Places input value in SC(3)

When COUNT = 4   `INPUT SC(4)`

   Places input value in SC(4)

When COUNT = 5   `INPUT SC(5)`

   Places input value in SC(5)

When COUNT = 6   `INPUT SC(6)`

   Places input value in SC(6)

If the scores had not been added in the input loop, the elements of the array could be totaled quickly after the values were entered.

```
40   '******** TOTAL THE ELEMENTS IN THE SC ARRAY **********
50   FOR COUNT = 1 TO 6
60       LET TOTAL = TOTAL + SC(COUNT)
70   NEXT COUNT
80   RETURN
```

To print all scores, a routine similar to the following might be used.

```
100  '******** PRINT ALL ELEMENTS OF THE SC ARRAY *********
110  FOR COUNT = 1 TO 6
120      PRINT SC(COUNT)
130  NEXT COUNT
140  RETURN
```

To print the scores in the reverse order from which they were input, use a routine similar to the following.

```
200  '*********** PRINT SCORES IN REVERSE ORDER ***********
210  FOR COUNT = 6 TO 1 STEP -1
220      PRINT SC(COUNT)
230  NEXT COUNT
240  RETURN
```

What changes would need to be made in the programs to handle more than six scores? Like 30 or 100?

A question has probably occurred to you by now—How many elements *are* there in the SC array? The answer is that the programmer defines the number of elements in the array before its first use with the DIM (DIMension) statement.

It was possible to omit the DIM statements in the examples thus far because, in the absence of a DIM statement, BASIC allocates ten elements. Even though elements 1–6 were used, #7, 8, 9, and 10 were still available. In fact, there is one more—element 0—but more about that later.

Dimensioning an Array

The DIM Statement—General Form

line number DIM array name(number of elements) . . .

The DIM Statement—Examples

```
100    DIM SCORE(100)
110    DIM NAM$(50)
120    DIM A(20),B(20),C(40),N$(50),P(10)

200    INPUT COUNT
210    DIM SC(COUNT)
```

The DIM statement allocates storage space for the specified number of elements and initializes each to zero. In the case of string arrays, each element is set to a null string (no characters).

Placement of the DIM statement is critical. DIM must be executed before any statement that references the array. Most programmers place all DIM statements at the start of the program, after the initial remarks and before the program mainline. The only exception to that practice would be something similar to the preceding example on lines 200 and 210, where the size of the array is determined during program execution.

One program may have multiple DIM statements, and one DIM statement may dimension multiple arrays. Either of these approaches is valid:

```
50    DIM APPLES(20), BANANAS(20), FRUIT$(40)
```

or

```
50    DIM APPLES(20)
60    DIM BANANAS(20)
70    DIM FRUIT$(40)
```

Each array may be dimensioned only once in a program. Any attempt to change the size of an array after its first use causes the error message, DUPLICATE DEFINITION.

The maximum number of elements in one array is 32767 (that familiar number again!). A more practical limit for programming with arrays is the memory size of the computer. Each array element (and each regular variable) causes memory to be set aside. Many large arrays can quickly take the entire memory of small computers.

Without a DIM statement, BASIC defaults to ten elements. However, *it is strongly recommended that all arrays be dimensioned, even those with ten elements or less.* Having the DIM statements appear together in the program is an aid to documentation and program debugging. The proposed ANSI standards for BASIC will require that all arrays be dimensioned.

As mentioned earlier, BASIC also allocates an element zero for each array. The statement

```
50    DIM SC(6)
```

actually defines seven elements: SC(0), SC(1), SC(2), SC(3), SC(4), SC(5), and SC(6). In actual practice, the 0th (say zeroeth) element is commonly ignored. If there is no need for an element zero, one of two approaches may be taken: (1) ignore element zero or (2) use the OPTION BASE statement, which defines the lower limit for array elements.

```
10   OPTION BASE 1
```

or

```
20   OPTION BASE 0 (the system default)
```

Line 10 declares that all program arrays will begin with element 1 (instead of zero). This could save space if the program uses many arrays. If the OPTION BASE statement is used, it must appear before any array is dimensioned or used.

More on Subscripts

A subscript (which may also be called an index) must reference a valid element of the array. Invalid subscripts include negative numbers and any number greater than the number of elements dimensioned. If a list contained ten names, it wouldn't make sense to ask, "What is the fifteenth name on the list?" Try asking for the -1st name or the $2\frac{1}{2}$th name on the list. BASIC rounds fractional subscripts and gives the error message, SUBSCRIPT OUT OF RANGE, for invalid subscripts.

Feedback

```
10   DIM A(20)
20   LET I = 10
```

After execution of the preceding statements, which of the following are valid subscripts?

1. A(20)   5. A(0)
2. A(I)   6. A(I-20)
3. A(I*2)   7. A(I/3)
4. A(I*3)   8. A(I/5-2)

Filling an Array with READ and DATA Statements

Using the READ to fill an array is similar to using the INPUT statement.

```
200   '****** FILL TEN-ELEMENT ARRAY WITH READ/DATA ********
210   DIM COST(10)
220   FOR INDEX = 1 TO 10
230      READ COST(INDEX)
240   NEXT INDEX
250   DATA 2.00,2.10,2.50,2.75,3.00,3.15,3.45,4.10,4.85,5.25
260   RETURN
270   '
400   '***** FILL ARRAY WITH READ/DATA UNTIL TERMINAL VALUE *
410   DIM COST(20)
420   LET INDEX = 1
430   READ COST(INDEX)
440   WHILE COST(INDEX) >= 0 AND INDEX < 20
445      LET INDEX = INDEX + 1
450      READ COST(INDEX)
460   WEND
470   DATA 2.00,2.10,2.50,2.75,3.00,3.15,3.45,4.10
475   DATA 4.85,5.25,5.85,6.45,-1
480   RETURN
```

Feedback

Use this statement for both problems:

```
10  DIM NAM$(50)
```

1. Using INPUT, write the statements that will request names from the keyboard, and fill the NAM$ array with those names until EOD is entered.
2. Write the READ/DATA statements necessary to READ names into the NAM$ array until EOD is read.

Parallel Arrays

Consider the test score example again. If keeping names along with the scores is desired, a second array is required, one for the set of scores and another for the set of names.

```
500  '****** READ DATA INTO PARALLEL ARRAYS *****************
510  DIM NAM$(6),SCORE(6)
520  FOR INDEX = 1 TO 6
530      READ NAM$(INDEX), SCORE(INDEX)
540  NEXT INDEX
550  DATA J. SPRAT,75,M. MUFFETT,80,L. BOPEEP,95,B. SHAFTOE,85
560  DATA L. BOYBLUE, 90, O. L. SHOE, 65
570  RETURN
```

	NAM$ ARRAY		SCORE ARRAY
(1)	J. SPRAT	(1)	75
(2)	M. MUFFETT	(2)	80
(3)	L. BOPEEP	(3)	95
(4)	B. SHAFTOE	(4)	85
(5)	L. BOYBLUE	(5)	90
(6)	O. L. SHOE	(6)	65

The elements in the two **parallel arrays** correspond; that is, the first name goes with the first score, second with second, and so forth. The complete list could be printed out, or any single element.

```
800  '********** PRINT LIST OF ALL NAMES AND SCORES ********
810  FOR INDEX = 1 TO 6
820      PRINT NAM$(INDEX), SCORE(INDEX)
830  NEXT INDEX
840  RETURN
850  '
1000  '************ FIND HIGH SCORE *********************
1010  LET HIGH.INDEX = 1
1020  FOR INDEX = 2 TO 6
1030      IF SCORE(INDEX) > SCORE(HIGH.INDEX)
              THEN LET HIGH.INDEX = INDEX
1040  NEXT INDEX
1050  '* NOW HIGH.INDEX HOLDS THE SUBSCRIPT OF THE HIGH SCORE
1060  PRINT "HIGHEST PERSON WAS " NAM$(HIGH.INDEX);
1070  PRINT " WITH A SCORE OF" SCORE(HIGH.INDEX)
1080  RETURN
```

Arrays Used for Accumulators

Array elements are regular variables, just like all variables used thus far. These subscripted variables may be used in any way chosen, such as for counters or total accumulators.

To demonstrate the use of array elements as total accumulators, eight totals will be accumulated. For the example, eight scout groups are selling raffle tickets. A separate total must be accumulated for each of the eight groups. Each time a sale is made, the number of tickets must be added to the correct total. The statement

```
50  DIM TOTAL(8)
```

will establish the eight accumulators.

Initializing the Array

Although all program variables are initially set to zero, it is often necessary to re-initialize variables. Such is the case when printing subtotals. After the subtotals are printed, the fields must be reset to zero. To zero out an array, each element must be individually set to zero.

```
100  '*************** ZERO OUT TOTAL ARRAY ****************
110  FOR INDEX = 1 TO 8
120      LET TOTAL(INDEX) = 0
130  NEXT INDEX
140  RETURN
```

Adding to the Correct Total

Assuming that a program inputs a group number and number of tickets, the problem is to add that ticket count to the correct total. The sales will be input in any order, with multiple sales for each group.

```
300  '******* INPUT GROUP NUMBER AND TICKET SALE ***********
310  INPUT "ENTER GROUP NUMBER ", GROUP
320  INPUT "NUMBER OF TICKETS SOLD ", SALE
330  RETURN
```

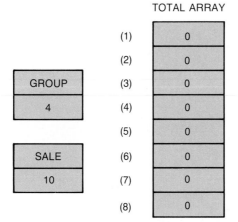

After execution of the input subroutine, GROUP holds the group number, and SALE holds the amount of this sale. Assume for the first sale that 4 was entered for the group number and 10 tickets were sold.

In order to add 10 to the group 4 total, use GROUP as a subscript to add to the correct TOTAL element.

```
310   LET TOTAL(GROUP) = TOTAL(GROUP) + SALE
```

Of course, there is always the danger that the user will incorrectly enter the group number. Since it is undesirable for the user to get the error message SUBSCRIPT OUT OF RANGE, the group number must be validated.

```
400   '* ADD TICKET SALE TO CORRECT TOTAL OR PRINT ERROR MSG *
410   IF GROUP >= 1 AND GROUP <= 8
          THEN LET TOTAL(GROUP) = TOTAL(GROUP) + SALE
          ELSE PRINT "INVALID GROUP NUMBER, RE-ENTER THIS SALE"
```

Using the group number as an index to the array is a technique called direct reference.

Direct Table Reference

There are many occasions when it is useful to use an input variable as a subscript to point to an array element. Another example of direct reference is the use of a table to look up the month names. If a month number is input (perhaps part of the date), the corresponding month name can be printed out.

When using tables for reference, it is necessary to *load* the table as an initialization step in the program. The entire table must be in memory and available during all processing.

```
400   '************** LOAD MONTH TABLE ********************
410   DIM MONTH$(12)
420   FOR MONTH.SUB = 1 TO 12
430       READ MONTH$(MONTH.SUB)
440   NEXT MONTH.SUB
450   DATA JANUARY, FEBRUARY, MARCH, APRIL, MAY, JUNE, JULY
460   DATA AUGUST, SEPTEMBER, OCTOBER, NOVEMBER, DECEMBER
470   RETURN
```

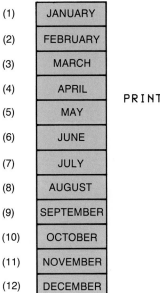

MONTH$ ARRAY

PRINT MONTH$ (MONTH.NUM)

Output: OCTOBER

Lookup by Direct Reference

The month number can be used to directly access (or look up) the correct array element. If the month number is input, it is a simple task to print out the corresponding month name.

```
500   '****** INPUT MONTH NUMBER AND PRINT MONTH NAME ******
510   INPUT "ENTER MONTH NUMBER ", MONTH.NUM
520   IF MONTH.NUM >= 1 AND MONTH.NUM <= 12
          THEN PRINT MONTH$(MONTH.NUM)
530   RETURN
```

If the user entered 10 for MONTH.NUM, then the tenth element of the MONTH$ array would be printed—which is OCTOBER.

Table Lookup— Serial Search

Things don't always work out so neatly as month numbers or group numbers that can be used to directly access the table. Sometimes a little work must be done to **look up** the correct value. Go back to the eight scout groups and their ticket sales. Now the groups are not numbered 1–8, but 101, 103, 110, 115, 121, 123, 130, and 145. The group number and the number of tickets sold will still be input, and the number of tickets will be added to the correct total. But, another step is needed—determine to which element of the SALES array to add.

The first step in the program will be to establish a parallel array with the group numbers. Then, before any processing is done, the group numbers must be loaded into the table.

```
50    DIM TOTAL(8), GR.NUM(8)
      ::
      ::
1500    '********** LOAD GROUP NUMBER ARRAY ****************
1510    FOR GR = 1 TO 8
1520        READ GR.NUM(GR)
1530    NEXT GR
1540    DATA 101,103,110,115,121,123,130,145
1550    RETURN
```

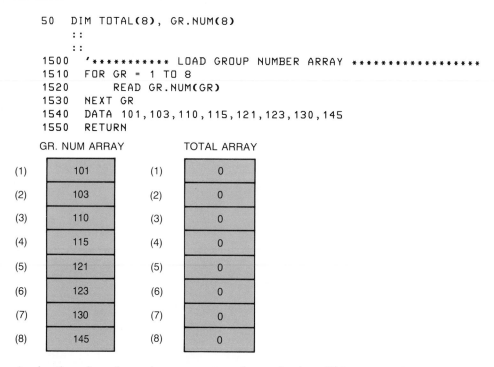

Again, the subroutine to input group number and sales will be executed.

```
3000    '****** INPUT GROUP NUMBER AND TICKET SALE ***********
3010    INPUT "ENTER GROUP NUMBER ", GROUP
3020    INPUT "NUMBER OF TICKETS SOLD ", SALE
3030    RETURN
```

The technique used is called **serial table lookup,** or **table search.** In the table lookup, the object is to find the element number (1–8) of the group number and use that element number as a subscript to the total table. So, if the third group number (110) is entered, the sale will be added to the third total. If the seventh group number (130) is entered, the sale will be added to the seventh total.

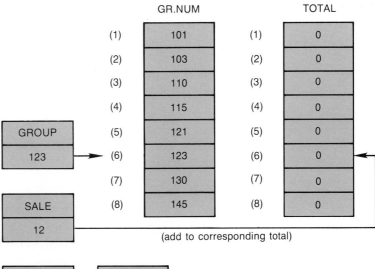

Figure 11.1
Diagram of arrays and fields for lookup.

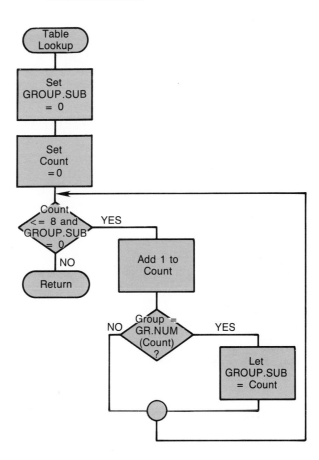

Figure 11.2
Flowchart of lookup logic.

When BASIC executes the statement

```
LET TOTAL(GROUP.SUB) = TOTAL(GROUP.SUB) + SALE
```

the value of GROUP.SUB must be a number in the range 1–8. The task for the lookup operation is to find the number to place in GROUP.SUB, based on the value of GROUP. Figure 11.1 shows the fields used for the lookup. Figure 11.2 shows the flowchart of the lookup logic.

Coding a Table Lookup

```
3600  '********** TABLE LOOKUP FOR GROUP NUMBER **********
3610  LET GROUP.SUB = 0            'INITIALIZE TO ENTER LOOP
3620  LET COUNT = 0               'BEGIN COUNTER AT ZERO
3630  WHILE COUNT <= 8 AND GROUP.SUB = 0
3640     LET COUNT = COUNT + 1
3650     IF GROUP = GR.NUM(COUNT)
            THEN LET GROUP.SUB = COUNT
3660  WEND
3670              '** GROUP.SUB NOW CONTAINS CORRECT ELEMENT
3680              '    NUMBER, OR ZERO, IF NO MATCH WAS FOUND
3690  RETURN
```

After execution of the LOOKUP subroutine, GROUP.SUB will hold the subscript corresponding to the GROUP that was entered. If the count went all the way to 8 and a match was not found, then GROUP.SUB will still hold 0. So, after the lookup, the program can test for 0 in GROUP.SUB. This only slightly changes the ADD subroutine.

```
3400  '* ADD TICKET SALE TO CORRECT TOTAL OR PRINT ERROR MSG *
3410  IF GROUP.SUB <> 0
         THEN LET TOTAL(GROUP.SUB) = TOTAL(GROUP.SUB) + SALE
         ELSE PRINT "INVALID GROUP NUMBER, RE-ENTER THIS SALE"
3420  RETURN
```

Example Program: Serial Table Lookup

Now the entire program can be put together.

Hierarchy Chart and Flowchart

Figure 11.3 (pp. 294–95) shows a hierarchy chart and a flowchart of the table lookup program.

Program Listing

```
100 ' PROGRAM TO DEMONSTRATE SERIAL TABLE LOOKUP OPERATION
110 '
120 '    TABULATES TOTAL SALES FOR EIGHT SCOUT GROUPS
130 '
140 '           PROGRAM VARIABLES
150 '
160 '  GR.NUM(8)        TABLE TO HOLD GROUP NUMBERS
170 '  TOTAL(8)         ARRAY TO HOLD 8 TOTALS
180 '  GROUP            GROUP NUMBER ON INPUT
190 '  GROUP.SUB        SUBSCRIPT TO ADD TO TOTAL TABLE
200 '  INDEX            INDEX OF LOOP
210 '  COUNT            LOOP COUNTER
220 '
230 '        DIMENSIONS
240 '
250 OPTION BASE 1
260 DIM GR.NUM(8),TOTAL(8)
270 '
500 '************** PROGRAM MAINLINE *********************
520 GOSUB 1000           'LOAD GROUP NUMBER TABLE
530 GOSUB 2000           'DETAIL PROCESSING
540 GOSUB 4000           'PRINT GROUP TOTALS
550 END
560 '
```

```
1000 '*********** LOAD GROUP NUMBER ARRAY ******************
1010 FOR GR = 1 TO 8
1020     READ GR.NUM(GR)
1030 NEXT GR
1040 DATA 101,103,110,115,121,123,130,145
1050 RETURN
1060 '
2000 '*************** DETAIL PROCESSING *******************
2010 GOSUB 3000                    'PRIMING INPUT FOR TICKET SALES
2020 WHILE SALE <> 0
2030     GOSUB 3200                'LOOK UP GROUP NUMBER
2040     GOSUB 3400                'ADD TO CORRECT TOTAL
2050     GOSUB 3000                'INPUT NEXT SALE
2060 WEND
2070 RETURN
2080 '
3000 '******* INPUT GROUP NUMBER AND TICKET SALE **********
3010 CLS
3020 LOCATE 4,15
3030 INPUT "ENTER GROUP NUMBER ", GROUP
3040 LOCATE 6,15
3050 INPUT "NUMBER OF TICKETS SOLD ", SALE
3060 RETURN
3070 '
3200 '*********** TABLE LOOKUP FOR GROUP NUMBER ***********
3210 LET GROUP.SUB = 0             'INITIALIZE TO ENTER LOOP
3220 LET COUNT = 0                 'BEGIN COUNTER AT ZERO
3230 WHILE COUNT <= 8 AND GROUP.SUB = 0
3240     LET COUNT = COUNT + 1
3250     IF GROUP = GR.NUM(COUNT)
             THEN LET GROUP.SUB = COUNT
3260 WEND
3270             '** GROUP.SUB NOW CONTAINS CORRECT ELEMENT
3280             '       NUMBER, OR ZERO, IF NO MATCH WAS FOUND
3290 RETURN
3300 '
3400 '***** ADD SALE TO CORRECT TOTAL OR PRINT ERROR MSG ***
3410 IF GROUP.SUB <> 0
         THEN LET TOTAL(GROUP.SUB) = TOTAL(GROUP.SUB) + SALE
         ELSE GOSUB 3510          'PRINT ERROR MESSAGE
3420 RETURN
3430 '
3500 '**************** PRINT ERROR MESSAGE ****************
3510 LOCATE 20,10
3520 PRINT "ERROR IN GROUP NUMBER, RE-ENTER THIS SALE"
3530 LOCATE 22,20
3540 PRINT "PRESS ANY KEY TO CONTINUE"
3560 LET D$ = INPUT$(1)
3570 RETURN
3580 '
4000 '*********** PRINT ALL GROUP TOTALS *****************
4010 CLS
4020 PRINT "   GROUP            SALES"
4030 FOR INDEX = 1 TO 8
4040     PRINT USING "    ###          #,### "; GR.NUM(INDEX),TOTAL(INDEX)
4050 NEXT INDEX
4060 RETURN
4070 '************ END OF PROGRAM ***********************
```

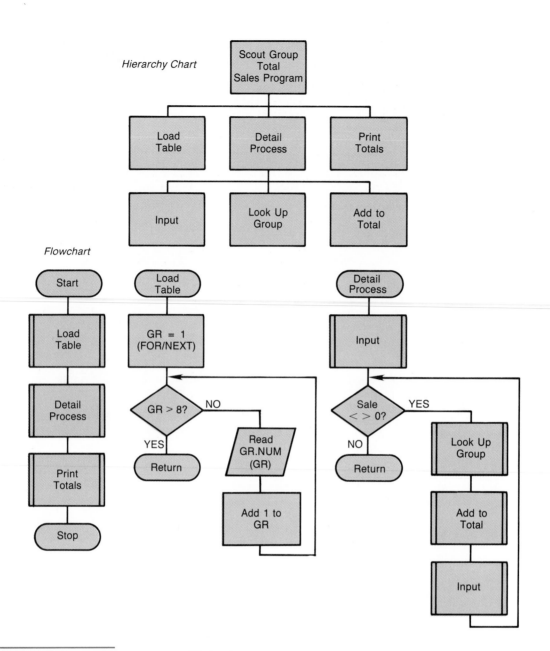

Hierarchy Chart

Flowchart

Figure 11.3
Hierarchy chart and flowchart of
table lookup program.

Figure 11.3—*Continued*

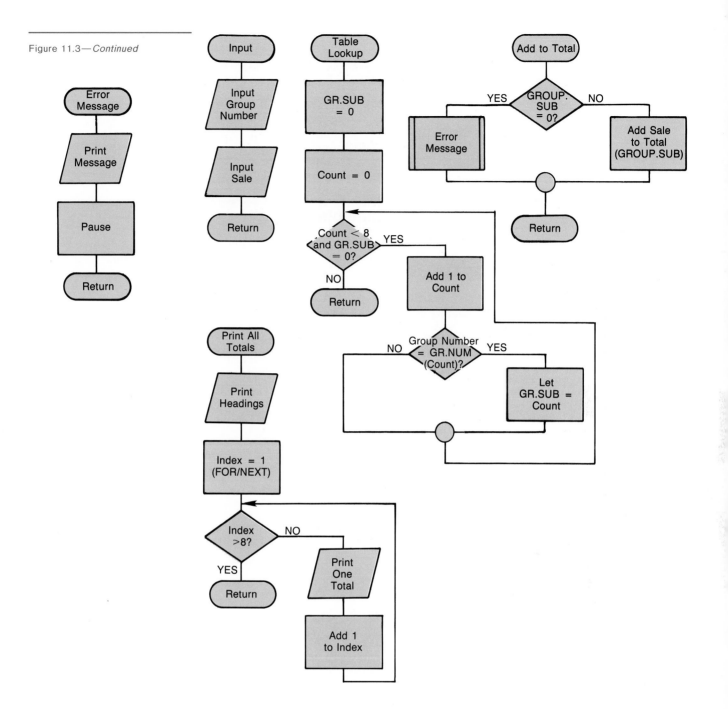

Table Lookup with String Data

The table lookup process works exactly the same way for string data as for numeric. However, sometimes a little caution is needed when looking up a name. The search is only successful on an exact match, character by character.

```
                          Joan  T.  Smith
does not match            JOAN  T.  SMITH
or                        Joan  T  Smith
or                        Joan  Smith
```

Programming Example

This program will keep a personal telephone number directory. A person's name will be entered, and their telephone number will be displayed on the screen.

Input

1. Names and telephone numbers to establish the table (directory).
2. During execution—one name for lookup.

Output

1. Telephone number—corresponding to name.
2. Error message, if name not in directory.

Pseudocode

1. Load the tables
2. Inquiry loop
   2.1 Input a name
   2.2 Loop until name = "END"
        2.2.1 Look up name
        2.2.2 If name found
                  then display it
                  else display error message
        2.2.3 Pause before clearing screen
        2.2.4 Input next name
3. End program

Hierarchy Chart and Flowchart

Figure 11.4 (pp. 298–99) shows both a hierarchy chart and a flowchart for the program.

Program Listing

```
100 '          PERSONAL  TELEPHONE  DIRECTORY
110 '
120 ' LOOK UP NAME AND PRINT PERSON'S TELEPHONE NUMBER
130 '
140 '          PROGRAM VARIABLES
150 '
160 '          NAM$(50)        TABLE TO HOLD NAMES
170 '          PHONE$(50)      TABLE TO HOLD PHONE NUMBERS
180 '          NM$             NAME FOR INQUIRY INPUT
190 '          NAM.SUB         SUBSCRIPT FOR CORRECT NUMBER
200 '          COUNT           LOOP COUNTER
210 '          MAX             MAXIMUM NUMBER OF NAMES
220 '
500 DIM NAM$(50), PHONE$(50)
505 '
```

```
510 '**************** PROGRAM MAINLINE ********************
520 GOSUB 1000                        'LOAD TABLES
530 GOSUB 2000                        'INQUIRY LOOP
540 CLS
550 END                               'END OF PROGRAM
560 '
1000 '************** LOAD TABLES **************************
1010 LET COUNT = 1
1020 READ NAM$(COUNT), PHONE$(COUNT)
1030 WHILE NAM$(COUNT) <> "END"
1040    LET COUNT = COUNT + 1
1050    READ NAM$(COUNT), PHONE$(COUNT)
1060 WEND
1065 LET MAX = COUNT - 1
1070 DATA LEANNE LOTT, 555-1234, JILL JAMES, 555-3225
1080 DATA GEORGE HILL, 555-9119, JOHN SHORT, 555-5926
1090 DATA BILL ROGERS, 555-2290, ANITA PAZ, 555-5611
1100 DATA ALICE ALLISON, 555-2345, HARRY HOLD, 555-4921
1110 DATA BOB STEP, 555-3333, CARL BROWN, 555-6543
1120 DATA END, END
1130 RETURN
1140 '
2000 '***************** INQUIRY LOOP *************************
2010 GOSUB 3000                       'PRIME INPUT
2020 WHILE NM$ <> "END"
2030    GOSUB 4000                     'LOOK UP NAME
2040    IF NAM.SUB <> 0
            THEN GOSUB 5000
            ELSE GOSUB 6000
2050    GOSUB 7000                     'PAUSE
2060    GOSUB 3000                     'INPUT NEXT NAME
2070 WEND
2080 RETURN
2090 '
3000 '************** INPUT A NAME ***************************
3010 CLS
3020 LOCATE 10,10
3030 INPUT "ENTER NAME, 'END' TO QUIT ", NM$
3040 RETURN
3050 '
4000 '*************** LOOKUP NAME ****************************
4010 LET NAM.SUB = 0                   'INITIALIZE TO ENTER LOOP
4020 LET COUNT = 0                     'BEGIN COUNT AT ZERO
4030 WHILE COUNT < MAX AND NAM.SUB = 0
4040    LET COUNT = COUNT + 1
4050    IF NM$ = NAM$(COUNT)
            THEN LET NAM.SUB = COUNT
4060 WEND
4070 RETURN
4080 '
5000 '************ PRINT PHONE NUMBER ***********************
5010 LOCATE 12,37
5020 PRINT PHONE$(NAM.SUB)
5030 RETURN
5040 '
6000 '************ PRINT ERROR MESSAGE **********************
6010 LOCATE 16,40
6020 PRINT "NAME NOT ON FILE"
6030 RETURN
6040 '
7000 '************ PAUSE ************************************
7010 LOCATE 22,40
7020 PRINT "PRESS ANY KEY TO CONTINUE . . .";
7030 LET D$ = INPUT$(1)
7040 RETURN
8000 '************ END OF PROGRAM ***************************
```

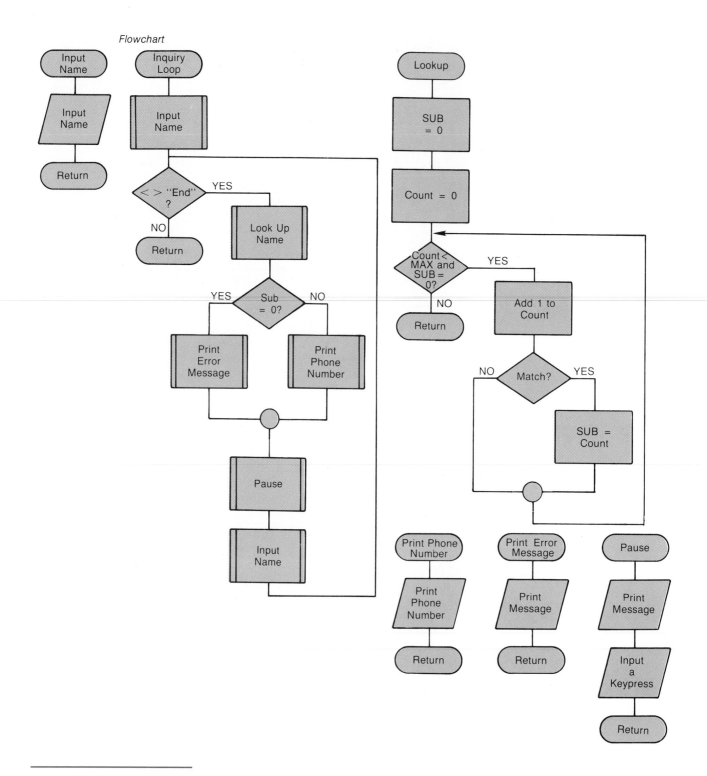

Flowchart

Figure 11.4
Planning for personal telephone
directory program.

Figure 11.4—*Continued*

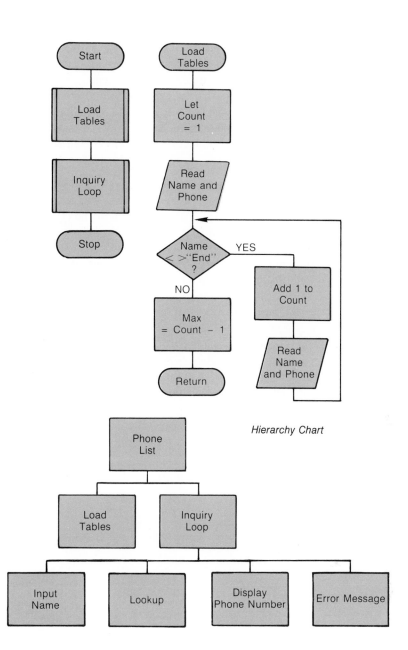

Hierarchy Chart

The serial search technique will work for any table, numeric or string. It is not necessary for the fields being searched to be arranged in any sequence. The comparison is done to one item in the list, then the next, and the next, until a match is found. In fact, it's possible to save processing time by arranging the table with the most-often-used entries at the top, so fewer comparisons must be made. When a table gets really large, say more than 100 items, the serial search can become extremely slow. For these large tables, a **binary search** may be the best solution.

Binary Search

In a binary search, it is not necessary to search the entire table for a match. The table entries are arranged in sequence—whether numeric or string. The search can be quickly narrowed to a particular section of the table.

The first step in the search process is to compare the **search argument** (field to be matched) to the middle table element. If the search argument is higher than the middle element, the first half of the table can be discarded. Then that second half is again divided in half, and the comparison is made to the middle element. Again, half of the remaining group is discarded. This process continues until the table is narrowed down to one element, or a *hit* is made sooner.

Searching in this manner may seem cumbersome, but it is actually quite efficient. To serially search a 1000 element table, an average of 500 comparisons would be required. For a binary search of a 1000 element table, a *maximum* of ten comparisons is required. If a high percentage of the items to be matched is not in the table, the advantage of a binary search increases dramatically.

Diagram of a Binary Search

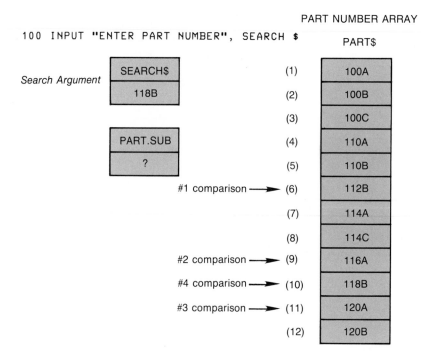

In the preceding example a twelve-element table of part numbers is searched. The search argument (part number to look up) is called SEARCH$. When the correct element is found, the subscript will be placed in PART.SUB. If no match is found, zero will be placed in PART.SUB to indicate that the part number is not in the table. Figure 11.5 shows the logic for a binary search.

Flowchart of Binary Search

Set upper limit for search to number of elements in array + 1

Set lower limit for search to zero

Set middle point to halfway between upper and lower limits (low + upper)/2

Is there a match at the middle element or a determination that there is no match?

While not finished:

If the search argument < middle element

then set new upper limit at middle

else set new lower limit at middle

Set new middle, halfway between lower and upper limits

While end

Finished. Now check to see why. (Was there a match or not?)

If no match found (middle will be equal to lower limit)

then let SUB = 0

else let SUB = middle

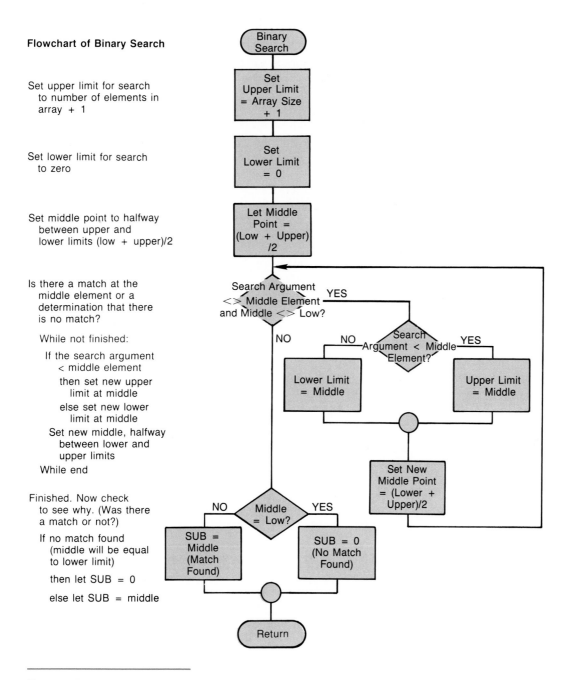

Figure 11.5
Flowchart of binary search.

Coding of Binary Search

The coding in the following subroutine could be used to replace the lookup subroutine in the preceding program. You will recall that the search argument was GROUP, and the table being searched was GR.NUM.

```
3200  '*********** BINARY SEARCH ****************************
3210  LET UPPER.LIMIT = 9        'ARRAY SIZE + 1
3220  LET LOW.LIMIT = 0
3230  LET MIDDLE = INT((LOW.LIMIT + UPPER.LIMIT) / 2)
3240  WHILE GR.NUM(MIDDLE) <> GROUP AND MIDDLE <> LOW.LIMIT
3250      IF GROUP < GR.NUM(MIDDLE)
              THEN LET UPPER.LIMIT = MIDDLE
              ELSE LET LOW.LIMIT = MIDDLE
3260      LET MIDDLE = INT((LOW.LIMIT + UPPER.LIMIT) / 2)
3270  WEND
3280  IF MIDDLE <> LOW.LIMIT
          THEN LET GROUP.SUB = MIDDLE
          ELSE LET GROUP.SUB = 0
3290  RETURN
```

Feedback

Write the BASIC statements to:

1. Set up a twenty-element array called K, and initialize each element to 100.
2. Divide all even-numbered elements in the K array by 2.
    [K(2), K(4), K(6), ... K(20)]
3. Subtract 1 from every element of the K array.
4. Print all elements of the K array, ten per line.
5. Dimension and load a table with the following data:
    50 DATA CANDY, ICE CREAM, POPCORN, GUM, COOKIES, GUM DROPS
6. How does a binary search differ from a lookup operation?
7. When would it be better to use a binary search?
8. When would it be better to use a serial search?

Summary

1. An array is a group of variables all referenced by the same name.
2. Arrays provide a means to hold multiple field values in memory at the same time.
3. The individual variables in an array are called elements.
4. To refer to an individual element in an array, a subscript is added to the array name. For this reason the elements are also referred to as subscripted variables.
5. Subscripted variables may be used exactly the same way as regular (unsubscripted) variables.
6. A subscript may be a constant, variable, or numeric expression. Any fractional subscript is rounded to the nearest integer.
7. A subscript cannot be a negative number or greater than the number of elements in the array.
8. The number of elements in an array is established by the DIM (DIMension) statement.
9. An array may be dimensioned for up to 32767 elements.
10. One program may have multiple DIM statements; one DIM statement may dimension multiple arrays.
11. The DIM statement for any array must be executed before any statement referencing that array.
12. If an array is not dimensioned before its first use, eleven elements are automatically defined—elements 0–10.

13. BASIC established arrays with an element 0. However, if the statement OPTION BASE 1 is used before the first DIM or array reference, all arrays will begin with element 1.
14. A variable may be used in the DIM statement as in DIM ARR(N). However, the size of an array cannot be changed once it has been established.
15. When the DIM statement is executed, BASIC allocates the storage for the variables and initializes them to zero. In the case of string arrays, the elements are initialized to null strings (no characters).
16. Array elements may be filled with READ/DATA statements, INPUT, or assignment statements.
17. In parallel arrays, the elements of one array correspond to those in another array.
18. Array elements may be used as accumulators.
19. When using an input data item for a subscript, the value should always be validated. Otherwise the user is apt to receive the system error message, SUBSCRIPT OUT OF RANGE.
20. Table elements may be accessed by direct reference, serial search (or lookup), and binary search.
21. For direct reference of a table, the actual subscripts (1–N) must be available.
22. In table lookup (serial search), multiple comparisons are made until the correct element is found.
23. The item to seek is called the search argument.
24. Table lookup requires an error handling routine in case a match is not found.
25. A search may be performed for numeric or string search arguments.
26. For a serial search, the table elements may be arranged in any order. However, for a binary search, the elements must be sorted in order.
27. A binary search should be considered for a large table (more than 100 elements) that can be arranged in sequence.

Programming Exercises

11.1. Write a program using single-dimension arrays to analyze an income survey. The statistics for each home include an identification code, the number of members in the household, and the yearly income.

INPUT: Use READ/DATA to enter the identification, annual income, and number of persons for each household. Use the test data provided.

OUTPUT: Produce a three-part report that shows:
1. A three-column table displaying the input data. The data will fit on one page.
2. A listing of the identification number and income for each household exceeding the average income.
3. The percentage of households having incomes below the poverty level.

The output must be nicely formatted with titles and column headings.

PROCESSING: Read the data into three arrays. *After* the arrays are filled, print out the data in three columns, showing the ID number, annual income, and number of persons. (Do *not* print the data as it is being read.)

Calculate the average income, and print one line for each household with income greater than average.

Calculate the poverty level for each household, and compute the percentage of households whose income falls below poverty level. The poverty level can be calculated as $8,000 for a family of one or two, plus $2,000 for each member more than two.

TEST DATA:

ID Number	Annual Income	Number of Persons
2497	$12,500	2
3323	13,000	5
4521	18,210	4
6789	8,000	2
5476	6,000	1
4423	16,400	3
6587	25,000	4
3221	10,500	4
5555	15,000	2
0085	19,700	3
3097	20,000	8
4480	23,400	5
0265	19,700	2
8901	13,000	3

11.2. Write a menu program to keep track of concert ticket sales by your club. Ticket prices are based on the section of the auditorium in which the seats are located. Your program should calculate the price for each sale, accumulate the total number of tickets sold in each section, display the ticket price schedule, and print a summary of all sales.

MENU: Clear the screen and print the menu with an appropriate title and these choices:
1. Calculate ticket sales
2. Display ticket prices
3. Print sales summary
4. Quit

The user should be prompted to enter a choice between 1 and 4. (Validate their response.) The menu will be redisplayed after execution of choices 1, 2, or 3.

Menu Item #1—Calculate ticket sales

This is an interactive display (no printer involved), designed to calculate and to display the total price for each sale. Request the section and number of tickets, look up the unit price, calculate the total price (number of tickets times the unit price), and print the sales total on the screen. The sales should be accumulated in a table for later printing.

Give the user the option of entering more sales or returning to the menu after each sale.

Menu Item #2—Display ticket prices

Display the table of ticket prices on the screen:

SECTION	TICKET PRICE
A	20.00
W	17.50
B	15.00
M	11.00

Menu Item #3—Print sales summary

Print out (on the printer) the summary of all ticket sales made. For each section, print the number of tickets sold and the dollar amount. Also, print report totals of number of tickets sold and total amount of money collected. The report must include appropriate title, column headings, and numeric alignment of columns of detail data and totals.

Menu Item #4—Quit

Print an appropriate message and end the program.

SPECIAL CONSIDERATIONS:

All screens should be well designed and printed with LOCATE (or HTAB/VTAB). Do not allow the output to scroll on the screen.

"Idiot proof" all input, so that invalid values will be found and "friendly" messages printed. Do not allow the user to receive BASIC error messages for numeric values out of range or a section not in the table.

11.3. Write a menu program that will keep track of a list of items. The item names will be entered from the keyboard. As each item name is entered, the list should be checked to see if that item has already been entered. If the item is not already on the list, add it to the list. If it already appears on the list, count it.

Use a string array to hold the item names and a parallel numeric array to hold the counts. Allow array space to hold 100 items.

MENU CHOICES:
1. Enter items
2. Print the item list and counts
3. Quit

Choice 1: Clear the screen and request input of an item. Allow entry of items until a terminal value is entered (perhaps END or QUIT). Redisplay the menu when the entry is complete. Assume that the user may again choose #1 and wish to add more items to the list.

Choice 2: Print a list of the items entered so far and the count of the number of times each has been entered. Be aware of the number of lines on the screen (generally 24), and do not print the list so fast that it scrolls off the top of the screen too quickly to read. If the list is long, print one screenfull and a message to press a key to continue.

Choice 3: Clear the screen and print an end-of-job message.

11.4. Write a program to look up state names and their two-letter abbreviations. Given a name, look up the abbreviation; given the abbreviation, look up the name. In the event that a match cannot be found for the state input, print an appropriate error message.

MENU CHOICES:
1. Find a state name from the abbreviation
2. Find the abbreviation from a state name
3. End the program

Choice 1: Clear the screen and request the two-character abbreviation. Print out the corresponding state name, and hold the screen by requesting a keypress. After a key is pressed, return to the menu.

Choice 2: Similar to choice 1, except request the state name and print out the abbreviation.

Choice 3: Clear the screen and print an end-of-job message.

TABLE DATA:

AL	Alabama	MT	Montana
AK	Alaska	NE	Nebraska
AS	American Samoa	NV	Nevada
AZ	Arizona	NH	New Hampshire
AR	Arkansas	NJ	New Jersey
CA	California	NM	New Mexico
CZ	Canal Zone	NY	New York
CO	Colorado	NC	North Carolina
CT	Connecticut	ND	North Dakota
DE	Delaware	CM	Northern Mariana Island
DC	District of Columbia	OH	Ohio
FL	Florida	OK	Oklahoma
GA	Georgia	OR	Oregon
GU	Guam	PA	Pennsylvania
HI	Hawaii	PR	Puerto Rico
ID	Idaho	RI	Rhode Island
IL	Illinois	SC	South Carolina
IN	Indiana	SD	South Dakota
IA	Iowa	TN	Tennessee
KS	Kansas	TX	Texas
KY	Kentucky	TT	Trust Territories
LA	Louisiana	UT	Utah
ME	Maine	VT	Vermont
MD	Maryland	VA	Virginia
MA	Massachusetts	VI	Virgin Islands
MI	Michigan	WA	Washington
MN	Minnesota	WV	West Virginia
MS	Mississippi	WI	Wisconsin
MO	Missouri	WY	Wyoming

11.5. In many applications, such as interest calculations, it is necessary to compute the exact number of days between two dates. Write a program that will compute the number of days between two dates in the same year, as well as print the number of days in any month.

Use an array to store the number of days in each month. Ignore leap year, and count twenty-eight days for February.

MENU CHOICES:
1. Find the number of days in a month
2. Find the number of days between two dates
3. Quit

After each menu choice is complete, the menu should be redisplayed.

Choice 1: Clear the screen and request input of a month name. Lookup and print the number of days in the month. Hold the output on the screen until a key is pressed.

Choice 2: Clear the screen and request input of two dates in the same year. Request the month name, spelled out, and the day. Using the month array, compute and print the number of days between the two dates. The ending date should be counted, but not the beginning date. Thus the number of days between January 1 and January 2 is 1. The number of days between January 15 and February 10 is 26 [(31 − 15) + 10].

Choice 3: Clear the screen and print a signoff message.

11.6. Write a program using single-dimension arrays to request a month of the year and print the holidays in that month. Allow for a maximum of three holidays in one month.

11.7. Write a program using single-dimension arrays to request the name of a city and print the corresponding zip code. If the city is not in the table, print a message telling the user that no zip code was found.

11.8. Write a program using single-dimension arrays to request the name of a state in the United States and print the corresponding capital. If the user types in a nonexistent state, print a message that there is no such state.

11.9. Write a program using single-dimension arrays to create a word guessing game.

INPUT: The user will input, from the keyboard, the word he thinks the "computer guessed."

OUTPUT: If the user guesses the word, print an appropriate message. If the user doesn't guess the word after three guesses, print the word the computer picked and print a message asking the user if he wants to play again.

PROCESSING:
1. Create a table with thirty words in it.
2. Use the randomize statement and the RND function for the computer's choice.

11.10. Write a program using single-dimension arrays to keep track of scores for the karate tournament for the Kiwi Karate Studio.

INPUT: Students' names will come from DATA statements. The scores will be input from the keyboard.

OUTPUT: Print a title, headings, student name, points for each event, total points, and which student was the grand champion.

PROCESSING:
1. The grand champion is the student with the most points.
2. Events:
   1. Sparring
   2. Open-hand Kata
   3. Weapons Kata
   4. Soft Kata
   5. Breaking
3. Not every student will participate in every event; some students may participate in only one or two.

TEST DATA:
Brian Boon
Chris Cook
Eric Mills
Mandy Moon
Nancy Noon
Scott Peck
Peter Smith
Sam Snoop
Trish Little

11.11. Write a program using single-dimension arrays to keep track of merchandise, prices, and the items that can be sold at the promotional price of three-for-the-price-of-two. Employees should be able to type in the merchandise code and receive the corresponding price and promotion.

INPUT: Merchandise code, price, and promo code will come from DATA statements.

OUTPUT: Print the price and promo for the item requested on the screen.

PROCESS: If the item is a promo item, print the savings for the customer if the item is purchased.

TEST DATA:

Item	Price	Promo	Item	Price	Promo
P–1600–24	4.39	3/2	KX–135–24	3.89	None
PO–135–24	2.99	3/2	KX–135–36	4.89	None
PO–135–36	3.18	3/2	PS–135–36	3.29	3/2
P2–110–12	1.99	3/2	PD–135–24	3.49	3/2
P2–110–24	2.99	3/2	PD–135–36	4.49	3/2
P2–126–24	2.99	3/2	PL–135–24	4.59	3/2
P2–135–24	3.89	3/2	PL–135–36	5.59	3/2
P2–135–36	4/38	3/2	PLA–594	7.99	None
P4–135–24	4.38	3/2	PMA–464	8.99	None
P4–135–36	5.38	3/2	PN–135–24	3.49	None
KA–135–24	3.09	None	PN–135–36	4.49	None
KA–135–36	4.09	None	PR–135–24	3.89	None
KB–110–24	3.20	None	PR–135–36	4.89	None
KB–135–24	4.09	None	P–DISK–15	2.49	3/2
KB–135–36	5.09	None	P–DISK–15–2	4.18	3/2
KF–135–24	5.99	None	P600	9.37	None
KM–135–24	6.09	None	PSX70	9.37	None
			PSPEC	9.37	None

11.12. Write a program using single-dimension arrays to find the mean, midrange, range, variance, and standard deviation of a set of 100 I.Q. scores.

INPUT: The I.Q. scores will come from DATA statements.

OUTPUT: The mean, median, midrange, range, variance, and standard deviation will be printed on the screen.

PROCESS:
1. Mean = total of all scores/number of scores.
2. Midrange = highest score + lowest score/2.
3. Range = highest value − lowest value.
4. Variance = number of scores * (sum of X^2) − (sum of X)^2/ number of scores * (number of scores − 1).
5. Standard deviation = square root of the variance.

11.13. Write a program using single-dimension arrays to find the critical value of the linear correlation coefficient and the linear correlation coefficient (r) for nine pairs of data and a significance level of .05.

INPUT: The table values and the nine pairs of data will come from DATA statements.

OUTPUT: The critical value, the linear correlation coefficient, and the type of correlation between the pairs of data should be output to the screen.

PROCESS:

1. r = number of pairs * sum of $x*y$ − (sum of x) * (sum of y) / the square root of [the number of pairs * (sum of x^2) − (sum of x)^2 − the square root of [the number of pairs * (sum of y^2) − (sum of y)^2].

2. The critical value should be looked up in the table below.

3. If the magnitude of r exceeds the critical value found in the table, there is a significant linear relationship between x and y.

   A. If the relationship is significant and r is positive, there is a positive linear correlation.

   B. If the relationship is significant and r is negative, there is a negative linear correlation.

4. If r is less than the critical value, there is no correlation.

TABLE OF CRITICAL VALUES   **PAIRS OF DATA**

N	.05	.01	X	Y
4	.950	.999	10	12
5	.878	.959	15	11
6	.811	.917	20	10
7	.754	.875	25	13
8	.707	.834	30	9
9	.666	.798	35	8
10	.632	.765	40	6
			45	4
			50	1

11.14. Write a program using single-dimension arrays to find the sum of x, the sum of y, the sum of $x*y$, the sum of x^2, the sum of y^2, and the sum of x^2*y^2.

INPUT: The numbers for x and y will come from DATA statements.
OUTPUT: Print the output on the printer as follows:

x	y	$x*y$	x^2	y^2	x^2y^2

Totals

TEST DATA:

x	y
10	12
9	14
7	17
4	19
2	15
1	10
11	21
3	2
8	8
5	7

11.15. Write a program using single-dimension arrays to do a binary search for a requested name and date of birth.

INPUT:
1. The list of names and birth dates will come from DATA statements. The names are given below, and you will need to make up corresponding birth dates.
2. The requested name will be input from the keyboard.

OUTPUT: Once you have found the name, print it and the corresponding birth date on the screen.

PROCESSING: Perform a binary search.

TEST DATA
Alan
Bob
Brian
Chris
Connie
Dave
Henry
John
Kevin
Luis
Mindy
Nancy
Peter
Rose
Rudy
Scott
Steve
Tom
Tony
Wendy
Zena

11.16. Write a program using single-dimension arrays to keep track of belt color, weapon specialty, and names of the students at the Kiwi Karate Studio.

INPUT:
1. Student name, belt color, and weapon will be read from DATA statements.
2. A request for a choice of a complete list of students or a single student will come from the keyboard.

OUTPUT:
1. If a complete list is requested, it should be printed on the printer.
2. If a single student is requested, it should be printed on the screen.

TEST DATA:

Name	Belt Color	Weapon
Aline Ash	Orange	Joto
Anu Brown	Black	Scye
Kim Cook	Blue	Manrici
Sandy Campbell	White	Samurai Sword
Alice Drake	Brown	Joto
Tag Garison	Brown	Samurai Sword
Kristen Bosco	Black	Nunchucks
Jim Snow	White	Manrici
Larry Robles	Blue	Joto

12 Advanced Array Handling

SWAP Statement

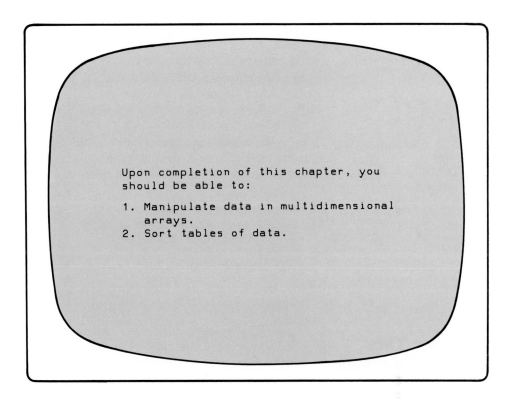

```
Upon completion of this chapter, you
should be able to:

1. Manipulate data in multidimensional
   arrays.
2. Sort tables of data.
```

Two-Dimensional Arrays

The arrays discussed in chapter 11 were one-dimensional arrays. Each element in the array is identified by one subscript, which indicates its position in the list. Often there is a need to identify data by two subscripts. Such is the case in tabular data, where data is arranged into rows and columns.

Many applications of two-dimensional tables may quickly come to mind—insurance rate tables, tax tables, addition and multiplication tables, postage rates, foods and their nutritive value, population by region, rainfall by state.

To define a *two-dimensional array* or **table,** the DIM statement specifies the number of rows and columns in the array.

```
10   DIM TABLE(4,6)
                 ↑ ↑
                 | Columns
                 Rows
```

This statement establishes an array of twenty-four elements, with four rows and six columns (assuming OPTION BASE 1). When referring to individual elements of the TABLE array, two subscripts must always be used. The first subscript should always be the row, the second the column. Figure 12.1 shows a diagram of this two-dimensional array.

The elements of the array may be used as any other variable—as accumulators, counts, reference fields for lookup, in statements like LET, PRINT, INPUT, READ; and forming conditions. Some valid references to TABLE include:

```
LET TABLE(1,2) = 0
LET TABLE(N+1,N-1) = N
LET N = TABLE(J,K/2)
IF TABLE(4,6) > 0 ...
READ TABLE(ROW,COL)
PRINT TABLE(ROW,COL)
```

Invalid references for the four-by-six table in figure 12.1 would include any negative subscript, the first subscript greater than 4, or the second subscript greater than 6.

Initializing Two-Dimensional Arrays

Although the array is initially set to zero, many situations require that an array be re-initialized—to zero or some other value. Nested loops are an ideal way to set each array element to an initial value.

```
1000   '********** INITIALIZE TWO-DIMENSIONAL ARRAY ************
1010   DIM TABLE(4,6)
1020   FOR ROW = 1 TO 4
1030      FOR COL = 1 TO 6
1040         LET TABLE(ROW, COL) = 0
1050      NEXT COL
1060   NEXT ROW
1070   RETURN
```

The LET statement on line 1040 will be executed twenty-four times, once for each element of TABLE. How can you confirm that?

A two-dimensional table can be filled with READ/DATA statements and nested loops. The programmer may choose to fill the table one row at a time or one column at a time, as long as the DATA statements are in the corresponding order. Figure 12.2 shows the array filled with values.

Figure 12.1
Two-dimensional array showing subscripts.

(1,1)	(1,2)	(1,3)	(1,4)	(1,5)	(1,6)
(2,1)	(2,2)	(2,3)	(2,4)	(2,5)	(2,6)
(3,1)	(3,2)	(3,3)	(3,4)	(3,5)	(3,6)
(4,1)	(4,2)	(4,3)	(4,4)	(4,5)	(4,6)

Figure 12.2
Array filled with values from data
statements.

(1,1)	(1,2)	(1,3)	(1,4)	(1,5)	(1,6)
20	45	1.2	7	6	1.6
(2,1)	(2,2)	(2,3)	(2,4)	(2,5)	(2,6)
12	-1	14	-17	19	-16
(3,1)	(3,2)	(3,3)	(3,4)	(3,5)	(3,6)
17.5	21	-2.5	21.3	5	3
(4,1)	(4,2)	(4,3)	(4,4)	(4,5)	(4,6)
19	-2.2	2.1	-3	8.6	9.8

```
200   '***** FILL A TWO-DIMENSIONAL TABLE, ONE ROW AT A TIME
210   FOR ROW = 1 TO 4
220      FOR COL = 1 TO 6
230         READ TABLE(ROW,COL)
240      NEXT COL
250   NEXT ROW
260   DATA 20,45,1.2,7,6,1.6,12,-1,14,-17,19,-16,17.5,21,-2.5
270   DATA 21.3,5,3,19,-2.2,2.1,-3,8.6,9.8
280   RETURN
```

Printing a Two-Dimensional Table

To print a two-dimensional table, again employ nested loops. Each execution of the PRINT statement (line 330) will print one element of the TABLE array.

```
300   '********** PRINT A TWO-DIMENSIONAL TABLE *************
310   FOR ROW = 1 TO 4
320      FOR COL = 1 TO 6
330         PRINT USING " ###.# "; TABLE(ROW,COL);
340      NEXT COL
350      PRINT
360   NEXT ROW
370   RETURN
```

Summing a Two-Dimensional Table

Tables may be summed in various ways. Either the columns or the rows of the array may be summed. Or, as in a crossfoot, the figures may be summed in both directions and the totals double-checked.

```
                                                    ROW
                                                    TOTALS
        20.0    45.0     1.2     7.0     6.0     1.6    80.8
        12.0    -1.0    14.0   -17.0    19.0   -16.0    11.0
        17.5    21.0    -2.5    21.3     5.0     3.0    65.3
        19.0    -2.2     2.1    -3.0     8.6     9.8    34.3
        ----    ----    ----    ----    ----    -----   -----
COLUMN
TOTALS  68.5    62.8    14.8     8.3    38.6    -1.6   191.4
                                                       ↑
                                                 crossfoot total
```

To sum the array in both directions, each column needs one total field and each row needs one total field. Two, one-dimensional arrays will work well for the totals. Figure 12.3 shows a diagram of the necessary arrays. The following DIM statement establishes the necessary total fields.

```
100   DIM ROW.TOT(4),COL.TOT(6)
400   '********** SUM TWO-DIMENSIONAL ARRAY ***************
420   FOR ROW = 1 TO 4
430      FOR COL = 1 TO 6
440         LET ROW.TOT(ROW) = ROW.TOT(ROW) + TABLE(ROW,COL)
450         LET COL.TOT(COL) = COL.TOT(COL) + TABLE(ROW,COL)
460      NEXT COL
470   NEXT ROW
480   '
```

Table Columns	(1)	(2)	(3)	(4)	(5)	(6)		ROW.TOT
Rows (1)	20	45	1.2	7	6	1.6	(1)	80.8
(2)	12	-1	14	-17	19	-16	(2)	11
(3)	17.5	21	-2.5	21.3	5	3	(3)	65.3
(4)	19	-2.2	2.1	-3	8.6	9.8	(4)	34.3
COL.TOT	68.5	62.8	14.8	8.3	38.6	-1.6		191.4
	(1)	(2)	(3)	(4)	(5)	(6)		GRAND.TOT

Figure 12.3
Summing an array into two, one-dimensional arrays. Each row is summed into the corresponding element of the ROW.TOT array. Each column is summed into the corresponding element of the COL.TOT array.

```
500  '************** SUM THE ROW TOTALS *******************
510  FOR ROW = 1 TO 4
520      LET GRAND.TOT = GRAND.TOT + ROW.TOT(ROW)
530  NEXT ROW
535  '
540  '************* SUM THE COLUMN TOTALS ****************
550  FOR COL = 1 TO 6
560      LET CHECK.TOT = CHECK.TOT + COL.TOT(COL)
570  NEXT COL
580  IF GRAND.TOT <> CHECK.TOT
                    THEN PRINT "THE PROGRAMMER BLEW IT"
590  RETURN
```

Feedback

Write the BASIC statements to:

1. Dimension the following table (call it GRID).

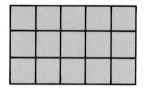

2. Set each element in the first row of GRID to 1.
3. Set each element in the second row of GRID to 2.
4. For each column of GRID, add together the elements in rows 1 and 2, placing the sum in row 3. (Even though the sum for every column will be 3, perform the addition operation for every column.)
5. Print the entire table.

Lookup Operation for Two-Dimensional Tables

To look up items in a two-dimensional table, use all three techniques learned in chapter 11—direct reference, binary search, and serial search. The limitations are the same as in a one-dimensional table.

1. Direct reference: Must have row and column subscripts readily available. For an example, the hours used for each of five machines (identified by machine numbers 1–5) and each of four departments (identified by department numbers 1–4) may be tallied. In the example, the number of hours (5) is added to the total for machine #4 in department #2.

Machine Table   *Departments*

	(1)	(2)	(3)	(4)
Machines (1)	0	0	0	0
(2)	0	0	0	0
(3)	0	0	0	0
(4)	0	5	0	0
(5)	0	0	0	0

MACH	DEPT	HRS
4	2	⑤

```
100    DIM MACHINE(5,4)

480    '******* INPUT DATA **********
500    INPUT "DEPARTMENT NUMBER"; DEPT
510    INPUT "MACHINE NUMBER"; MACH
520    INPUT "HOURS USED"; HRS

530    '**** ADD TO CORRECT TOTAL ****
540    LET MACHINE(MACH,DEPT) = MACHINE(MACH,DEPT) + HRS
```

2. Binary search: The elements to be searched must be in sequence in the table. When the table is large *and* in sequence, a binary search is the preferred technique.
3. Serial table lookup: This is the most common technique used for lookup.

Many two-dimensional tables used for lookup require additional one-dimensional tables to aid in the lookup process. For an example, use a shipping rate table (figure 12.4) to look up the rate to ship a package. In this example, a one-dimensional table holds the weight limits, and another holds the zones, as well as one for the five-by-four rate table.

As an initialization step, the three tables shown in figure 12.5 must be set up. The first step in the program would be to establish and fill the three arrays. The WT array perhaps needs a bit of explanation, since only four elements were dimensioned, and there are five rows in the rate table. However, the last row is open-ended; that is, any package heavier than 10 pounds will use the last row. No upper bound is required.

```
100    DIM RATE (5,4),WT(4),ZN$(4)
::
200    '*********** LOAD TABLES ********************
210    '          WT TABLE
220    FOR INDEX = 1 TO 4
230        READ WT(INDEX)
240    NEXT INDEX
250    DATA 1,3,5,10
260    '          ZONE TABLE
270    FOR INDEX = 1 TO 4
280        READ ZN$(INDEX)
290    NEXT INDEX
300    DATA A,B,C,D
310    '          RATE TABLE
320    FOR ROW = 1 TO 5
330        FOR COL = 1 TO 4
340            READ RATE(ROW,COL)
350        NEXT COL
360    NEXT ROW
370    DATA 1,1.5,1.65,1.85,1.58,2,2.4,3.05,1.71,2.52,3.1,4
380    DATA 2.04,3.12,4,5.01,2.52,3.75,5.1,7.25
390    RETURN
```

Advanced Array Handling

Figure 12.4
Shipping rate table.

Zone | **Rate Table**

Weight not to Exceed		A	B	C	D
	1 lb.	1.00	1.50	1.65	1.85
	3 lb.	1.58	2.00	2.40	3.05
	5 lb.	1.71	2.52	3.10	4.00
	10 lb.	2.04	3.12	4.00	5.01
any > 10 lb.		2.52	3.75	5.10	7.25

RATE ARRAY

	(1)	(2)	(3)	(4)
(1)	1.00	1.50	1.65	1.85
(2)	1.58	2.00	2.40	3.05
(3)	1.71	2.52	3.10	4.00
(4)	2.04	3.12	4.00	5.01
(5)	2.52	3.75	5.10	7.25

WT ARRAY

(1)	1
(2)	3
(3)	5
(4)	10

ZN$ ARRAY

(1)	A
(2)	B
(3)	C
(4)	D

Figure 12.5
Shipping rate table arrays. The two-dimensional RATE array is used to hold the rates. The two, one-dimensional arrays are used to hold the weight limits and the zones to be used for lookup.

In order to print the rate to ship a package that weighs 4 pounds to zone B, the correct row and column must first be found.

```
1000    '********** INPUT REQUEST **********************
1010    INPUT "ENTER WEIGHT OF PACKAGE ",WEIGHT
1020    INPUT "ENTER ZONE              ",ZONE$
1030    PRINT
1040    RETURN
```

To print the correct rate, these statements *could* be used:

```
500    LET ROW = 3
510    LET COL = 2
520    PRINT RATE(ROW,COL)
```

This will print the correct rate (2.52), but it is not a practical solution. In order to find the correct values for ROW and COL, a lookup operation must be done for each.

```
600    '************ FIND RATE IN TABLE ***************
610    GOSUB 2000               'FIND ROW
620    GOSUB 3000               'FIND COLUMN
630    IF COL <> 0
           THEN PRINT USING " ##.## "; RATE(ROW,COL)
           ELSE PRINT "INCORRECT ZONE"
640    RETURN
```

The following subroutines show the coding to look up the row and column before the rate is printed. For the row, an exact match is unnecessary, only a weight not greater than the limit for that row. Any package too heavy for row 4 is assigned to row 5.

```
2000    '*********** LOOKUP ROW ************************
2010    '** NOTE THAT ANY WT. > 4TH ELEMENT USES SUB OF 5 **
2020    LET ROW = 1
2030    WHILE WEIGHT > WT(ROW) AND ROW < 5
2040       LET ROW = ROW + 1
2050    WEND
2060    RETURN
2070    '
```

```
3000  '************* LOOKUP COLUMN *********************
3010  LET COL = 0                    'INITIALIZE TO BEGIN LOOP
3020  LET COUNT = 0                  'TO BEGIN
3030  WHILE COUNT <= 4 AND COL = 0
3035     LET COUNT = COUNT + 1
3040     IF ZONE$ = ZN$(COUNT)
              THEN LET COL = COUNT
3060  WEND
3070  RETURN
```

Multidimensional Arrays

Arrays may be defined for more than two dimensions. The need for *three-dimensional arrays* is fairly common. Although Microsoft BASIC allows dimensions as high as 255, rarely will there be more than three. Many versions of BASIC allow for only two dimensions.

Assume that for the shipping rate table, there were three different classes of shipping rates—Class I, II, and III. To manually look up the correct rate, first find the correct chart (Class I, II, or III), then find the correct weight and zone. Figure 12.6 illustrates the three-dimensional table. The dimension statement for this three-dimensional array looks like this:

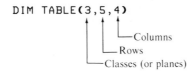

In the computer program, the lookup procedure would be done the same way as manually. Three lookup operations are needed in order to find the correct class, weight, and zone. The statement to print the rate is:

```
PRINT TABLE(CLASS, ROW, COL)
```

Now, assume a further revision to the shipping tables. The company has two classes of customers—regular and preferred. To reflect this, there are two complete sets of these tables. Figure 12.7 illustrates the four-dimensional rate table. The DIM statement for the four-dimensional table is:

```
DIM TABLE(2,3,5,4)
```

The subscripted variable to reference one element of the table is this:

```
TABLE(CUST, CLASS, ROW, COL)
```

To carry this example to an extreme, set up three different rate schedules, one for each of three different regions of the country. The five-dimensional table is illustrated in figure 12.8. The dimension statement is:

```
DIM TABLE(3,2,3,5,4)
```

Figure 12.6
Three-dimensional table. Each element can be identified by a class number as well as a row and column.

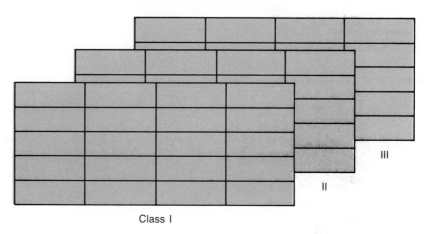

Class I

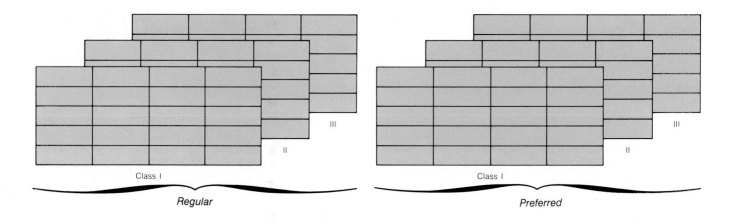

Figure 12.7
Four-dimensional table.

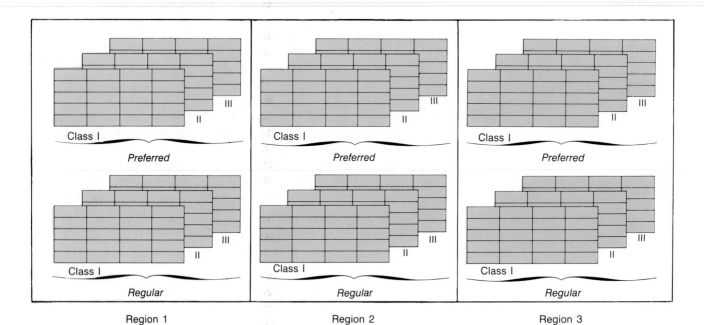

Region 1   Region 2   Region 3

Figure 12.8
Five-dimensional table.

A subscripted reference is:

```
TABLE(REGION, CUST, CLASS, ROW, COL)
```

The statement PRINT TABLE(1,2,1,2,3) would print the value for region 1, preferred customer, Class I, weight greater than 10 pounds, to zone C.

Programming Example:
Two-Dimensional Tables

Both temperature and wind cause heat loss from body surfaces. When the effects of temperature and wind are combined, the body feels colder than the actual temperature. Looking at the chart in figure 12.9, you can see that if the temperature is 10 degrees fahrenheit and the wind 20 mph, the temperature felt by the body is −24 degrees. For the computer program, input the temperature and wind speed, and display the wind-chill factor.

Wind Speed (MPH)	Actual Temperature in Degrees Fahrenheit							
	30	20	10	0	-10	-20	-30	-40
10	16	3	-9	-22	-34	-46	-58	-71
20	4	-10	-24	-39	-53	-67	-81	-95
30	-2	-18	-33	-49	-64	-79	-93	-109
40	-5	-21	-37	-53	-69	-84	-100	-115

Figure 12.9
Windchill table.

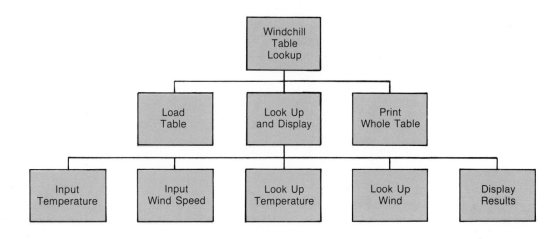

Figure 12.10
Hierarchy chart for windchill program.

When establishing two-dimensional tables for lookup, there is a choice of two distinct methods:

1. Establish one, two-dimensional table, four-by-eight
      one, one-dimensional table with four elements
         to hold the wind speeds
      one, one-dimensional table with eight elements
         to hold the temperatures
            or

2. Establish one, two-dimensional table, five-by-nine
      Use the top row for temperatures
      Use the first column for wind speeds

Since the three-array method was used in the earlier example, in this program the one-array approach will be selected.

This will be a menu program with choices:

1. Look up the windchill factor
2. Print the entire table
3. Quit

Hierarchy Chart Refer to figure 12.10.

Advanced Array Handling   319

```
110 ' PROGRAM TO LOOK UP WINDCHILL FACTOR, GIVEN TEMPERATURE, WIND SPEED
130 '
140 '          PROGRAM VARIABLES
160 '          CHILL(5,9)        WINDCHILL TABLE
170 '          WIND              WIND SPEED
180 '          TEMP              TEMPERATURE
190 '          COUNT             LOOP COUNTER FOR LOOKUP
200 '          CHOICE            MENU CHOICE
210 '          ROW               ROW SUBSCRIPT
220 '          COL               COLUMN SUBSCRIPT
230 '          F$, P$            PRINT IMAGES
240 '
250 DIM CHILL(5,9)

500 '*************** PROGRAM MAINLINE ***********************
510 GOSUB 1000                      'LOAD TABLE
520 GOSUB 2000                      'PRINT MENU
530 WHILE CHOICE < 3
540     ON CHOICE GOSUB 3000, 8000
550     GOSUB 2000                  'PRINT MENU AGAIN
560 WEND
570 END
1000 '***************** LOAD TABLE ***********************
1010 FOR ROW = 1 TO 5
1020     FOR COL = 1 TO 9
1030         READ CHILL(ROW, COL)
1040     NEXT COL
1050 NEXT ROW
1060 DATA 0,30,20,10,0,-10,-20,-30,-40
1070 DATA 10,16,3,-9,-22,-34,-46,-58,-71
1080 DATA 20,4,-10,-24,-39,-53,-67,-81,-95
1090 DATA 30,-2,-18,-33,-49,-64,-79,-93,-109
1100 DATA 40,-5,-21,-37,-53,-69,-84,-100,-115
1110 RETURN
1120 '
2000 '****************** PRINT MENU ***********************
2010 CLS
2020 LOCATE 4,32
2030 PRINT "WINDCHILL FACTOR"
2040 LOCATE 10,25
2050 PRINT "1. DISPLAY A WINDCHILL FACTOR"
2060 LOCATE 12,25
2070 PRINT "2. DISPLAY ENTIRE TABLE
2080 LOCATE 14,25
2090 PRINT "3. QUIT"
2100 LOCATE 17,29
2110 PRINT "ENTER SELECTION "
2120 LET CHOICE = 0
2130 WHILE CHOICE < 1 OR CHOICE > 3
2140     LOCATE 17,45
2150     LET CHOICE = VAL(INPUT$(1))
2160 WEND
2170 RETURN
2180 '
3000 '*********** DISPLAY A WINDCHILL FACTOR *****************
3010 GOSUB 4000                  'INPUT AND ROUND TEMPERATURE
3020 GOSUB 4500                  'INPUT AND ROUND WIND SPEED
3030 GOSUB 5000                  'LOOK UP TEMPERATURE
3040 GOSUB 5500                  'LOOK UP WIND
3050 GOSUB 6000                  'DISPLAY RESULTS
3060 RETURN
3070 '
4000 '*********** INPUT AND ROUND TEMPERATURE ***************
4010 CLS
4020 LET TEMP = 40
4030 WHILE TEMP < -40 OR TEMP > 30
4040     LOCATE 8,26
4050     INPUT "ENTER TEMPERATURE (+30 TO -40) "; TEMP
4060 WEND
4070 LET TEMP = FIX(TEMP/10 +.5 * SGN(TEMP))*10 'ROUND TO NEAREST 10
4080 RETURN
4090 '
```

```
4500 '************** INPUT AND ROUND WIND SPEED ***************
4510 LET WIND = 0
4520 WHILE WIND < 10 OR WIND > 40
4530    LOCATE 11,26
4540    INPUT "ENTER WIND SPEED (10 TO 40 MPH) "; WIND
4550 WEND
4560 LET WIND = FIX(WIND/10 +.5 * SGN(WIND))*10 'ROUND TO NEAREST 10
4570 RETURN
4580 '
5000 '************** LOOK UP TEMPERATURE ********************
5010   LET COL = 0                  'INIT TO ENTER LOOP
5020   LET COUNT = 1                'TO BEGIN CHECK (AT 2)
5030   WHILE COUNT < 9 AND COL = 0
5040      LET COUNT = COUNT + 1
5050      IF TEMP = CHILL(1, COUNT)
              THEN LET COL = COUNT
5060   WEND
5070   RETURN
5080 '
5500 '************** LOOK UP WIND SPEED *********************
5510 LET ROW = 0                    'INIT TO ENTER LOOP
5520 LET COUNT = 1                  'TO BEGIN CHECK (AT ROW 2)
5530 WHILE COUNT <= 4 AND ROW = 0
5540    LET COUNT = COUNT + 1
5550    IF WIND = CHILL(COUNT, 1)
            THEN LET ROW = COUNT
5560 WEND
5570 RETURN
5580 '
6000 '*************** DISPLAY WINDCHILL ********************
6010 CLS
6020 LOCATE 8,24
6030 PRINT "FOR A TEMPERATURE OF " TEMP
6040 LOCATE 10,24
6050 PRINT "AND A WIND OF " WIND " MPH"
6060 LOCATE 12,24
6070 PRINT"THE WINDCHILL FACTOR IS " CHILL(ROW, COL)
6080 LOCATE 22,40
6090 PRINT "PRESS ANY KEY TO CONTINUE . . ."
6100 LET D$ = INPUT$(1)
6110 RETURN
6120 '
8000 '*************** DISPLAY ENTIRE TABLE ******************
8010 CLS
8020 LOCATE 2,33
8030 PRINT "WINDCHILL TABLE"
8040 PRINT
8050 PRINT
8060 LET P$ = " ####"
8070 LET F$ = "            ### :"
8080 FOR ROW = 1 TO 5
8090    FOR COL = 1 TO 9
8100       IF COL = 1
               THEN PRINT USING F$; CHILL(ROW,COL);
               ELSE PRINT USING P$; CHILL(ROW,COL);
8110    NEXT COL
8120    PRINT
8130    PRINT
8140    IF ROW = 1
            THEN PRINT TAB(13) STRING$(60,"-")
8150 NEXT ROW
8160 LOCATE 22,40
8170 PRINT "PRESS ANY KEY TO CONTINUE . . .";
8180 LET D$ = INPUT$(1)
8190 RETURN
8200 '************** END OF PROGRAM ***********************
```

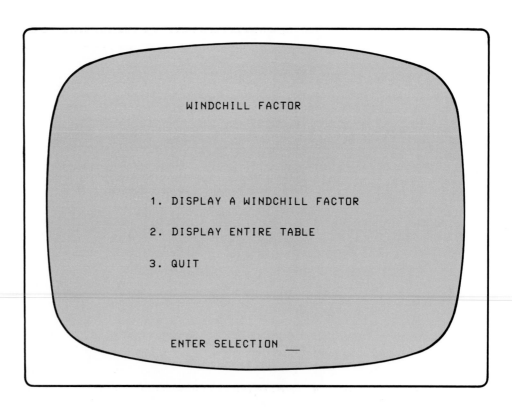

```
                    WINDCHILL FACTOR




          1. DISPLAY A WINDCHILL FACTOR

          2. DISPLAY ENTIRE TABLE

          3. QUIT




             ENTER SELECTION __
```

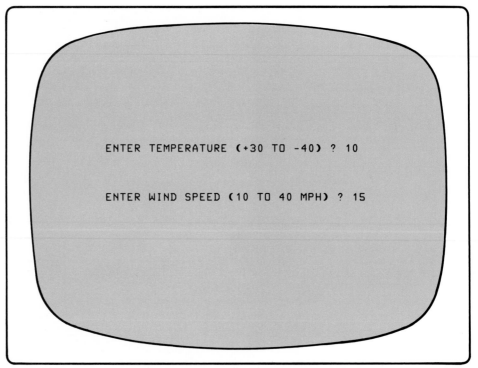

```
     ENTER TEMPERATURE (+30 TO -40) ? 10


     ENTER WIND SPEED (10 TO 40 MPH) ? 15
```

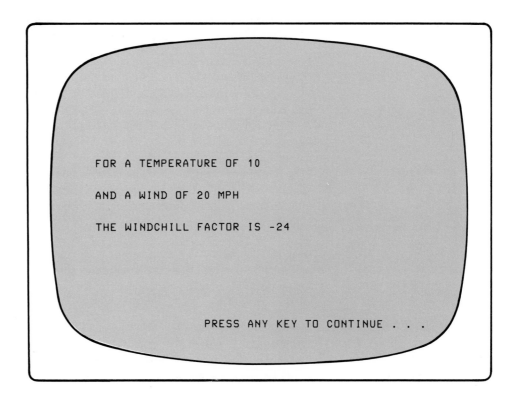

```
          FOR A TEMPERATURE OF 10

          AND A WIND OF 20 MPH

          THE WINDCHILL FACTOR IS -24




                              PRESS ANY KEY TO CONTINUE . . .
```

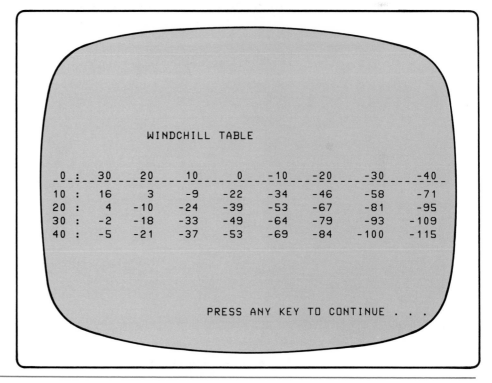

```
                    WINDCHILL TABLE


     _0_:__30____20____10_____0____-10____-20____-30____-40_
     10 :   16     3    -9   -22   -34   -46   -58   -71
     20 :    4   -10   -24   -39   -53   -67   -81   -95
     30 :   -2   -18   -33   -49   -64   -79   -93  -109
     40 :   -5   -21   -37   -53   -69   -84  -100  -115




                              PRESS ANY KEY TO CONTINUE . . .
```

Sorting

A common and useful technique in computing is **sorting**—rearranging table entries in alphabetic order, numeric order, by date, by time. Data can be arranged in *ascending* (low to high) or *descending* (high to low) order. Dates may be sorted by year, by month, by quarter, or any other convenient arrangement.

If a list is to be printed in a different order than it was input, it only makes sense that all data items must be in memory. The lowest entry can't be found unless all are checked. Is it any wonder then that sorting is covered in the unit on arrays? The data items to be sorted can be stored in an array and then rearranged or printed in any chosen order.

There are many methods used for sorting—some faster than others. Some are faster for short lists, others for long. Some can take advantage of lists already partially in order, others can't. Much research has been done and whole books written on sort algorithms and their relative merits.

In this text, two sort algorithms will be presented—the **bubble sort** and the **Shell sort.** The bubble sort is presented since it is relatively easy to understand. However, in real life it seldom will be used except to sort short lists of data. The more efficient Shell sort gains more advantage the more items there are to sort.

The Bubble Sort

In a bubble sort, adjacent entries are compared. If the first entry is larger than the second, the two entries are exchanged. This process is repeated many times, as the highest entries are moved to the highest position in the array. This process of "rising to the top" is the basis for the name "bubble" sort.

Sort Example

Original List	*Sorted List*
Collins	Allen
Bradley	Bradley
Turner	Collins
Allen	Norton
Norton	Turner

The Bubble Sort Process

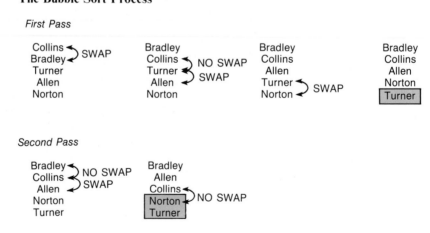

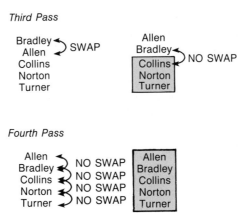

Third Pass

Bradley → SWAP
Allen ↗
Collins
Norton
Turner

Allen
Bradley ↘ NO SWAP
Collins ↗
Norton
Turner

Fourth Pass

Allen ↘ NO SWAP
Bradley ↗ NO SWAP
Collins ↗ NO SWAP
Norton ↗ NO SWAP
Turner ↗

Allen
Bradley
Collins
Norton
Turner

Notice that on the last pass, no exchanges were made. This is the signal that the sort is complete.

Coding for Bubble Sort

```
110 '************** BUBBLE SORT ****************************
120 LET MAX = ELEMENTS - 1       'ELEMENTS = # OF ELEM. TO SORT
130 LET SWAP.FLAG = 0
140 WHILE SWAP.FLAG = 0
150     LET SWAP.FLAG = 1
160     FOR SUB = 1 TO MAX
170         IF TABLE$(SUB) > TABLE$(SUB+1)
                THEN SWAP TABLE$(SUB), TABLE$(SUB+1):
                    LET SWAP.FLAG = 0
180     NEXT SUB
190 WEND
200 RETURN
```

What Happens in the Bubble Sort?

It can be seen from the diagram (p. 324) that the program goes through the entire list once for each element (less one). On the first pass, the highest element is placed in the highest position in the list. On the second pass, the second highest element is placed in the second highest position. This process continues until one complete pass is made with no elements changing place. In the program coding, two items may need explanation: The use of the field called SWAP.FLAG, and the new BASIC statement introduced on line 170, the SWAP statement.

SWAP.FLAG is used as a switch field (or flag). You recall that a switch is a variable that takes one of two possible values to indicate a condition. Here, when SWAP.FLAG = 0, it means that at least one more pass is needed. SWAP.FLAG is initially set to zero, so that the loop will be entered. Then, for each pass, the flag is set to 1 (line 150). If any exchange is made during the pass, the flag is set back to zero (line 170), saying, "A swap was made during this pass, so you must make at least one more pass to make sure the list is in order." As soon as one complete iteration of the WHILE loop is made (one pass) with no swap, the sort is complete. Figure 12.11 illustrates the logic of the bubble sort.

The SWAP Statement—General Form

line number SWAP variable1, variable2

The SWAP statement seems to be designed especially for the sort. It will exchange the values of two variables. The variables may be of any type (single-precision, double-precision, integer, or string) as long as the two variables are the same type. The two variable names must be separated by a comma.

The SWAP Statement—Examples

```
100    SWAP TABLE$(SUB), TABLE$(SUB+1)
200    SWAP X,Y
300    SWAP ARR(R,C), ARR(R+1,C)
400    SWAP A$, B$
500    SWAP I%, J%
```

Figure 12.11
Flowchart of a bubble sort.

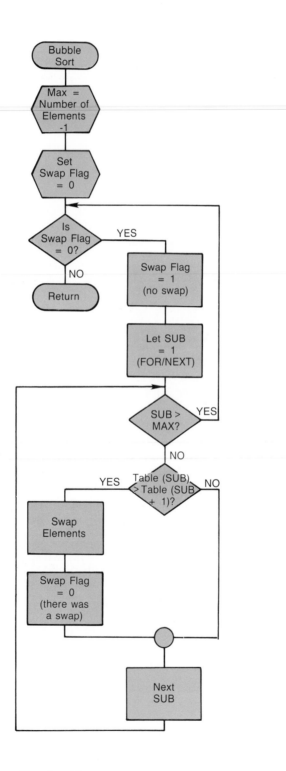

Example Program: The Bubble Sort

A program will be created to input a series of names until END is entered and to print out the list in alphabetic order.

Processing

1. Input names in a loop, counting the entries
2. Sort the list of names
3. Print out the sorted list

Hierarchy Chart

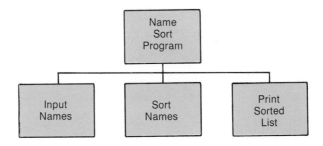

Program Listing

```
110 '       PROGRAM TO INPUT A SERIES OF NAMES, SORT THEM INTO
120 '          ALPHABETIC ORDER USING A BUBBLE SORT, AND PRINT
125 '          THE SORTED LIST
130 '
140 '             PROGRAM VARIABLES
150 '
160 '             COUNT           COUNT OF NAMES INPUT
170 '             LST$            ARRAY TO HOLD NAMES
180 '             SUB             SUBSCRIPT TO REF. NAMES
190 '             MAX             MAXIMUM # OF ENTRIES TO SORT
200 '             SWAP.FLAG       SWITCH FIELD
210 '                             1 = NO SWITCH MADE
220 '                             0 = SWITCH MADE THIS PASS
230 '
240 DIM LST$(50)
500 '************ PROGRAM MAINLINE ****************************
510 GOSUB 1000                    'INPUT NAMES
520 GOSUB 2000                    'SORT LIST
530 GOSUB 3000                    'PRINT SORTED LIST
540 END
1000 '*************** INPUT NAMES ****************************
1010 CLS                          'CLEAR THE SCREEN
1020 PRINT "ENTER NAMES, TYPE 'END' TO QUIT"
1030 LET COUNT = 1
1040 INPUT LST$(COUNT)
1050 WHILE LST$(COUNT) <> "END" AND COUNT < 50
1060    LET COUNT = COUNT + 1
1070    INPUT LST$(COUNT)
1080    IF COUNT = 50 AND LST$(COUNT) <> "END"
            THEN PRINT "SORRY, I CAN ONLY HANDLE 50 NAMES"
1090 WEND
1100 IF COUNT <> 50
            THEN LET COUNT = COUNT - 1 'DON'T COUNT "END"
1110 RETURN
1120 '
```

```
2000 '************** SORT THE NAMES ****************************
2020 LET MAX = COUNT - 1          'SET MAXIMUM ENTRIES TO SORT
2030 LET SWAP.FLAG = 0            'ENTER LOOP
2040 WHILE SWAP.FLAG = 0          'CONTINUE UNTIL NO SWAPS
2050    LET SWAP.FLAG = 1
2060    FOR SUB = 1 TO MAX
2070        IF LST$(SUB) > LST$(SUB+1)
                THEN SWAP LST$(SUB), LST$(SUB+1):
                    LET SWAP.FLAG = 0              'SWAP MADE
2080     NEXT SUB
2090 WEND
2100 RETURN
2110 '
3000 '*********** PRINT THE SORTED LIST *********************
3010 CLS
3020 PRINT TAB(24); "SORTED LIST"
3030 PRINT
3040 FOR SUB = 1 TO COUNT
3050      PRINT LST$(SUB)
3060 NEXT SUB
3070 RETURN
3080 '************ END OF PROGRAM ***********************
```

Sample Program Output

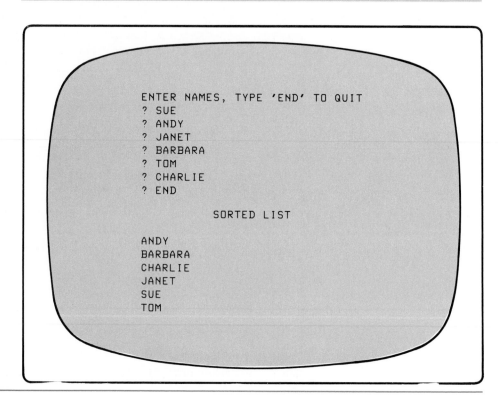

```
ENTER NAMES, TYPE 'END' TO QUIT
? SUE
? ANDY
? JANET
? BARBARA
? TOM
? CHARLIE
? END

            SORTED LIST

ANDY
BARBARA
CHARLIE
JANET
SUE
TOM
```

The Shell Sort

The bubble sort can work well for sorting short lists of data. However, for long data lists, the processing can be excessively slow. The Shell sort (named for its author, Donald Shell) has proven to be a much more efficient sort. The longer the list to be sorted, the greater the advantage. Table 12.1 shows a comparison of times.

Table 12.1.

Comparison of times using a bubble sort and a Shell sort, on an IBM-PC (sorting single-precision data items).

Number of Items	Bubble Sort	Shell Sort
10	1 sec.	1 sec.
20	5 sec.	3 sec.
50	28 sec.	17 sec.
100	1.8 min.	36 sec.
500	49.1 min.	5.2 min.
1000	3.3 hr.	13.2 min.

The Shell sort is similar to the bubble sort, except the comparisons and exchanges are made over a greater distance. Rather than compare and swap adjacent elements, a larger gap (distance between the elements) is used. To begin, the gap is equal to half the length of the list [GAP = INT(COUNT/2) where COUNT is the number of elements to be sorted].

Each time a pass is completed with no exchange, the GAP is divided in half, and the comparison and exchange process continues. The gap is continually halved, until it reaches 1. When the gap is at 1, adjacent elements are compared, and the sort proceeds in the same fashion as the bubble sort. Figure 12.12 details the Shell sort procedure graphically.

Pseudocode for the Shell Sort

```
Initialize the GAP at COUNT/2 (Where COUNT is the number of elements
    to sort)

LOOP WHILE GAP > 0
        Set SWAP.FLAG to 0 (to begin the loop process)
        LOOP WHILE SWAP.FLAG = 0 (repeat as long as any swaps made)
            Set SWAP.FLAG to 1 (to indicate NO swap made)
            FOR SUB = 1 TO (COUNT - GAP)
                IF element > element GAP distance apart
                    THEN SWAP elements
                        Set SWAP.FLAG to 0
                ENDIF
            NEXT SUB
        ENDLOOP
        Calculate new GAP as GAP/2 (a pass was made with no swap)
ENDLOOP
```

Figure 12.12
The Shell sort.

Count = 12   (items to sort)
  Gap = 6

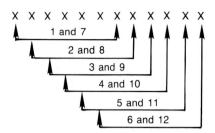

With Gap = 6, comparisons and exchanges
are made until a pass occurs where no
exchanges are made.

Then:
    Gap = INT(Gap/2)
    Gap = 3

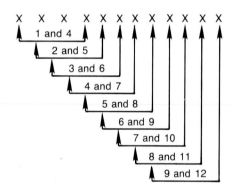

With Gap = 3, comparisons and exchanges
are made until a pass occurs where no
exchanges are made.

Then:
    Gap = INT(GAP/2)
    Gap = 1

and adjacent entries are compared and
exchanged, just as in the bubble sort.

Example Program: The Shell Sort

The previous sort example will be modified to replace the bubble sort with a Shell sort. Only the one subroutine (and a few remarks) need be changed.

Program Listing

```
100 '      PROGRAM TO INPUT A SERIES OF NAMES, USE A SHELL SORT TO
110 '      ARRANGE THEM IN ALPHABETIC ORDER, AND PRINT THE SORTED LIST
120 '
130 '            PROGRAM VARIABLES
140 '
150 '            COUNT              COUNT OF NAMES INPUT
160 '            LST$               ARRAY TO HOLD NAMES
170 '            SUB                SUBSCRIPT TO REF. NAMES
180 '            SWAP.FLAG          SWITCH FIELD
190 '                               1 = NO SWITCH MADE
200 '                               0 = SWITCH MADE THIS PASS
210 '
220 DIM LST$(50)
500 '************ PROGRAM MAINLINE *************************
510 GOSUB 1000                      'INPUT NAMES
520 GOSUB 2000                      'SORT LIST
530 GOSUB 3000                      'PRINT SORTED LIST
540 END
1000 '************** INPUT NAMES *************************
1010 CLS
1020 PRINT "ENTER NAMES, TYPE 'END' TO QUIT"
1030 LET COUNT = 1
1040 INPUT LST$(COUNT)
1050 WHILE LST$(COUNT) <> "END" AND COUNT < 50
1060     LET COUNT = COUNT + 1
1070     INPUT LST$(COUNT)
1080     IF COUNT = 50 AND LST$(COUNT) <> "END"
             THEN PRINT "SORRY, I CAN ONLY HANDLE 50 NAMES"
1090 WEND
1100 RETURN
1110 '
2000 '********* SHELL SORT TO SORT THE NAMES *****************
2010 IF COUNT <> 50
         THEN LET COUNT = COUNT - 1   'DON'T COUNT "END"
2020 LET GAP = INT(COUNT/2)
2030 WHILE GAP > 0                    'SET INITIAL GAP
2040     LET SWAP.FLAG = 0            'ENTER LOOP
2050     WHILE SWAP.FLAG = 0          'CONTINUE UNTIL NO SWAPS
2060         LET SWAP.FLAG = 1
2070         FOR SUB = 1 TO COUNT - GAP
2080             IF LST$(SUB) > LST$(SUB+GAP)
                     THEN SWAP LST$(SUB), LST$(SUB+GAP):
                         LET SWAP.FLAG = 0    'SWAP MADE
2090         NEXT SUB
2100     WEND
2110     LET GAP = INT(GAP/2)              'SET NEW GAP FOR NEXT PASS
2120 WEND
2130 RETURN
2140 '
3000 '************* PRINT THE SORTED LIST ****************
3020 PRINT TAB(24); "SORTED LIST"
3030 PRINT
3040 FOR SUB = 1 TO COUNT
3050     PRINT LST$(SUB)
3060 NEXT SUB
3070 RETURN
3080 '************ END OF PROGRAM *************************
```

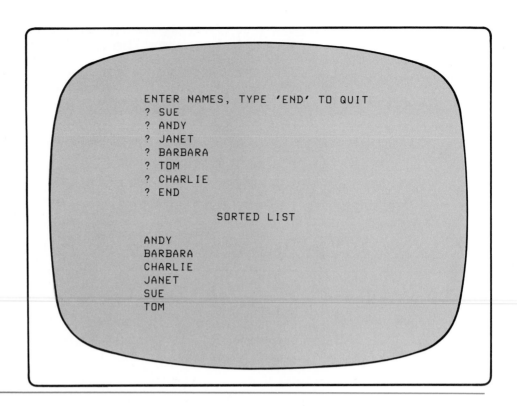

```
                    ENTER NAMES, TYPE 'END' TO QUIT
                    ? SUE
                    ? ANDY
                    ? JANET
                    ? BARBARA
                    ? TOM
                    ? CHARLIE
                    ? END

                              SORTED LIST

                    ANDY
                    BARBARA
                    CHARLIE
                    JANET
                    SUE
                    TOM
```

Multiple Fields to Be Sorted

A more realistic sort example would have additional fields to accompany each name. In the following example, each record consists of a name, date of last payment, and payment amount.

In a case such as this, the data will be read into three parallel arrays (one for the names, one for the dates, and one for the payments). If the records are sorted by the name field, the corresponding arrays must be kept in the same order as the names. Few modifications are required in our sort example program to accommodate the additional data.

Example Program:
Sorting a List with Additional Data Items

Program Listing

```
100 '    FURTHER VARIATION ON THE SORT PROBLEM. PROGRAM WILL
110 '      DEMONSTRATE SORTING A LIST (BY NAME FIELD) WHEN THERE
115 '      ARE ADDITIONAL FIELDS ALONG WITH THE NAME
120 '
130 '        PROGRAM VARIABLES
140 '
150 '        COUNT            COUNT OF NAMES INPUT
160 '        LST$             ARRAY TO HOLD NAMES
162 '        DAT$             ARRAY TO HOLD DATES
164 '        PMT              ARRAY TO HOLD PAYMENT AMOUNTS
170 '        SUB              SUBSCRIPT TO REF. ARRAYS
180 '        SWAP.FLAG        SWITCH FIELD
190 '                           1 = NO SWITCH MADE
200 '                           0 = SWITCH MADE THIS PASS
210 '
220 DIM LST$(50),DAT$(50),PMT(50)
```

```basic
500 '************* PROGRAM MAINLINE **************************
510 GOSUB 1000                        'INPUT NAMES
520 GOSUB 2000                        'SORT LIST
530 GOSUB 3000                        'PRINT SORTED LIST
540 END
1000 '*************** INPUT NAMES ***************************
1010 CLS
1030 LET COUNT = 1
1040 INPUT "NAME ('END' TO QUIT) ", LST$(COUNT)
1050 WHILE LST$(COUNT) <> "END" AND COUNT < 50
1052    INPUT "DATE OF LAST PAYMENT ", DAT$(COUNT)
1054    INPUT "PAYMENT AMOUNT       ", PMT(COUNT)
1056    PRINT
1060    LET COUNT = COUNT + 1
1070    INPUT "NAME ('END' TO QUIT) ", LST$(COUNT)
1080    IF COUNT = 50 AND LST$(COUNT) <> "END"
         THEN PRINT "SORRY, I CAN ONLY HANDLE 50 NAMES"
1090 WEND
1100 IF COUNT <> 50
         THEN LET COUNT = COUNT - 1   'DON'T COUNT "END"
1110 RETURN
1120 '
2000 '********** SHELL SORT TO SORT THE NAMES ****************
2020 LET GAP = INT(COUNT/2)
2030 WHILE GAP > 0                     'SET INITIAL GAP
2040    LET SWAP.FLAG = 0              'ENTER LOOP
2050    WHILE SWAP.FLAG = 0            'CONTINUE UNTIL NO SWAPS
2060       LET SWAP.FLAG = 1
2070       FOR SUB = 1 TO COUNT - GAP
2080          IF LST$(SUB) > LST$(SUB+GAP)
                  THEN GOSUB 2500      'SWAP ALL ELEMENTS
2090       NEXT SUB
2100    WEND
2110    LET GAP = INT(GAP/2)           'SET NEW GAP FOR NEXT PASS
2120 WEND
2130 RETURN
2140 '
2500 '*************** SWAP THE ARRAY ELEMENTS ****************
2510 SWAP LST$(SUB), LST$(SUB + GAP)
2520 SWAP DAT$(SUB), DAT$(SUB + GAP)
2530 SWAP PMT(SUB), PMT(SUB + GAP)
2540 LET SWAP.FLAG = 0                 'INDICATE SWAP MADE
2550 RETURN
2560 '
3000 '*************** PRINT THE SORTED LIST ****************
3020 PRINT TAB(34); "SORTED LIST"
3030 PRINT
3040 FOR SUB = 1 TO COUNT
3050    PRINT LST$(SUB), DAT$(SUB), PMT(SUB)
3060 NEXT SUB
3070 RETURN
3080 '************* END OF PROGRAM **************************
```

```
        ENTER NAME ('END' TO QUIT) SUE
        DATE OF LAST PAYMENT       3/15/86
        PAYMENT AMOUNT             50

        ENTER NAME ('END' TO QUIT) ANDY
        DATE OF LAST PAYMENT       3/1/86
        PAYMENT AMOUNT             15

        ENTER NAME ('END' TO QUIT) JANET
        DATE OF LAST PAYMENT       2/25/86
        PAYMENT AMOUNT             85

        ENTER NAME ('END' TO QUIT) BARBARA
        DATE OF LAST PAYMENT       3/14/86
        PAYMENT AMOUNT             20

        ENTER NAME ('END' TO QUIT) TOM
        DATE OF LAST PAYMENT       2/5/86
        PAYMENT AMOUNT             10
```

```
        ENTER NAME ('END' TO QUIT) CHARLIE
        DATE OF LAST PAYMENT       3/2/86
        PAYMENT AMOUNT             50

        ENTER NAME ('END' TO QUIT) END

                     SORTED LIST

        ANDY          3/1/86          15
        BARBARA       3/14/86         20
        CHARLIE       3/2/86          50
        JANET         2/25/86         85
        SUE           3/15/86         50
        TOM           2/5/86          10
```

Summary

1. In a one-dimensional array, each element is identified by one subscript. In a two-dimensional array, each element is identified by two subscripts.
2. A two-dimensional array can be pictured as a table with rows and columns.
3. In dimensioning and subscripting a two-dimensional array, the first subscript identifies the row, the second the column.
4. Nested loops are an ideal tool for processing two dimensional tables.
5. Two-dimensional tables may be used in table lookups and binary searches.
6. Arrays may be dimensioned for three or more dimensions (up to 255). A three-dimensional array requires three subscripts for reference to an array element.
7. Numeric or string data stored in an array may be sorted into ascending (low to high) or descending (high to low) sequence.
8. The bubble sort rearranges data elements by continually exchanging data elements until the highest elements are at the high end of the array.
9. The Shell sort is more efficient than the bubble sort, especially for long lists of data.
10. The SWAP statement is used to exchange the contents of two variables. The two variables must be the same type (string, single-precision, double-precision, or integer).

Programming Exercises

12.1. A club is raising funds through the sale of candies. They will be selling three different types—mints, peanut clusters, and English toffee. Write a program that will produce two reports, a detail of each sale and a summary report.

INPUT: Candy sales will be entered with READ/DATA statements. For each sale reported, an entry will be made containing the member name, type of candy sold, the quantity sold, and the date of sale.

PROCESSING: Use one-dimensional arrays to store the member names, candy types, and months of the year. Use a two-dimensional array to store the counts and the total sold per member.

Club Members	Types of Candies
DOUG	1 MINTS
MIMI	2 PEANUT CLUSTERS
KARL	3 ENGLISH TOFFEE
SCOTT	
JANNETTE	

OUTPUT: The detail report must contain the member name, the type of candy sold, and the quantity sold. Each line must also contain the date the sale was recorded with the month spelled out.

The summary report must contain the names of the members, the total count of each type sold per member, the total quantity sold per member, and the total of each type for the entire club.

TEST DATA: This data is supplied for test purposes. Remember, your program must be able to work for *any* data supplied, any month name, any quantity of these three candy types, and in any sequence entered.

Member (Names must be entered)	Type	Quantity	Date
KARL	1	3	3/21
KARL	3	5	3/21
MIMI	1	5	3/21
SCOTT	2	4	4/4
DOUG	3	3	4/4
DOUG	1	8	4/4
MIMI	1	8	4/11
KARL	2	4	9/11

SAMPLE PROGRAM OUTPUT USING TEST DATA:

SALES REPORT

NAME	TYPE	QUANTITY	DATE
KARL	MINTS	3	MARCH 21
KARL	TOFFEE	5	MARCH 21
MIMI	MINTS	5	MARCH 21
SCOTT	CLUSTERS	4	APRIL 4
DOUG	TOFFEE	3	APRIL 4
DOUG	MINTS	8	APRIL 4
MIMI	MINTS	8	APRIL 11
KARL	CLUSTERS	4	SEPTEMBER 11

SUMMARY REPORT

NAME	MINTS	CLUSTERS	TOFFEE	TOTAL
DOUG	8	0	3	11
MIMI	13	0	0	13
KARL	3	4	5	12
SCOTT	0	4	0	4
JANNETTE	0	0	0	0
TOTAL	24	8	8	40

12.2. A questionnaire has been sent to 100 households concerning the insulation of their homes. The form has fifteen questions, each with five possible answers. The possible responses are:

1. Always
2. Usually
3. Sometimes
4. Seldom
5. Never

What is needed is an item analysis that lists each question and the number of persons responding with choice 1, choice 2, choice 3, and so forth.

INPUT: The input data may come from DATA statements or INPUT statements. For each questionnaire received, enter a response (1–5) for each of the fifteen questions. Although 100 questionnaires were distributed, not all were returned. Test your program with different numbers of questionnaires returned.

Sample Data (Make up your own data to resemble the sample):
For each questionnaire

Question	Response
1	2
2	5
3	1
4	5
5	5
6	5
7	2
.	.
.	.
.	.
15	2

PROCESSING: Accumulate the number of each possible response for each question. Use a two-dimensional array for the accumulators.

Responses

Questions	(1)	(2)	(3)	(4)	(5)
(1)					
(2)					
(3)					
(4)					
(5)					
(6)					
(7)					
(8)					
(9)					
(10)					
(11)					
(12)					
(13)					
(14)					
(15)					

OUTPUT: Print an item analysis that shows the question number and the count of each possible response.

QUESTION	CHOICE 1	CHOICE 2	CHOICE 3	CHOICE 4	CHOICE 5
1	5	2	0	4	6
2	2	2	10	2	1
3	17	0	0	0	0
.	.	.	.	.	.
.	.	.	.	.	.
.	.	.	.	.	.

12.3. Students in a programming course have each taken three exams. Write an interactive program that will input each student's name and the three exam scores and will produce a listing showing each student's average and the class averages.

INPUT: Make up your own test data, similar to the data shown.

Name	Exam 1	Exam 2	Exam 3
Jan Shanks	80	75	92
Andy Mills	83	92	88
Ken Bird	72	65	80
.	.	.	.
.	.	.	.
.	.	.	.

Although the exact number of students is not known prior to entry, there will be no more than fifty students in the class. Be sure to INPUT all data into arrays before any calculations are done. Use a one-dimensional array for the student names, and a two-dimensional array to hold the exam scores.

CALCULATIONS: After inputting all data into the arrays, calculate the average for each student and the class average for each exam. Use two, one-dimensional arrays to store the averages.

OUTPUT: Print appropriate title and column headings and one detail line for each student. Each line must show the student name, three exam scores, and average score. At the bottom of the list, print a summary line that shows the average for each exam. Align the averages beneath their corresponding columns of data.

12.4. Modify the program in exercise 12.3 to print the list sorted into rank order. This places the student having the highest average at the top of the list, and the student with the lowest average at the bottom of the list.

12.5. Modify the program in exercise 12.4 to include a menu with these choices:

1. Enter student names and scores
2. Display data for one student on the screen
3. Print class list in rank order
4. Print class list in alphabetic order
5. Quit

12.6. Write a program that will generate a series of random integers in the range 1–50 and will count the number of times each of those integers occurs. Present a menu with these choices:

1. Generate random numbers
2. Print the set of random numbers
3. Print the counts in numerical order
4. Print the counts in rank order by occurrence
5. Quit

Choice 1: Generate random numbers.
Request input of how many numbers to generate. Then, using the RND function, generate the specified number of integers in the range 1–50, counting the number of occurrences of each integer. Hint: Set up a one-dimensional array of fifty elements, using element 1 to count the occurrences of the integer 1, element 2 to count the 2's, and so forth. Each time the program is run, it must generate a different set of random numbers (use RANDOMIZE).

Choice 2: Display the list of random numbers. If possible, print all the numbers on one screen rather than allow them to scroll.

Choice 3: Print the list of numbers and their occurrences.

```
NUMBER          OCCURRENCES
   1                 4
   2                 3
   3                 4
   4                 6
   .                 .
   .                 .
   .                 .
```

Choice 4: Print the list sorted by the number of occurrences with the numbers occurring most frequently at the *top* of the list.

Choice 5: Print an appropriate sign-off message.

12.7. Modify the program in exercise 12.6 to graph the output with a series of asterisks. For each integer (1–50), print asterisks corresponding to the number of times the integer occurred.

Sample Output

```
1 * * * *
2 * * *
3 * * * *
4 * * * * * *
  .  .
  .  .
  .  .
```

12.8. Modify the program in exercise 12.7 to print the graph turned sideways. Hint: Create a two-dimensional string array, fifty-by-fifty. First fill each array position with a blank space. Then store the appropriate number of asterisks in the correct positions.

Sample Output

```
            *
            *
  *     *   *
  *  *  *   *
  *  *  *   *
  *  *  *   *

  1  2  3  4  . . .
```

12.9. A program is needed to keep track of sales of computer software for five salespersons. The group is selling ten different products by item number. Accumulate sales statistics and print a summary report.

TABLES: Use DATA statements to set up the tables for lookup.

Product Table

Item #	Product name	Unit price
A101	Accounting Made Easy	125.00
A102	Credits and Debits and Stuff	75.00
A103	Accounting for Turtle Factories	200.00
A104	Accounting for Preschoolers	10.00
B101	Wordy Processing	150.00
B102	The Big Word	115.00
B104	Only Words	210.00
C201	Spelling Games	85.00
C203	Games of Chance	30.00
C205	Games of Skill	40.00

Salesperson Table

Salesperson Number	Salesperson Name
101	Dot Mannix
105	Daisy Wharton
114	Ian Jet
118	Kathy Baud
120	Al Grithom

INTERACTIVE PROGRAM OPERATION: During interactive program execution, request the salesperson number, the item number, and the quantity sold. For that sale, display the salesperson's name, item description, unit price, quantity sold, and extended price (quantity × unit price). Accumulate the quantity sold by item number and salesperson.

If an item number or salesperson number is not in the table, print an error message and allow re-entry of the data.

PRINTER OUTPUT: After all sales have been entered, print a summary report of the data. For each item number, print the item number, item name, number sold by each salesperson, the total units sold (for all salespersons), the unit price, and the total sales price of those items.

Report totals are required for the sales for each salesperson, as well as for the total units and total price. Design the output similar to this.

ITEM NO.	ITEM DESCRIPTION	PERSON 1	PERSON 2	PERSON 3	PERSON 4	PERSON 5	TOTAL UNITS	UNIT PRICE	SALES PRICE
XXXX	XXXXXXXXXXXXX	XXX	XXX	XXX	XXX	XXX	X,XXX	XXX.XX	X,XXX.XX
	TOTALS	XXXX	XXXX	XXXX	XXXX	XXXX	X,XXX		XX,XXX.XX

12.10. Write a program that will look up the distance between two cities by highway.

TABLE: Create the table with DATA statements.

Ref.	City
1	BOSTON
2	CHICAGO
3	DALLAS
4	LAS VEGAS
5	LOS ANGELES
6	MIAMI
7	NEW ORLEANS
8	TORONTO
9	VANCOUVER
10	WASHINGTON DC

	1	2	3	4	5	6	7	8	9	10
1	0	1004	1753	2752	3017	1520	1507	609	3155	448
2	1004	0	921	1780	2048	1397	919	515	2176	709
3	1753	921	0	1230	1399	1343	517	1435	2234	1307
4	2752	1780	1230	0	272	2570	1732	2251	1322	2420
5	3017	2048	1399	272	0	2716	1858	2523	1278	2646
6	1520	1397	1343	2570	2716	0	860	1494	3447	1057
7	1507	919	517	1732	1858	860	0	1307	2734	1099
8	609	515	1435	2251	2523	1494	1307	0	2820	571
9	3155	2176	2234	1322	1278	3447	2734	2820	0	2887
10	448	709	1307	2420	2646	1057	1099	571	2887	0

INTERACTIVE PROCESSING: Request input of the cities of departure and destination, and display the corresponding mileage. Format the screen so that the city names always appear in the same location, and data is not allowed to scroll.

    If either the departure or destination city is not in the table, print an error message. Be sure to clear the message for any further processing.

12.11   The Plain Wrap Auto Supply Store sells its own brand of spark plugs. In order to cross-reference to major brands, they keep a table of equivalent part numbers. They would like to computerize the process of looking up part numbers in order to improve their customer service.

TABLE:

Plain Wrap	Brand A	Brand C	Brand X
PR214	MR43T	RBL8	14K22
PR223	R43	RJ6	14K24
PR224	R43N	RN4	14K30
PR246	R46N	RN8	14K32
PR247	R46TS	RBL17Y	14K33
PR248	R46TX	RBL12-6	14K35
PR324	S46	J11	14K38
PR326	SR46E	XEJ8	14K40
PR444	47L	H12	14K44

INTERACTIVE PROGRAM EXECUTION: Request input of a manufacturer's code (A, C, or X) and the part number. Then display the corresponding Plain Wrap part number.

12.12.   Write a program that will allow for the input of names and print the list of names in alphabetical order. Use LINE INPUT so that names can be sorted by last name.

12.13.   Write a program that will generate thirty random numbers and perform a Bubble Sort of the numbers. Print the numbers on the screen before and after the sort.

12.14.   Write a subroutine to perform a Binary Search on the data sorted in exercise 12.12.

12.15.   Write a subroutine that will fill a 5 × 5 array with random numbers and print row and column totals.

12.16.   Write a program to print the sum and the average of each column in a 4 × 4 array. Use DATA statements to fill the array.

13 Sequential Data Files

OPEN Statement
CLOSE Statement
WRITE# Statement
PRINT# Statement
INPUT# Statement
EOF(n) Function
PRINT# USING Statement
KILL Statement
NAME Statement

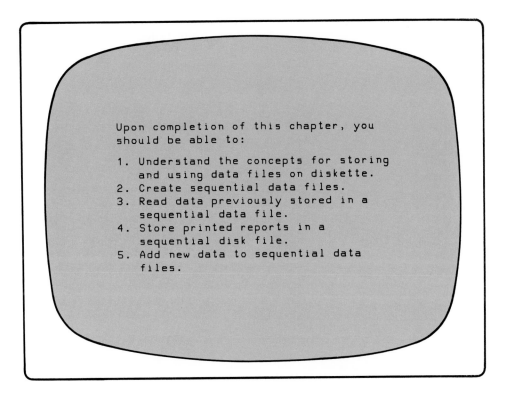

Upon completion of this chapter, you
should be able to:

1. Understand the concepts for storing
   and using data files on diskette.
2. Create sequential data files.
3. Read data previously stored in a
   sequential data file.
4. Store printed reports in a
   sequential disk file.
5. Add new data to sequential data
   files.

Introduction

All of the example programs written until now have had their data entered with INPUT, DATA, or LET statements. While this is satisfactory for many applications, there are many situations requiring large quantities of data.

Many computer applications require data to be saved from one program run to the next. Some examples are personal tasks such as budgeting, mailing lists, and sports team records and business applications such as inventory records, customer files, and master files. This chapter and the next deal with methods to store and access **data files** on diskette.

Diskette Storage

There are several popular sizes of diskettes, or floppy disks. The most common sizes are

8 inch—called diskettes
5 1/4 inch—called minidiskettes or minifloppies
3 1/2 inch—called microdiskettes

The following terminology applies equally to each of these sizes of diskettes.

The actual diskette is encased in an outer protective envelope. Figure 13.1 illustrates a floppy diskette and its covering. Data are stored along **tracks,** which are concentric circles on the surface of the disk (refer to figure 13.2). Each track is further broken down into **sectors.** See figure 13.3 for a diagram of tracks and sectors on diskette.

If you have done any comparison of disk capacity from one computer manufacturer to another, you may have been surprised to find disk storage capacities ranging anywhere from about 100,000 bytes (100 K bytes) to about 1,000,000 bytes (1 megabyte). The difference depends on the number of characters per sector and the number of sectors per track. Some common sector sizes are 512 bytes for IBM-PC diskettes, 256 bytes for Apple diskettes, 128 bytes for "standard" CP/M diskettes. When a file is stored, the required number of sectors are allocated. Whenever data is written to the disk or read from the disk, an entire sector is written or read.

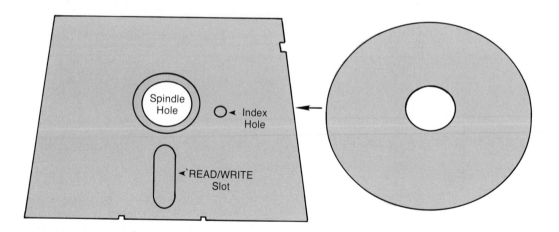

Figure 13.1
A floppy disk (diskette) in its
outer protective envelope.

Figure 13.2
Diskette showing tracks.

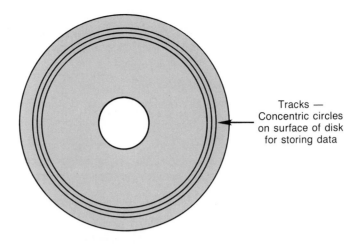

Tracks —
Concentric circles
on surface of disk
for storing data

Figure 13.3
One track divided into sectors.

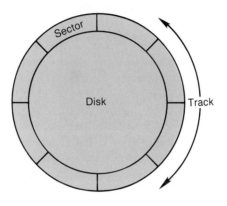

Data Files and Program Files

In diskette terminology, anything stored on the diskette is given its own unique name and called a file. Each program written and saved is called a *file*. However, these *program* files differ from the *data* files to be created now. One application will probably have one program file containing the program instructions, in addition to another file (or more) containing the actual data (names and addresses, inventory amounts, account balances, etc.).

For a list of the files stored on a diskette, use the FILES command.

```
FILES

COMMAND .COM    PROG1  .BAS    TEST    .DAT    BIGPROG .BAS
BASIC   .COM    PROG2  .BAS    MYDATA          LISTING .TXT
PROGRAM9.BAS
```

Recall from chapter 1 the naming rules for disk files: a one-to-eight-character name, optionally followed by a period and up to a three-character extension. The three-character extension is generally used to identify and group the files into types. Most BASIC program files end with .BAS. Some other common extensions are

.COM—Command files (programs that are ready to execute)
.ASM—Assembler program files
.OBJ—Compiled programs (object files)
.TXT—Text files (ASCII form, to be printed out)
.DAT—Data files

Note that file names may always be preceded by a drive specification. If the file resides on a drive other than the currently logged disk drive, include the drive and a colon.

```
A:MYFILE.DAT

B:DATAFILE
```

In order to discuss data files, some terminology must be agreed upon. The entire collection of data is called a **file.** The file is made up of **records**—one record for each entity in the file.

Examples: In a customer file, the data for one customer would be one record. In a name and address file, the data for one person is one record.

Each record can be further broken down into individual **fields** (also called **data elements**).

Examples: In the customer file, one customer record would have an account number field, a name field, an address field, perhaps a field to indicate credit rating, another to store the current balance, and another to store the date the account was opened. Each of these fields relates to the same customer.

The data stored in files is nearly always entered in an organized manner. Records may be stored in account number order, alphabetically by name, by date, or by the sequence in which they are received. One field in the record is the organizing factor for the file (such as account number, name, or date). This field, which is used to determine the order of the file, is called the **record key,** or *key field.*

A key field may be either a string or numeric field. In the customer file, if the records are in order by customer number, then customer number is the key field. If the order is based on customer name, then the name is the key field.

File Organizations

The manner in which data are organized, stored, and retrieved is called the *file organization.* BASIC supports two file organizations: **sequential** and **random.** A third file organization, called **indexed files,** is also popular in data processing applications. Indexed organization is supported by some other programming languages, such as COBOL, PL/I, and RPG. In BASIC, a combination of a sequential file, a table, and a random file can be used to create indexed files. The remainder of this chapter is devoted to sequential files; chapter 14 deals with random files and chapter 15 covers special file handling techniques including indexed files.

Feedback

1. What is a disk track?
2. What is a sector?
3. How many characters can be stored in one disk sector?
4. What is the difference between a program file and a data file?
5. For the file specification

   ```
   B:REPORT.PRT
   ```

   a. What does B: signify?
   b. What is .PRT?
6. Consider the situation in which an instructor stored data about the students in a class. For each student, the required data was name, identification number, five quiz scores, and three exam scores. The student data is in alphabetic order by student name.
   a. The student identification number is a _____ .
      (field, record, file)
   b. All of the data for one student is a _____ .
      (field, record, file)
   c. The key field is _____ .
   d. All of the data for all students is called a _____ .
      (field, record, file)

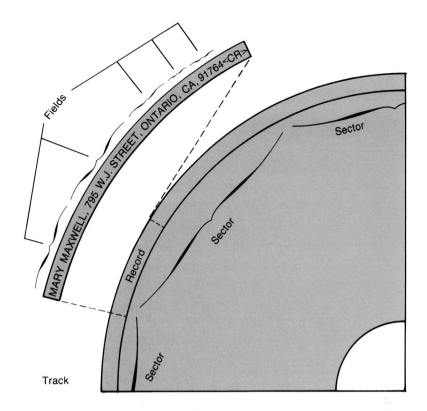

Figure 13.4
One record stored on a diskette.

Fields

MARY MAXWELL, 795 W.J. STREET, ONTARIO, CA, 91764<CR>

Sector

Sector

Record

Sector

Sector

Track

Sequential File Organization

Sequential files are the easiest to create and read in BASIC. Data elements (fields) are stored one after another in sequence. When the data is read *from* the disk, it must be read in the same sequence. Conceptually, a data file on the disk is similar to DATA statements in a program. In order to read any particular element of data, all fields preceding that one must be read first. As data elements are written on diskette, the fields are separated by commas. Records are generally terminated by a carriage return character. Figure 13.4 illustrates data fields stored on diskette.

As an example program, a name and address file will be created (for a person with few friends).

Sample Data

First Record

Name field:	Harry Maxwell
Address field:	795 W. J Street
City field:	Ontario
State field:	CA
Zip code field:	91764

Second Record

Name field:	Jennifer Helm
Address field:	201 Cortez Way
City field:	Pomona
State field:	CA
Zip code field:	91766

Third Record

Name field:	Craig Colton
Address field:	1632 Granada Place
City field:	Pomona
State field:	CA
Zip code field:	91766

This data stored in a disk data file would look like this:

Harry Maxwell,795 W. J Street,Ontario,CA,91764<CR>
Jennifer Helm,201 Cortez Way,Pomona,CA,91766<CR>
Craig Colton,1632 Granada Place,Pomona,CA,91766<CR>

Writing Data to a Disk File

Writing data to a disk file is similar to PRINTing data on the screen or printer. The data is *output* from the program. There are three steps necessary to place data on the disk.

1. *Open* the file. Before any data may be placed on the disk, the file must be opened as an *output file*.
2. *Write* the data elements to be stored.
3. *Close* the file. This should always be the last step in a program that handles disk data files.

Examine the following example program and the explanation of the individual program statements.

Example Program: A Sequential Disk File

Program Listing

```
10 '    PROGRAM TO CREATE A SEQUENTIAL DISK FILE
20 '       INPUTS NAMES & ADDRESSES
30 '       AND WRITES EACH ON THE DISK DATA FILE
40 '
500 '************* PROGRAM MAINLINE ************************
510 GOSUB 1000                    'OPEN FILE
520 GOSUB 2000                    'CREATE FILE
530 GOSUB 3000                    'CLOSE FILE
540 END
550 '
1000 '*********** OPEN FILE FOR OUTPUT ********************
1010 OPEN "O", #1, "NAMES.DAT"
1020 RETURN
1030 '
2000 '************** CREATE THE FILE *********************
2010 INPUT "ENTER NAME, 'END' TO QUIT ", NAM$
2020 WHILE NAM$ <> "END"
2030    INPUT "STREET ADDRESS ", ADDR$
2040    INPUT "CITY           ", CITY$
2050    INPUT "STATE          ", ST$
2060    INPUT "ZIP            ", ZIP$
2065    PRINT
2070    WRITE #1, NAM$, ADDR$, CITY$, ST$, ZIP$
2080    INPUT "ENTER NAME, 'END' TO QUIT ", NAM$
2090 WEND
2100 RETURN
2110 '
3000 '************** CLOSE THE FILE **********************
3010 CLOSE #1
3020 RETURN
3030 '************** END OF PROGRAM **********************
```

```
            ENTER NAME, 'END' TO QUIT Harry Maxwell
            STREET ADDRESS 795 W. J Street
            CITY            Ontario
            STATE           CA
            ZIP             91764

            ENTER NAME, 'END' TO QUIT Jennifer Helm
            STREET ADDRESS 201 Cortez Way
            CITY            Pomona
            STATE           CA
            ZIP             91766
```

```
ENTER NAME, 'END' TO QUIT Craig Colton
STREET ADDRESS 1632 Granada Place
CITY            Pomona
STATE           CA
ZIP             91766

ENTER NAME, 'END' TO QUIT END
OK
SYSTEM
A>TYPE NAMES.DAT
"Harry Maxwell","795 W. J Street","Ontario","CA","91764"
"Jennifer Helm","201 Cortez Way","Pomona","CA","91766"
"Craig Colton","1632 Granada Place","Pomona","CA","91766"
A>BASIC
```

Before any data file may be accessed (created or read), the file must be opened.

The OPEN Statement—General Form

Format 1:

line number OPEN, $\left\{ \begin{matrix} \text{"I"} \\ \text{"O"} \end{matrix} \right\}$, #filenumber, "file name"

Format 2:

line number OPEN "filename" FOR $\left\{ \begin{matrix} \text{INPUT} \\ \text{OUTPUT} \\ \text{APPEND} \end{matrix} \right\}$ AS #filenumber

Some versions of Microsoft BASIC allow only the first version of the OPEN statement, others allow a choice of either method. The elements shown in brackets are the *file mode*. The brackets indicate that a choice may be made, but that the entry is required.

The OPEN Statement—Examples

```
100    OPEN "O", #1, "DATAFILE"
or
100    OPEN "DATAFILE" FOR OUTPUT AS #1


200    OPEN "I", #2, "B:NAMES.DAT"
or
200    OPEN "B:NAMES.DAT" FOR INPUT AS #2
```

The first example (100) opens a file called DATAFILE as an output file, calling it file #1. The second example (200) opens a file on the B: drive called NAMES.DAT as an input file, calling it file #2.

File Mode	Explanation
"O"—OUTPUT	Data will be output from the program and written on the disk. This is used to create a data file.
"I"—INPUT	Data will be input into the program from the disk. This will read data previously stored on the disk.
APPEND	Data will be output from the program and written on the disk. The new data will be added to the *end* of a previously created data file.

Remember that a data file must *always* be opened prior to being used for output or input. When a data file is opened for output, the following actions are taken.

1. The directory is checked for the named file. If the file does not exist, an entry is created for this file. Note that if a file already exists, the old file contents will be lost. The new data will *replace* the previous contents of the file.
2. A **buffer** is established in memory. This is simply setting aside enough main storage to hold 128 bytes of data. As the program instructs BASIC to WRITE data on the disk, the data is actually placed in the buffer. Not until the buffer is filled is the data physically written on the disk.
3. A *file pointer* is set to the beginning of the file. The concept of a file pointer is similar to that in a DATA list in the program. The pointer is always updated to indicate the current location in the file.
4. The file is given a *file number* for future reference. In the example program, it was called file #1. Each file used in one program must be assigned a unique number; however, the numbers need not begin with #1. If you wish, you may

call the first file #3. The allowable range is from 1 to the maximum number of files allowed in a program. That value defaults to 3 unless a BASIC control command is given to increase the number of allowable files (see BASIC statement, appendix A).

At the conclusion of processing, the file should be closed.

The CLOSE Statement—General Form

```
line number CLOSE [#filenumber, ...]
```

The CLOSE Statement—Examples

```
500    CLOSE #1
600    CLOSE #1, #2, #3
700    CLOSE
```

The CLOSE statement is used to terminate processing of a disk file. When used without a file number (third example), all open files are closed. The CLOSE statement performs many "housekeeping" tasks:

1. Physically writes the last partially filled buffer on the disk. Data are placed in the buffer by the WRITE statement and are not written to the disk until the buffer is filled. Generally, there will be data in the buffer at the end of the program. That data must be written to the disk.
2. Writes an *End Of File mark (EOF)* at the end of the file.
3. Releases the buffer.
4. Releases the file number. The file number may be reused in another OPEN for a different (or the same) file.

Note that executing an END statement will automatically close all open files. However, it is *not* recommended procedure to rely upon this. If a program terminates in any manner other than an END statement, the files will remain open and probably be "garbaged." A good rule is always to explicitly CLOSE every file that has been opened in the program.

The WRITE# Statement—General Form

```
line number WRITE #filenumber, fields to write
```

Use the WRITE# statement to place data into a data file. Before the WRITE# statement can be executed, the file must be opened in output mode. The list of fields to write may be string and/or numeric expressions and may be separated by commas or semicolons.

The WRITE# Statement—Examples

```
1050    WRITE #1, ACCT, DESC$, UNIT, PRICE
2200    WRITE #3, A; B; C; D
3150    WRITE #2, NAM$, ADDR$, CITY$, ST$, ZIP$
```

The WRITE# statement outputs data fields to the disk. As you recall, those fields must have commas written between them as they appear on the disk. The WRITE# statement places commas between each element of data, encloses string data in quotation marks, and inserts a carriage return and a linefeed character after the last item in the list.

Sample name and address data written to the disk file by the WRITE# statement.

```
"HARRY MAXWELL","795 W. J STREET","ONTARIO","CA","91764"<CR><LF>
"JENNIFER HELM","201 CORTEZ WAY","POMONA","CA","91766"<CR><LF>
"CRAIG COLTON","1632 GRANADA PLACE","POMONA","CA","91766"<CR><LF>
```

Unfortunately, some versions of Microsoft BASIC do not have the WRITE# statement. For those, the PRINT# statement must be used.

The PRINT# Statement—General Form

line number **PRINT#** filenumber, list of expressions

PRINT# actually functions much like the PRINT statement. Each of the items to print are formatted the same as in a PRINT. There will be one space for the sign preceding positive numbers, and one space following the numbers. PRINT# does *not* place the necessary commas on the disk between the data items. It also responds to semicolons and commas in the print list just as if the data were going to the screen. So, any commas in the print list will be treated as TABs and cause extra spaces to be inserted between the data elements. Since commas must be written on the disk between the data elements, the commas must be explicitly written in the PRINT# statement.

The PRINT# Statement—Examples

```
1050    PRINT #1, ACCT; ","; DESC$; ","; UNIT; ","; PRICE
2200    PRINT #3, A; ","; B; ","; C
3150    PRINT #2, NAM$; ","; ADDR$; ","; CITY$; ","; ST$;
                        ","; ZIP$


4400    LET C$ = ","
4410    LET REC$ = NAM$ + C$ + ADDRS$ + C$ + CITY$ + C$ + ST$
4420    PRINT #2, REC$
```

The use of the PRINT# statement is not recommended unless the WRITE# statement is not available on your system.

Looking at the Data File on Diskette

Generally, the reason for writing data on diskette is the need to be able to read it in the future. The best way to check the data written on the disk is to write another program that reads the file and prints the contents. Such a program will soon be written.

A second way to "see" the data written on the disk is to use a DOS command, TYPE. To use an operating system command, it is necessary to terminate execution of the BASIC interpreter by keying in SYSTEM. When the system prompt appears, key in "TYPE filename".

A>	System prompt. The A> refers to the currently logged drive and may be another letter such as B> or C>.
A>TYPE filename	If the file is on a drive other than the currently logged drive, include the drive specification.
A>TYPE B:MYFILE.DAT	

To return to the BASIC interpreter, type the appropriate name for the system being used—generally one of these:

MBASIC	BASICA
MSBASIC	GBASIC
BASIC	GWBASIC

Feedback

1. Why must the data elements in a sequential disk file be separated by commas?
2. What is the purpose of the OPEN statement?
3. What would happen if the CLOSE statement were left out of a program?
4. You might choose a name for your data file without realizing that there was already a file on the disk with the same name. Your program would have an open statement, and a file by that name would already exist. What would happen?
5. What happens when a file is opened for output and the file is not already in the directory?
6. Can you name any reason for using the PRINT# statement rather than WRITE#?

Writing a Program to List the Data File

To read the data from the disk, an input operation is needed. The concept is similar to the READ statement, where each field read brings in the next element in the list. The steps to read data from the disk are

1. Open the file for input
2. Read the data from the disk (and print it on the screen or printer)
3. Close the file

Example Program: Reading the Name and Address File and Printing Address Labels

Program Listing

```
10 '   READ THE SEQUENTIAL NAME AND ADDRESS FILE
15 '   AND PRINT ADDRESS LABELS
20 '
500 GOSUB 1000                    'OPEN FILE
510 GOSUB 2000                    'PRINT LABELS
520 GOSUB 3000                    'CLOSE FILE
530 END
540 '
1000 '*********** OPEN FILE FOR INPUT ********************
1010 OPEN "I", #1, "NAMES.DAT"
1020 RETURN
1030 '
2000 '********** READ DATA FILE AND PRINT LABELS *************
2010 WHILE NOT EOF(1)
2020    INPUT #1, NAMES$, ADDRESS$, CITY$, STATE$, ZIP$
2030    LPRINT NAMES$
2040    LPRINT ADDRESS$
2050    LPRINT CITY$; ", "; STATE$; " "; ZIP$
2060    LPRINT: LPRINT
2070 WEND
2080 RETURN
2090 '
3000 '************** CLOSE THE FILE *********************
3010 CLOSE #1
3020 RETURN
3030 '*************** END OF PROGRAM *******************
```

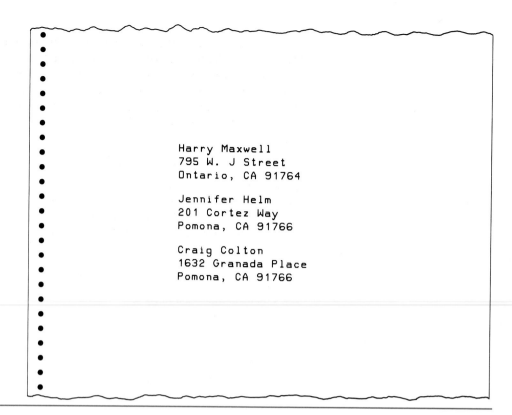

```
              Harry Maxwell
              795 W. J Street
              Ontario, CA 91764

              Jennifer Helm
              201 Cortez Way
              Pomona, CA 91766

              Craig Colton
              1632 Granada Place
              Pomona, CA 91766
```

A new BASIC statement (INPUT#), a new function [EOF(n)], and a file opened for input were illustrated in the sample program.

Opening a File for Input

When a data file is opened for input, there is a slight change in the functions performed by the OPEN. When a file was opened for output, a new directory entry was created if the file did not exist. If a file is opened for input, and the file does not exist, an error message is printed and the program terminated. The OPEN, then, performs these functions:

1. The directory is checked for the named file.
2. The buffer is established.
3. The file pointer is set to the beginning of the file.
4. The file is given a number for future reference.

The INPUT# Statement—General Form

line number I NPUT #filenumber, fields to read

The filenumber named on the INPUT# statement must be the number of a previously opened data file. The fields named should be separated by commas.

The INPUT# Statement—Examples

```
1100    INPUT #1, ACT, DES$, UNIT, PR
2500    INPUT #3, ALFA, BRAVO, CHARLIE, DELTA
3500    INPUT #2, NAMES$, ADDRESS$, CITY$, STATE$, ZIP$
```

The data on the disk are stored in a manner similar to the items on a DATA statement; that is, no variable names are associated with the data elements. It doesn't matter what variable names were used when the data was written to the disk. When the data elements are read from the disk, they may be called by the same variable names or completely different ones. In the example programs, the variable names were purposely changed to illustrate that point.

Finding the End of the Data File

There is more than one way to find the end of the data file. One way would be to keep reading until the data are exhausted. However, this will cause an error message and program cancellation. The second way to find the end of the data file was illustrated in the example program. The BASIC function EOF(n) was used to indicate the *end of file* condition.

The EOF(n) Function—General Form

```
EOF(filenumber)
```

This function returns *false* (0) as long as the end of file has not been found. As soon as the end of file mark has been found, the function returns *true* (-1).

The filenumber included in parentheses must be the file number of a currently open disk file. Notice that *no* number sign (#) is used in this function for file number.

The EOF(n) Function—Examples

```
600    WHILE NOT EOF(1)
1200   IF EOF(1)
       THEN . . .
1500   IF EOF(2) <> 0
       THEN . . .
```

Recall in the discussion of the CLOSE statement that one of the functions of the CLOSE is to write an end of file mark. That mark is actually an ASCII code 26, written after the last field of data.

Notice the placement of the test for end of file. There is *no* priming INPUT of the data. When data are being read with the INPUT# statement, the last read of *good* data also includes the EOF mark.

```
500    WHILE NOT EOF(1)
510        INPUT #1, NAM$
520        PRINT NAM$
530    WEND
```

A program in this form will read and print all good data and will *not* print anything for the EOF mark.

A third way to find the end of the data file is to place a terminal value there yourself. A common approach is to write some value such as EOF, END, or zero amounts at the end of the file when it is created. This technique would be quite similar to placing terminating data in a DATA list.

Example Program: Creating a File with Terminating Data

Program Listing

```
10  '   PROGRAM TO CREATE A SEQUENTIAL DISK FILE
20  '      INPUTS NAMES AND ADDRESSES
30  '      AND WRITES EACH ON THE DISK DATA FILE
40  '
50  '      ADDS TERMINATING DATA TO END OF FILE
60  '
500 '************* PROGRAM MAINLINE ***********************
510 GOSUB 1000                    'OPEN FILE
520 GOSUB 2000                    'CREATE FILE
530 GOSUB 3000                    'CLOSE FILE
540 END
550 '
1000 '*********** OPEN FILE FOR OUTPUT *******************
1010 OPEN "O", #1, "NAMES2.DAT"
1020 RETURN
1030 '
2000 '************* CREATE THE FILE **********************
2010 INPUT "ENTER NAME, 'END' TO QUIT ", NAM$
2020 WHILE NAM$ <> "END"
2030     INPUT "STREET ADDRESS ", ADDR$
2040     INPUT "CITY           ", CITY$
2050     INPUT "STATE          ", ST$
2060     INPUT "ZIP            ", ZIP$
2070     WRITE #1, NAM$, ADDR$, CITY$, ST$, ZIP$
2080     INPUT "ENTER NAME, 'END' TO QUIT ", NAM$
2090 WEND
2100 RETURN
2110 '
3000 '*************** CLOSE THE FILE *********************
3005 WRITE #1, "END", "END", "END", "END", "END"
3010 CLOSE #1
3020 RETURN
3030 '*************** END OF PROGRAM *********************
```

The program that reads the data file will test for the terminating data (written by line number 3005).

```
10   ' READ THE SEQUENTIAL NAME AND ADDRESS FILE
15   ' AND PRINT ADDRESS LABELS
20   '
30   '    TESTS FOR DUMMY TERMINATING DATA
40   '
499  '************ PROGRAM MAINLINE ********************
500   GOSUB 1000                     'OPEN FILE
510   GOSUB 2000                     'PRINT LABELS
520   GOSUB 3000                     'CLOSE FILE
530   END
540   '
1000  '************ OPEN FILE FOR INPUT ****************
1010   OPEN  "I", #1, "NAMES2.DAT"
1020   RETURN
1030   '
2000   '********** READ DATA FILE AND PRINT LABELS *********
2005   INPUT #1, NAMES$, ADDRESS$, CITY$, STATE$, ZIP$
2010   WHILE NAMES$ <> "END"
2030      LPRINT NAMES$
2040      LPRINT ADDRESS$
2050      LPRINT CITY$; ", "; STATE$; " "; ZIP$
2060      LPRINT: LPRINT
2065      INPUT #1, NAMES$, ADDRESS$, CITY$, STATE$, ZIP$
2070   WEND
2080   RETURN
2090   '
```

```
3000    '************** CLOSE THE FILE *******************
3010    CLOSE #1
3020    RETURN
3030    '************** END OF PROGRAM ******************
```

Storing Printed Reports

A common application for sequential data files is temporarily to store a printed report. The report may be completely formatted with titles, column headings, and page breaks and written to a disk file rather than a print file. Then, at a more convenient time, the disk file can be printed out.

There are several situations that might require that printed reports be stored on the disk and printed later. One reason might be that several computers share one printer. Or, sometimes one program may print multiple reports—perhaps a detail report and a summary report. One report could be printed as the program runs and the other stored on the disk.

Example Program: Store a Report on Disk

Program Listing

```
10 '   PROGRAM TO READ DATA AND CREATE A FORMATTED REPORT
20 '      THAT IS STORED ON A DISK DATA FILE
30 '
40 '            VARIABLES
50 '            TREE$             SPECIES OF TREE
60 '            COUNT             NUMBER OF TREES OF THAT SPECIES
70 '            TOTAL             REPORT TOTAL OF ALL TREES
80 '            T$,H$,D$,F$       PRINT IMAGES
90 '
100 '
500 '**************** PROGRAM MAINLINE ********************
510 GOSUB 1000                     'INITIALIZE
520 GOSUB 2000                     'PRINT HEADINGS
530 GOSUB 3000                     'PRINT REPORT
540 GOSUB 5000                     'TERMINATE
550 END
560 '
1000 '**************** INITIALIZE ***********************
1010 LET T$ = "         CITY TREE INVENTORY"
1020 LET H$ = "          SPECIES          COUNT"
1030 LET D$ = "         \         \      #,###"
1040 LET F$ = "             TOTAL = ###,###"
1050 OPEN "O", #1, "TREEREPT.PRT"
1060 RETURN
1070 '
2000 '**************** PRINT HEADINGS *******************
2010 PRINT #1, CHR$(12);        'ADVANCE TO TOP OF PAGE
2020 PRINT #1, T$               'PRINT TITLE
2030 PRINT #1, " "              'PRINT A BLANK LINE
2040 PRINT #1, H$               'PRINT COLUMN HEADINGS
2050 PRINT #1, " "              'PRINT A BLANK LINE
2060 RETURN
2070 '
3000 '**************** PRINT REPORT *********************
3010 GOSUB 4000                 'READ DATA
3020 WHILE TREE$ <> "END"
3030     LET TOTAL = TOTAL + COUNT
3040     PRINT #1, USING D$; TREE$; COUNT
3050     GOSUB 4000             'READ NEXT DATA
3060 WEND
3070 RETURN
3080 '
```

```
4000 '***************** READ TREE DATA *************************
4010 READ TREE$, COUNT
4020 DATA ALDER,100,ASH,225,BIRCH,75,ELM,305,EUCALYPTUS,145
4030 DATA LAUREL,90,MAPLE,250,OAK,125,SYCAMORE,275,WILLOW,110,END,0
4040 RETURN
4050 '
5000 '****************** TERMINATE ***********************
5010 PRINT #1, " "                 'PRINT A BLANK LINE
5020 PRINT #1, USING F$; TOTAL
5030 CLOSE #1
5040 RETURN
5050 '***************** END OF PROGRAM *********************
```

Running this program produces no visible output, except for the "disk busy" light on the disk drive. After the report has been saved in the disk file, the report may be printed with the DOS command TYPE or PRINT. (For CP/M, press CTRL-P and then the command "TYPE filename".)

```
SYSTEM
A>TYPE TREEREPT.PRT

        CITY TREE INVENTORY

    SPECIES           COUNT

    ALDER              100
    ASH                225
    BIRCH               75
    ELM                305
    EUCALYPTUS         145
    LAUREL              90
    MAPLE              250
    OAK                125
    SYCAMORE           275
    WILLOW             110

       TOTAL =      1,700
```

Another new statement was introduced in this program, the PRINT# USING.

The PRINT# USING Statement—General Form

line number PRINT #filenumber, USING "image string"; variables to print

The PRINT# USING Statement—Examples

```
1500   PRINT #1, USING P$; DESC$; AMT
2200   PRINT #3, USING "###.##"; X; Y; Z
```

The PRINT# USING is similar to the PRINT USING statement. All characters used to format the image string for PRINT USING are also valid for PRINT# USING. Notice the punctuation in the statement. A comma must follow the file number, and a semicolon follows the print image. The expressions to print must also be separated by semicolons.

Making Changes to the Data in Sequential Files

It is not a simple task to make changes in the data stored in a sequential file. Recall that opening the file for output places the file pointer at the start of the file, destroying any data in the file. There isn't any way to input data, make changes (like perhaps to change an address), and write the data back to the file. The only way to make changes in a sequential file is to create an entirely new file. Updating sequential files will be covered in chapter 15.

Adding Data to Sequential Files

At some time new names and addresses may need to be added to the end of a name and address file. How easy that will be depends on which version of Microsoft BASIC is used. Some versions have an *APPEND mode,* others do not. Both methods will be covered here.

APPEND Mode

Referring back to the format for the OPEN statement (p. 350), one of the options was to open the file in APPEND mode. When a file is opened for APPEND, the file pointer is placed at the *end* of the file in output mode. Then the WRITE# or PRINT# statement may be used to add data to the file.

Example Program:
Adding Data to a Sequential File with APPEND

Program Listing

```
110 '   PROGRAM TO APPEND DATA TO A SEQUENTIAL DISK FILE
120 '      INPUTS NAMES AND ADDRESSES
130 '      AND WRITES EACH AT THE END OF THE DISK DATA FILE
140 '
500 '************* PROGRAM MAINLINE *************************
510 GOSUB 1000                     'OPEN FILE
520 GOSUB 2000                     'ADD DATA TO THE FILE
530 GOSUB 3000                     'CLOSE FILE
540 END
550 '
1000 '********** OPEN FILE FOR OUTPUT ***********************
1010 OPEN "NAMES.DAT" FOR APPEND AS #1
1020 RETURN
1030 '
2000 '************* CREATE THE FILE ************************
2010 INPUT "ENTER NAME, 'END' TO QUIT ", NAM$
2020 WHILE NAM$ <> "END"
2030     INPUT "STREET ADDRESS ", ADDR$
2040     INPUT "CITY          ", CITY$
2050     INPUT "STATE         ", ST$
2060     INPUT "ZIP           ", ZIP$
2070     WRITE #1, NAM$, ADDR$, CITY$, ST$, ZIP$
2080     INPUT "ENTER NAME, 'END' TO QUIT ", NAM$
2090 WEND
2100 RETURN
2110 '
3000 '*************** CLOSE THE FILE ***********************
3010 CLOSE #1
3020 RETURN
3030 '************** END OF PROGRAM ***********************
```

Adding Data to the End of the File with No APPEND Available

If the APPEND mode is not available, the process of adding data to a sequential file becomes more complicated. The only options are to open the file for INPUT or OUTPUT, and both modes place the file pointer at the *start* of the file. In order to get the file in OUTPUT mode with the file pointer at the end of the file (for writing), the entire file must be copied to a new, temporary file.

The steps for appending data to a sequential data file (called MASTER.FIL) are:

1. Open MASTER.FIL for INPUT.
2. Open a second file, called TEMP.FIL, for OUTPUT.

3. Copy all data from MASTER.FIL to TEMP.FIL

   Loop until end of file
       INPUT from MASTER.FIL
       WRITE to TEMP.FIL
   End loop

4. Close MASTER.FIL
5. KILL MASTER.FIL
6. Now all data is in TEMP.FIL, the file pointer is at the end of the file in OUTPUT mode. Any new data may be added at the end of the file.

   INPUT new data from keyboard
   Loop until end of new data
       WRITE to TEMP.FIL
       INPUT new data from keyboard
   End loop

7. Close TEMP.FIL
8. Rename TEMP.FIL (to) MASTER.FIL

Example Program:
Adding Data to a Sequential File Without APPEND

Program Listing

```
110 '   PROGRAM TO APPEND DATA TO A SEQUENTIAL DISK FILE
115 '      WHEN THE APPEND STATEMENT IS NOT AVAILABLE
120 '       INPUTS NAMES AND ADDRESSES
130 '       AND WRITES EACH AT THE END OF THE DISK DATA FILE
140 '
500 '************* PROGRAM MAINLINE ************************
510 GOSUB 1000                      'OPEN FILES
515 GOSUB 1500                      'COPY OLD FILE TO TEMP FILE
517 GOSUB 1800                      'GET RID OF OLD FILE
520 GOSUB 2000                      'ADD DATA TO NEW FILE
530 GOSUB 3000                      'CLOSE NEW FILE
540 END
550 '
1000 '*************** OPEN BOTH FILES *********************
1010 OPEN "I", #1, "NAMES.DAT"
1015 OPEN "O", #2, "TEMP.DAT"
1020 RETURN
1030 '
1500 '*********** COPY OLD FILE TO TEMP FILE **************
1510 WHILE NOT EOF(1)
1520    INPUT #1, NAM$, ADDR$, CITY$, ST$, ZIP$
1530    WRITE #2, NAM$, ADDR$, CITY$, ST$, ZIP$
1540 WEND
1550 RETURN
1560 '
1800 '*********** GET RID OF OLD FILE ********************
1810 CLOSE #1
1820 KILL "NAMES.DAT"
1830 RETURN
1840 '
2000 '************** CREATE THE FILE *********************
2010 INPUT "ENTER NAME, 'END' TO QUIT ", NAM$
2020 WHILE NAM$ <> "END"
2030    INPUT "STREET ADDRESS ", ADDR$
2040    INPUT "CITY           ", CITY$
2050    INPUT "STATE          ", ST$
2060    INPUT "ZIP            ", ZIP$
2070    WRITE #2, NAM$, ADDR$, CITY$, ST$, ZIP$
2080    INPUT "ENTER NAME, 'END' TO QUIT ", NAM$
2090 WEND
2100 RETURN
2110 '
```

```
3000 '************** CLOSE THE FILE **************************
3010 CLOSE #2
3015 NAME "TEMP.DAT" AS "NAMES.DAT"
3020 RETURN
3030 '************** END OF PROGRAM **************************
```

Two new statements were introduced in this example program, KILL and NAME. KILL is a vicious way to delete a disk file, and NAME is used to rename a file.

The KILL Statement—General Form

line number KILL "filename"

The KILL Statement—Examples

```
100   KILL "MAST.DAT"
400   KILL "B:PROG5.BAS"
```

You will recall from chapter 1 that KILL may be used as a command without a line number. Now it is used as a statement in a program for delayed execution. KILL will delete a file from diskette. The file must be present and *not open* in order for the KILL to be successful.

The NAME Statement—General Form

line number NAME "old filename" AS "new filename"

The NAME Statement—Examples

```
500   NAME "TEMP.FIL" AS "MASTER.FIL"
600   NAME "A:COPY.DAT" AS "GOOD.DAT"
```

The NAME command simply changes the name of a disk file without moving the file or altering its contents in any way. The file named as "old filename" must exist on the disk, and the "new filename" must *not* exist in order for the NAME command to be successful.

Feedback

1. What happens if a file is opened for input, and the file does not exist?
2. What is the purpose of the file buffer?
3. Does the file number used for the INPUT# statement have to be the same as the file number used when the file was written? Why or why not?
4. How would you know what variable names to use when reading data from the disk?
5. Why is it not necessary to use a priming INPUT# when using the EOF(n) to test for end of file?
6. Why is it necessary to create a new file to make changes in a data file?
7. When appending data without the advantage of APPEND mode, why must the entire file be copied?

Summary

1. Data may be saved from one program run to the next by using data files on diskette.
2. The three most common sizes of diskettes, or floppy disks, are 8 inch, 5 1/4 inch, and 3 1/2 inch.
3. Data are stored along concentric circles, called tracks, on the surface of the diskette.
4. Each track on the diskette is divided into sectors. The sector size varies from one computer operating system to another.
5. Both program files and data files can be stored on a diskette.
6. Filenames may be one to eight characters in length optionally followed by a period and up to a three-character extension.
7. A file is a collection of records.
8. A record is a collection of fields (or data elements).
9. One field in each record is generally called the key field. This record key is the field used to determine the order for the file.
10. BASIC supports two file organizations: sequential and random.
11. Sequential files are always created and read in sequence. In order to read any data element in the file, all preceding elements must first be read.
12. In sequential files on diskette, commas must separate all fields, and a carriage return character separates records.
13. In order to read or write data in a disk file, the file must first be opened.
14. At the conclusion of processing, the data file must be closed.
15. When a data file is opened for output, certain actions occur:
    a. Check for existence of the file. Create an entry if it doesn't exist.
    b. Establish a file buffer.
    c. Set the file pointer to the start of the file.
    d. Establish a correspondence between the filename and the filenumber.
16. The close statement will accomplish these tasks:
    a. Write the last partial buffer to the disk.
    b. Write an End of File mark at the end of the file.
    c. Release the file buffer.
    d. Release the filenumber.
17. Data is written in the disk file with the WRITE#, PRINT#, or PRINT# USING statements.
18. The WRITE# statement is the most efficient of the datafile output statements. The data written on the disk with the WRITE# statement will have the necessary commas separating the fields and quotation marks surrounding string elements.
19. When placing data on the disk with the PRINT# statement, literal commas must be written between the fields of data.
20. In order to check the data written in a disk file, the DOS command, TYPE, may be used. It is necessary to key the command SYSTEM to exit BASIC before entering any DOS command.
21. A program may be written to print the contents of a data file. To accomplish this, the file must first be opened, then the data fields read and printed. At the conclusion of processing, the file must be closed.
22. When a data file is opened for input, the file must exist or an error message is printed and the program terminated.
23. The BASIC statement to read data from a disk file is the INPUT# statement.
24. The end of a data file is indicated with the EOF(n) function. The function returns a value of *false* as long as data remains in the file. When the End of File mark is read, the EOF(n) function returns a value of *true*.

25. Often sequential files are used to temporarily store printed reports.
26. The PRINT# USING statement can be used to store formatted data in a data file.
27. The only way to make changes in a sequential file with a BASIC program is to create a new file.
28. Data may be appended to the end of a sequential file with one of two methods. If the BASIC interpreter supports APPEND mode, this is the preferred method. After opening a file in APPEND mode, the file pointer is placed at the end of the file in output mode.
29. If the APPEND mode is not available, the entire file must be copied to a new file. The goal is to place the file pointer at the end of the file in output mode.
30. After the old file is copied to a new file, the old file can be deleted with the KILL statement.
31. The newly created file can be renamed to the same name as the old filename with the NAME command.

Programming Exercises

13.1. Write two programs: one to create a sequential data file, and the second to read the file and calculate commission amounts.

Program 1
INPUT: Input from the keyboard the salesperson's number, name, commission rate, and amount of sales.
OUTPUT: Create a sequential file that contains all input data.

Program 2
INPUT: The input data will be the sequential file created in the first program. Input fields are the salesperson's number, name, commission rate, and amount of sales.
OUTPUT: Print a report with a title and column headings. One detail line will be printed for each salesperson (each input record). The fields on the detail line are to be the salesperson's number, name, sales amount, commission rate, and commission amount.
CALCULATIONS: Compute the commission amount as the sales amount multiplied by the commission rate.
TEST DATA:

Salesman Number	Salesman Name	Sale Amount	Commission Rate
1245	HERMAN HOLLERITH	1157.85	6.5%
1386	BLAISE PASCAL	2540.00	5%
1457	CHARLES BABBAGE	1853.70	4%
1819	JOHN ATANASOFF	650.00	4%
1722	JOHN VON NEUMANN	1000.00	5%

13.2. This assignment entails writing five programs. The first will create a data file to be used by the other four programs. Each of programs 2 through 5 relies on the data file created by program 1. However, the latter four programs do not depend on each other in any way and need not *all* be written.

Program 1
Write a program to create a data file of the book inventory at an elementary school. For each book, store the title, author, grade level, and room location.
Data should be requested from the keyboard and written to the data file. You may make up your own data, find some "real-life" data, or use the test data provided.

TEST DATA:

Title	Author	Grade Level	Room Location
BIG TREES	COGSWELL	4	2
FANTASTIC FRIDAY	CASEY	5	4
FRIENDS	HANOVER	3	2
FUN WITH PHYSICS	HAU	6	1
JANE AND DICK	ADAMS	1	3
MAGICAL MICE	MANNY	5	4
SMALL WORLD	ZANE	5	5
TRY AGAIN	KANT	6	1

Program 2

A program is needed that prints out the entire file on the printer. Format the report with appropriate title and column headings. Add a line at the bottom of the report with a count of the number of books.

Program 3

The teachers need to find the titles at a particular grade level. Write a program that will INPUT a grade level number from the keyboard. Then read through the file, printing only the records matching the selected grade level. If there are no books on that level, print a message to that effect.

Program 4

Write a menu program that will print the entire file sorted into one of four different orders. For this program, the entire file must first be read into arrays. It can then be sorted into any sequence desired.

Menu:
1. Print book list by title
2. Print book list by author
3. Print book list by location
4. Print book list by grade level
5. Quit

Program 5

Write a menu program to access the book file.
Menu:
1. Display the book file on the screen
2. Print the book file on the printer
3. Add new books to the file
4. Quit

For choice 3 (add books), input new records from the keyboard, and add them to the end of the book file. The program should be able to move back and forth between the menu options; that is, add some records, display the file, add some more records, and display the file again.

13.3. When tables must be used in a program, a common approach is to store the tables in data files rather than in the program. This makes the table data independent from the program, which is preferable in two specific situations: (1) The table data must be used by more than one program; or (2) the table data must be changed periodically.

Modify the program in exercise 12.9 (p. 339) to store the two tables in data files. This will entail two small programs to INPUT the table data from the keyboard and write it to disk files. Create one file for the product table and another file for the salesperson table.

In the main (third) program, follow the specifications for the program in exercise 12.9. However, do *not* use DATA statements. Instead, read the data files to fill the tables.

13.4. Write a program to create a sequential data file for the video selection at Jose's Video Store as well as a listing of the data.

INPUT: Input from the keyboard the name of the video, the number of VHS copies available, and the number of BETA copies available.
OUTPUT:
1. Create a sequential file on disk.
2. Print a report with a title, column headings, the name of the video, number of VHS copies available, and number of BETA copies available. The report should be printed on the printer.

13.5. Write a program to create a sequential data file for a list of names.

INPUT: The names should come from INPUT statements.
OUTPUT: Create a sequential file on disk, and print the names on the screen.
PROCESSING: Give the user the option of printing the names sequentially or in alphabetical order.

13.6. Write a program to create a sequential employee file for Dan's Dance Studio.

INPUT: Employee name, address, phone number, account number, number of dependents, and pay rate should be input from the keyboard.
OUTPUT: Create a sequential file and print all the input information on the screen or printer depending on what the user wants.
PROCESSING:
1. Design a nice-looking screen for data entry.

Menu Options:
1. Enter employee information
2. Print file on screen
3. Print file on printer
4. Quit

13.7. Write a program to create an employee file for the employees at Gonzo's Gunite Company.

INPUT: Employee's name, address, phone number, employee number, number of dependents, marital status, and pay rate will be input from the keyboard.
OUTPUT: Create a sequential file on disk and print the entire employee file on the printer or one record on the screen, whichever the user wishes to do.
Menu Options
1. Add a record
2. Print file on printer
3. Display one record on the screen
4. Quit

13.8. Write a program to create a sequential file for the company information for Gonzo's Gunite Company's subcontracters.

INPUT: The company name, address, phone number, and representative should be input from the keyboard.
OUTPUT: A list of the companies and all the company information should be printed on the printer and a sequential file should be created on disk.
Menu Options
1. Add a record
2. Print file sequentially on printer
3. Print file in alphabetical order on printer
4. Quit

13.9. Write a program to create a sequential file to keep track of your stamp collection.

INPUT: The Scott's number, description, and value will be input from the keyboard.

OUTPUT: Output should be to the screen. The user should be able to display the entire file or just one record. Also, a sequential file should be output to disk.

Menu Options
1. Add a record
2. Display entire file
3. Display one record
4. Quit

TEST DATA:

Scott's No.	Description	Value
C13	65 c Green Graf Zeppelin	2700.00
C14	1.30 Brown Graf Zeppelin	5150.00
C15	2.60 Blue Graf Zeppelin	9000.00
15–16	3c, 5c Refugees	26.75
17–18	3c, 5c U.P.U.	30.00
19–20	3c, 5c Technical Assist	15.00
21–22	3c, 5c Human Rights	40.00
1455	8c Family Planning	8.75
1456	8c Glassmaker	.22
1460	6c Olympics-Bicycling	7.25
1461	8c Olympics-Bobsledding	8.75
1462	15c Olympics-Running	16.00
1470	8c Tom Sawyer	8.75
1471	8c Christmas Angel	8.75

13.10. Write a program to keep track of your software collection in a sequential file.

INPUT: Item No., description, publisher, and price will be input from the keyboard.

OUTPUT: Output should be to the screen. The user should be able to display the entire file or just one record. Also, a sequential file should be created on disk.

Menu Options
1. Add a record
2. Display entire file
3. Display one record
4. Quit

TEST DATA

Item No.	Description	Publisher	Price
208	Grand Bridge	Electric Inc.	59.95
209	Chess 1000	Electric Inc.	39.95
214	Resume Maker	InfoTron	49.95
203	Form and Tool	Black Corp.	95.00
218	Will Maker	No Press	49.95
238	Insect	IOU Software	99.00
202	Pro Grames	Delayed Microsys.	59.95
200	World of Golf	Electric Inc.	49.95
227	NewsLetter	Benson	99.95
240	Fast Mail	Sys. & Soft.	79.95
226	Squeeze	Turnover Pub.	79.95
100	Glu Master	Benson	59.95
213	The Tutor	No Soft.	94.95
216	Power Balance	Minds	49.95
223	Orbit Rider	Byte	49.95
217	Graph	New Soft.	97.60
211	Quacky DOS	Gaze Systems	69.95
224	Jet in the Air	subline Inc.	49.95
221	Disk Destroyer	No Soft.	59.95
121	Gee Wiz	Byte	39.95

13.11. Write a program to create a sequential checkbook file.

INPUT: Check number, transaction date, description of transaction, and payment amount will be input from the keyboard. Only the transaction date and amount will be input for deposits.

OUTPUT: Format the output and send it to the printer.

PROCESS:

1. When a check is written, subtract the amount from the current balance.
2. For a deposit, add the amount to the current balance.

Menu Options
1. Enter withdrawal
2. Enter deposit
3. Enter beginning balance
4. Print calculated checkbook
5. Quit

Note: Keep the beginning balance in a separate file.

13.12. Create a sequential file to keep track of your magazine collection.

INPUT: Magazine title, cover story, year, month, and comments you want to make about the issue should be input from the keyboard.

OUTPUT: Create a sequential file on disk. If the whole file is to be printed, it should be sent to the printer. If just one record is to be displayed, it should be displayed on the screen.

Menu Options
1. Add a record
2. Print entire file
3. Display one record
4. Quit

14 Random Data Files

OPEN Statement
FIELD Statement
LSET Statement
RSET Statement
MKS$ Function
CVS Function
GET Statement
PUT Statement

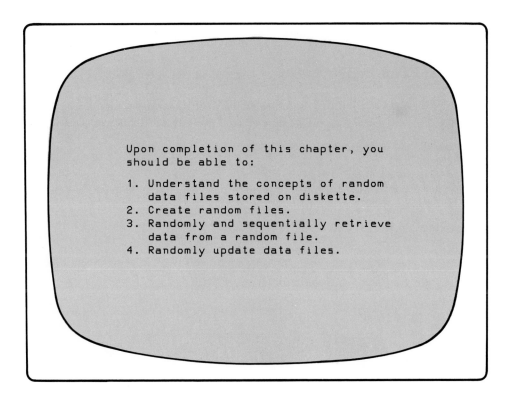

```
Upon completion of this chapter, you
should be able to:

1. Understand the concepts of random
   data files stored on diskette.
2. Create random files.
3. Randomly and sequentially retrieve
   data from a random file.
4. Randomly update data files.
```

Introduction

The two types of files supported by BASIC are sequential files and random files. Chapter 13 dealt with sequential files. In this chapter, the concept of random files will be developed.

The primary difference between sequential files and random files is that data may be written and read in any order in a random file. In sequential files, it was always necessary to start at the beginning of the file and proceed in order through the file.

Programs to handle sequential files are a little easier to code than those for random files, but generally the extra statements required for random files are well worth the effort. Random files offer greater speed as well as the capability for random access. Also, a random file will often use less disk storage space than the same data stored in a sequential file. This decrease occurs for two reasons—numeric data is stored in a special, compressed form, and there is no need to store commas between the fields of data.

Random Files

Random files can be visualized like a table, where each entry may be referenced by its relative position. Each entry in a file is one record, which is referred to by its record number. Figure 14.1 illustrates the table concept of random files. Any record in the file may be read or written without the necessity of reading the preceding records.

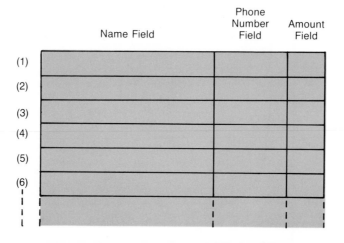

Figure 14.1
Layout of a random file. Each record consists of a name field, a phone number, and an amount field. The record is identified by its position in the file (record 1, record 2, etc.).

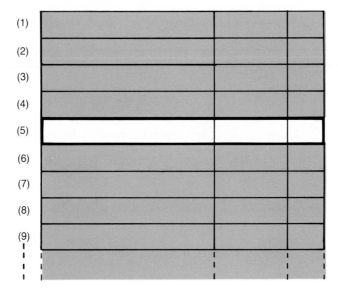

Figure 14.2
Writing record 5. The record is written into the fifth location in the file.

Creating a Random File

As an example, a program to keep track of concert ticket sales by the Contemporary Music Club will be developed. One record will be stored for each member, consisting of three fields—the member name, telephone number, and the number of tickets sold to date. The member number will be used as the record number in the file.

Random files may be *created* either sequentially or randomly. When creating the file for the Contemporary Music Club, the member names may be entered in sequential order (1, 2, 3, . . .) or in any random order. By specifying the record number (which is assigned as the member number), you may first write record #5, then #1, then #20, or any other order. When record #5 is written in the file, BASIC skips enough space for four records and writes in the fifth physical location. Record positions 1–4 remain empty until such time as records are written in those locations. See the diagram in figure 14.2.

Here are the steps necessary to write data in a random file. Each of the new statements will be explained in the sections that follow.

1. Open the file in random mode
2. Establish a record buffer (with the FIELD statement)
3. Loop until finished
    3.1   Input the record data from the keyboard
    3.2   Place the record data in the record buffer (with the LSET statement)
    3.3   Output the data in the record buffer to the disk (using the PUT statement)
    3.4   Ask the user if finished
4. Close the file
5. End

Opening a Random File

The OPEN statement for a random file is only slightly different from the OPEN for a sequential file. Rather than being opened for INPUT or OUTPUT, the file is opened in *RANDOM mode*. This will allow both input and output while the file is open. Additionally, the *record length* must be specified each time a file is opened.

The OPEN Statement for Random Files—General Form

> *Format 1:*
> line number OPEN "R", #filenumber, "filename", reclength
> *Format 2:*
> line number OPEN "filename" AS #filenumber LEN = reclength

The file mode, Random ("R"), indicates that both input and output may be performed on the file and that the records may be read or written in any sequence. In Format 1 of the OPEN statement, "R" is a required entry. However, in the second format, the mode does not appear. In this case, Random Mode is assumed.

The OPEN Statement for Random Files—Examples

```
100    OPEN "R", #1, "SALES.DAT", 100
100    OPEN "SALES.DAT" AS #1 LEN = 100

200    OPEN "R", #2, DAT.FILE$, REC.LENGTH
200    OPEN DAT.FILE$ AS #2 LEN = REC.LENGTH
```

Each of these pairs of OPEN statements has the same effect. Some versions of Microsoft BASIC allow only the first format; others offer a choice of the two methods. Before the OPEN in line 200 can be executed, the two fields DAT.FILE$ and REC.LENGTH must be given a value. This may be done with an INPUT statement to allow flexibility.

Fixed Record Size

To be randomly written or read, each record must be the same size. This is a departure from sequential files, in which records varied in size.

When a random file is opened, the size of the record is declared. The record length is the sum of the lengths of the individual fields that make up the record. The length of each field is defined in the FIELD statement, a new BASIC statement that will be covered shortly.

Fixed Field Size

In sequential files, fields (as well as records) are variable in length. In a field such as a name, only the required number of characters are stored, followed by a comma. In a random file, the name field must be the same length for all records. A short name will be padded with spaces to fill the field; a long name may be truncated to fit the field length. Numeric values are stored in a special compressed format using fixed length strings. Before the file can be created, some planning is required to choose the optimum field sizes.

Selecting and Defining Field Size and Record Length

Before the number of characters in a record can be determined, the length of each individual field must be established. In the BASIC program, after the file is opened, the FIELD statement declares the field lengths.

The FIELD Statement—General Form

```
line number FIELD #filenumber, fieldlength AS stringvar1,
            fieldlength AS stringvar2, . . .
```

The field statement establishes a *file buffer* in memory. The file buffer is the length of one record and is used as a temporary holding place for data as it is being read from or written to the disk file. One important fact must be noted: all fields named in the buffer must be *string* variables.

The FIELD Statement—Examples

```
1010    FIELD #2, 20 AS B.NAM$, 30 AS B.ADDR$, 15 AS B.CITY$,
        2 AS B.STATE$, 5 AS B.ZIP$
2000    FIELD #1, 30 AS B.MEMB$, 14 AS B.PHONE$, 4 AS
        B.TICKET$
```

The field names chosen in the examples all begin with *B* for consistency. Although BASIC makes no such requirement, a standard practice such as this makes programs easier to read and decipher. The buffer fields will be easily distinguished from any other program variables. Line 2000 establishes the file buffer for the club member example. The file buffer is illustrated in figure 14.3. Thirty characters were allocated for the member name field. You may choose to use fewer characters in order to save space; or, more characters may be necessary if some members have long names. Since the field size must be the same length, whether storing the name for J. Doe (six characters) or for Ebeneezer Abernathy Hornblower, Jr. (thirty-five characters), the length chosen will generally be a compromise. The phone number field was defined as fourteen characters in the form (XXX) XXX-XXXX, to allow space for an area code and number including the parentheses and hyphen.

The numeric field to store the number of tickets sold was defined as a four-character string. Due to the compressed form used for numeric values, all single-precision variables require four characters of storage in a random data file.

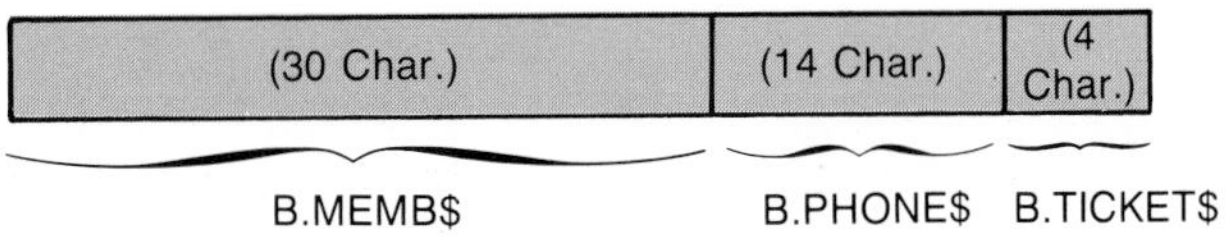

Figure 14.3

Club member file buffer. Forty-eight characters are allocated for the file buffer.

(30 Char.)	(14 Char.)	(4 Char.)
B.MEMB$	B.PHONE$	B.TICKET$

Using the File Buffer for Input and Output

The input/output statements for random file processing differ from those used for sequential files in several important respects. Data is read from the file with the GET statement and written with the PUT statement. The GET and PUT do not include a list of variables like the other I/O (input/output) statements you have seen.

```
100   GET #1, recno
200   PUT #1, recno
```

The *recno* field on these statements indicates the record number in the file to read or write.

```
500   GET #1, 5
```

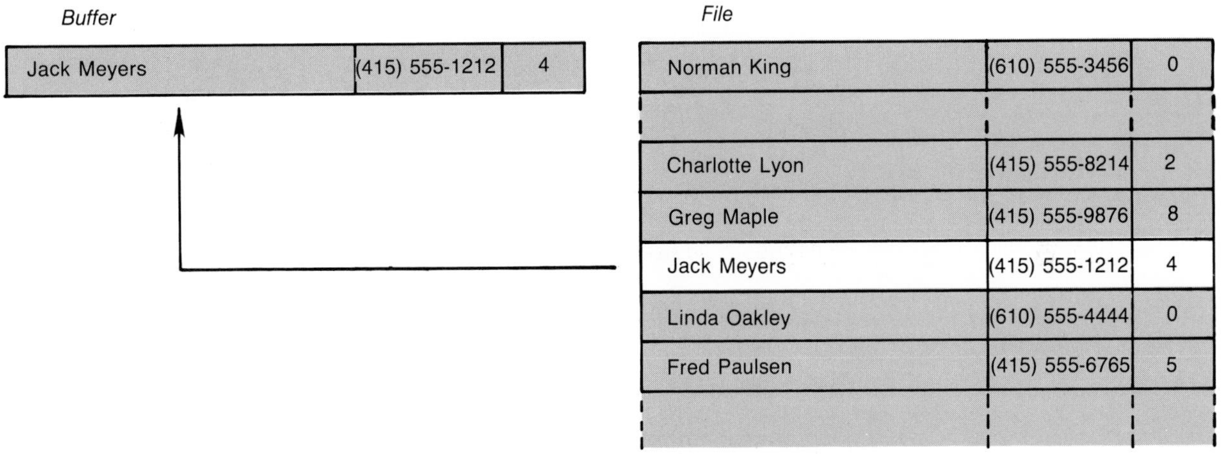

Buffer

Jack Meyers	(415) 555-1212	4

File

Norman King	(610) 555-3456	0
Charlotte Lyon	(415) 555-8214	2
Greg Maple	(415) 555-9876	8
Jack Meyers	(415) 555-1212	4
Linda Oakley	(610) 555-4444	0
Fred Paulsen	(415) 555-6765	5

When the statement

```
GET #1, 5
```

is executed, the entire record at location five is placed into the file buffer. Then the field names on the FIELD statement can be used to reference the data.

```
100   OPEN "R", #1, "MEMBER.DAT", 48
110   FIELD #1, 30 AS B.MEMB$, 14 AS B.PHONE$, 4 AS B.TICK$
::
::
200   INPUT "MEMBER NUMBER ", MEMB.NO  'SELECT MEMBER NUMBER
                                          TO READ
210   GET #1, MEMB.NO                  'READ SELECTED RECORD
::
::
400   PRINT MEMB.NO, B.MEMB$           'PRINT MEMBER NUMBER
                                        AND NAME
```

Similarly, when a record is written to the disk file with the PUT statement, the contents of the buffer are placed on the disk.

```
600   PUT #1, 2
```

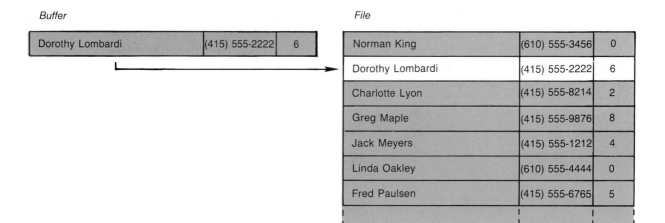

Before the record may be PUT into the file, the buffer must be filled with the correct data. Placing data in the buffer *cannot* be done with the familiar statements LET, INPUT, or READ. Instead, there are two new BASIC statements for placing data in a file buffer: the LSET and RSET statements. In actual practice, the RSET is seldom used and is included here for information only. Generally data file buffers will be filled with the LSET statement.

LSET (left-justify) places the data at the left of the receiving buffer field, filling any extra characters with blank spaces. RSET (right-justify) aligns the data at the right end of the field, filling any unused characters at the left of the field with spaces.

The LSET and RSET Statements—General Form

> line number LSET stringvar = string expression
> line number RSET stringvar = string expression

A string expression (literal, variable, or function) will be placed into the string variable named on the left of the equal sign. This string variable will be a field named in the FIELD statement.

The LSET and RSET Statements—Examples

```
100    LSET B.NAM$ = "SAM SPADE"
200    RSET B.NAM$ = "SAM SPADE"
300    LSET B.BOOK$ = BOOK$
400    LSET B.AMT$ = MKS$(AMT)
500    LSET B.ID$ = MID$(LONG$,2,5)
```

If the buffer field B.NAM$ were defined as twenty characters, the effect of the LSET and RSET statements in lines 100 and 200 would be:

    100   LSET B.NAM$ = "SAM SPADE"

> SAM SPADE

    200 RSET B.NAM$ = "SAM SPADE"

>   SAM SPADE

The choice of LSET or RSET determines which end of the receiving field will be padded with blanks. However, if the sending field is longer than the receiving field length, the excess characters will be truncated from the right end, whether LSET or RSET is used.

Using the Record Buffer for Numeric Data

Numeric data is handled in a unique manner in random files. Two statements have been made that may have given a clue. Recall that in the FIELD statement, all buffer fields *must* be string variables. In the discussion of the space used for random files, it was mentioned that numeric data is stored in a special, compressed format.

At the present time, the discussion will be limited to single-precision numeric values, by far the most common numeric type. Each single-precision numeric value will be converted into a four-character string variable before being placed into the record buffer. When numeric data is read *from* the file, it must be reconverted from its compressed, string form into its numeric equivalent. The number of digits in the numeric value is irrelevant—all numeric values require four characters of storage.

Conversion of Numeric Values to Compressed Strings

Two functions are provided for the numeric conversion. MKS$ (make single string) converts a numeric expression into a string. The reverse operation, CVS (convert to single), takes a string and converts it into single-precision numeric form.

The MKS$ and CVS Functions—General Form

```
MKS$(numeric expression)
CVS(string variable)
```

The MKS$ and CVS Functions—Examples

```
200    '*** CONVERT NUMERIC EXPRESSIONS TO STRINGS AND
                PLACE IN BUFFER
210    LSET B.AMT$ = MKS$(AMT)
220    LSET B.ANIMALS$ = MKS$(DOGS + CATS + ARMADILLOS)


400    '*** CONVERT COMPRESSED STRING DATA FROM BUFFER
                INTO NUMERIC VALUES
410    LET AMT = CVS(B.AMT$)
420    LET ANIMALS = CVS(B.ANIMALS$)
```

Reading and Writing the Random Data File

You can now set up one record and PUT (write) it into the random file.

```
100    OPEN "R", #1, "MEMBER.DAT", 48
110    FIELD #1, 30 AS B.MEMB$, 14 AS B.PHONE$, 4 AS B.TICK$
::
::
500    '******** INPUT DATA FROM KEYBOARD ****************
510    INPUT "MEMBER NUMBER ", MEMB.NO
520    INPUT "MEMBER NAME    ", MEMB$
530    INPUT "PHONE NUMBER   ", PHONE$
540    INPUT "TICKETS SOLD   ", TICK
::
::
```

```
600    '********* SET UP RECORD BUFFER ********************
610    LSET B.MEMB$   = MEMB$
620    LSET B.PHONE$  = PHONE$
630    LSET B.TICK$   = MKS$(TICK)
::
::
700    '*********** WRITE RECORD IN THE FILE *************
710    PUT #1, MEMB.NO
::
::
```

To read one record and print the contents of that record on the screen, add a little more coding.

```
1000   '************** ACCEPT INQUIRY *******************
1010   INPUT "ENTER MEMBER NUMBER ", MEMB.NO
::
::
2000   '***** READ CORRECT RECORD INTO THE BUFFER ********
2010   GET #1, MEMB.NO
::
::
3000   '******* DISPLAY THE RECORD ON THE SCREEN *********
3010   PRINT "MEMBER NAME    "; B.MEMB$
3020   PRINT "PHONE NUMBER   "; B.PHONE$
3030   PRINT "TICKETS SOLD   "; CVS(B.TICK$)
::
::
```

Notice that fields may be printed directly from the file buffer. While it isn't necessary to move the data to another field outside the buffer, *never* attempt to INPUT data directly into the file buffer field. BASIC will not produce an error message for this operation, but the buffer field will no longer be available to be used to transfer data into the file.

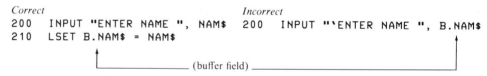

Correct
```
200   INPUT "ENTER NAME ", NAM$
210   LSET B.NAM$ = NAM$
```
Incorrect
```
200   INPUT "ENTER NAME ", B.NAM$
```
_____ (buffer field) _____

The GET Statement—General Form

| line number GET #filenumber [,recordnumber] |

The GET statement reads data from a random disk file and places the data into the file buffer established by the FIELD statement. After the GET is performed, the fields in the buffer may be used in other program statements such as PRINT or LET statements. When the record number is omitted from the statement, the *next* record is read from the file.

The GET Statement—Examples

```
600    GET #1, 4
875    GET #2, CUSTNO
900    GET #1
```

Either a variable or a constant may be used for the record number. Generally you will want to use a variable to allow selection of any record in the file.

```
1050   INPUT "ENTER CUSTOMER NUMBER ", CUSTNO
1060   GET #1, CUSTNO
```

The PUT Statement—General Form

> line number PUT #filenum [,recordnumber]

The PUT statement takes the contents of the file buffer (defined by the FIELD statement) and writes it on the disk. The *record number* determines the relative location within the file for the record. If the record number is omitted, the record will be placed in the next location after the last record PUT into the file. (This is not necessarily following the final record in the file, only the prior record PUT in this program run.)

The PUT Statement—Examples

```
1200    PUT #1, ACCT.NUM
1550    PUT #2, 1
1825    PUT #3
```

As with the GET, the record number may be a variable or a constant. Using a variable gives the most flexibility. Before a record may be PUT, the data must be placed in the buffer fields. Data may be transferred into the buffer fields with the LSET or RSET statements.

Printing Selected Records from a File

A program that *selectively* reads a particular disk record will follow this pattern:

1. OPEN the file
2. FIELD the record
3. Loop until finished
    - 3.1   INPUT (from keyboard) the desired record number
    - 3.2   GET the record
    - 3.3   Convert any compressed numeric fields to their numeric format (CVS)
    - 3.4   Print the record (on screen or printer)
    - 3.5   Ask user if finished
4. CLOSE the file
5. END

Example Program: Selectively Print One Record from a Random File

Program Listing

```
100 '      PROGRAM TO DEMONSTRATE THE SELECTIVE PRINTING OF
110 '          ONE RECORD IN A RANDOM FILE
120 '
130 '              PROGRAM VARIABLES
140 '
160 '    B.MEMB$             MEMBER NAME
170 '    B.PHONE$            MEMBER PHONE NUMBER
180 '    B.TICK$             NUMBER OF TICKETS SOLD
190 '    ANS$                ANSWER TO QUESTION
200 '
210 '
```

```
1000 '************** PROGRAM MAINLINE ***********************
1010 OPEN "R", #1, "MEMBER.DAT", 48
1020 FIELD #1, 30 AS B.MEMB$, 14 AS B.PHONE$, 4 AS B.TICK$
1030 CLS
1040 LET ANS$ = "Y"
1050 WHILE ANS$ = "Y" OR ANS$ = "y"
1060     PRINT
1070     INPUT "MEMBER NUMBER     ", MEMB.NO 'INPUT RECORD NUMBER
1080     GET #1, MEMB.NO              'READ CORRECT RECORD FROM FILE
1090     GOSUB 2000                  'PRINT THE RECORD
1100     INPUT "DISPLAY ANOTHER RECORD"; ANS$
1110 WEND
1120 CLOSE #1
1130 END
1140 '
2000 '***************** PRINT THE RECORD **********************
2010 PRINT
2020 PRINT "MEMBER NAME      "; B.MEMB$
2030 PRINT "PHONE NUMBER     "; B.PHONE$
2040 PRINT "TICKETS SOLD     "; CVS(B.TICK$)
2050 PRINT
2060 RETURN
2070 '****************** END OF PROGRAM **********************
```

Sample Program Output

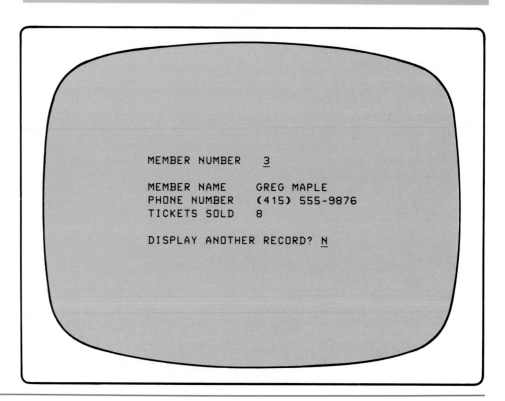

```
              MEMBER NUMBER    3

              MEMBER NAME      GREG MAPLE
              PHONE NUMBER     (415) 555-9876
              TICKETS SOLD     8

              DISPLAY ANOTHER RECORD? N
```

Printing Out an Entire File

A program that reads and prints all of the records in a random file in order would follow this pattern:

1. OPEN the file
2. FIELD the record
3. Loop until end of file
    - 3.1 GET a record
    - 3.2 Convert any compressed numeric fields to numeric data with CVS
    - 3.3 PRINT the fields from the file buffer
4. CLOSE the file
5. END

Finding the End of a Random Data File

Locating the end of a random file is another area where Microsoft BASIC varies from one implementation to another. The EOF function (used with sequential files) cannot be depended upon for random files in all versions of BASIC.

When a random file contains no **empty cells** (unused record numbers), the EOF function will correctly find the End Of File. However, if the file *does* contain unused record positions, the EOF function is inconsistent. End Of File will be correctly detected on the sixteen-bit version of BASIC (IBM-PC BASIC and MS-BASIC), but not on the eight-bit version (MBASIC), which runs on the Apple and other computers using CP/M.

Example Program: Printing an Entire Random File

Program Listing

```
100 '      PROGRAM TO DEMONSTRATE PRINTING AN ENTIRE RANDOM FILE
110 '         USING THE EOF FUNCTION FOR DETECTING END OF FILE
120 '      (NOTE: ANY UNUSED RECORD POSITIONS WILL PRINT GARBAGE)
130 '
140 '           PROGRAM VARIABLES
150 '
160 '    B.MEMB$            MEMBER NAME
170 '    B.PHONE$           MEMBER PHONE NUMBER
180 '    B.TICK$            NUMBER OF TICKETS SOLD
190 '
200 '
1000 '************** PROGRAM MAINLINE **********************
1010 OPEN "R", #1, "MEMBER.DAT", 48
1020 FIELD #1, 30 AS B.MEMB$, 14 AS B.PHONE$, 4 AS B.TICK$
1030 CLS
1040 WHILE NOT EOF(1)
1050       GET #1                   'READ NEXT RECORD FROM FILE
1060       GOSUB 2000               'PRINT THE RECORD
1070 WEND
1080 CLOSE #1
1090 END
1100 '
2000 '**************** PRINT THE RECORD ******************
2010 PRINT
2020 PRINT "MEMBER NAME     "; B.MEMB$
2030 PRINT "PHONE NUMBER    "; B.PHONE$
2040 PRINT "TICKETS SOLD    "; CVS(B.TICK$)
2050 PRINT
2060 RETURN
2070 '***************** END OF PROGRAM *******************
```

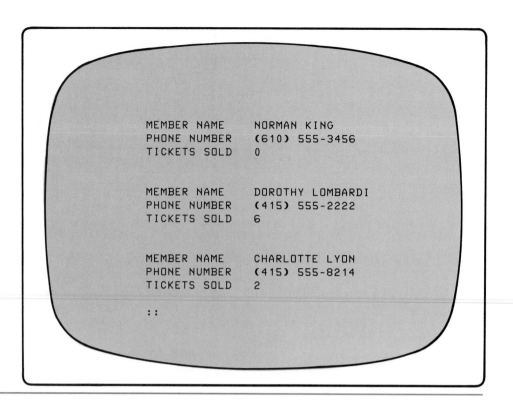

```
          MEMBER NAME    NORMAN KING
          PHONE NUMBER   (610) 555-3456
          TICKETS SOLD   0


          MEMBER NAME    DOROTHY LOMBARDI
          PHONE NUMBER   (415) 555-2222
          TICKETS SOLD   6


          MEMBER NAME    CHARLOTTE LYON
          PHONE NUMBER   (415) 555-8214
          TICKETS SOLD   2

       ::
```

The Unused Record Positions

The preceding sample program will work well for a data file with *no* empty record positions. However, another approach must be used when some record positions will be unused (empty cells). As mentioned earlier, writing a record in record position 5 (for example) does not disturb any other records. If *you* haven't written anything in positions 1–4, that doesn't mean that those positions are blank.

To understand why "garbage" may be found in the midst of a file, you must understand a little bit about how the operating system (DOS) saves and deletes files. When any files (programs or data files) are saved on a diskette, those sectors are reserved as "in use." When a file is deleted from the diskette, DOS frees those sectors to be reused, but the file is *not erased*. Therefore, all available diskette space that has been previously used will hold the remains of old files. When the record in position 5 is written, positions 1–4 may hold *anything*.

There are two possible solutions to this dilemma: (1) assign record numbers in sequence with no unused record positions, or (2) initialize all record positions before writing any good records in the file. The second solution is the one chosen for the sample program for the Contemporary Music Club's ticket sales.

Example Program: Random File Maintenance

Now the complete program can be written to handle the data for the Contemporary Music Club. Notice that the menu allows choices to add members, update ticket sales, selectively print the record of one member, print a list of all members, or initialize the file. A maximum file size of 100 records was chosen for the initialization process.

Hierarchy Chart

Refer to figure 14.4.

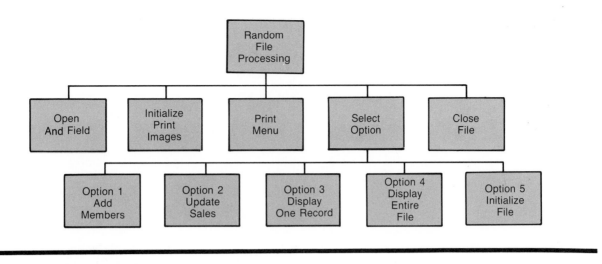

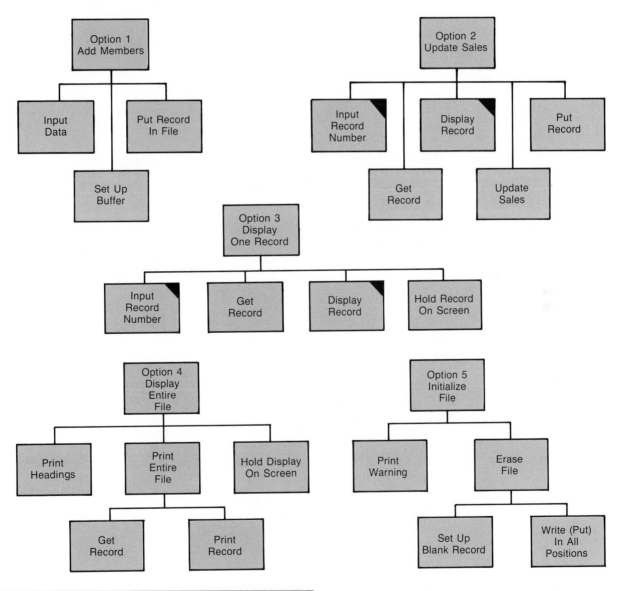

Figure 14.4
Hierarchy chart for random file processing program. Any
subroutines that are executed from more than one location are
shown with shaded corners. This indicates a shared module.

Flowchart   Refer to figure 14.5.

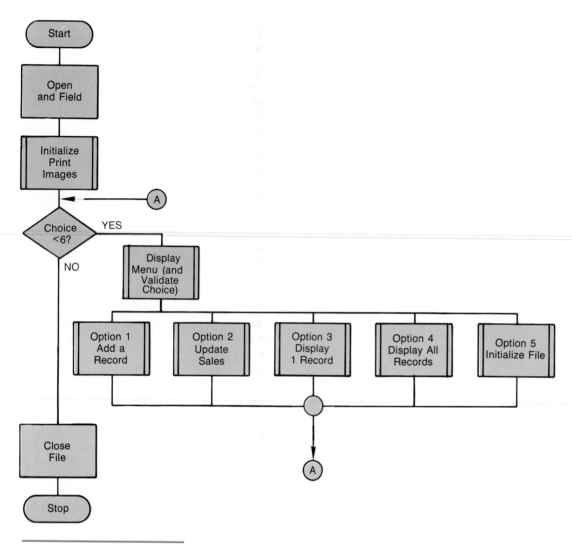

Chapter 14

Figure 14.5
Flowchart for random file
processing program.

Figure 14.5—*Continued*

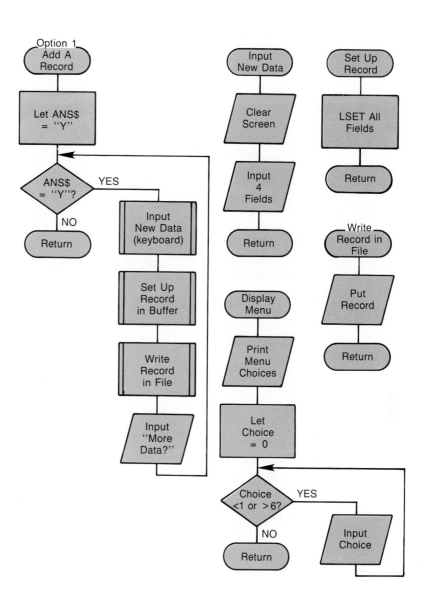

Figure 14.5—*Continued*

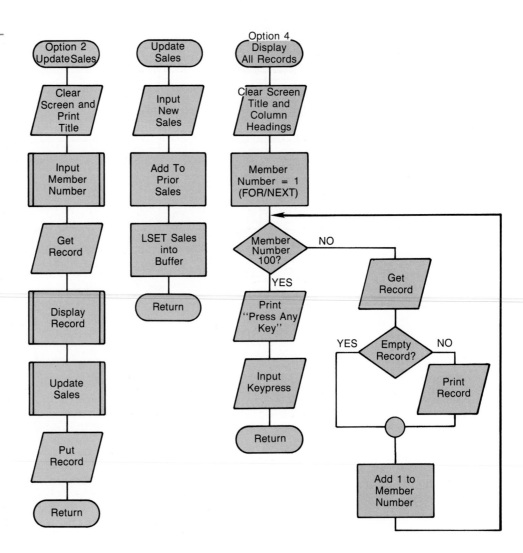

Figure 14.5—*Continued*

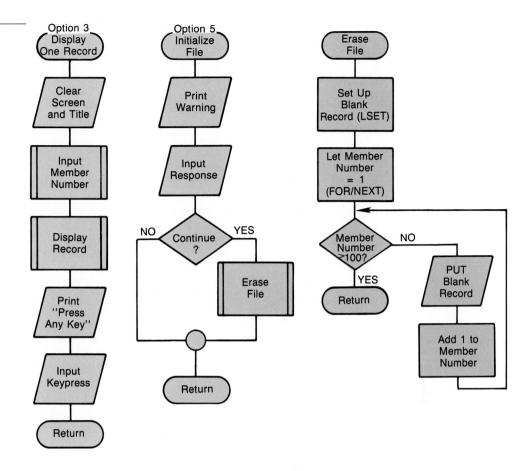

Program Listing

```
100 '       PROGRAM TO CREATE AND MAINTAIN A RANDOM DATA FILE
110 '          TO BE USED BY THE CONTEMPORARY MUSIC CLUB
120 '          FOR RECORDING MEMBER INFORMATION AND CONCERT
130 '          TICKET SALES
140 '
150 '              PROGRAM VARIABLES
160 '
170 '    MEMB.NO          MEMBER NUMBER (RECORD NUMBER)
180 '    MEMB$            MEMBER NAME
190 '    PHONE$           MEMBER PHONE NUMBER
200 '    TICK             NUMBER OF TICKETS SOLD
210 '    ANS$             ANSWER TO QUESTION
220 '    TITLE$           SCREEN TITLE
230 '    H$, T2$, D$      PRINT IMAGES
240 '    SALES            NEW SALES FOR UPDATE
250 '    CHOICE AND CHOICE$ MENU CHOICE
260 '
270 '              BUFFER FIELDS
280 '
290 '    B.MEMB$          MEMBER NAME
300 '    B.PHONE$         MEMBER PHONE NUMBER
310 '    B.TICK$          NUMBER OF TICKETS SOLD
320 '
330 '
```

```
1000 '************** PROGRAM MAINLINE **************************
1010 OPEN "R", #1, "MEMBER.DAT", 48
1020 FIELD #1, 30 AS B.MEMB$, 14 AS B.PHONE$, 4 AS B.TICK$
1025 GOSUB 1500                       'INITIALIZE PRINT IMAGES
1030 WHILE CHOICE < 6
1040     GOSUB 2000                   'MENU
1050     ON CHOICE GOSUB 3000, 4000, 5000, 6000, 7000
1060 WEND
1070 CLOSE #1
1080 CLS
1090 END
1100 '
1500 '****************** INITIALIZE PRINT IMAGES **************
1510 LET TITLE$ = "CONTEMPORARY MUSIC CLUB"
1520 LET T2$ = "CONCERT TICKET SALES"
1530 LET H$ =  "MEMBER        NAME                          TE
LEPHONE    TICKETS SOLD"
1540 LET D$ = "  ###       \                         \        \
           \       ####"
1550 RETURN
1560 '
2000 '****************** DISPLAY MENU ************************
2010 CLS
2020 PRINT
2030 PRINT TAB(29); TITLE$
2040 PRINT
2050 PRINT TAB(31); T2$
2060 PRINT
2070 PRINT TAB(21); "1. ADD MEMBERS TO FILE"
2080 PRINT
2090 PRINT TAB(21); "2. UPDATE TICKET SALES"
2100 PRINT
2110 PRINT TAB(21); "3. DISPLAY INFORMATION FOR ONE MEMBER"
2120 PRINT
2130 PRINT TAB(21); "4. DISPLAY INFORMATION FOR ALL MEMBERS"
2140 PRINT
2150 PRINT TAB(21); "5. INITIALIZE THE FILE"
2160 PRINT
2170 PRINT TAB(21); "6. QUIT"
2180 PRINT
2200 PRINT TAB(24); "ENTER CHOICE (1 - 6) ";
2210 LET CHOICE = 0
2220 WHILE CHOICE < 1 OR CHOICE > 6    'VALIDATE CHOICE
2230     LOCATE 19,44
2240     PRINT "    "
2250     LOCATE 19,44
2260     INPUT CHOICE$
2270     LET CHOICE = VAL(CHOICE$)
2280 WEND
2290 RETURN
2300 '
3000 '***************** ADD A RECORD TO FILE *****************
3010 LET ANS$ = "Y"
3020 WHILE LEFT$(ANS$,1) = "Y" OR LEFT$(ANS$,1) = "y"
3030     GOSUB 3200                   'INPUT DATA FROM KEYBOARD
3040     GOSUB 3400                   'SET UP RECORD BUFFER
3050     GOSUB 3600                   'WRITE RECORD IN FILE
3060     INPUT "ADD ANOTHER MEMBER"; ANS$
3070 WEND
3080 RETURN
3090 '
```

```
3200 '************* INPUT DATA FROM KEYBOARD ******************
3210 CLS
3220 INPUT "MEMBER NUMBER ", MEMB.NO
3230 PRINT
3240 INPUT "MEMBER NAME    ", MEMB$
3250 PRINT
3260 INPUT "PHONE NUMBER   ", PHONE$
3270 PRINT
3280 INPUT "TICKETS SOLD ", TICK
3290 PRINT :PRINT
3300 RETURN
3310 '
3400 '************* SET UP RECORD BUFFER ********************
3410 LSET B.MEMB$ = MEMB$
3420 LSET B.PHONE$ = PHONE$
3430 LSET B.TICK$ = MKS$(TICK)
3440 RETURN
3450 '
3600 '************** WRITE RECORD IN THE FILE ****************
3610 PUT #1, MEMB.NO
3620 RETURN
3630 '
4000 '************* UPDATE TICKET SALES ********************
4010 CLS
4020 PRINT TAB(29); TITLE$
4030 GOSUB 4400                    'INPUT VALID RECORD NUMBER
4040 GET #1, MEMB.NO               'READ CORRECT RECORD
4050 GOSUB 4600                    'DISPLAY THE RECORD
4060 GOSUB 4800                    'UPDATE THE SALES
4070 PUT #1, MEMB.NO               'REWRITE THE RECORD IN THE FILE
4080 RETURN
4090 '
4400 '*********** INPUT VALID RECORD NUMBER *****************
4410 PRINT
4420 INPUT "ENTER MEMBER NUMBER ", MEMB.NO
4430 WHILE MEMB.NO < 1 OR MEMB.NO > 100
4440    LOCATE 5,10
4450    PRINT "MEMBER NUMBER MUST BE IN THE RANGE 1-100"
4460    LOCATE 3,21
4470    INPUT "", MEMB.NO
4480    LOCATE 5,10
4490    PRINT "                                            "
4500 WEND
4510 RETURN
4520 '
4600 '************* PRINT THE RECORD *********************
4610 PRINT                        'DISPLAY RECORD ON SCREEN
4620 PRINT
4630 PRINT "MEMBER NAME     "; B.MEMB$
4640 PRINT "PHONE NUMBER    "; B.PHONE$
4650 PRINT "TICKETS SOLD    "; CVS(B.TICK$)
4660 PRINT
4670 RETURN
4680 '
4800 '************* UPDATE THE SALES *********************
4810 PRINT:PRINT
4820 INPUT "ENTER NEW SALES ", SALES
4830 LET SALES = SALES + CVS(B.TICK$)   'ADD PRIOR SALES TO NEW
4840 LSET B.TICK$ = MKS$(SALES)         'REPLACE SALES IN BUFFER
4850 RETURN
4860 '
```

```
5000 '********* DISPLAY ONE RECORD FROM THE FILE *************
5010 CLS
5020 PRINT TAB(29); TITLE$
5030 GOSUB 4400                      'INPUT VALID RECORD NUMBER
5060 GET #1, MEMB.NO                  'READ CORRECT RECORD FROM FILE
5070 GOSUB 4600                       'PRINT THE RECORD
5080 PRINT "PRESS ANY KEY TO CONTINUE";
5090 LET X$ = INPUT$(1)              'ALLOW DATA TO REMAIN ON SCREEN
5100 RETURN
5110 '
6000 '************* DISPLAY ALL RECORDS IN FILE *************
6010 CLS
6020 PRINT TAB(29); TITLE$
6030 PRINT
6040 PRINT TAB(12); H$
6050 PRINT
6060 FOR MEMB.NO = 1 TO 100
6070    GET #1, MEMB.NO
6080    IF LEFT$(B.MEMB$,1) <> " "
            THEN PRINT USING D$; MEMB.NO, B.MEMB$, B.PHONE$,
                    CVS(B.TICK$)
6090 NEXT MEMB.NO
6100 PRINT:PRINT
6110 PRINT "PRESS ANY KEY TO CONTINUE";
6120 LET X$ = INPUT$(1)
6130 RETURN
6140 '
7000 '******************** INITIALIZE THE FILE ****************
7010 CLS
7020 LOCATE 8,30
7030 PRINT "CAUTION, THIS WILL ERASE ALL MEMBER DATA IN THE FILE"
7040 PRINT
7050 PRINT
7060 INPUT "          DO YOU WISH TO PROCEED"; ANS$
7070 IF LEFT$(ANS$,1) = "Y" OR LEFT$(ANS$,1) = "y"
        THEN GOSUB 7200              'ERASE ALL RECORDS IN FILE
7080 RETURN
7090 '
7200 '*************** ERASE ALL RECORDS IN FILE **************
7220 LSET B.MEMB$ = " "
7230 LSET B.PHONE$ = " "
7240 LSET B.TICK$ = MKS$(0)
7250 FOR MEMB.NO = 1 TO 100
7260    PUT #1, MEMB.NO
7270 NEXT MEMB.NO
7280 RETURN
8000 '***************** END OF PROGRAM ********************
```

Sample Program Output

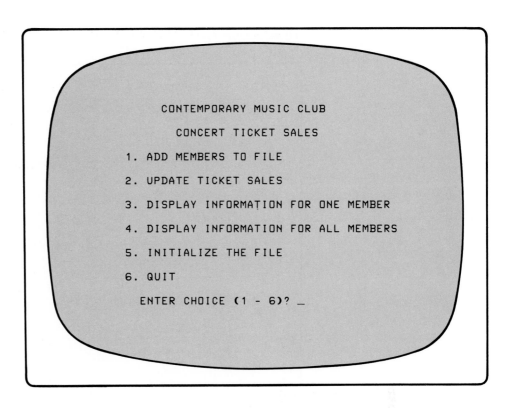

```
           CONTEMPORARY MUSIC CLUB

            CONCERT TICKET SALES

    1. ADD MEMBERS TO FILE

    2. UPDATE TICKET SALES

    3. DISPLAY INFORMATION FOR ONE MEMBER

    4. DISPLAY INFORMATION FOR ALL MEMBERS

    5. INITIALIZE THE FILE

    6. QUIT

       ENTER CHOICE (1 - 6)? _
```

Choice 1—Add Members to File

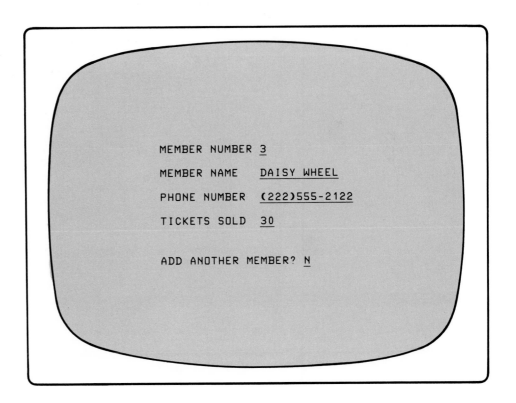

```
    MEMBER NUMBER 3

    MEMBER NAME   DAISY WHEEL

    PHONE NUMBER  (222)555-2122

    TICKETS SOLD  30


    ADD ANOTHER MEMBER? N
```

Choice 2—Update Ticket Sales

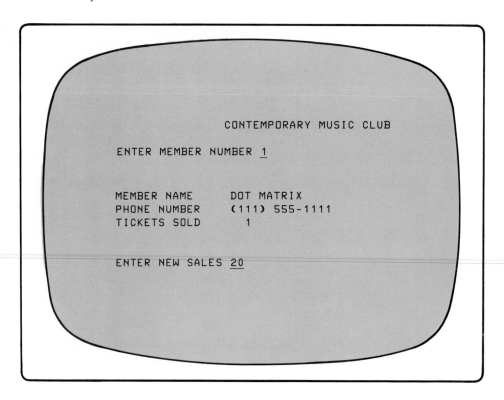

```
                    CONTEMPORARY MUSIC CLUB

   ENTER MEMBER NUMBER 1


   MEMBER NAME      DOT MATRIX
   PHONE NUMBER     (111) 555-1111
   TICKETS SOLD       1


   ENTER NEW SALES 20
```

Choice 3—Display Information for One Member

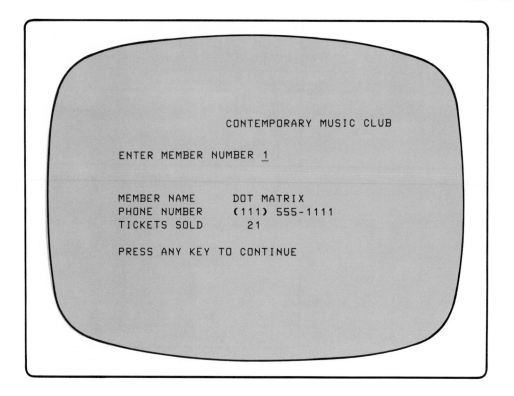

```
                    CONTEMPORARY MUSIC CLUB

   ENTER MEMBER NUMBER 1


   MEMBER NAME      DOT MATRIX
   PHONE NUMBER     (111) 555-1111
   TICKETS SOLD       21

   PRESS ANY KEY TO CONTINUE
```

Choice 4—Display Information for All Members

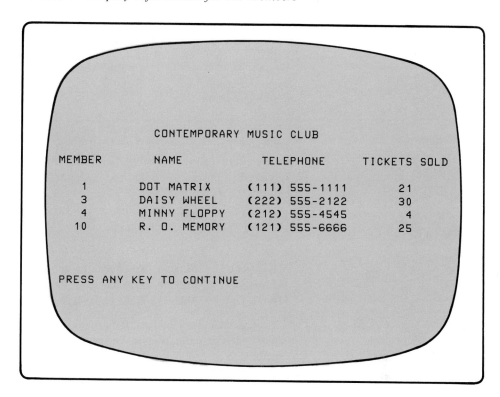

```
                CONTEMPORARY MUSIC CLUB

MEMBER        NAME          TELEPHONE        TICKETS SOLD

   1        DOT MATRIX     (111) 555-1111         21
   3        DAISY WHEEL    (222) 555-2122         30
   4        MINNY FLOPPY   (212) 555-4545          4
  10        R. O. MEMORY   (121) 555-6666         25


PRESS ANY KEY TO CONTINUE
```

Choice 5—Initialize the File

```
CAUTION, THIS WILL ERASE ALL MEMBER DATA IN THE FILE
         DO YOU WISH TO PROCEED? N
```

You will recall from chapter 10 that there are three types of numeric variables. Each type occupies a different number of bytes of storage.

Variable Type	Field Name Example	Bytes of Storage
integer	FLD%	2
single-precision	FLD!	4
double-precision	FLD#	8

In the absence of an explicit type definition, numeric variables default to single precision. The compressed form used for storing numeric values in data files is based on the internal storage format. Therefore, all integers require two bytes of storage, all single-precision variables require four bytes, and all double-precision variables require eight bytes.

BASIC provides three functions that convert the numeric variables into the string expressions needed for the file buffer.

Converting Numeric Expressions to Strings

MKI$(I%)	Make a two-character string from an integer expression
MKS$(S!)	Make a four-character string from a single-precision expression
MKD$(D#)	Make an eight-character string from a double-precision expression

The second set of functions takes a string and converts it back to its numeric equivalent. These functions do the reverse operation of the MKI$, MKS$, and MKD$ functions.

Converting Compressed Strings Back to Numeric Values

CVI(I$)	Convert a two-character string into an integer variable
CVS(S$)	Convert a four-character string into a single-precision variable
CVD(D$)	Convert an eight-character string into a double-precision variable

The field names shown in the preceding examples were chosen to demonstrate the use of the function. In actual practice, *any* variable names may be used, as long as the type (integer, single, or double) is consistent with the function.

Example Program Segment: Placing Numeric Data into a Record Buffer

Program Listing

```
100 FIELD #2, 2 AS B.INT$, 4 AS B.SING$, 8 AS B.DOUB$
..
..
..
500 '********* INPUT NUMERIC VALUES *****************
510 INPUT "ENTER AN INTEGER                 ", I.NUM%
520 INPUT "ENTER ANY NUMBER, 7 DIGITS OR LESS", S.NUM
530 INPUT "ENTER ANY NUMBER > 7 DIGITS       ", D.NUM#
..
..
..
600 '*********** MOVE FIELDS TO BUFFER **************
610 LSET B.INT$ = MKI$(I.NUM%)
620 LSET B.SING$ = MKS$(S.NUM)
630 LSET B.DOUB$ = MKD$(D.NUM#)
```

Example Program Segment:
Using Numeric Data Stored in a Random File

Program Listing

```
100 FIELD #2, 2 AS B.INT$, 4 AS B.SING$, 8 AS B.DOUB$
 ..
 ..
 ..
1000 '************ ACCEPT INQUIRY *******************
1010 INPUT "ENTER RECORD NUMBER TO READ ", REC.NO
 ..
 ..
2000 '**** RANDOMLY READ THE SELECTED DISK RECORD ****
2010 GET #2, REC.NO
 ..
 ..
3000 '**** CONVERT NUMERIC DATA TO USABLE FORM ******
3010 LET I.NUM% = CVI(B.INT$)
3020 LET S.NUM  = CVS(B.SING$)
3030 LET D.NUM# = CVD(B.DOUB$)
 ..
 ..
4000 '****** PRINT NUMERIC DATA FROM DISK RECORD *****
4010 PRINT I.NUM%, S.NUM, D.NUM#
 ..
 ..
```

Relative Size of Random Files vs. Sequential Files

As a general rule, random disk files take less space than sequential files on a diskette. There are two reasons for this size difference: (1) numeric data is stored in compressed form, and (2) it is not necessary to write commas between the fields of data and place the linefeed and carriage return characters between records.

However, for some files sequential organization will use less space than random. In a sequential file, string data fields are variable in length. Only as many characters as are necessary are written, followed by a comma. In a random file, the string data fields must be fixed in length, probably resulting in wasted space. If the majority of the fields in the record are variable length strings rather than numeric fields, it may be that the sequential file will occupy less space.

Feedback

1. Would BASIC be able to randomly read any record in the file if the records were not all the same length? Why or why not?
2. How is the record length specified for a random file?
3. How are the field lengths specified?
4. Explain how field lengths are determined for string variables. For numeric variables.
5. Explain the use of the record buffer for writing data on the disk.
6. How is the record buffer used for randomly reading a record from the file?
7. Use these statements for reference.

```
100   OPEN #2, "R", "INVEN.DAT", 14
110   FIELD #2, 10 AS B.DESC$, 4 AS B.QUANT$
```

Write the BASIC statements to accomplish the following:
a. Read the fourth record in the file INVEN.DAT, and print the description and quantity on the screen.
b. Input (from the keyboard) an item number, description, and quantity. Place the data into the file buffer, and write the record (using the item number for the record number).
c. List the entire INVEN.DAT file. Use the EOF function to find the end of file.

Summary

1. The records in a random file may be written and read in any order.
2. The advantages of using random files over sequential files include:
   a. capability for random access (rather than being limited to sequential access);
   b. random files are faster; and
   c. the random file will generally occupy less space on diskette.
3. Each record in a random file is referenced by its record number, which is its relative position in the file.
4. A random file may be created sequentially or randomly.
5. The file is opened in random mode ("R"), which allows for both input and output in any sequence.
6. All records in the file must be the same length. This record length is specified on the OPEN statement.
7. Each field within the record must be a fixed size. The size of the field is declared with the FIELD statement.
8. The file must be opened before a FIELD statement may be executed.
9. The FIELD statement establishes a record buffer, which is used to transfer data to and from the data file on diskette.
10. All variables that make up the record buffer must be string variables. Numeric data must be converted to strings in order to be placed in the buffer.
11. The I/O statements for a random file are GET and PUT.
12. When a GET is executed, the data is read from the data file and placed in the record buffer. A PUT takes the data in the buffer and writes it to the data file.
13. Both the GET and PUT statements include a record number. This is the indication of which record position should be read or written. When the record number is omitted, it will read or write the *next* record.
14. Data fields are placed in the buffer fields with the LSET statement.
15. Single-precision numeric variables must be converted to four-character compressed strings in order to be placed in the record buffer. The MKS$ function will "make single string" of a numeric variable. Then the resulting string may be LSET into a properly defined (four-character) buffer field.
16. To perform the reverse operation and convert a compressed string into its numeric value, the CVS (convert to single) function is used.
17. The EOF function may or may not function correctly in a random file. When the file has unused record positions, some versions of BASIC will incorrectly indicate End Of File prematurely.
18. When there are unused record positions in a file, the empty cells may contain garbage. Initializing the file to blank spaces will solve this problem.
19. When storing numeric variables in a data file, there are actually three choices, depending on the type of variable used. Integer variables require two bytes and use the MKI$ function. Single-precision variables require four bytes and use the MKS$ function. Double-precision variables require eight bytes and use the MKD$ function.
20. There are three complementary functions for converting the compressed strings back to numeric values. These are CVI (convert to integer), CVS (convert to single), and CVD (convert to double).

14.1. Establish a random file for reserving airplane seats. The plane has forty rows, numbered 1–40. Each row has six seats (three on each side of the aisle), referred to as A, B, C, D, E, and F.

Set up a random file of forty records. Each record will have six fields for the six seats. Make each field long enough to hold a passenger's name. Initially, each seat must be set to the value AVAILABLE. Then, as seats are assigned, place the name of the passenger in that field position.

Use a menu, with these choices:

1. Assign a seat
2. Display list of available seats
3. Print list of passengers with seat assignments
4. Initialize all seats as available
5. End

Choice 1: Prompt the user for a requested seat location. If that seat is available, assign the passenger to that seat. (Place the passenger's name in the corresponding field and rewrite the record.) If the seat is not available, the program might offer another choice or perhaps display the list of remaining available seats (menu choice 2).
Choice 2: Print out all seat locations that are still available. If no seats are available, print a message that the plane is full.
Choice 3: Print out the list of passengers along with their seat locations. This will be in seat-number order.
Choice 4: Print an appropriate sign-off message.

14.2. Modify the program in exercise 14.1 to print the passenger list in alphabetic order. This will require reading the entire file into arrays and sorting the data. The order of the file will remain unchanged (in seat-number order).

14.3. Modify the program in exercise 14.1 (or 14.2) to indicate which seats are next to windows or which are aisle seats. The aisle is in the middle of the plane, so seats A and F are window seats, and C and D are aisle seats. Allow the user to request any available window or aisle seat.

14.4. The company needs to store personnel records in a data file. Each employee will be assigned an employee number, beginning with number 1. Write a program that will create and update a random access file for storing personnel records.

PERSONNEL FILE: The fields in each personnel record should be name, address, social security number, marital status, exemptions, and department number.
MENU PROGRAM: The solution should be written as a menu program with options to create the file, to update individual records, to list the file on the printer, to display the file on the screen, or to quit.
  a. *Create the File*—Request input of each of the fields for each employee. The records should be assigned employee numbers, beginning with #1. Use the employee number as record number and write each record in the random file.
  b. *Update Option*—Request the employee number to update. Then display the data for that employee, and give the user the option of changing *no* fields if this is not the correct employee. Allow the user to change as many fields as desired for that employee. When all updates for that employee are complete, return to the menu.

c. *List the File on the Printer*—Design a report layout with an appropriate title. Create a company name.
d. *Display the File on the Screen*—Design a pleasing screen layout, and display all records.
e. *Quit*—Print a sign-off message.

INPUT DATA: Make up data for at least five employees. For each, enter the name, address, city, state, zip code, social security number, marital status, exemptions, and department number.

CHANGES: Make up changes to the file, testing all change options. List the file between changes to determine that the changes have been correctly made.

14.5. Modify the program in exercise 14.4 to include data validation and formatted screens for data entry.
   a. Data validation—both for the create and update.
      (1) Social security number—check for correct number of digits.
      (2) Marital status—check for M or S.
      (3) Exemptions—valid numeric characters, between 0 and 15.
      (4) Department number—the only valid department numbers are 40, 41, 45, 50, and 55.
   b. Formatted screens—make data entry easy and clear. Do not allow screens to scroll. Any error messages must be cleared after corrections are made.

14.6. Establish a random file to maintain inventory information for parts. The part numbers are in the range 1–100 and can be used as record numbers in the file.

Record Layout

Part number	integer
Description	25 characters
Unit price	single-precision
Quantity on hand	integer

Write the program as a menu, with these choices:
1. Increase part inventory
2. Decrease part inventory
3. Display parts inventory file on the screen
4. List parts inventory file on the printer
5. Initialize the parts inventory file
6. Sign off

Choice 1: Increase part inventory—Prompt the user for the part number. Then retrieve and display the part description, unit price, and quantity on hand. Then request input of the number of units to *add* to the inventory.

Choice 2: Decrease part inventory—Similar to choice 1, only enter number of units to *subtract* from inventory.

Choice 3: Display file on screen—Display a list of the entire file. However, do not list any part numbers that do not have data in the file (empty record positions). When a screenful of data has been printed, hold the display with the message: PRESS ANY KEY TO CONTINUE.

Choice 4: List file on printer—List the entire file on the printer, leaving out any part numbers for which there is no data (empty record positions). Format the report with an appropriate title and column headings. Multiple page output must have headings on each page with the page number on all pages.

Choice 5: After printing a warning message, initialize the entire file (record numbers 1–100). Numeric fields (part number, unit price, and quantity on hand) should be set to zero, the descriptions should be set to blanks. Then allow the user to enter data for part numbers, along with corresponding description, unit price, and quantity on hand. Part numbers may be entered in any order. Use the part number for record number.

Choice 6: Clear the screen and print an appropriate sign-off message.

PROGRAM TESTING: Run your program, selecting choice 5 to establish the file. Make up your own data, using noncontiguous part numbers such as 1, 5, 20, 25, 50, 100. Be sure to use record positions 1 and 100. Place sufficient parts in the file to test the multiple screen and multiple page options of menu choices 3 and 4.

Once the file has been established, select options to add parts, list the file, subtract parts, and list again, making sure that all requested changes are made.

ERROR CHECKING: Verify that requested part numbers are in the range 1–100 before attempting to read or write in the file. This must be done for menu choices 1, 2, and 5.

14.7. Modify the program in exercise 14.6 to include a formatted screen to make data entry easier and more clear. Do not allow screens to scroll. Any error messages must be cleared after corrections are made.

14.8. Modify the program in exercise 14.6 (or 14.7) to include a field for a reorder point in the file. Any inventory reduction that causes the quantity of a part to drop to or below the reorder point should cause a printed notice. Also, add a menu option to print a list of all items at or below the reorder point.

14.9. Modify the program in exercise 14.6 (or 14.7 or 14.8) to include an option to change the description or unit price (or reorder point from 14.8). Prompt the user for the part number, and display the corresponding data from the file. Then allow the user to change the required field(s).

14.10. Write a random file program to create a plane rental file for West End Airport Flight School. The program should have a menu with these options:

1. Add a record
2. Change a record
3. Delete a record
4. Print available planes on screen
5. Search for one plane
6. Quit

TEST DATA:

Plane Number	Plane	Rental Rate (dollars/hr)	Number Available
1	Cessna 152	26.90	8
2	Cessna 182	45.70	2
3	Piper Warrior	37.00	1
4	Cessna T120	91.00	1
5	Cessna 172	35.80	3
6	Cessna 150	24.00	2

14.11. Write a random file program to create and list a file for the students attending Dan's Dance Studio.

INPUT: Student's name and telephone number should be input from the keyboard.

OUTPUT: Create a random file on disk. Then print a list of the file on the screen.

Menu Options
1. Add a record
2. Change a record
3. Delete a record
4. View the file
5. Quit

14.12. Write a random file program to create a customer file for Jose's Video Store.

INPUT: Customer name, address, phone number, and status should be input from the keyboard.
OUTPUT: Create a random file on disk. Print the file on the printer if requested.
PROCESSING:
1. Status is either "NO DEBTS" or "OWES MONEY."

Menu Options
1. Add a record
2. Change a record
3. Delete a record
4. Print the file on the printer
5. Quit

14.13. Write a program to create a random file to keep track of Girl Scout Troup #21.

Input the Scout's number, name, age, and number of badges from the keyboard, and create a random file on diskette.

Allow the user to enter the Scout's number, and display that person's information on the screen or print the entire file on the screen.

Menu Options
1. Add a scout to the file
2. List all scouts
3. Display information for one scout
4. Quit

14.14. Write a program to create a random file for MacPac's division managers.

Input the division number, the division, and the manager's name and home phone number from the keyboard to create the file.

Allow the user to enter a division number and display the information for the corresponding manager.

Menu Options
1. Add records
2. View one record
3. Quit

TEST DATA:

Division #	Division	Manager's Name	Phone No.
1	Accounting	John Price	432–6542
2	Sales	Steve Johnstone	946–3749
3	Receiving	Marla Keating	720–4800
4	Shipping	Kim Smith	439–0000
5	Stock	Dave Sillo	987–9111

15

Additional File Handling Concepts

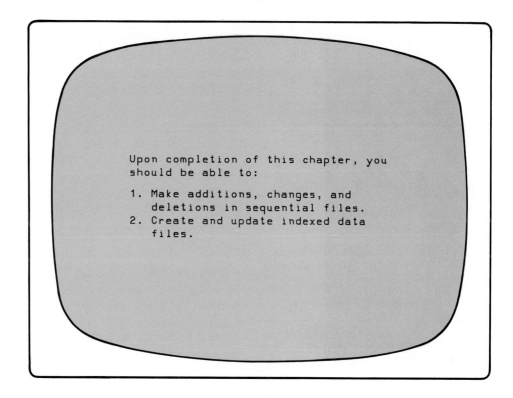

```
Upon completion of this chapter, you
should be able to:

1. Make additions, changes, and
   deletions in sequential files.
2. Create and update indexed data
   files.
```

Updating Sequential Files

Sequential files are not easily updated. A program may read a file (input) or write data in a file (output), but it cannot do both to one file. Therefore, if data in a file must be changed, it must be read from one file and written in another file. That new file must contain all data from the old file as well as any changes that were made.

Traditionally, sequential updates have been a *batch operation* (as opposed to an on-line, interactive process). A group of updates is accumulated and sorted into key sequence. Then the update program reads both the master file and the transaction file (which holds the updates). The program produces a new master file as well as an error report to indicate any updates that cannot be processed. Possible errors include changes or deletions for records that do not exist or records for addition that duplicate a record already in the file. This style of batch processing is not well suited for the interactive processing generally done on a microcomputer or for timesharing on a larger computer system.

One of the advantages of microcomputer processing (and timesharing) is the interactive nature of operations. The user will enter the update transactions from the keyboard. Since it is not reasonable to require the user to enter the transactions in key sequence, another method must be used.

When a sequential file must be updated, there are several different approaches available.

1. Allow the user to enter multiple transactions (adds, changes, deletes), and store these transactions in a separate file. The transaction file would need to be sorted into key sequence before the update program could be run. As mentioned earlier, this technique is used extensively for batch processing (as opposed to on-line, interactive processing). This is the method of choice when a majority of the records in the file must be updated.
2. For each transaction entered from the keyboard (add, change, or delete), process the entire file, creating a new file. This method *does* allow multiple changes to be made in an interactive mode. However, this technique is reasonable only for a relatively small file. To read and write every record in a large file for each transaction would be extremely slow.
3. Read the entire file into arrays in memory. Then data may be added, deleted, or changed in the arrays. At the conclusion of processing, the entire file must be rewritten. This method will work only for a small file. Since the arrays must all be held in the main storage of the computer, the limiting factor is main storage size.
4. Use a random file. For a file that must be updated often, random organization is generally the best choice.

Each of the update choices has major drawbacks; but there are occasions when a file simply must be sequential and must be updated.

Although BASIC *can* be used for batch processing, in reality it seldom is. Either choice #2 or #3 above could be used for interactive updating. The array method (#3) *cannot* be used on a large file, and the single transaction method (#2) *should* only be used for a relatively small file requiring few updates.

In this text, the single transaction method (#2) will be demonstrated. Remember that an entirely new file will be created for *every transaction* entered.

In the example, the key field will be an item number. Therefore the master file must be in sequence by item number.

```
ITEM      ITEM                    ITEM
NUMBER DESCRIPTION                PRICE

101,"CARDS - ALL OCCASION",1.75
102,"CARDS - ALL OCCASION",2.45
105,"CARDS - BIRTHDAY",1.5
110,"FOLDING NOTES",2.05
114,"POST CARDS",3.5
122,"STATIONERY",2
125,"STATIONERY",3.25
136,"ENVELOPES",1.85
```

Adding a Record

Record Added from Keyboard

```
ITEM      ITEM                    ITEM
NUMBER DESCRIPTION                PRICE

108,"CARDS - HUMOROUS",4.5
```

New Master File

```
ITEM      ITEM                    ITEM
NUMBER DESCRIPTION                PRICE

101,"CARDS - ALL OCCASION",1.75
102,"CARDS - ALL OCCASION",2.45
105,"CARDS - BIRTHDAY",1.5
108,"CARDS - HUMOROUS",4.5
110,"FOLDING NOTES",2.05
114,"POST CARDS",3.5
122,"STATIONERY",2
125,"STATIONERY",3.25
136,"ENVELOPES",1.85
```

The steps necessary to add a record are:

1. Open the old master file for input
2. Open the new master file for output
3. Input the new record from the keyboard (record to be added)
4. LOOP until end of old master file
    4.1 Read a record from the old master file
    4.2 Compare the item number from the new record with the item number from the master file. The new record should be inserted when the master item number is higher than the new item number.
        IF master item number > new item number
            THEN write new record in new master file
                    set switch field to indicate that the add has been made
    4.3 Write the record from the old master file into the new master file
5. Close both files
6. Kill the old master file
7. Rename the new master file to be the current master file
8. Stop

Example Subroutines: Adding a Record to the File

Program Listing

```
1000 '*********** ADD A RECORD TO THE FILE ********************
1010 OPEN "I", #1, "ITEMS.DAT"
1020 OPEN "O", #2, "ITEMS.TMP"
1030 LET ADDED.SW = 0              'SET SWITCH FOR NO ADD YET
1040 GOSUB 2000                    'INPUT DATA FOR NEW RECORD
1050 WHILE NOT EOF(1)
1060    INPUT #1, ITEM1, DESC1$, PRICE1
1070    IF ITEM1 >= ITEM2 AND ADDED.SW <> 1
            THEN GOSUB 2200        'WRITE THE NEW RECORD
1080    WRITE #2, ITEM1, DESC1$, PRICE1
1090 WEND
1100 IF ADDED.SW <> 1
        THEN GOSUB 2200            'WRITE THE NEW RECORD AT END OF
                                   FILE
1110 CLOSE #1, #2
1120 KILL "ITEMS.DAT"             'REMOVE OLD MASTER FILE
1130 NAME "ITEMS.TMP" AS "ITEMS.DAT" 'NEW FILE IS NOW MASTER
1140 RETURN
1150 '
2000 '************** INPUT THE NEW RECORD *****************
2010 CLS
2020 PRINT:PRINT:PRINT
2030 PRINT TAB(30); "ADD AN ITEM TO THE FILE"
2040 PRINT:PRINT
2050 INPUT "ITEM NUMBER      ", ITEM2
2060 PRINT
2070 INPUT "ITEM DESCRIPTION ", DESC2$
2080 PRINT
2090 INPUT "ITEM PRICE       ", PRICE2
2100 RETURN
2110 '
2200 '**************** WRITE THE NEW RECORD *****************
2210 IF ITEM1 <> ITEM2
        THEN WRITE #2, ITEM2, DESC2$, PRICE2
        ELSE GOSUB 2400           'ERROR - DUPLICATE KEY FIELD
2220 LET ADDED.SW = 1             'SET SWITCH TO INDICATE RECORD
                                  ADDED
2230 RETURN
2240 '
2400 '************** ERROR--DUPLICATE KEY FIELD *************
2410 PRINT: PRINT: PRINT
2420 PRINT TAB(15); "ERROR--THIS ITEM NUMBER IS ALREADY IN THE FILE"
2430 RETURN
```

Deleting a Record

When deleting a record from the file, it is also necessary to rewrite the entire file. However, the deleted record will be left out of the new file. In all other respects, the new file will be an exact copy of the old file. The master file must be read until a match is found—that is, the item number of the master record matches the item number to be deleted.

Example Subroutines: Deleting a Record from the File

Program Listing

```
3000 '*********** DELETE A RECORD FROM THE FILE **************
3010 OPEN "I", #1, "ITEMS.DAT"
3020 OPEN "O", #2, "ITEMS.TMP"                    -
3030 LET DEL.SW = 0               'SET SWITCH OFF FOR NO DELETE YET
                                  'INPUT ITEM NUMBER TO DELETE
3040 GOSUB 4000
3050 WHILE NOT EOF(1)
3060    INPUT #1, ITEM1, DESC1$, PRICE1
```

```
3070     IF ITEM1 <> ITEM2
            THEN WRITE #2, ITEM1, DESC1$, PRICE1
            ELSE LET DEL.SW = 1
3080 WEND
3090 IF DEL.SW <> 1
        THEN PRINT "ERROR - ITEM NOT IN FILE"
3100 CLOSE #1, #2
3110 KILL "ITEMS.DAT"              'REMOVE OLD MASTER FILE
3120 NAME "ITEMS.TMP" AS "ITEMS.DAT" 'NEW FILE IS NOW MASTER
3130 RETURN
3140 '
4000 '********** INPUT ITEM NUMBER TO DELETE ****************
4010 CLS
4020 PRINT:PRINT:PRINT
4030 PRINT TAB(30); "DELETE A RECORD FROM THE FILE"
4040 PRINT:PRINT
4050 INPUT "ITEM NUMBER TO DELETE"; ITEM2
4060 PRINT:PRINT
4070 RETURN
```

Changing a Record

To change the data in a record in the master file, the item number of the changed data must match an item number in the file. The file must be read until a match is found, and the new (changed) data will replace the old data. The new master file will contain all of the data from the old file with the exception of the changed data.

Example Subroutines: Changing Data in a File

Program Listing

```
5000 '********** CHANGE A RECORD IN THE FILE ******************
5010 OPEN "I", #1, "ITEMS.DAT"
5020 OPEN "O", #2, "ITEMS.TMP"
5030 LET CHANGE.SW = 0              'SET SWITCH FOR NO CHANGE YET
5040 GOSUB 6000                     'INPUT NEW DATA (FOR CHANGE)
5050 WHILE NOT EOF(1)
5060    INPUT #1, ITEM1, DESC1$, PRICE1
5070    IF ITEM1 <> ITEM2
            THEN WRITE #2, ITEM1, DESC1$, PRICE1
            ELSE WRITE #2, ITEM2, DESC2$, PRICE2: LET CHANGE.SW = 1
5080 WEND
5090 IF CHANGE.SW <> 1
        THEN PRINT "ERROR - ITEM NOT IN FILE"
5100 CLOSE #1, #2
5110 KILL "ITEMS.DAT"              'REMOVE OLD MASTER FILE
5120 NAME "ITEMS.TMP" AS "ITEMS.DAT" 'NEW FILE IS NOW MASTER
5130 RETURN
5140 '
6000 '********** INPUT CHANGED DATA ***********************
6010 CLS
6020 PRINT:PRINT:PRINT
6030 PRINT TAB(30); "CHANGE DATA IN THE FILE"
6040 PRINT:PRINT
6050 INPUT "ITEM NUMBER       ", ITEM2
6060 PRINT
6070 INPUT "ITEM DESCRIPTION ", DESC2$
6080 PRINT
6090 INPUT "ITEM PRICE        ", PRICE2
6100 PRINT:PRINT
6110 RETURN
```

Example Program: Adding, Changing, and Deleting Records in a Sequential File

The program to utilize these subroutines can best be done with a menu. The user will be given a choice of the desired function, and the correct subroutine will be performed.

Program Menu

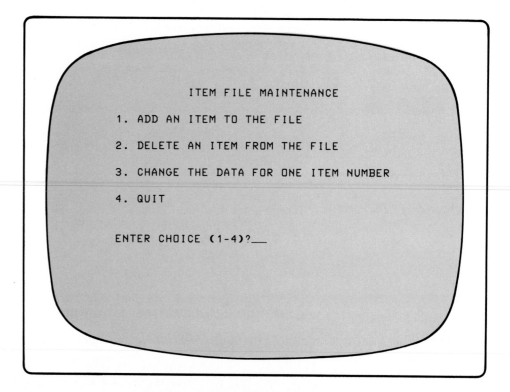

```
                ITEM FILE MAINTENANCE

    1. ADD AN ITEM TO THE FILE

    2. DELETE AN ITEM FROM THE FILE

    3. CHANGE THE DATA FOR ONE ITEM NUMBER

    4. QUIT


    ENTER CHOICE (1-4)?__
```

Program Listing

```
100 'PROGRAM TO UPDATE A SEQUENTIAL DATA FILE
110 '   UPDATES ARE ENTERED IN AN INTERACTIVE MODE,
120 '   WITH MENU SELECTION OF UPDATE FUNCTION
130 '
140 ' MASTER FILE IS ITEMS.DAT
150 ' TEMPORARY FILE FOR UPDATE IS ITEMS.TMP
160 '
170 '                PROGRAM VARIABLES
180 ' ITEM1          ITEM NUMBER FROM (OLD) MASTER FILE
190 ' DESC1$         ITEM DESCRIPTION FROM (OLD) MASTER FILE
200 ' PRICE1         ITEM PRICE FROM (OLD) MASTER FILE
210 ' ITEM2          ITEM NUMBER FOR RECORD TO UPDATE
220 ' DESC2$         ITEM DESCRIPTION FOR NEW OR CHANGED RECORD
230 ' PRICE2         ITEM PRICE FOR NEW OR CHANGED RECORD
240 ' ADDED.SW       SWITCH FIELD TO INDICATE THAT ADD WAS MADE
250 ' CHANGE.SW      SWITCH FIELD TO INDICATE THAT CHANGE WAS MADE
260 ' DEL.SW         SWITCH FIELD TO INDICATE THAT DELETE WAS MADE
270 '                SWITCHES -- 0 = NO ACTION
275                              (ADD, CHANGE, OR DELETE)
280 '                            1 = ACTION TAKEN
290 '
300 '
500 '**** SEQUENTIAL FILE MAINTENANCE--PROGRAM MAINLINE ******
510 WHILE CHOICE <> 4
520     CLS
530     GOSUB 800                'PRINT MENU
540     ON CHOICE GOSUB 1000,3000,5000
550 WEND
560 CLS
570 END
580 '
```

```
 800 '************** PRINT THE MENU AND GET CHOICE ************
 810 PRINT:PRINT
 820 PRINT TAB(30); "ITEM FILE MAINTENANCE"
 830 PRINT:PRINT:PRINT
 840 PRINT TAB(15); "1. ADD AN ITEM TO THE FILE"
 850 PRINT
 860 PRINT TAB(15); "2. DELETE AN ITEM FROM THE FILE"
 870 PRINT
 880 PRINT TAB(15); "3. CHANGE THE DATA FOR ONE ITEM NUMBER"
 890 PRINT
 900 PRINT TAB(15); "4. QUIT"
 910 PRINT:PRINT
 920 PRINT TAB(15); "ENTER CHOICE (1 - 4)";
 930 INPUT CHOICE$
 940 LET CHOICE = VAL(CHOICE$)
 950 RETURN
 960 '
1000 '*********** ADD A RECORD TO THE FILE ****************
1010 OPEN "I", #1, "ITEMS.DAT"
1020 OPEN "O", #2, "ITEMS.TMP"
1030 LET ADDED.SW = 0              'SET SWITCH FOR NO ADD YET
1040 GOSUB 2000                    'INPUT DATA FOR NEW RECORD
1050 WHILE NOT EOF(1)
1060     INPUT #1, ITEM1, DESC1$, PRICE1
1070     IF ITEM1 >= ITEM2 AND ADDED.SW <> 1
             THEN GOSUB 2200       'WRITE THE NEW RECORD
1080     WRITE #2, ITEM1, DESC1$, PRICE1
1090 WEND
1100 IF ADDED.SW <> 1
         THEN GOSUB 2200           'WRITE THE NEW RECORD AT END OF FILE
1110 CLOSE #1, #2
1120 KILL "ITEMS.DAT"             'REMOVE OLD MASTER FILE
1130 NAME "ITEMS.TMP" AS "ITEMS.DAT" 'NEW FILE IS NOW MASTER
1140 RETURN
1150 '
2000 '*************** INPUT THE NEW RECORD ****************
2010 CLS
2020 PRINT:PRINT:PRINT
2030 PRINT TAB(30); "ADD AN ITEM TO THE FILE"
2040 PRINT:PRINT
2050 INPUT "ITEM NUMBER      ", ITEM2
2060 PRINT
2070 INPUT "ITEM DESCRIPTION ", DESC2$
2080 PRINT
2090 INPUT "ITEM PRICE       ", PRICE2
2100 RETURN
2110 '
2200 '**************** WRITE THE NEW RECORD ****************
2210 IF ITEM1 <> ITEM2
         THEN WRITE #2, ITEM2, DESC2$, PRICE2
         ELSE GOSUB 2400           'ERROR - DUPLICATE KEY FIELD
2220 LET ADDED.SW = 1             'SET SWITCH TO INDICATE RECORD ADDED
2230 RETURN
2240 '
2400 '************** ERROR--DUPLICATE KEY FIELD *************
2410 PRINT: PRINT: PRINT
2420 PRINT TAB(15); "ERROR--THIS ITEM NUMBER IS ALREADY IN THE FILE"
2430 RETURN
2440 '
```

```
3000 '*********** DELETE A RECORD FROM THE FILE **************
3010 OPEN "I", #1, "ITEMS.DAT"
3020 OPEN "O", #2, "ITEMS.TMP"
3030 LET DEL.SW = 0               'SET SWITCH OFF FOR NO DELETE YET
3040 GOSUB 4000                   'INPUT ITEM NUMBER TO DELETE
3050 WHILE NOT EOF(1)
3060    INPUT #1, ITEM1, DESC1$, PRICE1
3070    IF ITEM1 <> ITEM2
           THEN WRITE #2, ITEM1, DESC1$, PRICE1
           ELSE LET DEL.SW = 1
3080 WEND
3090 IF DEL.SW <> 1
        THEN PRINT "ERROR--ITEM NOT IN FILE"
3100 CLOSE #1, #2
3110 KILL "ITEMS.DAT"             'REMOVE OLD MASTER FILE
3120 NAME "ITEMS.TMP" AS "ITEMS.DAT" 'NEW FILE IS NOW MASTER
3130 RETURN
3140 '
4000 '*********** INPUT ITEM NUMBER TO DELETE *****************
4010 CLS
4020 PRINT:PRINT:PRINT
4030 PRINT TAB(30); "DELETE A RECORD FROM THE FILE"
4040 PRINT:PRINT
4050 INPUT "ITEM NUMBER TO DELETE"; ITEM2
4060 PRINT:PRINT
4070 RETURN
4080 '
5000 '********** CHANGE A RECORD IN THE FILE *****************
5010 OPEN "I", #1, "ITEMS.DAT"
5020 OPEN "O", #2, "ITEMS.TMP"
5030 LET CHANGE.SW = 0            'SET SWITCH FOR NO CHANGE YET
5040 GOSUB 6000                   'INPUT NEW DATA (FOR CHANGE)
5050 WHILE NOT EOF(1)
5060    INPUT #1, ITEM1, DESC1$, PRICE1
5070    IF ITEM1 <> ITEM2
           THEN WRITE #2, ITEM1, DESC1$, PRICE1
           ELSE WRITE #2, ITEM2, DESC2$, PRICE2: LET CHANGE.SW = 1
5080 WEND
5090 IF CHANGE.SW <> 1
        THEN PRINT "ERROR - ITEM NOT IN FILE"
5100 CLOSE #1, #2
5110 KILL "ITEMS.DAT"             'REMOVE OLD MASTER FILE
5120 NAME "ITEMS.TMP" AS "ITEMS.DAT" 'NEW FILE IS NOW MASTER
5130 RETURN
5140 '
6000 '********** INPUT CHANGED DATA ***************************
6010 CLS
6020 PRINT:PRINT:PRINT
6030 PRINT TAB(30); "CHANGE DATA IN THE FILE"
6040 PRINT:PRINT
6050 INPUT "ITEM NUMBER        ", ITEM2
6060 PRINT
6070 INPUT "ITEM DESCRIPTION ", DESC2$
6080 PRINT
6090 INPUT "ITEM PRICE         ", PRICE2
6100 PRINT:PRINT
6110 RETURN
6120 '*************** END OF PROGRAM ************************
```

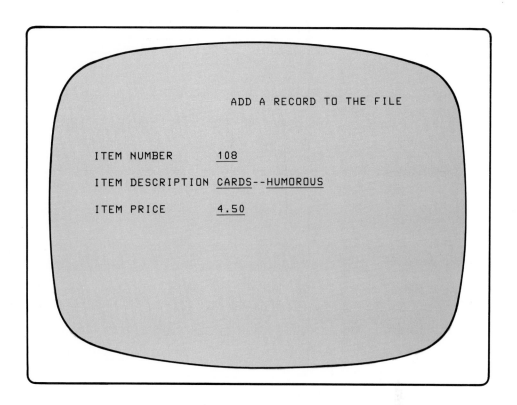

ADD A RECORD TO THE FILE

ITEM NUMBER   108

ITEM DESCRIPTION CARDS--HUMOROUS

ITEM PRICE   4.50

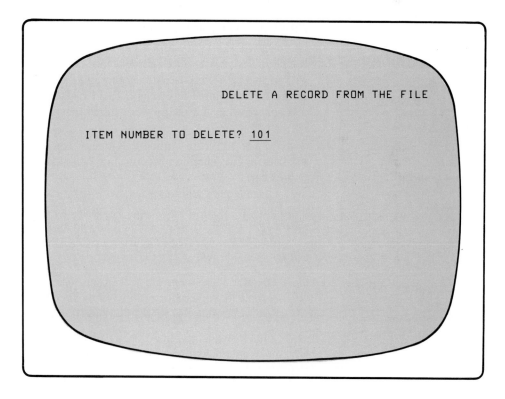

DELETE A RECORD FROM THE FILE

ITEM NUMBER TO DELETE? 101

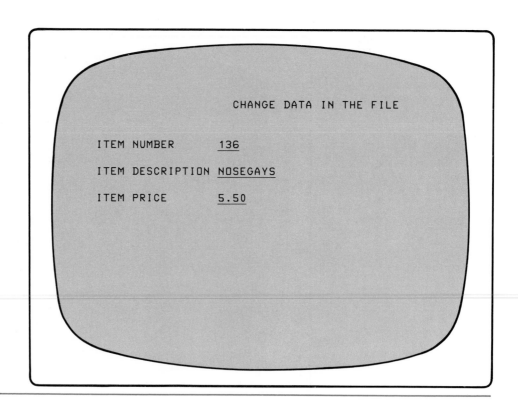

```
                             CHANGE DATA IN THE FILE


        ITEM NUMBER          136

        ITEM DESCRIPTION  NOSEGAYS

        ITEM PRICE           5.50
```

Indexing Files

When files must be updated, random file organization is generally the preferred approach. However, the limitations of random files sometimes make their use difficult.

The Random File

Random files must be accessed by record number. Ideally, those record numbers begin with #1 and proceed consecutively through the number of records in the file. A file may certainly have unused record positions. However, each unused record location requires disk space just as if a record were stored there.

More often than not, the key fields associated with files do not lend themselves to conversion to record numbers. Numeric key fields such as account numbers, item numbers, or customer numbers or alphabetic key fields such as names are common in data files.

One common solution is to use an *index* for the data file. The index is an array that holds the key fields. For any access to the data file, the array is used to look up the record number. Then a random read may be initiated to retrieve the correct record. This concept is illustrated in figure 15.1. The steps to retrieve one record from the file would be:

1. The user enters item #114.
2. A table lookup produces a match on the fifth element.
3. Record position 5 is randomly read from the file.

The technique of using tables to look up the record number is called indexing files and is commonly used to allow random access by any record key. Although the record number (for a random file) must always be numeric, the key field may be either numeric or string. A table lookup works equally well for numeric or string data.

The Index File

A second file must be used to store the index table. In previous programs, when a table was used for lookup, the table data was read from DATA statements in the program. Since the index table will be changed as records are added and deleted, the data to fill the table must be stored in a data file between program runs. For each run of the program, an initialization step must be to read the index file into the array. At the termination of a program run, the index array must be rewritten in the index file.

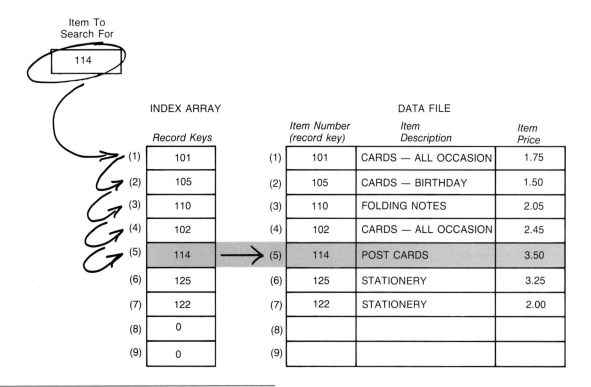

Figure 15.1

Using an index to find the record. Each position of the index array is checked for a match. When a hit is made, the corresponding record is read from the random file.

INDEX FILE		DATA FILE		
Record Keys		Item Number (record key)	Item Description	Item Price
101	(1)	101	CARDS — ALL OCCASION	1.75
105	(2)	105	CARDS — BIRTHDAY	1.50
110	(3)	110	FOLDING NOTES	2.05
102	(4)	102	CARDS — ALL OCCASION	2.45
114	(5)	114	POST CARDS	3.50
125	(6)	125	STATIONERY	3.25
122	(7)	122	STATIONERY	2.00
0	(8)			
0	(9)			

Figure 15.2

The index file and the data file. The record keys in the index file are in the same sequence as those in the primary data file.

Two Files

An indexed file will always have two parts: (1) the *primary data file*, which will be a random file, and (2) the *index file*, which will be a sequential file. Figure 15.2 illustrates the two files to be used. Note that the record keys in the index file are in the same sequence as those in the primary data file.

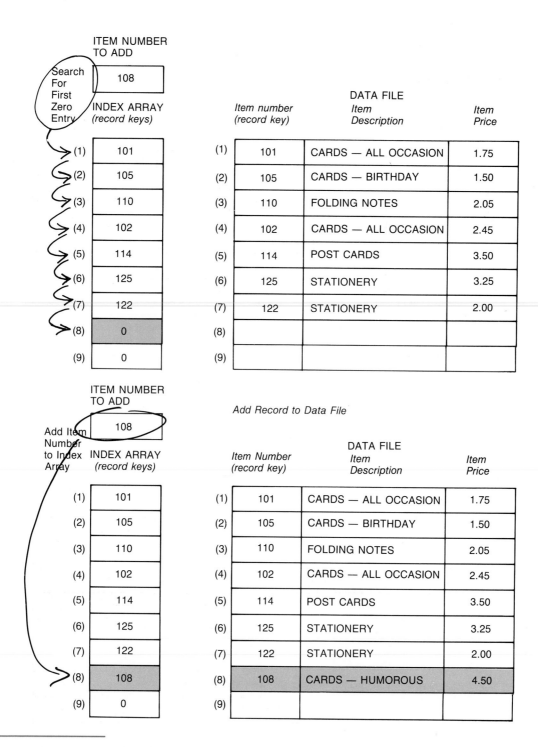

Figure 15.3
Adding a record to the file.

Using the Index to Access the File

Initially, all elements of the index array are set to zero. When a record is added to the file, an empty record position must be found to hold the new record. The index array is searched for the first zero entry (which indicates an available slot). Then the record is written in the data file at that record position, and the corresponding array element is set to the record key. See the illustration of record addition in figure 15.3.

ITEM NUMBER TO DELETE

Look Up Item Number in the Index Array

	125

INDEX ARRAY (record keys)

(1)	101
(2)	105
(3)	110
(4)	102
(5)	114
(6)	125
(7)	122
(8)	108
(9)	0

DATA FILE

	Item Number (record key)	Item Description	Item Price
(1)	101	CARDS — ALL OCCASION	1.75
(2)	105	CARDS — BIRTHDAY	1.50
(3)	110	FOLDING NOTES	2.05
(4)	102	CARDS — ALL OCCASION	2.45
(5)	114	POST CARDS	3.50
(6)	125	STATIONERY	3.25
(7)	122	STATIONERY	2.00
(8)	108	CARDS — HUMOROUS	4.50
(9)			

ITEM NUMBER TO DELETE

Change the Item Number to Zero

	125

INDEX ARRAY (record keys)

(1)	101
(2)	105
(3)	110
(4)	102
(5)	114
(6)	0
(7)	122
(8)	108
(9)	

DATA FILE

	Item Number (record key)	Item Description	Item Price
(1)	101	CARDS — ALL OCCASION	1.75
(2)	105	CARDS — BIRTHDAY	1.50
(3)	110	FOLDING NOTES	2.05
(4)	102	CARDS — ALL OCCASION	2.45
(5)	114	POST CARDS	3.50
(6)	125	STATIONERY	3.25
(7)	122	STATIONERY	2.00
(8)	108	CARDS — HUMOROUS	4.50
(9)	0		

Figure 15.4
Deleting a record from the file.

Records to be deleted are not actually erased from the file. Instead, the index entry for the deleted record is set to zero. The zero index entry flags that location as available. (In some applications, a delete *does* actually cause blank spaces to be written in the record position.) A delete operation is shown in figure 15.4.

Establishing the Index File

A one-time initialization program must establish the index file before the first run of the program that accesses the primary data file. Alternately, the index file (which is only a series of zero fields) may be created with an editor.

One important step is to establish the maximum file size. The number of elements chosen for the index array will determine the maximum number of records the file may hold. For the example program, the number 100 has been chosen.

```
100    'INITIALIZE INDEX FILE
110    'A ONE-TIME OPERATION
120    OPEN "O", #2, "ITEM.NDX"
130    FOR SUB = 1 TO 100
140          WRITE #2, 0
150    NEXT SUB
160    CLOSE #2
170    END
```

Programming Example

The item file from the sequential update program has been changed to an indexed file. By entering an item number (the record key), any record may be retrieved from the file. A record may be displayed, added, deleted, or changed.

Pseudocode

1. Open and field the random file
2. Initialize the index array
   2.1 Open the index file for input
   2.2 Read the entire file into the index array
   2.3 Close the index file
3. LOOP until menu option #5 (QUIT) chosen
   3.1 Display the menu and input choice
   3.2 Execute the correct subroutine:
        3.2.1 Display a record
        3.2.2 Add a record
        3.2.3 Delete a record
        3.2.4 Change a record
4. Rewrite the index file
   4.1 Open the index file for output
   4.2 Write the entire index array into the index file
   4.3 Close the index file
5. Close the random file
6. Stop

Display a Record Subroutine

1. Input the item number to display
2. Look up the item in the index array
   Use a table lookup, setting FOUND.SW = 1 when a match is found, FOUND.SW = 0 when no match found. When a match is found, POSN will hold the record position to be used for the random read.
3. IF the item number was found (FOUND.SW = 1)
        THEN read the record and display it
        ELSE display an error message
4. Hold the record (or the error message) on the screen until a key is pressed
5. Return

Add a Record Subroutine

1. Input the data for the new record
2. Look up the item number (checking for a duplicate). FOUND.SW = 1 means that a match was found (duplicate record), FOUND.SW = 0 means that the record can be added.
3. IF a match was found (FOUND.SW = 1)
   THEN print an error message
   ELSE add the record
      3.1 Search the index array for the first zero entry (set POSN to the first available record position)
      3.2 Save the item number in the index array
      3.3 LSET the fields into the buffer
      3.4 PUT the record
4. Return

Delete a Record Subroutine

1. Input the item number to delete
2. Look up the item number in the index array. FOUND.SW = 1 means a match was found, FOUND.SW = 0 means that no match was found. POSN will hold the record position where the match was found.
3. IF the record was found
   THEN delete the record
      3.1 Read the record and display it on the screen
      3.2 Request verification of delete
      3.3 IF verified
          THEN set index array element to zero
          ELSE print an error message
4. Return

Change a Record Subroutine

1. Input the item number to change
2. Look up the item number in the index array. FOUND.SW = 1 means a match was found, FOUND.SW = 0 means that no match was found. POSN will hold the record position where the match was found.
3. IF the record was found
   THEN change the record
      3.1 Read the record and display on the screen
      3.2 Input new description
      3.3 Input new price
      3.4 IF the data was changed,
          THEN LSET into buffer
      3.5 Rewrite the record (PUT)
   ELSE print an error message
4. Return

Program Listing

```
100 '       INDEXED FILE MAINTENANCE PROGRAM
110 '         MENU SELECTION TO CHOOSE ACTION:
120 '          1) DISPLAY DATA FOR ONE ITEM
130 '          2) ADD AN ITEM TO THE FILE
140 '          3) DELETE AN ITEM FROM THE FILE
150 '          4) CHANGE THE DATA FOR AN ITEM
160 '          5) QUIT
170 '
180 '                     PROGRAM VARIABLES
190 '
200 '      ITEM           ITEM NUMBER
210 '      DESC$          ITEM DESCRIPTION
220 '      PRICE          ITEM PRICE
230 '      B.ITEM$        ITEM NUMBER--BUFFER
240 '      B.DESC$        ITEM DESCRIPTION--BUFFER
250 '      B.PRICE$       ITEM PRICE--BUFFER
260 '      MAX            MAXIMUM NUMBER OF RECORDS IN FILE
270 '      INDEX(MAX)     INDEX ARRAY
280 '      FOUND.SW       SWITCH USED TO INDICATE A MATCH FOUND IN INDEX
290 '                     1 = MATCH FOUND, 0 = NO MATCH FOUND
300 '      POSN           POSITION FOR RECORD KEY IN INDEX AND FILE
310 '      ANS$           RESPONSE TO CONFIRM DELETE
320 '      X$             DUMMY VARIABLE FOR KEYPRESS
330 '
500 '****** INDEXED FILE MAINTENANCE--PROGRAM MAINLINE ********
510 LET MAX = 100                   'ESTABLISH MAXIMUM FILE SIZE
520 GOSUB 1000                      'INITIALIZE RANDOM FILE
530 GOSUB 1200                      'INITIALIZE INDEX
540 WHILE CHOICE <> 5
550     CLS
560     GOSUB 2000                  'PRINT MENU
570     ON CHOICE GOSUB 3000,4000,5000,6000
580 WEND
590 GOSUB 7000                      'REWRITE INDEX ARRAY IN INDEX FILE
600 CLOSE #1                        'CLOSE RANDOM FILE
610 CLS
620 END
630 '
1000 '*************** INITIALIZE RANDOM FILE ******************
1010 OPEN "R", #1, "ITEM.DAT"
1020 FIELD #1, 4 AS B.ITEM$, 20 AS B.DESC$, 4 AS B.PRICE$
1030 RETURN
1040 '
1200 '*************** INITIALIZE INDEX ********************
1210 DIM INDEX(MAX)                 'ESTABLISH INDEX ARRAY
1220 OPEN "I", #2, "ITEM.NDX"
1230 FOR SUB = 1 TO MAX             'FILL THE INDEX ARRAY WITH ITEM
1240     INPUT #2, INDEX(SUB)       'NUMBERS FROM THE INDEX FILE
1250 NEXT SUB
1260 CLOSE #2
1270 RETURN
1280 '
2000 '*************** PRINT THE MENU AND GET CHOICE ************
2010 PRINT:PRINT
2020 PRINT TAB(30); "ITEM FILE MAINTENANCE"
2030 PRINT:PRINT:PRINT
2040 PRINT TAB(15); "1. DISPLAY THE DATA FOR ONE ITEM"
2050 PRINT
2060 PRINT TAB(15); "2. ADD AN ITEM TO THE FILE"
2070 PRINT
2080 PRINT TAB(15); "3. DELETE AN ITEM FROM THE FILE"
2090 PRINT
2100 PRINT TAB(15); "4. CHANGE THE DATA FOR ONE ITEM NUMBER"
2110 PRINT
2120 PRINT TAB(15); "5. QUIT"
2130 PRINT:PRINT
2140 PRINT TAB(15); "ENTER CHOICE (1 - 5)";
2150 INPUT CHOICE$
2160 LET CHOICE = VAL(CHOICE$)
2170 RETURN
2180 '
```

```
3000 '********** DISPLAY AN ITEM FROM THE FILE ****************
3010 GOSUB 3200                      'INPUT ITEM NUMBER TO DISPLAY
3020 GOSUB 3600                      'LOOK UP ITEM IN INDEX
3030 IF FOUND.SW = 1
        THEN GOSUB 3400
        ELSE GOSUB 3800              'DISPLAY RECORD (OR ERROR MSG)
3040 LET X$ = INPUT$(1)              'HOLD FOR KEYPRESS
3050 RETURN
3060 '
3200 '*********** INPUT ITEM NUMBER TO DISPLAY ****************
3210 CLS
3220 PRINT:PRINT:PRINT
3230 PRINT TAB(30); "DISPLAY AN ITEM FROM THE FILE"
3240 PRINT:PRINT
3250 INPUT "ITEM NUMBER TO DISPLAY"; ITEM
3270 RETURN
3280 '
3400 '****** GET A RECORD AND DISPLAY ON SCREEN ***************
3410 GET #1, POSN
3420 PRINT:PRINT
3430 PRINT TAB(20); "ITEM NUMBER       "; CVS(B.ITEM$)
3440 PRINT
3450 PRINT TAB(20); "ITEM DESCRIPTION  "; B.DESC$
3460 PRINT
3470 PRINT TAB(20); "ITEM PRICE        "; CVS(B.PRICE$)
3480 PRINT:PRINT
3490 RETURN
3500 '
3600 '*********** LOOK UP ITEM NUMBER IN INDEX ****************
3610 LET FOUND.SW = 0               'SET SWITCH FOR NO MATCH FOUND
3620 LET POSN = 0                   'SET TO BEGIN AT START OF INDEX
3630 WHILE POSN < MAX AND FOUND.SW = 0
3640    LET POSN = POSN + 1
3650    IF INDEX(POSN) = ITEM
           THEN LET FOUND.SW = 1  'A MATCH IS FOUND
3660 WEND
3670 RETURN
3680 '
3800 '********** PRINT ERROR MESSAGE ********************
3810 PRINT:PRINT
3820 PRINT "ERROR: THIS ITEM IS NOT IN THE FILE"
3830 LET X$ = INPUT$(1)             'HOLD FOR KEYPRESS
3840 RETURN
3850 '
4000 '*********** ADD A RECORD TO THE FILE ****************
4010 GOSUB 4200                     'INPUT NEW RECORD
4020 GOSUB 3600                     'CHECK INDEX FOR DUPLICATE
4030 IF FOUND.SW = 1
        THEN GOSUB 4800
        ELSE GOSUB 4600             'ADD THE RECORD IF NOT A DUPLICATE
4040 RETURN
4050 '
4200 '************** INPUT THE NEW RECORD ****************
4210 CLS
4220 PRINT:PRINT:PRINT
4230 PRINT TAB(30); "ADD AN ITEM TO THE FILE"
4240 PRINT:PRINT
4250 INPUT "ITEM NUMBER       ", ITEM
4260 PRINT
4270 INPUT "ITEM DESCRIPTION ", DESC$
4280 PRINT
4290 INPUT "ITEM PRICE        ", PRICE
4300 RETURN
4310 '
```

```
4600 '********** FIND THE FIRST EMPTY ENTRY IN THE INDEX ********
4610 LET POSN = 1                    'BEGIN WITH POSITION 1
4620 WHILE INDEX(POSN) <> 0 AND POSN < MAX
4630      LET POSN = POSN + 1        'FIND FIRST ZERO ENTRY IN INDEX
4640 WEND
4650 'POSN POINTS TO EMPTY RECORD POSITION UNLESS FILE IS FULL
4660 IF POSN = MAX AND INDEX(POSN) <> 0
         THEN GOSUB 4900
         ELSE GOSUB 4700            'ADD THE RECORD
4670 RETURN
4680 '
4700 '******** SET UP AND WRITE NEW RECORD *********************
4710 LET INDEX(POSN) = ITEM         'SAVE ITEM NUMBER IN INDEX
4720 LSET B.ITEM$ = MKS$(ITEM)      'SET UP FIELDS IN BUFFER
4730 LSET B.DESC$ = DESC$
4740 LSET B.PRICE$ = MKS$(PRICE)
4750 PUT #1, POSN                   'WRITE THE RECORD IN THE FILE
4760 RETURN
4770 '
4800 '************** ERROR--DUPLICATE KEY FIELD **************
4810 PRINT: PRINT: PRINT
4820 PRINT TAB(15); "ERROR--THIS ITEM NUMBER IS ALREADY IN THE FILE"
4830 LET X$ = INPUT$(1)             'HOLD MESSAGE FOR KEYPRESS
4840 RETURN
4850 '
4900 '************** THE FILE IS FULL ************************
4910 PRINT "ERROR - RECORD CANNOT BE ADDED"
4920 PRINT:PRINT
4930 PRINT "THE FILE IS FULL"
4940 LET X$ = INPUT$(1)             'HOLD MESSAGE FOR KEYPRESS
4950 RETURN
4960 '
5000 '*********** DELETE A RECORD FROM THE FILE **************
5010 GOSUB 5200                     'INPUT ITEM NUMBER TO DELETE
5020 GOSUB 3600                     'LOOK UP ITEM NUMBER IN INDEX
5030 IF FOUND.SW = 1
         THEN GOSUB 5400
         ELSE GOSUB 3800            'DELETE THE RECORD (IF IT EXISTS)
5040 RETURN
5050 '
5200 '*********** INPUT ITEM NUMBER TO DELETE ***************
5210 CLS
5220 PRINT:PRINT:PRINT
5230 PRINT TAB(30); "DELETE AN ITEM FROM THE FILE"
5240 PRINT:PRINT
5250 INPUT "ITEM NUMBER TO DELETE"; ITEM
5270 RETURN
5280 '
5400 '************** DELETE THE RECORD **********************
5410 GOSUB 3400                     'GET RECORD AND DISPLAY ON SCREEN
5420 PRINT TAB(20); "DELETE THIS RECORD (YES TO CONFIRM)";
5430 INPUT ANS$
5440 IF ANS$ = "YES" OR ANS$ = "yes"
         THEN LET INDEX(POSN) = 0
5450 RETURN
5460 '
6000 '********** CHANGE A RECORD IN THE FILE *****************
6010 GOSUB 6200                     'INPUT ITEM NUMBER TO CHANGE
6020 GOSUB 3600                     'LOOK UP ITEM NUMBER IN INDEX
6030 IF FOUND.SW = 1
         THEN GOSUB 6400
         ELSE GOSUB 3800            'CHANGE FIELDS (IF RECORD EXISTS)
6040 RETURN
6050 '
```

```
6200 '*********** INPUT CHANGED DATA ***************************
6210 CLS
6220 PRINT:PRINT:PRINT
6230 PRINT TAB(30); "CHANGE DATA IN THE FILE"
6240 PRINT:PRINT
6250 INPUT "ITEM NUMBER TO CHANGE ", ITEM
6270 RETURN
6280 '
6400 '***************** CHANGE THE DATA *********************
6410 GOSUB 3400                    'DISPLAY THE RECORD
6420 INPUT "NEW DESCRIPTION (PRESS ENTER FOR NO CHANGE) ", DESC$
6430 PRINT:PRINT
6440 INPUT "NEW PRICE (PRESS ENTER FOR NO CHANGE) ", PRICE$
6450 IF DESC$ <> ""
        THEN LSET B.DESC$ = DESC$ 'CHANGE THE DESCRIPTION
6460 IF PRICE$ <> ""
        THEN LSET B.PRICE$ = MKS$(VAL(PRICE$)) 'CHANGE PRICE
6470 PUT #1, POSN                  'REWRITE THE RECORD IN THE FILE
6480 RETURN
6490 '
7000 '*********** REWRITE INDEX ARRAY IN INDEX FILE ***********
7010 OPEN "O", #2, "ITEM.NDX"
7020 FOR SUB = 1 TO MAX
7030    WRITE #2, INDEX(SUB)
7040 NEXT SUB
7050 CLOSE #2
7060 RETURN
7070 '*************** END OF PROGRAM ***********************
```

Sample Program Output

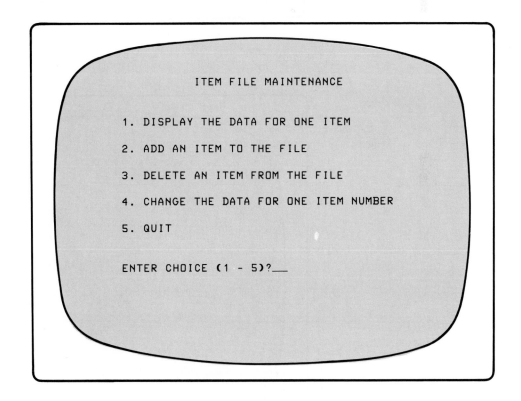

```
                ITEM FILE MAINTENANCE


    1. DISPLAY THE DATA FOR ONE ITEM

    2. ADD AN ITEM TO THE FILE

    3. DELETE AN ITEM FROM THE FILE

    4. CHANGE THE DATA FOR ONE ITEM NUMBER

    5. QUIT


    ENTER CHOICE (1 - 5)?__
```

Choice 1

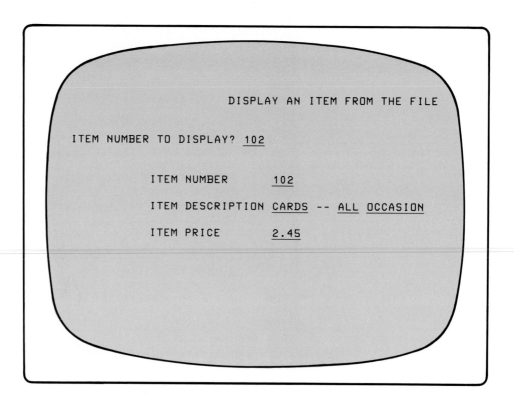

```
                              DISPLAY AN ITEM FROM THE FILE

ITEM NUMBER TO DISPLAY? 102


           ITEM NUMBER        102

           ITEM DESCRIPTION CARDS -- ALL OCCASION

           ITEM PRICE         2.45
```

Choice 2

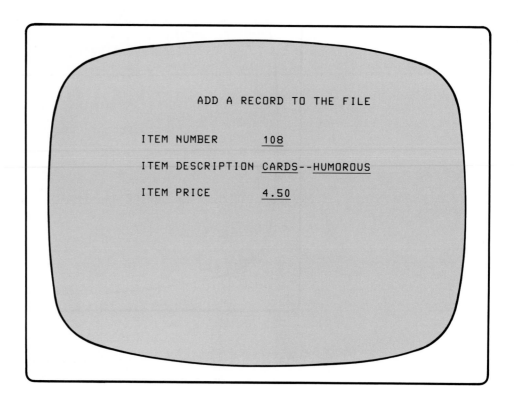

```
                    ADD A RECORD TO THE FILE


           ITEM NUMBER        108

           ITEM DESCRIPTION CARDS--HUMOROUS

           ITEM PRICE         4.50
```

Choice 3

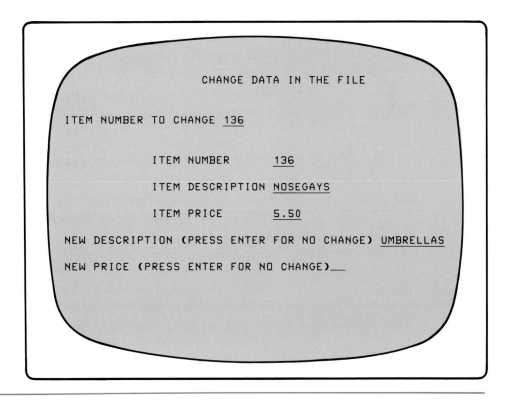

```
                    DELETE A RECORD FROM THE FILE


ITEM NUMBER TO DELETE? 101


              ITEM NUMBER        125

              ITEM DESCRIPTION STATIONERY

              ITEM PRICE         3.25
```

Choice 4

```
                    CHANGE DATA IN THE FILE


ITEM NUMBER TO CHANGE 136


              ITEM NUMBER        136

              ITEM DESCRIPTION NOSEGAYS

              ITEM PRICE         5.50

NEW DESCRIPTION (PRESS ENTER FOR NO CHANGE) UMBRELLAS

NEW PRICE (PRESS ENTER FOR NO CHANGE)___
```

Summary

1. To update a sequential file, an entirely new file must be created.
2. In batch processing, updated transactions are accumulated. Then, the transactions are sorted and all updates are applied in a group.
3. The interactive style of program execution generally used with BASIC programming is not conducive to batch updates.
4. There are two methods of sequential updates that *do* allow for interactive program execution. However, neither should be used on a large file or one needing frequent updates. The two methods are:
   a. For each transaction (add, change, or delete), create an entirely new file.
   b. Read the file into arrays in memory, do all updating in the arrays, and rewrite the file when finished.
5. Files that need frequent updating should be organized as a random file, if possible.
6. When a record key field of a file cannot be used as a relative record number, indexed files may be used.
7. An indexed file actually consists of two files:
   a. A random file for the data records.
   b. An index file, which holds the record keys and their corresponding record number. The index file is generally stored in a sequential file and read into an array at the beginning of any program that accesses the primary file.

Programming Exercises

15.1. *Sequential Update*—Write a program to update the sequential file created by the program in exercise 13.1 (p. 363) (salesperson file). The program must be able to add new salespersons, delete salespersons, or change the data for any salesperson. Fields that may be changed are the name, sales amount, and the commission rate (*not* the salesperson number). Any new salespersons are to be added in order by the salesperson number (the key field). Use the listing program written for exercise 13.1 to verify that all changes are correctly made.

15.2. Combine the two programs written for exercise 13.1 with exercise 15.1 in a menu program, which will create the file, add records, delete records, change records, and list the file.

15.3. Modify the program in exercise 15.1 (or 15.2) to make the change routine easier to operate. After the user has entered the salesperson number of the record to change or delete, display the old data for that person on the screen. For a change, allow the user to accept or change each field (except the key field). For the delete, display a message and allow the user to verify that the correct record is being deleted.

15.4. Modify the program in exercise 15.1 (or 15.2 or 15.3) to include screen formatting. Do not allow any screens to scroll.

15.5. *Sequential Update*—Write a program that will allow changes to be made in the book file created by the program in exercise 13.2 (p. 363). Since the file is in alphabetic order by book title, the title is the key field. The program must allow new books to be added to the file (in sequence), books to be deleted from the file, or the room location of any book to be changed.

15.6. *Sequential Update*—Write a program that will allow changes to be made in the two table files created by the program in exercise 13.3 (p. 364).

PRODUCT TABLE: Products may be added or deleted, or the price of any item may be changed. The table file is in order by item number (and must remain that way).

SALESPERSON TABLE: Salespersons may be added to the table file, deleted from the file, or the name may be changed.

15.7. *Indexed File*—Change the organization of the salesperson file created by the program in exercise 13.1 and updated by the program in exercise 15.1. Use the salesperson number as the key field, and establish an index file for random access.

Use a menu with these choices:
1. Display data for a salesperson
2. Add a salesperson to the file
3. Delete a salesperson from the file
4. Change a salesperson's name
5. Change a sales amount
6. Change a commission rate
7. Quit

15.8. *Indexed File*—Change the organization of the book file from the programs in exercises 13.2 and 15.5 to an indexed file. The key field is the book title. See the program in exercise 15.5 for the update program requirements.

15.9. *Indexed File*—Modify the program in exercise 14.4 (personnel file, p. 395) to create an indexed file. Rather than assign sequential employee numbers as in the program in exercise 14.4, use the employee name as the key field. Follow the specifications shown to include file creation, updating, and listing. Additionally, include an option to add an employee to the file.

15.10. The Perfect Picture Company has had some problems with customers who write bad checks. The area office has sent out a list of customers who have written bad checks, so that the sales clerks will not accept any more checks from those people. Write a program to create an indexed file to aid the credit checking. Use the customer last name as the record key.

MENU CHOICES
1. *Check credit for a customer*—Input the customer last name. Display a list of all customers in the file with that last name. If that name is not on file, print a message to that effect.
2. *Display the file*—Display the entire file on the screen. Be sure to hold the screen for a keypress, so that names do not scroll by too quickly to be read.
3. *Add a customer to the file*—Input last and first name, placement date, check date, and check number from the keyboard. Add the customer to the file.
4. *Delete a customer from the file*—Input the last and first name from the keyboard. Display the entire record on the screen and ask the clerk to verify the delete.
5. *Change customer information*—Input the customer last name. Display the data on the screen and allow the user to change fields.
6. *Quit.*

TEST DATA:

Last Name	First Name	Placement Date	Check Date	Check No.
Jones	Ray	2–14–88	2–5–88	121
Smith	Andy	3–21–88	3–2–88	83
Brown	Barbara	5–8–88	5–1–88	301

16 Color and Pixel Graphics

Upon completion of this chapter, you should be able to:

1. Differentiate between low-resolution, medium-resolution, and high-resolution graphics.
2. Control the colors on the display screen.
3. Draw points, lines, circles, and other shapes, using the special graphics commands in medium- and high-resolution graphics.
4. Use graphics to draw line charts, bar charts, and pie charts.
5. Scale graphs to world coordinates.
6. Save and reload graphic images.

Introduction to Graphics

Computer graphics may be undertaken strictly for fun or to make program output more understandable. Businesses use graphics to convert columns of numbers into meaningful visual displays as line graphs, bar charts, and pie charts.

Microsoft BASIC offers several modes for displaying graphics. Each mode has its own distinct rules, statements, advantages, and disadvantages. The choices are also expanded by the possible hardware configurations. The graphics capabilities of computers vary greatly, depending on the display adapter installed and the monitor type in use. In release 3.2 of Microsoft BASIC, the number of graphics modes was increased from three to seven, with the addition of four modes designed to take advantage of enhanced color hardware. Table 16.1 shows the seven graphics modes.

Table 16.1.
Graphics modes.

Three standard modes for standard color hardware and BASIC prior to release 3.2.

	Low Resolution (Text)	Medium Resolution	High Resolution
Screen mode	0	1	2
Resolution	80 Horizontal 25 Vertical or 40 Horizontal 25 Vertical	320 Horizontal 200 Vertical	640 Horizontal 200 Vertical
Color	16 Foreground 8 Background 16 Border	4 at a time from 1 of 2 sets called palettes	None

Four additional modes for enhanced hardware and BASIC release 3.2.

	Medium Resolution	High Resolution	Enhanced High Resolution	Monochrome High Resolution
Screen mode	7	8	9	10
Resolution	320 Horizontal 200 Vertical	640 Horizontal 200 Vertical	640 Horizontal 350 Vertical	640 Horizontal 350 Vertical
Color	16	16	16 (at one time from a choice of 64)	None

Overview of the Four Screen Resolutions for Graphics

The diagram in figure 16.1 shows the four screen resolutions available for graphics.

Low-Resolution or Text Mode Graphics

The normal operating mode of the video display terminal (VDT) is text mode. Each position on the screen (40 or 80 characters by 25 lines) may display any one of the printable ASCII characters. Pictures and graphs may be drawn using letters, digits, special characters (such as * ! # ?), or with additional graphics characters referred to as the IBM extended graphics symbols.

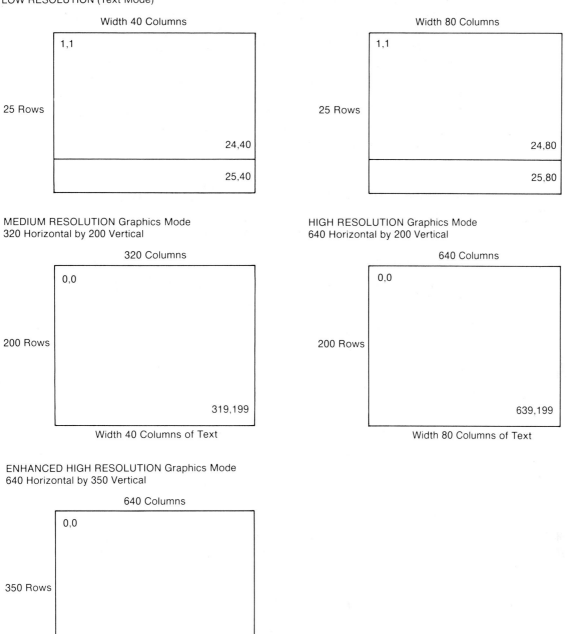

LOW RESOLUTION (Text Mode)

Width 40 Columns

1,1

25 Rows

24,40

25,40

Width 80 Columns

1,1

25 Rows

24,80

25,80

MEDIUM RESOLUTION Graphics Mode
320 Horizontal by 200 Vertical

320 Columns

0,0

200 Rows

319,199

Width 40 Columns of Text

HIGH RESOLUTION Graphics Mode
640 Horizontal by 200 Vertical

640 Columns

0,0

200 Rows

639,199

Width 80 Columns of Text

ENHANCED HIGH RESOLUTION Graphics Mode
640 Horizontal by 350 Vertical

640 Columns

0,0

350 Rows

639,349

Width 40 Columns of Text

Figure 16.1
The four screen resolutions available for graphics.

The COLOR statement may be used to display text characters in sixteen colors, the background in any of eight colors, and the screen border in any of eight colors. The COLOR statement may also be used on color or black-and-white monitors to provide reverse image, underlining, high-intensity, and blinking characters.

Note: The screen border is sometimes called the overscan area. It appears around the edges of the screen area used for text. No border area is available on EGA hardware.

Medium-Resolution Graphics

In medium **resolution** graphics, the screen is divided into small blocks called **pixels** (for picture elements). There are 320 horizontal positions and 200 vertical positions on the screen. The increased number of picture elements provides for greater picture quality through higher resolution, at the cost of color choices. With standard color hardware and medium-resolution graphics, only four different colors may be used on the screen at any one time.

Several new BASIC statements are available to draw points, lines, circles, arcs, and boxes. These statements are available in black-and-white as well as in color.

High-Resolution Graphics

High resolution provides twice as many pixels on the screen (640 horizontal by 200 vertical) at the cost of color. Unless you are using *enhanced* color hardware, you will be limited to black and white even on a standard color monitor. High-resolution pictures consist of more dots than those drawn with medium resolution and can therefore have smoother curves and rounder circles. Most of the graphics statements available in medium-resolution mode are also available in high resolution, with the notable exception of the color commands.

Enhanced High-Resolution Graphics

With the proper hardware (EGA adapter, enhanced color monitor with switch set for 350 rows), a fourth resolution mode is possible. See figure 16.1 for a diagram that shows the highest resolution possible for Microsoft BASIC graphics.

Software Requirements for Graphics

To do either medium- or high-resolution graphics, the advanced version of Microsoft BASIC is needed. On an IBM computer, load BASICA. On compatible computers, use GWBASIC (i.e., Gee Whiz). The additional graphics modes to support enhanced graphics hardware are found in release 3.2 or later.

Hardware Requirements for Graphics

For computers with the monochrome display adapter (MDA) and monochrome monitor, the only graphics possible are low-resolution text graphics. A monochrome monitor with a Hercules Graphics Adapter is capable of producing all three types of graphics, but without color. To get the full effect of all graphics commands requires a color monitor and either a color graphics adapter (CGA) or an enhanced graphics adapter (EGA). The hardware requirements are summarized in table 16.2.

Printing Graphics Images

Medium- and high-resolution graphics are intended for the screen. In these modes the Shift-PrtSc key combination will not transfer a graphics image to the printer unless a special DOS utility program has been executed *before* loading BASICA. With the DOS master diskette in the A: drive, type

```
A>GRAPHICS
A>BASICA
```

When the GRAPHICS program has been executed before BASICA, the Shift-PrtSc key combination will send the graphics images to the printer correctly.

Note: These commands are for the IBM-PC and compatible dot matrix printers. Many other computers and printers have similar utilities.

Table 16.2.
Hardware requirements for graphics.

Display Adapter	Monitor	Graphics Possible	Screen Mode
Monochrome (MDA)	Monochrome	Low-res text only	0
Hercules graphics	Monochrome	Low-res, medium-res, high-res (no color)	0,1,2
Color graphics adapter (CGA)	Composite black-and-white	Low-res, medium-res, high-res (no color	0,1,2
Color graphics adapter (CGA)	Standard color	Low-res or medium-res (with color), or high-res	0,1,2
Enhanced graphics adapter (EGA)	Standard color	Low-res, medium-res, or high-res	0,1,2, 7,8
Enhanced graphics adapter (EGA)	Enhanced color	Low-res, medium-res, or high-res	0,1,2 7,8,9
Enhanced graphics adapter (EGA)	Monochrome	Low-res, medium-res, or high-res (no color)	0,10

Low-Resolution, Text Mode Graphics— Screen Mode 0

Low-resolution graphics are also called text or block graphics. These are the only graphics possible on a computer with a monochrome display adapter and screen. Text graphics are drawn with symbols such as letters, digits, and special characters. Some elementary text graphics were presented in chapter 8. You will recall that there are twenty-four lines on the screen, plus the twenty-fifth line that may be used after KEY OFF is executed. Each line may consist of either forty or eighty characters, depending on the setting of the width (WIDTH 40 or WIDTH 80).

Each character is drawn with dots in a block that is eight dots wide by eight dots tall. The dots that form the character itself are called the **foreground.** The dots surrounding the character are called the **background.**

Color Graphics

With a color monitor and a color graphics adapter (CGA), beautiful things are possible. The foreground may be displayed in any of sixteen colors, the background in any of eight colors, and the border (area around the edge of the screen) in any of sixteen colors. Additionally, the foreground characters can be made to blink, for a total of thirty-two possible color choices. Table 16.3 shows these thirty-two color possibilities.

Some experimentation is necessary to select the best color combination for any task. The actual colors and intensities will vary depending on the display adapter, the monitor, and its adjustment, and may not match the names given. The border area does not display on monochrome or EGA monitors. You may want to try different combinations to find those most pleasing to you.

Use the COLOR statement to select the colors to display. You may select any of the thirty-two color choices shown in table 16.3 for the foreground. You may choose colors 0–7 for the background, and colors 0–15 for the border.

Table 16.3.
Color available in low-resolution text mode.

Color Number	Color	Color Number	Color
0	Black	16	Blinking black
1	Blue	17	Blinking blue
2	Green	18	Blinking green
3	Cyan	19	Blinking cyan
4	Red	20	Blinking red
5	Magenta	21	Blinking magenta
6	Brown	22	Blinking brown
7	White	23	Blinking white
8	Gray	24	Blinking gray
9	Light blue	25	Blinking light blue
10	Light green	26	Blinking light green
11	Light cyan	27	Blinking light cyan
12	Light red	28	Blinking light red
13	Light magenta	29	Blinking light magenta
14	Yellow	30	Blinking yellow
15	High-intensity white	31	Blinking high-intensity white

The COLOR Statement in Low-Resolution, Text Mode—General Form

line number   COLOR   [Foreground][,[Background][,Border]]

When any parameter is omitted that selection will remain unchanged.

The COLOR Statement in Low-Resolution, Text Mode—Examples

```
100   COLOR 7,0      'White characters on black background
200   COLOR 15,1     'High-intensity white on blue background
300   COLOR 4        'Red characters, unchanged background
400   COLOR ,3       'Unchanged foreground, cyan background
500   COLOR ,,2      'Unchanged foreground and background,
                      green border
600   COLOR 0,7      'Reverse image, black characters on
                      white background
```

Example Program: Display Any Color Combination

Program Listing

```
100 ' Demonstrate COLOR statement
102 ' Select any color combinations
104 '
110 CLS:KEY OFF                          'Clean screen
120 INPUT "Foreground color (0-31)"; FOREGROUND
130 WHILE FOREGROUND >= 0 AND FOREGROUND <= 31
140     INPUT "Background color (0 - 7)"; BACKGROUND
150     INPUT "Border color (0 - 15)"; BORDER
160     COLOR FOREGROUND,BACKGROUND,BORDER
170     LOCATE 12,25
180     PRINT STRING$(5,254); " This is it "; STRING$(5,254)
190     LOCATE 1
200     INPUT "Foreground color (0-31, any other number to quit)";FOREGROUND
210 WEND
215 COLOR 7,0                            'Return to white on black
220 END
```

Program Output

You must try this one for yourself.

It seems that some versions of BASIC are capable of some additional color choices that are not documented in the manual. You may want to experiment with undocumented color choices outside the ranges listed. What happens when a background color greater than seven is selected?

The Bar Chart Program Revisited

With the addition of color, the bar chart program from chapter 8 can be upgraded to be more visually pleasing. We have added scaling to the program, so that the chart will fill the screen even with very large or small numbers.

Example Program: A Bar Graph Using Graphic Text Characters

Program Listing

```
100 ' Program to print a bar chart, using graphic text characters
110 '
120 '                     Program Variables
130 '   PIC$                 Character used to print bars for chart
140 '   MONTH$               Names of months, from DATA list
150 '   HOWMANY              Number of hamburgers sold for each month
160 '   COUNT                Counter for loops
170 '   MAXSALES             Highest value to graph
180 '   SCALEFACTOR          Ratio to fit values on screen
190 '
500 ' *********************** MAINLINE ***************************
510 GOSUB 600                   'INITIALIZE
520 GOSUB 800                   'PRINT HEADING
530 GOSUB 1000                  'PRINT DETAIL DATA
540 GOSUB 1200                  'PRINT SCALE
550 END
600 ' *********************** INITIALIZE ***************************
610 LET PIC$ = CHR$(219)        'CHARACTER TO USE FOR BARS
620 LET MAXSALES = -1
630 READ MONTH$,HOWMANY         'READ DATA LIST
640 WHILE MONTH$ <> "END"       '  TO FIND MAXIMUM DATA VALUE
650     IF HOWMANY > MAXSALES
            THEN LET MAXSALES = HOWMANY
660     READ MONTH$,HOWMANY
670 WEND
680 LET SCALEFACTOR = MAXSALES/70 'SCALE TO 70 CHARACTERS ON SCREEN
690 RESTORE                      'RESET DATA POINTER
700 RETURN
```

```
800 ' ************************* PRINT HEADING ****************************
810 CLS: KEY OFF                      'CLEAN SCREEN
820 LOCATE 4,25: PRINT "HAMBURGER SALES"
830 PRINT:PRINT:PRINT
840 RETURN
1000 ' ********************** PRINT A BAR CHART **********************
1010 READ MONTH$, HOWMANY
1020 WHILE MONTH$ <> "END"
1024     LET PRETTY = PRETTY + 1            'CHOOSE THE NEXT COLOR
1025     COLOR PRETTY                       'SET COLOR FOR NEXT LINE
1030     PRINT MONTH$; TAB(10)
1040     FOR COUNT = 1 TO INT(HOWMANY / SCALEFACTOR +.5)
1050       PRINT PIC$;                      'PRINT THE BAR
1060     NEXT COUNT
1070     PRINT:PRINT
1080     READ MONTH$, HOWMANY
1090 WEND
1100 RETURN
1200 ' ********************** PRINT SCALE ***************************
1205 COLOR 7,0                        'RETURN TO BLACK & WHITE
1210 PRINT TAB(9);CHR$(179);          'START SCALE LINE
1220 FOR COUNT = 1 TO 10
1230     PRINT STRING$(6,196);CHR$(179); 'SEGMENTS OF LINE
1240 NEXT COUNT
1250 PRINT TAB(3);
1260 FOR COUNT = 0 TO MAXSALES STEP MAXSALES/10
1270     PRINT USING "  #####"; COUNT;      'PRINT NUMBERS
1280 NEXT COUNT
1290 RETURN
1300 ' ****************** DATA FOR HAMBURGER SALES *******************
1310 DATA JUNE,250,JULY,500,AUGUST,450,SEPTEMBER,200,END,0
1320 '**************** END OF DATA ****************************
```

Program Output

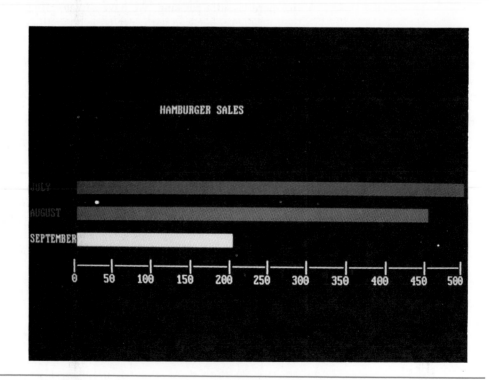

Switching Between Modes—The SCREEN Statement

The SCREEN statement is used to switch between low-resolution, medium-resolution, and high-resolution modes. Until this point, the SCREEN statement was unnecessary, since low-resolution text mode is the default. From this point on, we will always include a SCREEN statement in each graphics program.

The SCREEN statement does several things: It sets the mode, clears any prior COLOR statements, and clears the screen.

The SCREEN Statement—General Form

```
line number   SCREEN   Mode [,Colorburst]
```

The values for mode are:

0 = Low-Resolution Text Mode
(width 40 or 80)
up to 16 colors
1 = Medium-Resolution Mode
(320 × 200)
4 colors at one time
2 = High-Resolution Mode
(640 × 200)
no color

Note: The rest of the Modes require an EGA display adapter and BASIC 3.2 or later.

7 = Medium-Resolution Mode
(320 × 200)
with up to 16 colors
8 = High-Resolution Mode
(640 × 200)
with up to 16 colors
9 = Enhanced High-Resolution Mode
(640 × 350)
with up to 16 colors
10 = Monochrome graphics
(640 × 350)
on a monochrome monitor with an EGA adapter

Colorburst is an expression designed to turn color on or off for composite monitors. The effects vary with the type of monitor and display adapter in use and the graphics mode selected. In Text Mode, a zero value disables color, and a nonzero value enables color. In Medium Resolution, the effects are reversed: A zero value should enable color, and a nonzero value disable color. In reality, for most hardware configurations, Colorburst has no effect and can be ignored.

The SCREEN Statement—Examples

```
100 SCREEN  0        'Switch to Text Mode
200 SCREEN  1,0      'Switch to Medium-Resolution Mode,
                        colors enabled
300 SCREEN  1,1      'Switch to Medium-Resolution Mode,
                        colors disabled (on some monitors)
400 SCREEN  2        'Switch to High-Resolution Mode
500 SCREEN  7        'Switch to Medium-Resolution Mode,
                        full color, EGA hardware only
600 SCREEN  8        'Switch to High-Resolution Mode
                        full color, EGA hardware only
```

Medium-Resolution Graphics— Screen Mode 1

In medium resolution graphics (Screen Mode 1), the number of pixels (picture elements) on the screen is increased to 320 horizontal by 200 vertical. The price we must pay for the increased detail is the loss of some color choices. The LOCATE and PRINT statements may also be used to mix text and graphics. Any characters printed will appear in width 40.

Color in Medium Resolution— Screen Mode 1

Only four different colors may be displayed on the screen at any one time. The colors are chosen from one of two sets, called palettes (like the artist's palette). For each palette, you select the background color, and the other three colors are fixed. After you have chosen the palette (with the COLOR statement), subsequent plotting instructions select the color from the palette. Table 16.4 shows the two palettes and their color choices.

The format and use of the COLOR statement is different in Medium Resolution than in Text Mode. COLOR selects the background color and the palette (0 or 1).

The COLOR Statement in Medium Resolution Mode—General Form

```
line number   COLOR   [Background][,[Palette]]
```

The choices for Background are any color 0–15. Palette should have a value of 0 or 1, however any even number will select palette zero, and any odd number will select palette one.

When any parameter is omitted, that selection will remain unchanged.

The COLOR Statement in Medium Resolution Mode—Examples

```
150   COLOR 0,0    'Select background black, palette zero
                    (green, red, and brown)
250   COLOR 9,0    'Select background light blue, palette
                    zero (green, red, and brown)
350   COLOR ,1     'Leave the background unchanged select
                    palette one (cyan, magenta, white)
450   COLOR 0      'Change background to black, leaving
                    palette unchanged
550   COLOR 14,1   'Select background yellow, palette one
                    (cyan, magenta, white)
```

If color plotting is desired, the COLOR statement must be executed prior to any of the plotting instructions such as PSET, LINE, and CIRCLE. When CLS is executed after a COLOR statement, the entire screen will change to the background color. An interesting phenomenon occurs when a COLOR statement changes the palette after colors have already been plotted on the screen: The entire screen changes to the new palette. Green becomes cyan, red becomes magenta, brown becomes white, and the new background color replaces the old.

Table 16.4.
Two palette choices in medium-resolution mode.

Palette color	Palette 0	Palette color	Palette 1
0	Background (any color 0–15)	0	Background (any color 0–15)
1	Green	1	Cyan
2	Red	2	Magenta
3	Brown	3	White

After specifying a color palette, we will want to draw on the screen. We will look at three instructions to draw—PSET (for Point Set), LINE, and CIRCLE. Each of these statements specifies a screen location with two numbers called coordinates. The first coordinate is the horizontal position across the screen, generally referred to as X, which may be any number from 0 to 319. The second coordinate is the vertical position down the screen, called Y, which ranges from 0 to 199. Therefore the upper left corner of the screen is position 0,0, and the lower right corner is position 319,199.

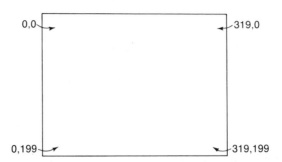

Plotting Points—The PSET and PRESET Statements

The PSET, or Point Set, instruction is used to turn on or off individual pixels on the screen. In addition, each point may be set to any of the four colors on the current palette. PRESET resets the point and can be used to erase a point.

The instruction:

```
200 PSET (50,100)
```

turns on the point at horizontal (X) position 50 and vertical (Y) position 100.

To plot points in color, be sure to place a COLOR statement before the first PSET statement. The statements

```
300 SCREEN 1
310 COLOR 0,0
320 PSET (120,10),2
```

turn on medium resolution graphics, set the background color to 0 (black), select palette 0 (green, red, brown), and then plot a point in red (palette color 2) at horizontal (X) position 120 and vertical (Y) position 10.

The PSET and PRESET Statements—General Form

```
line number   PSET (X, Y) [, Palette.color]
line number   PRESET (X, Y) [, Palette.color]
```

The value for X is the horizontal position across the line (0–319 for medium resolution, 0–639 for high resolution). The value for Y is the vertical position down the screen (0 to 199). The Palette.color option refers to the four possible choices on the previously selected palette, and must have a value 0–3. Omitting the Palette.color parameter has different effects depending on whether a COLOR statement was previously executed. If no COLOR statement precedes the PSET statement, the point will be plotted in white on black. If a palette has been selected with a COLOR statement, and the Palette.color parameter is omitted, the point will be plotted in Palette.color 3.

A point may be erased with either the PSET or the PRESET statement. If Palette.color 0 is selected on a PSET statement, the point will be plotted in the background color, effectively erasing the point. PRESET automatically resets the point to the background color.

```
550  PSET (0, 0) 'Plot a point in the upper left corner
650  PSET (ACROSS, DOWN) ,2           'Plot a point in
                                       Palette.Color 2
700  PRESET (ACROSS, DOWN)            'Erase the point
                                       plotted in line 650
750  PSET (LEFT+OFFSET, TOP+OFFSET) 'Plot a point at the
                                       location calculated
```

Example Program: Plotting Points

Program Listing

Can you tell what this program will do? Try it to see.

```
200 ' Program to plot points
205 '
210 SCREEN 1                         'MEDIUM RESOLUTION
220 COLOR 0,1                        'BACKGROUND BLACK, PALETTE 1
230 CLS:KEY OFF                      'CLEAN SCREEN
235 LOCATE 1,1
240 INPUT "Horizontal position (0 - 319): ", HORIZ
250 INPUT "Vertical position (0 - 199): ", VERT
260 PSET (HORIZ,VERT), 1             'PLOT POINT IN COLOR 1 - CYAN
270 END
```

Using Relative Coordinates

We have been plotting points with their absolute screen coordinates, without regard for the last point plotted. Rather than specify the location for each point with its X and Y screen coordinates, we can instead specify a relative position—how far from the last point plotted. Adding STEP to the PSET command changes the coordinates to relative. The statement

```
265 PSET STEP (5, 2), 1
```

plots a point five pixels to the right and two pixels down from the last point plotted, in Palette.color 1.

Example Program: Plotting Points with Relative Coordinates

Program Listing

```
200 ' Program to plot points using STEP for relative position
210 '
220 SCREEN 1                         'MEDIUM RESOLUTION
230 CLS:KEY OFF                      'CLEAN SCREEN
240 PSET (0,200)                     'SET INITIAL POINT IN LOWER LEFT CORNER
250 FOR COUNT = 1 TO 200
260    PSET STEP (2, -1)             'EACH POINT RIGHT BY 2, UP BY 1
270 NEXT COUNT
280 END
```

Program Output

Drawing Lines

We can draw lines on the screen by plotting individual points. But a much easier method exists. The LINE statement draws a line from one screen point to another—in color or black and white. The statement

```
300 LINE (0,0) - (100,100)
```

draws a line from point 0,0 (upper left corner) to point 100,100 (100 pixels over, 100 pixels down). Adding color to the statements

```
200 SCREEN 1
210 COLOR 9,0
220 LINE (0,0) - (100,100), 1
```

draws the line in green (Palette.color 1) on a light blue background.

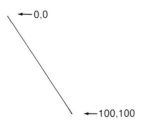

You may also use the LINE statement to draw boxes, solid or open. When "B" is specified, BASIC uses the two coordinates as corners for a box. And including "BF" makes the Box Filled with the same color used for plotting.

```
400 SCREEN 1                        'MEDIUM RESOLUTION
410 CLS: KEY OFF                    'CLEAN SCREEN
420 COLOR 0,1                       'SELECT PALETTE
430 LINE (20,10) - (30,25), 1, BF   'DRAW A FILLED BOX
```

These statements will draw a solid filled box with upper left corner at position 10,10 and lower right corner at position 20,50. Can you tell what color the box will be? Note that when you omit the color parameter, two commas are required:

```
430 LINE (10,10) - (20,50),,BF 'DRAW A FILLED BOX
```

The LINE Statement—General Form

| line number   LINE   [(X.Start, Y.Start)] - (X.End, Y.End) [,[Palette.color] [,B [F]]] |

X.Start and Y.Start specify the coordinates for the beginning of the line; X.End and Y.End specify the coordinates for the point at the end of the line. The X coordinates may range from 0 to 319 in medium resolution (0–639 in high resolution). The Y coordinates range from 0 to 199.

The LINE Statement—Examples

```
125   LINE (0,0) - (100,100)          'Draw a diagonal line
225   LINE (X,Y) - (X+10, Y+15) , 3, B 'Draw an open box
325   LINE (X.PT, Y.PT) - (X.PT - 20, Y.PT - 12)
425   LINE - (NEW.X, NEW.Y), 1        'Draw from the last
                                       point referenced to
                                       a new point
525   LINE (10,10) - (200,100),,BF 'Draw a solid box in
                                       default color
```

Connecting Lines

A line may be drawn from the last point plotted to a new location without specifying the starting location.

```
450 LINE - (60,80)
```

draws a line from the last point plotted to a new point at position 60,80.

Drawing Circles

The circle statement can be used to draw circles, ellipses, or arcs. To draw a circle, you must specify the center point and the radius in pixels. Optionally, you may also specify a color for the circle. The statement

```
300 CIRCLE (160,100),50,2
```

draws a circle with its center point at 160,100 (center of the screen in medium resolution), radius of 50 pixels across, in Palette.color 2. Note that BASIC will adjust for the shape of the pixels and make the circle round. So a radius of 50 will produce a circle 100 pixels wide and fewer pixels vertically, depending on the resolution chosen.

CIRCLE may also be specified with relative coordinates as described in the PSET statement. The statement:

```
400 CIRCLE STEP (5,10), 50
```

draws a circle with its center five pixels to the right and ten pixels down from the last point referenced. When a circle is drawn, BASIC treats the center of the circle as the last point referenced.

Example Program: The Step Option

Example Listing

```
400 ' Draw two circles, illustrating the STEP option
410 SCREEN 1: CLS: KEY OFF          'CLEAN SCREEN
420 CIRCLE (160,100), 50
430 CIRCLE STEP (5,10), 50
```

Program Output

Drawing Arcs of a Circle

You may also use the CIRCLE statement to draw parts of a circle, by specifying the beginning and ending points of the arc. The endpoints for the arc are determined by a measurement in radians counterclockwise from the 0 or 2 PI point. The angle reference is illustrated in the following figure.

The statements

```
480 SCREEN 1
490 LET PI = 3.141593
500 CIRCLE (160,100), 50, 2, 0, PI
```

draw the top half of a circle, beginning at the right side (angle 0) and proceeding over the top to the left side (angle PI). The arc will be drawn in Palette.color 2, with a radius of 50 pixels.

Another parameter on the CIRCLE statement changes the aspect ratio and can be used to draw ellipses and elliptical arcs. The aspect ratio refers to the comparative length of a radius drawn on the horizontal to a radius drawn vertically. When this parameter is omitted, the aspect ratio is assumed to be 1, and the figure drawn is a circle. When the aspect ratio is less than 1, the elliptical figure will be wider than it is tall on the screen. When the aspect ratio is greater than 1, the ellipse will display on the screen taller than it is wide.

Example Program: Three Figures

Program Listing

```
100 'Draw three figures with different aspect ratios
110 SCREEN 1: CLS: KEY OFF          'MEDIUM RESOLUTION CLEAN SCREEN
120 CIRCLE (100,50), 20             'CIRCLE
130 CIRCLE (150,50), 20,,,, .5      'ELLIPSE
140 CIRCLE (200,50), 20,,,, 1.5     'ELLIPSE
```

Program Output

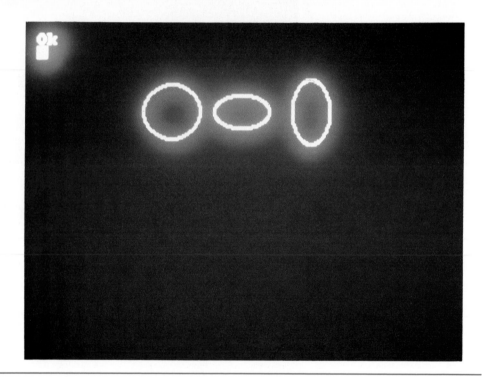

Example Program: Shapes Drawn with CIRCLE

Program Listing

```
100 ' Program to display a Happy Face, using the CIRCLE statement
110 '
200 SCREEN 1:CLS:KEY OFF              'SET UP SCREEN IN MEDIUM RES
210 LET PI = 3.141593                'DEFINE CONSTANT
220 CIRCLE (160,100),60              'DRAW OUTER CIRCLE
230 CIRCLE (160,100),40,,PI*1.2,PI*1.8  'DRAW MOUTH
240 CIRCLE (140,90),5                'DRAW LEFT EYE
250 CIRCLE (180,90),5                'DRAW RIGHT EYE
```

Program Output

Segments of a Pie

An arc may be drawn with its endpoints connected to the center of the circle, creating a slice of pie. If the endpoint is given as a negative number, a radius will be drawn from the end point to the center point.

> *Note:* The minus sign preceding the end point is strictly to specify the radius, *not* to indicate a negative *angle*.

Example Program: Pie Segment

Program Listing

```
500 SCREEN 1: CLS: KEY OFF
505 LET PI = 3.141593
510 CIRCLE (50,100), 30,, -PI/2, -PI
```

These pie segments can be used to create pie charts.

Example Program: Pie Chart

Program Listing

```
100 ' A Piece of Pie
110 SCREEN 1: CLS: KEY OFF        'MEDIUM RESOLUTION, CLEAN SCREEN
120 LET PI = 3.141593
130 CIRCLE (160,100), 20,, -PI/2, -2*PI
140 CIRCLE STEP (5, -4), 20,, -2*PI, -PI/2
```

Program Output

Combining plotting instructions and LOCATE and PRINT can produce a chart with labels and legends.

Example Program: Labeled Pie Chart

Program Listing

```
100 ' A Piece of Pie
110 SCREEN 1: CLS: KEY OFF      'MEDIUM RESOLUTION, CLEAN SCREEN
120 LET PI = 3.141593
130 CIRCLE (160,100), 20,, -PI/2, -2*PI
140 CIRCLE STEP (5, -4), 20,, -2*PI, -PI/2
150 LOCATE 14, 10
160 PRINT "HOUSING";
170 LOCATE 11, 25
180 PRINT "FOOD";
190 LOCATE 24
200 END
```

Program Output

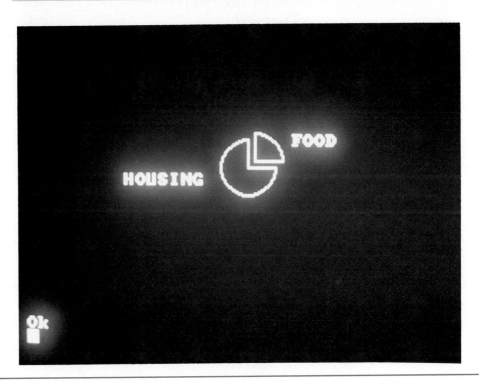

The CIRCLE Statement—General Form

> line number CIRCLE (X, Y), Radius [, Palette.color
> [, Start.angle, End.angle [,Aspect.ratio]]]

X and Y specify the coordinates of the center of the circle, and Radius defines the radius in pixels on the horizontal axis. The Palette.color chooses a color from a previously selected palette, and may be 0–3. If Palette.color is omitted, the circle will be drawn in Palette.color 3 when a COLOR statement has been executed, or in white if not.

If Start.angle and End.angle are included, an arc will be drawn. Negative numbers for the angles will link the ends of the arc to the center of the circle.

The Aspect.ratio determines the shape of the figure drawn.

The CIRCLE Statement—Examples

```
400 CIRCLE (10, 20), 5   'Circle with center on 10,20 with
                             a radius of 5 pixels
450  CIRCLE (X, Y), RADIUS, COLOR, P.START, P.END, SHAPE
500  CIRCLE (X, Y), 100, 2, 0, PI/2  'Plot an arc with a
                                  radius of 100
```

Painting the Figures

After you have drawn figures on the screen, you may fill them with the PAINT statement. PAINT specifies a point within the figure to fill, the color to use, and the color that forms the boundary for filling. Carefully choose the correct boundary, and do not have any breaks in the boundary —otherwise, the color will "bleed" into other figures, and may fill the entire screen.

The PAINT Statement—General Form

```
line number   PAINT (X, Y)   [[, Fill.color][,Boundary.color]]
```

Both Fill.color and Boundary.color must be chosen from the current palette. The coordinates X and Y specify a point *within* the figure to fill. (Do not specify a point that is *on* the boundary.) If the Fill.color is omitted, it will default to the foreground color. PAINT may also be used to draw solid shapes in black and white.

The PAINT Statement—Examples

```
200 PAINT (10, 20)      'Paint with the default, foreground color
250 PAINT (X, Y), 1, 2  'Paint with Palette.color 1, the
                         figure formed with color 2
```

Example Program: Using PAINT to Fill Shapes

Program Listing

```
100  ' Program to demonstrate the use of PAINT
110  '    It draws circles and boxes, then fills them with color
120  '
130 SCREEN 1: KEY OFF            'MEDIUM RESOLUTION CLEAN SCREEN
140 COLOR 9,0:CLS                'YELLOW BACKGROUND, PALETTE 0
150 ' ********************* DRAW THE FIGURES  *********************
160 LET X.CORNER = 10
170 LET Y.CORNER = 10
180 FOR FIGURE = 1 TO 3          'DRAW THREE FIGURES
190                              'DRAW A BROWN CIRCLE
200    CIRCLE (X.CORNER + 30, Y.CORNER + 25), 25, 3
210                              'DRAW A GREEN BOX AROUND THE CIRCLE
220    LINE (X.CORNER, Y.CORNER) -(X.CORNER + 60, Y.CORNER + 50), 1, B
230    LET X.CORNER = X.CORNER + 100
240 NEXT FIGURE
250 LINE (1,1) - (278, 68),2,B 'DRAW A RED BOX AROUND ALL THREE FIGURES
260 LOCATE 23                    'MOVE THE CURSOR OUT OF THE WAY
270 LET PAUSE$ = INPUT$(1)       'PAUSE TO SEE OPEN FIGURES ON SCREEN
```

```
280 ' ********************** PAINT THE FIGURES **************************
290 ' Use a point within the first circle, using a boundary of brown
300 PAINT (40, 35), 2, 3          'PAINT THE CIRCLE RED
310 ' Use a point within the second circle, but a boundary of green
320 PAINT (140, 35), 2, 1         'PAINT THE SQUARE RED
325 ' Use a point within the third circle, but a boundary of red
330 PAINT (240, 35), 1, 2         'PAINT THE ENTIRE OUTER BOX WITH GREEN,
340 '                              UP TO ALL RED BOUNDARIES AROUND THE
350 '                              FILLED CIRCLE AND SQUARE
360 END
```

Program Output

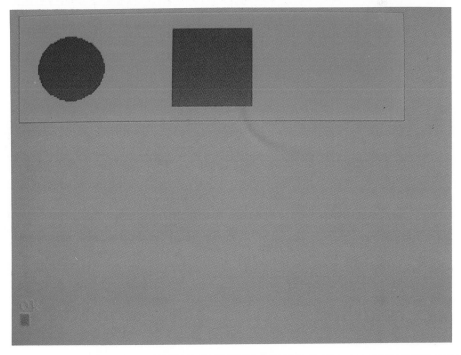

Clipping

What would happen if you drew a circle so close to the edge of the screen that the entire circle would not fit? In many programming languages and other versions of BASIC, the picture will "wrap around" to the opposite edge of the screen, producing some strange-looking results. In Microsoft BASIC, the graphics image is "clipped" so that any points beyond the limits of the screen will not appear. **Clipping** is done automatically by BASIC for any graphics image (not just circles).

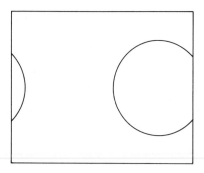

Circle "Wrapped"

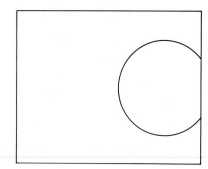

Circle "Clipped"

World Coordinates— Scaling the Screen to Fit the Numbers at Hand

When we wish to plot graphs on the screen, seldom do our values fit neatly in the ranges allotted (0–320 horizontal by 0–199 vertical). Converting from the numbers we have to the screen coordinates requires some mathematics. Fortunately, Microsoft BASIC has given us a tool that performs the necessary calculations with ease. We refer to the values to plot as the **world coordinates**, or their location in the "real" world. The world coordinates are mapped to screen coordinates by the WINDOW statement.

The WINDOW Statement— General Form

```
line number   WINDOW   (W.left, W.top) - (W.right, W.bottom)
```

The first set of numbers gives the world coordinates to assign to the top left corner of the screen. The second set of numbers defines the coordinates of the lower right corner.

The WINDOW Statement—Examples

```
400 WINDOW (0, 0) - (100, 100) 'Redefines screen to 100 x 100
500 WINDOW (-20, 15) - (20, -15) 'Places 0,0 at the center
                       of the screen with positive values up
                       and to the right, negative values down
                       and to the left
```

After execution of the WINDOW statement, the screen may be used to display any values in the range defined, without the need for conversion to screen coordinates. Example line 500 will be of particular interest to mathematicians, because now a function may easily be graphed using the familiar mathematical notation that has zero at the center. Note that any values outside the range defined will be clipped.

Example Program:
Plotting a Function with World Coordinates

Program Listing

```
100 ' Plot a function using standard mathematical notation for coordinates.
110 '   In order to make 0,0 at the center of the screen, negative values
120 '   for X go to the left and positive values are right. For Y, positive
130 '   values are plotted in the top half of the screen, negative values in
140 '   the bottom half.
150 SCREEN 1: KEY OFF: CLS              'Clean screen
160 LET W.LEFT = -10                    'Minimum X value (left)
170 LET W.RIGHT = 10                    'Maximum X value (right)
180 LET W.TOP   = 5                     'Maximum Y value (up)
190 LET W.BOT   = -5                    'Minimum Y value (down)
200 WINDOW (W.LEFT, W.TOP) - (W.RIGHT, W.BOT) 'Map new coordinates to screen
210 FOR X.CORD = W.LEFT TO W.RIGHT STEP .1
220    LET Y.CORD = SIN(X.CORD)         'Find the sine of a new X coordinate
230    PSET (X.CORD, Y.CORD)            'Plot one point of the sine wave
240 NEXT X.CORD
250 END
```

Program Output

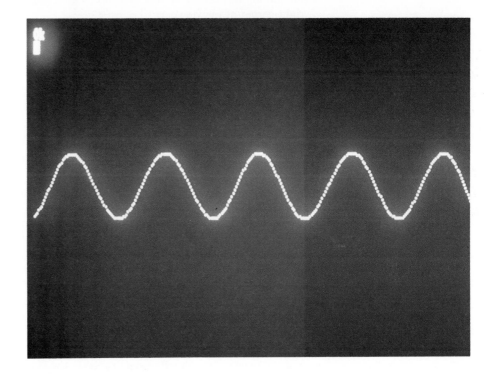

Viewports—
Using Only a Part
of the Screen

At times you may want to use an area smaller than the entire screen for your graph. You may want to draw multiple graphs on the screen at once. The VIEW statement provides a method to define a rectangular area for graphing, called a **viewport.** This viewport may be any size, up to the dimensions of the full screen. Combining VIEW with WINDOW allows you to define the location on the screen, and then adjust the coordinates of the area to the problem at hand.

The viewport established by the VIEW statement may also be colorful. When a palette is active (COLOR has been executed), you can set the background color of the viewport, as well as an optional border around the viewport.

The VIEW Statement—General Form

```
line number   VIEW   (V.left, V.top) - (V.right, V.bottom)
                     [,[Color] [, Boundary]]
```

The View coordinates given are the actual screen coordinates of the area you wish to use for graphing. The first set of numbers gives the screen coordinates to use for the top left corner of the viewport. The second set of numbers defines the lower right corner of the viewport.

The VIEW Statement—Examples

```
100 VIEW (0, 0) - (160, 99) 'Makes viewport in upper left
                                 quarter of the screen
150 VIEW (60, 20) - (260, 179) 'Creates large viewport in
                            the center of the screen
200 VIEW (10, 10) - (20, 20), 1, 2 'Viewport of color 1
                            from the current palette, outlined in
                            color 2
250 VIEW (200, 100) - (319, 199),,3 'Creates a viewport
                            and draws a box around it in color 3
                            from the current palette
```

After a VIEW statement has been executed, a CLS statement only clears the viewport, not the entire screen. To clear the screen manually, press CTRL-HOME. You can clear the viewport by executing another VIEW statement. VIEW by itself (no paramenters) resets the screen to its normal mode.

```
300 VIEW      'Reset the viewport to use the entire screen
```

Combining the SCREEN, VIEW, and WINDOW statements gives great flexibility in drawing graphs. Be sure to specify the statements in the correct order:

```
100 SCREEN 1                   'Selects medium resolution
                                graphics
110 VIEW (20,10) - (60,100),,3 'Sets aside screen area
                                and draws a box around it
120 WINDOW (1,100) - (500,0)   'Establishes world coordinates
                                within the viewport
```

Note: If color is desired, the COLOR statement should appear between the SCREEN statement and the VIEW statement.

Example Program: A Bar Chart Program with Viewport and World Coordinates

Program Listing

```
100 ' ** Program to plot any five values in a viewport in the center of
110 '     the screen. The viewport is always scaled to the current data
120 '     with the WINDOW statement.
130 '
500 '***************************** Mainline *****************************
510 GOSUB 1000                        'Input the values to plot
520 GOSUB 2000                        'Setup and scale the viewport
530 GOSUB 3000                        'Plot the values
535 GOSUB 3500                        'Draw scale on Y axis
540 GOSUB 4000                        'Cleanup the screen
550 END
1000 ' ******************** Input Values to plot *********************
1010 CLS
1020 FOR COUNT = 1 TO 5
1030    PRINT "VALUE # "; COUNT;
1040    INPUT "", VALUE(COUNT)
1050    IF VALUE(COUNT) > HIGHEST
           THEN LET HIGHEST = VALUE(COUNT)
1060    IF VALUE(COUNT) < LOWEST
           THEN LET LOWEST = VALUE(COUNT) 'Zero if no negative values
1070 NEXT COUNT
1080 RETURN
2000 ' ********************* Setup the screen ***********************
2010 SCREEN 1: KEY OFF
2020 COLOR 0,1
2030 ' *******Set Viewport to use a box in the center of the screen *******
2040 VIEW (80, 50) - (240, 150), 2, 3
2050 ' ** Scale the viewport Y axis to the current data **
2060 ' ** X axis scaling allows for 5 bars, + 0.5 for spacing
2070 WINDOW (.5, HIGHEST) - (6, LOWEST)
2080 RETURN
3000 '********************** Plot the values ************************
3010 FOR COUNT = 1 TO 5
3020    LET HEIGHT = VALUE(COUNT)
3030    LINE (COUNT, HEIGHT) - (COUNT + .5, 0) ,,BF 'Bar is filled box
3040 NEXT COUNT
3050 RETURN
3500 ' *************** Label the Y axis to show the scaling ***************
3510 ' ** Find the range between ticks
3520 LET TICK.RANGE = (HIGHEST - LOWEST) / 4
3530 LET TICK.ROW = 150/8         'Lower edge of viewport, 8 pixels per row
3535 LET TICK.VALUE = LOWEST      'Print the lowest value first
3540 FOR COUNT = 1 TO 5           'Divide the viewport into five sections
3550    LOCATE TICK.ROW, 2        'Place the label on the screen row
3560    PRINT USING "####.# -"; TICK.VALUE;
3570    LET TICK.ROW = TICK.ROW - 3   'Find the next higher row for label
3575    LET TICK.VALUE = TICK.VALUE + TICK.RANGE 'What value to print
3580 NEXT COUNT
3590 RETURN
4000 '********************** Clean up the screen **********************
4010 LET DUMMY$ = INPUT$(1)        'HOLD FOR KEYPRESS
4020 SCREEN 0: WIDTH 80: KEY ON: CLS
4030 RETURN
4040 '********************** End of Program **********************
```

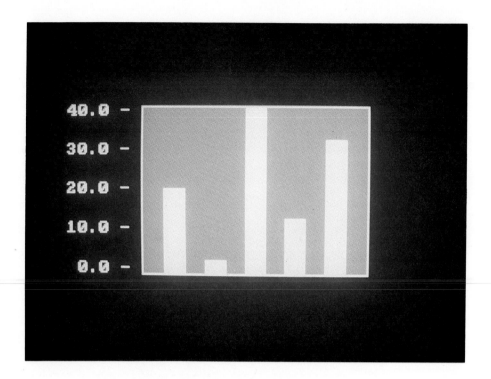

High-Resolution Graphics— Screen Mode 2

The rules and statements for high-resolution graphics (Screen Mode 2) are the same as those for medium resolution, with three exceptions: 1) No color is allowed in high resolution; 2), the number of pixels is doubled; and 3), any text printed will be in width 80, rather than 40.

You may use the PSET, PRESET, LINE, and CIRCLE statements in high resolution, leaving out the Palette.color parameter. Note that a comma must still be included when omitting the color, as BASIC determines the parameters by their position in the statement.

```
100 LINE (X, Y) ,, B
```

The *X* coordinate may range from 0–639 in high resolution, but the *Y* coordinate remains the same (0–199).

Windows and viewports work as well in high resolution as in medium resolution. In fact, it will be a rare occasion when you want to draw a graph *without* using windows and viewports; they are what make the whole operation reasonable.

Some experimentation may be necessary to determine which resolution looks best. In both modes, pixels are taller than they are wide, but the effect is more pronounced in high resolution than in medium.

Creating Pie Charts

To produce pie charts, a little math is required. The angles are measured in radians rather than in degrees. Finding the location to place the legends can cause some headaches.

Radians
When using degree measurement, a circle has 360 degrees. A half-circle, then, is 180 degrees.

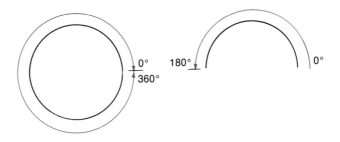

In radian measurement, the term π is the fraction 3.141593. A complete circle is $2\ \pi$ radians, so a half-circle is π radians.

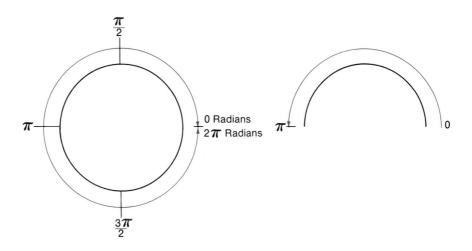

Therefore, if the number of degrees is known, you can convert to radian measurement with this calculation:

$$\text{Radians} = \text{Degrees} / 180$$

Finding Points around the Circle

If you want to place labels on the pie chart, you must find a point midway in the pie section but located on a larger (imaginary) circle outside the chart. A little trigonometry can be used to find the points, but another wrinkle makes it even more interesting. Since pixels are taller than they are wide, an adjustment must be made. For high resolution, a ratio of .46 works well.

The X coordinate can be found by multiplying the radius by the cosine of the angle that is the midpoint of the section:

```
200 LET X.COORD = RADIUS * COS ((START.ANGLE + END.ANGLE) / 2)
```

If pixels were square, the Y coordinate would be found by multiplying the radius by the sine of the angle. However, we must adjust for the shape. In high res, use this statement

```
210 LET Y.COORD = RADIUS * SIN((START.ANGLE + END.ANGLE) / 2) * 0.46
```

Combining LOCATE and PRINT with Graphics Statements

In both medium- and high-resolution graphics, you may combine pictures with text. Use LOCATE and PRINT to place text on the screen. Remember that in medium resolution the screen is in WIDTH 40, and in high resolution the text will appear in WIDTH 80. At times you may need to convert from *XY* screen coordinates to a row or column number for printing. Each character is eight pixels wide by eight pixels tall. So the formulas for converting from *XY* pixel locations to rows and columns are

```
ROW    = 1 + Y.COORDINATE/8
COLUMN = 1 + X.COORDINATE/8
```

Example Program:
A Pie Chart Program in High Resolution Graphics

Program Listing

```
100 ' Program to plot a Pie Chart, using high-resolution graphics
110 '
120 '           PROGRAM VARIABLES
130 '
140 '    CLASS           Counter for 4 classifications
150 '    HOWMUCH         Value to plot for each segment
160 '    LABEL$          Label for pie segment
170 '    START.POINT     Beginning angle for pie segment, in radians
180 '    END.POINT       Ending angle for pie segment, in radians
190 '    SHARE           Size of pie segment, in radians
200 '    X.CORD          X coordinate for placing segment label
210 '    Y.CORD          Y coordinate for placing segment label
220 '    ROW             Row for printing segment label
230 '    COL             Column for printing segment label
240 '    PI              Constant, 3.141593
250 '
500 ' ********************** MAINLINE **************************
510 GOSUB 700                      'Initialize
520 GOSUB 1000                     'Print heading
530 GOSUB 2000                     'Plot pie segments
540 LOCATE 23,1                    'Place cursor out of the way
550 END
700 ' ********************** INITIALIZE ***********************
710 SCREEN 2: CLS: KEY OFF         'Clean screen
720 WINDOW (-320, 100) - (319, -100) 'Make 0,0 in center of screen
730 LET PI = 3.141593
740 FOR CLASS = 1 TO 4             'Add up all values to plot
750    READ HOWMUCH,LABEL$
760    LET TOTAL = TOTAL + HOWMUCH
770 NEXT CLASS
780 RESTORE
790 RETURN
1000 ' ********************** PRINT HEADINGS *******************
1010 LOCATE 2,33
1020 PRINT "OFFICE EXPENSES"
1030 RETURN
2000 ' ******************** PLOT PIE SEGMENTS ******************
2010 LET END.POINT = 0
2020 FOR CLASS = 1 TO 4
2030    READ HOWMUCH,LABEL$        'Read data values
2040    GOSUB 2200                 'Calculate share of pie
2050    CIRCLE (0,0), 100,, -START.POINT, -END.POINT
2060    GOSUB 2400                 'Print label for segment
2070 NEXT CLASS
2080 RETURN
```

```
2200 ' ****************** CALCULATE SHARE OF PIE ******************
2210 LET START.POINT = END.POINT
2220 LET SHARE = HOWMUCH / TOTAL * 2 * PI
2230 LET END.POINT = START.POINT + SHARE
2240 IF CLASS = 4
         THEN LET END.POINT = 2 * PI 'Take care of rounding errors
2250 RETURN
2400 ' ***************** PRINT LABEL FOR SEGMENT ******************
2410 ' Find the location on a circle of radius 120 for the end
2420 '  point for the label for each segment.
2430 ' For the Y coordinate, use a correction of 0.46 for pixel
2440 '   shape.
2450 LET X.CORD = 120 * COS((START.POINT+END.POINT)/2)
2460 LET Y.CORD = 120 * SIN((START.POINT+END.POINT)/2) * .46
2470 LET ROW = 13 - Y.CORD/8          'Each row made up of 8 pixels
2480 LET COL = 41 + X.CORD/8          'Each column is 8 pixels wide
2490 IF COL <= 40
         THEN LET COL = COL -LEN(LABEL$) 'print label to left of spot
2500 LOCATE ROW,COL: PRINT LABEL$
2510 RETURN
3000 ' ********************** DATA TO GRAPH **********************
3010 DATA 25,Utilities,60,Rent,15,Office Expense,5,Telephone
3020 ' ********************** END OF DATA **********************
```

Program Output

Enhanced Graphics Modes—Screen Modes 7, 8, and 9

To take advantage of the enhanced graphics modes, you must have the correct hardware and software. For software, use release 3.2 or later of either IBM's BASICA or Microsoft's GWBASIC. For the hardware, you must have an EGA display adapter. Connected to the EGA display adapter you may have a standard color display monitor for screen modes 7 or 8. Screen mode 9 requires an enhanced color display monitor attached to the EGA display adapter.

The primary advantage of using the enhanced modes is the addition of color. Both medium- and high-resolution graphics can be done in sixteen colors. Table 16.5 shows the capabilities and requirements for the enhanced modes.

With the addition of the new color capabilities, we also have a new way to specify colors. You may use any of the plotting instructions, specifying a color to display. However, the color that will actually appear when any color number is selected is not fixed (as it is in low-resolution text graphics). You are allowed to assign colors to color numbers. This concept is similar to the palette selected for screen mode 1. Once the palette colors were selected, any subsequent plotting instructions were to use "the first color from the palette," or "the second color from the palette." The color numbers we call Palette.color are referred to as Attributes in the BASIC Reference Manual. In screen mode 1, four attributes were allowed. In screen modes 7, 8, and 9, we can use sixteen attributes. Colors are assigned to their attributes with a PALETTE statement.

The PALETTE Statement—General Form

```
line number  PALETTE  [Attribute, Color]
```

The Attribute must be an integer in the range 0–15 generally. (The range is limited to 0–3 in screen mode 1 or in screen mode 9 if the EGA has no more than 64K of memory; for screen mode 2 the attribute range limit is 0–1.) The value for Color must be an integer. Its legal values are also dependent on the screen mode. For screen modes 1, 2, 7, and 8 the range is 0–15. For screen modes 0 and 9 the allowable range for Color is 0–63.

The PALETTE statement can only be used when an EGA display adapter is present in the computer.

Table 16.5.
Enhanced graphics modes.

Screen Mode	Hardware	Colors
7 Medium-resolution (320 × 200)	EGA adapter, standard or enhanced monitor	16
8 High-resolution (640 × 200)	EGA adapter, standard or enhanced monitor	16
9 Enhanced high-resolution (640 × 350)	EGA adapter, standard or enhanced monitor	16
10 Monochrome high-resolution (640 × 350)	EGA adapter, standard or enhanced monitor	16

```
100 SCREEN 8              'Select high-resolution enhanced color
100 PALETTE 0, 1          'Assign color 1 (blue) to attribute 0
110 PSET (X,Y), 0         'Plot a blue point

200 SCREEN 7              'Select medium-resolution enhanced color
210 PALETTE 5, 14         'Assign color 14 (yellow) to attribute 5
220 CIRCLE (X,Y), 20, 5   'Plot a yellow circle of radius 20

350 PALETTE               'Reset all attributes to their default
```

The PALETTE statement may be used to change the color of something previously displayed on the screen.

```
300 SCREEN 8                    'Select high resolution enhanced color
310 LINE (250, 50) - (390, 150), 2, BF 'Draw a box in color 2
320 PRINT "Press any key to continue"
330 LET DUMMY$ = INPUT$(1)            'Wait for a keypress
340 PALETTE 2, 4               'Change color 2 to 4 (red)
```

Saving and Restoring Graphic Images

At times it may be useful (and a big time saver) to save a screen image in a disk file. At a future time (or in another program) the image may be reloaded and displayed on the screen.

Understanding the statements necessary to save and reload screen images would require a lengthy discussion on the memory layout of the computer, how it is addressed, and the hexadecimal number system, which are beyond the scope of this book. However, the statements are easy to code and may be included in a program as they are given here.

After the image has been drawn on the screen, execute the DEF SEG (Define Segment) and BSAVE (Binary Save) commands. These statements will specify the area of memory to save, the size, and the name of the disk file you wish to use for the picture. The numbers to use vary depending on the graphics adapter on your computer. The file name must conform to DOS naming standards. If the three-character extension is omitted, ".BAS" will be used.

Standard Color Graphics system (color or black-and-white monitor):

Save a screen image calling it "SCREEN1" on the disk:

```
100 DEF SEG = &HB800
110 BSAVE "SCREEN1" , 0, &H4000
```

And later (perhaps in another program) include these lines to recall the image and display it on the screen:

```
200 DEF SEG = &HB800
210 BLOAD "SCREEN1", 0
```

Monochrome system with a Hercules Graphics Adapter:

Save a screen image calling it "SCREEN2" on the disk:

```
100 DEF SEG = &HB000
110 BSAVE "SCREEN2" , 0, &H8000
```

And later, probably in another program, include these lines to recall the image and display it on the screen.

```
200 DEF SEG = &HB000
210 BLOAD "SCREEN2", 0
```

Many screen images may be saved to the disk in separate files. Reloading them in rapid succession can produce animation effects (limited by the speed of the disk drive).

Summary

1. There are several graphics modes: low-resolution, medium-resolution, high-resolution, and enhanced high-resolution. The BASIC statements operate differently in each mode.
2. In low resolution, or text graphics, thirty-two colors may be displayed on the screen.
3. Medium resolution provides 320×200 pixels on the screen. Only four colors may be displayed at any one time.
4. High resolution provides 640×200 pixels, with no color possible.
5. In low resolution, the COLOR statement specifies the colors for the foreground, background, and border.
6. The SCREEN statement is used to set the graphics mode.
7. In medium-resolution mode, colors are chosen from one of two palettes. The COLOR statement is used to select the palette.
8. The PSET, PRESET, LINE, and CIRCLE statements may be used in medium- and high-resolution modes.
9. Shapes may be filled in with the PAINT statement.
10. When graphics are specified for a location off the screen, the shape is clipped so that only the visible portion is displayed.
11. The coordinates of the screen may be adjusted to conform to the problem at hand (called world coordinates) by using the WINDOW statement.
12. The VIEW statement provides a way to select an area of the screen to use for graphics.
13. Text characters may be mixed with pixel graphics. In medium-resolution mode, text will be WIDTH 40; in high-resolution, characters will display in WIDTH 80.
14. With an EGA (enhanced graphics adapter) and an enhanced color display monitor attached to a computer, four additional graphics modes are allowed. These modes provide for full color use in medium- and high-resolution graphics.
15. The PALETTE statement provides a method to select colors but is available only on computers that have an EGA display adapter.
16. Graphics images may be saved in a disk file and recalled for later use.

Programming Exercises

16.1. Draw three solid squares on the screen using the LINE command.

16.2. Using only the circle command, draw a border around the screen.

16.3. Draw a line from the top left corner to the bottom right corner and another line from the top right corner to the bottom left corner of the screen.

16.4. Create a pie chart to represent the calculated data from program 2.14 (Budget Report).

16.5. Write a program using any of the graphics commands to draw a house and background scenery on the screen.

16.6. The perfect picture company wishes to put a glamorous advertisement in every popular magazine to promote its film. Create a design for the ad using any graphics commands you wish.

16.7. Write a program using the PAINT statement to paint the entire screen eight different colors. Hold the screen for a keypress between colors.

16.8. Write a program using the PSET and PRESET statements to print a blinking dot on the screen.

16.9. Using any of the graphics statements discussed thus far, write a program that will create a weekly material log screen for data entry. Design the form to fit on the screen and include the following input areas:

1. Title
2. Week ending date
3. Signature
4. Employee number
5. Cost code
6. Description
7. Order number
8. Quantity
9. Job number
10. Department

16.10. Write a program that will draw five circles, with a radius of 21, on the screen. Then use the PAINT statement to fill each circle.

16.11. Write a program to create a bar chart to depict the percentage of karate matches won by each karate student at the Kiwi Karate Studio.

INPUT: Data will come from DATA statements.
OUTPUT:
  1. Output should be to the screen.
  2. Print a title on the chart.
  3. Label both the x and y axis.
PROCESS:
  1. The x-axis will be the Student's last name.
  2. The y-axis will be the percentage of matches won.
  3. Percentage won = matches won/total matches.
  4. Use the LINE statement to create the bars.
TEST DATA:

Name	Number of Matches	Matches Won
Brian Boon	5	0
Chris Cook	6	5
Eric Mills	4	4
Mandy Moon	7	6
Nancy Noon	10	7
Scott Peck	8	7
Peter Smith	9	9
Sam Snoop	12	6
Trish Little	20	20

16.12. Using the PSET statement, graph the following ellipse:

$$\frac{X^2}{4} + \frac{Y^2}{9} = 1$$

INPUT: After the above ellipse is plotted, the user should have the option of graphing an ellipse with different intercepts.
OUTPUT: Display the ellipse on the screen.
PROCESS:

1. Equation of an ellipse $= \frac{X^2}{a^2} + \frac{Y^2}{b^2} = 1$

2. To graph an ellipse, plot the four intercepts a, −a, b, and −b, and sketch an ellipse through the intercepts.

3. Since a and b are squared in the equation and not in the problem given, you must take the square root of the numbers to obtain a and b. e.g., a = the square root of 4.

16.13. Write a program using VIEW, WINDOW, and CIRCLE to print a happy face on the screen, in the middle of the window.

16.14. Write a program to randomly place circles on the screen with lines connecting the center of the circles.

16.15. Write a program using PSET and PRESET to create the effect of a moving dot. The dot should keep moving until a key is pressed.

Appendixes

Appendix A
Summary of Commands for BASIC, MS-DOS, PC-DOS, and CP/M

Summary of Commands

There are two levels of commands needed to run BASIC programs. The BASIC interpreter has one set of commands, and the computer's operating system has another, different set. The commands you must use depend upon whom you are addressing.

After BASIC has been loaded and is running, all commands must be addressed to the BASIC interpreter. When BASIC is not running, commands go to the operating system. The commands specify operations to perform such as running programs, copying files, and displaying files.

BASIC Commands

In BASIC, a command is a directive issued at the command level; that is, a command does *not* have a statement number. A command is executed as soon as it is entered. Actually, many BASIC statements may be issued at the command level. Such statements as LET and PRINT are executed immediately if entered without a statement number. This can be handy for program debugging, but these program statements are not considered commands and will be omitted from the list.

Rules for Filenames in BASIC Commands

1. A filename must be enclosed in quotes.
2. A filename may be one to eight characters, followed by an optional period and a one-to-three-character extension.
3. BASIC will supply an extension of .BAS for any filename that does not already have an extension.
4. Anywhere a filename is called for, a diskette drive designation may also be supplied. (Ex: "A:MYPROG" "B:NAMES.DAT")

Table A.1.
Summary of BASIC commands.

Command	Action
AUTO linenumber,increment	Automatically generates line numbers. If line number and/or increment are omitted, defaults to begin at 10, increment by 10.
CONT	Continues program execution after a BREAK, STOP, or END. Usually used for debugging.
DELETE line1–line2	Deletes specified program lines. May delete one line or a range of lines.
EDIT linenumber	Enters Edit Mode for changing program lines.
FILES	Lists the diskette directory.
KILL "filename"	Deletes a file from diskette.

Command	Action
LIST	Lists program on the screen.
LIST line1–line2	Lists specified lines on the screen.
LLIST	Lists program on the screen.
LLIST line1–line2	Lists specified lines on the printer.
LOAD "filename"	Loads a program file from diskette.
MERGE "filename"	Merges a saved program from diskette with the program in memory. The program on diskette must have been saved with "FILENAME",A option (ASCII file).
NAME "old filename" AS "new filename"	Renames a file on diskette.
NEW	Erases the program in memory.
RENUM newnum,oldnum,increment	Renumbers program lines. If omitted, newnum defaults to 10, oldnum defaults to the first program line, and increment defaults to 10.
RESET	Reinitializes diskette directory information. Generally used after changing diskettes.
RUN	Executes the current program.
RUN "filename"	Loads a program file from diskette into memory and executes it.
RUN linenumber	Begins execution of the program with the specified line number.
SAVE "filename"	Saves the program in memory onto the diskette under the given filename.
SAVE "filename",A	Saves the program in memory onto the diskette in ASCII format. Useful if another editor will be used, or if program will be MERGEd.
SYSTEM	Exits BASIC, returning to the operating system. Closes any open files.
TRON, TROFF	Turns trace on or off.
TRACE, NOTRACE	Turns trace on or off for some systems.

Operating System Commands— MS-DOS, PC-DOS, CP/M

The operating system is the master program, which controls execution of all other programs. Each operating system has its own set of commands for requesting actions to be performed.

The two most common operating systems for microcomputers are CP/M and MS-DOS (which is also IBM's PC-DOS). There are many similarities between the two operating systems. Some of these similar features will be covered first. Then the specific commands for each will be explained.

The Logged Drive

Each disk drive is designated by a letter and a colon. The first drive is always called A:, the second (if present) is B:. Any more disk drives on the system will be designated C:, D:, etc.

One of the drives is designated the "logged drive"; that is, any commands, files, or programs are expected to come from that drive.

A>   This is the system prompt, which also indicates that drive A: is the logged drive.

To log the B: drive:

A>B:<ENTER>   Now the system prompt indicates that B: is the logged drive.
B>

All commands refer to the logged drive unless otherwise stated.

Filenames

Filenames may be one to eight characters with an optional period and a one-to-three-character extension. Filenames may include letters, digits, and special characters. Characters which are *not* legal in filenames are:

< > . , : = ; * ? [ ]

Filenames may include an optional drive designation.

```
A:PROG1.BAS
B:LISTER.COM
```

File Extensions

The three-character extension is often used to designate the file type.

```
.COM—executable program
.BAS—BASIC program
.DAT—data file
```

Table A.2. MS-DOS and PC-DOS commands.	Command	Action
	BASIC BASICA MSBASIC GWBASIC	Begin execution of the BASIC interpreter. May be any one of these commands, depending on the system in use.
	BASIC [/F:*number of files*] [/S:*maximum record size*]	The optional entries (/F: and /S:) allow a change in the number of files that may be open in one program and the maximum size of the record buffer for random files. When these entries are omitted, the number of files defaults to 3, and the maximum record size is set at 128 bytes.
	CLS	Clear the display screen.
	COPY oldfilename newfilename	Copy diskette files. COPY B:MYFILE A: Copies the file called MYFILE from the B: drive to the A: drive. COPY B:PROG1.BAS A:PROG1.BAK Copies a file called PROG1.BAS on the B: drive to the A: drive and renames it to PROG1.BAK.

	Command	Action
Table A.2.—*Continued* **MS-DOS and PC-DOS commands.**	**DEL** filename	Delete a file from diskette.
	DIR	Display the diskette directory on the screen.
	ERASE filename	Delete a file from diskette.
	FORMAT	Initialize a diskette. Will erase any data already stored on the diskette.
		FORMAT B: Initialize a diskette on the B: drive.
	RENAME oldname newname	Rename a file on diskette.
	TYPE filename	Display the contents of a data file on the screen.

Output Control

Command	Action
CTRL-S or **CTRL-NUMLOCK**	Temporarily suspend output. (Toggles on and off.)
CTRL-P or **CTRL-PRTSC**	Send screen output to printer. (Toggles on and off.)

Disk drive and filename naming conventions are the same in CP/M as in MS-DOS.

	Command	Action
Table A.3. **Summary of CP/M commands.**	**BASIC** **MBASIC** **MSBASIC** **GBASIC** **GWBASIC**	Begin execution of the BASIC interpreter. The specific command used depends on the system in use.
	BASIC [**/F:** *number of files*] [**/S:** *maximum record size*]	The optional entries (/F: and /S:) allow a change in the number of files that may be open in one program and the maximum size of the record buffer for random files. When these entries are omitted, the number of files defaults to 3, and the maximum record size is set at 128 bytes.
	DIR	Display the diskette directory of the logged drive on the screen.
		A>DIR produces the directory of the diskette on the A: drive.
		A>DIR B: produces the directory of the diskette on the B: drive.
	ERA filename	Erase (delete) a file from diskette.
	FORMAT	Initialize a diskette. Erases any data that was on the diskette.
		A>FORMAT B: Initializes the diskette on the B: drive.

Table A.3.—*Continued*	Command	Action
Summary of CP/M commands.	P I P newfile = oldfile	Copy files from one diskette or device to another.
	A>PIP A:MYFILE = B:	
		Copies filename MYFILE from B: drive to A: drive.
	A>PIP A:PROG1.BAK = B:PROG1.BAS	
		Copies a file called PROG1.BAS on the B: drive to the A: drive and renames it to PROG1.BAK.
	REN newname = oldname	Rename diskette files.
	TYPE filename	Display the contents of a data file on the screen.
	Output Control	
	CTRL-S	Temporarily suspend output. To restart, press CTRL-S again. (Toggles on and off.)
	CTRL-P	Send output to the printer. All output for the screen will also appear on the printer. (Toggles on and off.)

Diskette Switching

    CP/M keeps an image of the diskette directory in memory. If a diskette is switched, the directory must be updated. To update the directory when in CP/M, press CTRL-C. If the diskette is switched during operation of BASIC, type the BASIC command RESET.

CP/M Error Messages

BDOS ERR ON A:BAD SECTOR	May be:
	1. No disk in drive
	2. Disk door not closed
	3. Disk inserted improperly
	4. Bad disk
BDOS ERR ON A:R/O	R/O means Read Only May be:
	1. The diskette was changed, but CTRL-C was not pressed (or RESET typed in BASIC).
	2. There is a write-protect tab on the diskette notch.

Appendix B
Editing Program Lines

The process of making changes in a BASIC program is called editing, and there is more than one way to do the editing. The biggest difference in commands is found between the versions of Microsoft BASIC that run on eight-bit computers (running CP/M) and those running on sixteen-bit computers (using MS-DOS, CP/M-86, or PC-DOS). The methods used to add lines and delete lines are the same for all versions of BASIC. The differences lie in the methods used to make changes to existing lines.

Adding Program Statements— All Versions

A new statement can be added anywhere in a BASIC program by typing a new line number and the BASIC statement. The new line number must fall between the two line numbers that will precede and follow the new statement.

Example

```
LIST
100    PRINT "FIRST LINE"
110    PRINT "LAST LINE"
```

Added line:

```
105    PRINT "THIS LINE WILL PRINT IN THE MIDDLE"
```

```
LIST
100    PRINT "FIRST LINE"
105    PRINT "THIS LINE WILL PRINT IN THE MIDDLE"
110    PRINT "LAST LINE"
```

Deleting Program Statements— All Versions

Any program line may be deleted by typing the statement number and pressing the ENTER/RETURN key.

Example

```
LIST
200    PRINT "GOOD LINE"
210    PRINT "GARBAGE"
220    PRINT "GREAT LINE"
```

To delete line 210, type

```
210<ENTER>
```

```
LIST
200    PRINT "GOOD LINE"
220    PRINT "GREAT LINE"
```

Editing Program Statements

The advantages of editing can be seen when it is necessary to make changes in existing program lines. Of course, the entire line can be retyped, but editing provides for making changes *without* retyping.

In order to be useful, an editor must provide for certain basic operations:

1. Moving the cursor to the desired location
2. Inserting characters
3. Deleting characters
4. Changing (replacing) characters
5. Locating characters

The method used to edit (change) existing program lines depends on the version of BASIC in use. If you are using the version of Microsoft BASIC designed to run on eight-bit computers with CP/M, see Edit Mode, page 468.

I. The BASIC Editor for the IBM-PC and Compatibles

The BASIC editor allows you to edit any line, anywhere on the screen. This means that you may list a program and then move the cursor to the desired location and make changes. However, you must be sure to press the ENTER key *on that line* in order for the changes to take effect.

The editor is considered a "screen line editor." This means that a change may be made anywhere on the screen, but to only one line at a time. Although you must press ENTER on the changed line, you may do so with the cursor anywhere on the line; it is not necessary to move the cursor to the end of the line.

One further point must be made. In prior versions of BASIC, screen editing was not possible. Instead, a set of editing commands was provided to enter Edit Mode, insert and delete, search, extend, etc. Even though screen editing is far more convenient, the old line editor is still available for use. If you wish, you may use any of the editing subcommands found in Table B.1 in addition to the editing methods explained below.

II. Moving the Cursor

The arrow keys are used to move the cursor to the desired location.

→	Move one character to the right.
←	Move one character to the left.
↑	Move one position up.
↓	Move one position down.
HOME or CTRL-L	Move the cursor to the upper left corner of the screen.
CTRL-HOME or CTRL-L	Clear the screen and move the cursor to the upper left corner (same action as CLS).
CTRL- → or CTRL-F	Move the cursor to the next word.
CTRL- ← or CTRL-B	Move the cursor to the preceding word.
END or CTRL-N	Move the cursor to the end of the statement; useful for adding characters to the end of the line.
→| or CTRL-I	Tab right. Move cursor to the next tab location (every eight characters). The tab key performs differently when in Insert Mode. Then it inserts blank spaces up to the next tab location rather than skip over the characters.

III. Inserting Characters—Insert Mode

1. Entering Insert Mode

INS or CTRL-R	Pressing the Insert key (or CTRL-R on some computers) switches the state of Insert Mode. If Insert Mode was off, it will be turned on. If Insert Mode was on when the key was pressed, it will be turned off. In Insert Mode, any characters typed at the cursor location will be inserted. Any characters to the right of the cursor will be moved further to the right to make room for the inserted characters.

2. Exiting Insert Mode

INS	Pressing the INS (Insert) key a second time exits Insert Mode. Also, pressing any cursor movement key or the ENTER key turns off Insert Mode.

IV. Deleting Characters

DEL or CTRL-H	Delete the character at the current cursor location. Any characters to the right of the cursor will be moved left by one position.
← (Backspace)	Delete the last character typed. From anywhere on the line, the character to the left of the cursor will be deleted. All characters from the cursor location to the end of the line will be moved left by one position.
CTRL-END or CTRL-E	Delete from the cursor location to the end of the line.

V. Changing Characters

Typing new characters on top of old characters will do a replace. Recall that for *any* changes to actually be made in the program line, ENTER must be pressed.

VI. Cancelling a Line

ESC or CTRL-U or CTRL-[	Erase the current line from the screen. However, this does not remove the line from the program in memory. Handy for typing a new line or listing or running the program without the necessity of moving the cursor to a blank line at the bottom of the screen.
CTRL-BREAK or CTRL-C	Cancel any editing on the current line. This does not erase the line from the screen as ESC does.

VII. Moving Around the Screen

The screen editor provides for creating and changing lines on the screen. Program lines are not actually made a part of the current program in memory until the ENTER key is pressed. This is true for typing a line for the first time or for editing a line already entered.

Using the screen editor makes it easy to go back and change characters in the first part of the current line. While typing the current line, the cursor may be moved to a prior line, a change made (and the ENTER key pressed), and then returned to complete the current line. Any of the cursor movement keys may be used when moving about, such as the arrow keys, tab keys, HOME, or END.

VIII. Edit Mode—Eight-Bit Version of BASIC

If you are using one of the earlier versions of Microsoft BASIC designed to run on eight-bit computers under CP/M, you have available a line editor for changing program lines. In this editor, you enter Edit Mode and then use a variety of subcommands for inserting, deleting, and changing program lines. Note that the instructions for adding new lines and deleting entire lines are found in the preceding section (page 465).

IX. Entering Edit Mode

1. Syntax error in the program. If a syntax error occurs when running a program, BASIC automatically enters Edit Mode.

```
10   RIM THIS IS A REMARK
RUN
?Syntax error in 10
OK
10 __
```
┗━━━━━━━━ cursor here in Edit Mode

2. To edit a particular line number, type

```
EDIT line number
```

Example

```
EDIT 20<ENTER>
20 __
```
┗━━━━━━━━ cursor here in Edit Mode

3. To edit a line just completed, type

```
EDIT .
```

The period symbol means "the current line" and may be entered in place of a line number.

```
50   PRINT OOPS! I FORGOT THE QUOTE"<ENTER>
EDIT .
50 __
```
┗━━━━━━━━ cursor here in Edit Mode

X. Moving the Cursor to the Desired Location

To move the cursor to the right, press the space bar.

```
10 __
```

Press the space bar once:

```
10   R__
```

And again:

```
10   RI__
```

Each press of the space bar moves the cursor one position to the right and reveals the next character (to view the entire line, see the L subcommand). The cursor may be moved multiple spaces (and reveal multiple characters) by entering a number before pressing the space bar:

```
EDIT 10
10 __
```

To move the cursor fifteen characters right, type:

```
15<space bar>
10 RIM THIS IS A R __
```

XI. Inserting Characters—Insert Mode

To insert characters, first move the cursor to the location where the new characters must be inserted. In Insert Mode, any characters typed will be inserted into the line. Any remaining characters in the line will be moved to the right to make room for the new text.

1. Entering Insert Mode.
    With the cursor in the desired location, press the I key.

    ```
    50   PRINT OOPS! I FORGOT THE QUOTE"
    EDIT 50
    50 PRINT __
    ```

    Press I (for insert), then the quote.

    ```
    50   PRINT "__
    ```

    Any further characters typed will also be inserted here (including spaces). In order to stop inserting, you must exit Insert Mode.

2. Exiting Insert Mode.
    a. Press the Escape key <ESC>. Insert Mode will be terminated, but it will remain in Edit Mode so that other changes may be made to the statement.
    b. Press the ENTER key. This will terminate both Insert Mode and Edit Mode on the current line.

3. Inserting at the end of a line.
    Characters may be added at the end of a line by entering the X (eXtend) subcommand (from anywhere in the line). The cursor will move to the end of the line, and Insert Mode entered.

    ```
    EDIT 90
    90 __
    ```

    To insert characters at the end of the line, type

    ```
    X
    90 PRINT "THIS LINE IS TOO__
    ```
    ↑
    cursor here in Insert Mode

XII. Deleting Characters

1. One or more characters may be deleted. First move the cursor to the character to be deleted and press the D key (for Delete).

    ```
    100   PRINT "EXXTRA"
    EDIT 100
    100   PRINT "EX__
    ```

    Press the D key, and the deleted character is shown enclosed in backslashes.

    ```
    100   PRINT "EX\X\__
    ```

2. To delete multiple characters, type a number before the D key.

```
100   PRINT "EXXXXTRA
EDIT 100
100   PRINT "EX__
```

To delete three characters, type

```
3D
```

```
100   PRINT "EX\XXX\__
```

3. To delete characters at the end of a line, use the H (*Hack*) subcommand. Typing H will delete all characters to the right of the cursor and enter Insert Mode. This is useful for changing text at the end of a line.

4. Another method for deleting multiple characters is shown in section VI— Locating Text with the K (*Kill*) subcommand.

XIII. Changing (Replacing) Characters

1. To change a character, first move the cursor to the correct position. Then press the C key (for *Change*), and then type the new (changed) character.

```
10   RIM THIS IS A REMARK
EDIT 10
10 R__
```

To change the I to E, place the cursor on the I, and type

```
CE
10 RE__
```

2. Changing multiple characters. A number may be typed before the C subcommand. To change four characters, type 4C and the four new characters.

```
80   PRINT "I CHANGED MY MIND"
EDIT 80
80   PRINT "I CHANGED MY __
```

To change four characters, place the cursor on the first character, and type

```
4CWORD
80   PRINT "I CHANGED MY WORD__
```

XIV. Locating Text

1. To quickly move the cursor to a particular character, use the S (*Search*) subcommand.

```
10   PRINT "THIS MUST BE AN ERRROR"
EDIT 10
10 __
```

To move the cursor to the first occurrence of the letter R, type

```
SR
```

```
10   P__
```

Another SR will move to the next occurrence of the letter R.

```
10   PRINT "THIS MUST BE AN E__
```

Or, alternately, to move to the second or third occurrence of the character, use a number before the subcommand S.

```
EDIT 10
10 __
```

To find the third occurrence of the letter R, type

```
3SR

10   PRINT "THIS MUST BE AN ER__
```

2. A second subcommand can be used to search for a character. The K (*K*ill) subcommand deletes all characters from the current cursor location up to the named character.

```
100   PRINT "THIS MUST GO"
EDIT 100
100   PRINT "__
```

To delete the word THIS (everything from the cursor to the first occurrence of the letter M), type

```
KM

100   PRINT "\THIS \__
```

XV. Exiting and Restarting Edit Mode

1. Edit mode may be exited from anywhere on the line by pressing the ENTER key. The remainder of the line will be printed.

2. The E (*E*xit) subcommand also exits Edit Mode, but does not print the remainder of the line.

3. Typing Q (*Q*uit) exits Edit Mode without saving any of the changes that were made to the line during Edit Mode.

4. Typing L (*L*ist) will list the remainder of the line and replace the cursor at the start of the line while remaining in Edit Mode. The L subcommand is useful to view the entire line before beginning to edit.

```
EDIT 60
60 __
```

To view the line, type

```
L
60   PRINT "THIS LINE MUST BE CHANGED"
60 __
     └cursor here in Edit Mode
```

5. The A (*A*bandon) subcommand allows you to restart the editing of that line. Typing A from anywhere on the line will restore the original line and place the cursor at the beginning of the line.

Table B.1.
Summary of edit subcommands in BASIC-80.

Moving the Cursor	
space bar	Move to the right.
←	Move to the left.
Insert Mode	
I	Enter Insert Mode at the cursor location.
ESC	Exit Insert Mode.
ENTER	Exit Insert Mode and Edit Mode (saves all changes made).
X	Extend the line. Moves the cursor to the end of the line and enters Insert Mode.

Table B.1.—*Continued*
Summary of edit subcommands in BASIC-80.

Moving the Cursor

Deleting Characters

D	Delete the character at the cursor location.
nD	Delete n characters.
H	Delete all characters from the current cursor location to the end of the line and enter Insert Mode.

Changing Characters

C	Allow the character at the cursor location to be replaced.
nC	Allow n characters to be replaced.

Locating Characters

S	Search for the occurrence of a character and move the cursor to the position preceding the character.
nS	Search for the nth occurrence of the character.
K	Kill (delete) all characters between the cursor and the named character.
nK	Kill all characters between the cursor and the nth occurrence of the character.

Exiting and Restarting Edit Mode

ENTER	Exit Edit Mode and print the remainder of the line (saves all changes made).
E	Exit Edit Mode but do not print the remainder of the line (saves all changes).
L	List the remainder of the line and restart editing at the start of the line (handy to view the line before editing).
A	Restart editing at the start of the line (does not save any changes made so far).

Appendix C
The ASCII Code

ASCII CODE	CHARACTER	CONTROL CHARACTER	ASCII CODE	CHARACTER	ASCII CODE	CHARACTER
0	(null)	NUL	43	+	86	V
1	☺	SOH	44	,	87	W
2	☻	STX	45	-	88	X
3	♥	ETX	46	.	89	Y
4	♦	EOT	47	/	90	Z
5	♣	ENQ	48	0	91	[
6	♠	ACK	49	1	92	\
7	(beep)	BEL	50	2	93	]
8	■	BS	51	3	94	∧
9	(tab)	HT	52	4	95	—
10	(line feed)	LF	53	5	96	`
11	(home)	VT	54	6	97	a
12	(form feed)	FF	55	7	98	b
13	(carriage return)	CR	56	8	99	c
14	♫	SO	57	9	100	d
15	☼	SI	58	:	101	e
16	►	DLE	59	;	102	f
17	◄	DC1	60	<	103	g
18	↕	DC2	61	=	104	h
19	!!	DC3	62	>	105	i
20	¶	DC4	63	?	106	j
21	§	NAK	64	@	107	k
22	▬	SYN	65	A	108	l
23	↨	ETB	66	B	109	m
24	↑	CAN	67	C	110	n
25	↓	EM	68	D	111	o
26	→	SUB	69	E	112	p
27	←	ESC	70	F	113	q
28	(cursor right)	FS	71	G	114	r
29	(cursor left)	GS	72	H	115	s
30	(cursor up)	RS	73	I	116	t
31	(cursor down)	US	74	J	117	u
32	SPACE		75	K	118	v
33	!		76	L	119	w
34	"		77	M	120	x
35	#		78	N	121	y
36	$		79	O	122	z
37	%		80	P	123	{
38	&		81	Q	124	¦
39	'		82	R	125	}
40	(		83	S	126	~
41	)		84	T	127	⌂
42	*		85	U		

ASCII CODE	CHARACTER	ASCII CODE	CHARACTER	ASCII CODE	CHARACTER
128	Ç	171	½	214	π
129	ü	172	¼	215	╫
130	é	173	¡	216	╪
131	â	174	«	217	┘
132	ä	175	»	218	┌
133	à	176	▒	219	█
134	å	177	▒	220	▄
135	ç	178	▓	221	▌
136	ê	179	│	222	▐
137	ë	180	┤	223	▀
138	è	181	╡	224	α
139	ï	182	╢	225	β
140	î	183	╖	226	Γ
141	ì	184	╕	227	π
142	Ä	185	╣	228	Σ
143	Å	186	║	229	σ
144	É	187	╗	230	μ
145	æ	188	╝	231	τ
146	Æ	189	╜	232	Φ
147	ô	190	╛	233	θ
148	ö	191	┐	234	Ω
149	ò	192	└	235	δ
150	û	193	┴	236	∞
151	ù	194	┬	237	$\varnothing$
152	ÿ	195	├	238	$\in$
153	Ö	196	─	239	$\cap$
154	Ü	197	┼	240	$\equiv$
155	¢	198	╞	241	$\pm$
156	£	199	╟	242	$\geq$
157	¥	200	╚	243	$\leq$
158	Pt	201	╔	244	$\lceil$
159	f	202	╩	245	$\rfloor$
160	á	203	╦	246	$\div$
161	í	204	╠	247	$\approx$
162	ó	205	═	248	$\circ$
163	ú	206	╬	249	$\bullet$
164	ñ	207	╧	250	$\cdot$
165	Ñ	208	╨	251	$\sqrt{}$
166	ª	209	╤	252	n
167	º	210	╥	253	2
168	¿	211	╙	254	■
169	⌐	212	╘	255	(blank 'FF')
170	¬	213	╒		

Appendix D
Testing and Debugging Techniques

A computer is supposed to produce correct results. However, too often the output is not correct. Many beginning programmers believe that if the program runs, it must be finished. But all aspects of the output must be carefully checked before a program can be turned over to a user. All available methods should be used to verify the correctness of the program output.

Use Test Data

One method of verifying the correctness of program output is to run the program with test data. This is data that will produce known results. If test data is carefully designed, the chances are good that any program errors will be found.

Many times a program will work correctly for all "normal" inputs; but when given extreme values, errors pop up (sometimes not until a program has been in use for weeks or months). In selecting test data, be sure to exercise all options of a program. If a discount is given for sales of 100 or more units, be sure to test 99, 100, and 101 as well as 0—perhaps even a negative number.

A pattern that will fit many programs is one in which there are three distinct cases to validate. These three cases correspond to the beginning, middle, and end. In testing, make sure that the normal cases will be correctly handled (the middle). Then determine "Will the first input and/or calculation be handled correctly?" Then, "What will happen when the last record is read?"

Any situation that is a potential for error should be carefully checked. In a program with subtotals, be sure to check the first record, the last, the last record of one group, and the first record of the next group.

Use a Calculator

The calculator method of checking output may seem tedious, but it is definitely worth the trouble. It may be necessary to verify an entire report with the calculator; or it may be enough to validate only certain test cases. In a report that calculates gross pay for employees, use the calculator to verify at least one of each possibility—one person with 0 hours, one with less than 40 hours (if that is the cutoff point for overtime); one with exactly 40 hours; one with a fraction of an hour overtime (worked 40.5 hours); and one with a large amount of overtime (worked 55 hours).

Develop a Proofreader's Eye

A calculator won't help much for alphanumeric data. The way to catch errors is to carefully proofread all output, comparing the output to the input or to the desired output, if available. Proofreading is a skill that improves with practice.

Bugs in the Program

Only when all output has been carefully checked and proven correct is the program ready to go. If any errors are found, these are called program **bugs.** The process of locating and correcting the errors is called **debugging.**

Debugging Methods

1. *Printing Intermediate Values.* Inserting extra print statements in a program can greatly aid the debugging process. If a value is input correctly but something goes wrong somewhere in the calculations, extra print statements can pinpoint the location of the error. Of course, any extra print statements added for debugging purposes should be removed after the error is located.

Example

```
500   ' PROGRAM TO DEMONSTRATE INTERMEDIATE PRINT STATEMENTS
510   READ AMT
520   WHILE AMT <> 0
530      LET TOTAL = TOT + AMT
540        READ AMT
550   WEND
560   PRINT "THE TOTAL IS "; TOTAL
570   DATA 12,20,45,60,16,0
580   END
RUN
THE TOTAL IS 16
```

Sixteen is not the expected answer for the total. For debugging purposes, a print statement will be placed in the loop to see the intermediate values for TOTAL.

```
535   PRINT "TOTAL =    "; TOTAL '*** DEBUGGING LINE

LIST
500   ' PROGRAM TO DEMONSTRATE INTERMEDIATE PRINT STATEMENTS
510   READ AMT
520   WHILE AMT <> 0
530      LET TOTAL = TOT + AMT
535        PRINT "TOTAL = "; TOTAL '*** DEBUGGING LINE
540        READ AMT
550   WEND
560   PRINT "THE TOTAL IS "; TOTAL
570   DATA 12,20,45,60,16,0
580   END
RUN
TOTAL = 12
TOTAL = 20
TOTAL = 45
TOTAL = 60
TOTAL = 16
THE TOTAL IS 16
```

At this point, it is obvious that the total has the same value as AMT for each iteration of the loop. The total is not accumulating. Determining exactly what is happening should help pinpoint the problem. Can you see it? The culprit is line 530, where TOT was used in place of TOTAL.

2. *Stopping Program Execution to Examine Variables.* Two BASIC statements have been provided that allow for selectively stopping and restarting program execution. The statement STOP may be placed anywhere in a BASIC program. The contents of program variables may then be printed in immediate mode (at the command level). Program execution may then be resumed with the CONT (Continue) statement. When a STOP statement is encountered in program execution, execution halts and a message is printed:

Break in linenumber

If a PRINT statement is entered without a line number, it will be executed immediately. This is called immediate mode. The value of any variable may be printed while the program is stopped.

Typing the command CONT will then continue program execution. BASIC will not allow a continue if any program lines have been edited since the break. CONT may also be used to resume a program that has been halted by a CTRL-BREAK (or CTRL-C).

Example

```
500    ' PROGRAM TO DEMONSTRATE THE STOP STATEMENT
510    READ AMT
520    WHILE AMT <> 0
530        LET TOTAL = TOT + AMT
540        READ AMT
550    WEND
560    PRINT "THE TOTAL IS "; TOTAL
570    DATA 12,20,45,60,16,0
580    END
RUN
THE TOTAL IS 16
```

The STOP statement may be placed at a strategic spot in the program.

```
535        STOP    '*** DEBUGGING LINE

LIST
500    ' PROGRAM TO DEMONSTRATE THE STOP STATEMENT
510    READ AMT
520    WHILE AMT <> 0
530        LET TOTAL = TOT + AMT
535        STOP '*** DEBUGGING LINE
540        READ AMT
550    WEND
560    PRINT "THE TOTAL IS "; TOTAL
570    DATA 12,20,45,60,16,0
580    END

RUN
Break in 535

PRINT TOTAL
 12
OK


PRINT AMT
 12
OK

PRINT TOT
 0
OK

CONT
Break in 535
```

3. *Using a Trace.* At times it is difficult to follow the flow of control of a program. Was the subroutine actually executed? A trace can be most useful here.

    When a program is being traced, the statement number of each line prints as the statement is executed. The trace output appears on the screen mixed with any PRINT output from the program.

    The BASIC statements that turn trace mode on and off are TRON and TROFF (TRACE and NOTRACE in some versions). These statements may be entered as statements in the program with line numbers or may be entered from the command level without statement numbers.

The most common form of the trace is to type the command TRON (or TRACE) and then RUN. When the program has completed, TROFF (or NOTRACE) must be entered. However, if only a portion of the program is in question, TRON and TROFF (TRACE and NOTRACE) may appear at the start and end of the suspect routine. The trace statements may also appear multiple times in one program.

Example

```
1000    ' PROGRAM TO DEMONSTRATE THE USE OF A TRACE
1010    GOSUB 2000                      'PRIMING READ
1020    WHILE PERSON$ <> "END"
1030        GOSUB 3000                  'CALCULATIONS
1040        GOSUB 4000                  'OUTPUT
1050        GOSUB 2000                  'READ NEXT DATA
1060    WEND
1070    END
2000    '*************** PROGRAM INPUT *************************
2010    READ PERSON$, SOLD, COLLECTED
2020    DATA PAT, 0, 0, PETE, 4, 2, PAM, 0, 2, END, 0, 0
2030    RETURN
3000    '**************** CALCULATIONS ***********************
3010    LET DUE = SOLD - COLLECTED
3020    RETURN
4000    '****************** OUTPUT ****************************
4010    PRINT PERSON$, SOLD, DUE
4020    RETURN
4030    '**************** END OF PROGRAM **********************

TRON
OK
RUN
[1000][1010][2000][2010][2020][2030][1020][1030][3000][3010]
[3020][1040][4000][4010]PAT          0            0 [4020]
[1050][2000][2010][2020][2030][1020][1030][3000][3010]
[3020][1040][4000][4010]PETE         4            2 [4020]
[1050][2000][2010][2020][2030][1020][1030][3000][3010]
[3020][1040][4000][4010]PAT          0           -2 [4020]
[1050][2000][2010][2020][2030][1060][1070]
```

4. *Combining Methods for Postponed Debugging.* Sometimes the best method of debugging is to get away from the computer for a while, let the problem percolate in your brain, and come back to it later. Then, having the proper tools can be invaluable.

   Before stopping a debugging session, print some listings.

   A. LPRINT a complete, current listing of the program.
   B. Place a STOP statement in a strategic location in the program—in a place where you suspect the problem to lie. The location chosen might be right after the calculations, or perhaps after input has occurred.
   C. Turn on the trace option with TRON.
   D. Press CTRL-PRTSC. This turns on printer echo, so that everything that appears on the screen will also appear on the printer.
   E. Run the program.
   F. When the STOP occurs, verify that the execution is in the spot you want to check. This can be done by looking at the trace line numbers and the program listing.
   G. Do you wish you knew for sure the value of any variables at this time? Are any input values suspect? Or any calculations strange? If so, type PRINT variablename.
   H. Turn off printer echo by typing CTRL-PRTSC again.
   I. Now, take your listings, leave the computer, and give it some time. The printer output can be used later for debugging, away from the computer.

Appendix E
Answers to Chapter Feedback

Chapter 1, Feedback, p. 26

1. HALF A LOAF IS BETTER THAN NONE
2. HALF,   MY EYE
3. HAWKS 0   DOVES 0
4. 1   2   3   4   5
   6   7   8   9   10
5. Same as #4.
6. In line 10, RAM should be REM.
7. In line 60, the colons must be replaced by semicolons or commas.
8. In line 110, the INPUT statement must name a variable. It is not legal to place the actual number (the 1) on an INPUT statement.
9. Line 230 must say *PRINT* rather than PT.
10. The use of a variable name must be consistent. Change line 310 to:

        310 INPUT AGE

    (The problem could also be corrected by changing line 320 to PRINT A.)
11. What will print is not the numbers 1, 2, 3, but the contents of the variables ONE, TWO, and THREE. Unless a value has been assigned to the variables, each has the value zero.
12. The numbers will not all print on the same line. Since the numbers are separated by commas, they will print in the print zones. Only five numbers will be printed on one line.
13. The sum was not calculated. Add a line to the program:

        525   LET SUM = NUM1 + NUM2

Chapter 2, Feedback, p. 33

PORCUPINE.PIE	valid
COUNT#1	invalid—illegal # imbedded in name
ETC...	valid
A2	valid
2A	invalid—must begin with a letter
PRINT	invalid—reserved word

Chapter 2, Feedback, p. 36

1. 18
2. 1
3. 6
4. 5
5. 22
6. 2048
7. 22
8. 38
9. Valid
10. Invalid. The variable must appear to the left of the equal sign.
11. Valid

12. Valid
13. Invalid. Any calculations must appear on the right side of the equal sign. The results of the calculation are then assigned to the variable named on the left of the equal sign.
14. Invalid. No operations are assumed in BASIC. If multiplication is needed, it must be stated. Without an operational sign, this will generate a syntax error.
    150 LET ANS = NUM * (NUM - 1)
15. Valid

Chapter 2, Feedback, p. 37

1. Valid
2. Valid
3. Invalid—$ must be rightmost character.
4. Valid
5. Invalid—$ must be rightmost character.
6. Invalid—PRINT is a reserved word.
7. Invalid—PAY.CLASS is numeric. The value "M" cannot be assigned to a numeric variable.
8. Invalid—The value must be enclosed in quotation marks.
    `510 LET SSNO$ = ``550-51-5257''`
9. Valid
10. Invalid—The string literal ("SAMMY") must appear to the right of the equal sign, the variable to the left.
    `530 LET PERSON$ = "SAMMY"`

Chapter 2, Feedback, p. 44

1. ```
   100 INPUT "ENTER CLASS NAME ", CLASS$
   110 INPUT "ENTER THE CLASS COUNT ", COUNT
   ```

2. ```
   200 'INPUT NAME AND ADDRESS
   210 INPUT "ENTER NAME ", NAM$
   220 INPUT "ADDRESS      ", ADDR$
   230 'PRINT NAME AND ADDRESS ON PRINTER
   240 LPRINT NAM$ 250 LPRINT ADDR$
   ```

3. Note: Quotation marks will be needed around the data when it is input in order to accept the comma.

   ```
   300   INPUT "ENTER THE DATE, SURROUNDED BY QUOTATION MARKS ", DAT$
   ```

Chapter 2, Feedback, p. 46

1. Subroutines are a good way to group statements that together perform one function. Subroutines are also useful when a task must be performed from more than one location in a program.
2. Execution returns to the statement immediately following the GOSUB.
3. Try this on the computer.
4. No limit.

5. a. ```
      HELLO FROM LINE 100
      HELLO FROM LINE 200
      HELLO FROM LINE 120
      HELLO FROM LINE 200
      HELLO FROM LINE 140
      ```

   b. ```
      START HERE
      Undefined line number in 310
      ```

```
c. PRINTED BY LINE 400
   PRINTED BY LINE 500
   PRINTED BY LINE 540
   PRINTED BY LINE 610
   PRINTED BY LINE 590
   PRINTED BY LINE 560
   PRINTED BY LINE 520
   PRINTED BY LINE 420
```

```
d. ENTER FIRST NUMBER 1
   ENTER SECOND NUMBER 2
   ENTER THIRD NUMBER 3
   THE SUM IS 6
   THE SUM IS 6
   ENTER FIRST NUMBER 1
   ENTER SECOND NUMBER 2
   ENTER THIRD NUMBER 3
   RETURN without GOSUB in 340
```

Have you figured out why the strange results here? Look for END and RETURN statements.

Chapter 3, Feedback, p. 63
1. True
2. True
3. True
4. False
5. False
6. True
7. True
8. True
9. True
10. True

Chapter 3, Feedback, p. 65
1. True
2. False
3. True
4. False
5. True
6. No possible value of X satisfies the condition.
7. Any value for Y in the range 1–10 would make the condition true.

Chapter 3, Feedback, p. 71
1.
```
10 'PROGRAM TO PRINT NAME 5 TIMES
20 WHILE COUNT < 5
30    PRINT "LOUIE LOOP"
40    LET COUNT = COUNT + 1
50 WEND
60 END
```

2.
```
100 ' PRINT THE NUMBERS 1 - 10
110 WHILE NUMB < 10
120    LET NUMB = NUMB + 1
130    PRINT NUMB
140 WEND
150 END
```

3.
```
200 ' INPUT AND PRINT PARTICIPANT NAMES
210 INPUT "ENTER NAME (TYPE 'QUIT' TO END) ", NAM$
220 WHILE NAM$ <> "QUIT"
230    LPRINT NAM$
240    INPUT "ENTER NAME (TYPE 'QUIT' TO END) ", NAM$
250 WEND
260 END
```

4. None—assuming that Z = 0, the loop would never be entered.
5. X = 5   `*****`
   X = 10   `*********`
   X = 1   `*`
   X = 0   No output

Chapter 3, Feedback, p. 82

1. `25 25.4  25.40  25.396`

2.
```
FROGS      10
TOADS       5
POLLIWOG   75
```

3.
```
THE SCORE IS 12 FOR THE ROVERS
THE SCORE IS  6 FOR THE BRAVES
THE SCORE IS %125 FOR THE AMAZING AMAZ
```

4. `JOEY        SPENT    2.00 ON GUM`

5. Illegal function call—error message. The two variables must be reversed on line 830 to match the print image.

Chapter 3, Feedback, p. 85

1.
```
******$1.00
$250,000.00
******$0.60
**$1,000.00
%$123,456,789.00
```
2.
```
    4.0     50.5-  100.6-     0.0
    4.0+    50.5-  100.6-     0.0+
   +4.00   -50.45  %+100.63    +0.00
      $4.00      -$50.45    -$100.63     $0.00
  $    4.00  $  -50.45  $ -100.63 $    0.00
```

Chapter 3, Feedback, p. 85

1. Placing all print images at the beginning of the program will make them easier to find and to alter.
2. The actual print statements will be shorter, cleaner, and easier to read.
3. If a line is to be printed on both the screen and the printer, the print image can be shared.
4. It would be possible to change a print image during program execution, based on a condition in the program.

Chapter 4, Feedback, p. 101

1. `THE FROGS HAVE IT`
2. `IT'S THE TOADS & POLLIWOGS`
3. `IT'S TRUE`

```
4.    300 'COMPARE THE RELATIVE PRICES OF APPLES & ORANGES
      310 INPUT "HOW MUCH ARE THE APPLES"; APPLE
      320 INPUT "HOW MUCH ARE THE ORANGES"; ORANGE
      330 IF APPLE > ORANGE
          THEN
              PRINT "THE APPLES COST MORE"
          ELSE
              PRINT "THE ORANGES COST MORE"
      340 END
```

Chapter 4, Feedback, p. 107

```
100    IF K > 0
          THEN
              PRINT "THE ACCOUNT IS POSITIVE":
              LET K = 0:
              LET K.COUNTER = K.COUNTER + 1
          ELSE
              PRINT "THE ACCOUNT IS NOT POSITIVE"
```

Or, an alternate solution:

```
100    IF K > 0
          THEN GOSUB 200
          ELSE PRINT "THE ACCOUNT IS NOT POSITIVE"
::
::
199    RETURN
200    '***** POSITIVE BALANCE *****
210    PRINT "THE ACCOUNT IS POSITIVE"
220    LET K = 0
230    LET K.COUNTER = K.COUNTER + 1
240    RETURN
```

Chapter 4, Feedback, p. 115

1.   a. The variable types do not match in the READ and DATA statements. One way to correct:

```
40    DATA JOHN, 4, MARTHA, 5
```

   b. Out of data error. Another value is needed in the DATA list.
   c. In order to read a date (with an imbedded comma), quotation marks are needed.

```
70    DATA HUMPTY DUMPTY, "JAN. 15, 1990"
```

   d. No error will be generated, but only the first two values in the data list will be read.
   e. This will print the word "END" at the bottom of the list. A priming read is needed to eliminate the last line.

2.   ```
     50 READ ST.TIME$, END.TIME$
     60 DATA "1:25", "2:45"
     ```

Note: Quotation marks are needed because of the colons in the string values.

3.   ```
     200 READ WORD$
     210 WHILE WORD$ <> "END"
     220     PRINT WORD$
     230     LET WORD.COUNT = WORD.COUNT + 1
     240     READ WORD$
     250 WEND
     260 PRINT "THE NUMBER OF WORDS IS"; WORD.COUNT
     270 DATA list of words, separated by commas
     280 DATA END
     ```

Chapter 5, Feedback, p. 137

1. The term *top-down* means to break the program into its individual functions. The top-down idea can best be illustrated with a hierarchy chart, where each level shows breaking the program into successively smaller parts. Structured programming includes the top-down concept, as well as several other ideas and guidelines intended to produce "good" programs. The standards include rules for flow of control, module formation, and coding guidelines such as indentation, variable names, and remarks.
2. Short variable names do indeed make programs more concise. However, the programs will be more cryptic and difficult to read, debug, and maintain.
3. A subroutine that adds to subtotals, prints a detail line, and reads data would most likely be an example of poor cohesion.

Chapter 6, Feedback, p. 148

1. Each page after the first will have headings and one detail line.
2. It will generally be much faster to skip to the new page rather than print blank lines.
3. There are 66 lines, assuming 6 lines to the inch.
4. Detail lines are the lines printed for each iteration of the program. One input record generally produces one detail line. The other lines are heading lines, total lines, etc.

Chapter 6, Feedback, p. 155

1. The field used to determine the timing of the subtotals is called the *control variable*. When the control variable changes (or breaks), it is time to print subtotals.
2. In the detail calculations, add to two fields. In the control break, add to two report totals, and zero out the two subtotal fields.
3. Change the two print images ST\$ and RT\$ to include an average field, and change the LPRINTs for the subtotals and report totals to include the averages.

```
6520   LPRINT USING ST$; CAL.SUBTOT, GROUP.AVG
7020   LPRINT USING RT$; CAL.TOT, REPORT.AVG
```

Add the lines to calculate the group average:

```
5015   LET GROUP.COUNT = GROUP.COUNT + 1
6512   LET GROUP.AVG = CAL.SUBTOT / GROUP.COUNT
```

In the subtotal routine, add these lines:

```
6545   LET REPORT.COUNT = REPORT.COUNT + GROUP.COUNT
6555   LET GROUP.COUNT = 0
```

Add this line just before printing the report totals:

```
7015   LET GROUP.AVG = CAL.TOT / REPORT.COUNT
```

4. A second control variable (the division) and a division subtotal variable are needed. When the division changes, division subtotals are printed, added into the group subtotals, and zeroed out. When the group number changes, first a division control break is done, then a group control break. At the end of the report, the division subtotals, group subtotals, and report subtotals are printed.

Prime read
While not end of data
    Add to division subtotals
    Print detail line
    Read next data

>> If new division
>> > Print division subtotals
>> > Add division subtotals to group subtotals
>> > Let division subtotals = 0
>> If new group
>> > Print group subtotals
>> > Add group subtotals to report totals
>> > Let group subtotals = 0
> EndWhile
> Print report totals

Chapter 7, Feedback, p. 175

1.
```
10 CLS
20 LOCATE 12,36
30 PRINT "YOUR NAME"
```

2.
```
100 'PRINT A BOX IN THE CENTER OF THE SCREEN
110 CLS
120 LOCATE 10, 35
130 PRINT "*********"
135 LOCATE 11, 35
140 PRINT "*         *"
145 LOCATE 12, 35
150 PRINT "*         *"
155 LOCATE 13, 35
160 PRINT "*         *"
175 LOCATE 14, 35
180 PRINT "*********"
190 ' NOW INPUT IN THE CENTER OF THE BOX
200 LOCATE 12, 38
210 INPUT NUMBER
```

Chapter 7, Feedback, p. 189

1. When using an INPUT$ or INKEY$ function, it may be necessary to make the cursor visible with the LOCATE statement.
2. Hopefully, you thought of several ways. Here are two:

```
500    PRINT STRING$(40, "=")
510    PRINT STRING$(40, 61)
```

3. Convert the numeric variable to a string. Then the LEN function can be used. However, the string will include one character for the sign.

```
550    LET DIGITS = LEN(STR$(NUM)) - 1
```

4. A common use of the VAL function is to convert data from a string variable to a numeric variable after validity checking.
5. INKEY$ does not halt program execution to input characters. It also does not require the ENTER key to be pressed, as does the INPUT statement.
6. Although neither INKEY$ nor INPUT$ require the ENTER key to be pressed, there is an important difference between the two. INPUT$ halts program execution and INKEY$ does not. So INKEY$ would be used when execution is not to be halted.
7. Since INPUT$ *does* halt program execution, it would be used when the input must take place before any further operations occur. INPUT$ is handy in the situation of the message: PRESS ANY KEY TO CONTINUE.
8.
```
10 '  READ AND PRINT, RIGHT-JUSTIFIED
20 READ FRUIT$
```

```
     30 WHILE FRUIT$ <> "END"
     40     PRINT TAB(30 - LEN(FRUIT$)+1); FRUIT$
     50     READ FRUIT$
     60 WEND
     100 DATA FIG, WATERMELON, PINEAPPLE, PLUM, MANGO, END
  9. DOG
 10. 100 INPUT P$
     110 LET PER = INSTR(P$,".")
     120 PRINT MID$(P$,PER+1)
 11. 100 INPUT P$
     110 LET PER = INSTR(P$,".")
     120 IF PER > 0
         THEN
             PRINT MID$(P$,PER+1)
 12. 200 LPRINT CHR$(12);        'ADVANCE PAPER TO TOP-OF-PAGE
 13. 400 LET CHAR$ = INPUT$(1)
     410 WHILE CHAR$ <> "*"
     420     PRINT CHAR$;
     430     LET CHAR$ = INPUT$(1)
     440 WEND
```

Chapter 9, Feedback, p. 225
1. The most common use of the ON...GOSUB statement is for menu programs.
2. 3—Branch to subroutine at line 625
   0—"Fall through" to the statement immediately following the ON...GOSUB statement
     5—Same as 0
   −1—Same as 0
3. Each subroutine must have a RETURN statement.
4. When the RETURN is encountered, control will pass to the first statement following the ON...GOSUB.

Chapter 10, Feedback, p. 257
1. a. Correct
   b. Incorrect. Line 150 must be NEXT A.
   c. Two errors here: The FOR statement must have a variable for the index (rather than 4). The NEXT statement is also incorrect. FOR is a reserved word that cannot appear in a NEXT statement.

   ```
   200  FOR INDEX = 1 TO 10 STEP 2
   250  NEXT INDEX
   ```

   d. Correct
   e. Correct
   f. For this to work, it needs a negative STEP. As it is, the loop will never be entered, since 10 is already greater than 1.

2.
   ```
   500 ' PRINT THE NUMBERS 3-100
   510 FOR INDEX = 3 TO 100 STEP 3
   520     PRINT INDEX
   530 NEXT INDEX
   ```

3.
   ```
   700 ' PRINT 10 LINES
   710 FOR COUNT = 1 TO 10
   720     PRINT "THIS IS A LARK"
   730 NEXT COUNT
   ```

4. a.
```
    BICYCLE         150
    TRAIN           65
    BALL            1.5
    NERD            .27
    GAME            6.95
                    223.72
```
    b. 10
        12
        14

    c. ********

5.

	Loop Iterations	Index after Loop Completion
a.	4	14
b.	10	0
c.	7	6.5
d.	0	5
e.	3	4

Chapter 10, Feedback, p. 260

1.
```
    2               1
    2               2
    2               3
    5               1
    5               2
    5               3
```

2. a.
```
    *****
    **
    *********
    ******
    *
```

    b. The PRINT on line 560 is needed to force the next output to another line. Without it, all the stars would appear on one line.

```
    ***********************
```

Chapter 10, Feedback, p. 265

1. Integer variables can be used anywhere whole units are being counted (people, accounts, balls, etc.). The index of a FOR/NEXT loop is a good candidate for integer variables.
2. Double precision will hold more digits accurately than single precision.
3. Calculations are quicker with single-precision variables than with double. Also, single-precision variables use half as much storage as double.

Chapter 10, Feedback, pp. 275-276

1. a. 2   e. illegal function call
    b. 2   f. 4
    c. 2   g. 4
    d. 3   h. -1

2. a. 5   c. ****
    b. 20   d. YES PLEASE

3. A dummy argument holds the place for an actual argument. At the time the function is executed, the actual argument will take the place of the dummy argument.
4. There is no limit to the number of operations in the expression. The only limit is the 255-character line length.
5. Left as a thought-provoking exercise.

Chapter 11, Feedback, p. 286

1. Valid
2. Valid
3. Valid
4. Invalid. I*3 is 30, which is too large to be used as a subscript in this array.
5. Valid. The array actually has an element 0.
6. Invalid. No negative subscripts are allowed.
7. Valid. The result will be rounded, so this is a reference to A(3).
8. Valid. The resulting subscript will be 0.

Chapter 11, Feedback, p. 287

1.
```
100 INPUT "ENTER NAME, TYPE 'EOD' TO QUIT ", ANAME$
110 LET SUB = 1
120 WHILE ANAME$ <> "EOD"
130     LET NAM$(SUB) = ANAME$
140     LET SUB = SUB + 1
150     INPUT "ENTER NAME, TYPE 'EOD' TO QUIT ", ANAME$
160 WEND
```

Or, an alternate approach, which will place EOD into the highest array element:
```
200 LET SUB = 1
210 INPUT "ENTER NAME, TYPE 'EOD' TO QUIT ", NAM$(SUB)
220 WHILE NAM$(SUB) <> "EOD"
230     LET SUB = SUB + 1
240     INPUT "ENTER NAME, TYPE 'EOD' TO QUIT ", NAM$(SUB)
250 WEND
1020 NEXT
```

2.
```
100 READ ANAME$
110 LET SUB = 1
120 WHILE ANAME$ <> "EOD"
130     LET NAM$(SUB) = ANAME$
135     LET SUB = SUB + 1
140     READ ANAME$
150 WEND
300 DATA SAM,JOE,PETE,DAN,MELVIN,EOD
```

Or, an alternate approach, which will place EOD into the highest element:
```
200 LET SUB = 1
210 READ NAM$(SUB)
220 WHILE NAM$(SUB) <> "EOD"
230     LET SUB = SUB + 1
240     READ NAM$(SUB)
250 WEND
300 DATA SAM,JOE,PETE,DAN,MELVIN,EOD
```

Chapter 11, Feedback, p. 302

1.
```
300 DIM K(20)
310 FOR SUB = 1 TO 20
320     LET K(SUB) = 100
330 NEXT SUB
```

2.
```
400 ' DIVIDE EACH EVEN NUMBERED ELEMENT BY 2
410 FOR SUB = 2 TO 20 STEP 2
420     LET K(SUB) = K(SUB) / 2
430 NEXT SUB
```

3.
```
500 ' SUBTRACT 1 FROM EVERY ELEMENT
510 FOR SUB = 1 TO 20
520     LET K(SUB) = K(SUB) - 1
530 NEXT SUB
```

4.
```
600 ' PRINT ALL 20 ELEMENTS, 10 PER LINE
610 FOR SUB = 1 TO 20
620    PRINT K(SUB);
630    IF SUB = 10
          THEN PRINT        'BEGIN NEW LINE
640 NEXT SUB
```

Alternate approach:
```
700 ' PRINT ALL 20 ELEMENTS, 10 PER LINE
710 FOR BEGIN = 1 TO 11 STEP 10
720    FOR SUB = BEGIN TO BEGIN + 10
730       PRINT K(SUB);
740    NEXT SUB
750    PRINT
760 NEXT BEGIN
```

5.
```
10 ' DIMENSION AND FILL A TABLE
20 DIM GOODIES(6)
30 FOR SUB = 1 TO 6
40    READ GOODIES(SUB)
50 NEXT SUB
60 DATA CANDY, ICE CREAM, POPCORN, GUM, COOKIES, GUM DROPS
```

6. In a serial search, every element of the table is checked for a match. In a binary search, the number of elements to search is repeatedly divided in half until a match is found.

7. A binary search should be used when the table is large and can be arranged in sequence.

8. A serial search may be used for small tables or when the most popular elements can be placed at the beginning of the list.

Chapter 12, Feedback, p. 314

1.
```
10 DIM GRID(3,5)
```

2.
```
50 FOR COL = 1 TO 5
60    LET GRID(1,COL) = 1
70 NEXT COL
```

3.
```
100 FOR COL = 1 TO 5
110    LET GRID(2,COL) = 2
120 NEXT COL
```

4.
```
150 FOR COL = 1 TO 5
160    LET GRID(3,COL) = GRID(2,COL) + GRID(1,COL)
170 NEXT COL
```

5.
```
200 FOR ROW = 1 TO 3
210    FOR COL = 1 TO 5
220       PRINT GRID(ROW,COL);
230    NEXT COL
240    PRINT
250 NEXT ROW
```

Chapter 13, Feedback, p. 346

1. A disk track is one of the concentric circles on the disk surface used for storing data.

2. A sector is a segment of a track.

3. The number of characters per sector differs with the operating system in use. CP/M uses sectors of 128 characters, while MS-DOS uses 512 characters per sector.

4. A program file holds executable BASIC statements. A data file holds actual data to be used by a program.

5. a. B: signifies that the file is stored on the diskette in the B drive.
    b. .PRT is the file extension, which is generally used to group programs into like types.
6. a. File
    b. Record
    c. Student name
    d. File

Chapter 13, Feedback, p. 353

1. When the file is read into a program, the fields must be delimited (separated). The commas indicate where one field stops and another starts.
2. The primary function of the OPEN statement is to make the file available for processing. If the file is to be input, it must be found on the diskette. If the program is going to create the file, a new directory entry must be created and space allocated for the new file.
3. The consequence of omitting a CLOSE depends on how the program ends. If an END statement is executed, BASIC will automatically CLOSE the file. If the file is not closed, data will likely be lost at the end of the file.
4. This is a good way to lose a file. The new data will replace the data in the previously existing file.
5. A new directory entry will be created for the new file.
6. The PRINT# statement should *only* be used on a system that lacks the WRITE# statement.

Chapter 13, Feedback, p. 361

1. An error message will be generated.
2. The file buffer is used to temporarily hold the data coming from or going to the diskette. When the data is physically written on the diskette, only whole sectors are written. Data is "saved up," until a full sector can be written. The same is true for reading data from the diskette. An entire sector is read into the buffer. Then the data is actually passed to the program as the INPUT# statements are executed.
3. A file number is in effect only for the duration of the program. The file number is *not* stored with the file. Each program that accesses the file may refer to the file with a different file number.
4. It is not necessary to know the variable names when reading data from a file. The variables may be called by different names when they are read. The concept is similar to the data in DATA statements. Each field is assigned to the next variable in the sequence named.
5. The EOF(n) function evaluates TRUE when the last *good* data is read. The final data may be processed after it is read, before termination of the loop.
6. Sequential files can be opened for INPUT or OUTPUT, but not both at the same time. It is not possible to read a record, make changes in the data, and write it back in the file.
7. To add data to the end of a file, the file must be open in the OUTPUT mode with the pointer at the end of the file. If APPEND mode is not available, the only way to accomplish this task is to write the entire file. After the file is copied, the pointer is then at the end of the new file, ready to add any new records.

Chapter 14, Feedback, p. 393

1. The only way BASIC has to find any record in the file is to count the number of bytes from the beginning of the file. If the records were not all the same length, this would not be possible.
2. The record length is specified in the OPEN statement.
3. The field lengths are specified in the FIELD statement.

4. For string variables, the length chosen should be as long as the longest value expected to be in the field. For numeric data, fixed length strings must be established. Integers require two bytes, single-precision variables require four bytes, and double-precision variables require eight bytes.

5. When a record is written to the disk, the contents of the record buffer are output from the program. Before the record can be written, the data must be placed into the buffer with the LSET (or RSET) statement.

6. When a record is read from the disk (GET), the record is placed in the file buffer. Then the field names specified in the FIELD statement are used to refer to the data.

7. a.
```
200 ' READ AND PRINT THE 4TH RECORD
210 LET REC = 4
220 GET #2, REC
230 LET QUANT = CVS(B.QUANT$)
240 PRINT B.DESC$, QUANT
```
   b.
```
400 'BUILD A NEW RECORD
405 '
410 'INPUT THE DATA
415 '
420 INPUT "ITEM NUMBER      ", ITEM
430 INPUT "DESCRIPTION      ", DESC$
440 INPUT "QUANTITY         ", QUANT
450 '
460 ' SET UP BUFFER
470 '
480 LSET B.DESC$ = DESC$
490 LSET B.QUANT$ = MKS$(QUANT)
500 '
510 ' WRITE THE RECORD IN THE FILE
520 '
530 PUT #2, ITEM
```
   c.
```
600 ' LIST THE ENTIRE FILE
610 '
620 LET ITEM = 1
630 WHILE NOT EOF(2)
640      GET #2, ITEM
650      LET QUANT = CVS(B.QUANT$)
660      PRINT ITEM, B.DESC$, QUANT
670      LET ITEM = ITEM + 1
680 WEND
```

Appendix F
Summary of Reserved Words in BASIC

These words are reserved by BASIC and cannot be used as variable names. However, reserved words may be imbedded within a variable name. When using the reserved words in their intended fashion, be sure to properly delimit them (with spaces or other special characters required by statement syntax).

Not all of these words are reserved by all versions of Microsoft BASIC, but avoidance of the entire list will provide a measure of compatibility if the program is moved from one version to another.

ABS	ELSE	LPOS	RIGHT$
AND	END	LPRINT	RMDIR
ASC	ENVIRON	LSET	RND
ATN	EOF	MERGE	RSET
AUTO	EQV	MID$	RUN
BEEP	ERASE	MKD$	SAVE
BLOAD	ERDEV	MKDIR	SCREEN
BSAVE	ERL	MKI$	SGN
CALL	ERR	MKS$	SHELL
CDBL	ERROR	MOD	SIN
CHAIN	EXP	MOTOR	SOUND
CHDIR	FIELD	NAME	SPACE$
CHR$	FILES	NEW	SPC(
CINT	FIX	NEXT	SQR
CIRCLE	FNXXXXXX	NOT	STEP
CLEAR	FOR	OCT$	STICK
CLOSE	FRE	OFF	STOP
CLS	GET	ON	STR$
COLOR	GOSUB	OPEN	STRIG
COM	GOTO	OPTION	STRING$
COMMON	HEX$	OR	SWAP
CONT	IF	OUT	SYSTEM
COS	IMP	PAINT	TAB(
CSNG	INKEY$	PALETTE	TAN
CSRLIN	INP	PEEK	THEN
CVD	INPUT	PEN	TIMER
CVI	INSTR	PLAY	TIME$
CVS	INT	PMAP	TO
DATA	IOCTL	POINT	TROFF
DATE$	KEY	POKE	TRON
DEF	KILL	POS	USING
DEFDBL	LEFT$	PRESET	USR
DEFFN	LEN	PRINT	VAL
DEFINT	LET	PSET	VARPTR
DEFSEG	LINE	PUT	VIEW
DEFSNG	LIST	RANDOMIZE	WAIT
DEFSTR	LLIST	READ	WEND
DEFUSR	LOAD	REM	WHILE
DELETE	LOC	RENUM	WIDTH
DIM	LOCATE	RESET	WINDOW
DRAW	LOF	RESTORE	WRITE
EDIT	LOG	RESUME	XOR
		RETURN	

Appendix G
Simulating IF-THEN-ELSE and WHILE/WEND for Other BASIC Versions

Writing BASIC Programs without IF-THEN-ELSE or WHILE/WEND

To write BASIC programs without the IF-THEN-ELSE statement, a combination of two statements must be used—the IF-THEN statement and the GOTO statement.

The IF-THEN Statement—General Form

```
Format 1
    line number IF  <condition> THEN  <line number>
```

The condition is evaluated for *true* or *false*. When the condition tests *true*, the program will branch to the line number named after the word THEN. If the condition is *false*, the program will not branch, but continue with the next line following the IF statement.

```
Format 2
    line number IF  <condition> THEN  <statement>
```

The condition is evaluated for *true* or *false*. When the condition tests *true*, the statement following the THEN is executed.

Note: Format 2 is not available on all versions of BASIC. Format 1 is the only truly standard form of the IF statement.

The IF-THEN Statement—Examples

```
Format 1
    100   IF X > Y THEN 150
    200   IF NAM$ = "END" THEN 500
Format 2
    1000   IF GRADE > 60 THEN PRINT "YOU PASSED"
    1500   IF COUNTY$ = "LA" THEN LET TAX.RATE = .065
```

Coding IF-THEN-ELSE Logic

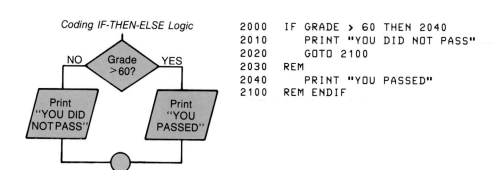

Coding IF-THEN-ELSE Logic

```
2000   IF GRADE > 60 THEN 2040
2010      PRINT "YOU DID NOT PASS"
2020      GOTO 2100
2030   REM
2040      PRINT "YOU PASSED"
2100   REM ENDIF
```

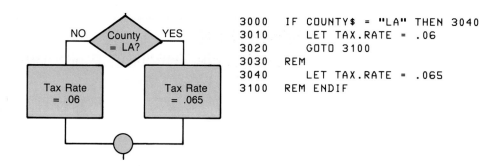

```
3000     IF COUNTY$ = "LA" THEN 3040
3010         LET TAX.RATE = .06
3020         GOTO 3100
3030     REM
3040         LET TAX.RATE = .065
3100     REM ENDIF
```

Coding Loops Without the WHILE/WEND

Whenever a loop appears in a program, there must always be a decision—"Should the loop be executed again?" That decision is made by the WHILE statement in Microsoft BASIC. If the WHILE statement is not available, the same logic may be coded with a combination of the IF-THEN and a GOTO.

For programs to be properly structured, the loop decision must be made at the top of the loop or the bottom of the loop (*never* in the middle of the loop). The best practice is to place the decision (IF statement) at the top of the loop. At the bottom of the loop, always code a GOTO back to the decision. An examination of the flowchart in figure G1 and coding below will reveal that the two program versions do *exactly* the same thing and that both follow the flowchart.

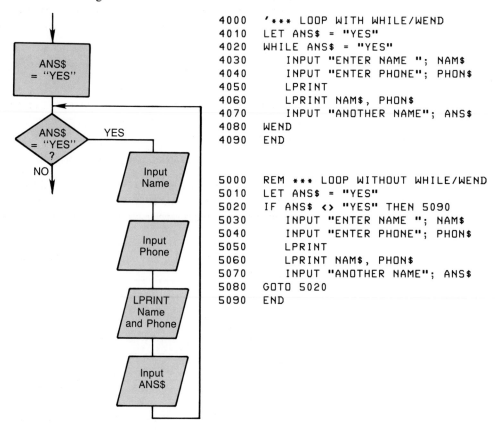

```
4000     '*** LOOP WITH WHILE/WEND
4010     LET ANS$ = "YES"
4020     WHILE ANS$ = "YES"
4030         INPUT "ENTER NAME "; NAM$
4040         INPUT "ENTER PHONE"; PHON$
4050         LPRINT
4060         LPRINT NAM$, PHON$
4070         INPUT "ANOTHER NAME"; ANS$
4080     WEND
4090     END


5000     REM *** LOOP WITHOUT WHILE/WEND
5010     LET ANS$ = "YES"
5020     IF ANS$ <> "YES" THEN 5090
5030         INPUT "ENTER NAME "; NAM$
5040         INPUT "ENTER PHONE"; PHON$
5050         LPRINT
5060         LPRINT NAM$, PHON$
5070         INPUT "ANOTHER NAME"; ANS$
5080     GOTO 5020
5090     END
```

Indentation

The indentation shown for IF-THEN-ELSE logic and for loops is strongly recommended to improve program readability.

Appendix H
Using Special Functions of Printers

Special Printer Functions

Most printers available for use on microcomputers have capabilities beyond straight text printing. Many dot matrix printers have multiple character sets such as italics, condensed printing, or extrawide characters. Features that may often be switched include line length, margins, tabs, underlining, vertical and horizontal spacing, and proportional spacing.

You have already seen how a special, nonprinting character can control the printer. In chapter 6, you learned to send the printer a form-feed character, CHR$(12), to cause the paper to advance to the top of the next page. CHR$(12) is generally accepted as the form-feed. Most other special characters are *not* standard, however. Each printer manufacturer chooses a set of control codes that control the specific functions of that printer.

Some printer manuals clearly demonstrate the method of controlling the special features. Others print tables of codes and leave it to the programmer to figure out. A term often used is "escape sequence." This refers to a sequence of characters, preceded by the Escape character [CHR$(27)—refer to the ASCII code chart in appendix C]. For example, if your printer manual requires an ESC (Escape) and a "Q" to turn on a feature, the statement would be similar to:

```
1050   LPRINT CHR$(27); "Q"
```

The examples that follow are for Epson printers (also, the IBM dot matrix printer). For any other printer, consult your printer manual for the correct codes. The examples are intended as a guideline to help you figure out how to use the specific codes for your printer.

```
100   LPRINT CHR$(27); CHR$(87); CHR$(1) 'TURN ON DOUBLE WIDE
                                          CHARACTERS
110   LPRINT "BIG TITLE"
120   LPRINT CHR$(27); CHR$(87); CHR$(0) 'TURN OFF DOUBLE WIDE
                                          CHARACTERS
130   LPRINT
140   LPRINT "REGULAR SIZE"
150   LPRINT CHR$(15)                    'TURN ON CONDENSED MODE
155   LPRINT
160   LPRINT "DOWNRIGHT SMALL"
170   LPRINT
180   LPRINT CHR$(18)                    'TURN OFF CONDENSED MODE
190   LPRINT "BACK TO NORMAL"; CHR$(27); CHR$(45); CHR$(1);
             "UNDERLINED "; CHR$(27); CHR$(45); CHR$(0);
             "AND NOT UNDERLINED"

RUN
```

BIG TITLE

REGULAR SIZE

DOWNRIGHT SMALL

BACK TO NORMAL <u>UNDERLINED</u> AND NOT UNDERLINED

Example Program: Controlling Many Printer Features

Program Listing

```
100 '        PROGRAM TO USE THE SPECIAL FUNCTIONS OF THE EPSON
105 '        PRINTER
110 '
120 '        MAY BE USED AS A STAND-ALONE PROGRAM, OR INDIVIDUAL
130 '          SUBROUTINES MAY BE INCLUDED IN PROGRAMS
140 '

1000 '*************** PROGRAM MAINLINE ********************
1010 WHILE CHOICE <> 16
1020     GOSUB 1500                'DISPLAY MENU AND INPUT CHOICE
1030     ON CHOICE GOSUB 2000, 2100, 2200, 2400, 2600, 2800, 3000,
                      3200, 3400, 3600, 3800, 4000, 4200, 4400, 4600
1040 WEND
1050 CLS
1060 END

1500 '************** DISPLAY MENU AND INPUT CHOICE ***********
1510 CLS
1520 PRINT TAB(24); "EPSON PRINTER SPECIAL FUNCTIONS"
1530 PRINT:PRINT
1540 PRINT TAB(15); "1.   TURN ON  COMPRESSED CHARACTER MODE"
1550 PRINT TAB(15); "2.   TURN OFF COMPRESSED CHARACTER MODE"
1560 PRINT TAB(15); "3.   TURN ON DOUBLE WIDTH PRINTING"
1570 PRINT TAB(15); "4.   TURN OFF DOUBLE WIDTH PRINTING"
1580 PRINT TAB(15); "5.   TURN ON EMPHASIZED MODE"
1590 PRINT TAB(15); "6.   TURN OFF EMPHASIZED MODE"
1600 PRINT TAB(15); "7.   TURN ON SUPERSCRIPT MODE"
1610 PRINT TAB(15); "8.   TURN ON SUBSCRIPT MODE"
1620 PRINT TAB(15); "9.   TURN ON DOUBLE STRIKE MODE"
1630 PRINT TAB(14); "10.   TURN OFF SUPERSCRIPT, SUBSCRIPT, AND DOUBLE
STRIKE"
1640 PRINT TAB(14); "11.   TURN ON ITALIC CHARACTER SET"
1650 PRINT TAB(14); "12.   TURN OFF ITALIC CHARACTER SET"
1660 PRINT TAB(14); "13.   RESET LINE LENGTH"
1670 PRINT TAB(14); "14.   SET NUMBER OF LINES PER PAGE"
1680 PRINT TAB(14); "15.   TURN OFF ALL SPECIAL FUNCTIONS"
1690 PRINT TAB(14); "16.   EXIT PROGRAM"
1700 PRINT:PRINT
1710 PRINT TAB(19); "ENTER CHOICE (1-16)";
1720 INPUT CHOICE$
1730 LET CHOICE = VAL(CHOICE$)
1740 RETURN

2000 '********** TURN ON COMPRESSED MODE *****************
2010 LPRINT CHR$(15);
2020 RETURN

2100 '********** TURN OFF COMPRESSED MODE ****************
2110 LPRINT CHR$(18);
2120 RETURN
```

```
2200 '********** TURN ON DOUBLE WIDTH PRINTING ****************
2210 LPRINT CHR$(27); CHR$(87); CHR$(1);
2220 RETURN


2400 '********** TURN OFF DOUBLE WIDTH PRINTING ***************
2410 LPRINT CHR$(27); CHR$(87); CHR$(0);
2420 RETURN


2600 '********** TURN ON EMPHASIZED MODE *******************
2610 LPRINT CHR$(27); CHR$(69);
2620 RETURN


2800 '********** TURN OFF EMPHASIZED MODE ******************
2810 LPRINT CHR$(27); CHR$(70);
2820 RETURN
3000 '********** TURN ON SUPERSCRIPT MODE ******************
3010 LPRINT CHR$(27); CHR$(83); CHR$(0);
3020 RETURN


3200 '********** TURN ON SUBSCRIPT MODE *******************
3210 LPRINT CHR$(27); CHR$(83); CHR$(1);
3220 RETURN


3400 '********** TURN ON DOUBLE STRIKE MODE ***************
3410 LPRINT CHR$(27); CHR$(71);
3420 RETURN


3600 '*** TURN OFF SUPERSCRIPT, SUBSCRIPT, AND DOUBLE STRIKE ***
3610 LPRINT CHR$(27); CHR$(72);
3620 RETURN


3800 '********** TURN ON ITALIC CHARACTER SET ***************
3810 LPRINT CHR$(27); CHR$(52);
3820 RETURN


4000 '********** TURN OFF ITALIC CHARACTER SET **************
4010 LPRINT CHR$(27); CHR$(53);
4020 RETURN


4200 '********** RESET LINE LENGTH ********************
4210 CLS
4220 PRINT:PRINT:PRINT
4230 PRINT TAB(15); "RESET LINE LENGTH"
4240 PRINT
4250 PRINT TAB(10); "NUMBER OF CHARACTERS FOR LINE LENGTH";
4260 INPUT LENGTH
4270 LPRINT CHR$(27); "Q"; CHR$(LENGTH);
4280 RETURN


4400 '********** SET NUMBER OF LINES PER PAGE ****************
4410 CLS
4420 PRINT:PRINT:PRINT
4430 PRINT TAB(15); "HOW MANY LINES PER PAGE";
4470 INPUT LINES
4480 PRINT
4490 INPUT "DO YOU WANT TO SKIP OVER PERFORATIONS (Y/N)"; ANS$
4500 INPUT "ALIGN PRINTER FOR FIRST LINE AND PRESS RETURN"; X$
4510 LPRINT CHR$(27); "C"; CHR$(LINES);
4520 IF ANS$ = "Y"
        THEN LPRINT CHR$(27); "N"; CHR$(6);
4530 RETURN


4600 '********** TURN OFF ALL SPECIAL FUNCTIONS **************
4610 ' RESETS ALL SPECIAL MODES TO POWER UP STATE (INCLUDING TOF)
4620 LPRINT CHR$(27); CHR$(64);
4630 RETURN
4700 '************ END OF PROGRAM ********************
```

Appendix I
Error Trapping, CHAIN, and COMMON

Error Trapping

When errors occur in program execution, a BASIC error message is printed. Common error messages seen by programmers include SYNTAX ERROR and ILLEGAL FUNCTION CALL, which are both caused by misuse of the BASIC language. It goes without saying that all programmer errors will be removed from a program before it is turned over to a user.

There are some errors that may occur when the user runs the program. The user may neglect to switch on the printer, the printer may be out of paper, the door of the diskette reader may be open, or the wrong disk inserted. BASIC also prints error messages for this type of error and halts program execution. A complete list of all possible errors can be found in a BASIC manual. See table I.1 for a partial listing of common errors.

A BASIC program may intercept the error conditions, handle the situation, and resume processing. Having the program take care of the error condition (rather than allow BASIC to send the standard system message) is called error trapping. To accomplish the error trapping, two new BASIC statements are needed—ON ERROR and RESUME—and two BASIC variables—ERR and ERL.

The ON ERROR Statement—General Form

line number **ON ERROR GOTO** line number of error routine

For error trapping to occur, the ON ERROR statement must be executed before any error condition occurs. Therefore, it is recommended that the ON ERROR statement appear at the beginning of the program. If any error occurs later in the program, the subroutine named on the ON ERROR statement will be executed.

The ON ERROR Statement—Example

```
500    '********** PROGRAM MAINLINE **************
510    ON ERROR GOTO 10000
520    ...
::
599    END
10000   '******** ERROR HANDLING SUBROUTINE ******
::
::
```

If any error occurs during program execution (including syntax errors), control will pass to line 10000. In the error handling subroutine, the error numbers may be checked, messages printed to the user, and a decision may be made to continue processing or to abort the program.

Determining the Cause of the Error— ERR and ERL

Two BASIC supplied variables are available to indicate the cause and location of any error. When an error condition occurs, BASIC places the error code into the variable ERR, and the offending line number into the variable ERL.

ERR and ERL—Program Variables

```
10050   IF ERR = 2
            THEN PRINT "THIS IS A PROGRAMMER CAUSED SYNTAX ERROR":
                PRINT "ERROR OCCURRED AT LINE"; ERL
10080   IF ERR = 71
            THEN PRINT "CHECK THE DISKETTE DRIVE"
```

Table I.1.
Common error codes.

Number	Message
1	NEXT without FOR
2	Syntax error
3	RETURN without GOSUB
4	Out of data
5	Illegal function call
6	Overflow (The number computed is too large to fit into the the variable type being used.)
9	Subscript out of range
11	Division by zero
19	No RESUME (The error trapping routine has been entered, but it does not contain a RESUME statement.)
25	Device fault (A hardware error.)
27	Out of Paper (Either the printer is out of paper or not switched on.)
53	File not found (The file specified does not exist.)
57	Device I/O error (An error on an I/O device—some systems return this error for disk drive door open or disk not inserted in drive—see error 71.)
58	File already exists
61	Diskette full
70	Disk Write Protect (An attempt was made to write on a disk that is write-protected.)
71	Disk not ready (The disk drive door is open or a diskette is not in the drive—see error 57 above.)

The RESUME Statement

```
line number RESUME
line number RESUME NEXT
line number RESUME line number for continuation
```

The RESUME statement is used to continue program execution after an error occurs. The statement appears only in an error-handling subroutine.

The first example (RESUME by itself) will resume execution at the statement that caused the error. The RESUME NEXT will resume execution at the statement immediately following the one that caused the error. The third example, "RESUME line number," will resume execution at the named line number.

```
10050   IF ERR = 27
            THEN PRINT "CHECK THE PRINTER":
                 RESUME
```

What If You Don't Want to RESUME?

Some error conditions can be handled by the program, others cannot. You would not want to check for every possible error condition in your program. The statement

```
ON ERROR GOTO 0
```

turns off error trapping. If there is an error condition that has not been resolved (with a RESUME), BASIC will print the system error message and halt execution.

Any error handling subroutine should include two elements:

1. What to do for specific errors.
   Check error codes
   Print messages
   Perhaps await a keypress
   RESUME
2. What to do for any other error.
   ON ERROR GOTO 0

Example Program: Error Trapping

Program Listing

```
500 '**************** PROGRAM MAINLINE *********************
510 ON ERROR GOTO 10000        'TRAP ANY ERRORS
515 '**** GENERATE SOME ERRORS TO TEST PROGRAM ****************
520 OPEN "I", #1, "TESTFILE"   'NONEXISTENT FILE
530 LPRINT "TO THE PRINTER"      'WITH PRINTER TURNED OFF
600 END


10000 '*************** ERROR TRAPPING ROUTINE ******************
10010 '
10020 '*************** DISK DRIVE NOT READY ********************
10030 IF ERR = 71 OR ERR = 57
          THEN PRINT "CHECK DISKETTE DRIVE, AND PRESS ANY KEY TO CONTINUE"
              LET X$ = INPUT$(1): RESUME
10050 '*************** WRONG DISK MOUNTED *********************
10060 IF ERR = 53
          THEN PRINT "THE FILE NEEDED FOR THIS PROGRAM IS NOT ON THE DISK":
          PRINT "MOUNT THE CORRECT DISK,": LET X$ = INPUT$(1): RESUME
10100 '**** PRINTER OFF OR OUT OF PAPER *********************
10110 IF ERR = 27
          THEN PRINT "CHECK THE PRINTER, AND PRESS ANY KEY TO CONTINUE":
              LET X$ = INPUT$(1): RESUME
```

```
10200 '********** ANY OTHER ERROR ****************************
10210 CLOSE                          'CLOSE ALL FILES BEFORE STOPPING
10220 ON ERROR GOTO 0
10230 '************* END OF PROGRAM **************************
```

Note for Printer Errors: The error condition 27 (printer out of paper or not ready) may or may not occur, depending on the specific computer system running. Many computers have both hardware and software enhancements that temporarily store output destined for the printer. These *buffers* and *spoolers* send an indication to BASIC that the printed output has been properly received, even though the printer may be switched off. BASIC cannot detect this condition.

Linking Programs Together

Programs vary in size from a few lines to many hundreds of lines. As programs grow in size, the limits of main storage can quickly be exceeded. If a program is too large to fit in the computer's memory, *none* of the program will be loaded. BASIC cannot load and run a partial program.

There *is* a solution to the problem of program size, however. BASIC will allow one program to load and run another program. So several small programs may be written to solve one large problem.

The BASIC statement that loads and runs other programs is CHAIN. The original program, which contains the CHAIN statement, is called the "chaining" program. The secondary program is called the "chained-to" program.

The CHAIN Statement—Simplified Form

line number CHAIN filename

The CHAIN Statement—Examples

```
100    CHAIN "PROGRAM2"
500    CHAIN "B:MENU"
700    CHAIN "A:PART2.OVL"
```

When a CHAIN statement is encountered in program execution, the chained-to program is loaded into memory and execution begun. The new (chained-to) program replaces the old (chaining) program in memory.

Note that the CHAIN is a one-way operation. Since the chaining program has been replaced, control will not return to the old program after completion of the new program. If it is necessary to return, another CHAIN must be executed at the completion of the chained-to program.

A common use for the CHAIN statement is in menu programs. The menu is written as a separate program. Each of the menu choices would also be written as a separate program. The menu program determines the function to be performed and chains to the correct subprogram. At the conclusion of the subprogram, a CHAIN must be executed to return to the menu.

The contents of program variables from the chaining program will *not* be available in the chained-to program with the form of the CHAIN shown in the examples. When the values in variables must be passed to the chained-to program, there are two choices available depending on whether *all* variables or just some are needed.

When all of the variables must be passed to the chained-to program, the ALL option of the CHAIN statement can be used.

Passing All Variables

```
200    CHAIN "PROG2",,ALL
```

The ALL statement will preserve all variables and make them available in the chained-to program. Note that two commas are required before the word ALL. This is due to the fact that one option of the CHAIN has been left out. The omitted option will be explained soon.

Passing Some Variables

Variables may be passed on an individual basis by using the COMMON statement. The COMMON statement appears in the chaining program and names any variables and/or arrays to be passed to the chained-to program.

The COMMON Statement—General Form

```
line number COMMON  list of variables
```

When an array is to be passed, the name must appear with empty parentheses.

The COMMON Statement—Examples

```
200   COMMON PART, QUANT, TABLE()
210   CHAIN "LOOKUP"
```

This example chains to the program called LOOKUP on the currently logged drive and passes the array TABLE along with the variables PART and QUANT.

A COMMON statement may appear anywhere in a BASIC program as long as it precedes the CHAIN statement. However, it is strongly recommended that COMMON appear at the start of a program (along with the DIM statements). Multiple COMMON statements may be used in one program. One variable name may not be repeated in a second COMMON statement.

Chaining to a Specified Line Number

When a program has been chained-to, execution begins with the first program statement. Ordinarily, this is the preferred location. However, on occasion it may be necessary to begin execution at a statement number other than the first one. This would be the case when one program calls a second, and execution must return to the statement immediately following the CHAIN. Chaining to a specific line number is the option omitted earlier (in the discussion of ALL).

The CHAIN Statement—General Form

```
line number CHAIN  program name [,[line number to begin execution] [,ALL]]
```

The CHAIN Statement—Examples

```
400   CHAIN "MESSAGES",,ALL
500   CHAIN "MAIN",1100,ALL
800   CHAIN "PARTB",2200
```

The first example chains to the program MESSAGES passing all variables. Execution will begin at the first program line.

The second example passes all variables to the program MAIN, but begins execution with line 1100 in the chained-to program.

The third CHAIN statement begins execution at line 2200 in the program PARTB. No variables have been passed. If the contents of any variables are needed in the chained-to program, the chaining program must include a COMMON statement.

Example Programs: Using CHAIN and COMMON

The example program system is a menu program with four relatively independent program modules. In addition to the menu program and four menu choices, a sixth program has been written to handle any error processing. Each of the programs has an error trap (ON ERROR statement). Rather than repeat the error checking routines in each program, each chains to the program ERRS.

The six programs comprise a system for display and maintenance of a sequential library file.

Hierarchy Chart:
Private Library System

Each of the programs in figure I.1 is shown in one box. Since the error routine is executed from more than one location, it is shown with a shaded corner to indicate a shared module.

Program Listing

```
100 '    PROGRAM TO DEMONSTRATE THE USE OF CHAIN AND COMMON
110 '        ERROR TRAPPING IS ALSO INCLUDED
120 '
130 '                    PROGRAM VARIABLES
140 '
150 '    CHOICE              NUMERIC FORM OF MENU CHOICE
160 '    CHOICE$             ALPHANUMERIC FORM OF MENU CHOICE
170 '    PROG$               PROGRAM NAME TO PASS TO ERROR SUBPROGRAM
180 '

500 '*************** MENU PROGRAM MAINLINE ******************
510 COMMON PROG$
520 ON ERROR GOTO 10000
530 LET CHOICE = 0
540 WHILE CHOICE <> 5
550     GOSUB 1000                 'PRINT MENU AND INPUT CHOICE
560     IF CHOICE = 1
            THEN CHAIN "SELLIST"
570     IF CHOICE = 2
            THEN CHAIN "TITLLIST"
580     IF CHOICE = 3
            THEN CHAIN "AUTHLIST"
590     IF CHOICE = 4
            THEN CHAIN "FILEADD"
600 WEND
610 CLS
620 END

1000 '************* PRINT MENU AND INPUT CHOICE **************
1010 CLS
1020 PRINT TAB(30); "PRIVATE LIBRARY MENU''
1030 PRINT: PRINT
1040 PRINT TAB(20); "1. PRINT LIST ARRANGED BY SELECTION NUMBER"
1050 PRINT
1060 PRINT TAB(20); "2. PRINT LIST ARRANGED BY TITLE"
1070 PRINT
1080 PRINT TAB(20); "3. PRINT LIST ARRANGED BY AUTHOR"
1090 PRINT
1100 PRINT TAB(20); "4. ADD NEW TITLES TO FILE"
1110 PRINT
1120 PRINT TAB(20); "5. QUIT"
1130 PRINT:PRINT
1140 PRINT TAB(23); "ENTER SELECTION ";
1150 INPUT "", CHOICE$
1160 LET CHOICE = VAL(CHOICE$)
1170 RETURN
```

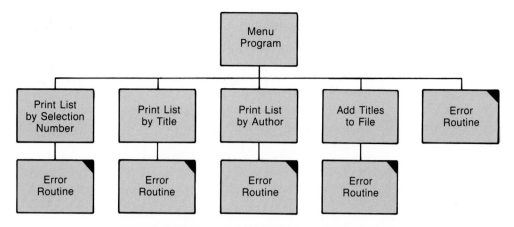

Figure I.1

Hierarchy chart for the library system programs. Each of the programs is shown in one box. Since the error routine is executed from more than one location, it is shown with a shaded corner, to indicate a shared module.

```
10000 '*************** ERROR ROUTINE ***************************
10010 LET PROG$ = "MENU"
10020 CHAIN "ERRS"
10030 '*************** END OF PROGRAM ***********************


100 ' SUBPROGRAM "SELLIST"
110 ' THIS PROGRAM IS CHAINED TO BY PROGRAM "MENU"
120 ' PERFORMS MENU FUNCTION #1, TO PRINT THE FILE BY
130 '      SELECTION NUMBER (NATURAL ORDER FOR THE FILE)
140 '
150 ' ERROR TRAPPING IN THIS PROGRAM CAUSES THE ERROR SUB-PROGRAM
160 '     TO BE CHAINED TO
170 ' AFTER NORMAL TERMINATION OF THIS PROGRAM, THE MENU PROGRAM
180 '     WILL AGAIN BE CHAINED TO
500 '******** SUBPROGRAM "SELLIST" MAINLINE ******************
510 COMMON PROG$
520 ON ERROR GOTO 10000
530 OPEN "I", #1, "LIBRARY.DAT"
540 GOSUB 1000                    'INITIALIZE PRINT IMAGES
550 GOSUB 2000                    'PRINT HEADINGS
560 WHILE NOT EOF(1)
570     INPUT #1, SELECTION, TITLE$, AUTHOR$
580     LPRINT USING D$; SELECTION, TITLE$, AUTHOR$
590 WEND
600 CLOSE #1
610 CHAIN "MENU"
620 END


1000 '*************** INITIALIZE PRINT IMAGES *****************
1010 LET T$ = "          LIBRARY LISTING BY SELECTION NUMBER"
1020 LET H$ = " SELECTION   TITLE                      AUTHOR"
1030 LET D$ = "   ###      \                      \ \         \"
1040 RETURN


2000 '*************** PRINT HEADINGS ***********************
2010 LPRINT T$
2020 LPRINT
2030 LPRINT
2040 LPRINT H$
2050 LPRINT
2060 RETURN


10000 '*************** ERROR TRAP ROUTINE ******************
10010 LET PROG$ = "SELLIST"      'PASS NAME OF CHAINING PROGRAM
10020 CHAIN "ERRS"               'CALL ERROR SUBPROGRAM
10030 '*************** END OF PROGRAM ********************
```

```
100 ' SUBPROGRAM "TITLLIST"
110 ' PRINTS A LIST BY TITLE
120 '
130 ' STUB MODULE TO TEST SYSTEM

135 '*********************************************************
140 COMMON PROG$
150 ON ERROR GOTO 10000
160 CLS
170 PRINT "PRINT LIST BY TITLE"
180 PRINT:PRINT
190 PRINT "PROGRAM NOT YET WRITTEN"
200 PRINT:PRINT
210 PRINT "PRESS ANY KEY TO CONTINUE"
220 LET X$ = INPUT$(1)
230 CHAIN "MENU"

10000 '************* ERROR ROUTINE *************************
10010 LET PROG$ = "TITLLIST"
10020 CHAIN "ERRS"
10030 '************* END OF PROGRAM *************************


100 ' SUBPROGRAM "AUTHLIST"
110 ' PRINTS A LIST BY AUTHOR
120 '
130 ' STUB MODULE TO TEST SYSTEM

135 '*********************************************************
140 COMMON PROG$
150 ON ERROR GOTO 10000
160 CLS
170 PRINT "PRINT LIST BY AUTHOR"
180 PRINT:PRINT
190 PRINT "PROGRAM NOT YET WRITTEN"
200 PRINT:PRINT
210 PRINT "PRESS ANY KEY TO CONTINUE"
220 LET X$ = INPUT$(1)
230 CHAIN "ENU"

10000 '************* ERROR ROUTINE *************************
10010 LET PROG$ = "AUTHLIST"
10020 CHAIN "ERRS"
10030 '************* END OF PROGRAM *************************


100 ' SUBPROGRAM "FILEADD"
110 ' ADDS TITLES TO THE FILE
120 '
130 ' STUB MODULE TO TEST SYSTEM

135 '*********************************************************
140 COMMON PROG$
150 ON ERROR GOTO 10000
160 CLS
170 PRINT "ADD TITLES TO THE FILE"
180 PRINT:PRINT
190 PRINT "PROGRAM NOT YET WRITTEN"
200 PRINT:PRINT
210 PRINT "PRESS ANY KEY TO CONTINUE"
220 LET X$ = INPUT$(1)
230 CHAIN "MENU"
```

```
10000 '************* ERROR ROUTINE ****************************
10010 LET PROG$ = "FILEADD"
10020 CHAIN "ERRS"
10030 '************* END OF PROGRAM *************************



100 '          SUBPROGRAM "ERRS"
110 '
120 '  SUBPROGRAM TO DO ERROR HANDLING FOR ALL PROGRAMS IN SYSTEM
130 '
140 '  THIS PROGRAM IS CHAINED TO BY "SELLIST", "TITLLIST",
150 '  "AUTHLIST", AND "FILEADD"
160 '
170 '  AFTER DETERMINATION OF THE ERROR, CONTROL IS PASSED BACK TO
180 '       THE MENU PROGRAM (BY CHAINING BACK)
190 '


500 '**************** SUBPROGRAM "ERRS" MAINLINE *************
510 CLS
520 PRINT:PRINT:PRINT
530 PRINT TAB(25); "ERROR CONDITION EXISTS"
540 PRINT:PRINT:PRINT
550 IF ERR = 71 OR ERR = 57
        THEN GOSUB 2000              'DISKETTE DRIVE NOT READY
560 IF ERR = 53
        THEN GOSUB 3000              'FILE NOT FOUND
570 IF ERR = 27
        THEN GOSUB 4000              'PRINTER NOT READY
580 IF ERR <> 71 AND ERR <> 57 AND ERR <> 53 AND ERR <> 27
        THEN GOSUB 5000
590 CLOSE                            'CLOSE ALL FILES (SAFETY PRECAUTION)
600 CHAIN "MENU"
610 END


1000 '****************** PAUSE ****************************
1010 PRINT:PRINT:PRINT
1020 PRINT TAB(25); ". . . PRESS ANY KEY WHEN READY TO CONTINUE"
1030 LET X$ = INPUT$(1)
1040 RETURN


2000 '************* DISKETTE DRIVE NOT READY ******************
2010 PRINT TAB(20); "CHECK THE DISKETTE READER"
2020 PRINT
2030 PRINT TAB(20); "IS THERE A DISKETTE IN THE DRIVE?"
2040 PRINT
2050 PRINT TAB(20); "IS THE DOOR CLOSED COMPLETELY?"
2060 GOSUB 1000                      'PAUSE
2070 RETURN


3000 '*********** DATA FILE NOT FOUND *******************
3010 PRINT TAB(20); "THE DATA FILE NEEDED FOR YOUR PROGRAM WAS"
3020 PRINT TAB(25); "NOT FOUND ON THE CORRECT DRIVE"
3030 GOSUB 1000                      'PAUSE
3040 RETURN


4000 '************* PRINTER NOT READY *******************
4010 PRINT TAB(20); "CHECK THE PRINTER"
4020 PRINT:PRINT
4030 PRINT TAB(20); "IS IT TURNED ON, WITH PAPER PROPERLY INSTALLED?"
4040 GOSUB 1000                      'PAUSE
4050 RETURN
```

```
5000 '******** UNIDENTIFIED ERROR, NOT CORRECTABLE BY USER ****
5010 PRINT
5020 PRINT TAB(25); "E R R O R     E R R O R"
5030 PRINT:PRINT:PRINT
5040 PRINT "COPY THE FOLLOWING INFORMATION AND DELIVER TO PROGRAMMER:"
5050 PRINT
5060 PRINT TAB(15); "ERROR NUMBER "; ERR
5070 PRINT
5080 PRINT TAB(15); "AT LINE NUMBER "; ERL
5090 PRINT
5100 PRINT TAB(15); "IN PROGRAM "; PROG$
5110 GOSUB 1000                'PAUSE
5120 RETURN
5130 '************* END OF PROGRAM *************************
```

Sample Program Output

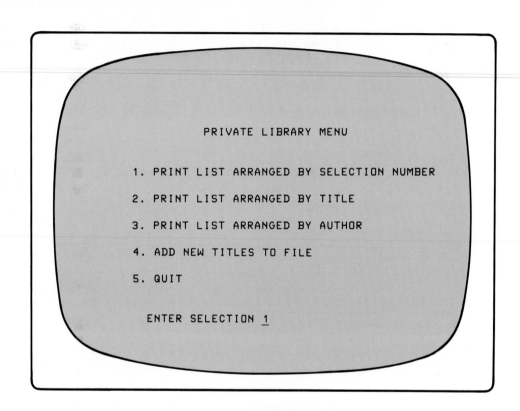

```
              PRIVATE LIBRARY MENU


     1. PRINT LIST ARRANGED BY SELECTION NUMBER

     2. PRINT LIST ARRANGED BY TITLE

     3. PRINT LIST ARRANGED BY AUTHOR

     4. ADD NEW TITLES TO FILE

     5. QUIT


     ENTER SELECTION 1
```

Output From Menu Choice 1—On Printer

```
                LIBRARY LISTING BY SELECTION NUMBER

     SELECTION    TITLE                    AUTHOR

        101       ROOTS                    HALEY
        102       THE HOBBIT               TOLKIEN
        103       RUBEN, RUBEN             DE VRIES
```

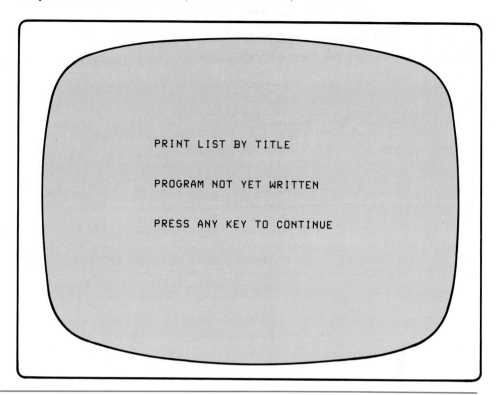

```
PRINT LIST BY TITLE

PROGRAM NOT YET WRITTEN

PRESS ANY KEY TO CONTINUE
```

Testing the Error Conditions

Any error condition may be "turned on" with the ERROR statement. This statement simulates the error condition and must follow the ON ERROR statement.

The ERROR Statement—General Form

```
line number ERROR  error number
```

The ERROR Statement—Example

```
525   ERROR 27
```

By placing this statement in one of the library system programs, the error trap for error number 27 can be tested.

Example Subroutine: Simulating an Error Condition

Program Listing

```
100 '   SUBPROGRAM "TITLLIST"
110 '   PRINTS A LIST BY TITLE
120 '
130 ' STUB MODULE TO TEST SYSTEM

135 '**************************************************************
140 COMMON PROG$
150 ON ERROR GOTO 10000
160 CLS
170 PRINT "PRINT LIST BY TITLE"
180 PRINT:PRINT
190 PRINT "PROGRAM NOT YET WRITTEN"
200 PRINT:PRINT
210 PRINT "PRESS ANY KEY TO CONTINUE"
220 LET X$ = INPUT$(1)
225 ERROR 27
230 CHAIN "MENU"
10000 '************* ERROR ROUTINE **************************
10010 LET PROG$ = "TITLLIST"
10020 CHAIN "ERRS"
10030 '************* END OF PROGRAM *************************
```

The addition of line 225 should invoke the ON ERROR statement, branch to line number 10000 and chain to program ERRS. The error message for error number 27 should then appear on the screen. Any of the error conditions may be set on in any of the programs to thoroughly test all routines.

Developing Programs Using the CHAIN Statement— A Word of Advice

One small word of advice is in order for the person writing programs using the CHAIN. *ALWAYS* save your program before any test run. It can be extremely frustrating to spend time working out the details of a program and lose it. When a CHAIN statement is executed, the program in memory is *replaced* by the new program. If the current program has not been saved before the CHAIN, it will be lost.

A good way to force a SAVE before any RUN is to include a SAVE statement at the beginning of your program. This is for testing and debugging only and must be removed for a working program.

```
10   SAVE "MENU"
100 '    PROGRAM TO DEMONSTRATE THE USE OF CHAIN AND COMMON
110 '         ERROR TRAPPING IS ALSO INCLUDED
120 '
130 '                    PROGRAM VARIABLES
500 '**************** MENU PROGRAM MAINLINE ******************
510 COMMON PROG$
520 ON ERROR GOTO 10000
530 LET CHOICE = 0
540 WHILE CHOICE <> 5
550     GOSUB 1000                    'PRINT MENU AND INPUT CHOICE
560     IF CHOICE = 1
            THEN CHAIN "SELLIST"
570     IF CHOICE = 2
            THEN CHAIN "TITLLIST"
580     IF CHOICE = 3
            THEN CHAIN "AUTHLIST"
590     IF CHOICE = 4
            THEN CHAIN "FILEADD"
600 WEND
610 CLS
620 END
```

```
10 SAVE "ERRS"
100 '          SUBPROGRAM "ERRS"
110 '
120 '   SUBPROGRAM TO DO ERROR HANDLING FOR ALL PROGRAMS IN SYSTEM
::
::
```

Appendix J
Summary of BASIC Statements and Functions

BASIC statements.

Statement	Effect
BEEP	Beeps the speaker.
BEEP [pitch] [,duration]	Beeps the speaker in MBASIC. Pitch and duration are in the range 0–255.
BLOAD "filename" [,offset]	Loads into memory a file that has been previously saved with BSAVE.
BSAVE "filename", offset, length	Saves an area of memory into a disk file.
CALL numvariable [(variable[,variable] . . .)]	Calls an assembly language subroutine.
CHAIN "filename" [,linenumber] [,ALL]	Loads and runs another program. Execution begins at the first line of the chained program, unless a line number is specified. The ALL parameter passes all program variables to the chained program.
CIRCLE (X, Y), radius [,palette.color [,start.angle, end.angle [,aspect.ratio]]]	Draws a circle in medium- or high-resolution graphics modes.
CLOSE #filenum	Closes a file.
CLS	Clears the screen.
COLOR [foreground] [,[background] [,border]]	Sets colors in text mode (low resolution).
COLOR [background] [,[palette]]	Sets color choices in medium-resolution graphics mode.
COMMON variable [, variable2,...]	Passes variables to the chained program.
DATA constant [,constant2,...]	Provides the constants to be read by READ statements.
DATE$ = date.string	Sets the current date.
DEF FN name(argument(s)) = expression	Defines a function for later execution.
DEF DBL letter [-letter] [,letter [-letter]]	Declares that variables beginning with the named letters will be double-precision.

DEF INT letter [-letter] [,letter [-letter]]
: Declares that variables beginning with the named letters will be integer.

DEF SEG [= segment.start]
: Defines the beginning of the current segment of memory for subsequent BLOAD, BSAVE, CALL, PEEK, or POKE.

DEF SNG letter [-letter] [,letter [-letter]]
: Declares that variables beginning with the named letters will be single-precision.

DEF STR letter [-letter] [,letter [-letter]]
: Declares that variables beginning with the named letters will be string variables.

DIM array name(number of elements) [,array2(elements),...]
: Establishes the number of elements and allocates storage for arrays.

DRAW string
: In graphics mode, draws an object using a graphics definition language. (Not covered in this text, consult your manual.)

END
: Stops execution of the program and closes all files.

ERASE arrayname [,arrayname]
: Eliminates arrays from memory

FIELD #filenum, fieldlength as stringvariable [, fieldlength as stringvariable2,...]
: Establishes field names and lengths for random file buffer.

FOR loop index = initial value TO test value [STEP increment]
: Controls execution of a loop.

GET #filenum [,recordnumber]
: Reads data from a random file. If the record number is not specified, the *next* record is read.

GOSUB linenumber
: Begins execution of a subroutine. The RETURN statement returns from the subroutine.

GOTO linenumber
: Branches to the specified line number.

HOME
: Apple MBASIC. Clears the screen.

HTAB position
: Apple MBASIC. Moves the cursor to horizontal column position on the line.

IF condition THEN statement(s) [ELSE statement(s)]
: Performs the statement(s) following THEN when the condition evaluates *true*. Performs the statements following the ELSE (if included) when the condition evaluates *false*.

INPUT [;] ["prompt";] variable [,variable2,...]
: Inputs data from the keyboard. If a prompt is included, it prints before the input occurs.

INPUT #filenum, variable [,variable2,...]
: Reads data from a sequential data file.

KEY OFF
: Turns off function key display.

KEY ON	Turns on function key display.
KEY LIST	Lists the current function keys.
KEY keynumber, string	Sets a function key to a new series of keystrokes.
KILL "filename"	Deletes a file from disk.
LET variable = expression	Evaluates the expression and assigns the result to the variable.

LINE [(X.start, Y.start)]—(X.end, Y.end) [,[palette.color] [,B[F]]]
    Draws a line in medium- or high-resolution graphics modes.

LINE INPUT [;] ["prompt";] stringvariable
    Inputs all characters (limit 255) typed at the keyboard. Accepts all characters including commas and colons, until ENTER is pressed.

LINE INPUT #filenumber, stringvariable
    Reads characters from a disk file until a carriage-return character is encountered (up to 255 characters). All characters including delimiters will be placed into stringvariable.

LOCATE row, column [,cursor]	Places the cursor at the row and column position specified. The optional cursor parameter controls the visibility of the cursor.
LPRINT items to print	Prints data on the printer. Items are separated by commas or semicolons.

LPRINT USING "stringliteral"; items to print
LPRINT USING stringvariable; items to print
    Prints data on the printer, according to the format specified in the string literal or variable.

LSET stringvariable = stringexpression
    Left-justifies the string expression in the string variable.

MID$(stringvariable, start position, number of characters) = stringexpression
    Replaces part of a string variable with the string expression.

NAME "old filename" AS "new filename"
    Renames a disk file.

NEXT [loop index]	Terminates a FOR...NEXT loop.

ON ERROR GOTO line number
    Enables program error trapping and specifies the line number of the error handling routine.

ON numeric expression GOSUB list of line numbers
    Evaluates the numeric expression and begins execution of the subroutine specified.

ON numeric expression GOTO list of line numbers
    Evaluates the numeric expression and branches to the corresponding line number.

OPEN mode, #filenum, "filename"
Opens a sequential data file. Mode must be "I" for input files or "O" for output files.

OPEN "filename" FOR mode AS #filenum
Alternate format. Opens a sequential data file. Mode must be INPUT, OUTPUT, or APPEND.

OPEN "R", #filenum, "filename", reclength
Opens a random data file.

OPEN "filename" AS #filenum, LEN = reclength
Alternate format. Opens a random data file.

OPTION BASE number
Sets the minimum value for array subscripts. Must be 0 or 1.

PAINT (X, Y) [[,fill.color] [,boundary.color]]
Fills an area on the screen with the selected color, in medium-resolution graphics mode.

PLAY string
Plays music specified in string. A special music definition language includes letters for notes, length, tempo, rests, and speed.

POKE memory.offset, value
Writes a value (range 0–65535) into the byte specified by offset, in the current memory segment. The current segment is set by DEF SEG.

PRESET (X, Y) [, palette.color]
Resets a point in medium- or high-resolution mode graphics.

PRINT items to print
Displays data on the screen. Items to print may be separated by semicolons or commas (with different results).

PRINT USING "string literal"; items to print
PRINT USING stringvariable; items to print
Displays data on the screen, according to the format specified in the string literal or variable.

PSET (X, Y) [, palette.color]
Draws a point in medium- or high-resolution mode graphics. Note that color is valid only for medium resolution.

PUT #filenum [,recordnumber]
Writes data from a file buffer into a random file in the record number named. If the record number is omitted, the record is written in the *next* position.

RANDOMIZE [numeric expression]
Reseeds the random number generator. If the expression is omitted, a seed is requested from the keyboard.

READ variable [,variable2,...]
Reads constants from DATA statements into the variable(s) named.

REM remark
Inserts a remark into the program. An alternate format allows substitution of a single quote (') for the word REM.

RESTORE	Resets the DATA pointer to the beginning of the program so that data may be reread.
RESUME RESUME NEXT RESUME linenumber	Resumes execution after error trapping with ON...GOTO.
RETURN	Returns from a subroutine to the statement immediately following the GOSUB.
RSET stringvariable = stringexpression	Right-justifies the string expression in the string variable.
SCREEN [mode] [,[colorburst] [, [active.page] [,visual.page]]]	Sets the screen mode for low-, medium-, or high-resolution modes.
SHELL [command string]	Allows execution of DOS commands, programs, and batch files.
SOUND frequency, duration	Generates sound through the speaker. Frequency range 37–32767, duration range .0015–65535.
STOP	Halts program execution. May be resumed with a CONT command.
SWAP variable1, variable2	Exchanges the contents of the two variables.
TIME$ = string	Sets the current time. Form of string is "hh:mm:ss".
VIEW (V.left, V.top) — (V.right, V.bottom) [,[palette.color] [,boundary]]	Defines a rectangular viewport for drawing graphs in medium- or high-resolution graphics modes.
VTAB linenumber	Apple MBASIC. Moves the cursor to the line number specified.
WEND	Terminates a WHILE/WEND loop.
WHILE condition	Begins a program loop. The statements in the loop will be repeated as long as the condition evaluates *true*.
WIDTH 40	Sets the screen width to 40 characters.
WIDTH 80	Sets the screen width to 80 characters.
WIDTH "LPT1:", linelength	Sets the length of the line on the printer.
WINDOW (W.left, W.top) — (W.right, W.bottom)	Redefines the coordinates of the screen or viewport in medium- or high-resolution graphics. Scales the area to World Coordinates.
WRITE #filenum, variable [,variable2,...]	Writes data in a sequential data file.

Function	Returns

Note: All functions that have a $ in the function name return strings. Numeric function names always return numeric values.

Function	Returns
ABS(X)	Absolute value of X.
ASC(X$)	ASCII code number of the first character of X$.
ATN(X)	Arctangent of X in radians.
CDBL(X)	Double-precision value of X.
CHR$(X)	The character represented by the ASCII code number X.
CINT(X)	X rounded to an integer.
COS(X)	Cosine of X in radians.
CSNG(X)	Single-precision value of X.
CVD(X$)	Double-precision numeric equivalent of an eight-byte string.
CVI(X$)	Integer numeric equivalent of a two-byte string.
CVS(X$)	Single-precision numeric equivalent of a four-byte string.
EOF(filenum)	True at the end of a sequential file.
EXP(X)	e to the power of X.
FIX(X)	Truncated integer portion of X.
HEX$(X)	A string that represents the hexadecimal value of X.
INKEY$	One character from the keyboard, or a null string if no key has been pressed. Does not suspend program execution.
INPUT$(X)	A string of characters from the keyboard, X characters in length. Suspends program execution.
INSTR([B,] X$,Y$)	Position in X$ where substring Y$ begins. Optional B gives starting search position within X$.
INT(X)	Largest integer in X.
LEFT$(X$,N)	Leftmost N characters of X$.
LEN(X$)	Number of characters in X$.
LOC(filenumber)	Record number of last record read or written in a random file.
LOF(filenumber)	Number of bytes in the file.
LOG(X)	Natural logarithm of X.
LPOS(1)	Current position of the print head within the printer buffer for LPT1.

MID$(X$,B [,N])	Substring of X$, beginning in position B for a length of N.
MKD$(D)	Eight-byte string from a double-precision numeric value.
MKI$(I)	Two-byte string from an integer numeric value.
MKS$(S)	Four-byte string from a single-precision numeric value.
OCT$(X)	A string that represents the octal value of X.
PEEK(X)	The byte read from memory location X.
PMAP(coordinate, selection)	Corresponding physical screen coordinate or world coordinate. Coordinate may be X or Y. Selection: 0 = map world coordinate x to screen x 1 = map world coordinate y to screen y 2 = map screen coordinate x to world x 3 = map screen coordinate y to world y
POS(X)	Current horizontal (column) position of the cursor.
RIGHT$(X$,N)	Rightmost N characters of X$.
RND[(X)]	A random number between 0 and 1.
SGN(X)	Sign of X. 1 = positive; -1 = negative; 0 = zero.
SIN(X)	Sine of X in radians.
SPACE$(N)	A string of N spaces.
SPC(N)	N spaces inserted in a PRINT or LPRINT statement.
SQR(X)	Square root of X.
STR$(X)	The string representation of X.
STRING$(N,C$) STRING$(N,X)	A string of N length comprised of the single character C$ or ASCII code number X.
TAB(X)	Print pointer moved to position X on the line. For PRINT and LPRINT.
TAN(X)	Tangent of X in radians.
TIMER	Number of seconds elapsed since midnight or a system reset.
USR	Calls an assembly language subroutine.
VAL(X$)	Numeric value of X$.

Glossary

Accumulator

A numeric variable used to accumulate a sum such as a total field.

Algorithm

A step-by-step procedure for solving a problem.

Append

To add data to the end of a sequential file.

Argument

The value(s) supplied to a function in order for the function to perform its specified operation.

Arithmetic expression

A numeric value, which may be one variable or constant or a series of constants, variables, functions, and arithmetic operators.

Arithmetic operator

The symbols used for arithmetic operations: + - * / ∧

Array

A group of variables referenced by a single name. To use any one individual variable (element), a subscript must be used.

ASCII

American Standard Code for Information Interchange. The code used by microcomputers to store characters. Each character (letter, digit, special symbol) is represented by a unique number. *See* appendix C.

Background

Each character on the screen is drawn in a box nine dots by nine dots. The dots that form the characters are called foreground, those surrounding the character are the background. *See also* Foreground.

Binary search

A method used to locate a particular value in a sorted array by repeatedly dividing the array in half and discarding the portion that does not contain the value until a match is found.

Bubble sort

A method used to sort numeric or alphanumeric data, where adjacent elements are continually compared and swapped until they are in the desired sequence.

Buffer

An area of computer memory set aside to hold a record immediately before it is placed on the disk and immediately after it is read from the disk.

Bug

A program error.

Byte

One character of storage.

Character

A single letter of the alphabet, a numeric digit, or a special symbol (such as $, % *).

Clipping

In graphics mode, any dots specified that would be outside the screen area (or the current viewport) are not plotted.

Cohesion

A measure of how well the statements of a program module are related to one another and the function being performed.

Collating sequence

The order, or precedence, of characters that determines their order for comparing or sorting operations.

Compiler

Software that converts high-level programming languages to the machine code necessary for program execution. The entire program is converted before execution begins. *See* Interpreter.

Computer program

A series of instructions written in a programming language and arranged in a sequence that will cause the computer to solve a particular problem.

Concatenation

Combining two or more strings, thus making a longer string.

Constant

A numeric or character string value that does not change during program execution.

Control break

A point during processing when a special event occurs such as subtotals being printed.

Control variable

The variable used to determine the timing of a control break.

Counter

A numeric variable used to count.

Coupling

A measure of the interdependence of program modules. Modules should be loosely coupled, which is to say that each should stand alone as much as possible.

CP/M

(Control Program/Microcomputers) An operating system for microcomputers written by Digital Research, Inc.

Cursor

Generally a flashing character such as an underline or block that indicates where the next typed character will appear on the screen.

Data element

One variable or field.

Data file

A collection of data records stored on a disk.

Data terminator

A special item of data that indicates the end of the input data. Also called a sentinel or trailer.

Debugging

Finding and correcting the errors in a computer program.

Delimiter

A character such as a comma or semicolon used to separate fields.

Detail line

A line that is displayed for each record processed.

Disk Operating System (DOS)

Operating system software that determines how the diskettes are to be formatted and accessed.

Diskette

A floppy disk.

Documentation

Written explanations of the development, design, coding, and operation of a program or system.

Dummy variables

The variables named in a DEF FN statement that establish the relationships to be assigned to the function arguments. Also, a variable used in a location where it is required to use a variable name, but the contents of that variable are of no consequence in the program.

Echo

Display of characters on the screen as they are being keyed.

Empty cell

An unused record position in a random file.

Execution

The actual carrying-out of the program instructions.

E (Exponential) notation

The method of displaying numeric data similar to scientific notation where the exponent and fraction are shown. Generally used for extremely large or extremely small numbers.

Field

A subdivision of a record. One variable.

File

A group of logically related records.

Flag

See Switch.

Floppy disk

A disk made of magnetizable material used to store programs and data for later retrieval.

Flowchart

A pictorial representation of program logic using a set of standard symbols. Used to plan the logic of a program as well as to document a completed program.

Foreground

The actual characters printed or points plotted on the screen. *See* Background.

Function

A prewritten subprogram that performs an operation and furnishes (returns) one value. Many functions are supplied with BASIC, others are written by the programmer. *See* User-defined function.

GIGO

(*Garbage-In Garbage-Out*) A phrase meaning that output can be no more accurate than the input fed into the computer.

Hierarchy chart

A pictorial representation of the organization of program modules that shows program functions layered in a top-to-bottom, general-to-detail fashion. Used for program planning as well as documentation. Sometimes called a top-down chart.

Hierarchy of operations

A set of rules that determines the order in which arithmetic operations are carried out.

Indexed file

A random file that has a separate table of key values called an index. The index is used to look up the record number, given the key value.

Input

The items of data needed by a computer program to perform its operations.

Integer

A whole number.

Interactive

A conversational mode of operation, where there is a dialogue between the program and the operator.

Interpreter

The system software that translates program statements into the corresponding machine instructions for execution. Statements are decoded and executed one statement at a time. *See also* Compiler.

Iteration

One pass or repetition of a loop.

K

Used to indicate the capacity of computer storage, 1K = 1024 characters. Example: 64 K = 65,536 characters of storage.

Line counter

A numeric variable used to count the number of lines printed and determine the timing for a new page.

Line number

The number that precedes each statement. Line numbers determine the sequence of statement execution.

Literal

A string constant. A series of alphabetic characters, digits, and special symbols enclosed in quotation marks.

Logical operator

AND, OR, and NOT. Can be used in combination with the relational operators to form compound conditions.

Lookup

Find a match for a value in a table. Also called a search.

Loop

A series of repeated program steps.

Mainline

The top level module of a program controlling execution of the other program modules.

Menu

A list of choices displayed to the user.

Modular programming

The process of creating a program by first breaking a problem down into smaller parts, writing subprograms to solve those smaller problems, and combining the subprograms into one functioning unit.

Module

A component of a program designed to perform one task.

MS-DOS

An operating system for microcomputers produced by Microsoft Corp.

Nested loops

Loops contained within other loops.

NULL string

A string containing no characters. An empty string.

Operating system

The control program that supervises computer operations.

Output

The result of program execution displayed on an output device such as the screen or printer.

Page counter

A numeric variable used to count the number of pages and print the page number at the top of each page.

Parallel arrays

Two or more arrays that have elements that correspond to one another.

PC-DOS

The disk operating system used on an IBM-PC.

Pixel

Picture element. One of the individual dots used to form a character or a graphics image.

Precision

A measure of correctness indicating the number of digits that can be held accurately.

Print image

The string used for formatting printed output in a PRINT USING statement.

Processing

The manipulation of data provided as input in order to generate output; includes calculating, summarizing, classifying, sorting, and storing.

Program planning

Developing the program logic necessary to solve the problem before coding is begun. It may be done with a flowchart, hierarchy chart, pseudocode, or other planning methods.

Prompt

A message to the user indicating the desired response.

Pseudocode

English-like statements that describe the logic of a program. Used as a planning tool.

Random data file

A collection of data records organized in such a way as to allow any record to be retrieved or written without disturbing the other records.

Real number

A number that has a fractional part (digits to the right of the decimal point).

Record

A group of related data elements or fields. Generally, the data used for one iteration of a program.

Record key

A control field within a record that identifies that record uniquely. The organizing factor of the file.

Relational operators

The symbols used for comparisons: $>$, $>=$, $<$, $<=$, $=$, $<>$.

Reserved words

Words that have special meaning to BASIC and cannot be used as variable names.

Resolution

A term that is used to define the clarity or sharpness of an image, based on the number of pixels used to form the image. A screen that displays 640 pixels horizontally is said to have higher resolution than one that displays 320 pixels. *See also* Pixel.

Search argument

The item of data that must be matched in a table search.

Sector

One segment of a track on diskette. Depending on the operating system, one sector may hold 128 characters, 256 characters, or 512 characters.

Sentinel

A special item of data that indicates the end of the input data. Also called a data terminator.

Sequential file

A group of related records organized so that the records must be written or retrieved one after another in sequence. *See* Data file.

Shell sort

A method used to sort numeric or alphanumeric data. The sort algorithm was named for its creator, Donald Shell, and is more efficient than a bubble sort.

Sort

Arranging the elements of an array into ascending or descending numeric or alphabetic sequence.

String

A variable or constant consisting of letters, digits, or special symbols.

Structured programming

A method of program design, coding, and testing designed to produce programs that are correct, easy to read, and easy to maintain.

Stub

A program module for which the code has not yet been written, designed to allow the program to be tested in its present state.

Subroutine

A program module that is executed by a GOSUB statement and exited with a RETURN.

Subscript

A numeric value identifying a specific element of an array.

Subscripted variable

One element of an array.

Switch

A variable used to indicate a program condition. The only two values assigned to the variable are 1 or 0 for switch ON or OFF. Also called a flag.

Syntax

Rules that must be followed while coding program instructions, similar to grammatical rules for the English language.

Table

An array.

Table lookup or search

A method of locating a particular value in an array by comparing the search argument to each element of the array until a match is found.

Top-down programming

A method of designing a program that first looks at the entire problem, then multiple levels, breaking the problem into smaller and smaller parts. Illustrated with a hierarchy chart.

Track

One of the concentric circles on a diskette on which data is stored. A track is divided into sectors.

Trailer

A special item of data that indicates the end of the input data. Also called a data terminator or sentinel.

User

A person who needs and uses the information produced by the computer system. The person who operates the computer.

User-defined function

A function that has been constructed by the programmer and coded with a DEF FN statement.

Variable

A storage location in main memory whose contents may change during program execution.

Viewport

A rectangular portion of the screen used to draw an image in medium- or high-resolution graphics.

VTOC

*V*isual *T*able *O*f *C*ontents. *See* Hierarchy chart.

World coordinates

Numbers to plot based on their actual values, rather than on the screen coordinates. Provides a means to draw graphs without converting coordinates from their "real world" values to the dimensions of the screen.

Credits

Table of Contents

Page vii left: courtesy of Texas Instruments, **right:** courtesy of Hewlett Packard Company; **page viii left:** courtesy of Apple Computer, Inc., **right:** courtesy of Hewlett Packard Company; **page ix top left:** © Bob Coyle, **bottom left:** courtesy of Hitatchi, **right:** courtesy of Hewlett Packard Company; **page x top left:** courtesy of Apple Computer, Inc., **bottom left:** courtesy of Radio Shack, A Division of Tandy Corporation, **top right:** courtesy of IBM, **bottom right:** courtesy of Hewlett Packard Company; **page xi top left:** courtesy of The Voice Connection, **bottom left:** © Bob Coyle, **right:** courtesy of Hewlett Packard Company; **page xii top:** courtesy of AT&T, **bottom:** courtesy of IBM.

Chapter 1

Page 2 top: courtesy of IBM, **left:** courtesy of Hewlett Packard Company, **right:** courtesy of Texas Instruments; **page 4:** Reprinted with permission of Compaq Computer Corporation. All Rights Reserved; **page 5:** © Bob Coyle; **page 6 top:** courtesy of Apple Computer, Inc., **bottom:** courtesy of Hewlett Packard Company; **page 7 top:** courtesy of Hewlett Packard Company, **left & middle:** courtesy of Apple Computer, Inc., **right:** courtesy of the Voice Connection; **page 14:** © Bob Coyle.

Chapters 8 and 16

© Wm. C. Brown Publishers, Photographed by Bob Coyle.

Index

Summary of BASIC Statements

Statement	Effect	Text Page #
ON ERROR GOTO line number	Enables program error trapping and specifies the line number of the error handling routine.	493
ON numeric expression GOSUB list of line numbers	Evaluates the numeric expression and begins execution of the subroutine specified.	224
ON numeric expression GOTO list of line numbers	Evaluates the numeric expression and branches to the corresponding line number.	509
OPEN mode, #filenum, "filename"	Opens a sequential data file. Mode must be "I" for input files or "O" for output files.	342
OPEN "filename" FOR mode AS #filenum	Alternate format. Opens a sequential data file. Mode must be INPUT, OUTPUT, or APPEND.	342
OPEN "R", #filenum, "filename", reclength	Opens a random data file.	363
OPEN "filename" AS #filenum, LEN = reclength	Alternate format. Opens a random data file.	363
OPTION BASE number	Sets the minimum value for array subscripts. Must be 0 or 1.	278
PAINT (X, Y) [[,fill.color] [,boundary.color]]	Fills an area on the screen with the selected color, in medium-resolution graphics mode.	434
PRINT items to print	Displays data on the screen. Items to print may be separated by semicolons or commas (with different results).	23
PRINT USING "stringliteral"; items to print PRINT USING stringvariable; items to print	Displays data on the screen, according to the format specified in the string literal or variable.	78
PSET (X, Y) [, palette.color]	Draws a point in medium- or high-resolution mode graphics. Note that color is valid only for medium resolution.	425
PUT #filenum [,recordnumber]	Writes data from a file buffer into a random file in the record number named. If the record number is omitted, the record is written in the *next* position.	369
RANDOMIZE [numeric expression]	Reseeds the random number generator. If the expression is omitted, a seed is requested from the keyboard.	260
READ variable [,variable2,...]	Reads constants from DATA statements into the variable(s) named.	112

(continued from inside front cover)